INTERNET
POLITICS

States, Citizens, and New Communication Technologies

Andrew Chadwick

Royal Holloway College, University of London

NEW YORK   OXFORD

OXFORD UNIVERSITY PRESS

2006

Oxford University Press, Inc., publishes works that further Oxford University's objective of excellence in research, scholarship, and education.

Oxford   New York
Auckland   Cape Town   Dar es Salaam   Hong Kong   Karachi
Kuala Lumpur   Madrid   Melbourne   Mexico City   Nairobi
New Delhi   Shanghai   Taipei   Toronto

With offices in
Argentina   Austria   Brazil   Chile   Czech Republic   France   Greece
Guatemala   Hungary   Italy   Japan   Poland   Portugal   Singapore
South Korea   Switzerland   Thailand   Turkey   Ukraine   Vietnam

Copyright © 2006 by Oxford University Press, Inc.

Published by Oxford University Press, Inc.
198 Madison Avenue, New York, New York 10016
http://www.oup.com

Oxford is a registered trademark of Oxford University Press

Library of Congress Cataloging-in-Publication Data

Chadwick, Andrew.
   Internet politics : states, citizens, and new communication technologies / Andrew Chadwick.
      p. cm.
   Includes bibliographical references and index.
   ISBN-13: 978-0-19-517773-2 (alk. paper)
   ISBN-10: 0-19-517773-8 (alk. paper)
   1. Internet in public administration. 2. Internet in political campaigns. 3. Political
participation—Technological innovations. 4. Information technology—Political aspects. 5.
Information society. I. Title.

JF1525.A8C43 2006
320'.0285'4678—dc22   2005050892

Printing number: 9 8 7 6 5 4 3 2 1

Printed in the United States of America
on acid-free paper

INTERNET POLITICS

CONTENTS

FIGURES,
TABLES, AND EXHIBITS

FIGURES

TABLES

EXHIBITS

ABBREVIATIONS AND ACRONYMS

ACLU   American Civil Liberties Union

APC   Association for Progressive Communications

APEC   Asia-Pacific Economic Co-operation

ARPA   Advanced Research Projects Agency

ARPANET   Advanced Research Projects Agency Network

ASCII   American Standard Code for Information Interchange

ASEAN   Association for South East Asian Nations

BBC   British Broadcasting Corporation

BEV   Blacksburg Electronic Village

CCTV   Closed Circuit Television

CDA   (U.S.) Communications Decency Act (1996)

CIA   (U.S.) Central Intelligence Agency

CIPA   (U.S.) Children's Internet Protection Act (2000)

CITU   (U.K.) Central Information Technology Unit

CPSR   Computer Professionals for Social Responsibility

DNS   Domain Name System

DRM   Digital Rights Management

DSL   Digital Subscriber Line

EDT   Electronic Disturbance Theater

EFF   Electronic Frontier Foundation

EU   European Union

EU15   European Union 15 member states, 1995–2004

EZLN   Ejército Zapatista de Liberación Nacional

FBI   (U.S.) Federal Bureau of Investigation

FCC   (U.S.) Federal Communications Commission

FEC   (U.S.) Federal Election Commission

FOSS   Free and Open-source Software Movement

FTP   File Transfer Protocol

G8 DOT Force   G7/8 Digital Opportunity Taskforce

GAC   Governmental Advisory Committee (of ICANN)

GATS   General Agreement on Trade in Services

GBDE   Global Business Dialogue on E-commerce

GIIC   Global Information Infrastructure Commission

GSA   (U.S.) General Services Administration

HHI   Herfindahl-Hirschman Index

HTML   Hypertext Markup Language

IANA   Internet Assigned Numbers Authority

ICANN   Internet Corporation for Assigned Names and Numbers

IETF   Internet Engineering Task Force

IMF   International Monetary Fund

IPTO   Information Processing Techniques Office

IRC   Internet Relay Chat

ISOC   Internet Society

ISP   Internet Service Provider

ITU   International Telecommunication Union

MIT   Massachusetts Institute of Technology

NAFTA   North American Free Trade Agreement

NGO   Nongovernmental Organization

NSA   (U.S.) National Security Agency

NSF   (U.S.) National Science Foundation

NSFNET   (U.S.) National Science Foundation Network

NTIA   (U.S.) Department of Commerce National Telecommunications and
Information Administration

OECD   Organization for Economic Co-operation and Development

OMB   (U.S.) Office of Management and Budget

PAC   Political Action Committee

PRI   Partido Revolucionario Institucional (Mexico)

RFID   Radio Frequency Identification

RIAA   Recording Industry Association of America

RIPA   (U.K.) Regulation of Investigatory Powers Act (2000)

TCP/IP   Transmission Control Protocol/Internet Protocol

TIA   (U.S.) Total Information Awareness Program

TIPS   (U.S.) Terrorism Information and Prevention System

TRIPS   Trade Related Agreement on Intellectual Property Rights

UCLA   University of California, Los Angeles

UCSB   University of California, Santa Barbara

UN   United Nations

UNICT   United Nations Information and Communication Technology Taskforce

UNSD   United Nations Statistical Division

USDA   (U.S.) Department of Agriculture

VPN   Virtual Private Network

W3C   World Wide Web Consortium

WBG   World Bank Group

WEF   World Economic Forum

WELL   Whole Earth 'Lectronic Link

WIPO   World Intellectual Property Organization

WSIS   World Summit on the Information Society

WTO   World Trade Organization

XML   Extensible Markup Language

ACKNOWLEDGMENTS

No book is the product of a single individual. Countless authors and institutions have been formative in my approach to Internet politics, and I would like to begin by thanking the growing legion of Internet scholars around the globe; without you, this book could not have been written.

I would like to express special gratitude to all at the Oxford Internet Institute, particularly Bill Dutton, Victoria Nash, Stephen Coleman, Ralph Schroeder, Adrian Shepherd, John Taylor, Chris Marsden, Miriam Lips, Deborah Wheeler, Arthur Bullard, James Boon, Ruth Hayward, and Linda Frankland, for their encouragement and advice and financial and administrative support during the Visiting Fellowship, which gave me the time, space, and intellectual stimulation necessary to bring this book to fruition.

Themes and ideas presented here have been trailed at several conferences and workshops, including the American Political Science Association Annual Meeting (2001); the Canada-Europe Parliamentary Association seminar in the Canadian House of Commons (2002); the U.K. Political Studies Association Annual Conference (2003 and 2005); an impromptu session organized by the Congressional Research Service Science and Technology Policy Section, while I was conducting field research in Washington, D.C. (spring 2004); and several events at the Oxford Internet Institute during 2003 and 2004. I would like to thank the participants in those sessions as well as the following, who, perhaps unwittingly, directly shaped this book with advice, encouragement, or information along the way: Richard Allan, Christine Bellamy, Matt Bonham, Robin Brown, Lincoln Dahlberg, Todd Davies, Mary Francoli, Dave Garson, Rachel Gibson, Elizabeth Gorgue, Chip Hauss, Richard Heffernan, Oliver James, Steven Kennedy, Brian Loader, Helen Margetts, Christopher May, Alister Miskimmon, Ted Nelson, Eli Noam, Pippa Norris, Derek Parkinson, Chris Paterson, Bert Rockman, Alice Robbin, Kenneth Rogerson, Lee Salter, Mike Saward, Jeff Seifert, Amy Spinetta, James Stanyer, Tom Steinberg, Paul A. Taylor, Steven Ward, Darrell West, Graham Wilson, Yorick Wilks, and Steve Woolgar. A period as a Visiting Scholar at the American Political Science Association Centennial Center in Washington, D.C. (organized by Sean Twombly), was immensely helpful.

My sincere thanks go to the seven anonymous referees who commented on the original book proposal and the four anonymous readers who undertook the task of reviewing the manuscript. They have undoubtedly improved the book. I also owe a considerable debt to several cohorts of students in my undergraduate and postgraduate courses at Royal Holloway, University of London, as well as my inspirational doctoral students.

Acknowledgments

The relationship between author and publisher is an essential ingredient in producing any book, and I have been fortunate enough to have worked with an excellent team at OUP: Peter Labella, Sean Mahoney, Celeste Alexander, and Shiwani Srivastava in New York and Sue Dempsey in Oxford. My special thanks go to Peter Labella, for his enthusiasm for the subject, judicious combination of patience and eagerness, and spookily British sense of humor about the freezing New England winter—all qualities that greatly assisted this transatlantic effort.

Despite forecasts of its demise, the library continues to be the hub of academic life—a good case study in institutional adaptation. Staff at the following helped with the research process, the most crucial aspect of any book: the Bedford and Founders Libraries at Royal Holloway, University of London; the British Library of Political and Economic Science at the London School of Economics; and the University of London Library at Senate House. A special thank you must go to the long-suffering interlibrary loans department at Royal Holloway, for putting up with my ridiculously burdensome requests for books and articles, and the library staff responsible for interfacing Royal Holloway's networks with now-indispensable global e-journals systems.

In sections of the book I have made use of data from the Pew Internet and American Life Project. In accordance with its guidelines, I would like to state that the Project bears no responsibility for the interpretations or conclusions based on my analysis of the data.

Internet politics is a fast-moving area. Factual material can quickly become outdated. Fortunately, I can try to offset this when updating the accompanying website. But any errors or shortcomings in this book are, of course, my own.

Last, but by no means least, I would like to thank my family and friends outside academia, for continually resisting the urge to tell me to "get a proper job."

Andrew Chadwick

INTERNET POLITICS

INTRODUCTION

Information is the oxygen of the modern age. It seeps through the walls topped by barbed wire, it wafts across the electrified borders.

—RONALD REAGAN, *speech in London, June 1989*

CHAPTER OVERVIEW

This introductory chapter briefly sets out the book's organizing perspective before discussing some of the main characteristics of the Internet, including its size and scope and how it differs from other forms of media, notably the press and television. The chapter also provides a summary guide to the rest of the book.

In the developed world, the Internet is now ubiquitous. The issue is no longer *whether* politics is online, but *in what form and with what consequences?* Even in the developing world, the Internet is diffusing at a breathtaking rate. My aim in this book is to provide a clear, accessible, and comprehensive overview of the politics of the Internet—one that synthesizes the best contemporary scholarly research rather than the hype and speculation that bedevils both mainstream media coverage and the "gray literature" of consultants, think tanks, corporations, and self-appointed experts. The overriding question driving my account is this: is the Internet, by reconfiguring the relations between states and between citizens and states, causing fundamental shifts in patterns of governance? Put more bluntly, is the Internet changing how we do politics and how we think about politics? To address these issues, I focus on key contemporary debates about the role and influence of the Internet and related technologies on the values, processes, and outcomes of public bureaucracies; representative institutions, including political parties and legislatures; pressure groups; social movements; and global governance institutions. I also examine persistent and controversial policy problems brought up by the Internet: the digital divide; the governance of the Internet itself; the tensions between security and privacy; and the economic power of the Internet media sector. The approach is mostly comparative. I draw on examples from around the world, but in order to make the material familiar to my intended readership, my principal focus is on the politics of the United States and Britain.

WHY INTERNET POLITICS?

Over the last decade, political actors of all kinds have become much more closely involved in the production, consumption, and regulation of information and communication technologies than they were when the Internet first emerged. This is not to say that states were not involved in the Internet's development. As we shall see in chapter 3, the U.S. federal government played an influential role in fostering computer networking during the 1960s. However, only in the last few years have political actors sought to harness its potential, regulate it, and sanction the development of new legal regimes to deal with its various by-products, like copyright infringement, new economic monopolies, or privacy and surveillance issues. This book is about this changing terrain. Its organizing assumption is that the Internet is now more heavily politicized than at any time in its short history, and this trend is only likely to intensify.

This politicization—a struggle for control, coupled with new uses of its technologies for political ends—is what will condition the Internet's development in the coming years. Political actors are increasingly attempting to use the Internet to enhance their presence and legitimize their activities in ways that are genuinely new but which still have affinities with older media strategies long ago designed for traditional print and broadcast media. States are increasingly attempting to regulate social and political behavior online and are monitoring the use of the Internet by groups and movements considered to be a threat to political stability and the interests of key economic actors. In the meantime, such economic actors are themselves lobbying governments to act to protect their positions. States are seeking to use the Net to position themselves in civil societal networks, to plug their actions into currents of political opinion which, in postindustrial societies, are increasingly intertwined with lifestyle choices and consumer values—both important drivers of the contemporary Internet (Bennett, 1998). At the same time, the networks of Internet-based movements and subcultures are continuing to thrive and expand away from states.

The often tense relationship between states and their civil societies will continue to cause political antagonisms. Linkages between existing political structures and these movements, sometimes stimulated from above, sometimes from below, are forming, as developments like e-democracy and Internet-enabled grassroots mobilization are energizing traditional forms of civic engagement. Similar processes of politicization are occurring at the international level and are clustering around the vexed issue of how to govern and regulate the Internet itself, the increasingly important digital divide between the developed and the developing countries, as well as threats to state security, real and imagined, from global terrorist networks. Political actors are much more intelligent in their use of the Internet than they were during its early days. Yet in the final analysis, the Net is not as easy to control as other aspects of civil society, and its fluid, dynamic nature is what makes the subject so fascinating.

The politics of the Internet are shot through with tensions, paradoxes, and contradictions. How are we able to make sense of them? How can we cut a path through the jungle? In this book, I try to cut such a path in two ways. First, I focus on political institutions. In the sphere of politics, as Philip Agre (2002) argues, institutions vary from the instantly recognizable—parties, executives, legislatures, interest groups, international organizations, social movements—to those that are less visible but still crucial, such as law, electoral processes, parliamentary procedure, norms of civility, or bureaucratic rules, to mention but a few. Such political institutions play an important role in shaping perceptions, define what is possible, and contribute to the creation and maintenance of political identity. A key point here is that institutions are generally persistent; they last because they are perceived as necessary for the achievement of specific goals. This is not to say that institutions do not change or even break down, but it is to argue that the kinds of changes that are produced by new technologies should not be seen as self-evident and will inevitably be refracted through the lenses of existing institutional practices. In part 2 of the book, I examine how some of the central institutional features of politics are being affected by the Internet.

This focus on institutions, though important, does not, however, tell us the whole story about Internet politics. First, there is much in the argument that the Internet has so far proved to be a major source of institutional innovation. Although what happens politically on the Internet maps onto existing non-Internet institutional forms, the Net has created new types of rules, norms, procedures, and social goals. In other words, the Net is itself a source of institutional innovation; it creates some new institutions of its own. Indeed, though it might be stretching the point, I would argue that the ways in which the Internet organizes and reorganizes systems of communication renders it an institutional form in its own right. As Lance Bennett has argued with reference to new forms of global activism, communicative practices "also operate as social organizational resources" (Bennett, 2003a: 150). In other words, they can have the force of institutions. Focusing on pre-Internet institutions alone might risk missing out on exploring these new dimensions of institutionality.

There is a second reason why an institutional focus might prove limiting: it often tends to encourage a singular focus on a particular institution or maybe how a couple of institutions (for example, parliaments and executives) interact. This kind of approach tends to obscure how policy problems emerge from a more complex context of cross-cutting jurisdictions involving different institutional players with different motivations. In such cases it pays to focus on the set of *issues* that bring different political actors together to argue, set the agenda, establish new institutions, and compete for scarce resources. In part 3, I turn to a consideration of the most controversial Internet policy issues that have emerged and are still evolving.

WHAT IS THE INTERNET? TWO PRELIMINARY ANSWERS

Like any communication medium, the Internet has been the subject of a wide variety of interpretations, and the most important contours of this debate are explored throughout the rest of the book. There are, however, some basic features of the Internet that are useful to grasp at the outset. In the next chapter, I consider some conceptual tools in more detail, and in chapter 3 I trace the history of the Internet. But it will be useful here to answer the question "What is the Internet?" by reflecting on how it differs from other forms of media.

A Technical Answer

We can provide what we might term a technical answer by focusing on what really allows the Internet to work in the way that is does: networks, common technical standards, and protocols.[1] The Internet is not a single entity but a collection of entities, a relatively decentralized network of networks. This network of networks joins together hundreds of millions of computing and communication devices of varying types, running various software programs. Due to the way Internet communication is designed, particularly the way in which data is split into small chunks before being transmitted, you do not need a direct connection to another computer to successfully send and receive information, and you do not need to know the precise route through which your message should be sent. What allows these different computers and networks to communicate are common standards and software protocols. There are many different ways of using the Internet, but one thing they all have in common is that they must interface with these established standards and protocols. As the Internet has developed since the 1960s, these have been consciously designed, adopted, and refined. Development has historically been open to all those with an interest in a particular area and the technical ability to contribute. Once adopted, these standards and protocols are published and remain in the public realm, making it very difficult for any single entity, be it a corporation or a state, to exert decisive control over how and for what purpose the Internet is used. This, in a technical sense, is the Internet.

A Comparative Answer

If we depart from this rather brief technical definition of the Internet as a network of networks, we might begin to think about providing a second answer to the question. We can do this by comparing the Net with other types of communication media. Throughout history, when new communication technologies have emerged, commentators have tended to try to understand them in terms of what came before. Printed books were compared with handwritten manuscripts, telegrams were compared with letters, the telephone with telegrams, radio with newspapers, television with radio. The Internet has not been immune from this type of understanding, with good reason. Like other media, it borrows heavily from its predecessors in terms of the organization of its content, its visual genres, and how it may be used.

In other respects, though, the Net is very different from other forms of mass communication (newspapers, radio, and television) and personal communication (like the telegram and the telephone). Consider the kinds of networks of communication that these older technologies establish. Newspapers, radio, and television, at least in the days before the World Wide Web started to change how they operate, were predominantly "one-to-many" media. A single information product is created by a relatively restricted group of people (journalists, program makers) and distributed to large numbers of people (readers, listeners, and viewers). At the same time, telegrams and the telephone were

---

[1]**Technical standards and protocols:** agreed-upon principles and rules, sanctioned by the Internet Society (ISOC), that govern common ways of communicating on Internet networks.

predominantly "one-to-one" forms of communication. You usually establish a direct connection with another person to hold a telephone conversation. There are some important exceptions to these models. Newspapers have always had letters pages, radio and television have long featured phone-in shows, and other types of interactivity have been made possible by the rise of digital cable and satellite technology. Even telephones may be used to hold conference calls involving several participants. But as a shorthand description of how these pre-Internet media worked, "one-to-many" and "one-to-one" do a pretty good job.

Now, consider the Internet in light of this approach. Technologies such as email, chat, and instant messaging allow one-to-one forms of communication. Web pages and online document and file repositories involve one-to-many communication. We need to go further, though, if we are to encompass all of the communication that occurs on the Internet. This is where two further categories come in handy: "many-to-many" and "many-to-one." Through technologies like Usenet,[2] discussion boards, mailing lists, weblogs (blogs),[3] and peer-to-peer networks,[4] the Net facilitates "many-to-many" communication in which large numbers of people simultaneously produce and receive information. Email, feedback forms, and online polls allow "many-to-one" communication by giving many users the chance to send information directly to the producer of a website, the author of a message on a discussion board, or a politician.

Again, as with newspapers, radio, and television, there are exceptions to the rules, and in the case of the Internet, these exceptions are important because they complicate matters still further. Email, for instance, is used for more than one-to-one communication, because it is increasingly employed for promotional purposes, such as political advertising, as a one-to-many medium. It is even possible to use instant messaging and chat in this way. A web page may appear at first glance to be a simple one-to-many device, but often web pages are composed of information, such as news feeds, from many different sources that have been brought together by automated scripts that dynamically update content without human intervention. Web pages may also contain discussion forums alongside more traditional forms of content. Understood in this way, they start to resemble many-to-many communication. Internet radio that is interactively shaped by listeners who choose which songs to be added to the playlist in real time complicates

---

[2]**Usenet:** The multiple networks and host computers that allow asynchronous newsgroup discussions to take place. Newsgroups are online discussion and bulletin boards. In the early 1980s, there were a few dozen such groups. Now there are at least one hundred thousand, though many of these are unofficial and not carried by all newsgroup providers.

[3]**Blogs:** Websites containing postings, usually in reverse chronological order. Blog software allows individuals or groups to post news items quickly and easily using a simple web browser interface. Most include search functions, systems of categorization, and cross-referencing. They also include simple means by which readers can post reactions to others' comments and automate the sharing of news and others' blog entries (see also chapters 6, 7, and 12).

[4]**Peer-to-peer networks:** A network without a server, in which all connected computers have theoretical equality. These may be small, connecting as few as two computers in an organization. More often, and controversially, they may consist of millions of users involved in anonymous file sharing across the Internet. The absence of a central server makes genuine peer-to-peer networks very difficult to monitor and virtually impossible to close down (see also chapter 12).

the traditional one-to-many characteristics of that medium. The spread of broadband[5] connectivity means that broadcast-quality audio and video can now be transmitted using the Internet. Political advertisements designed for television are now a common feature of the websites of political parties and presidential candidates. It is likely that some parts of the web will start to resemble traditional broadcast television channels in the near future as broadband connections speed up.

These and other phenomena point to the relatively complex nature of the Internet as a communication medium or, rather, set of media. Some of these are facets of convergence—the idea that the Internet is developing into a giant grid which will eventually carry all forms of electronic communication. But one does not have to subscribe to convergence theory to see that the Net already mixes attributes from most previous forms of communication.

All of this has implications for the kinds of authority and control that may be exercised over the Internet and the levels of resistance that may be achieved by less-powerful groups, whose voices may be absent from mainstream channels like the press and television. Ordinary citizens and the politically marginalized are no longer wholly dependent upon the ways in which the traditionally dominant broadcast media construct their identities or selectively frame political grievances. Political communication on the Internet becomes, in the words of Douglas Kellner, "more decentered and varied in its origins, scope and effects" (1999:103). The relative speed and fluidity of cyberspace sometimes allows marginal groups to thrust their agenda into the political mainstream (Mitra, 2001:34). The authoritative status of powerful institutional players, be they governments, corporations, or mainstream media, has been loosened.

For some, the very notion of authoritative communication has been challenged (Mitra, 2001). Institutional power in the offline world certainly travels over to the online world, but power in cyberspace is much more fragile and contingent. The website of a major media corporation, like CNN, for instance, may be located toward the center of the Internet's constellation of news websites, but for many readers it is simply a staging post on a journey through a whole range of seemingly marginal sites. In fact, media organizations facilitate this when they deliberately provide follow-up links in their stories, pointing the reader to a collection of different sources, encouraging her to explore the issues for herself. Cyberspace also messes with many of the traditional spatial and temporal rhythms of news production, allowing outsider groups to intervene where the major media players leave gaps (Leizerov, 2000:466). Compared with the relatively passive consumption of broadcasting, cyberspace is a more interactive and participatory communication ecosystem in which it becomes more difficult for the powerful to intervene to draw discussion to a close.

Comparing the Internet with other media also reminds us that some media are easier to regulate than others. In the past, states have dealt with the emergence of new media by developing policies and regulatory structures suited to the particular problems brought up by the technologies and the contexts in which they are used. At the same time, there are usually prevalent economic structures that tend to shape access to media.

---

[5]**Broadband:** very high speed data networks that make it possible to deliver broadcast- or near-broadcast-quality audio and video across the Internet.

Television, for example, is a highly restricted and regulated form of media, not only in those countries, like Britain, where there are powerful state-owned broadcasting organizations (the BBC), but also in countries (for example, the United States) where television companies are mostly privately owned. States use laws and standards to regulate the content of television, to varying extents depending on national contexts, and the costs of starting and running a television company are huge—a fact which excludes the vast majority of people. There are ongoing debates about the role of private companies in broadcasting, for instance in Italy, where Silvio Berlusconi has used his ownership of television stations to help his own political career. In countries with strong state-owned broadcast networks, there are always debates about the power of governments to determine content. But despite these familiar policy problems, regulating television is actually pretty straightforward in comparison with the Internet. Television is primarily a one-to-many medium, with high entry costs and, despite the emergence of satellites and the globalization of the entertainment industry, is often very "national" in its orientation, especially if we consider popular programming such as news, drama, and sports.

In contrast, it is very difficult for governments to regulate and control access to Internet content. Some governments have tried and have achieved surprising successes, most notably, as we shall see in chapter 11, in authoritarian systems such as China and Singapore. Physical seizure of computers is one option, as is state rationing of access to telecommunication infrastructure. But, as Michael Froomkin puts it, "What most governments still cannot effectively do, short of full-time keystroke, screen capture, or processor-level surveillance, is prevent even a slightly motivated person from accessing material available online" (2003:780). There are well-known technical fixes for state censorship, such as using proxy servers, encryption, and other anonymity tools to route around controls. This is not to say that the Internet cannot be regulated, as has often been claimed. Rather, the comparative difficulty of regulating it depends upon the continuation of its current standards and protocols. And, as we shall see in chapters 9 and 10, these are ultimately determined not by any single national government, but by nonstate actors at the international level, organized in bodies such as the Internet Engineering Task Force (IETF), the International Telecommunication Union (ITU), and the Internet Corporation for Assigned Names and Numbers (ICANN).

Returning to our question "What is the Internet?," if we combine the technical answer and the comparative answer above, we have the formulation in exhibit 1.1. Brief definitions such as this must carry a health warning. One of the challenges of studying Internet politics is the fact that the technology is continually evolving. Many of the assumptions about how the Internet worked ten years ago, both in terms of its speed,

EXHIBIT 1.1. WHAT IS THE INTERNET?

The Internet is a network of networks of one-to-one, one-to-many, many-to-many, and many-to-one local, national, and global information and communication technologies with relatively open standards and protocols and comparatively low barriers to entry.

accessibility, and typical software applications, are steadily being eroded. It is therefore important to be aware of a number of transitional trends that developed countries are currently experiencing (Wellman et al., 2003). Such trends are already having an impact on expectations about the social and political impact of the Internet.

First, as broadband connections increase, the era of bandwidth[6] scarcity is drawing to a close. The Internet is moving from a primarily textual and still-picture medium toward a richer form, in which text, still graphics, audio, and video communication frequently converge as a matter of course. Second, permanent broadband connections make the Internet much more like an everyday utility, like electricity. They also root Internet forms of communication more securely in everyday life. No longer having to "log on" by dialing up to an Internet service provider (ISP) means greater fluidity of movement between communications in the proximate environment and those which occur across the Internet. The perceived differences between face-to-face and electronic communication over distance are likely to soften. The diffusion of wireless devices— cell phones and handheld computers—is accentuating this. A third trend is that Internet technologies increasingly allow minute levels of personalization (Wellman et al., 2003). This creates a radically individualized environment in which it is more difficult for policy makers to count on a coherent national, or even local, political community that it can assume has been exposed to broadly similar media content. Again, wireless connectivity intensifies personalization because it is based on the assumption of connecting discrete individuals rather than households or other physical locations. Fourth, within developed countries, the digital divide is starting to narrow. While digital inequality will undoubtedly continue, the simple conception of the digital divide as being based upon those who have access to the Internet and those who do not is decreasing in significance. The Internet is no longer restricted to nerds, geeks, and techies and is continuing to diffuse at a remarkable rate. Single-country studies such as those produced by the respected Pew Internet and American Life Project document how time spent online has increased in recent years and how applications like email and instant messaging have now eclipsed the telephone as the principal means of communication for some social groups.

Despite forecasts of the Internet's demise, in fact these trends point to a future in which more and more aspects of communication become dependent upon the Internet. Visions of the Internet-enabled toaster during the dotcom bubble of the late 1990s were clearly ludicrous, but increasingly many communication technologies will overlap or converge on Internet forms of delivery and communication, if they haven't done so already. For example, cell phones increasingly interface with the Internet. Cable television companies already package Internet access with their television products and have started to use Internet networks to broadcast. Telecommunications operators now deliver television and video over copper-wired Digital Subscriber Line (DSL) networks originally designed for simple telephony. Owners of the TiVo personal video recorder are now using the Internet to program their boxes from remote locations and share recordings and photographs with others using the Internet. Meanwhile, Microsoft is

---

[6]**Bandwidth:** a term used to refer to the speed at which information may travel across a network. High bandwidth network connections allow for faster transmission of information.

investing heavily in its bid to introduce computers to the living room through its Media Center software. These and many other developments are being reinforced by the development of a new version of the Internet Protocol, IPv6, which will make it easier for a range of disparate devices to communicate across Internet networks. Convergence upon the Internet seems to be well underway. Hence my decision to entitle this book *Internet Politics*, rather than "new media politics" or "information society politics."

THE SIZE AND SCOPE OF THE INTERNET

If defining the Internet is fraught with pitfalls, so is assessing its size and scope. Most of the problems arise from the fluidity of the medium itself. Websites come and go, so how reliable is a snapshot? Measuring the different types of communication that occur across the Net, from email to chat to simple web browsing, is incredibly difficult, due the transient nature of many of these forms of activity. Chat, for instance, is often nothing more than flows of data. These challenges are very real but they have not deterred people from attempting to estimate the Internet's reach. The blunt fact is that there is never likely to be universal agreement on how to measure such a complex phenomenon; the best we can do is provide a number of different estimates. In chapter 4, I analyze the digital divide in terms of global disparities in Internet access as well as more subtle differences within the developed world. But it pays to consider a few inescapable facts and trends at this introductory stage in our journey.

An effective and reasonably accurate way of measuring the growth of the Internet is the Internet Domain Survey host count. A host is usually a single device connected to the Internet or a machine that acts as several hosts through a method known as virtual hosting. The advantage is that measuring hosts connected to the Net gives us an idea of the physical extent of the global network. However it does not, on its own, tell us anything accurate about user numbers.

Figure 1.1 reveals the massive growth in hosts connected to the Internet since the early 1990s. In January 1991, there were about 376,000 hosts around the globe. By 1995, there were around 5.8 million. In January 2000, just before the height of the dotcom era,

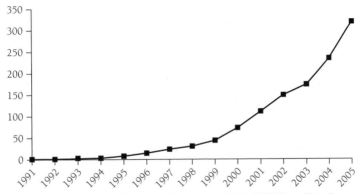

Figure 1.1. Estimated Internet host count, 1991–2005 (in millions).
Source: Internet Systems Consortium, 2005.

Table 1.1. Estimated Global Internet Users in 2002 and 2004

Survey	Global Users 2002	Global Users 2004
ITU	627 million	676 million*
CIA World Factbook	604 million	Not updated
NUA	606 million	Not updated
Internet World Stats	587 million	798 million
Computer Industry Almanac	665 million	945 million
Mean	**618 million**	**806 million**

Sources: Analysis of data from ITU, 2004a; U.S. Central Intelligence Agency (CIA), 2003; *Computer Industry Almanac,* 2004; NUA, 2004.

Note: *Based on 2003 projections.

the host count had increased more than sixfold, to 72 million. But perhaps the most staggering fact is that, since 2000, the Internet has continued to grow at a massive pace, reaching around 233 million hosts in January 2004. Growth is even more impressive if we go back to the 1980s. This graph does not show data for that decade, but the Internet Systems Consortium surveys do go back that far, and they estimate that there were just 562 hosts connected globally in 1983 (Internet Systems Consortium, 2005).

Internet size can also be understood in terms of user numbers. The problems here are manifold. Reputable global surveys that publish their methodology are thin on the ground. There is very little reliable historical data that go back much further than 1998, and surveys differ in how they define an active user. For example, some identify "active users" as those who may go online every day or as little as twice a month, while other surveys define "active users" as those who have only accessed the Internet once in the last three months. Some surveys include children, while others use different age cutoff points. Some include those who use the Net only at work, while others only record usage in the home.

A common response to this methodological minefield is the one adopted by organizations that aggregate other surveys in order to arrive at an educated guess at the global Internet population. The ITU survey adopts such an approach. Its methodology is open to criticism, but its data have been used for several years as basic indicators of global user numbers. Another alternative is the U.S. Central Intelligence Agency (CIA) *World Factbook,* but this publication only started to collect usage data in 2000.

To give a flavor of how Internet user number data can vary, consider the examples for 2002 and 2004, taken from some of the most well-known sources (table 1.1). These figures vary tremendously, but perhaps it is more surprising that they are so alike. There is a rough trend here, which is that global user numbers in 2004 were around the 800 million mark. The global population, according to the *CIA World Factbook* of 2003, is estimated at 6.3 billion. Thus, in 2004, about 13 percent of the world population were Internet users, variously defined.

Single-year data provide crude snapshots, but what about the growth in user numbers over time? Probably the most reliable and complete data over a period of years derive from the ITU's annual surveys (figure 1.2). In 1991, there were just 4.4 million users. By 1995, this had increased nearly tenfold, to 40 million. At the height of the dotcom boom in 2000, there were 399 million users. By 2003, the last year for which we have ITU figures, this had swollen to 676 million. This chart reveals spectacular growth

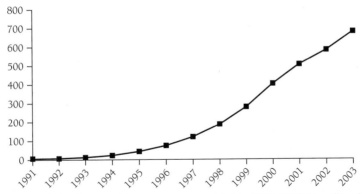

Figure 1.2. Estimated Internet users worldwide, 1991–2003 (in millions).
Source: ITU, 2005.

in user numbers since the mid-1990s, but more interestingly, it also broadly matches the trends that we observed above in the data for host counts.

These two very rough ways of measuring the Internet—hosts and ITU user data—give us an idea of its size and phenomenal growth. However, they also reveal the Net to be very much a minority pursuit, judged in terms of the percentage of the global population defined as users. But a word of caution is necessary: beyond this they tell us very little. There are many other revealing ways of measuring Internet diffusion and use that will help us understand the debate over the digital divide between the information haves and have-nots. These will be covered in some detail in chapter 4.

Once again, though, when considering these big picture numbers, it pays to think about the real significance of the Internet in comparison with other forms of media. According to the ITU, in 2002 there were an estimated 1.62 billion television receivers in the world—nearly ten times the number of hosts (machines) connected to the Internet and almost three times the number of Internet users (International Telecommunication Union, 2003d). At first glance, then, television is a much bigger global medium than the Internet. However, this assumption misses a crucial difference between the two. While a computer connected to the Net grants you potential (if not actual) access to all parts of a global network, owning a television does not. You may view television programs that have been imported from another country by a company based in your own. If you have relatively sophisticated satellite technology, you may even be able to watch simultaneously as programs are broadcast in other countries around the world. Yet the former relies on national gatekeepers—those who run the national television company in question—while the latter is not a widespread practice. What makes the Internet entirely different is its potentially global user base. Despite the fact that the vast majority of the world's inhabitants lack access, it is the largest *global* communication medium, by a long way.

OUTLINE OF THE BOOK

This book is divided into three broad sections, which I have labeled "Contexts," "Institutions," and "Issues and Controversies."

The first section provides a series of contexts within which Internet politics may be understood. We begin with chapter 2, which outlines some concepts and themes which underpin the material in the book. It briefly discusses two dominant conceptual understandings of the relationship between technology and politics—technological determinism and social determinism—before defining a middle-way approach. It then goes on to explore eight key themes for understanding Internet politics that recur throughout the rest of the text: decentralization; participation; community; globalization; postindustrialization; rationalization; governance; and libertarianism.

Chapter 3 provides a brief history of the Internet. Its diverse range of actors, interests, and institutions, its paradoxes and ideological clashes, preface many of the issues that are covered in the rest of the book. The chapter illustrates how a curious mixture of technical innovation, state control, voluntarism, do-it-yourself "home-brew" culture, transnational collaboration, and commercial competition have conditioned the Internet's technical and political development.

The last of the contextual chapters (chapter 4) examines the digital divide—probably one of the most commonly used phrases in academic and popular writing about the Internet. As we shall discover, there is not a single divide but several. Yet the concept remains a useful shorthand term for the persistent inequalities that exist between the info-rich and the info-poor, both in terms of the global divisions among the developed, the developing, and the least-developed countries as well as those within even the most advanced postindustrial nations like the United States.

The second section of the book covers the Internet's impact on core political institutions. Chapter 5 considers the potential for the Internet to enhance community cohesion, political deliberation, and participation through what is now commonly termed "e-democracy." It begins by tracing the origins of contemporary arguments in favor of using technology to increase civic engagement. It then considers a range of examples and trends in this area, including community networks, the development of online political communities, and attempts by governments to involve citizens in policy making through online mechanisms. Finally, I provide an assessment of e-democracy, focusing on two key concepts: social capital and the public sphere.

The topic of chapter 6 is e-mobilization—a shorthand term for uses of the Internet by interest groups and social movements for political recruitment, organization, and campaigning. The chapter is structured around three main themes: organizational change among traditional interest groups; new forms of transnational mobilization; and "pure" Internet forms of direct action using methods that only apply in the online world. In the final section of the chapter, I assess interpretations of the difference the Internet makes in this sphere.

We then move on to chapter 7, in which I consider the impact of the Internet on parties and election campaigning. Following a contextual discussion of recent challenges to political parties, I examine the evolution of online campaigning in the United States and the United Kingdom. An extended case study of the 2003–2004 primary and presidential campaigns illustrates several key shifts in this area. Finally, I assess how and why the Internet might be reconfiguring election campaigning by focusing on three themes: party competition, power diffusion, and institutional adaptation.

In chapter 8, the last of those dealing with the Internet's impact upon institutions, I examine e-government. I begin by considering the origins of e-government in the new public management ideas of the 1990s. Then, I examine some of its tensions and paradoxes, by concentrating on four main themes: cost reduction, coordination, effectiveness, and democratization. The last of these is particularly important: is e-government about better government or better democracy? The chapter concludes by discussing some interpretations of how the Internet may be reconfiguring power relations, both within bureaucracies and between bureaucracies and other parts of the political system.

Part 3 of the book examines four persistent issues and controversies that have accompanied the Internet's development.

Chapter 9 looks at the recent emergence of a new global information society regime. This is composed of a range of international organizations, nongovernmental actors, and business associations whose main aim is to influence the frameworks within which Internet policy discussions will occur over the coming years. At present, the global agenda is split between those who argue that the Internet and other information and communication technologies should form part of a socially responsible approach to development and those who wish to open up markets in developing countries for information technology and e-commerce companies in the developed world to exploit. Many of these organizations appear at various points throughout the subsequent chapter—on the rise of Internet governance—so this also serves as a preliminary roadmap.

Chapter 10 examines recent international attempts to provide a governance structure for the Internet, particularly the emergence and current workings of what many commentators perceive to be a new regulatory regime or even global government for policing the Internet: the deeply controversial Internet Corporation for Assigned Names and Numbers (ICANN). The chapter traces the emergence of Internet governance from a policy crisis in the late 1990s involving a range of different political actors. I examine how the emerging system is being shaped, how actors in the global system are increasingly attempting to regulate and steer the Internet, and some of the implications for its future development.

Chapter 11 explores how the Internet reconfigures the relationship between surveillance, privacy, and security. It considers state-initiated surveillance in two distinct though interrelated forms. Intrastate surveillance concerns attempts by states to monitor the Internet use of their populations, as a way of dealing with harmful content, crime, subversion, and terrorism. Interstate surveillance concerns states' roles in the international sphere, where they attempt to monitor external threats to national security by intercepting global Internet communications or defending themselves against (or even launching their own) "cyberwarfare" attacks. The chapter also considers how businesses use the Net to gather, process, match, and integrate personal information. The line between state and corporate surveillance is itself blurring, as states seek to extend their reach through methods such as data mining. The Internet is implicated in all of these areas, either as an object of surveillance or as part of the infrastructure which allows law enforcement and corporate actors to more efficiently distribute information around information systems. Such developments have important implications for individual privacy.

In chapter 12, I consider whether the Internet is changing the political economy of the media and entertainment industries. This is a potentially vast area, so I focus on three particularly controversial themes: ownership in the Internet media sector; the production and distribution of news; and the politics of intellectual property. To illuminate these areas, the chapter adopts a critical political economy perspective, which involves a focus on how economic inequalities shape the range of media content available in market-based societies. My overriding question is whether the Internet is reinforcing or threatening established economic inequalities in the broader media. Is it having a leveling effect by creating opportunities for new market entrants to spoil the party of the big media companies? Is it creating a newly diverse and pluralistic media landscape? Or are Internet media simply "business as usual"?

In the final chapter, I take a brief look at the likely short-to-medium-term future of Internet politics. My strategy there is to attempt to trace forward some of the key developments that we have encountered throughout the book.

Discussion Points

- Why is it so difficult to define the Internet?
- How does the Internet differ from other media?
- Is media convergence a myth?
- Why is measuring the size and scope of the Internet problematic?

Further Reading

A highly readable introduction to the Internet, including its technical characteristics (which I cover in more detail in chapter 3), can be found in Naughton, 1999. Kellner, 1999, is a lively essay on the Internet's potential to diffuse political power in comparison with other media. On the political importance of technical standards, see Froomkin, 2003. Wellman et al., 2003, provides a good overview of trends toward convergence and its effects in embedding the Internet in everyday life, as does the Convergence Center, Syracuse University, at http://dcc.syr.edu. For Internet and other technology diffusion statistics, the best place to start is the ITU website at http://www.itu.int.

PART I

CONTEXTS

INTERNET POLITICS

Some Conceptual Tools

Tear up what you know or think you know about politics. It's all changing.
— DICK MORRIS, 1999

Politics on the Internet is politics as usual.
— MICHAEL MARGOLIS AND DAVID RESNICK, 2000

CHAPTER OVERVIEW

The aim of this chapter is to outline some concepts and themes which underpin Internet politics. It briefly discusses two dominant understandings of the relationship between technology and political life, technological determinism and social determinism, before defining a middle-way approach. It then goes on to explore eight key themes for understanding Internet politics that recur throughout the rest of the book: decentralization; participation; community; globalization; postindustrialization; rationalization; governance; and libertarianism.

In the previous chapter we briefly examined the nature of the Internet and some aspects of its growth and scale. But making sense of the politics of the Internet also requires that we think about both the nature of technology and broader conceptual debates about its impact. This is especially important for a technology whose emergence has sparked off a whole range of discussions about its potential to cause radical transformations.

THE POLITICAL NATURE OF TECHNOLOGIES

In what sense can a technology or set of technologies be said to be political or have political consequences? Obviously this is a huge issue and cannot be dealt with in its entirety here. However, it will help to sketch out the broad contours of the position that informs my own approach because it gives an indication of the kinds of questions and issues that I consider important in this book.

There is a long-running debate, conducted across all of the social sciences, about the nature of technology and the role it plays in social, economic, and political life (Feenberg, 1999). Since the nineteenth century, this has most often been couched in broad terms as a battle between technological determinism and social determinism. By technological determinism, I mean the view that "technology develops as the sole result of an internal dynamic and then, unmediated by any other influence, molds society to fit its patterns" (Winner, 1988:35). By social determinism, I mean the view that technologies are neutral tools and that non-technological forces such as social class, political power, or even individual personalities have an independent effect on how they are designed and controlled. Some writers have demonstrated that the dispute between the two approaches can be traced back to ancient times, and most philosophical traditions contain some reference to the role played by new forms of technology in altering or sustaining particular social, economic, and political institutions (Mumford, 1967; Winner, 1977).

Technological Determinism

Technological determinism often gets a bad press, but in fact it has a long and venerable history (Roe Smith and Marx, 1994). For some, many of the most eloquent statements of technological determinism can be found in the writings of Karl Marx, whose entire theory of history, and of social and political development, was based on the notion that the material basis of society is the primary motor of social, economic, and, ultimately, political change. At the same time, however, it is important to recall that Marx was also concerned with agency: the ways in which humans, acting in concert, can sometimes shape social processes. Thus, even though Marxism may be seen as technologically determinist, it is more subtle than is usually recognized when it comes to understanding how humans mold technological change.

More recently, a rash of optimistic writings has emerged which claim that new communication technologies have ushered in a new age, an information society which differs fundamentally from the societal orders of the past (Webster, 2002). As Christopher May has argued, many accounts presume that certain technologies "embody specific norms" (May, 2002:25). It has been claimed, as we shall see, that the Internet embodies values like freedom, community, equality, altruism, and democracy. At the same time, it has been argued that the Internet embodies values like social control, discipline, and hierarchy. Whatever the content, it is the *idea* that technological forms have their own inherent properties and that these are beyond the scope of human intervention which characterizes technological determinism. There are those who argue that such is the pervasiveness of technologies: their inherent properties can be used to predict future social, economic, and political change.

Social Determinism

Lining up against much-maligned technological determinism is the more popular social determinist perspective, sometimes known as the "social shaping of technology" approach (Mackenzie and Wajcman, 1999). Most closely associated with a group of post-war writers such as Lewis Mumford (1967) and Jacques Ellul (1964), in its undiluted form, this presumes that specific technologies do not in themselves matter much at all. Social scientists, it is assumed, merely need to reconstruct the social context of technological change to explain all that is considered to be important. Using the example of the Internet again, the social determinist argues that it is nothing particularly distinctive or new and that we can make sense of its effects by referring to preexisting models of social and political change. If technology is presumed to be nothing special, we need only examine the social forces that produced it—the power struggles and the influential groups, classes, individuals, and institutions which initiated and subsequently shaped technological change. This does not mean that there are not going to be disputes about the impact of the Internet. It does mean, however, that those disputes will tend to center on the usefulness of competing, often very general models of social scientific explanation. In other words, technology becomes just another policy area, like transport, health, or agriculture, for instance.

Having It Both Ways: Political Technologies in Political Contexts

While this simple conflict between technological and social determinism might make comfortable and familiar reading, it does not get us very far in making sense of the politics of the Internet. It is simply too convenient to assume, as do technological determinists, that the technology is all that matters and that we can understand its effects by examining its innate properties. It is equally problematic to go along entirely with the social determinists and assume that the features of a technology have no bearing on how it may be used politically. Instead, we can arrive at a more fruitful and illuminating position—one that recognizes that technologies have political properties while simultaneously placing their use in political contexts. We can do so by drawing upon the ideas of the political theorist Langdon Winner (see exhibit 2.1).

EXHIBIT 2.1. POLITICAL TECHNOLOGIES IN POLITICAL CONTEXTS: LANGDON WINNER'S PERSPECTIVE

"The things we call 'technologies' are ways of building order in our world. Many technical devices and systems important in everyday life contain possibilities for many different ways of ordering human activity. Consciously or unconsciously, deliberately or inadvertently, societies choose structures for technologies that influence how people are going to work, communicate, travel, consume, and so forth over a very long time. In the processes by which structuring decisions are made, different people are situated differently and possess unequal degrees of power as well as unequal levels of awareness. . . . The issues that divide or unite people in society are settled not only in the institutions and practices of politics proper, but also, and less obviously so, in tangible arrangements of steel and concrete, wires and semiconductors, nuts and bolts."

Source: Quoted from Winner, 1988:43.

Winner argues that there are two senses in which technologies can have political properties. First, there are examples where "the invention, design or arrangement of a specific technical device or system becomes a way of settling an issue in the affairs of a particular community." Second, there are "inherently political technologies": man-made systems that appear to require or be strongly compatible with particular kinds of political relationships (Winner, 1988:36).

The first of these categories is the least controversial. It is the argument that technologies structure and sometimes inhibit types of social and political action. To push the argument a stage further, as Winner does with his second category, is more difficult. To argue that "some technologies are by their very nature political in a specific way" (Winner, 1988:36) requires an accompanying view of technology as being quite inflexible. If the adoption of a particular technology is very likely to produce a particular social and political effect, we need to demonstrate the way that technology works internally: how certain forms of working with it are made easier than others and how the easiest or most effective ways of using it in practical, "operational" terms tend to facilitate regular, patterned, and predictable social and political outcomes.

To take one brief example, a common complaint about the Internet is that it corrodes social interaction because it is not user friendly and tends to make individuals behave in non-intuitive, or even divisive, socially destructive ways. Yet technicians may not prove too receptive to arguments about sociality and community if such values appear to threaten their expertise and the viability of the technologies themselves. It may be that "operational necessity" means that the smooth technical running of a computer system takes precedence over such social and political costs. Of course, some technicians, such as hackers or those involved with the free and open-source software (FOSS) movement, seek to enshrine values like community, democracy, equality, and freedom in the design of their software, but the principle is the same (see also chapter 12). In these types of cases, it seems helpful to acknowledge that the technologies themselves can have political characteristics, not in an absolute sense, but in terms of the constraints they impose in their everyday use—how they narrow opportunities and marginalize alternatives.

These two ways of understanding the political nature of technologies may not help in all circumstances. There may be instances where there is nothing inherently political—in Winner's second sense—about a given technology, such that it becomes necessary to take one step back and examine, in social determinist fashion, the power struggles that take place external to the technology itself. Equally, there may be occasions when a failure to grasp how a technology shapes human behavior means that we miss what is significant about a given situation. But at the very least we can begin to understand new communication technologies as political artifacts which exist in political contexts in a way that does not collapse one category into the other and which avoids many of the simplistic assumptions of technological determinism. We can think about how technologies that have certain affordances can nevertheless become the subject of what Andrew Feenberg terms "democratic rationalizations": positive human interventions that can alter how a technology works in practice (1999). It may be possible to analyze the politics of the Internet without much discussion of the technologies themselves. It may even be easier to do so, but my guiding assumption is that many of the issues around the politicization of the Net arise from the nature of the technology itself and how this, in part, structures social and political action.

Code as Law

Langdon Winner engages with a long-running historical debate about the inherent properties of technology in all of its forms, not just the Internet. But during the 1990s, a group of scholars began to focus on the nature of the Internet as a new and distinctive technology of communication. Seeking also to understand how the Internet facilitates and constrains certain forms of political behavior, such writers as Lawrence Lessig (1999), Andrew Shapiro (1999), William Mitchell (1995), Joel Reidenberg (1998, 2004), and James Boyle (1997) have argued that the technological architecture of the Net—what Reidenberg labeled "lex informatica" and Lessig called "code"—must be seen as inherently political. Lessig writes: "In real space we recognize how laws regulate—through constitutions, statutes and other legal codes. In cyberspace we must understand how code regulates—how the software and hardware that make cyberspace what it is *regulate* cyberspace as it is" (1999:6). The technological architecture of the Internet makes behavior more or less "regulable." In the "code is law" approach, however, technology is powerful but not uncontrollable; it can be designed by human intervention to embody certain values. Yet, once designed in, such values continue to exert their influence long after the founding moment.

So, once more, we see a virtuous path between technological and social determinism. The Internet is an inherently political set of technologies, but its politics are subject to decisions made in supremely political contexts. Those who own the means of architectural production—the corporations and governments who determine the types of technologies that operate in the software and hardware of the Net—emerge as new types of power brokers. This is because such forces, though they will inevitably be resisted and challenged, are often able to determine the components of network architecture that may subsequently be used to regulate behavior. And increasingly, as Reidenberg argues, regulation of behavior can be all the more effective if it works through preemptive or automated means (2004:4).

The code school uses many different examples to illustrate its argument, and I add many more throughout this book, but for now, consider Lessig's comparison of two university computer networks in the 1990s—at Chicago and Harvard (Lessig, 1999:26–28). The University of Chicago's network allowed for anonymous connections to the Internet. Users could communicate with each other anonymously and their activities were not monitored. In contrast, to access Harvard University's network, users were compelled to register their computers, anonymous communication was not permitted, and all online behavior could potentially be monitored and traced back to an individual computer. The architecture of these networks was determined by policy choices made by the senior management of the two universities. While Chicago's leaders recognized the value of anonymous communication, based, according to Lessig, on a sympathetic understanding of the First Amendment to the U.S. Constitution, Harvard's decided that it was more important to be able to trace the activities of individual users. In Chicago's case, excluding the requirement that individuals submit identifying information about themselves makes it much more difficult to determine the type of data they are producing and exchanging. Chicago's network made it relatively difficult to regulate online behavior; Harvard's made it relatively straightforward. The point is that the architecture of these two very different networks produces certain outcomes.

EIGHT KEY THEMES

If technologies have political properties but must also be situated within political contexts, we also need a broader range of concepts for making political sense of the Internet. New theoretical approaches are appearing all the time in the area of Internet studies, but when it comes to its political impact, we can identify some hardy perennials that are likely to be relevant for many years to come. An excellent distillation of these has been provided by information scientist Philip Agre (2002). The remainder of this chapter uses some of Agre's "common proposals" as its point of departure but reworks and augments them with a more explicit consideration of the international sphere of politics. In total, I sketch out eight key conceptual themes.

1. Decentralization

In the mid-1990s, when *Wired* magazine, a siren of the new economy, was founded, it became fashionable to predict the ways in which the Internet would remove intermediaries from social, economic, and political processes. "Disintermediation," one of the more useful jargon terms that emerged during the dotcom hype of the 1990s, was first used to describe the impact on stockbroker firms of the spread of technology in the stock market, but in general it came to refer to the ways in which networks can reduce the need for those who have some pre-Internet claim to expert knowledge or a traditional market position not based on the use of technology. The dotcom firm that delivered your groceries would put the complacent supermarket out of business. The sparky new online news site, set up—supposedly—at very little cost, would end the dominance of traditional newspapers, television, and radio. The fusion of online political communities with e-voting mechanisms would undermine traditional political intermediaries like parties, interest groups, legislatures, and bureaucracies. For the first time in history, it was argued, the Internet would provide the technology required to link a politically active cyber civil society and more formal decision-making processes once controlled by elite political gatekeepers. Such gatekeepers could find themselves automated out of existence by Internet-mediated opinion (Agre, 2002:312).

Yet while the Net is slowly changing the nature of the links between citizens and the established political process as well as the way we consume goods and services, it is by no means clear that gatekeepers and intermediaries are being undermined. Old intermediaries have found their skills highly relevant to the Internet age. In some cases, new intermediaries are mushrooming. Consultants specializing in spreading the gospel of e-government, e-democracy, or online campaigning abound. The political blogging explosion of the 2004 U.S. presidential election, while it energized ordinary citizens, also brought new intermediaries into the campaign process in the form of skilled and highly motivated individuals like Zephyr Teachout, who managed the technology and much of the strategy underlying Howard Dean's online campaign (McCullagh, 2004; see also chapter 7). Even academics are positioning themselves as new intermediaries, using the Internet to create networks and move out of the ivory tower into the world of think tanks and policy. Intermediaries seem here to stay.

Despite some of the problems with disintermediation theory, there is a lot of mileage in less-sweeping ideas about the Internet's effects on social and political power.

It has long been claimed that the technical architecture of the Internet will cause a power shift as the resources required for mass communication become increasingly diffused throughout societies. In this view, the Net emerges as a reaction against conglomeration and oligopoly in the global media sector as well as the "professionalization" of media management by political actors. In economic terms, as we saw in the introductory chapter, web technologies lower barriers to entry by making publishing resources much more widely available. The Net is supposed to create a reasonably level playing field on which a more diverse range of opinions can compete and flourish. The power of large media organizations and political communications professionals to shape public opinion will be steadily diluted as self-publishing by a multitude of groups and individuals becomes the norm. Pluralist group politics returns to its roots as the reflection of an active civil society characterized by rapid mobilization of opinion using information technology. Networked forms of political organization come to predominate over older hierarchical forms. In the words of Lawrence Grossman (1995:49), this "is likely to extend government decision making from the few in the center of power to the many on the outside who may wish to participate." It is possible to see the extent—and the limits—of such decentralizing effects in many of the areas we will encounter in the rest of this book, but consider two here: one institutional and the other policy related.

Compared with traditional mass media, the Internet is *potentially* a much cheaper form of communication. The word *potentially* is italicized deliberately because this point is not as straightforward as it might appear. The professionalization of web-based politics has massively increased costs since the early days of the mid-1990s, and though it is relatively simple to establish a website, this is no guarantee that users will flock to it or that it will be taken as seriously as a site that has been developed by a dedicated team of web designers using the latest hardware and software. At the same time, however, expensive websites are not always perceived as better than their low-cost counterparts, nor are complex sites always as effective as those that are basic but easily navigable (Nielsen, 1999). The rise of political blogging has been based upon very simple text-based sites that are quick to load and easy to use. It is also the case that a website is still much cheaper than a series of television advertisements, the costs of which are more than 2 million dollars for a month-long series of short spots on national networks (Stromer-Galley, 2000a:44). Once again, though, there are contradictory pressures here: the 2000 U.S. presidential campaign saw the convergence of television advertising with website content. During the 2004 campaign, with broadband connectivity required to display decent video increasingly widespread, television advertisements were very prominent on the candidates' sites (see chapter 7). In fact, the presence of such ads arguably drives traffic to sites because it makes them more appealing to those who are not motivated to wade through the text of blogs.

In policy terms, one much-publicized example of potential power diffusion is the entertainment industry, which has been forced to react to the phenomenon of Internet file sharing (see chapter 12). Whether file sharing, or "Napsterization," is a political movement is open to dispute (Barbrook, 2000; May, 2002:100), but it is clear that large numbers of those who share files on peer-to-peer networks do so with the specific intention of reducing the influence of global entertainment conglomerates such as Sony, AOL Time Warner, or BMG. They are in part driven by a different model of music distribution in which artists are able to sell their products directly to their fan base through digital networks rather than agree to restrictive contract agreements. For some, Napsterization, by diffusing the power to create music and reach an audience, is an assault on some of the core practices of contemporary capitalism.

Problems, however, abound with this form of optimism. The technology itself may provide opportunities for power shifts, but this needs to be situated within the wider configuration of institutional sources of power outside the Net. We come back to the problem of disintermediation. Record companies' power to shape popular tastes rests on their institutional location at the center of precisely those informational networks that matter to that particular industry. They have at their disposal forms of knowledge, expertise, and wealth that are not distributed evenly throughout society. The same goes for more mainstream forms of political behavior. While the Net may enable more rapid mobilization of political support, we need to consider whom the mobilization benefits most. Existing power brokers are often just as likely to have their position enhanced by the Net as they are to have it reduced as a result of competition with smaller or newly emergent players. In the international sphere, too, it is by no means settled that the Internet diffuses power. In authoritarian states, for example, it has been argued that the free flow of information can assist democratic opposition with attacks on the regime, but it is just as likely that such regimes will use technical means such as filtering and site blocking as well as physical means such as restricting telecommunication access or closing down cybercafés to offset these new effects. Institutions that have preexisting power resources at their disposal can prove remarkably skillful at adapting to changes in their external environments. As I write, the major record companies are in the midst of launching legal music download sites that will no doubt prove highly profitable.

A final point about the theme of decentralization is that although widespread use of the Internet is a relatively recent development, the use of computers is not. It should therefore come as no surprise that older assumptions from studies of the computerization of organizations have also become embedded in many contemporary interpretations of the Internet. Most closely associated with the so-called Irvine School of the 1970s (named after researchers mainly based at the University of California–Irvine), the reinforcement model points to the multiple ways in which new technologies are adapted to conform with existing power structures (Danziger et al., 1982). Put simply, those in positions of power are likely to shape the adoption and implementation of a new information and communication system in such a way that it serves to enhance rather than undermine their power. Such technologies *reinforce* inequalities of power based upon other sources, such as an individual's or group's position in a formal hierarchy and their expertise, experience, or control over strategically more significant areas of decision making. Though the original Irvine approach did suggest that comparatively less-hierarchical organizations would also mold information and communication technologies in their own image, usually such models measure the normative hope that the Internet will decentralize power against the reality that it reinforces an undesirable status quo, and several studies have been quick to expose the sometimes stubborn mature of unequal pre-Internet power structures (e.g., Bimber and Davis, 2003; Margolis and Resnick, 2000).

2. Participation

Even casual Internet browsers soon come to recognize that much of what goes on in cyberspace is talk. Hundreds of thousands of forums have sprung up, in which people in their diverse identities can argue, compete, collaborate, or simply share thoughts. Workers, citizens, consumers, criminals, techies, obsessives—you name it, there is a place in cyberspace for your particular fix. But when it comes to politics, the spontaneous emergence of online discussion speaks to many deep-seated anxieties about the character of contemporary liberal democracy as well as ancient concerns in political philosophy regarding the possibility of sweeping away representative democracy and establishing a direct democracy in its place. The turn toward deliberative models of democracy that began during the 1970s and 1980s with the work of writers such as Benjamin Barber and Jurgen Habermas together with the switch of emphasis in the writings of classical pluralists such as Robert Dahl often mentioned the potential of new technologies for realizing the dream of increased citizen engagement (Barber, 1984; Dahl, 1989; Habermas, 1962 [1989]). Barber's *Strong Democracy* has been particularly influential for a generation of students of politics attempting to come to terms with one of the central issues of contemporary liberal democratic politics: apathy.

Online forums have been celebrated by many as free public spheres of political deliberation—a "civic commons" in cyberspace (Blumler and Coleman, 2001; Klein, 1999)—but they have also been criticized for the poor quality of interaction they create as well as their tendency to produce a plurality of deeply segmented political associations. Cass Sunstein (2001), in a highly influential theory, calls online forums "echo chambers." These corrode democracy, he argues, because in the online world it is much more likely that we will seek out like-minded people and have our views reinforced rather than challenged by alternative perspectives.

Sunstein's theory is in fact very similar to early communication research by writers such as Paul Lazarsfeld, Bernard Berelson, and Wilbur Schramm. In their pioneering audience studies of the 1940s, Lazarsfeld and his colleagues came to the conclusion that messages received during election campaigns did not often change voters' minds. Instead, they tended to reinforce previously held views. Also, those who were already interested in politics tended to use the media to reinforce that interest, while those who were less interested tended to avoid political coverage (Lazersfeld et al., 1944; Schramm and Roberts, 1971). Although the model of media effects in this early research has long been heavily criticized for its simple "hypodermic needle" approach, which looked for immediate changes of opinion following the "injection" of a specific item of information, the concept of reinforcement still casts a huge shadow over much contemporary writing about all forms of media. Its attractiveness is partly explained by the fact that it draws attention to some basic questions about the role that increased political information on the Internet might play in reducing political apathy and increasing political participation.

Since the emergence of the Internet, several writers have revisited the concept of reinforcement to guide their empirical research. And many have concluded that increasing the amount of political information available online does not necessarily contribute to higher levels of civic engagement. In the early wave of Internet politics research during the late 1990s, it almost became conventional wisdom that political information on the Net was more likely to be sought and used by those already interested in politics (Hill and Hughes, 1998; Davis, 1999). This dovetailed with previous arguments about the effects of radio, television, and the press. The problem with such perspectives now is that they largely based their analyses on the relatively static and top-down styles of websites that characterized politicians' approaches in the mid-1990s. Based as they were on a quasi-broadcasting model of communication, it is easy to see how such sites might not pull individuals into the political process. The long-term impact of the U.S. primary and presidential campaigns of 2003–2004 is difficult to gauge, but it seems clear that a new form of online campaigning based upon more interactive forms of communication, particularly blogs, creates a different sort of environment—one which appears to have lowered levels of apathy and increased citizen participation. But we do not have to rely on very recent events to make the case: one of the most successful online deliberative forums, Minnesota E-democracy (covered in chapter 5), is based almost entirely on discussions using email.

3. Community

Most of the claims about the Internet's role in promoting political participation rest on an underlying view of community. In this perspective, the Internet is medication for the perceived ills of modern society: isolation, fragmentation, competitive individualism, the erosion of local identities, the decline of traditional religious and family structures, and the downplaying of emotional forms of attachment and communication. As Robert Putnam's (2000) highly influential "bowling alone" thesis contends, the United States, along with other developed states, has witnessed a decline in social capital during the last thirty years (see also chapter 5). The nostalgic search for intimacy (Agre, 2002:312) in modern life is exhibited everyday in chat rooms, discussion boards, and personal home pages. Some advocates of participatory democracy argue that strong community prefigures strong democracy. Thus, political apathy is a result of the withering away of community. Reinvent community in cyberspace, the argument goes, and greater levels of political participation will follow.

Related to such claims is the view that online forms of interaction have an intrinsically egalitarian quality usually absent from the real world. This is due to the fact that the traditional signs of social inequality—particularly gender, ethnicity, and age, but also regional accents and physical disabilities—are hidden from participants in a predominantly textual environment. Cyberspace, it is maintained, is not tarnished by the forms of prejudice that proliferate in visual culture. An enduring catchphrase comes from Peter Steiner's famous 1993 New Yorker cartoon depicting two dogs at a computer desk. The caption? "On the Internet, nobody knows you're a dog."

There are several problems with the vision of the Internet as the enabler of community, but perhaps the biggest is that life online exhibits many of the social pathologies communitarians wish to transcend. It has been argued that the ties that bind members of a virtual community are not as strong as the old ties of family, locality, religion, or even political structures like local party and lobby group associations. The Net, in this view, takes the impersonality of modern society to a new level, substituting a diluted form of community and social capital for the real things (Doheny-Farina, 1996).

The best we can hope for, in a striking concept invented by Barry Wellman, is a hybrid form of networked individualism (Wellman et al., 2003).

Networked individualism is actually a reasonably optimistic view of the world. But other writers have pointed to features of online communities that are far from ideal. Face-to-face interaction usually imposes the well-known demands of basic civility; the removal of such discipline from the online environment makes it much easier to express views that are on the margins of social and political acceptability. Racism, sexism, and all manner of other prejudices flourish online, where individuals can hide behind the cloak of anonymity or pseudonymity, both widely accepted practices in cyberspace.

Sunstein's (2001) view of online echo chambers is also relevant here. While new and strong communities have emerged, they are often highly segmented. Yet much depends upon what is perceived as a desirable basis for community. Sunstein's underlying assumption is that a healthy public sphere is a universal one in which opinions clash and conventional wisdom is challenged. This is very much rooted in notions about the competition of ideas (albeit in the context of underlying consensus) that has proved dominant in Western liberalism. But others might see this as missing the point. Identity is a source of cohesion in any community, and some research has demonstrated that online interactions are often characterized by elaborate identity construction rituals, rule writing, and enforcement (Smith and Kollock, 1999). In the end, promoting community and social capital through social cohesion may inevitably undermine Sunstein's ideal of a common public sphere of political debate.

4. Globalization

Since the 1990s, the social sciences have been awash with this wildly popular idea. There are many competing definitions of globalization, but one of the most useful comes from David Held and colleagues, who see it as "a process (or set of processes) which embodies a transformation in the spatial organization of social relations and transactions, generating transcontinental or interregional flows and networks of activity, interaction and power" (Held et al., 1999:16). In basic terms, globalization is best seen as a set of processes rather than any final state. The Internet's contribution here is far from straightforward. In several respects it builds upon the effects of previously new technologies—mass air transport or television are good examples. Yet in other ways it obviously increases opportunities for forms of communication that are not predicated on the idea of a national community. Thus, there are genuinely robust reasons for setting many, though certainly not all, aspects of the politics of the Internet in the context of globalization.

Forecasters of the "death of distance" argue that the Net creates the conditions for a truly global, twenty-four/seven market where geographical proximity becomes less and less relevant (Cairncross, 1997). Governments, in this view, are unable to intervene to prevent the flow of information and capital across national boundaries. Instead, they must succumb to a global neoliberal consensus by reducing their own national regulatory burdens if they are to flourish in the global economy. This is a decidedly economic perspective—albeit one with distinct political implications—but there are, of course, different schools of globalization theory focusing on different aspects of the phenomenon, including political, cultural, military, and even migratory trends.

Consider three of these, the political, the cultural, and the military, in relation to the Internet. In addition to the debate about whether governments are no longer able to effectively regulate markets in the interests of national social goals, there are a whole host of issues surrounding the free flow of information as well as the new forms of global governance regimes that have emerged in response to the death of distance argument. An excellent example here is the regulation of certain technical aspects of the Internet itself, particularly the standards-setting process. As we shall discover in chapters 9 and 10, since the late 1990s, a nascent governance regime for the Internet has emerged, involving a wide variety of international organizations such as the United Nations (UN), the International Telecommunications Union (ITU), a new body known as the Internet Corporation for Assigned Names and Numbers (ICANN), and the World Intellectual Property Organization (WIPO). States as well as business actors have reacted to the Internet in diverse ways, sometimes seeking to free up communication in the interests of promoting global e-commerce markets while at other times attempting to exert national regulatory leverage.

As we shall see in chapters 4 and 9, similar complexities arise if we examine the Internet's contribution to cultural globalization. One approach perceives the relatively unconstrained nature of Internet communication as creating a kind of global cosmopolitanism in which cultures intermingle and fuse. Another sees the Net as the ultimate tool for the export of Western values around the world. Yet another points to the potential for non-Western cultures to establish and maintain their own identities in an online environment as well as their capacity to subvert and adapt Western media values for their own purposes.

When it comes to military globalization, analysts of new surveillance technologies point to the ways in which the compression of time and distance permits new forms of social control based on omnipresent private and public forms of monitoring our everyday lives (Lyon, 2003; see also chapter 11). In this view, global electronic networks may play an integrative role, as those already powerful actors in the global system are able to be all-seeing. Analyses of the role of communication in imperialism have long pointed to the center's desire to extend its control over the periphery through the construction of more efficient forms of transport, like railroads and telegraphy (Innis, 1951).

Another way of perceiving the Internet's contribution to globalization requires us to think not just about distance but about space and place. The spatial aspects of politics have often been neglected, ironically, perhaps, because the development of new communication technology is said to render place less significant. But control over the physical spaces in which political contestation occurs remains an important power resource (Leizerov, 2000:467). It is an obvious but important observation that protestors seeking to influence a political institution usually focus their physical efforts on campaigning near to its physical location; it is equally obvious to observe that the vast majority of public spaces and buildings are fortified against unwanted physical invasion. Thus, while there are what we might term "natural" limits on political space, such as the physical geography that separates nations or localities within nations, there are also deliberately constructed restrictions on physical political spaces. The Internet reduces such spatial constraints. While cyberspace is a space where boundaries and topography exist, they are much weaker constraints on behavior than those in the physical world. This opens up new possibilities for forms of political action that subvert attempts by the powerful to control the spaces in which politics is conducted as well as reconfigure the "geography of access" (Lin and Dutton, 2003:132), for example, by enabling those involved in local campaigns to more easily follow and contribute when they migrate to national or even transnational levels (see chapter 6).

5. Postindustrialization

If the concept of globalization has proved popular in Internet studies, it is rapidly being joined by postindustrialization. A growing number of scholars, foremost among them Ronald Inglehart (1997, 1999), Anthony Giddens (1991), Ulrich Beck (1999), Alberto Melucci (1989, 1996), Lance Bennett (1998, 2003b), and Pippa Norris (2002a), point to the postindustrial characteristics of contemporary societies. The concept of post-industrialism first rose to prominence with Daniel Bell's writings of the early 1970s (Bell, 1973). More recently, as applied to politics, this thesis holds that as Western societies witness a decline in the authority of traditional institutions, including religious organizations but also trade unions, political parties, and government itself, individuals retreat further into their own private spheres, becoming less obviously politically engaged in the sense of participating in the large-scale structures of liberal democracy. For Inglehart, political struggles in advanced industrial nations increasingly center upon post-material issues, such as demands to protect the environment or to participate in decision-making processes in areas of society traditionally dominated by hierarchical structures, like the workplace, for example (Inglehart, 1997, 1999). Crucially, however, Inglehart maintains that the commitment to democracy among the citizens of Western nations remains high; it is the institutional manifestations of these commitments that are changing. Although there may be widespread distrust of established political institutions, underlying belief systems give rise to new forms of participation and protest that increasingly occur outside of older, less-flexible forms of political organization.

Some, notably Lance Bennett, have adapted postindustrial theory for interpreting Internet-enabled citizen activism. In Bennett's perspective, individual political identity derives not from relatively fixed, collective institutional sources but is increasingly a matter of self-expression and lifestyle choice. Politics is now much more intertwined with practices that have traditionally been perceived as less political, such as consumption, recreation, personal communication, and the manipulation of symbolic forms in genres such as advertising and corporate branding. These areas of life become politically contestable, while older areas of contestation are said to be diminishing in importance. In this new environment, powerful corporations become the targets of "globalization from below" (Kellner, 1999) by "a class of ordinary citizens who increasingly see the sites of their political action as ranging from local to global without necessarily passing through national institutions on the way" (Bennett, 1998, 2003b: 27). Politics becomes, in part, subject to the same dynamics as lifestyle choices. Individuals constantly engage in processes of reinvention and frequently engage in cross-cultural "raids" in order to navigate their own personal path through contentious everyday encounters.

Central to the new lifestyle politics are more spontaneous, less hierarchical network forms of organization (see chapter 6). It is through decentralized and flexible linkages that individuals come to form political alliances, often across national boundaries, in ways that cut across diverse campaigns and causes. The Internet allows for mobilization based upon these diverse and fragmented political identities, as individuals join many more groups and movements in the online world than they would ever consider offline (Bennett, 2003a: 147). Many of the participants in action against global neoliberalism, for instance, do not appear to see a contradiction between their national political apathy (not voting in elections) and their transnational engagement. Recent examples of lifestyle politics include the anti-sweatshop movement against Nike, initially coordinated by an online network, Global Exchange; the anti–genetically modified foods campaign aimed at Monsanto; and the global campaign against Microsoft, largely coordinated online by an alliance named Netaction.

The use of lifestyle values in appeals for mobilization has also led some to speak of a new political culture based in part upon a cultural turn in politics (Clark and Hoffman-Martinot, 1998). Unlike traditional media, the Net seems particularly well-suited to the rapid diffusion of simple yet powerful ideas that seem to crystallize particular social concerns. In this sense, the Internet could be said to subvert some of the trends set in place during the 1980s—the period in which televised forms of politics became consolidated. Claims for a new political culture are often vague and have not gone uncontested (Scott and Street, 2000; Stolle and Hooghe, 2004). But irrespective of whether there is a fundamental qualitative shift in the politics of Western nations, it is clear that the Internet reduces the levels of expertise and professional knowledge required for the production of cultural forms of political appeal, narrowing the traditional gap between oppositional voices and the institutionally produced messages of powerful groups.

6. Rationalization

So far, our conceptual discussion has mainly revolved around debates about the Internet's capacity for loosening political processes by diffusing power, making politics more flexible and pluralistic, or by creating diverse communities. But there are also concepts which stress the Internet's role in generating new, more efficient forms of social control. Since the 1950s, computerization, not just of government and politics but of many aspects of society, has been proposed as a solution to countless ills. This tied in with the rise of so-called scientific administration and a general current in the social sciences towards what was known as the end of ideology thesis (Bell, 1960). Computing was seen as a part of the end of ideology because it held out the promise of information abundance as a pragmatic route to objectively better solutions to social and economic problems. These, it was often claimed, would be guided by systematic knowledge rather than irrational ideological belief systems. These kinds of arguments concern technology's role in rationalization and are highly relevant for aspects of Internet politics, especially e-government, e-campaigning, and surveillance (see chapters 7, 8, and 11).

Rationalization has long been used as a broad, critical term in the social sciences. In the sense pioneered by Max Weber (1947), it refers to a set of ideas which inspired the emergence of rules-based organizations based upon rational calculation, planning, and control. Bureaucracies—organizations that generally require individual adherence to formal rules rather than the expression of emotion or creativity—are a classic symptom of rationalization. The various technologies of surveillance and measurement upon which large organizations depend reflect its incessant logic. Some writers, most notably the sociologist George Ritzer, argue that rationalization has become the dominant force in contemporary life. Ritzer uses the fast food industry as an extreme example of this in action, as every step in the production process is "scientifically" controlled in the pursuit of maximum efficiency (Ritzer, 1993).

Rationalization through the use of the Internet affects politics at many different levels. E-government may be seen as a continuation of rationalizing tendencies, as indeed may e-commerce. This is because they, like fast food restaurants, are based upon the efficient control and automation of as many aspects of the production process as possible. Research on election campaigning suggests that the use of databases to rapidly process massive quantities of data about voter intentions is now taken for granted as part of fighting a campaign (Howard and Milstein, 2003). The sheer physical amount of stored and easily retrieved information about voter opinion makes it much easier to target, or "narrowcast," to specific groups of voters. Highly tailored email messages can be produced through the use of data-mining systems that correlate a voter's lifestyle choices with a specific component of a candidate's policy platform. In much the same way that private companies track how users navigate around their websites, government agencies now identify those areas of their sites that attract the most interest. Online behavior patterns can be used to generate tailored email messages that mention policy issues in which a voter is interested. Special sections of candidates' sites that specifically cater to the press and broadcasters are now common. These are just a few examples of the Internet's role in surveillance—a classic form of Weberian rationalization which I explore in detail in chapter 11.

7. Governance

The concept of rationalization leads us to consider a related one—governance. The governance approach in political science, which first emerged in the 1990s, insists that power struggles can no longer be understood by a narrow focus on the core executive and the traditional institutions of central government. Instead, we need to appreciate how states have changed their modes of operation during the last twenty to thirty years. The issue has been neatly crystallized by Jon Pierre and Guy Peters (2000:1), who argue that "unlike the narrower term of 'government' [governance] cover[s] the whole range of institutions and relationships involved in the process of governing." The main question is "how the centre of government interacts with society to reach mutually acceptable decisions, or whether society actually does more self-steering rather than depending upon guidance from government" (Peters, 2000:36). This draws our attention to the complex, often decentralized mixture of public and private actors, state-civil society relations, and competing values which inform the politics of the Internet.

When stripped down to its essentials, the study of politics is about the study of power. There is nothing new in this. But understanding how power relationships have evolved and how they work out in day-to-day political interaction is very difficult due to their inherent complexity. Making sense of this complexity is even more challenging today, as state and nonstate political actors are enmeshed in a multiplicity of different ways and at a variety of different levels, from the local to the national, the supranational to the international (Richards and Smith, 2002:14). This emphasis on the multiplicity of policy levels and arenas and the centrality of networks is especially useful for examining Internet politics and policy. The politics of the Internet are played out in the interaction between states and citizens, public and private actors, in a variety of arenas, some of which do not even appear to be political—on the surface at least.

The main advantage of the governance approach is the recognition that networks, interaction, and participation are increasingly important characteristics of contemporary politics (Kooiman, 1993:4, 2002). The Internet is facilitating, reinforcing, and often reconfiguring these trends. The networked character of much contemporary political activity renders the government paradigm less helpful than it perhaps once was. State sovereignty is still alive and well. However, as we shall see throughout this book, states are but one type of actor in the political process, and the Internet sometimes unleashes forces which threaten their authoritative status. Governments and legal regimes cannot always deal with the implications of the Internet in the "command and control" modes of the past, though they will undoubtedly try. Understanding the politics of Internet technologies—their usage, distribution, design, and regulation—requires us to think in terms of the diverse actors, new communities, interests, and interdependencies they foster.

8. Libertarianism

Finally, if this tour through some of the key conceptual discussions about the Internet has demonstrated its complex and contradictory nature, one of its most powerful ideological strands needs to be acknowledged: libertarianism. Despite the U.S. federal government's heavy involvement in fostering the early development of its technologies and the encroachment of the market since the 1990s, the Net has long been perceived as a realm of relative freedom from both government and corporate control, a space in which the kinds of large power structures which predominate in the real space of modern societies have a weaker grip. In both positive and pejorative senses, the term "cyberlibertarianism" frequently appears in both popular and academic writing about the Internet. The nature, meaning, and prevalence of such libertarianism is essential to understanding many of the fault lines of Internet politics.

One of the finest distillations of cyberlibertarian ideology can be found in John Perry Barlow's famous "Declaration" (exhibit 2.2). First published in 1996, this iconoclastic statement has proved inspirational for large numbers of campaigners involved in Internet policy issues. Barlow's background as one of the lyricists for the psychedelic rock band the Grateful Dead hints at his rebellious approach. Along with Mitch Kapor, Barlow founded the Electronic Frontier Foundation (EFF) in 1990—a lobby group that campaigns on a number of issues related to privacy, intellectual property, freedom of communication, and Internet governance. Barlow and Kapor, along with other San Francisco Bay Area figures such as Kevin Kelly, Douglas Rushkoff, and Louis Rossetto, were also instrumental in founding *Wired* magazine in 1993. *Wired*'s approach is eclectic, but it has always been held together by its broadly libertarian stance.

The extent to which libertarianism is the default ideology of the Internet has been the subject of fierce debate. The scientists and engineers involved in laying the foundations of its technologies may have had a vision of unfettered communication and information sharing, but their passion was matched by entrepreneurs that sought to make profits from the new medium. It is this incursion of capitalist values that some writers seek to expose in their critiques of cyberlibertarian ideology (Borsook, 2000; Barbrook

EXHIBIT 2.2. JOHN PERRY BARLOW, "A DECLARATION OF THE INDEPENDENCE OF CYBERSPACE"

"Governments of the Industrial World, you weary giants of flesh and steel, I come from Cyberspace, the new home of Mind. On behalf of the future, I ask you of the past to leave us alone. You are not welcome among us. You have no sovereignty where we gather.

We have no elected government, nor are we likely to have one, so I address you with no greater authority than that with which liberty itself always speaks. I declare the global social space we are building to be naturally independent of the tyrannies you seek to impose on us. You have no moral right to rule us nor do you possess any methods of enforcement we have true reason to fear.

Governments derive their just powers from the consent of the governed. You have neither solicited nor received ours. We did not invite you. You do not know us, nor do you know our world. Cyberspace does not lie within your borders. Do not think that you can build it, as though it were a public construction project. You cannot. It is an act of nature and it grows itself through our collective actions.

You have not engaged in our great and gathering conversation, nor did you create the wealth of our marketplaces. You do not know our culture, our ethics, or the unwritten codes that already provide our society more order than could be obtained by any of your impositions.

You claim there are problems among us that you need to solve. You use this claim as an excuse to invade our precincts. Many of these problems don't exist. Where there are real conflicts, where there are wrongs, we will identify them and address them by our means. We are forming our own Social Contract. This governance will arise according to the conditions of our world, not yours. Our world is different.

Cyberspace consists of transactions, relationships, and thought itself, arrayed like a standing wave in the web of our communications. Ours is a world that is both everywhere and nowhere, but it is not where bodies live.

We are creating a world that all may enter without privilege or prejudice accorded by race, economic power, military force, or station of birth.

We are creating a world where anyone, anywhere may express his or her beliefs, no matter how singular, without fear of being coerced into silence or conformity.

Your legal concepts of property, expression, identity, movement, and context do not apply to us. They are all based on matter, and there is no matter here.

Our identities have no bodies, so, unlike you, we cannot obtain order by physical coercion. We believe that from ethics, enlightened self-interest, and the commonweal, our governance will emerge.

Our identities may be distributed across many of your jurisdictions. . . .

We will create a civilization of the Mind in Cyberspace. May it be more humane and fair than the world your governments have made before."

Source: Quoted from Barlow, 1996a.

EXHIBIT 2.3. INTERNET LIBERTARIANISM AS THE CALIFORNIAN IDEOLOGY

"The Californian ideologues preach an anti-statist gospel of hi-tech libertarianism: a bizarre mish-mash of hippie anarchism and economic liberalism beefed up with lots of technological determinism. . . . This new faith has emerged from a bizarre fusion of the cultural bohemianism of San Francisco with the hi-tech industries of Silicon Valley. Promoted in magazines, books, television programs, websites, newsgroups and net conferences, the Californian Ideology promiscuously combines the free-wheeling spirit of the hippies and the entrepreneurial zeal of the yuppies. This amalgamation of opposites has been achieved through a profound faith in the emancipatory potential of the new information technologies. In the digital utopia, everybody will be both hip and rich. Not surprisingly, this optimistic vision of the future has been enthusiastically embraced by computer nerds, slacker students, innovative capitalists, social activists, trendy academics, futurist bureaucrats and opportunistic politicians across the USA. . . . On the one hand, they cannot challenge the primacy of the marketplace over their lives. On the other hand, they resent attempts by those in authority to encroach on their individual autonomy. . . . Although they enjoy cultural freedoms won by the hippies, most of them are no longer actively involved in the struggle to build 'ecotopia'. Instead of openly rebelling against the system, these hi-tech artisans now accept that individual freedom can only be achieved by working within the constraints of technological progress and the 'free market.' In many cyberpunk novels, this asocial libertarianism is personified by the central character of the hacker, who is a lone individual fighting for survival within the virtual world of information. . . . Who would have thought that such a contradictory mix of technological determinism and libertarian individualism would become the hybrid orthodoxy of the information age?"

Source: Quoted from Barbrook and Cameron, 1996.

and Cameron, 1996). In an influential essay, Richard Barbrook and Andy Cameron dissect the principal components of what they see as the Californian ideology (see exhibit 2.3).

Barbrook and Cameron's tone may be scathing, but note their acknowledgment that the concern for the democratization of organizational life, first shared by the New Left social movements of the 1960s and '70s, permeates Internet libertarianism as much as the distaste for state regulation of markets. In other words, it appears that there is as much room for John Perry Barlow's spirited "Declaration" as there is for Bill Gates's Microsoft.

One of the problems with arguing that the Internet is dominated by cyberlibertarianism stems from the fact that there are many different forms of libertarianism. The term can have several different meanings, not all of which are compatible. In philosophy, libertarianism has most often been portrayed as the antithesis of determinism. Pure libertarians posit that human agency—the ability to shape future events free from structural or historical constraint—is the guiding force in all spheres of life. Human behavior cannot, therefore, be understood in simple causal terms. Pure determinists, on the other hand, have argued that humans have little or no means of intervening to off-set what are seen as the crushing effects of large structures, be they cultural, political, economic, or even biological. Behavior can be seen as the relatively predictable outcome of the causal impact of such structures.

The dominant meaning of libertarianism in contemporary politics turns this philo-sophical distinction into a normative argument for removing government from as many areas of life as possible. Deriving much of its original force from the seventeenth-century political theorist John Locke, political libertarians see government as inherently coercive and in need of constitutional restraint. They favor free and competitive markets over both state control and private monopoly and assert the right of the individual to control her own destiny in all areas of life but especially in the enjoyment of property. The Lockean insistence on the right to life, liberty, and property has thus given suste-nance to a strong variety of conservative anti-statism. Postwar thinkers such as Robert Nozick (1974) and Friedrich Hayek (1944) inspired the free market ideology of the Conservative and Republican governments of Thatcher, Reagan, and Bush in the 1980s, with their aim of rolling back the state. Nozick, Hayek, and a swathe of others argue for a minimal state—one that exists only to maintain order and uphold the rule of law that governs market competition.

Of course, in U.S. electoral politics, libertarianism may be most readily associated with the Libertarian Party. Founded in Colorado in 1971, the Libertarians' platform is based on "individual freedom and personal responsibility, a free market economy of abundance and prosperity [and] a foreign policy of non-intervention, peace and free trade" (U.S. Libertarian Party, 2005). The party, which tends to campaign against tax in-creases, government regulation of business, and infringements on personal and civil lib-erties, has never had a candidate elected to major public office, though its positions on a range of issues have sometimes found favor among diverse sections of U.S. society, from those opposed to gun control to gay and lesbian activists.

In fact, the combination of anti-state and free-market themes in the Libertarian Party's ideology often make uncomfortable bedfellows. Economic libertarians who may otherwise be conservative in matters of lifestyle rub shoulders with those free speech radicals who wish to assert their rights to live their lives as they choose. It is this kind of problem which points to one of the central difficulties with pinning down the mean-ing of libertarianism, even in the most abstract sense. Fundamentally, libertarians are concerned with extending freedoms, but the kinds of freedoms which one libertar-ian values may differ markedly from those valued by another. It is for this reason that some observers have argued that the term "libertarianism" is itself devoid of useful meaning unless it is tagged on to some other ideological term as a means of making sense of a particular strand within a larger historical tradition. Thus, we can speak of libertarianism in some overarching or neutral sense as the advocacy of freedom from restraint while recognizing that there can be libertarian conservatism, libertarian social-ism, libertarian feminism, libertarian environmentalism, and so on (Greenleaf, 1983; Cohen, 1995).

Libertarianism's contested nature applies just as much to its manifestations on the Internet as it does to its appearances in other areas of politics. In other words, "cyberlibertarianism," which I see as a legitimate term to describe an important strand of thinking about the role, purpose, and effects of the Internet as well as a much more diffuse but still significant cultural component of Internet use that touches almost all Net users at some stage, encompasses an assortment of perspectives that differ according to the types of freedoms they prioritize. There are powerful currents of cyberlibertarianism that celebrate heroic entrepreneurs and decry state regulation of the market. There are equally significant currents of opinion that promote the spontaneous, devolved, and self-organizing character of networks and the opportunities for do-it-yourself forms of organization that empower communities and the excluded and that also condemn the new concentrations of economic power that the Internet has produced in market sectors such as software, for example. Cyberlibertarianism as hatred of market regulation by government can be found throughout cyberspace yet so can cyberlibertarianism as distrust of political and corporate elites or fear of increases in public and private surveillance. Cyberlibertarianism as profit-seeking entrepreneurialism fuels technological innovations such as wireless networking (WiFi) as a new way to open up a consumer market for broadband or file-sharing software such as Napster and Kazaa as a means of introducing a new delivery channel for the sale of music and film. Yet cyberlibertarianism as a critique of government inaction and large telecommunication companies' lack of concern for rural communities also drives the establishment of nonprofit WiFi networks, while the dominance of the "big five" global entertainment companies in the music and film industries leads many to perceive file sharing as a means of subverting corporate power, fostering artistic diversity, or creating a new gift economy as an oasis of self-organized altruism in a desert of possessive individualism.

It is impossible to arrive at some overarching generalization about the character of Internet libertarianism because libertarianism is itself a contradictory concept unless disaggregated and qualified. But when compared with non-Internet policy issues, diverse forms of libertarianism appear to be much more prevalent in guiding the opinions and actions of Internet activists. From the protracted debate about Internet governance to issues of censorship, surveillance, intellectual property, the power of transnational corporations, international organizations, and political and bureaucratic elites, libertarian values often come to the fore in the online sphere.

Conclusion

Internet politics is a new and fast-moving area, but as this chapter has demonstrated, there are several perennial conceptual debates underlying almost all of the scholarly research in the field. It also seems clear that although the focus of this book is on the politics of the Internet, it is impossible and unwise to approach this subject wearing disciplinary blinders. Debates about the political properties of technology are inherently cross-disciplinary. While most if not all of the eight key themes identified have a foot in my disciplinary home, political science, they also draw upon a range of ideas from sociology, communication, economics, business, and management. What they all have in common is trying to arrive at a richer conceptual understanding of the impact of the Internet.

Discussion Points

- Are some technologies more democratic than others?
- In what circumstances would a social determinist perspective on technology make better sense than a technological determinist approach?
- Assess the arguments for and against the view that the Internet diffuses political power.
- How useful is the concept of postindustrialization for understanding Internet politics?
- Is libertarianism the Internet's default ideology?
- Is the Internet necessarily a global medium?

Further Reading

Abramson et al. (1988) had much to say about the kind of conceptual thinking that would be required for making sense of how interactive media disrupt assumptions about political communication. Agre (2002) does a superb job of condensing the core themes of what he calls "real-time politics" as well as outlining his own "institutionalist" approach.

On the relationship between technology and politics, Winner's essay is a wonderfully clear and concise exploration of the main issues (Winner, 1988), while Lessig's 1999 theory of code is a must-read.

The most forthright statement of the segmented pluralism argument is Sunstein, 2001. Davis, 1999, and Bimber and Davis, 2003, are good examples of reinforcement theory. Smith and Kollock, 1999, is still the best source for exploring the dynamics of virtual communities. See Bennett, 1998, 2003b, and Norris, 2002a, for postindustrial politics. A classic theory of transnational communication is Innis, 1951. Ritzer, 1993, is a provocative account of rationalization, while Barbrook and Cameron, 1996, is an illuminating if critical discussion of cyberlibertarianism. The literature on governance varies from the broad to the highly specialized, but a good accessible starting point is Pierre and Peters, 2000.

NETWORK LOGIC

A Political Prehistory of the Internet

The irony is that in all its various guises—commerce, research, and surfing—the web is already so much a part of our lives that familiarity has clouded our perception of the web itself. To understand the web in the broadest and deepest sense, to fully partake of the vision that I and my colleagues share, one must understand how the web came to be.

—TIM BERNERS-LEE, 1999

CHAPTER OVERVIEW

This chapter provides a brief history of the Internet. Its diverse range of actors, interests, and institutions, its paradoxes and ideological clashes, preface many of the issues that are covered in the rest of the book. The chapter illustrates how a curious mixture of technical innovation, state control, voluntarism, do-it-yourself "home-brew" culture, transnational collaboration, and commercial competition have conditioned the Internet's technical and political development.

If we are to make sense of how politics and the Internet have become so intertwined, we need to take a brief journey through its mazy history. The Net's origins have attained almost mythical status in recent times, and peeling off rose-tinted layers of exaggeration can be difficult. Different stories emphasize different individuals, institutions, and technologies. It would be impossible to do justice to the story's full complexity here, but we will cover the main developments. From a social scientist's perspective, the central questions are those we would expect to ask of any potentially significant change, namely (a) which actors, interests, and institutions have had the most influence on how the Internet developed and (b) what kind of technologies, organizational values, and ideologies have underpinned it?

The prehistory of the Internet is not simply a timeline of technological inventions, though many popular and highly readable accounts tell it that way. Technological advances need to be considered, but we need to situate such changes within the context of decisions on the kinds of values that the technologies were designed to enshrine. Only then will we be able to appreciate the curious mixture of technical innovation, state control, voluntarism, transnational collaboration, and commercial competition that make the Net what it is today (the leading accounts, upon which I draw here, are Castells, 2000b:45–54; Hafner and Lyon, 1996; Gillies and Cailliau, 2000; Hauben and Hauben, 1997; Leiner et al., 2000; Margolis and Resnick, 2000:25–51; Martin, 1998; Naughton, 1999; Randall, 1997; Salus, 1995; Winston, 1998).

NETWORK LOGIC

During the 1950s and 1960s, almost all large-scale computing involved the use of mainframes.[1] A typical mainframe system required users to write tailor-made programs to instruct a computer processor to carry out a specific task. Programming was a technical skill but it was also incredibly slow and laborious. Up-front investment costs were often very high, and such systems were inflexible and usually impossible to upgrade without expensive hardware alterations. By the late 1960s, however, time-sharing computing began to change the way mainframes were used. Time sharing meant that processor time could be shared by multiple users, each of whom would be completing a different task. By apportioning processor time intelligently, time-sharing mainframes allowed for multiple input terminals, each receiving feedback according to the specific tasks being performed.

What appears on the surface (and at the time) to have been an important but strictly technical innovation had widespread social, economic, and political implications. The logic of networking, facilitated in part by nascent operating systems like UNIX (invented at Bell Labs in 1969 but not widely used until the 1980s), began to be embedded in the ways that people actually used computers. Computer use was democratized, in the sense that individuals using these machines started to enjoy greater autonomy and began to customize their own approach to their work (Margolis and Resnick, 2000:26).

It is now well known that the Internet was sparked off, somewhat paradoxically, by an act of state intervention. The potential for time sharing to effect a fundamental shift in the way people interacted with computers was spotted by Joseph C. R. Licklider (known as "Lick" to his friends and colleagues), a computer scientist based at the Massachusetts Institute of Technology (MIT). Licklider had a fascination with psychology, stemming from his undergraduate degree and early career experiments in the psychoacoustics of speech. When this was merged with his interest in time-sharing computers, the result was an influential essay entitled "Man-Computer Symbiosis" (1960). In this Licklider outlined, in visionary fashion, what he called "thinking centers": a new form of human-computer interaction involving collaboration across networks to solve common technical problems. In 1962, Lick joined the U.S. Department of Defense for a

---

[1]**Mainframes:** Large computers that act as centralized locations of processor power. Usually found in large organizations such as firms or public sector institutions. Mainframes are often perceived to be an obsolete technology due to the emergence of client-server systems and the spread of the Internet. Client-server systems are based upon multiple PCs connected together in networks and do not rely upon mainframes (though many large organizations use both).

two-year shift as director of the Command and Control Research Division of the Advanced Research Projects Agency (ARPA)—a federal agency that specialized in developing cutting-edge technologies with military relevance. Following the symbolic renaming of the Command and Control Research Division to the Information Processing Techniques Office (IPTO), Licklider soon began to use his position and contacts to foster interest in the development of networks. This was achieved by funding basic research projects at the leading computer science research centers in the United States at the time—Stanford University, the University of California campuses at Los Angeles (UCLA), Berkeley, and Santa Barbara (UCSB), along with Utah University and MIT.

ARPA in the Department of Defense had been set up in reaction to the Soviet Union's early space program of the 1950s, particularly the momentous launch of *Sputnik* in 1957, but, as Hauben and Hauben (1997) argue, the military aspects of its activity were often little more than a backdrop to proceedings. ARPA's organizational culture was infused with a combination of state-sponsored military necessity and a freewheeling but serious spirit of scientific inquiry. With Licklider in charge, the latter, it seems, usually prevailed. By 1966, when Robert Taylor took charge of IPTO, Licklider's ideas had become influential throughout ARPA and its research programs. Thus, when Taylor looked for a way to streamline and integrate the various research projects scattered around U.S. universities, he was able to convince ARPA's director, Charles Herzfeld, to fund a network of between four and twelve mainframes. Together, they drew upon the skills of Lawrence Roberts, at that time working at MIT's Lincoln Laboratory (founded as a federal government research center in 1951 to work on defense technologies). During the next three years, Roberts worked on developing what was to become ARPANET—the precursor of the Internet.

NETWORK BUILDING IN THE SHADOW OF THE COLD WAR STATE: ARPANET

ARPANET's origins in the heart of the U.S. cold war defense establishment undoubtedly influenced the kind of project it became. Yet it did so in ways that are not at all obvious. Given that these events took place during the 1950s and '60s—the heyday of the power elite theory popularized by C. Wright Mills (1956)—we might expect to find the U.S. military and the Department of Defense exerting an iron grip on the ARPANET, restricting its work to the promotion of national security. American society, under the influence of what some called the "military-industrial complex"—a term used to describe the overlap of interests between the military, big corporate capital, and state agencies dependent upon scientists and high-tech weapons manufacturers—could have been presented with an ARPANET designed to increase surveillance and military effectiveness. After all, it is part of the mythology of the Net that it was designed to withstand a nuclear war. In fact, according to some accounts, this was only the aim of Paul Baran's work in the same area for the RAND Corporation and not the aim of ARPANET (Margolis and Resnick, 2000:29). Yet, if anything, it was not militarism which had the lasting influence but the spirit of technological advance and the different kind of elitism that usually accompanies it. In other words, the technocratic nature of the U.S. state at the height of the cold war permitted the kind of research and development that enabled Lawrence Roberts's network to be developed. A team of bright and motivated technicians, engineers, and academics with sufficient public and private funding were operating in the shadow of the cold war state, but enough light was let in for them to see the wider significance and pure science of their endeavors.

This point is aptly illustrated by the attraction of Internet communication's foundation—packet switching[2] technology, invented by Leonard Kleinrock at MIT in 1961. The long-term implications of adopting this as the basis for ARPANET were enormous, because its inherently decentralized and virtually uncontrollable nature would define the kind of medium that the Net would eventually become. The paradox of packet switching is that its flexible yet robust characteristics were attractive to the Department of Defense and the scientific community but for different reasons. Inspired by Licklider's ideology of free communication and network building among like-minded scientists, Lawrence Roberts and the teams of graduate students which formed the Network Working Group continued to build a surprisingly open network technology during an era of historically high levels of state-sponsored surveillance.

By the end of the 1960s, a simple prototype packet-switching network was in place, the nodes of which were based at Stanford, UCSB, UCLA, and Utah. By 1971, this had expanded to fifteen nodes and twenty-three host computers; by 1972, forty computers were connected (Margolis and Resnick, 2000:31). Faced with increasing difficulties associated with communication across this growing network, effort focused on developing new standards and protocols that would allow greater numbers of computers to be added. This fell to Steve Crocker, a UCLA graduate student who had studied under Leonard Kleinrock.

The way in which Steve Crocker went about his job of developing the software that would allow ARPANET to expand is fascinating because it tells us much about the kinds of values that suffuse the contemporary Internet. Rather than have ARPA's Network Working Group develop protocols independently and impose them upon the rest of the network, Crocker proceeded by issuing "Requests for Comments" (Crocker, 1969). These were designed to encourage people from around the participating institutions to get involved with the development process. Though at times chaotic, the system proved a success, not only as a democratic and participatory device that would legitimize ARPANET in the minds of its key developers but also as a simple way of introducing "blue skies" ideas.

The first successful email program was added to the ARPANET network in 1972 and soon resulted in an explosion of communication. But despite this and other successes, the absence of a simple and elegant means of joining together multiple networks of different types remained. It was with this in mind that Robert Kahn and Vinton Cerf started work in 1972 on the idea of open networking architecture. The aim was to

---

[2]**Packet switching:** Essentially a superbly efficient way of delivering data across a widely dispersed network. It works by breaking up data into discrete chunks and attaching a label to each chunk before sending it off across the network to be reassembled at the other end. The radical feature of this approach was that the separate packets of data did not have to travel by the same route but would, in a seemingly organic fashion, find any available route to their destinations.

EXHIBIT 3.1. TCP/IP AND THE FOUNDING VALUES OF INTERNET TECHNOLOGY

- Each distinct network would have to stand on its own and no internal changes could be required to any such network to connect it to the Internet.
- Communications would be on a best effort basis. If a packet didn't make it to the final destination, it would shortly be retransmitted from the source.
- Black boxes would be used to connect the networks; these would later be called gateways and routers. There would be no information retained by the gateways about the individual flows of packets passing through them, thereby keeping them simple and avoiding complicated adaptation and recovery from various failure modes.
- There would be no global control at the operations level.

Source: Quoted from Leiner et al., 2000.

---

design a protocol such that "individual networks may be separately designed and developed and each may have its own unique interface which it may offer to users and/or other providers, including other Internet providers" (Leiner et al., 2000). This was to become the software foundation of the Net: Transmission Control Protocol/Internet Protocol (TCP/IP).[3] It was based on four principles that are essential for understanding the values that underpinned it (exhibit 3.1).

On the surface, these might be perceived as dry, technical specifications and nothing more. But to see them in this way is to ignore the values contained within them. The idea of the Internet as potentially capable of limitless expansion is contained in the first principle. The second principle points toward its relatively robust and flexible nature. The third and fourth principles speak to the lack of centralized control and the difficulty of monitoring data traffic for surveillance purposes. It should come as no surprise that many of the issues and controversies of the contemporary Internet are crystallized to some extent in Robert Kahn's early declaration of the founding values of TCP/IP. Kahn and his colleagues believed that the efficiency of the network itself was of paramount importance, but they also devised a set of protocols that would make it very difficult to exert central control over the content of the data packets flowing around it.

We can add to these principles a belief in developing the Internet through international collaboration and the perceived necessity of converging standards and protocols. Between 1974 and 1980, TCP/IP was further refined under the aegis of an International Networking Group at research centers at Stanford, University College London, Bolt, Beranek, and Newman (a private research consultancy), the French Cyclades team (funded by the French state), and researchers working on the specifications for Local Area Networks at Xerox's Palo Alto Research Center (PARC), just south of San Francisco, in

---

[3]**Transmission Control Protocol/Internet Protocol (TCP/IP):** A label of convenience describing the two main ways of handling data on the Internet and other networks. There are in fact other protocols bundled with TCP/IP, but TCP and IP are the most important.

what would soon become known as Silicon Valley (Castells, 2000:47). Thus, teams working across international boundaries in specific mileux of innovation were a decisive feature of the Internet in its initial phases. As we shall see in chapter 10, devising mechanisms for continuing international standards and regulating the global nature of the Net have long caused political problems. However, the technological convergence fostered by such collaboration quickly became one of the driving forces behind the Net's further development in the 1980s. For instance, when, in 1983, TCP/IP was modified to make it work with UNIX by ARPA-funded researchers at Berkeley, uptake of both exploded. In keeping with the public spiritedness of Steve Crocker's Requests for Comments, the source code for UNIX was made freely available for other network operators to use and customize—a move which highlights a further important strand in the history of the Net: the voluntarist ethic of hacker culture.

Do-It-Yourself and Hacker Culture in the 1970s and '80s

Despite the seemingly generous intentions of its architects, ARPANET was still the network of defense contractors and a few elite research universities at the end of the 1970s. However, Dennis Hayes's invention of the dial-up modem on his dining room table in 1977 caused ripples throughout hobbyist computer culture. The emergence of the first small-scale personal computers in the mid-1970s spawned a lively "home brew" subculture of computer clubs around the United States and Europe, brought together by such publications as *Byte* magazine. Founded in 1975 by Carl T. Helmers, *Byte* featured the strap-line: "Computers—The World's Greatest Toy!" on its first cover as well as celebratory articles on "software hackers" and "hardware hackers" (Helmers, 1975). Similar inspiration was provided by publications such as Ted Nelson's *Computer Lib/Dream Machines*, a manifesto for "New Freedoms through Computer Screens," published the same year (Nelson, 1975). Personal computer users armed with modems caused unofficial networks such as FIDONET to proliferate in the late 1970s. Taking usage of the early modem to its limits, two Chicago friends, Ward Christensen and Randy Suess, assembled the first computerized bulletin board system from an assortment of soldered-together chips and floppy disk drives (Christensen and Suess, 1989). They, too, freely distributed the software for managing the bulletin board system in the hope that it would be rapidly adopted. Similar sentiments were at work among students at Duke University and the University of North Carolina in 1979, when they developed a customized version of UNIX to run a bigger bulletin board system that would prove much more scalable.[4] The software required for running what became known as Usenet was freely distributed. During the early 1980s, several other networks sprang up. Mainly centered on academic institutions (places often filled with experimentalists),

---

[4]**Scalability:** A property of computer applications that are designed to be used by many individuals simultaneously. Refers to the ability of a system to "scale up" or "scale down" according to fluctuations in user numbers. Network architecture that is not scalable is of little use for Internet applications because it is more likely to fail when large numbers attempt to use the network.

they included CSNET for computer scientists, THEORYNET at Wisconsin, and MEDLINE, which linked Johns Hopkins University researchers to the National Library of Medicine.

Once again, however, the contradictory nature of the Internet's development was in evidence. For while do-it-yourself hacker culture started to loosen the dominance of the state and the scientific establishment, fostering the creation, by the late 1980s, of what Howard Rheingold would famously term online "virtual communities" (Rheingold, 1993), participation using these technologies was still restricted to the technically literate and those with enough spare cash (and time) to spend on the arcane first generation of personal computers. Bulletin board systems might have seemed friendly enough places for the initiated, but they were forbidding for those who had little knowledge of computers. The use of graphics was in its infancy (though important steps were taken with the rise to prominence of Apple's Macintosh in 1984 and its subsequent influence on rival Microsoft). Personal computer processing power was very rudimentary, though again, this issue was dissolving as rapid progress in the manufacturing of microchips was made in the 1980s. Still, user-initiated information searches were virtually impossible on the Net of the early 1980s because each connected computer had only its numeric IP address[5] to identify it on the network. It was not until 1983, when TCP/IP was declared as the official standard for ARPANET and new, more compatible methods for routing email and allocating addresses via the Domain Name System (DNS)[6] were implemented, that we can start to see the relatively user-friendly characteristics of the Internet as we now know it.

The DNS, which initially created the domain suffixes .com, .gov, .net, .org, .mil, and .edu and which subsequently allowed for country-level domains such as .uk or .ca, proved to be a highly significant stage in the evolution of a more intuitive communication network. When governments, corporations, interest groups, social movements, and political parties started to go online in the 1990s, they found it a surprisingly simple way of alerting citizens and consumers to their existence.

The adoption of TCP/IP as an overarching set of protocols for Internet communication also allowed disparate networks to join together with ARPANET. But fear of the destabilizing effect of such developments led the Department of Defense to create MILNET, the successor to ARPANET, as a separate network. What was left over formed the open Internet for the rest of the 1980s. This was greatly expanded, with significant investment by the U.S. government's National Science Foundation (NSF) providing for the addition of the high-speed NSFNET academic and research backbone in 1985.

---

[5]**IP address:** Internet Protocol address—a unique numeric sequence which all computers on the Internet have (as a fixed address) or are assigned by their Internet service provider when users connect (a dynamic address). While a simple and elegant means of connecting large numbers of computers together, critics argue that the IP address system is a flaw in the Internet's design due to its privacy implications. IP addresses can often easily be traced, and a surprising amount of information can be gleaned about the user of a particular computer.

[6]**Domain Name System (DNS):** A crucial element in the building and maintenance of the World Wide Web, DNS converts domain names (such as http://www.google.com) into less intuitive numerical addresses (in Google's case, 216.239.39.101, among others). DNS is dependent on the correct functioning of several DNS root servers dotted around the Internet, most of which are concentrated in the United States.

THE NET WIDENS

A massive influx of government investment during the 1980s began to raise policy issues around what is now known as Internet governance (see chapter 10). Again, these reveal the clash of ideologies and organizational values. The introduction of the DNS made the Net a much more radical prospect. Its more flexible design and relative simplicity allowed for a rapid expansion of user numbers and content. This coexisted in tension with the restricted nature of Internet participation that had been the norm during the heyday of ARPANET in the 1970s. Still, at this time the major power brokers in the Internet community were those state-sponsored and academic scientists and researchers using the Internet as an end in itself rather than as the means toward some goal, such as commerce. The response to the emergent problems of Internet governance, initiated by these groups, was the creation of an Internet Advisory Board in 1983. This consisted of the heads of a number of devolved task forces, each of which was responsible for overseeing particular aspects of Internet policy (Margolis and Resnick, 2000:37). The most important of these was the Internet Engineering Task Force (IETF), which exists to this day as the supreme standards body for the Net.

Despite the relatively ad hoc and informal nature of this structure of governance, a throwback to the 1970s when Vinton Cerf and his colleagues had set about designing the principles of open networking, it was still ultimately operating under the aegis of the U.S. government. Public investment in the Internet by the NSF had strings attached. The NSF was keen to ensure that the expanded networks would join up academic institutions across the United States at least and would allow for further expansion into Europe, which came later in the 1980s when seven European countries were encompassed. The NSF did not at this stage envisage explicitly commercial uses of the network, and it even attempted to restrict these via its centrally enforced Acceptable Use Policy banning commercial transactions. But, as Margolis and Resnick have argued, this was in fact vague enough to be subverted in most cases and allowed for such a wide range of uses that it became difficult to enforce. The end result was that the academic, state- sponsored Internet became fused with various private and commercial networks, owned and maintained by large corporations such as IBM, MCI, UUNET, and PSINET (Margolis and Resnick, 2000:38). The involvement of private business interests in the governance of the Net was underway. This chaotic and often uneasy relationship between states, the scientific and research community, and businesses, which saw the future economic benefits of providing Internet services to consumers, continued until the mid-1990s, when the NSFNET backbone was fully privatized and handed over to private network carriers.

THE WEB

By the late 1980s, the number of computers connected to the Net had increased rapidly, but the problems of accessibility and ease of use remained much the same as in 1969. The final phase of our prehistory deals with the solution to this problem: the World Wide Web. The advent of the web in 1990 allowed for the convergence of several of the developments we have considered so far. The Internet itself was already in place in terms of connectivity; the growth of personal computing and the widespread adoption of computers in firms and government was already underway and was to be consolidated with the rise to global dominance of the Microsoft Windows operating system. A small but important subculture of virtual communities based around Usenet and related bulletin board systems existed. Missing from this picture, though, were three features that are now taken for granted as part of the early-twenty-first-century Internet: a significant business presence; a significant political presence; and a mass user base. The new accessibility of the Internet provided by the introduction of the web and the graphical browser was to ensure the emergence of each of these three ingredients—in developed countries at least—by the late 1990s.

The concept of the World Wide Web effectively predates the activities of Tim Berners-Lee and Robert Cailliau at the CERN Laboratories in Geneva, though these individuals are often credited with its invention. The idea of hypertext links owes much to Ted Nelson's vision in *Computer Lib/Dream Machines* (1975), which, as we have seen, was influential for the hobbyist computer subculture of the 1970s. Berners-Lee and Cailliau took this inspiration and created a viable system of textual markers that could be used to "tag" existing forms of data, including still images and text and eventually digital sounds and video. Hypertext Markup Language (HTML), when married with a new Hypertext Transfer Protocol (HTTP),[7] provided the basis for the creation of web browser software. The prototype for the latter was designed by Marc Andreesen, a student working at the University of Illinois National Center for Supercomputer Applications. Andreesen produced a rudimentary but relatively stable piece of software called Mosaic, which was designed to run on individual computers and display websites. In the tradition of the Net, he published the browser on the web for others to download free of charge. Other browsers were in existence at the time, but Mosaic was set for notoriety when it came to the attention of Jim Clark, then head of a software company in Silicon Valley. Clark and Andreesen formed Netscape in 1994, and it rapidly became the most widely used piece of browser software until it was finally eclipsed by Microsoft's Internet Explorer in the late 1990s. Improvements in computing power, especially server hardware and security, continued apace during the 1990s, allowing the Internet to evolve into a more graphical medium and web browsers to be used for direct commercial transactions. The "web" became synonymous with the "Net," even though stalwarts correctly insist that a distinction be drawn between the wider Internet—including Usenet, Internet Relay Chat (IRC),[8] Instant Messaging, and

---

[7]**Hypertext Markup Language (HTML) and Hypertext Transfer Protocol (HTTP)**: Both are essential features of the World Wide Web, enabling a diverse array of materials to be presented in a cross-compatible and accessible format: the web page. HTML contains a large number of tags that instruct web browser software how to display pages. HTTP is the communication protocol that allows computers with web browsers to communicate with web servers (the physical location of the files and pages that make up a website).

[8]**Internet Relay Chat (IRC)**: The earliest online chat system. Often, but not necessarily, it consists of web browser–based interfaces that allow users to come together in synchronous, or real-time, interaction across the Internet or Intranets. Users converse by typing lines of text. They may also share files (such as documents, images, audio, and video) in chat channels. Discussions may be one-to-one (private chat) or based on themes in chat rooms. Unlike Usenet, IRC is relatively fast moving and technically difficult to monitor by legal authorities. Such attributes make it attractive to hackers but also to criminals and terrorists.

File Transfer Protocol (FTP)[9] and those portions of it that are designed to be viewed using a graphical browser.

By the mid-1990s, the increasingly global nature of the Net posed a real problem for the ways in which it was "governed." Despite the fact that an Internet Advisory Board had, since 1983, been led by technicians, there were now radically different user constituencies with competing visions of what the future should entail. The scientific and research community was joined by major telecoms providers, hardware manufacturers, software companies, media firms, and government representatives in forming the Internet Society (ISOC) in 1992. The Internet Advisory Board was absorbed into ISOC. Of equal significance, and a development which signaled the commercial expansion into cyberspace during the 1990s, was the creation of the World Wide Web Consortium (W3C) in 1994. Headed by Tim Berners-Lee and based at MIT, CERN (the Centre Européen pour la Recherche Nucleaire), and the French National Institute for Research in Computing and Automation, W3C contains a large but still elite membership of government agencies, businesses, and nonprofit organizations. However, the dominant players are those commercial actors in the telecoms, financial services, media, and publishing businesses who wish to shape the future development and adoption of web standards (Salter, 2004).

Global expansion of the Net rendered U.S. national regulation less effective and less relevant to the needs of users in other countries. To fill the vacuum, a number of voluntary regulatory bodies, consisting of the same alliance of interests that founded the W3C, were established. As the Net continued to expand from the mid-1990s onward, it became vital to exert some form of control over the assignment of domain names. Like much else in relation to the Internet, what might appear to be a simple technical matter soon became deeply politicized, as companies lobbied for their favored name in cyberspace and to protect their intellectual property in trademarks. Such matters had originally been handled by a voluntary body known as the Internet Assigned Numbers Authority (IANA) along with the private companies, Network Solutions, Inc. (now Verisign), and telecoms giant AT&T. A huge international row over the governance and regulation of the Net ensued. (We pick up the contemporary story of Internet governance in chapter 10.)

CONCLUSION

If this has been the prehistory of the Internet, then it is fair to say that its current history begins in the 1990s, when use exploded and the commercial, educational, and government users began to multiply at a rapid rate. In 1991, the NSF announced that it would

---

[9]**File Transfer Protocol (FTP):** Widely used in the early days of the Internet and still alive and well, FTP was designed to simplify the transfer of large files between FTP servers and other computers. Many FTP servers are "anonymous": they do not require a password to retrieve files. Others do require a password, usually because the information contained on such servers is sensitive or illegal. FTP is less intuitive and user friendly than web-based interfaces and often requires some basic technical knowledge of the required commands. However, once the basics are mastered, anyone with an Internet-connected computer can set up an FTP server and share files. In the mid-1990s, such usage expanded as the chief means of trading MP3 audio files and copyrighted software before peer-to-peer networks expanded.

permit commercial transactions over the Net for the first time—a move which angered many of the academics and researchers but really gave recognition to practices that had started to mushroom since the 1980s. But the Net's expansion, and the arrival of new actors and interests, should not blind us to the continuities with the early days. As we have seen, the competing values of state control, technocracy, cold war paranoia, scientific endeavor, community building, the hacker subculture, commercialism, and the ways in which these have given birth to, and subsequently conditioned, technological innovations like TCP/IP and the browser have made the Internet the curious and contradictory medium that it is and will continue to be.

When it comes to analyzing the ways in which the relations between citizens and states are being changed by the Net, we would do well to remember that new political practices do not emerge out of the blue but build upon the foundations that have been laid in the past. Imagining what it is possible to do with network technologies—now the stuff of political initiatives the world over—has been substantially conditioned by the ways in which the technological infrastructure has itself developed. Equally, the foundations upon which the Internet rests and which have shaped its diffusion stretch far beyond the story told here, as we shall see in our third and final contextual chapter on the digital divide.

Discussion Points

- How has the historical development of the Internet shaped its contemporary characteristics?

- Is TCP/IP a radical communication technology?

- How important is the do-it-yourself, or hacker, ethos for making sense of the Internet's development?

- Assess the impact of the World Wide Web and the graphical browser on the diffusion of the Internet.

Further Reading

Writing on the origins of the Internet is something of a cottage industry. There are many useful works, but an excellent place to start is an essay by some of those who developed the core technologies: Leiner et al., 2000.

John Naughton, 1999, is a highly readable and enthusiastic account that encompasses a great amount of historical detail. The author also has a blog. Hafner and Lyon, 1996, captures the spirit of scientific endeavor, as does Hauben and Hauben, 1997. Margolis and Resnick's book (2000) contains an excellent distillation of the main events and themes.

To get a flavor of the ideas which continue to inspire many Internet technicians, see Licklider, 1960, and Nelson, 1975. On the web more specifically, see Berners-Lee, 1999, and Gillies and Cailliau, 2000. Winston, 1998, puts the story in a *much* deeper historical context.

ACCESS, INCLUSION, AND THE DIGITAL DIVIDE

I'm sceptical of the entire digital divide concept. . . . There have been and will continue to be many gaps—between those who knew how to farm and those who did not in the Agriculture Age; those who could fix an engine and those who could not in the Industrial Age; and those who could use a computing appliance and those who could not in the Information Age.

—BENJAMIN M. COMPAINE, 2001

Some would suggest that information and communication technology is a luxury for the poor, especially in the developing world. However . . . it is in effect becoming the electricity of the informational era, that is, an essential medium that supports other forms of production, participation, and social development.

—MARK WARSCHAUER, 2003

CHAPTER OVERVIEW

Inequalities in Internet access and use are shaped by broader social inequalities. The "digital divide" is probably one of the most commonly used phrases in academic and popular writing about the Internet—but not without good reason. As we shall discover, while there is not a single divide but several, the concept is a useful shorthand term for the persistent inequalities that exist between the info-rich and the info-poor. These may be viewed in terms of the global divisions between the developed, the developing, and the least-developed countries as well as those within even the most advanced post-industrial nations. This area has generated a voluminous and still expanding literature in recent years. Scholars rarely agree on how the digital divide should be measured, if at all, and there is even less agreement about its overall significance. It would be impossible to do justice to all of the nuances of the debate here. Rather, I have two main aims. First, I provide an up-to-date "big picture" of the digital divide at the global level and explore some of the major scholarly explanations of its contours. Second, I provide some illustrations of the issues that have arisen *internal* to countries in the developed world, through an extended case study of the most intensively studied country in this field: the United States.

Information and communication technologies have always have been precious social, economic, and political resources, and unequal access to their production and consumption has been a source of division and conflict since ancient times. In the developed world, the Internet is rapidly becoming socially embedded at all levels, from the local through the national to the transnational. It increasingly shapes how people interact in many areas of their lives, as workers, consumers, citizens, students, family members, or even personal diarists. Yet in the least-developed countries, the majority of people have yet to use a telephone, and if current trends continue, many will never have the opportunity.

In the second half of the twentieth century, as international organizations like the United Nations (UN) increasingly shaped the international development agenda, information and communication technologies were widely vaunted as a means to spur economic development for those countries left behind by the wave of industrialization that swept the now-developed world in the nineteenth and early twentieth centuries (Mowlana, 1997). The arrival of the Internet in the 1990s intensified these concerns. Inequalities in access to traditional media and household technologies have long been part of the global system, and it would be foolish to imagine that the Internet will be any different. A crucial question, however, is to what extent does it *matter* that large sections of the global population are excluded from this technology?

DOES THE DIGITAL DIVIDE MATTER?

Some argue that the digital divide is of little social significance, because it will be resolved once the natural play of market forces makes Internet access available to all who want it (Brady, 2000; Compaine, 2001); because there are more pressing problems facing today's societies, like poverty, hunger, and disease (Brady, 2000; Gates, 2000); or perhaps because computers and the Net are akin to other luxury commodities that will never be equally distributed. Hence the view of Michael Powell, chairman of the U.S. Federal Communications Commission (FCC): "I think there is a Mercedes divide. I'd like to have one; I can't afford one" (quoted in Warschauer, 2003:217).

Yet the Internet *is* different. Inequalities in access to technology matter if we start from the assumption that many developed regions of the world are moving, in the words of Manuel Castells, toward a "form of social organization in which information generation, processing, and transmission become the fundamental sources of productivity and power" (Castells, 2000:21). Castells, building upon Daniel Bell's (1973) influential take on post-industrialism, labels this new type of social organization "informationalism."

In the second half of the twentieth century, developed countries gradually increased their exports of knowledge-intensive products and services, while the poorer parts of the developing world, particularly Africa, fell ever further behind in terms of high-tech research and development. Many developing countries are dependent upon selling primary commodities whose market value has steadily dwindled (Warschauer, 2003:19). If the less-developed countries are unable to play a role in the structures of informationalism, and if global development strategies organized by bodies such as the UN do not take the Internet into account, developing countries may find that they "arrive" in terms of industrial development only to find the game has moved on. In other words, the previously developed countries will have become informational, their societies, economies, and political systems saturated with jobs and other social roles that require the ability to use advanced information and communication technologies. In this scenario, the digital divide comes to define a binary world of wealthy, postindustrial/informational societies on the one hand and poor, industrial, or semi-industrial societies on the other.

First-order resources like food, clothing, and shelter are undeniably crucial, but focusing attention solely on these risks a divided and unstable future. As Lisa Servon puts it, "poor people [may] have what they need to survive, but will never be able to get ahead. Resources such as IT can function as ladders with which people can exit poverty" (2002:20). Information and knowledge, and the way they are communicated, are also cultural assets. As Leigh Keeble and Brian Loader have argued, "they enable us to create our identities, develop a shared sense of community and gain an understanding of communities which are different from ourselves" (2001:2).

Both globally and within nations, Internet diffusion may have powerful effects in areas such as education, health care, labor productivity, democratization, citizenship, social cohesion, and integration with the world economy, but new gaps between the rich and the poor will need to be narrowed (Kraemer and Dedrick, 2001; Warschauer, 2003; Wilhelm, 2001; World Summit on the Information Society, 2003). As Joo-Young Jung and colleagues state in response to the view of Michael Powell: "The failure to own a Mercedes does not lead to impediments to job, educational and civic opportunities, whereas the failure to obtain appropriate Internet-related skills is likely to limit these opportunities" (Jung et al., 2001:508). Thus, the digital divide is clearly different from the "Mercedes divide." It matters.

PHYSICAL ACCESS AND BEYOND

Most fundamentally, the digital divide is about physical access to the Internet and its related hardware and software. Some corporate leaders, governments, and even researchers assume that it is *solely* about physical access. Hence the myriad studies which map out inequality in access along racial, income, education, geographical, or gender lines but the lack of studies which explore how social differences in skills shape what people are actually able to *do* when they are online. Measuring physical access is vital for understanding and assessing the digital divide, and a good deal of this chapter is devoted to this, but it is not the whole story. Some of the writing about the Internet spends too much time glorifying technology and tends to lose sight of those prevented from using it effectively. Excitement about advances in scale, speed, and functionality can often cloud judgments about whether and how such technology will actually be used by people in their daily lives. We need to remember that behind the computers, high-speed data networks, and telecommunication there are real people trying to make worthwhile use of those services and technologies to which they have access (Selwyn, 2004:347). Often assumptions have been guided by what Mark Warschauer (2003:31) terms "devices and conduits" approaches, the belief that overcoming the digital divide is simply about providing people with computers and an ISP account, or what Nicholas Garnham terms "technological fetishism," the view that "more," "newer," and "better" technologies will somehow miraculously overcome the problems of unequal access and how that access is shaped by power relations (quoted in Dutton, 1999:77). While a basic understanding of the inequalities in physical access is essential, we also need to consider that they are "embedded in a complex array of factors encompassing physical, digital, human and social resources and relationships" (Warschauer, 2003:6).

Fortunately, there are several approaches that can help here. For instance, Jan van Dijk and Kenneth Hacker (2003:315) argue that there are four principal barriers to real Internet access at the individual level:

- Lack of elementary digital experience caused by lack of interest, computer anxiety, and unattractiveness of the new technology ("mental access").
- No possession of computers and network connections ("material access").
- Lack of digital skills caused by insufficient user-friendliness and inadequate education or social support ("skills access").
- Lack of significant usage opportunities ("usage access").

Similarly, in their detailed study of the United States, considered later in this chapter, Karen Mossberger, and colleagues (2003:9) distinguish between:

- the access divide: inequalities in the basic availability of computers and Internet;
- the skills divide: inequalities in technical competence and information literacy;
- the economic opportunity divide: inequalities in the extent to which individuals are able to use information for the purposes of social advancement, such as getting a new job; and
- the democratic divide: divisions between those able to use the Internet for enhancing their political participation and influence (for the concept of "democratic divide," see also Norris, 2001).

By way of illustration, consider the following example. Those who argue against the significance of the digital divide often claim that the Internet's basic role in providing access to information has empowered citizens. In this view, quick and easy access to information provides us with the resources needed to make informed decisions in areas where we previously had to rely on expert, or "professional," intermediaries. There are many areas in which the flood of newly available data is causing changes: health, for example, where the expertise of medical professionals is being disputed by patients armed with information about their condition downloaded from the Internet. However, if we dig a little deeper, precisely how empowerment occurs is less straightforward. Much online health information is incomprehensible to the vast majority of citizens. This derives from its properties as scientific information that must be interrogated in the context of highly specialized types of knowledge. While there are many opportunities to gain social support from laypersons and fellow sufferers online, these do not unfortunately dissolve the basic divide between those who have the knowledge required to interpret the medical information and those who do not.

Another reason why it is important to consider issues beyond the divide in physical access involves thinking about how the Internet differs from other media. Many begin from the assumption that overcoming the digital divide is about giving disadvantaged groups the opportunity to become *consumers* of information and online services. While this is important, it is perhaps more important that we reduce inequalities in the *production* of content. The Internet dramatically lowers barriers to entry into the marketplace of ideas. Yet there are vast regions around the world and large swathes of the populations of wealthy countries whose cultures are not adequately reflected in the online environment. As Andy Carvin puts it: "The Internet may feel like a diverse place, but when compared with the wealth of diversity and knowledge reflected by humanity in the real world, it's still pretty weak" (2002:253). The content divide reinforces the physical access divide, creating a vicious circle of exclusion. Creating more diverse and relevant content involves equipping disadvantaged groups with physical access and skills, but those groups are likely to be uninterested in acquiring skills if there is little awaiting them in the online environment (Servon, 2002:7).

Going beyond the simple devices and conduits model is difficult due to the relative lack of research, but there is an emerging consensus that scholars must do so if we are to make sense of how the digital divide is likely to evolve in future.

The Global Digital Divide

The global digital divide is very real and can be measured with some accuracy, but before we proceed, a few health warnings about Internet user statistics are necessary. All numbers in this field are based on estimates. It is incredibly difficult to gather accurate data in such a fast-moving area, and until recently, some countries were not particularly systematic in their attempts to measure user numbers. At the time of writing (early 2005), the most reliable and up-to-date country-by-country figures come from the 2002 International Telecommunication Union (ITU) statistics and the Millennium Indicators Database maintained by the UN Statistical Division (UNSD) (ITU, 2004b; UNSD, 2004). The ITU is the UN agency responsible for collecting data on telecommunication infrastructure. In the past, researchers used the "how many online?" data produced by NUA, an Irish market research company. However, following NUA's demise in 2002, some time after it stopped updating its database, the ITU/UN figures became the most authoritative. They have been collected for many years, so the ITU data also enable us to see how Internet use has grown over time. We are now in the position of being able to assess its diffusion over a period of about seven years, from its initial mid-1990s rise to popularity in the developed world. Another advantage is that the ITU is an official body: it will continue to gather annual statistics in the years ahead, making it possible to measure future trends.

The ITU estimates are often a little conservative, especially compared with other aggregated sources of data, such as those from the *Computer Industry Almanac*. In an area that has been plagued by hype, this is probably a strength. One final word of caution: at first glance, these figures might appear low. But bear in mind that the ITU measures Internet users per 100 inhabitants. Thus, it estimates that in the United States in 2002 there were 55 users per 100 inhabitants, whereas the University of California–Los Angeles (UCLA) World Internet Project put the figure at 71 percent of the population (UCLA Center for Communication Policy, 2003). But the ITU's measure avoids some of the disadvantages of comparing countries that use different age thresholds for their population measures. This can be significant, because many countries do not even collect data for those under eighteen (or even twenty-one), yet in some countries, Internet use among teenagers is already at saturation levels (in the United States, 97 percent of twelve to fifteen-year-olds use the Internet (UCLA Center for Communication Policy, 2003:21). There are a whole host of other reasons why measuring Internet diffusion can be mysterious alchemy (see Minges, 2000), but the key issue is whether we can get a decent basic picture of what is occurring over time, and the ITU data serve this purpose.

As figure 4.1 reveals, the global digital divide is severe. Since 1995, the United States and Canada, northern Europe, and Australia and New Zealand have soared above other regions in levels of Internet penetration. Interestingly, western European countries have lagged behind, a point explored further below. But the most depressing headline from this chart is the vast number of countries grouped together in the regions at

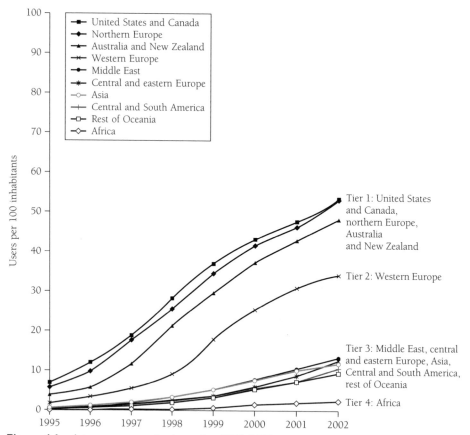

Figure 4.1. Internet penetration by region, 1995–2002. *Sources:* Analysis and adaptation of data from ITU, 2004b. The *CIA World Factbook 2004* was used to fill a small number of gaps in the 2002 data. (Countries excluded due to very incomplete data: Afghanistan, American Samoa, Andorra, Anguilla, Aruba, Bhutan, British Virgin Islands, Cayman Islands, Chad, Congo, D.R. Congo, Gibraltar, Iraq, Libya, Liechtenstein, Marshall Islands, Martinique, Monaco, Montserrat, Myanmar, Nauru, Netherlands Antilles, Nieue, Niger, Northern Mariana Islands, Tajikistan, Turkmenistan, Tuvalu.)

the bottom: the Middle East, central and eastern Europe, Asia, Central and South America, the rest of Oceania (i.e., excluding Australia and New Zealand), and Africa. It is possible to identify a tentative four-tier global stratification model, with the United States and Canada, northern Europe, and Australia and New Zealand grouped together at the top, before the step down to western Europe, then central and eastern Europe, the Middle East, Asia, Central and South America, the rest of Oceania, and finally Africa.

Some might put a positive spin on these figures by pointing out that the difference between the regions at the top and bottom is narrowing. For instance, in 1998, Internet penetration in the United States and Canada, at 28.2 users per 100 inhabitants, was a hundred times greater than in Africa, at 0.28. By 2002, however, this gap had narrowed, with the United States and Canada having "only" about twenty-three times more users than Africa (see figure 4.2). Some might take hope from this trend, but even if it continues—and that is very uncertain, as we shall see below—the developing countries are likely to be a long way behind for many years to come. With some exceptions, such as Guyana (14 percent), Mauritius (10 percent), and Reunion (20 percent), in 2002 the vast majority of African countries struggled to gain penetration levels of more than a couple percent. Even South Africa, once thought of as an Internet success story, saw 2002 user levels stagnate at around the 7 percent mark (ITU, 2004b).

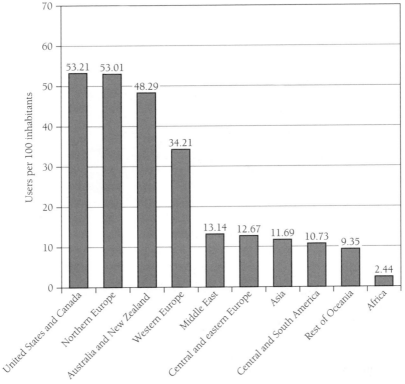

Figure 4.2. Internet penetration by region, 2002. *Sources:* Analysis and adaptation of data from ITU, 2004b. The *CIA World Factbook 2004* was used to fill a small number of gaps in the 2002 data.

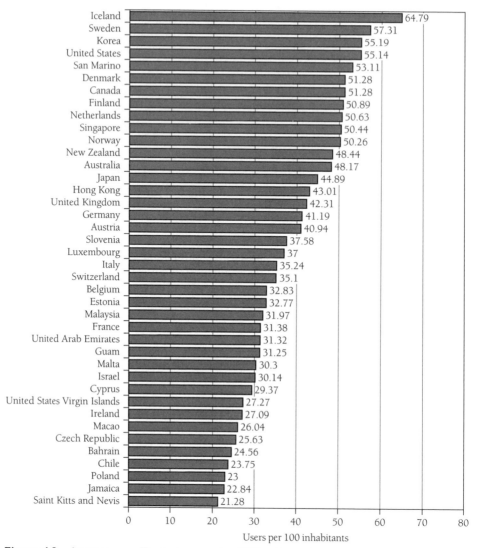

Figure 4.3. Internet users: Top forty countries, 2002. *Sources:* Analysis and adaptation of data from UNSD, 2004. The *CIA World Factbook 2004* was used to fill a small number of gaps in the 2002 data.

Figure 4.3 presents the top forty countries by Internet penetration for 2002—the most recent year for which we have reliable data. While we should be careful about drawing too many conclusions from such league tables, this gives us an idea of the kinds of countries that are in the avant garde—and the remarkable differences between them. While the northern European countries like Sweden, Denmark, Finland, and Iceland, together with the United States, Canada, and Korea, blaze the trail, there are some surprising countries toward the top of the list, such as Slovenia, which comes ahead of Italy, and Estonia, which comes above France. Noticeable for their absence from the top forty are Portugal and Spain, which each had penetration rates of just 19 percent in 2002, and Greece, which props up the European Union 15 (EU15) countries with just 13 percent.

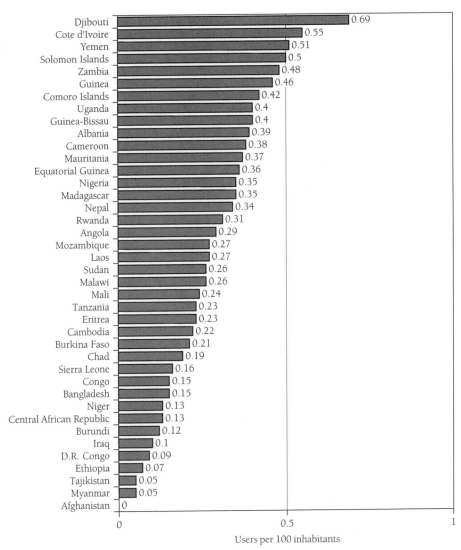

Figure 4.4. Internet users: Bottom forty countries, 2002. *Sources:* Analysis and adaptation of data from UNSD, 2004. The *CIA World Factbook 2004* was used to fill a small number of gaps in the 2002 data.

A more depressing tale is told by figure 4.4—the bottom forty countries. The former Stalinist state of Albania aside, these are drawn overwhelmingly from Africa, with a few Middle Eastern countries such as Iraq and Yemen making an appearance. Note that in 2002 all but four of the countries in the bottom forty have penetration levels of less than half a percent. These countries are among the most troubled parts of the globe and will continue to lag far behind for many years to come.

What does it mean to say that some countries lag behind? Fundamentally, it assumes an underlying evolutionary model of diffusion. Scholars who study the diffusion of technological innovations often identify the so-called S-curve model (Rogers, 1995).

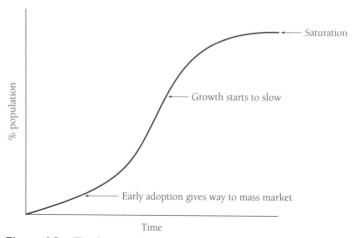

Figure 4.5. The S curve of technology diffusion.

The spread of older technologies such as radio and television indicates a general pattern: in the opening stages a few "early adopters" with sufficient wealth and knowledge start to use a technology. With successful innovations, demand for the technology increases, the costs of production and risks of innovation decrease, and a growth spurt occurs as more and more people become adopters. Finally, as diffusion reaches saturation levels, the rate of growth starts to plateau. Displayed as a schematic chart, a pure S-curve model looks like figure 4.5.

An optimistic S-curve model would predict that the Internet will eventually reach saturation levels of diffusion, in much the same way as has already occurred with televisions, radios, or washing machines (in developed societies). In this interpretation, as market saturation approaches, demand falls, as do prices, and this allows even the poorest groups in society—and the poorest countries in the world—to afford access. Such groups or countries may be the last to adopt—the so-called "laggards"—but they benefit from cheaper prices in the long run and may even experience diffusion growth rates that outstrip those in the pioneer countries. This is because they can implement innovations "off the shelf," without having to spend vast amounts on their own research and development costs. They can simply plug in to networks that have already been generated, at substantial cost, by the early adopters.

This "late-comer advantage" has been proposed by some economic historians as a general pattern of global industrialization, pointing to a future in which the developing countries rapidly catch up with today's developed countries over the next half-century (e.g., Lucas, 2000). From this optimistic perspective, all societies will eventually converge on a saturation point at the top right-hand corner of the S-curve chart. However, as Pippa Norris has pointed out, there is an alternative stratification S-curve model (2001:31). In this perspective, there will be no convergence because developed countries with built-in advantages, such as greater wealth, will always be ahead of the poorer countries. It may be that the real market for Internet access in developing countries will always be restricted to a small elite. Alternatively, it may be that the diffusion process takes so long that it ceases to have any significance. As the famous economist

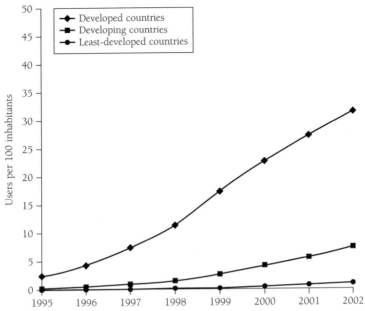

Figure 4.6. Internet penetration by level of development, 1995–2002.
Sources: UNSD, 2004. The *CIA World Factbook 2004* was used to fill a small number of gaps in the 2002 data. (Countries excluded due to very incomplete data: Afghanistan, American Samoa, Andorra, Anguilla, Aruba, Bhutan, British Virgin Islands, Cayman Islands, Chad, Congo, D.R. Congo, Gibraltar, Iraq, Libya, Liechtenstein, Marshall Islands, Martinique, Monaco, Montserrat, Myanmar, Nauru, Netherlands Antilles, Nieue, Niger, Northern Mariana Islands, Tajikistan, Turkmenistan, Tuvalu.)

    Note: Development categorizations provided by the UN. "Japan in Asia, Canada and the United States in northern America, Australia and New Zealand in Oceania, and Europe are considered developed regions or areas. In international trade statistics, the Southern African Customs Union is also treated as a developed region and Israel as a developed country; countries emerging from the former Yugoslavia are treated as developing countries; and countries of eastern Europe and the former U.S.S.R. countries in Europe are not included under either developed or developing regions" (UNSD, 2004). The least-developed countries are mainly drawn from Africa but include some Asian countries.

J. M. Keynes is reported to have said: "in the long run, we are all dead." A stratification model also highlights the fact that the digital divide is a moving target. As technologies change, new inequalities emerge, as some have greater functionality than others.

    Let us briefly explore the S-curve model by comparing the diffusion of the Internet with overall levels of development. The concept of development is highly contentious and open to multiple interpretations, but the UN categorizes countries according to its own criteria as "developed," "developing," and "least developed" (for further explanation, see the note to figure 4.6). What emerges when we compare Internet penetration over time for these three categories? As we would expect, developed countries exhibit higher levels of Internet penetration than the developing and least developed (figure 4.6). This is another confirmation of the regional patterns we saw in figure 4.1.

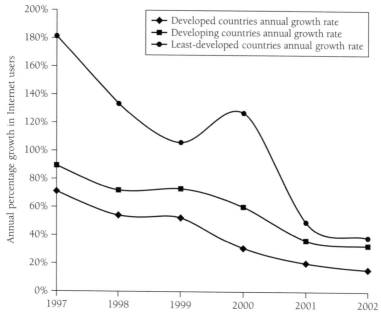

Figure 4.7. Annual growth rate in Internet users by level of development, 1996–2002. *Sources:* UNSD, 2004. The *CIA World Factbook 2004* was used to fill a small number of gaps in the 2002 data. (Countries excluded due to very incomplete data: Afghanistan, American Samoa, Andorra, Anguilla, Aruba, Bhutan, British Virgin Islands, Cayman Islands, Chad, Congo, D.R. Congo, Gibraltar, Iraq, Libya, Liechtenstein, Marshall Islands, Martinique, Monaco, Montserrat, Myanmar, Nauru, Netherlands Antilles, Nieue, Niger, Northern Mariana Islands, Tajikistan, Turkmenistan, Tuvalu.)
   Note: Development categorizations provided by the UN. See note to figure 4.6 for definitions.

Yet if we dig a little deeper and examine the annual growth rates for these three categories of country (figure 4.7), an unexpected and more worrysome trend emerges: growth rates appear to have stalled in the developing and least-developed countries.

Why is this significant? While we might expect the levels of growth to tail off in the developed world as diffusion starts to approach saturation levels at the peak of the S curve, to find this occurring in the developing and least-developed countries so early is extraordinary. It could be argued that we should not read too much into these figures, especially given the erratic trends in the least-developed countries (notice the "hump" in the curve for the year 2000 in figure 4.7). But an erratic trend is not a firm upward trend, and this is at average penetration levels of less than 1 percent, compared with 31 percent for the countries in the developed category. Even the UN's middle category of developing countries only managed penetration rates of around 7 percent by 2002. At best, this points to an unpredictable stop-start approach to growth in the poorer regions of the world over the coming years. We may see years of very high growth rates, such as occurred in 2000, followed by much weaker growth. At worst, even though the head-line growth rate in the developing countries continues to be impressive (39 percent in 2002), the steep decline since 2000 points to a likely widening of the digital divide in

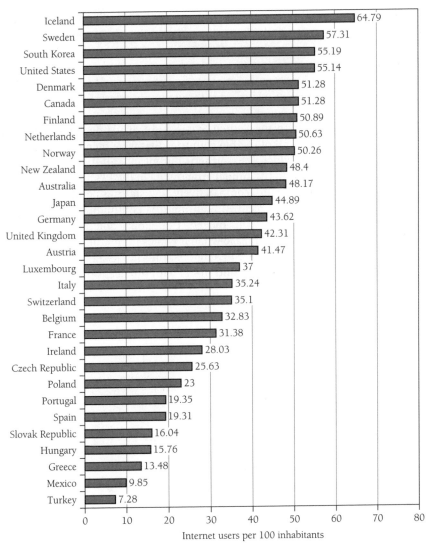

Figure 4.8. Internet penetration: OECD countries, 2002. *Source:* Analysis and adaptation of data from ITU, 2004b.

years to come. This pattern would not have been discernible without the time series data from the ITU.

Even within the developed regions there are marked disparities. This can be seen clearly in figure 4.8 covering the Organization for Economic Co-operation and Development (OECD) countries—the world's thirty richest nations. Surprisingly large differences exist within the OECD, with Turkey displaying an abysmally low penetration level of just 7 percent and very wealthy societies such as Switzerland, Belgium, and France appearing surprisingly low down the list. A common assumption is that relatively wealthy western European countries can be grouped together with the United

States and Canada. But to do so would be partly misleading. As figure 4.1 and the 2002 snapshot provided in figure 4.2 (the first two figures in this chapter) revealed, western Europe, which in those cases excludes northern European countries with high access levels that are EU members (Denmark, Finland, Norway, and Sweden), has always lagged behind the United States and Canada and continues to do so. Indeed, by 2002 there were possible signs that diffusion rates throughout western Europe were starting to plateau (figure 4.2).

Comparing the EU15 with the United States and Canada does not substantially alter the picture (the EU15 is all of the EU countries that were members from 1995 up to the 2004 enlargement, in which the northern European countries are of course included). As figure 4.9 illustrates, the annual growth rate in the EU has been higher over the years, which is explained by its comparatively low starting point in 1995. But in 2001 the United States started to recover, pointing to a continuing disparity between penetration levels in the medium term. Indeed, U.S. global dominance remains pronounced. Though it stands in fourth place when it comes to Internet penetration, other numbers tell a different story. A quarter of all global Internet users reside in the United States. China and Japan are in joint second place, with 9 percent of the world's online

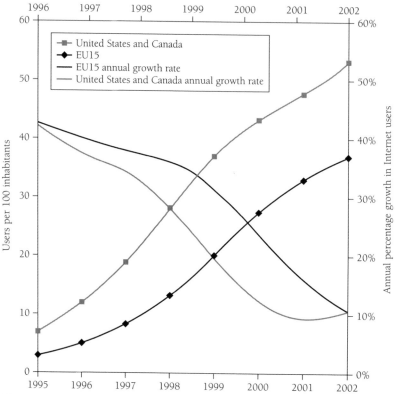

Figure 4.9. Internet penetration and growth rates in the EU and the United States and Canada, 1995–2002. *Source:* ITU, 2004b.
Note: Top x-axis begins at 1996 because it represents annual growth point for 1995–96.

population, though China, with a population of 1.3 billion, is clearly punching below its weight (ITU, 2004b). Thus, global inequalities in Internet access, between the developed and developing regions and between countries within the developed regions, are inescapable trends that are likely to remain with us for at least the next decade.

Explaining the Global Digital Divide

Describing the digital divide is one thing, explaining it quite another. From the discussion above, it seems clear that greater Internet penetration is associated with higher levels of economic development. It should be no surprise, then, to find that all of the major studies, including those that use sophisticated multivariate statistical analysis, have found this to be the case (Bauer et al., 2002; Drori and Jang, 2003; Hargittai, 1999; Lucas and Sylla, 2003; Norris, 2001; Robison and Crenshaw, 2002). Unlike descriptive statistics (simple measurements like those above), multivariate analysis allows scholars to isolate the influence of different variables. By using statistical controls, it is possible to disentangle influences and arrive at firmer conclusions about those that are genuinely significant. This is especially important for Internet access, where variables like economic development, computer ownership, telephone penetration, levels of education, literacy, and so on are likely to be related to each other. In other words, countries with higher per capita GDP—a simple measure of economic development—are statistically more likely to have higher literacy rates than poorer countries, but how can we assess the relative influence of per capita GDP versus literacy on levels of Internet diffusion? Scholars use multivariate analysis to try to answer such puzzles. Now, the social sciences are a broad church, but quantitative methods are not everybody's gospel. Therefore, no knowledge of multivariate methods is required for understanding my discussion below. It is much more important for our purposes that we summarize the findings of the major studies as a means of painting the big picture.

Probably the most categorical finding that economic development influences Internet access globally comes from Henry Lucas and Richard Sylla's analysis of World Bank data. They found that higher levels of economic development and telecommunication infrastructure (measured by telephone penetration) were strongly associated with Internet penetration, while literacy levels were also significant, though to a lesser extent (Lucas and Sylla, 2003:13). There are enormous differences in access to basic telephone service around the world. In 2001, Luxembourg, Norway, Sweden, and Iceland topped the global rankings, with over 150 lines and cellular subscribers per 100 inhabitants. The United Kingdom (136) and the United States (113) fall in the top forty countries, whereas Cameroon (3), Pakistan (3), and Niger (0.3) feature in the bottom forty (UNSD, 2004). In most countries, televisions outstrip telephone access (Warschauer, 2003:37). Pundits may point to a future in which wireless access via mobile devices will become the norm, and it is true that mobile phone, satellite, and wireless network technology is making inroads into the world's poorest regions, bypassing many of the costly pitfalls associated with establishing wired infrastructure. In sub-Saharan Africa, for example, cellular subscribers now far outnumber fixed lines (Støvring, 2004:21). However, the vast majority of the world's Internet users continue to access it via a computer attached to a physical wired network, whether old-fashioned dial-up or broadband DSL and cable (Polikanov and Abramova, 2003:45). After many

EXHIBIT 4.1. EXPLAINING THE GLOBAL DIGITAL DIVIDE: KEY VARIABLES

- *Economic development variables* other than GDP, such as economic inequality, energy consumption, proportion of the workforce in the service sector, and connectedness with global markets.
- *Specific technology infrastructure variables,* such as the penetration of telephones, computers, televisions and radios.
- *Relevant policy variables,* such as the level of competition in a country's telecommunication market, whether its telecommunication infrastructure is a public or private monopoly, or national commitment to an ideology of science- and technology-driven development
- *Human capital variables,* such as education, ethnic homogeneity, English-language proficiency, population density, basic literacy, and electronic literacies, meaning the skills required to effectively and meaningfully interact, use, and produce content using the Internet.
- *Political variables,* such as differing levels of democratic development or a country's connections with international organizations.

Sources: Analysis and summary of Bauer et al., 2002; Drori and Jang, 2003; Hargittai, 1999; Lucas and Sylla, 2003; Norris, 2001; Robison and Crenshaw, 2002; Warschauer, 2003.

years of delay, mobile phone networks are only just beginning to be upgraded to accept high-speed data traffic, even in many of the most advanced countries, and the bandwidth available across mobile connections is far below what can be achieved through fixed-line broadband. Also, wireless network access is only suitable for relatively small geographical areas, while satellite installations are plagued by reliability problems and high up-front costs. Thus, economic and infrastructural differences are likely to remain the major explanation for differences in Internet diffusion around the world for many years.

But is this the whole story? Perhaps not. The large gaps between some of the most advanced postindustrial nations of the OECD (see figure 4.8)—countries that are in many other ways quite similar—hint that there could be several other influences at work. To try to get to grips with this diversity, studies have assessed the effects of a range of possible variables. These can be grouped into six main categories (exhibit 4.1). Let us now consider the findings of these studies in more detail.

It is reasonable to assume that Internet access is shaped by the cost of a computer and subscribing to an ISP. These costs vary quite markedly, even among the wealthy OECD countries. Historically, national telecommunication sectors developed as public or private monopolies. However, during the 1980s, the emergence of neoliberal economic policies led many countries to privatize and deregulate their telecommunication sectors in the hope of increasing competition, fostering innovation, and bringing down prices. This vision is now globally dominant, especially in the development programs of the World Bank (Støvring, 2004). So it is worth considering whether a country's telecommunication policy is likely to have an effect on its levels of Internet access. The short answer is that it does. In her study of the OECD countries, Eszter Hargittai found that, after economic wealth (defined as per capita GDP), the competitiveness of the telecommunication market was the second major variable affecting Internet access. Thus, countries with high levels of Internet penetration are more likely to be wealthy, but those that are wealthy *and* have a competitive telecommunication market are *much* more likely to have higher penetration rates. Those countries with privately owned telecommunication infrastructures are (in theory) more likely to exhibit lower access charges, as competition forces companies into a scramble to attract customers (Hargittai, 1999). Findings from a similar study of the EU and the United States by Johannes Bauer and colleagues reinforce this: widespread personal computer diffusion as well as local loop unbundling (allowing multiple companies to compete in supplying telecommunication to customers at the local level) produce low ISP costs and higher levels of access (Bauer et al., 2002:133).

This goes some way toward explaining why the United States, Korea, and northern European countries such as Finland and Sweden display such high levels of Internet penetration. All of these have very competitive telecommunication markets. Finland is a particularly interesting case. Its very high penetration levels stem from its deregulated telecommunication market and high density of phone lines. Compare these countries with France, which falls surprisingly low in the OECD rankings. Despite liberalization reforms during the late 1990s, France still has a monopoly market structure in telecommunication, dominated by France Telecom. For many years this kept prices high and encouraged conservatism about the Internet, exhibited most notably in the continuation of the state's popular Minitel system, first introduced in 1982. Minitel provided a basic textual information service accessed via dumb terminals and was not connected to the broader Internet. While French subscribers may now access it using the Internet, Minitel's presence contributed to delays in the diffusion of the broader Internet (Hargittai, 1999:713).

When it comes to developing countries, the irony is that the true costs of computer equipment and ISP accounts can be incredibly high. Household income is much lower, the infrastructure less reliable, and the markets often smaller and too widely dispersed. The UN *Human Development Report* of 1999 estimated that the average American can afford to buy a computer with just one month's salary. The average Bangladeshi would require eight years' worth of earnings (quoted in Lucas and Sylla, 2003:4). Russians wishing to use the Internet would have to pay the equivalent of $121 a month in 1999—some 485 times more in real terms than those living in Finland (Lucas and Sylla, 2003:15). Reliable global data on ISP costs are only just emerging, and it seems that relative disparities may be closing: by 2002, twenty hours of monthly Internet access in India was "only" seventeen times more expensive than in the United Kingdom (Basu, 2004:118). Yet it seems likely that these costs will continue play a significant role in excluding poorer countries, where Internet access is likely to remain an expensive luxury service, restricted to metropolitan elites (Oyelaran-Oyeyinka and Adeya, 2004). Optimists point out that public access sites such as cybercafés are proliferating across many African countries, but there is growing evidence that these tend to be concentrated in major cities and are mostly used by the wealthy and educated in any case (Mwesige, 2004).

Inequalities in computer ownership and Internet access are also closely related to inequalities in access to traditional media (Norris, 2001:54). Overall, those countries that have long been excluded from radio, television, and a vibrant press are currently adding exclusion from the Internet to their plight. In her analysis of the global digital divide, Pippa Norris considers several other variables which we might expect to have an influence on access: levels of investment in technology research and development; human capital indicators, including adult literacy and levels of secondary education; and democratization indicators drawn from the internationally recognized Freedom House index, which grades countries according to their protection of rights and civil liberties. Norris found that all of these variables are strongly correlated with both new media *and* old media penetration. Yet after statistical controls were introduced, only per capita GDP and investment in research and development were significant influences (66). Though the conclusion that a country's level of democratization is not related to Internet diffusion has been contradicted by Kristopher Robison and Edward Crenshaw's huge cross-country analysis (2002), this is a major finding. It suggests that the digital divide in Internet access merely extends older media technology divides, not only reinforcing but amplifying long-term inequalities between the developed and developing regions. This interpretation would go some way toward explaining the stalling annual growth rate for the developing and least-developed countries we saw in figure 4.7 previously.

The lesson here would appear to be that a country must privatize and deregulate its telecommunication sector if it is to jump on the escalator of growing Internet access. Yet despite the pattern in the OECD, we should be careful about transferring this assumption to all societies. In some cases, privatization may make matters worse. A *purely* market-based approach may result in large swathes of the population, such as those living in rural areas, being denied access, because there are insufficient user numbers for companies to turn a profit. Such cases of market failure have traditionally been offset by government intervention in the form of publicly owned corporations or subsidies that may encourage wider diffusion. Even in the United States, widely considered to be the epitome of deregulated telecommunication, universal service strictures are in place to safeguard telephone penetration in rural areas and a federal e-rate program exists to subsidize cheaper Internet connectivity for public schools, colleges, and libraries.

The global applicability of the "privatize and deregulate" assumption appears even weaker if we consider other variables, such as the role that governments have played in driving forward a science- and technology-centered approach to economic and social development or how domestic demand for the Internet might be conditioned by the extent to which a country is culturally integrated into the broader global system. Finland may have a highly competitive Internet market, but it was also one of the first countries to launch a national program to get people online in 1994. It has also been suggested that the presence of high-tech companies such as Finland's Nokia and Sweden's Ericsson have had an effect by positioning technology research and development at the center of those economies. Alternatively, departing from a "world polity" perspective, Gili Drori and Yong Suk Jang (2003:155) argue that higher numbers of scientific and educational initiatives and stronger ideological commitment to the global information society are more important for predicting which countries have more sophisticated information and communication technology bases. Drori and Jang's is a persuasive interpretation: in 2003 the ITU published its Digital Access Index, comparing countries across a range of indicators. This revealed rapid growth in connectivity in countries that had explicit technology-related development policies, such as Malaysia with its Multimedia Super Corridor, the United Arab Emirates' Dubai Internet City project, and the Cyber City in Mauritius (ITU, 2003). These findings would appear to reinforce the view that governments can make a difference.

At the same time, however, we need to be careful about the underlying impact of such national initiatives, because there is evidence that inequalities caused by uneven development can have a braking effect on Internet diffusion (Robison and Crenshaw, 2002:355). An excellent example is India. During the 1990s, India's technology sector, particularly software and information services, expanded dramatically. By 1996, it was worth around $1.2 billion annually and by 2000 was growing at a rate of 50 percent a year. Over the last ten years, large numbers of Western firms, such as Motorola, HP, Citibank, Yahoo!, and Dell have outsourced chunks of their software development, customer support, and back-office functions to Indian companies, resulting in cost savings of as much as 50 percent. India's advantages include widespread use of English, the nine-hour time difference from U.S. Eastern Standard Time, but above all, the relatively low labor costs (which are nevertheless high by Indian standards). Successive Indian governments have played significant roles in fostering these sectors, for instance, by providing incentives to Californian firm Silicon Graphics to establish a presence in Bangalore and by encouraging intensive engineer training programs in schools and colleges (May, 2002:136–37). The problem, however, is that most of this activity has been concentrated in just a few sectors, notably software, and a few parts of the country, principally the major regions of Bangalore, Delhi, Hyderabad, and Madras, which have seen immense changes and a virtuous circle of ever-increasing development (Lal, 2001). Yet for the vast majority of India's rural poor, what goes on in Bangalore, which describes itself as "India's Silicon Valley," is still largely irrelevant (Mahara, 2002).

Another example is Mexico, which liberalized its information technology sector upon joining the North American Free Trade Agreement (NAFTA) in the mid-1990s. NAFTA opened up the Mexican market to an influx of transnational computer manufacturers, and this has stimulated Internet diffusion and the high-tech sector. But Mexico has little hardware or software production capacity of its own. Its role in global networks of production is often little more than a cheap assembly line that puts together components manufactured elsewhere (Dedrick et al., 2001). Similar patterns of uneven development due to integration into the global IT market are occurring in countries such as Brazil (Tigre and Botelho, 2001), China (Giese, 2003), and Egypt (Warschauer, 2003:23). National programs of technology-driven economic development may turn out to be less transformational than was once assumed.

What about some of the other global digital divide variables, such as language, literacy, and education? Given the dominance of the English language on the Internet, it is often assumed that an inability to speak English is a major contributor to inequalities of access. Perhaps this explains the variations between the otherwise similar OECD countries. It may potentially account for the relatively low access levels in countries such as France, Spain, Italy, and Greece, where less emphasis is placed on acquiring English-language skills, than in the northern European countries like Finland, Denmark, and Sweden. In all of the major studies to date, however, English proficiency was found to be only weakly related to higher levels of access. A surprising finding from Hargittai's study is that it did not make much difference across the OECD countries when compared with her "killer" variables of wealth and telecommunication policy (1999:710). Similarly, Robison and Crenshaw, assuming that proximity to Anglophone culture would increase Internet penetration, assessed the influence of former British colonial rule, only to find that it made little difference (2002:354).

On the one hand, this seems counterintuitive, given that around 80 percent of websites are in English. It has long been argued that the technological building blocks of computers and the Internet discriminate against non-Roman languages (Jordan, 2001:5). This is due to the fact that they were initially based upon the American Standard Code for Information Interchange (ASCII), which only specifies 256 characters. This creates problems for languages such as Japanese, for instance, which uses over 7,000 characters. On the other hand, we know that the most popular use of the Internet is for personal communication via email rather than browsing for information via the web (UCLA Center for Communication Policy, 2003). Seen in this light, the language barrier does not figure as a major deterrent to going online. It is just as easy to email your mother in French as it is in English. And recent changes to browser software have made it easier to display non-Roman languages, as has the development of Unicode, which allows for 65,536 characters, as a replacement for ASCII.

Of course, we need to bear in mind that Hargittai's study only had aggregate data for the OECD. Given that only around 6 percent of the world's population speaks English as a first language and about another 19 percent speaks it as a second language or knows some English (Warschauer, 2003:95–96), there are likely to be many hundreds of millions of individuals around the world for whom the lack of content in their own language is a major deterrent. Judged against the numbers of Arabic speakers, there is not much Internet content available in Arabic, for example. The truth is that we still know very little in concrete terms about the impact of language worldwide.

If the evidence on English-language proficiency appears fuzzy, much the same can be said of basic literacy. Some level of literacy is required for effective use of any medium, but it is especially important for the Internet, which remains dominated by textual content despite the proliferation of graphics and multimedia. As mentioned above, although Lucas and Sylla (2003) found literacy had some influence, in Norris's 2001 study it ceased to be significant after controlling for other variables. While this may be the case in these macro-level studies, literacy rates do vary dramatically, and it is difficult to imagine that these inequalities do not have an impact. Some developed countries such as Italy, Spain, Singapore, South Korea, and Greece enjoy near universal literacy, while many developing countries languish in the middle range of around 50–60 percent, including India and Egypt. Most of the least-developed countries have literacy rates around 20 percent (UNSD, 2004). There is also a significant gender gap, with women trailing men in many countries, sometimes by as much as 30 percent.

Part of the problem with simple measures of literacy is that they do not allow for consideration of the more fine-grained inequalities that emerge from the unequal distribution of effective literacy skills. Tim Jordan has argued that the effects of English-language dominance on the Internet go beyond simple proficiency, to encompass "cultural norms of communication" that exclude non-Westerners, such as competitive individualism, libertarianism, and a relish for confrontation that seems natural in the Anglo-American world but which serves to alienate those from cultures where consensus or social solidarity is a more prevalent value. Jordan uses the example of Japanese cultural norms, which value not open confrontation but slow consensus building to avoid embarrassing those whom a decision goes against (2001:6). There are also a range of electronic literacies based upon skills specific to the Internet and computer-mediated communication. It is not simply a question of being able to read and write. Instead, advanced skills are often required for readers to create and distribute their own content and to assess others' content in context. Being able to locate and interrogate texts and to respond appropriately and effectively to others are arguably much more important in the online environment than elsewhere, due to the sheer volume of information and the relative absence of gatekeepers able to sift trustworthy information from the rubbish (Silverstone, 2004). Indeed, Robert Fortner has written of a "pleonastic divide," referring to those who are excluded by the sheer *excess* of available information. Fortner argues that this leads many to tune out because they give up trying to decide what is valuable and what is not (Fortner, 1995; Warschauer, 2003:41–46, 114; see also Shenk, 1997; van Dijk and Hacker, 2003:324).

Such factors are difficult to quantify and can only be fully unearthed using ethnographic methods. However, one likely indication of the effects of cultural norms and literacies lies in the gross inequalities in the *production* of online content. Attempts have been made to map global inequalities in this area. For example, research by Matthew Zook (2001) revealed that 55 percent of the world's Internet domain names (e.g., www.google.com) were registered in the United States. Germany and the United Kingdom came next, with just 7 percent, folllowed by Canada, with 5 percent. These figures accurately portray what must be obvious to the majority of Internet users: U.S. content is predominant. There is much less web-based information in areas like health, education, weather, the environment, and the local economy that is intelligible and useful to those in developing countries. Over time, as other countries start to catch up, this gap is likely to diminish, but the advantages of being the first mover in so many areas will undoubtedly remain for some time, and this is likely to be a major area of conflict in future years.

Finally, literacy skills are in large part dependent upon access to education. While evidence from some studies (e.g., Norris, 2001) indicates that education is less significant than we might think, qualitative approaches (e.g., Warschauer, 2003) have argued otherwise. Indeed, it is possible that after economic development, education becomes a major influence, as Kristopher Robison and Edward Crenshaw found in their ambitious assessment of more than a dozen global variables. They conclude:

> education is an important catalyst in the formation of post-industrial technologies and social structures. If the manipulation, consumption, and production of the *cyber* are quickly replacing the manufacture of "real" goods as the principal key function of post-industrializing societies, then education operates for post-industrialization very much as cheap labor did for industrialization. (2002:356)

Education provides individuals with transferable skills in using computers and office software. Diffusion theorists argue that it also oils the wheels of innovation by providing a less conservative audience for new ideas (Rogers, 1995).

The main causes of the global digital divide in Internet access thus appear to be economic, though there is an emerging consensus that other significant influences include infrastructural capacity, telecommunication policy, levels of literacy (both basic and electronic), and country-level ideologies of national technology-led development. There is also evidence that education exerts a "supercharging" effect on levels of Internet diffusion in those countries that already score highly in terms of economic development and level of democratization (Robison and Crenshaw, 2002:352). There is less certainty about the direct influence of a country's level of democratic development or the predominance of the English language in the online environment.

Neat conclusions, especially from the kinds of quantitative macro-analyses considered above, must always be seen as tentative. Quantitative studies are largely governed by the range and availability of data at the global level, and there will always be arguments about how best to measure the digital divide. Some may suggest that it cannot be measured, but this is, of course, a cheap criticism: studies of global stratification must necessarily use large aggregate data sets. Although more fine-grained qualitative studies provide a rich variety of case studies from several countries, they can always be challenged on the grounds that the digital divide is a global phenomenon about which we cannot generalize without truly global data. In the end, much more research is required in this area if we are to make sense of how the global digital divide is continuing to evolve. For now, however, let us descend from the global level to focus on the inequalities internal to nations by examining the digital divide in the United States.

THE DIGITAL DIVIDE IN A HYPERDEVELOPED COUNTRY: THE UNITED STATES

The centrality of high-tech research and development for the U.S. economy has led one writer to describe it as a hyperdeveloped country (Suchman, 2002). It is here, perhaps more than anywhere, that speculation about the shift toward Castells's (2000) informationalism has been most prevalent. For example, the U.S. Bureau of Labor Statistics estimates that eight of the ten fastest-growing occupations through 2010 will be computer related (Mossberger et al., 2003:64). For this reason, combined with the fact that much of the single-country evidence about the societal influence of the Internet has been generated in or about the United States, it makes an excellent case study in state-of-the-art knowledge about the digital divide.

The United States is also experiencing a number of shifts that make it an even more interesting country to watch over the next few years. There are geographical enclaves where Internet penetration levels are extremely high. As an example, in the area around San Jose, California—the major city in Silicon Valley—it approaches 90 percent. This might appear an unusual example, but there are many other areas with similar rates, including Austin, Texas; Salt Lake City, Utah; Phoenix, Arizona; Long Island, New York; Orange County, California; and Boston (Ness, 2003). The United States is also experiencing rapid changes in usage patterns, due to the huge growth in broadband connections. By August 2004, more than half of those connecting from home in the United States did so using a broadband connection—an increase of 47 percent since August 2003 (Nielsen/Netratings, 2004). This points toward the emergence of a new divide between those who have always-on, high-speed access to rich multimedia content integrated into their everyday lives and those stuck in a 1990s time warp, logging on using dial-up modems.

As we saw in figure 4.1, Internet use has grown at a tremendous rate in the United States. At the time of writing (early 2005), the latest reliable figures for Internet use come from the Pew Internet and American Life Project and the UCLA Internet Report. In June 2004, the Pew Project found that 63 percent of the U.S. population was online (Rainie, 2004), whereas at the end of 2003, UCLA found the figure to be 71 percent (UCLA Center for Communication Policy, 2003). The majority of other surveys indicate that two-thirds of the US population regularly use the Internet. When asked if they had used the Internet "yesterday," 53 percent of Americans replied that they had (Pew Internet and American Life Project, 2004b). A quarter of U.S. homes have two computers, while 10 percent have three or more (UCLA Center for Communication Policy, 2003:26).

As we saw in our global comparisons above, these are very high levels of penetration. Yet user numbers have grown at only modest levels since 2001. This has led some commentators to speculate that the Net is unlikely to reach full saturation levels of over 90 percent but might instead peak at its present figure, which is about the level of penetration for cable television. If we bundle satellite television viewers in with cable viewers, those who pay an extra fee for their television reaches 80 percent, suggesting that Internet use might reach that sort of level in the next five to ten years. Still, Lee Rainie and Peter Bell of the Pew Project argue that it is likely to take another half-generation for Internet penetration to reach the levels for television (98 percent) and telephones (94 percent) (Rainie and Bell, 2004:47). In passing, we may note that usage levels for television and phone differ very little according to household income and many other demographic indicators (Warschauer, 2003:31), but as we shall see, Internet use is very different in this regard.

In the United States, the digital divide emerged as a policy concern as soon as the Internet started to diffuse. In 1995, the Department of Commerce's National Telecommunications and Information Administration (NTIA) produced a landmark survey entitled *Falling through the Net* (U.S. Department of Commerce/NTIA, 1995). This highlighted divisions between the info-rich and the info-poor across America, based upon age, geography, gender, race, and ethnicity. Between 1995 and 2000, the NTIA published a further three reports, all of which revealed huge annual growth in those going online but the persistence of social inequalities shaping access. The one demographic that bucked the trend was gender. All of the NTIA reports signaled a narrowing of the gender divide in access. This is of course very different from other areas, such as education and the labor market, where men far outnumber women in technology-related subjects and jobs, or the ways in which uses of the Internet are, like other domestic technologies, shaped by gender roles (Van Zoonen, 1992, 2002). But in terms of simple access, the gender divide in the United States is insignificant.

Other social indicators continued to be relevant in shaping inequalities in Internet access (U.S. Department of Commerce/NTIA, 1997, 1999, 2000). President Clinton's administration made much of the shift towards what would become known in popular political discourse as the new economy. The federal government argued that being denied access implied losing a number of important skills. It was widely felt that the United States would fall behind other nations if large sections of its society could not take advantage of the opportunities offered by the Internet. As a result, a number of policy responses were designed to combat the digital divide, most notably the $2.25 billion e-rate program, which subsidized access in rural areas and public schools, and two other small federal initiatives: the Technologies Opportunities Program (TOP) and the Community Technology Centers (CTC) initiative (Mossberger et al., 2003:3; see also Servon, 2002).

This policy agenda started to unravel, however, with the election of the Bush administration in 2000. A new, much more optimistic NTIA report, entitled *A Nation Online*, was published in 2002 (U.S. Department of Commerce/NTIA, 2002). This painted a rosy picture of Americans rapidly taking up the Internet and using it productively in their daily lives. There is much substance to this view, and it has been shared in large part by the Pew Project reports since 2002. But while usage did undoubtedly surge in the late 1990s, it was difficult to avoid the persistence of numerous divides, especially those based upon race, education, and income, and these were often glossed over by the NTIA as temporary phenomena that the market would eventually resolve. *A Nation Online* was also slightly misleading, because it measured access to the Internet from all locations, including work and the home, whereas previous reports had measured access only from the home. Not only is measuring all access likely to produce higher figures, because those in low-income households are more likely to use the Internet at work or in a public place such as a library or cybercafé, it also skates over the fact that access at work is a much more restrictive experience than in the home (Mossberger et al., 2003:19; Selwyn, 2004:347).

While the NTIA surveys are the most widely cited, there were a range of other studies conducted during the 1990s. In their helpful review of the eight major analyses, Karen Mossberger and colleagues found that all revealed gaps based on education and age, all but one emphasized the income gap, half reported gaps based on race and ethnicity, while none raised concerns over gender. In addition, a range of other variables have been identified as shaping access: parental presence, with single-parent households having lower levels of access; mental and physical disabilities, with nondisabled groups being more likely to go online; geography, with rural areas scoring lower than urban and suburban areas; and employment status, with those in work more likely to use the Net than the unemployed (Mossberger et al., 2003:23). Looking at table 4.1, one thing seems certain: these aspects of the digital divide have not disappeared.

Table 4.1 shows that in 2004 there are sizeable differences in Internet access by race. 67 percent of white Americans use the Net, compared with just 43 percent of African Americans. The age divide persists too: only a quarter of those over sixty-five go online, while more than three-quarters of those aged eighteen to twenty-nine do so. Indeed, this divide would be much greater if the lower age bracket included younger teenagers, since among that group usage has already achieved saturation levels of around 97 percent (UCLA Center for Communication Policy, 2003). But perhaps the two most startling divides are based on income and education. For households earning above $75,000, access is approaching saturation point (89 percent), but for low-income households (below $30,000), this falls to just 44 percent. Average household income in the United States is $43,300 (U.S. Census Bureau, 2004), indicating that income is still a barrier to access for a sizeable minority of Americans. Educational attainment appears to be an even more significant factor, with those holding a college degree

Table 4.1. Demographics of U.S. Internet Users, 2004

Demographic	Percentage Online
Women	61%
Men	66%
Age	
18–29	78%
30–49	74%
50–64	60%
65+	25%
Race/ethnicity	
White, non-Latino	67%
African American, non-Latino	43%
Latino	59%
Community type	
Urban	62%
Suburban	68%
Rural	56%
Household income	
Less than $30,000 per year	44%
$30,000–$50,000	69%
$50,000–$75,000	81%
More than $75,000	89%
Education	
Less than high school	32%
High school	52%
Some college	75%
College +	88%

Source: Pew Internet and American Life Project, 2004a.

being almost three times as likely to use the Internet as those who failed to graduate from high school.

Explaining the Digital Divide in the United States

How can we explain these inequalities? It may seem self-evident that age, income, education, and race have an influence, but in this area, just as with the global digital divide, we face the problem of identifying the relative influence of different variables. This is because demographic variables are often strongly related, so it is difficult to assess the differences that really matter or how much independent strength an individual variable really has. For example, in the United States, income, race, and educational attainment are all related. It is therefore difficult to know which of these is more significant in shaping access. If we simply compare them one by one, we are likely to overstate an individual variable's influence. Consider table 4.2, which is a survey of surveys of the access divide in the United States for 2001–2002. This was the last time we had a convergence of reliable data across three separate national studies: the Department of Commerce's *A Nation Online*, the Pew Project's report on the digital divide, and Karen Mossberger and colleagues' Kent State University survey.

As is evident, all three of these studies reveal gaps based on education, income, age, race, and ethnicity. I have included simple mean figures in the far right column for

Table 4.2. The Access Divide in the United States: A Survey of Surveys (in percentages)

Internet Access	Department of Commerce/ NTIA, Sept. 2001[1]	Pew, May 2002[2]	Kent State Survey, July 2001[3]	Mean
Education gap (high school diploma versus college degree)	41	37	21	33
Income gap (below versus above $30,000 a year)	35[a]	37	24	32
Age gap (see notes)	28[b]	22[c]	24[d]	25
Race gap (African American versus white)	20	15	17	17
Ethnicity gap (Latino versus white)	28	6	13	16

Sources: [1]U.S. Department of Commerce/NTIA, 2000; [2]Lenhart et al., 2003; [3]Mossberger et al., 2003. Table adapted from Mossberger et al., 2003.

Notes: Dates in the table are when the surveys were carried out.

The Kent State survey measured Internet access at home, whereas the Department of Commerce/NTIA and Pew surveys measured use at any location.

The Kent State survey data are more robust, because they are probabilities from multivariate analysis, using controls for overlap between factors such as race, education, and income.

[a]Below versus above $35,000.

Age gap: Use extra caution in considering these figures, because different intervals are used in each survey: [b]18–24-year-olds versus over 50-year-olds. [c]18–29-year-olds versus 50–64-year-olds. [d]Average 28-year-old versus average 61-year-old.

convenience. However, the most important thing to bear in mind when reading this table is that the Kent State study is the only one to use controls that allow us to more accurately assess the extent of the gaps. Thus, while all of these studies basically concur (in itself a powerful finding), the Kent State figures are more robust than the NTIA's *A Nation Online* and the Pew Project's special report on the digital divide. This is because these are "purer" figures that control for other influences. Only those variables that the Kent State survey found to be statistically significant are included in the table: education, income, age, race, and ethnicity. The Kent State survey found inequalities in income, followed by age and education, are most important, but unlike many other surveys discovered that race and ethnicity do exert significant influences on access. Race and ethnicity still shape the access divide, and the gaps cannot all be explained by differences in education and income (Mossberger, 2003:30). My own simple mean scores for the survey of surveys places the education gap at the top of the list, followed by income, then age, race, and finally ethnicity. The educational divide is thus a long-standing trend (see also Katz and Rice, 2002:40).

These are the factors shaping the basic access divide, but what do we know about some of the individual-level barriers that we also considered at the global level earlier in the chapter, such as language, basic literacy, and electronic literacy? Research on this area is fairly thin, but what little we do know points, rather depressingly, to a reinforcement of the basic access divide. The Kent State survey asked respondents if they would need assistance carrying out basic computer tasks such as using a mouse and keyboard, using email, or using the computer to find information on the web. It found a significant skills divide. Age and education were the most important predictors of needing assistance, followed by income, race, and ethnicity. Gender did not influence skill levels

(Mossberger et al., 2003:47). The skills divide thus reinforces the access divide and may go some way toward explaining it. Those who lack basic computer and Internet skills are less likely to consider accessing the Internet at all, but even when they do, they may find it a frustrating experience and may restrict their use to basic functions.

Skill levels and different real-world uses of the Internet must also be placed in a broader social and historical context, as is demonstrated by a study of different ethnic neighborhoods in Los Angeles—part of the broader Metamorphosis project at the University of Southern California (Jung et al., 2001). This developed a comprehensive Internet Connectedness Index which integrates a range of factors. These include how long a person has had a computer in the home; the breadth of tasks people conduct online; the number of different places an individual connects, such as home, work, or cybercafés; the breadth of goals people typically try to achieve, such as recreation, keeping up with events, making new friends, and so on; the range of online venues people visit, such as forums, chat rooms, and so on; the extent to which people actually interact with others online; the existence of generally positive or negative attitudes to cyberspace; and the extent to which people felt dependent on their computer and the Internet. Taken together, these form a fairly sophisticated means of measuring differences in the richness of Internet connections that can also be related to traditional demographic variables such as age, race, income, education, and gender.

The results of the Los Angeles study indicate that the social groups that generally enjoy greater access levels—white, well-educated, younger individuals with above-average incomes—are also more likely to engage in a broader range of online activities and enjoy a much richer and more socially useful online environment. The broader implication of this conclusion is that even as America reaches saturation levels of Internet access, there is likely to be a divide between those able to use the Internet for developing their knowledge, their personal, social, and professional networks, and those who simply use it primarily for entertainment purposes (see also Bonfadelli, 2002). Differential patterns of Internet use may come to resemble differences in television viewing and newspaper reading. In the United States, the demographics that shape Internet access and use (as defined in the Los Angeles Metamorphosis study) also shape patterns of television viewing, with higher-income, more-educated households more likely to watch news and current affairs programming, for instance.

While those lacking skills are less likely to make productive uses of the Net, it is also more likely that they will stop going online. The United States and many of the other countries at the forefront of the Internet wave have a number of so-called Internet dropouts: those who connected but decided to stop going online. The first study to identify this group was James Katz and Ronald Rice's series of surveys conducted between 1995 and 2000 (2002:67–81; but see also Wyatt et al., 2002). Katz and Rice broadly approach the issue of the digital divide in terms of a tradition in communication studies known as "uses and gratifications." This method assumes that individuals will tend to make use of media in ways that fit with the other aspects of their lives. They will have certain psychological needs for information and communication and will seek out media that meet them. Dropouts are significant because their existence suggests that Internet diffusion may not reach full saturation levels due to certain inherent barriers that make it different from television, radio, and other household technologies. Dropouts are also intriguing from the perspective of policy solutions to the digital divide, because they point to a group of people for whom the Internet has little everyday relevance, especially as an entertainment medium, compared with other conduits, particularly television. This highlights a possible future divide between those who are able to take advantage of the many other spillover benefits of the Internet besides entertainment, such as knowledge seeking, networking, content creation, using the Net for political influence, and so on and those who stick with passive, one-to-many media like television. Dropouts also alert us to the fact that Internet use tends to come on top of other forms of media. There are very, very few households in the developed world that have a computer and Internet access but do not have a television set or radio. The costs of accessing the Internet—ISP bills, continuous hardware and software upgrades, additional time spent dealing with problems with the computer, and so on—are additional to the other demands on our wallets and time.

Dropouts make up a surprisingly large proportion of nonusers. Katz and Rice found that around one-fifth of those who had used the Internet reported that they had now stopped. This group is more likely to be under forty-years-old, be on a low income, lack a college degree, have fewer computer skills, and slightly more likely to be female and African American. The most powerful influences are age and education. Given that the age variable can be explained by the relatively transient nature of young peoples' lives, such as moving around the country for college or after graduation, getting married, and so on, it would appear that education and income once again feature as the killer variables in the United States. Dropouts were also more likely to express feelings of being rushed or overloaded with work, suggesting that Fortner's pleonastic divide (mentioned previously) is significant here (Fortner, 1995; Katz and Rice, 2002:68–78). When it comes to the reasons why people stopped going online, 23 percent said that they had "lost access" due to moving house or job, but 16 percent indicated that the main reason was cost, while 15 percent suggested the Net was "too hard or complex" and 12 percent claimed it was "not interesting." This final response would fit well with a uses-and-gratifications approach because it suggests that the hype about the Internet being a "must-have" technology may not have reached a significant minority of the population for whom it is largely irrelevant. It might be suggested that Internet dropouts are a temporary phenomenon, but more recent surveys from the Pew Project reveal that they still form around 17 percent of current nonusers. Some 25 percent of people say they stopped going online "for an extended period," and a fifth of nonusers actually live in homes with an Internet connection. More than half of nonusers have no desire to go online, and there is considerable churn in the online population (Rainie and Bell, 2004:47–48).

It is also possible to apply uses-and-gratifications theory to the age divide. It has been argued, for example, that it is perfectly understandable that the elderly are less likely to adopt the Internet because their range of social goals is typically narrower than those of younger age groups. It is also the case that older people are more likely to worry about their privacy and susceptibility to social risks such as online fraud (Loges and Jung, 2001). In other words, there may be little reason to expect that, as time passes, the age divide will narrow as those who are currently middle-aged take their Internet habits into old age. It could be argued that elderly people tend to withdraw from society in general and may simply drop the Internet because it is no longer as relevant to their lives as it once was. It is far too early to tell whether the generational divide will exhibit secular decline or if it will persist as a cyclical feature of United States and other societies.

At the other end of the spectrum from the dropouts, of course, lie those with many years of online experience. Once again, this indicates a potentially important shift in the nature of the digital divide. Evidence suggests that levels of experience are crucial determinants of the number of activities that users typically undertake online. "Serious" uses of the Net increase dramatically with experience: individuals are more likely to integrate it into their everyday lives, have more trust in online transactions, and are more comfortable using it as a means of serious communication (Rainie and Bell, 2004:49). This "experience effect" is significant because it reinforces the skills divide identified previously. If we know that skills and confidence increase with experience, over time this will open up an even greater divide between users and nonusers.

The Broadband Effect

The United States and several other countries, especially South Korea, Hong Kong, Canada, and Sweden, have recently experienced massive growth in broadband usage (ITU, 2003a; Lee et al., 2003; Nielsen/Netratings, 2004). Already more than half of Americans with Internet access in the home go online with a high-speed broadband connection, and if we add those with fast connections at work, it is clear that broadband diffusion is occurring rapidly. Again, based on what we know from research evidence, we need to ask why this is significant.

A basic answer is that the broadband divide accentuates the access divide. Broadband adoption is highest among under-thirty-five-year-olds with college education and is heavily influenced by household income. Average monthly broadband bills are around $40; 47 percent of adopters have income of over $75,000. Broadband bucks the trend toward ever cheaper, even free (based on privacy selling or compulsory advertisement exposure) dial-up access and potentially creates many new pay-per-view opportunities for existing media companies. As Tim Luke (2000:5) puts it, "In a market economy based on pay-per-view, information inequality has always been assumed to be a fact of life." Broadband prices will come down over time, but then there will be slow broadband and fast broadband. The new geographical divide in broadband access is particularly worrying because the gap had been narrowing during the dial-up era (Servon, 2002:35). Once again, we find that the digital divide is a moving target.

There is also an important geographical element to the U.S. broadband divide. Urban and suburban residents are almost three times more likely to have broadband at home than their rural counterparts. While some of this difference may be accounted for by the fact that those living in rural areas tend to be older, less educated, and less wealthy than those in suburban and urban areas, there is a persistent infrastructural divide: high-speed connections are less prevalent in rural areas (Horrigan, 2004:4, 7). This is an old problem of market failure in telecommunication. Given a free market, companies will inevitably chase customers in wealthier suburban areas with reasonable population density and will neglect inner-city and rural locations (Stolfi and Sussman, 2001:55).

The significance of broadband also lies in the kinds of activities in which people with fast, always-on connections typically engage. They tend to create their own content and tailor and manage the content of others according to their own needs (Horrigan and Rainie, 2002). Content creation is the key here. The broadband versus dial-up divide reinforces the divide between those who are actively involved in creating web pages and blogs, contributing to discussion forums, sharing files, managing their own news feeds via news aggregator software, for example, on the one hand, and those for whom the Net is a much more disjointed, passive experience on the other. Again, this trend is reinforced by the fact that there is strong evidence that broadband use tends to displace other media consumption, particularly television viewing. A Pew Project survey in 2002 found that 37 percent of those with broadband stated that time spent watching television had declined, while 18 percent reported spending less time reading newspapers (Horrigan and Rainie, 2002:25). The UCLA survey of 2003 found that very experienced Internet users on average watched television for six hours a week less than nonusers (UCLA Center for Communication Policy, 2003:33).

CONCLUSION

Debates about the extent and significance of the digital divide are likely to continue for many years to come. As we have seen, those countries on the wrong side of the global divide typically exhibit low levels of economic development, poor telecommunication infrastructure, and low levels of education. In one sense, of course, these conclusions are not surprising. Social scientists have long known that global economic inequality leads to inequalities in other areas. But we now have the benefit of a first wave of rigorous studies that have quantified, albeit tentatively, the impact of different variables. This is not to say that these are the final word: far from it. New divides continue to emerge, because information and communication technologies are different from simpler, stabler technologies such as televisions and (fixed-line) telephones. Computers, printers, monitors, scanners, and operating systems and other software are in a continual process of evolution. Fast broadband connections that allow viewers to watch television through their Internet connection are common in Korea and Japan but are unlikely to reach most of Africa for many, many years. In India, as we saw above, Bangalore's software sector has grown enormously since the 1990s, but the benefits for the rest of Indian society have been minimal.

In the United States, meanwhile, there is a clear experiential divide, with those who have used the Internet for five years or more being much more adept at exploiting its potential than those who have recently gone online, and a content creation divide, with wealthier, more-educated white households more likely to have broadband and a richer variety of socially purposive online networks. These kinds of trends suggest that the Internet is different from other technologies. While it may take some time to adjust to speaking on the telephone or changing the channel on your television, these are basic skills that are easily learned. The importance of education as a variable in almost all of the literature suggests that higher-level skills are required to use the Internet effectively.

Some have argued that the simplification of computers will make skills much less relevant (Compaine, 2001). The point-and-click interface, is, after all, much easier for the novice to navigate than old text-based operating systems. Computer interfaces and Internet software have become simpler. But it is uncertain how much simpler personal computers and even mobile devices will become before they cease to be the multifunction technologies that they are at present and start to resemble technologies that are purely designed for entertainment. The digital divide is most relevant, not because access to entertainment should be more equally distributed (though that is important in an informational era where the media and entertainment industries assume a more important position). Rather, it is about reducing inequalities in access to information that can be used to improve social mobility in the context of the particular society in which an individual finds herself.

Our exploration of the digital divide in the hyperdeveloped world reveals the persistent effects of income, education, age, race, and ethnicity in shaping Internet access and use. It would be naive to believe that inequalities will somehow wither away in a society in which computers and Internet access are ubiquitous. The transition from predominantly rural and agricultural societies toward predominantly urban and industrial ones during the Industrial Revolution generated many new forms of social division, as did the transition to post-industrialism/informationalism. The decline of traditional blue-collar industrial jobs and the transition to a knowledge economy in which the service sector is central should not blind us to the ways in which inequalities can emerge within even the most advanced nations. Robert Reich, one-time economic adviser to Bill Clinton and influential theorist of the changing labor market, argues that informationalism rests upon an elite stratum of symbolic analysts—those with the education and skills to plan, design, and strategically implement the fruits of their knowledge (Reich, 1991). This group includes software engineers, marketing and PR professionals, financial experts, even academic researchers. But not everyone can be a symbolic analyst. There will still be a need for routine production work (administrative assistance, data entry, call center work, and so on) in the Reichian vision. Thus, while the majority of jobs will require the use of information and communication technologies, the ways in which these are actually used will differ markedly across these occupation groups and will also continue to be shaped by demographic factors.

Globally and within countries, the digital divide is in a constant state of flux. But it is less certain that it is withering as diffusion increases. In fact, growth rates in Internet diffusion in the developing and least-developed parts of the world stalled at the turn of the century. As we saw from the very latest figures from the United States, the income, age, and education divides are still with us, almost ten years from the Internet's takeoff in the mid-1990s. Does the digital divide decrease as diffusion increases, either globally or within an advanced post-industrial democracy such as the United States? The evidence so far suggests not.

This chapter has focused on the social and economic factors shaping Internet access and, in turn, how Internet use reinforces older inequalities. Next, we consider its potential role in enhancing community and increasing political participation.

Discussion Points

- Does the digital divide matter?
- What are the main causes of the global digital divide?
- Do higher levels of Internet diffusion reduce the digital divide, either within or between countries?
- Are there new digital divides opening up within developed countries?
- Is the digital divide ever likely to narrow significantly?

Further Reading

My approach to the global digital divide was influenced by Pippa Norris's and Mark Warschauer's excellent and wide-ranging analyses (Norris, 2001; Warschauer, 2003). Of the more specialized cross-national studies considered here, Kristopher Robison and Edward Crenshaw, 2002, is a useful if demanding place to start, while Eszter Hargittai's (1999) influential study of OECD countries crystallizes many of the important issues.

Currently the best scholarly analysis of the U.S. context is provided by Karen Mossberger et al. (2003). While this uses advanced statistical methods, no knowledge of these is required for understanding what is an impeccably clear book.

There is a wealth of data on the digital divide in the U.S. The best place to start is the Pew Internet and American Life Project website (http://www.pewcenter.org), where reports are arranged chronologically and a large spreadsheet containing time series data going back to the 1990s can be downloaded free of charge. This is a superb resource. A more-detailed set of time series data can be found in the five U.S. Department of Commerce/NTIA reports from 1995 to 2002.

PART II

INSTITUTIONS

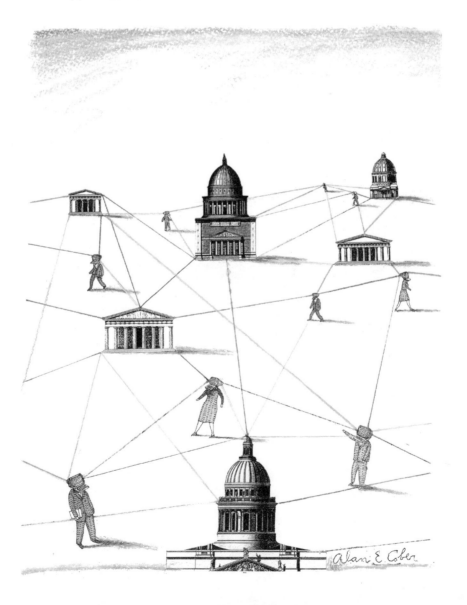

COMMUNITY, DELIBERATION, AND PARTICIPATION

E-democracy

There can be no strong democratic legitimacy without ongoing talk.
—BENJAMIN BARBER, 1984

Unplanned, unanticipated encounters are central to democracy itself.
—CASS SUNSTEIN, 2001

CHAPTER OVERVIEW

This chapter considers the Internet's role in enhancing community cohesion, political deliberation, and participation, or what is now often termed "e-democracy." It begins by tracing the origins of contemporary arguments in favor of using technology to increase civic engagement. It then considers a range of examples and trends in this area, including community networks, the development of online political communities, and attempts by governments to involve citizens in policy making through online mechanisms. The chapter then provides an assessment of e-democracy, focusing on two key concepts: social capital and the public sphere.

The Internet's potential for increasing political participation has been debated for over a decade (Barber, 1997; Browning, 1996; Van de Donk et al., 1995). But explorations of the democratic potential of other new communication technology go back even further (Arterton, 1987; Barber, 1988; Dutton, 1992; Dutton and Guthrie, 1991; Etzioni et al., 1975; Hollander, 1985; Laudon, 1977; McLean, 1989; Sterling, 1986). In the early 1970s, conference phone calls, interactive cable television, and portable video cameras were seen as the revolutionary route to grassroots citizen activism and a more democratic system of media production based upon the involvement of community groups in program making. The public access, or "guerrilla television," movement of the early 1970s, focused around counter-cultural publications like the magazine *Free Software*, saw new technology as a means of countering what members perceived to be the narrowness of mainstream media (Price and Wicklein, 1972; Shamberg, 1971). Columbus, Ohio, was an exciting place to live in 1977, when the QUBE interactive cable system was introduced, allowing citizens to participate in instantaneous opinion polls and local planning meetings. It is easy to smirk at these and many other failed experiments. But for many commentators, the false starts of the past (QUBE closed in 1984) are fading from memory, and, for good or ill, real-world developments are beginning to catch up with the vision. A consideration of e-democracy is a good place to start this section of the book, because many of the debates in this area have focused on how the Internet may be affecting the social foundations of citizenship, or in other words, what happens before individuals choose to become involved in interest groups, social movements, and political parties or interact with government agencies using e-government.

E-democracy has provoked much theoretical discussion but very little in the way of concrete success. Its central concerns certainly predate those of e-government (very much a creature of the twentieth-century administrative state—see chapter 8), and it conjures up all manner of dilemmas around the possibility of direct democracy, universal political participation, and popular sovereignty. Yet e-democracy is no longer the domain of theoretical speculation and utopian dreams. Its main themes are increasingly embedded in political practice. They have been exhibited in a wide variety of national and local experiments, in many different settings, using different forms of computer-mediated communication. These vary, from the 1980s and 1990s experiments in Santa Monica, California (Dutton and Guthrie, 1991), to the mid-1990s emergence of Minnesota E-democracy (Dahlberg, 2001a), to the very recent prelegislative consultations and other experiments in Britain (e.g., McIntosh et al., 2003) and other initiatives in countries as diverse as Canada, Australia, the Netherlands, Germany, France, Italy, Sweden, Denmark, Finland, and Estonia (Coleman and Gøtze, 2001:36–45). To a greater or lesser extent, these experiments have been concerned with promoting political participation *outside* of formal elections. In other words, they have been about policy deliberation, collaborative information sharing, building social capital, and plugging civil societal networks into established representative and administrative processes at both local and national levels.

THEORETICAL FOUNDATIONS

The U.K. Hansard Society—one of the key movers in operationalizing e-democracy—defines it as follows:

> The concept of e-democracy is associated with efforts to broaden political participation by enabling citizens to connect with one another and with their representatives via new information and communication technologies. (Hansard Society, 2003)

This broad, simple-yet-clear definition points to the horizontal linkages between citizens in civil society as well as the vertical linkages between civil society and policy makers. Among other definitions, Kenneth Hacker and Jan van Dijk's (2000:1) view of what they term "digital democracy" stands out:

> a collection of attempts to practise democracy without the limits of time, space, and other physical conditions, using information and communications technology or computer-mediated communication instead, as an addition, not a replacement, for traditional . . . political practices.

While both of these definitions rightly stress the role of new communication technologies, the theoretical underpinnings of e-democracy are far from new. Political theorists have been preoccupied with the problem of political participation since the birth of democracy. The participatory realm of the Athenian *agora*, a forum in which citizens (excepting women and slaves) would come together to exchange goods, watch a play, and—most importantly—discuss politics, has long been held up as a normative ideal to which all democracies should aspire. In the modern period, this preoccupation with involving citizens in political decision making paralleled the rise of liberal democratic politics. During the period from the late eighteenth to the early nineteenth century, political philosophers such as Jean-Jacques Rousseau (1712–78), Alexis de Tocqueville (1805–59), and Tom Paine (1737–1809) grappled with the central problem of representative democracy: how to enhance the influence of citizens between elections. For Rousseau, the answer lay in developing forms of self-government that became known as direct democracy. This meant rule through regular referendums on as many individual issues as possible rather than the bluntness and infrequency of general elections (Rousseau, 1762 [1968]). For Tocqueville, the solution was to enhance citizen participation in civil society. Impressed by what he saw in America during his travels of the 1820s, Tocqueville believed that a vital civil society of competing interest groups, newspapers, and philanthropic associations acted as both a check on government and as a means of civic education for citizens (Tocqueville, 1835–40 [2003]. For Paine, a radical deeply suspicious of all forms of government authority, only the combination of an active civil society with a recognition of inalienable individual rights would suffice (Paine, 1791–92 [1984]).

The concern with political participation has ebbed and flowed but was ever-present during the period of liberal democratic consolidation in the West. The rise of the modern bureaucratic state, which occurred broadly from the mid-nineteenth to the mid-twentieth centuries, only compounded the perceived problems of representative democracy—the weakness of ties between citizens and their elected representatives and the rise of technical expertise in policy making. Early responses to this came in the form of the pluralism espoused by British scholars and political activists G. D. H. Cole (1888–1959) and Harold Laski (1893–1950). They and others argued that the growth of the state had to be checked by myriad freely formed civil associations in which citizens could participate and use to bring policy recommendations up to the level of government (Hirst, 1989). Cole's and Laski's "guild socialist" ideas were briefly influential during the 1920s but soon died out. In the United States, meanwhile, philosophical pragmatists such as John Dewey (1859–1952) and George Herbert Mead (1863–1931) questioned the scientific basis of political knowledge and called for a politics of experimentation and practically oriented deliberation (Dewey, 1927; Mead, 1930).

By the 1960s, however, a new current in political theory started to question the stilted nature of political participation. Inspired in part by the oppositional social movements of the 1960s, particularly the feminist, civil rights, and peace movements, as well as a rediscovery of Rousseau's ideas, a collection of political theorists, including Benjamin Barber, C. B. Macpherson, Carole Pateman, and Jürgen Habermas, set about establishing a new agenda for participatory democracy that has persisted well into the twenty-first century (Barber, 1984; Habermas, 1962 [1989]; Macpherson, 1977; Pateman, 1970).

At the same time, partly as a reaction to the rise of neoconservative individualism during the 1980s, many sociologists and political scientists, most notably Amitai Etzioni, Robert Bellah, and James Fishkin, started to reconsider the concept of community. In *Habits of the Heart*, which took its title from one of Tocqueville's phrases, Bellah and his colleagues bemoaned the intensification of individualism in American society and called for a new communitarian ethic (Bellah et al., 1985; see also Etzioni, 1995). Thinkers such as Etzioni have argued that strong, emotionally powerful community bonds based around family and locality have declined. James Fishkin, meanwhile, contributed to the deliberative turn in political science by advocating new forms of opinion polling which rested upon citizens coming together to discuss issues. Echoing themes in Benjamin Barber's (1984) model of "strong democracy," Fishkin argues that "deliberative polling" has an educative effect, forcing citizens to reconsider preconceived opinions, and is thus superior to the usual individualist methodology that dominates traditional opinion polling (Fishkin, 1991).

In the eyes of participatory democrats and new communitarians, political deliberation is thus perceived as having a transformational influence on citizens. Contrary to liberal individualist perspectives which assume that citizens' political views are predetermined by their interests, deliberative democrats tend to argue that views are, and ought to be, molded by our creative interactions with others. We discover legitimate solutions to political problems by engaging in deliberation. Barber summarizes this difference between the politics of "bargaining and exchange" and the politics of transformation very neatly:

> The basic difference between the politics of bargaining and exchange and the politics of transformation is that in the former, choice is a matter of selecting among options and giving the winner the legitimacy of consent, whereas in the latter, choice is superseded by judgment and leads men and women to modify and enlarge options as a consequence of seeing them in new, public ways. . . . For this reason, there can be no strong democratic legitimacy without ongoing talk. Where voting is a static act of expressing one's preference, participation is a dynamic act of imagination that requires participants to change how they see the world. Voting suggests a group of men in a cafeteria bargaining about what they can buy as a group that will suit their individual tastes. Strong democratic politics suggests a group of men in a cafeteria contriving new menus, inventing new recipes, and experimenting with new diets in the effort to create a public taste that they can all share and that will supersede the conflicting private tastes about which they once tried to strike bargains. Voting, in the bargaining model, often fixes choices and thereby stultifies the imagination; judging, in the model of strong democracy, activates imagination by demanding that participants reexamine their values and interests in light of all the inescapable others—the public. (Barber, 1984:136–37)

Thus, political knowledge is discursive, contingent, and changeable; it emerges through interaction with others.

At the level of political and social theory, this body of big ideas has provided the roots of many attempts to use Internet technologies to enhance political participation, deliberation, and community. But two conceptual offshoots have proved particularly resilient: social capital and the public sphere.

Social Capital

Advocating participatory democracy and putting it into practice are, of course, hugely different. Participatory democracy has faced numerous challenges at both the scholarly and practical levels. Many authors have pointed to the steady decline in civic participation, especially in the United States (Verba et al., 1995). The most influential attempt to explain this decline in recent times may be found in the writings of Robert Putnam, whose research on the concept of social capital looms large over debates about the desirability, feasibility, and likely effects of e-democracy (Putnam, 1993, 1995, 2000). Putnam defines social capital as "the features of social organization such as networks, norms, and trust that facilitate co-ordination and co-operation for mutual benefit" (1995:66). This approach assumes that participation in civic associations, whether they are overtly political, like parties, quasi-political, like labor unions, or even nonpolitical, such as gardening groups or bowling leagues, enhances overall levels of political awareness and efficacy. Civic associations thus create social capital. Why?

Putnam argues that participation in civic associations increases levels of trust between citizens, and trust enhances political self-confidence. By coming face-to-face with other citizens, we learn the skills of negotiation, tolerance, and creative problem solving that are essential to the functioning of democracy. We also learn the value of reciprocity: the assumption that our contributions to the community will be reciprocated at some stage in the future. When such an assumption becomes the norm among members of a community, generalized reciprocity exists. Without this, trust and community wither on the vine.

Societies that exhibit dense networks of civic associations, even if the majority of them are not overtly political, are more likely to have high levels of reciprocal trust and efficacy. Most controversially, Putnam argues that during the postwar period, in many societies but particularly the United States, involvement in civic associations, and therefore the amount of social capital, has gradually declined. While the actual number of civic associations has increased, Putnam and his teams of researchers have found that either the intensity of involvement or the overall numbers of individuals involved have declined, and in some cases both of these trends may be observed. The popular "bowling alone" thesis takes its name from Putnam's finding that while the number of individuals bowling has remained steady, amateur bowling leagues have declined.

Explanations for the decline of civic life are manifold. Higher levels of civic engagement tend to be associated with age, higher levels of education, belonging to the racial majority, regular church attendance, and employment (Shah, McLeod, and Yoon, 2001:465). For Putnam, a major explanation is the retreat into the domestic sphere encouraged by the widespread diffusion of television. Other scholars have argued that the nature of television itself has steadily changed during the postwar period, as "soft" news, infotainment, and commercialization have edged out the media as a civic educator. Another influential interpretation is Ray Oldenburg's "third places" thesis (1997). Oldenburg argues that since the 1950s, planners and architects have failed to incorporate what he terms "great good places" in their suburban development schemes. Great good places provide meeting spaces away from work and the home. They may be public or perhaps semipublic spaces, such as cafés, bars, and hair salons, but the key point is that they regularly bring us into contact with others and encourage serendipitous encounters that extend our social ties. Although Putnam has only briefly speculated about the role of the Internet in relation to social capital, the interpretation of television's deleterious effects combined with the overall simplicity of the concept make it a highly attractive context for research on the Internet's potential to enhance democracy (Weber et al., 2003).

The Public Sphere

An equally influential approach to understanding the role of communication in encouraging citizen engagement is Jürgen Habermas's concept of the Public sphere (Habermas, 1962 [1989]). Habermas argued that the development of early-modern capitalism during the eighteenth century heralded a new era of communication based around a culture of enlightened, critical, and reasoned public debate among the propertied middle class. This culture was based upon an independent, privately owned press, the reading of political periodicals, and political discussion in physical spaces such as coffeehouses, salons, and pubs. It encouraged rational forms of political deliberation away from the tentacles of state control and allowed public opinion to develop (1962 [1989]:27). According to Habermas, this public sphere developed in western Europe during the eighteenth century, reached its high point during the mid-nineteenth century, and subsequently declined during the late nineteenth and early twentieth centuries, as it became increasingly tamed by the growth of private media oligopolies and the rise of the modern bureaucratic state.

Habermas originally insisted that the public sphere was a historical phase rather than a tool to judge all communication, but his concept has largely been developed in this latter sense. Some scholars have adapted the model of the public sphere to take into account the possibility of *multiple* public spheres. For instance, Nancy Fraser (1992) terms these "subaltern counter-publics"—groups and movements' own distinctive channels of communication—while John Keane (2000) has distinguished between micro-, meso-, and macro-public spheres, which he claims operate at the subnational, national, and transnational levels, respectively (see also Herbst, 1994). Overall, however, most scholars have deserted Habermas's empirical claims altogether and use the public sphere as a normative ideal which may be used to judge the existing communication structures of contemporary societies. Often this approach involves bringing in concepts from Habermas's more general theories of discourse and deliberation, which attempt to provide criteria for what he terms rational-critical discourse (e.g., Benhabib, 1996; Blaug, 1997; Chambers, 1996; Curran, 1991; Dahlberg, 2001a, 2001b; Dahlgren, 2000; Friedland, 2001).

Lincoln Dahlberg, a scholar who has used Habermasian theory to appraise the role of Internet, extracts six main conditions that e-democracy schemes must try to fulfill if they

EXHIBIT 5.1. RATIONAL DELIBERATION: CONDITIONS OF THE PUBLIC SPHERE

- **Autonomy from state and economic power:** Discourse must be based on the concerns of citizens as the public rather than driven by powerful corporate media or political elites.

- **Reason rather than assertion:** Deliberation involves engaging in reciprocal critique of normative positions that are provided with supporting reasons rather than dogmatically asserted.

- **Reflexivity:** Participants must critically reflect on their cultural values, assumptions, and interests as well as the larger social context and the effects these have on their own views.

- **Ideal role taking:** Participants must attempt to understand the argument from the other's perspective. This requires a commitment to an ongoing dialogue with difference in which interlocutors respectfully listen to each other.

- **Sincerity:** Each participant must make a sincere effort to make known all information—including true intentions, interests, needs, and desires—as relevant to the particular problem under consideration.

- **Discursive inclusion and equality:** As far as possible, every person affected by the issues under consideration is equally entitled to participate in deliberation.

Source: Adapted from Dahlberg, 2001a, 2001b.

are to genuinely create deliberative public spheres in the Habermasian sense (exhibit 5.1). Even before the Internet rose to prominence there were attempts to apply the public sphere framework to concrete instances of communication (Eley, 1992; Schudson, 1991). However, much like "social capital," the term crops up in all manner of places and guises in the writing on e-democracy (Abouchar and Henson, 2000; Papacharissi, 2002). This is not without good reason, because, despite criticisms of its vagueness, it does provide a suggestive means of thinking about the potential of the Internet to enhance political participation. Central to its power is the idea of autonomous spheres of communication in which citizens can freely engage in reasoned debate away from the controlling influence of the state, large media corporations, and structures of social inequality that impinge on their daily lives. The idea of citizens deliberating in freely formed associations in civil society before taking that knowledge up to the level of government recalls the direct democracy of ancient Athens but updates this for the contemporary period by focusing on the inescapability of mediation. The Internet emerges as a communications medium uniquely suited to providing multiple arenas for public debate that are relatively spontaneous, flexible, and above all, self-governed (Dahlgren, 2000). Citizens that have progressively shrunk into their respective private spheres as the historical public spheres collapsed are, in the Habermasian interpretation, once again able to emerge as a public force.

These two conceptual offshoots of theories of participatory democracy have been highly influential in shaping not only the practice of e-democracy experiments but also how we interpret them. Later in this chapter I will revisit these two themes—social capital and the public sphere—as part of a general appraisal of e-democracy. But now, let us consider the main themes and trends in this area.

LOCAL E-DEMOCRACY: COMMUNITY NETWORKS

Community networks first emerged during the 1970s but proliferated in many liberal democracies during the 1990s, as the costs of software, computers, and networking equipment began to fall. Early networks, such as the Berkeley Community Memory Project in northern California, used basic technologies such as text-based bulletin boards and email, and conscious efforts were made to locate public access terminals in physical public spaces like shops, community centers, and libraries. Bruce Tonn and his colleagues provide a useful working definition of a community network as "a computer-based system or set of systems designed to meet the social and economic needs of a spatially-defined community of individuals." Such networks are distinct from others in cyberspace because "they serve on-the-ground communities rather than communities that are not defined by spatial boundaries" (Tonn et al., 2001:201–2). Although they differ substantially, most community networks incorporate three main features: a high-speed network offered free of charge or at a subsidized rate to households; some form of community technology center, often based in a community building; and an emphasis on creating content specific to the local community (Pinkett and O'Bryant, 2003:188). They may be run by a nonprofit body, a public private partnership, a local or state government, or even local newspapers, tourist organizations, and other businesses. Amsterdam's Digital City project, at one stage the largest civic network in Europe with over fifty thousand members, was created by community activists and hackers and only had loose affiliations with official government structures (Brants et al., 1996). Indeed, its anarchic and sometimes libertine nature was often celebrated.

The recent rise of e-government (see chapter 8) has spurred subnational governments to improve their online presence, but these initiatives are often built upon previous non-governmental networks and thus continue to involve nonprofit organizations and other forms of alliance. For example, Southern California's Santa Monica Public Electronic Network, a pioneering community network established in 1986, has been converted into the city of Santa Monica's official portal but builds upon the public-private and voluntary structures that formed its early foundation. Today's community networks are more technologically sophisticated than their antecedents, but by handing to ordinary people the power to shape the production of information about their local community, they are essentially based upon the same voluntaristic principles. Almost all community networking projects have been inspired by the idea that virtual community can improve geographical communities by creating new social ties and reciprocal trust: the ingredients of social capital.

Community networks' rise to prominence has been caused by a range of factors. While they are geographically specific, many of the experiments nevertheless take their inspiration from figures such as Howard Rheingold (1993) and William Mitchell (1995), whose writings on virtual communities generated ripples of excitement when they first appeared in the mid-1990s. Rheingold was a participant in one of the first successful online communities, the Whole Earth 'Lectronic Link (WELL), which was founded by Stewart Brand and Larry Brilliant in 1985 in the San Francisco Bay Area. Much of the discussion that took place among the eight thousand participants in the WELL was not formally political, and Rheingold himself was often more fascinated by the social aspects of such virtual communities than he was by their potential to affect broader political processes. Indeed, this dislocation between the social or community-building aspects of virtual communities and the larger context of political life, which involves real-world institutions such as parties, interest groups, and legislatures, has arguably proved to be a fatal weakness in most e-democracy experiments to date. Nevertheless, the idea of ordinary people escaping the bonds of their isolated suburban existence to come together to share ideas, debate with each other, and create qualitatively new communities exerted a hold on the imagination of many political activists and scholars influenced by the participatory democracy revival. Celebrators of virtual communities argued that new communities of interest would increasingly become the norm, freeing us from the bonds of stifling neighborhood and family ties.

Aside from the influence of groups like the WELL, other factors spurred the development of community networks. First, there has long been a perception that e-democracy pioneers could contribute to an incremental learning process which would help future projects avoid the pitfalls of the past. Inspired by the reasonably successful early examples such as Santa Monica's Public Electronic Network (Dutton and Guthrie, 1991) as well as enthusiasts such as Doug Schuler, who was involved in establishing the Seattle Community Network in 1994, many other community activists and volunteers have established local experiments (Schuler, 1996). Second, the use of information technology in local governance increased radically during the 1990s. This gave rise to brigades of new policy entrepreneurs working in the sphere of government technology, not to mention a legion of third sector organizations like think tanks, nonprofits, and individual campaigners such as Steven Clift, coordinator of Minnesota E-democracy, who all contributed to the fervor. Third, increased funding from public sector institutions, particularly in Europe, where the EU's Information Society Project Office has played a role in many schemes, has created a relatively favorable context for innovation (Tambini, 1999:307).

According to the Association for Community Networking, a U.S.-based umbrella organization that focuses on nongovernmental networks, there are currently over one hundred fifty community networks in the United States alone (Association for Community Networking, 2004). A 2001 snapshot estimated that there were over fifty networks in the United Kingdom and around sixty in Canada (Pigg, 2001:508). These figures almost certainly underestimate the true number of networks in these countries. There is also some ambiguity about whether local government websites count as community networks, especially since the rise of e-government now means that all state, city, and municipal governments have an online presence incorporating transactions and services. Given that the vast majority of e-government sites are not interactive and few are explicitly community oriented (Musgrave, 2004), there is now a case to be made for distinguishing between grassroots community networks and those that are run by government. Over time, it is likely that this distinction will become more sharply drawn.

Typical networks include those in Seattle; Boulder; Blacksburg, Virginia; Roxbury, in Boston; and Ennis, in County Clare, Ireland. For example, the Boulder Community Network provides free web space to local nonprofit groups, information on a wide range of services like voter registration and volunteering, as well as a local service exchange scheme, allowing Boulder residents to exchange time and expertise. It also provides a massive compendium of locally specific links. The Seattle Community Network has similar features and also has a history of requesting commentary on local issues such as transportation. I consider Blacksburg, Camfield, and Ennis in more detail below, but for many other examples, see Tonn et al., 2001.

At first glance, the view that joining together citizens who already happen to live in the same neighborhood might appear to be missing the point. Why not try to encourage "real" interaction in physical civic spaces? Many of the proponents of community networks come from a background in urban planning and are therefore acutely aware of the history of attempts to generate community through the built environment. But it is an underlying analysis of the ways in which contemporary life erodes the capacity for civic participation and community building in traditional physical spaces that shapes the drive to use the Internet. Some community networks scholars point to some of the rather prosaic characteristics of social life in postindustrial democracies that constrain our ability to be good, active citizens. For example, Tonn and Petrich (1998) distill five categories of constraints on citizenship:

- work-related constraints—long and irregular hours, multiple jobs, company transfers;
- consumerism constraints—time spent on consuming goods and services, especially entertainment;
- social capital constraints—local social networks are insufficient to create community;
- personal constraints—fear of reprisals from other community members and lack of confidence and skills;
- built environment constraints—suburbanization, lack of meeting places away from home and work, and car-oriented planning.

The social forces that produce these constraints on civic engagement are, of course, fairly specific to developed countries. But the important point is that they derive from powerful long-term trends upon which traditional methods of real-world policy intervention seem to have had limited effect. In the eyes of their proponents, community networks can dilute these constraints (exhibit 5.2).

To what extent have community networks fulfilled their promise? Unfortunately, there are few systematic evaluation studies in this area. There is much anecdotal evidence and hype, but here I have decided to focus on examples that have been the subject of published scholarly research.

Not surprisingly, grand ambitions raise expectations and often mean that many community networks have disappointed. Despite their enthusiasm, in their survey of forty examples in the United States, Bruce Tonn and colleagues (2001:207) found that only around 10 percent were making any efforts to involve citizens in dialogue or

EXHIBIT 5.2: THE ARGUMENT IN FAVOR OF COMMUNITY NETWORKS

"Community networks can allow people to contribute to public discussions asynchronously according to their own schedules and not the schedules set for the convenience of city councils and government officials. Enlightened employers could allow employees the use of computers at work to allow employees to participate remotely but in real time in electronic town hall meetings and chat discussions. Well-designed community networks could help people build their own capacities to meet their citizenship obligations (e.g., through online citizenship certificate programs) and provide users with links to educational resources pertinent to ongoing discussions. People may find that contributing to online discussions causes less anxiety than in-person participation because there is no risk of immediate face-to-face personal confrontation. . . . Community networks as 'great good places' need, first and foremost, to be places that foster community-based dialogue. . . . Community networks need to facilitate collaboration between members of the community. Economic collaboration is one important area (e.g., through online cooperatives or services swapping). Another would be collaborative efforts on new developments (e.g., where a new grocery store should be located, how the brownfield should be redeveloped). Community networks can provide the homes for online, continuously evolving community histories. Special attention can be paid to disadvantaged and senior communities. Community networks can help people find mentors and allow young people to become more involved in community life. Community networks can be places where people share life's lessons. Education should also be fostered by community networks. These are the kinds of characteristics that community networks could possess to help improve community life."

Source: Quoted from Tonn et al., 2001:203–4.

comment on local development issues, though there were exemplary cases where this was occurring, such as in Boulder or Seattle. Official government sites were particularly underdeveloped in this sphere. Most community networks are simply portals with collections of links to other community sites. They are unlikely to be a destination, more a place citizens pass through on their way to other sites. Nevertheless, other in-depth studies have revealed a complex mixture of outcomes. Consider three examples.

Blacksburg Electronic Village

Officially launched in 1993 to cater to the small town of Blacksburg, Virginia, the Blacksburg Electronic Village (BEV) is probably the most researched community network in the world, largely due to its proximity to Virginia Tech (Casalegno, 2001; Cohill and Kavanaugh, 2000). Initially a public-private partnership involving Bell Telephone, Virginia Tech's outreach program, and the Blacksburg Town Council, by 1998 the telecommunication infrastructure had been privatized, though the provision of information in the network continues to emerge from a mixture of public and private sources. In 2004, Internet penetration in Blacksburg was extremely high, reaching 87 percent of residents. Over 60 percent use broadband connections (Blacksburg Electronic Village, 2004).

Blacksburg deliberately positioned itself as a test bed for piloting features that it was hoped would be borrowed by other community networks. Among the more noteworthy are its strong emphasis on local economic development, and relatively cheap Internet services, particularly its web-hosting packages and high-speed networks (for traffic that stays within Blacksburg). Containing sections such as the Village Mall, Government, Organizations, Education, and Arts/Entertainment and an impressive calendar of local events, the dominant approach of the BEV is to mirror real-world community institutions and patterns of behavior. The most commonly used services are email, web browsing, and discussion groups. Over 60 percent of the community members regularly take part in online discussion forums (Casalegno, 2001:22).

One of the more significant achievements of the BEV is the Seniors Group. This appears to have emerged spontaneously, and in time developed from an initial phase of simple message exchange into more-detailed discussions, links with other online groups, such as a youth project, and eventually real-world meetings. Levels of trust and cooperation in the Seniors Group eventually led to mobilization against plans by Virginia Tech and car manufacturers Ford, Chrysler, and GM to build a pilot scheme for an automated "smart road" linking Blacksburg and Inter-state 81 (Casalegno, 2001:27). Although these protests did not deter the smart road project, this example provides some evidence of community networks increasing political participation.

There is some consensus that the Blacksburg project has proved successful. However, it needs to be emphasized that the town of Blacksburg is itself highly unrepresentative of the rest of "small-town America." Twenty-two thousand of its twenty-six thousand residents are students or staff at Virginia Tech. Given that the university is a pioneer in high technology and has one of the most wired campuses in the United States, if not the world, this gives the project a highly favorable ecosystem. The same cannot be said of Roxbury, Boston.

Camfield Estates–MIT C3 Project

The Camfield Estates–MIT Creating Community Connections Project was started in 2000 as a partnership between the Camfield Tenants Association and Massachusetts Institute of Technology (MIT). Based upon an agenda to "build community, empowerment and self-sufficiency amongst the residents" of Camfield Estates, a housing development in Roxbury, Boston, the project involves a number of public, private, and nonprofit sector organizations, including the Massachusetts Housing Finance Agency, the Kellogg Foundation, Hewlett-Packard, RCN Telecom, Microsoft, and ArsDigita (Pinkett and O'Bryant, 2003:187). Its emphasis on informational self-sufficiency is one of several unique features.

In contrast with Blacksburg, the population of Camfield Estates consists predominantly of low- to moderate-income African American families, among which there is a high proportion of single-parent households. Significantly, Camfield Estates was a participant in the U.S. Department of Housing and Urban Development's demonstration-disposition program of the 1990s, under which public housing was renovated and sold back to residents' associations. In 1997, residents were temporarily relocated, their homes demolished and new ones built on the site. In 2000, residents moved back onto the Estates, and by 2001, a new nonprofit Camfield Tenants Association assumed ownership of the properties. These significant social and political shifts created an interesting environment for the creation of a new community network. MIT researchers Randall Pinkett and Richard O'Bryant had the opportunity to assess the state of the community before and after the launch of the new network.

The project is based around three main principles. First, it is asset based. In other words, it seeks to build upon the repertoire of skills and knowledge that already exists in the community. A comprehensive asset mapping exercise took place in 2001–2002, which resulted in the creation of Geographic Information Systems, with interactive maps depicting where local residents could find particular skills, services, and people. Second, it is internally focused. It seeks to create homegrown solutions to problems rather than bringing in people from outside the locality. Finally, it is driven by the goal of creating relationship networks among the community members (Pinkett and O'Bryant, 2003:192).

The project is based around ArsDigita Corporation's Community System. This is an open-source software platform that makes it relatively easy for ordinary web users to create their own web content, online discussion forums, and chat rooms. The result is a diverse array of communication tools, resulting in a community intranet,[1] including resident profiles detailing the formal and informal skills held by residents, event calendars, email lists, discussion forums, news and announcements, chat servers, "job and volunteer opportunity postings, online resumes, personal home pages, web portals ('MyCamfield'), electronic commerce, and more" (Pinkett and O'Bryant, 2003:198).

How has the project fared? Evaluations indicate several positive effects in creating social capital: interaction among residents increased; social networks became denser; and involvement in politics increased as did awareness of city of Boston services and individual self-confidence. The most popular aspects of the website were the personal resident profiles, the events calendar, and the discussion forums (Pinkett and O'Bryant, 2003:203). Although we need to be cautious in interpreting these results—the evaluation only included twenty-six households—the data indicate that the project was successful in building community and moderately successful in fostering civic engagement. A more complex pattern emerges from our third example.

Ennis Information Age Town

Launched in 1997 following a £15 million investment from Irish telecommunication company Eircom, Ennis's community network was designed to make the small town in the west of Ireland an Internet laboratory. The main aim was to establish a state-of-the-art Internet infrastructure and assess the effects on the ordinary lives of Ennis residents. The project was the focus of a fair amount of media hype, much of it whipped up by Eircom's public relations team. Nevertheless, the company kept its word, investing

---

[1]**Intranet:** a network that exists internal to an organization but is built on similar principles and technologies as the Internet.

millions in hardware, software, and training, including providing households with free or subsidized computers with Internet access (Bannon and Griffin, 2001:43).

By 2004, however, the network had come to resemble a standard portal. There are multiple directories, for example, but nothing that the local phone book does not provide. Apart from an email directory, opportunities for interaction among Ennis citizens are minimal (Ennis Information Age Town, 2004). Research by scholars at the nearby University of Limerick argues that the emphasis in this and similar projects is on "market liberalization and competition, with relatively little space or resources being given to improve social or community services" (Bannon and Griffin, 2001:36). It also appears that training in the use of computers was in limited supply. For example, one of the aims was to allow the unemployed to sign in electronically to receive their benefits using the new computers and broadband Internet connections provided by the project. In the end, due to frustration with the technology, many gave up on this and returned to the traditional regular trips to the welfare office. By casting their state-of-the-art computers aside, unemployed residents could be assured that their signing in was effective. They could also return to using the regular visits to overcome social isolation (Warschauer, 2003:4).

As these three examples illustrate, Internet-based community networks have not proved an unqualified success. Blacksburg is probably the most successful to date, but arguably this was an environment which already exhibited high levels of social capital before the network emerged. At the same time, however, the Roxbury case does illustrate the difference a community network can make in a dramatically different neighborhood. The case of Ennis conveys a different problem: the tendency for goals like increasing community and participation to become narrowly defined by the organizers of the network itself. One of the problems with very local e-democracy projects like this is that they will always to some extent be constrained by geography itself. The same cannot be said of virtual political communities.

VIRTUAL POLITICAL COMMUNITIES

There are hundreds of thousands of online virtual communities. Usenet alone now consists of over one hundred thousand groups. Corporate content providers such as Yahoo!, Microsoft Network, AOL, and Google host tens of thousands of online communities. Some are established centrally by the companies themselves; others are set up by groups of people wanting a place to meet online to discuss common interests. Many newspapers, television, and radio companies now provide opportunities for readers, viewers, and listeners to engage with program makers and each other. Dotcom success story eBay relies upon community discussion and rating schemes to construct an elaborate though still fragile environment of online trust (Boyd, 2002). Countless other e-commerce sites host online discussion forums to encourage users of their products to help each other out. Website-hosting companies such as Geocities (now owned by Yahoo!) encourage those establishing websites to cluster with similar sites. Central and local government agencies and legislatures have, slowly but surely, started to experiment with online forums. The majority of interest groups and other citizen associations have message lists of one kind or another. It is impossible to know how many non-institutional email-only discussion lists exist, but the numbers probably run into the tens of thousands. Weblogs link to other weblogs in endless circles but also cluster in identifiable ways. Consider the data from the Pew Internet and American Life Project (tables 5.1–5.3).

As tables 5.1–5.3 demonstrate, the most successful growth industry on the Internet is talk. It is difficult not to enthuse about the sheer quantity of it that takes place online, and all the signs are that the levels will increase. People spend more time with friends and relatives using relatively simple technologies like email and bulletin boards than they do buying goods and services (Horrigan et al., 2001:2). Spaces for deliberation that

Table 5.1. Group Memberships on the Internet

The Kinds of Groups Internet Users Contact	% of Internet Users Who Have Contacted Group
Trade association or professional group	50
A group for people who share a hobby or interest	50
A fan group of a particular team	31
A fan group of a television show or entertainer	29
A local community group or association	29
A group of people who share a lifestyle	28
A support group for a medical condition or personal problem	28
A group of people who share beliefs	24
A political group	22
A religious organization	21
A sports team or league in which one participates	20
Ethnic or cultural group	15
Labor union	6

Source: Adapted from Horrigan et al., 2001.

Table 5.2. Why People Communicate with Online Groups

The Reasons Cited for Emailing an Online Group	% Who Say It Is Important
Getting general membership news and information	76
Getting involved with or learning more about group activities	71
Discussing issues with others	68
Creating or maintaining relationships with others in group	49

Source: Adapted from Horrigan et al., 2001.

Table 5.3. Connectedness through the Internet

Those Who Say Their Use of the Internet has Helped Them "a lot" or "some" to	% Who Say It Is Important
find people or groups who share their interests	49
become more involved with organizations or groups to which they already belong	40
connect with people of different ages or generations	37
find people or groups who share their beliefs	32
connect with people from different economic backgrounds	29
connect with people from different racial or ethnic backgrounds	27
connect with groups based in their local community	26

Source: Adapted from Horrigan et al., 2001.

are relatively unconstrained by corporate and state influence and which have been inspired by the need for increasing citizen deliberation have opened up, leading to some hyperenthusiastic commentaries about the potential of the Internet in bringing about true participatory democracy (e.g., Grossman, 1995). Nevertheless, away from the hype, there have been genuinely significant developments in this area. Probably the most successful example is Minnesota E-democracy.

From Community to Politics: Minnesota E-democracy

Many community network experiments have been driven by attempts to increase civic engagement, but most have been inspired by a social rather than a political agenda. There has often been a missing link between community participation and more formal political concerns. In many respects, these projects can hardly be blamed for this, because they are based on the idea of "building from below." Just as models of social capital maintain that civic engagement starts with trust built up through "nonpolitical" activities, so it is the case that community networks seek to empower people by widening and deepening their social networks.

However, another strand of e-democracy has attempted to "connect the dots" between social networks and broader political processes while remaining independent of government, parties, or interest groups. Foremost among these is Minnesota E-democracy, one of the world's largest subnational-level political discussion forums.

Established in 1994, Minnesota E-democracy is a nonprofit organization based around a central email discussion list—MN-Politics-Discuss. Email was deliberately chosen as the main communication tool due to its popularity, ease of use, and low bandwidth demands and the fact that it is difficult to ignore, requires effort to subscribe, and appears to have norms of civility that are less prominent in other online spaces, such as Usenet (Dahlberg, 2001b: 624). Although email lists can be tightly controlled by requiring that all messages go through a single moderator's mailbox, the Minnesota team has generally refrained from heavily moderating the lists. Discussions have been monitored, and moderators intervene to uphold rules and occasionally steer the discussion, but participants are encouraged to obtain advice from others via private email before posting messages that they think might be unsuitable. There have been some changes since the project first began. The discussions are now hosted by Yahoo! Groups and can be accessed via a web interface as well as email.

Unlike many virtual communities, Minnesota E-democracy is dominated by discussion of issues affecting Minnesota, though national and international issues inevitably leaked into the discussions, resulting in the creation of a new national and world list, MN-Politics-National. However, the membership of the Minnesota list remains steady at around the five hundred mark, and the project remains remarkably faithful to its original aims, which are

- to strengthen, expand, and diversify citizen engagement through effective and meaningful online discussions and two-way information exchange on public issues;
- to increase the use and relevancy of democratic information resources that inform citizens about elections, governance, the media and public affairs and help us meet public challenges;

- to build and sustain the unique citizen-based "E-Democracy" model, so active citizens anywhere can join us and work to improve the outcomes of citizen participation in governance and public life in their communities and nations. (Minnesota E-democracy, 2004)

Minnesota's model has transferred to other areas, including Chicago, and there are also separate issue lists for Minnesota's major cities. It has also been adopted by several other experiments, including a similar one in Iowa, the now-defunct U.K. Online Citizens' Democracy, and Canada's Nova Scotia Electronic Democracy Forum.

FROM POLITICAL NETWORKS TO POLICY INFLUENCE?

Minnesota E-democracy provides spaces for citizen deliberation away from formal political institutions, but recently there has been a small but significant shift toward attempting to plug such networks into formal political processes. These are initiatives that attempt to provide a bridge between the kinds of associations and deliberations among citizens which take place spontaneously every day on the Net—and formal structures of governance which can provide an interface with decision-making processes. The recent participatory turn in political theory discussed in the opening sections of this chapter has generated a range of non-Internet methods for involving citizens in policy making at various organizational levels in many liberal democratic political systems. These include citizens' juries, people's panels, local policy forums, focus groups, deliberative polling, mini-referendums, and petitions (Coleman and Gøtze; 2001:14; Ryfe, 2002). However, e-democratic projects have introduced the Internet into this already-rich variety of experiments. These have generally adopted two broad models.

Consultative Models

Consultative approaches stress the communication of citizen opinion to government. They tend to assume that information is a resource which can be used to provide better policy and administration. By using the speed and immediacy of electronic networks, governments can seek voter opinion on particular issues to guide policy making.

Probably the best example of the consultative model in action is the U.S. federal government's e-rule-making program (Coglianese, 2004a, 2004b; Shulman et al., 2003). This is designed to allow interest groups, social movements, and individual citizens to comment on department and agency rules as they are being developed. Such rules are less headline-grabbing than laws originating in Congress, but they can often have huge impacts on ordinary citizens. Over one hundred federal bodies issue a total of over four thousand rules each year. The requirement that agencies consider submitted comments on draft rules is not new—it was mandated by the Administrative Procedures Act of 1946. However, until citizens started to submit comments online in the late 1990s, the procedure for making them was incredibly cumbersome and largely remained the preserve of political consultants and professional lobby organizations. The dockets, or files, containing relevant background documentation and comments—in effect the paper trail that leads to the formation of a rule—were housed in huge government archives seldom visited by ordinary citizens.

E-rule-making was pioneered by the Department of Agriculture (USDA), which, in 1998, launched its National Organic Program for the development of regulations on organic food. The USDA received 277,000 comments, covering a wide range of issues and concerns. A similar exercise involving rules on the Roadless Area Conservation Initiative in 1999 saw the Department of the Interior and the Forest Service inundated with over a million postcards or form letters, sixty thousand original letters, and ninety thousand emails. Other departments and agencies, especially the Environmental Protection Agency (EPA) and the Department of Transportation, hosted a variety of forms of e-rule making during the early 2000s. In 2002, in an attempt to diffuse the innovation throughout the entire federal government, the Office of Management and Budget started to develop a central rule-making portal—www.regulations.gov. The portal is managed by a lead agency—the EPA—and provides a simple, unified front-end to a wide variety of specific e-rule-making processes, though not all departments and agencies have moved their e-rule making permanently online. It is intended that the regulations.gov portal will eventually integrate all federal departments and agencies, though there has been some resistance to this from within some departments and agencies (Chadwick, 2004).

Significant as it undoubtedly is, e-rule making is a consultative model of e-democracy. The system as it stands is based on a patchwork of different methods, including email and web forms. Citizens who submit to bodies that only accept emails are unable to read the comments of others. The web form submission procedure does allow one to read others' comments, but these are presented in chronological list format rather than the threaded format that predominates in most online discussion forums. There are no plans to switch to a fully interactive threaded format across the board (Chadwick, 2004).

Deliberative Models

While consultative e-democracy mostly stresses the vertical flows of government-citizen communication, deliberative models conceive of a more complex horizontal and multi-directional interactivity. These models are thinner on the ground than their consultative counterparts. As I have argued, many of the community network–style attempts at e-democracy have been weak on plugging into local political structures. Examples from North Jutland, Denmark (aimed at nonvoters), Kalix, Sweden (town planning), and Scotland (aimed at eleven-to-eighteen year-olds) have been evaluated, but their role in relation to institutional politics is unclear. For example, the Jutland scheme strictly ruled out "providing answers to citizens' problems" (Coleman and Gøtze, 2001:44) and tended to be dominated by local politicians rather than ordinary members of the public (Jensen, 2003).

Somewhat surprisingly, the United Kingdom has been a pioneer in experimental attempts to integrate deliberative forums and consultation exercises directly into policy discussions (Hansard Society, 2000, 2003). The U.K. Hansard Society, a nonprofit body that aims to promote active citizenship and parliamentary government, uses the term "e-democracy" to refer to the direct integration of citizens' online deliberations to inform the behavior of elected representatives in a nonbinding way. It is designed to enhance, not supplant, traditional representative institutions. The society has been conducting small-scale experiments in online consultation since the late 1990s, including a discussion on floods and a path-breaking forum on experiences of domestic violence, involving over two hundred women in interactive discussion. Many had never used the Internet before and accessed the discussion through women's refuges or public libraries (Hansard Society, 2000). Exhibit 5.3 briefly outlines a fascinating case study: the online evidence and discussion forum on the Draft Communications Bill, set up

EXHIBIT 5.3. COMMBILL.NET

A joint committee of the House of Commons and the House of Lords was established in May 2002 to examine the British government's Draft Communications Bill. The bill (now law) was an overhaul of media and telecommunication regulatory structures with far-reaching consequences, including the abolition of the Office of Telecommunications (OFTEL), the Independent Television Commission, the Broadcasting Standards Commission, and the Radio Authority and their replacement by a new Office of Communication (OFCOM). In other words, this was a genuinely significant piece of legislation.

The online forum was set up in collaboration with the Parliamentary Office of Science and Technology (POST) on June 10, 2002, and discussions lasted until July 9, 2002 (Joint Committee on the Draft Communications Bill, 2003). The technology used was a simple and reasonably intuitive web-based threaded forum of the kind that has proliferated on political and nonpolitical websites. Live webcasts of the evidence sessions were made available on the www.parliamentlive.tv website and on the digital television channel BBC Parliament. Discussion was prestructured around five main areas of the committee's work and initially stimulated by short articles written by committee members. The forum attracted 373 participants who together posted 222 messages. The content of many (but not all) messages was presented to the committee as weekly summaries that were also published on the forum site. In this way, the online debate fed organically into the committee debate and vice versa. This continual interaction between the committee and the forum participants allowed committee members to use material gathered from the forum in their questions to "real" witnesses as they progressed and in their final report.

The forum created reasonably high levels of interactivity, as measured by the number of replies to previous messages. However, the committee's final report noted that evidence of what it terms community building was less obvious in this case than previous forums, "possibly due to the abstract nature of the issues" (Joint Committee on the Draft Communications Bill, 2003: annex 5). Nevertheless, the online method proved useful for nonaligned individuals and smaller bodies, such as charities and community broadcasters, to air their views. While the witness sessions involved representatives from the state-controlled BBC and large media and telecommunication corporations—ITV, Sky, AOL, BT, Telewest, NTL, and Vodafone among many others—these groups largely chose not to get involved in the online forum.

Sources: Summarized from Chadwick, 2003; Coleman, 2004; U.K. Parliament Joint Committee of the Draft Communications Bill, 2003.

under the aegis of a Joint Committee of the U.K. Parliament and the Hansard Society in 2002. Commbill.net was the first genuine attempt to integrate an online forum with established prelegislative arrangements (exhibit 5.3).

Commbill.net was a limited experiment but one that paved the way for other online consultations that plugged directly into existing parliamentary and departmental procedures, such as the month-long e-discussion on foreign policy conducted by the Canadian federal government in November 2004 (Canada Department of Foreign Affairs and International Trade, 2004). The significance of such initiatives lies in the fact that they converge what some, in the past, have dismissed as impractical or even utopian arguments about e-democracy with very traditional processes of policy making. Moreover, in the case of Commbill, by involving the executive and legislature, this form of convergence arguably defuses the criticism that executive-managed consultations marginalize elected representatives.

Assessing E-democracy

With the notable exceptions of some community networks—Minnesota E-democracy, e-rule making, and Commbill.net—the road to e-democracy is littered with the burnt-out hulks of failed projects. Reasons for this have varied but usually involve a combination of poor funding, unrealistic expectations, inappropriate technology, internal disputes, and a lack of clear objectives. In the case of community networks, the most commonly cited reason is that they have been insufficiently embedded in the kinds of goals people pursue in geographical communities. They have often been driven by an emphasis on simply getting people to use new technology rather than solving the real problems of a community (Bannon and Griffin, 2001:40).

Many e-democracy programs have been based upon idealized conceptions of citizenship. The Santa Monica Public Electronic Network suffered from problems with abusive messages, which led many to desert the discussion groups. Although local politicians were keen to take part in discussions in the project's early years, their enthusiasm waned over time (Docter and Dutton, 1998). Once the initial excitement has died down, many communities exhibit burn out as activist volunteers become disillusioned and drift away, only to be replaced a few years later by the next wave of enthusiasts. Over time, this leads to what Bill Dutton terms "innovation amnesia" (1999:82). Also, some participate in civic networks for "nonpolitical" reasons: they may be taking advantage of a generous offer of a free computer, seeking entertainment, or trying to secure a place for their child in a good local school. While social capital theorists would argue that such participation will contribute in the long run to political engagement, the links may sometimes be tenuous. In some cases, households take up the offer of free computers and network access but then drift off into their own private spheres. Building the infrastructure seems to be no guarantee that it will be used for community building. A further problem derives from the diffusion of the Internet. Many of the community networks were established when the technology was in its infancy. They are victims of their own success, as users have migrated to private sector ISPs and the bigger world of the open Internet. Stephen Doheny-Farina argues that the local orientation of community networks increasingly has little purchase in the globalized communication environment, where we are all essentially nomadic, free to roam around to much more exciting environments than our neighborhood (Doheny-Farina, 1996).

A community network will only thrive if there is a degree of convergence between real-world infrastructure and the technology network. All communities possess a civic communications infrastructure that predates the Internet. It comprises a familiar mixture of formal public arenas like town halls; informal "great good places" like parks, coffee shops, and bars; informal neighborhood networks based around social support and gossip; libraries and other information repositories; and local old media such as newspapers, radio, and television (Pigg, 2001:516; see also Friedland, 2001; Matei and Ball-Rokeach, 2003). Many online community networks would be found wanting when judged against this rich mixture. For example, research on the Missouri Express network concludes that it has "not made much progress in creating a community information infrastructure that looks like the one existing before the electronic network project was established" (Pigg, 2001:518–19). The Missouri Express consisted of an advanced and diverse set of electronic tools for deliberation, including special newsgroups, email discussion lists, web forums, feedback forms, and chat servers. Yet few of these arenas are used for community-oriented deliberation. A recent survey of community networks in Italy reveals similar trends, as municipal governments "still find great difficulties in adopting bilateral modes of communication with citizens" (Berra, 2003:223).

But before we prematurely consign e-democracy to the dustbin of history, let us assess it in greater depth. We can do so by revisiting the two resilient concepts (outlined earlier) that have guided research on the phenomenon: social capital and the public sphere.

Social Capital Revisited

Social capital and civic engagement may be powerfully suggestive concepts, but they are incredibly difficult to identify, let alone measure (Foley and Edwards, 1999). Some social psychologists were quick to pounce on the idea of the Internet as a force for good in this sphere. In a famous article, which has subsequently been heavily revised by the authors themselves, Robert Kraut and his colleagues argued that the Internet was an antisocial medium that generated feelings of isolation and even depression among those who use it, mainly because it took up valuable time that would otherwise be spent in real-life interactions with family and friends (Kraut et al., 1998).

Other early studies concurred that users, especially those who spent many hours online, tend to lose contact with their proximate social environment. Political scientists Norman Nie and Lutz Erbring published controversial findings from a survey undertaken by Stanford University's Institute for the Quantitative Study of Society in 2000. This concluded that Netizens were "home alone and anonymous" (Nie and Erbring, 2000:26). However, their reinforcement of Kraut and colleagues' earlier research was on shakier foundations once Kraut and his colleagues revisited their sample of surfers, only to find that that the Internet was actually proving to be socially and psychologically beneficial (Kraut et al., 2002).

Findings contradicting Nie and Erbring also come from a range of data-intensive studies in the United States and across Europe, such as James Katz and Ronald Rice's national surveys from 1995 and 2000 (2002); Lori Weber and colleagues' analysis of three huge opinion surveys in which they were able to assess the effects of the Internet on levels of political participation (2003); Dhavan Shah and colleagues' study differentiating between types of Internet use (Shah, Kwak, and Holbert, 2001); and Pippa Norris's European opinion study (2001). Katz and Rice found that well-established influences on community involvement such as age, income, and education were more significant than Internet use (2002:160). Weber and colleagues found that engagement in online activity "significantly affects" formal political participation beyond voting, such as signing petitions, letter writing, attending rallies, and so on, even when controlling for race, education, age, gender, and membership in local groups and hobby clubs (2003:32). Shah and colleagues discovered that those who seek out political information online are more likely to have high levels of social capital, whereas those who primarily use the Internet for social recreation are likely to have lower levels (Shah, Kwak, and Holbert, 2001:154). Perhaps more significant was the finding that using the Internet to exchange political information creates higher levels of trust than uses of traditional print and broadcast news media (Shah, McLeod, and Yoon, 2001). And in a withering critique of Nie and Erbring's Stanford study, Jonathan Gershuny (2003:165) argues that the view that the Internet displaces time that would otherwise be used for community-building activities fails to recognize that many of the activities on which we spend time online are actually for the purposes of organizing and extending our community ties.

Nie and Erbring's (2000) data were drawn from individual responses to national random samples. They share this approach, and their pessimism, with those scholars that have tried to isolate the effects on political engagement of increases in the quantity of political information provided by the Internet (Bimber, 2001; Scheufele and Nisbet, 2002). But there is more to the Internet than simply increasing the amount of political information available to citizens.

Studies of the Net's effects on actual social networks have tended to be quite positive. For example, in his study of Netville (a pseudonym), a Toronto suburb with broadband, Keith Hampton found that sociality increases with Internet use. Internet users knew three times as many local people as nonusers and were more likely to talk to their neighbors and to invite them round to their homes (2003). Extending such themes into the political sphere, Anabel Quan-Haase and colleagues found that those who use the Internet often are more likely to be positive about their online communities and see them as a useful means of interaction (2002). In her study of a community network and an Internet café in Skarpnäck, a relatively poor Stockholm suburb, Sara Ferlander found that while the community network failed to achieve its objectives and was wound up after two years, the Internet café prevailed and succeeded in increasing the levels of social capital. The Internet café was regarded as a useful physical meeting place as well as a provider of access to cyberspatial interaction. Ferlander's study is especially convincing because it was able to measure social capital before and after the technological innovations were introduced (Ferlander, 2003; Ferlander and Timms, 2001). Before the Internet café, Skarpnäck was an area with little sense of community, high levels of distrust, and few structures of social support.

These findings fit with patterns established in other successful local projects. In the "digital town" of Parthenay, in western France, Internet access points were deliberately located in well-known public spaces like the town hall. Teams of community workers were permanently on-site to provide guidance and support (Hervé-Van Driessche, 2001).

This would seem to confirm the view that such networks are more likely to succeed if they map onto real-world information infrastructures: in Skarpnäck's case, one of Oldenburg's (1997) "great good places," in Parthenay's, a public, political venue.

Some scholars of social networks, particularly Barry Wellman, insist that the decline of public or great good places does not necessarily mean that our social network ties have diminished. Wellman maintains that Internet forms of communication, which are based in the home, often fill the gap left by the decline of real-world community. In other words, we still create and belong to informal communities, but these are increasingly mediated through email, instant messaging, and online discussion forums. Perhaps those who emphasize the importance of place and face-to-face contact are missing the point (Wellman and Gulia, 1999:188).

Much stems from how we interpret social ties and their contribution to civic engagement. The social capital approach tends to privilege "strong," face-to-face ties over supposedly "weaker," electronically mediated ties. Yet research from the uses and gratifications tradition in political communication has long argued that people choose different forms of communication based upon their assessment of what they might achieve by using them. From this perspective, virtual engagement can occur through seemingly passive mediated encounters such as watching television news. Such experiences allow citizens to create their own cognitive maps of the larger political sphere, which they then feed into their real-world citizen engagement (Shah, McLeod, and Yoon, 2001:470).

In addition, Mark Granovetter's influential "strength of weak ties" theory (1973) argues that, for the achievement of some tasks, such as acquiring new information, weaker ties are in fact better because they increase the size of the information pool from which an individual can draw when deciding how to act. Remaining within a group based on strong ties is less effective for gaining new information, because there is little likelihood that new resources will flow into it. Keith Hampton's research on Netville reveals how email created "large, dense networks of relatively weak social ties" that nevertheless enabled local collective action against the housing developer and consortium by disgruntled residents (Hampton, 2003:418). Even more radically, Caroline Haythornthwaite has elaborated on the importance of "latent ties"—those that are technically possible but "not activated by social interaction" (2002:389). Individuals belonging to the same organization or electronic network such as an email list have latent ties established for them by the communication infrastructures of the organization or simply the technical capacity of the communication system, such as the presence of a shared email address book. When latent ties are activated, they become weak ties and may eventually turn into strong ties.

Social capital theory's relevance for the Internet may also be criticized for failing to understand that the traditional limits to community formation have withered. Community no longer requires geographical proximity. The assumption that simply living close to others is what makes a community is flawed. Communities, especially ones organized around political issues, are forged through shared interests and beliefs. Their success or failure over time depends upon the intensity of interest of their members (Baker and Ward, 2002:210; Wellman et al., 2003). The extent to which individuals perceive it to be worthwhile to contribute to a community may not derive from the fact that it consists of members of their street but because ten residents of the street share an interest in model railroads, or the films of Quentin Tarantino, or many other things. This is not to argue that physical communities do not matter. Neighbors share an interest in maintaining the pleasant aspects of the neighborhood, so it is more likely, for instance, that a community will be formed around projects such as planting trees or fighting local development plans. But local communities are not the homogenous entities that they once were and are no longer based upon the kinds of very local physical constraints that created the much-romanticized community ethos of eighteenth-century New England towns, for example (Tambini, 1999:324). The typical communities of today are communities of interest, which bring together those with shared passions, or communities of practice, whose force derives from the fact that participants are attempting to achieve something concrete, such as getting their job done. In other words, localities are themselves no longer purely local, and there are flaws in trying to understand community and political identity as primarily local phenomena (Meehan, 1993).

Indeed, there is a case to be made that local community networks are new, or at least hybrid, forms of social and political organization. Many localities will lack resources and skills. For some, the point is that the Internet can be used to access information resources from *outside* the community if those resources are lacking within. In the relatively poor regions of southern Italy, for example, community networks are seen as playing a role in regional development. In the absence of a developed industrial base, such networks aim to pull in expertise from outside the immediate area (Berra, 2003:219). In Bologna, the civic network was established during a period when the city was expanding to encompass several existing municipalities. Local politicians wanted a means of integrating citizens from these areas into their political orbit (Morison and Newman, 2001:176). Those groups that share a common condition, such as the disabled, accident victims, and so on, may not have social ties that are connected to their experiences, especially in their local communities, or if they do, they may find them difficult to forge. Similarly, there are those that have similar social and economic interests, such as geographically dispersed farmers, but location militates against collective action. The network thus acts as a means of building a new political community outside the constraints of geography.

Once again, however, before we get carried away with this argument, we face a contradiction, because many successful e-democracy projects *have* been geographically specific. As we saw earlier, the Camfield Estates–MIT project deliberately sought to construct a databank of local assets, which were seen as essential precursors for the formation of communities of interest. One of the earliest discussion topics on the Santa Monica PEN was homelessness. Over time, this led to the creation of a number of projects aimed at homeless people in the area (Rogers and Malhotra, 2000:23; Schalken, 2000:154–68). Purely virtual communities—ones not rooted in geography—may lack the types of commitment that are required for the creation and maintenance of "real" communities. It is too easy to exit a virtual community. As a result, membership can be fleeting. The kinds of shared understandings and loyalties that develop over time in real communities are difficult to replicate in such a fluid environment.

E-democracy programs that are autonomous or which have only weak links with real governance structures also face problems of institutionalization. They can be perceived as transient, without any real credibility or claim to be representative. However, once again, this needs to be traded off against the constraints that will inevitably be placed upon official e-democracy networks that are closely aligned with government. In Bologna, for example, discussion groups on its Iperbole civic network have been routinely censored by local officials, while a local planning consultation in Esslingen, Germany, was resisted by local administrators due to the amount of time it absorbed (Märker et al., 2001:272; Tambini, 1999:316, 320). Reactions to these forms of gatekeeping are what have spurred many community activists to try to establish networks from below. In Parthenay, France, community members were encouraged to use free web space to create their own local content. The town mayor deliberately wished to avoid this function falling into the hands of the town council (Hervé-Van Driessche, 2001:10–11). And due to pressure from below, Bologna's civic network eventually expanded its interactive features, creating multiple discussion forums and allowing citizens to comment on municipal proposals through its Democracy Online program (Berra, 2003:227; Coleman and Gøtze, 2001:36).

A final point here is that there is an important and sometimes overlooked distinction between two forms of social capital: "bridging" (or inclusive) and "bonding" (or exclusive). While bridging social capital is created in networks that are heterogeneous, "outward-looking and encompass people across diverse social cleavages," bonding social capital networks are homogeneous, "inward looking, and tend to reinforce exclusive identities" (Putnam, 2000:22). This distinction has important implications for understanding the contribution of the Internet to the creation or destruction of social capital (Norris, 2002b). It is easy to see how online interaction can create new forms of bonding social capital, because it provides many more opportunities for people to seek out those who share the same passions, beliefs, and interests. Bridging social capital is a more difficult prospect. But even this may also increase as a result of the diffusion of the Internet. Why? The answer lies in the type of networking that the Internet permits. Bonding social capital is less dependent upon media than its bridging counterpart; it is more likely to depend upon real-world interactions among family members and members of close-knit communities that are geographically concentrated. Bridging social capital, on the other hand, is more likely to be the product of ties that are established across social and geographical divides. Such ties are easier to establish and maintain using the Internet, which undermines the effects of distance on community formation and creates communities that are much more permeable. Evidence from a 2001 survey of Internet users' membership of community groups indicates that both of these forms of social capital are enhanced (Norris, 2002a:11). It is thus possible that the Internet may contribute to bridging political divides that are geographically embedded—between urban and suburban areas or areas of a city (or even a country) informally segregated along ethnic or religious lines.

Bringing people into contact with those they would not normally encounter in geographical spaces also has implications for our second concept: the public sphere.

The Public Sphere Revisited

In considering Habermas's (1962 [1989]) ideal of a public sphere of communication free from both corporate and state power, it pays to think about the characteristics of many online communities.

First, online talk mirrors talk in our everyday lives; it is often banal, sometimes gossipy, periodically awkward and conflictual, and only sporadically political in the formal sense. Sadly, as in real life, we may also find that our views are simply ignored. The relatively open, unstable, and ruleless nature of virtual communities might accentuate some of these aspects. Flaming and "trolling" (posting deliberately stupid or pointless messages designed to get a response) are often mentioned as particularly problematic (Abouchar and Henson, 2000). The majority of Usenet posts appear to go unanswered (Smith, 1999:210), and there is some evidence that the online forums of politically marginalized groups are most susceptible to these uncivic practices (Herring et al., 2002).

Second, AOL, Microsoft, Yahoo!, and so on are large media corporations who use community discussions as a means of increasing revenue by delivering eyeballs to advertisers. Companies who wish to make money selling advertising space will inevitably focus on providing space for popular communities, and these are not likely to be political—at least not in the narrow sense—in their orientation. They will also occasionally intervene to remove communities that they think may deter advertisers.

Third, segmented discussion forums are often best seen as semipublic spaces (Polletta, 1999). While membership of these is not physically restricted, it is de facto restricted because outsiders are discouraged from entering a space if they do not fit in. This is how many Internet discussion forums function. They are in principle open to all, but their specialized nature excludes many.

Finally, many government sites are more geared toward legitimizing government decisions and operate much more stringent forum policies as a result. They are often more about professional communication and service delivery and less about encouraging critical citizen deliberation (Chadwick, 2001; Chadwick and May, 2003; Musso et al., 2000).

Thus, many virtual communities are constrained by a mixture of private and public forms of power. In other words, they do not always fulfill the criteria for the public sphere identified by Habermas.

It is no accident that some of the most successful Internet media and e-commerce companies, such as AOL, Microsoft Network, or eBay, place the development of communities at the center of their business models. AOL is an excellent example of how private companies have developed new public spaces in the form of bulletin boards and chat rooms. Yet we need to be aware of some of the limitations of such spaces, and this requires us to consider how the technologies used by AOL have shaped the types and extent of communication that take place there (see exhibit 5.4). AOL's version of community thus designs out some of the unpredictability of political interaction in real space (see also Noveck, 2000:21).

Much of this makes sense if we consider why AOL and many other private companies encourage interaction in online discussion forums in the first place. Such devices mesh perfectly with firms' business goals. Steven McLaine (2003) has argued that the Internet enables the "commodification of community." Using examples drawn from online ethnic community sites such as AsianAvenue.com, BlackPlanet.com, and MiGente.com, McLaine shows how potentially "dangerous" political content is often subordinated to more "acceptable" discussion threads about music, fashion, and other lifestyle issues that can easily be tied in with advertiser demands (McLaine, 2003). Joshua Gamson argues that this trend is even more conspicuous in mainstream gay and

EXHIBIT 5.4. POLITICAL COMMUNITY ON A LEASH: AOL

"There are places in AOL where people can gather; there are places where people can go and read messages posted by others. But there is no space where everyone gathers at one time, or even a space that everyone sooner or later must pass through. There is no public space where you could address all members of AOL. There is no town hall or town meeting where people can complain in public and have their complaints heard by others. There is no space large enough for citizens to create a riot. The owners of AOL, however, can speak to all. Steve Case, the 'town mayor,' writes 'chatty' letters to the members. AOL advertises to all its members and can send everyone an email. But only the owners and those they authorize can do so. The rest of the members of AOL can speak to crowds only where they notice a crowd. And never to a crowd greater than twenty-three. . . .

That only twenty-three people can be in a chat room at once is a choice of the code engineers. While their reasons could be many, the effect is clear. One can't imagine easily exciting members of AOL into public action. One can't imagine easily picketing the latest pricing policy. There are places to go to complain, but you have to take the trouble to go there yourself. There is no place where members can complain en masse.

Real space is different in this respect. Much of the free speech law is devoted to preserving spaces where dissent can occur—spaces that can be noticed, and must be confronted, by nondissenting citizens. In real space there are places where people can gather, places where they can leaflet. People have a right to the sidewalks, public streets, and other traditional public forums. They may go there and talk about issues of public import or otherwise say whatever they want. Constitutional law in real space protects the right of the passionate and the weird to get in the face of the rest. But no such design is built into AOL."

Source: Quoted from Lessig, 1999:69.

lesbian online communities such as PlanetOut and Gay.com, where, he maintains, the Internet contributes to "the transformation of gay and lesbian media from organizations answering at least partly to geographical and political communities into businesses answering primarily to advertisers and investors," where "consumption-as-liberation ideologies" prevail (Gamson, 2003:260, 272). By slavishly focusing on consumer identities, such community sites have little space for political discussion and, ironically, are perhaps less useful for political mobilization than their old media equivalents like newsletters and paper magazines, which deliberately fused gay lifestyle issues with serious political content. Moreover, such sites are increasingly owned and controlled not by minority groups themselves but by large general media conglomerates that recognize the value of tailoring their products for such niche markets.

At the same time, however, there are several reasons why we should not be too pessimistic. Some authors have argued that understanding the political significance of online minority communities calls for an expanded conception of what we mean by "political." In an analysis of African American websites, Rohit Lekhi argues that despite their seemingly apolitical flavor, they in fact foster cultural identities that are counter to dominant white culture. This, Lekhi suggests, is in keeping with a long-established oppositional African American traditions which fuse cultural and political expression (2000:96). The variety and quality of political deliberation mirrors what occurs offline. Criticisms of the online environment (e.g., Barber, 1997; Streck, 1998; Wilhelm, 2000:86–104) often spring from idealized conceptions of the quality of real-world political talk. Anyone who has attended PTA or local town meetings that have descended into slanging matches will report that face-to-face politics has few obvious claims to superiority over its online counterpart. Asynchronous methods, such as email or forums, allow participants the time to reflect before sending a response; they introduce constraints that soften some of the problems of offline interaction. Studies of the kinds of interactions that actually take place in online communities have also revealed sophisticated informal mechanisms used to get around the limitations of computer-mediated communication, including cultivating online personalities, inventing new forms of rules and expressions such as written codes of conduct like FAQs (Frequently Asked Questions), the now-ubiquitous emoticons, and humorously discussing how the online environment can create misunderstandings (Bakardjieva and Feenberg, 2002:184).

It also pays to consider how online community environments have shifted since the early days of Usenet. Applications like instant messaging, Yahoo! Groups and phpBB (open source forum software) now consist of many features that are designed to recreate the conditions of community. Unlike open Usenet groups, other environments allow users to set up profiles, establish group boundaries, check on activity levels of other participants, combine asynchronous and synchronous discussion, and keep long-term selective archives (Bakardjieva and Feenberg, 2002:189). Moreover, more radical approaches suggest that liberation from our physical constraints, whether they be of bodily, geographical, or social origin, is the principal attraction of virtual communities (Turkle, 1996; see also Bakardjieva, 2003). Neighborhoods may provide social support, but they may also be information-poor, stifling, and conformity inducing. It has also been argued that the sometimes heated and relatively ruleless nature of online political discussion is in fact more conducive to democratic deliberation because it subverts the constraints of politeness that influence face-to-face discussion. Citizens can be more forthright in cyberspace (Papacharissi, 2004). In the end, media corporations and governments play a constraining role but cannot control all aspects of virtual community interaction. In fact, the record so far suggests that content providers and ISPs are very reluctant to become involved in regulation of speech in their communities.

As we saw in chapter 2, an influential approach in this area is Cass Sunstein's (2001) view that the Internet creates an "echo chamber" effect, where one's views are seldom if ever challenged in the self-created universe of the *Daily Me* (see also Levine, 2002). Sunstein argues that people will, given the choice, seek out those of like-minded opinion and avoid exposure to dissonant ideas. This interpretation seriously jeopardizes the idea of the public sphere as a space in which those with different perspectives are able to come together to deliberate. It is an elegant argument, but little systematic evidence is offered to support it. In fact, there is emerging evidence from studies of online political discussion that diversity of opinion is one of its attractions. Jennifer Stromer-Galley's analysis of online discussion forums in Yahoo! and on Usenet found that while individuals are not always happy to be exposed to opinions that are radically different from their own, they do encounter differences and often see such clashes as one of the benefits of political discussion online. Moreover, some participants are exposed to a greater range of views than they would find in their everyday lives. One respondent said: "There's a different culture on Usenet. Living in Alabama means living in a world where certain prejudices are completely ingrained into the culture. Usenet has a completely different culture which is often refreshing, given the face-to-face options around Alabama" (Stromer-Galley, 2003:8–9). More research is needed in this area, but Sunstein's thesis may become less secure as time passes.

Like almost all of the examples considered in this chapter, Minnesota E-democracy has been the subject of scholarly analysis rather than mere speculation. This allows us to appraise its success in promoting citizen deliberation. Lincoln Dahlberg's studies (2001a; 2001b) found that the carefully constructed and strictly enforced rules kept discussions on topic and encouraged participants to substantiate their claims rather than simply assert opinions. Although dogmatic assertions appeared, he also found evidence that participants were willing to modify their positions once they had engaged in discussion with others. The fact that the MN-Politics-Discuss list was reserved for Minnesotans contributed to a sense of community, which made it easier for participants to put themselves in the positions of others when responding to comments. Unusual among virtual communities, participants were required to use their real names and sign every post with a real email address, full name, and city of residence. This increased the levels of sincerity and therefore trust. The only major downsides to Dahlberg's findings are first, that those who are politically active offline are also most likely to dominate discussion on the email lists. There was a notable bias toward "politically active, educated, white males," and a masculine style of political argument was also observed. Second, the nongovernmental and nonprofit nature of the project was continually in jeopardy due to the costs of the web hosting and time spent moderating (Dahlberg, 2001b:625–27). Now that the lists are hosted by Yahoo! Groups, banner advertisements appear on the pages, and Yahoo! obviously sees the participants as potential subscribers to its other services. Thus, some commodification of the e-democracy experience has occurred. Nevertheless, Dahlberg, taking themes from Habermas, concludes that the project has contributed to the creation of a genuinely deliberative space in which people come together for reasoned debate about political issues. It goes some way toward recreating some of the characteristics of Habermas's idealized public sphere.

When it comes to those e-democratic projects that have tried to bridge the divide between civil society and politics, the record is a little stronger. As the U.S. e-rule making and U.K. Commbill examples demonstrate, these are pulling citizens into spheres where their deliberations are likely to influence the development of policy. Although this may only occur at the margins, in mature liberal democracies, such marginal changes are significant. These innovations point to the future routinization of what has been termed "participatory policy analysis." Capitalizing on nonexpert input may create more legitimate polices with broader support among the public (Kakabadse et al., 2003:56). Preliminary evaluations of e-rule making have revealed that federal agencies are encountering contradictory shifts. On the one hand, it merely enhances the ability of those specialist lobby groups and their legal teams to influence rule making. In some highly specialized areas, where rules can run to many pages of indecipherable references and cross-references to other rules, there are thus likely to be reinforcement effects.

However, there is also evidence that the range of voices has increased and that many citizens have commented in an individual capacity or as representatives of a locality that may be particularly affected by a regulatory change (Stanley et al., 2004).

This is not to deny that there are certain endemic problems with both consultative and deliberate models of e-democratic policy influence. Some of the celebrated examples from recent years, such as Canada's Energy Technology Futures consultation, soon flickered out. Those who give feedback in deliberative forums and who contact government with their views may be self-selected, technology-literate groups whose views and prejudices may not be representative of citizens as a whole. Indeed, the ability to use technology in the manner proposed is unevenly spread through government itself as well as civil society. There are also many old problems with direct democracy (McLean, 1989)—notably the difficulty of framing policy alternatives in ways which will solicit broadly comparable (and informed) responses and the possibility that both government and organized groups may be able to mobilize electronic campaigns to further their own aims (through question rigging) or may only seek consultation in certain policy areas or with certain groups. For example, the local e-polling system being developed by Greece only allows for simple yes/no responses to a series of closed rather than open-ended questions (Bouras et al., 2003). Indeed, it also becomes possible for government to poll relatively small sections of the electorate and, in turn, "narrowcast" information back. Government may be able to define the interests of a particular group in a particular way and keep that strategy hidden from other potentially affected interests (Abramson et al., 1988:49–54; Van de Donk et al., 1995:24). Government agencies also face huge practical issues when they are swamped by hundreds of thousands of citizen submissions, a factor which has led the e-rule-making project team into an eager search for content management systems that will automate the process of aggregating comments (Chadwick, 2004).

CONCLUSION

It pays to situate any appraisal of the Internet's impact on community, political deliberation, and participation in the context of its embeddedness in everyday life and how the functions of various media differ. Earlier forecasts that the Internet would destroy or radically transform community contain grains of truth, but a far more convincing perspective is that the Net supplements community (Wellman et al., 2003:9). It is an extra means of communication that can be used to maintain social ties or extend them when we wish. Political and other interests have transferred online, while the new experiences and views to which people are exposed online transfer into the offline world.

Is the Internet increasing or decreasing social capital and opportunities for political participation? The answer is that it appears to be doing both but not, perhaps, in the ways that many commentators have assumed. Communities of interest may tend toward being homogeneous echo chambers decried by Sunstein (2001), though, as we saw, even this claim is empirically contested. Yet even if it stands, we need to remember that individuals rarely have just one interest. The broader Internet community-scape is highly diverse and pluralistic, and it includes local, national, and transnational elements. Overall, e-democracy is producing more complex, rather than simply more or less, community, deliberation, and political participation.

One of the difficulties in studying this area is the dead weight of exaggeration and false dichotomies. Skeptics have often slain "straw men," such as those who supposedly claim that representative democracy would be entirely swept away by the Internet. Very few advocates of e-democracy have gone this far. Even writers that have categorically stated that the technical barriers to direct democracy are dead and buried have accompanied this with all manner of reflections on the nontechnical impediments (e.g., Budge, 1996). In fact, as in other areas of this book, the Internet encourages hybridity. E-democracy augments and in some cases destabilizes existing political arrangements. There is still a missing link between e-democratic activity in civil society and policy making that takes place in formal institutional spheres, but, as we have seen, some efforts are being made in this direction. Indeed, it is in this latter sphere that we may expect to see decisive shifts over the next few years.

Discussion Points

- What are the philosophical origins of e-democracy?
- Is geographical community and face-to-face interaction essential for democracy?
- Do virtual communities help or hinder democratic politics?
- Why is it so difficult to be an active citizen? Will the Internet help?
- Do corporate sector discussion forums provide deliberative public spheres?
- How useful are the concepts of social capital and the public sphere for interpreting the Internet's impact on democratic politics?

Further Reading

For participatory theories of democracy, the best places to begin are Barber, 1984, Fishkin, 1991, and Pateman, 1970. The influence of communitarianism is best captured by reading Bellah et al., 1985. For the concept of social capital, see Putnam, 1993, 1995, and 2000, and for a highly readable analysis of the constraints on active citizenship, see Tonn and Petrich, 1998. For the public sphere, see Habermas, 1962 [1989]. For overviews of its relevance for e-democracy, see Dahlberg, 2001a, and Papacharissi, 2002.

Good overviews of community networks are Tambini, 1999, and Tonn et al., 2001. On e-rule making, Shulman et al., 2003, is an excellent introduction, while Commbill.net is considered in Chadwick, 2003, and Coleman, 2004. Useful places to start for assessments of e-democracy that have wider relevance are Hampton, 2003, and Docter and Dutton, 1998. Sound quantitative studies of the Internet's impact on civic engagement include Weber et al., 2003, and Shah, Kwak, and Holbert, 2001.

INTEREST GROUPS AND SOCIAL MOVEMENTS

E-mobilization

Evolving technologies reduce substantially the costs of communicating with large audiences. At a minimum, a single farmer with an inexpensive PC, widely available software, and a low-cost ISP can make a web page viewable by millions. If the farmer spends more, he can buy an electronic mailing list that allows him to send messages to thousands of potential contributors. . . . Now it is possible for this farmer to apply social pressure in a way that his grandfather would have thought unimaginable. Something fundamental has changed.

—ARTHUR LUPIA AND GISELA SIN, 2003

There is a difference between street and online protest. I have been chased down the street by a baton-wielding police officer on horseback. Believe me, it takes a lot less courage to sit in front of a computer.

—MEMBER OF THE HACKTIVIST GROUP CULT OF THE DEAD COW
(Quoted in Weisenburger, 2001)

CHAPTER OVERVIEW

This chapter analyzes e-mobilization—shorthand for uses of the Internet by interest groups and social movements for political recruitment, organization, and campaigning. It is structured around three main themes: organizational change among traditional interest groups; new forms of transnational mobilization; and "pure" Internet forms of direct action, which use methods that only apply in the online world. In the final section of the chapter, we assess various interpretations of the difference the Internet makes in this sphere.

Communication technologies have long been powerful factors shaping political mobilization (Jones, 1994:152–53). For example, during the late 1980s democratic uprisings in the former Eastern bloc countries, overseas satellite television broadcasts informed dissidents of events media in their own countries refused to report. Fax machines were employed by Chinese students during the pro-democracy demonstrations in 1989; they were also used to shore up support for Boris Yeltsin's fledgling transitional regime during the attempted Russian coup of 1991. Steep reductions in the size and cost of hand-held video cameras made reporting from far-flung locations much easier for Western journalists during the early 1990s. Ironically, the same video technology made possible the amateur taping of Los Angeles police officers' beating of African American Rodney King, which, following the involved officers' acquittal in 1992, led to widespread rioting—some of the worst ever witnessed in the United States. There are many other examples of communication making a difference in this area, but the key issue here is whether the Internet's status as a complex, many-to-many medium marks it as more radical than these prior technologies. To date, the impact has been felt in three main areas.

First, many traditional groups with a predominantly national focus have gone on-line to augment their offline strategies, by exploiting new ways to reach out to supporters and the media or put pressure on political elites. On the surface, this does not substantially differ from traditional campaign methods, such as letter writing, phone canvassing, mail-outs, newsletters, and petitions, and the targeting of the old press and broadcast media. On closer scrutiny, however, it seems clear that the Internet is affecting the ways that traditional groups campaign. The Net has spurred changes that allow groups to capitalize on its potential for recruitment, fund-raising, organizational flexibility, and efficiency.

The second type of e-mobilization takes a transnational form. Campaigns that transcend the boundaries of a single nation-state existed long before the rise of the Internet. However, it is undeniable that during the last ten years transnational campaigns have proliferated, and the vast majority of these have involved significant use of the Internet.

Finally, groups and movements' online activity sometimes takes the form of direct action. This usually involves exploiting the technical properties of the Internet itself to achieve a set of political goals. Often referred to as "hacktivism" (which conflates the terms "hacker" and "activism"), this is a genuinely new form of mobilization that was brought into existence by computers and the Internet: it uses methods that only apply in the online world.

INTEREST GROUPS AND SOCIAL MOVEMENTS AS AGENTS OF MOBILIZATION

Political scientists have long sought to draw a distinction between interest groups and social movements. Differences between the two have been mapped along several dimensions, but these usually boil down to levels and foci of participation and influence. The orthodoxy is that interest groups deliberately work within established political institutions while social movements mobilize for collective action away from, but often as a means of exerting pressure on, policy elites. But in the last decade or so, some scholars have argued that the utility of this distinction has declined (Burstein, 1998; Burstein and Linton, 2002:12). In terms of their goals, constituencies of support, tactics, and policy impact, interest groups and social movements are said to be converging and are often treated this way by scholars. Social movements are becoming institutionalized in conventional policy making, while interest groups now often make appeals for mobilization that reach far beyond their restricted membership bases. In their review article, Paul Burstein and April Linton (2002:12) found little evidence that the distinction helped us to make sense of what both groups and movements actually *do*, because the boundaries between them have blurred. More helpful, therefore, is a dual focus on both interest groups and social movements as examples of mobilization (see also Brainard and Siplon, 2002:145). Arguably, the Internet has only accelerated these trends toward convergence, because it has created an environment in which organizational adaptation and experimentation is almost routine. However, as we shall see, in some cases the outcomes of these forces are often not genuinely new forms of political mobilization but are best understood as hybridized combinations of preexisting forms.

Precursors

The contemporary history of e-mobilization arguably begins with two celebrated campaigns from the early 1990s: the MarketPlace and Clipper Chip protests (Gurak, 1997, 1999). During 1990, an association of liberal computer scientists, Computer Professionals for Social Responsibility (CPSR), spearheaded an online campaign against the deployment of a new piece of software called Lotus MarketPlace: Households. The software, an early example of data mining, was developed by Lotus Corporation in alliance with consumer credit company Equifax. It involved the production and distribution of a CD-ROM linking individual names and addresses with consumers' past credit reports, purchases, and other demographic information. But Lotus was forced to cancel its plans due to sustained pressure from around thirty thousand activists who used email, Usenet groups such as misc.consumers, comp.society and comp.org.eff.talk together with rudimentary websites warning about the threats the database posed to individual privacy. More significantly, the campaign brought in other groups, including the newly founded Electronic Frontier Foundation (EFF)—now a significant lobbying presence on most Internet policy matters—and large numbers of outside supporters, whose interest was spurred by the publication of an article by John Wilke in the *Wall Street Journal* publicizing the CPSR's grievances. Wilke's views were reproduced, commented on, and augmented by thousands of individuals as the message circulated around public and corporate networks, including Lotus's own email network. In January 1991, less than a year after the initial announcement, Lotus and Equifax, fearing sustained negative publicity and the likelihood of congressional scrutiny, cancelled the project.

The Clipper Chip campaign of 1993–94 was sparked off by the Clinton administration's announcement of April 1993 that the U.S. National Security Agency (NSA) had developed hardware encryption chips for digital networks. Defended by the administration as a measure to protect communications in the interests of commercial and national security, the proposal was immediately leapt upon by an ad hoc coalition of privacy activists, computer scientists, and Internet libertarians, including the EFF. Most controversial was the so-called key escrow system: the chip would be compulsory for all networks and would be deployed in such a way that the NSA would retain a "master key" which it could use to decrypt intercepted communications as part of its remit. Many of the activists that had been drawn to the MarketPlace campaign became involved in the Clipper Chip protests on the same grounds: they perceived it as a threat to privacy as well as a badly executed encryption policy. The CPSR, the EFF, and the Association for Computing Machinery provided some organizational focus, but the campaign was effectively a loose network, rapidly mobilized through email, Usenet, and FTP download sites. The White House became the target of the first sustained email and electronic petition campaign in U.S. history. The petition, handled by the CPSR, secured forty to fifty thousand signatories (Gurak and Logie, 2003:30). Despite this groundswell of support, the Clipper Chip standard was officially adopted in February 1994. Yet the campaign was perceived by many commentators to be a glimpse of the future of Internet-enabled political mobilization.

The MarketPlace and Clipper Chip cases exhibited several key features of e-mobilization that would become common by the early 2000s. First, they demonstrated the speed with which events could move in the new online environment. In both cases, it took less than a day for people to become aware of the campaigns and to start contributing to the discussion. Second, they revealed untapped support for campaigns against Internet-specific privacy threats emerging from the corporate sector or government. The Net served as a means of rapidly mobilizing this new constituency. Third, as Gurak and Logie argue, the ethos of the online communities that developed during these campaigns was fairly coherent (Gurak and Logie, 2003:31). Establishing a shared sense of purpose proved relatively painless. Most contributors were technically literate and correctly assumed that other campaigners would be able to understand the specialist arguments around data protection and cryptography. Finally, email allowed protestors to circumvent many of the hierarchical structures of established interest groups, government, and large corporations. For example, once the Lotus CEO's email address was circulated, many protestors wrote directly to him. It seems hard to imagine now, but the shock at the flood of messages he received was instrumental in his decision to cancel MarketPlace.

ORGANIZATIONAL CHANGE AMONG TRADITIONAL INTEREST GROUPS

The MarketPlace and Clipper Chip protests are fascinating because they were genuinely new forms of networked political mobilization that would have been difficult to establish without the Internet. Along with other campaigns—against the U.S. Communications Decency Act of 1996 (Pal, 1998) or less-high-profile examples that relied heavily on email, such as Boston's Telecommunications Policy Roundtable campaign to influence other aspects of the U.S. Telecommunications Act of 1996 (Klein, 1999)—they are genuinely significant. Yet despite the excitement they generated, not to mention the inspiration they provided for similar technology-related campaigns, such as privacy groups' successful online protests against Intel's inclusion of unique hardware identifiers in its Pentium III processors in 1999 (Leizerov, 2000), these types of action were often dismissed as unrepresentative. There are notable exceptions, such as Wilmington, North Carolina, residents' protests against the nature of an urban redevelopment program in 1995 (Mele, 1999), but most of these early examples featured computer-literate groups protesting in areas related to their profession.

In the short space of a few years, however, Internet-mediated campaigns have mushroomed. They have sprung up right across the political spectrum, in almost all liberal democratic—and even authoritarian—political systems. By the early 2000s, most if not all major interest groups in the United States had established online presences and were using email, websites, bulletin boards, and instant messaging to organize existing supporters, fund-raise, and reach out to old and new constituencies of support.

Email is now ubiquitous in the vast majority of interest groups. It accelerates communication between national leaders and local branches and enhances the experience of ordinary grassroots members by facilitating cheap and regular communication on a scale that would have been impossible using older methods. Web-based forums allow ordinary members of a group to establish discussion topics away from the disciplinary control of the leadership. Feedback from such forums may then be used to inform policy at the center. The Internet amplifies, accelerates, and, in some ways, transforms communication within a group's internal organization, but it also changes the relationship between one group or movement's network and those of its potential competitors or collaborators. The Internet also affects the relationship between groups and movements and their principal targets: government, citizens, and the mainstream media.

But before we are swept away on a tide of novelty, it pays to consider just how the Internet has changed group and movement politics. Media depictions of Internet-enabled political action tend to focus on spectacular incidents rather than the more prosaic aspects of online political participation (Postmes and Brunsting, 2002:293). However, explaining the long-term significance of the Internet in this sphere must incorporate consideration of the kinds of mainstream interest groups that are such crucial actors in liberal democratic political systems. If it can be demonstrated that mainstream interest groups—the staples of modern liberal democracy—are adapting to new information and communication technologies, some of the more grandiose claims regarding the novelty of Internet-enabled mobilization will perhaps be much easier to swallow.

In a groundbreaking study of the impact of the Internet on American politics, Bruce Bimber deliberately places new online movements in the context of a focus on traditional, long-established groups. While new single-issue campaigns readily lend themselves to Internet-based forms of mobilization, changes in older groups really demonstrate the power of the new medium. The Internet, Bimber argues, provokes internal organizational adaptation as well as innovation in the ways in which groups gather support and use it to influence legislation and rule-making processes. In fact, these two developments—organizational change and external mobilization—are inextricably linked. There are many examples of these phenomena, including online coordination by the U.S. National Association of Manufacturers, which preempted many liability lawsuits in the build up to the "millennium bug" deadline of January 1, 2000, or the National Coalition against Domestic Violence's successful mobilization of supporters to lobby Congress to complete the five-year reauthorization of the 1994 Violence against Women Act—a campaign in which over one hundred fifty thousand emails were sent by citizens to members of Congress (Bimber, 2003:114–16). But one of Bimber's cases stands out for its illustration of the relationship between organizational change and capacity to mobilize: Environmental Defense. Let us consider it in a little more detail.

Environmental Defense

Environmental causes have often been framed as inherently global, but the fact remains that the constellation of green groups and movements differs markedly from country to country due to the "backyard" nature of many of the issues. In the United States, there is a long tradition of environmental lobbying, dating back to at least the 1890s, when the Sierra Club was founded. Despite being controversial, the discourse of environmentalism—at least in its moderate "light green" guise—has long been part of the mainstream of U.S. political debate. Many environmentalist groups have enjoyed periods of substantial, if unspectacular, citizen support. Environmental Defense, set up as the Environmental Defense Fund in 1967, is one such group. In 1998, it had a staff of 170, a membership of three hundred thousand, and an annual budget of $24 million. Until recently, it specialized not in citizen mobilization, but in litigation and lobbying at the legislative level. The old Environmental Defense Fund was certainly not a grassroots organization (Bimber, 2003:138).

In recent years, however, the group has reinvented itself to capitalize on the Internet's capacity for recruitment and mobilization. In 1999, the group's leadership launched a new website, radically slimmed down its core staff to just twenty- to twenty-five full- and part-timers, and effectively became a grassroots organization with a web-based strategy of information gathering and dissemination together with a new conception of membership. The group based its new approach on the insight that most citizens become interested in the environment when it "goes backyard." It used its website to find out what its members and other nonmember supporters perceived to be high-priority environmental concerns, then ruthlessly focused its activities around a set of core themes, like clean air and pesticides. Rather than focus solely on its full members, however, the group used the website to reach out to citizens wanting information on a specific issue and those who were often only willing to volunteer help on specific campaigns. In the past, such transient supporters would not have been highly prized by any interest group, but especially not among environmentalists, who often pride themselves on the commitment of their supporters. The new Internet form of organization put an end to this form of snobbery, however, and quickly led to a reassessment of what it means to be a member or a supporter among the broader environmental movement. Now, Bimber argues, most environmental groups are "operating with two distinct classes of membership": new cohorts of affiliate members sit alongside traditional dues-paying members. The new cohorts are not required or even expected to make financial contributions but may be drawn upon for specific campaigns using email. The reduction in membership revenues was thus balanced by the reduction in the costs of mobilizing support on specific issues. Environmental Defense is now able to use its database to target specific groups of members (Bimber, 2003:144, 146). It also has a more pluralistic approach to mobilization; it tends to ask those who have expressed an interest in a particular issue to respond to calls for action, as in 2001, when it requested that a carefully selected group of eight thousand of its one hundred thirty thousand affiliate members lobby the White House in protest at new relaxed proposals on carbon dioxide emissions. In the same year, the group generated twelve thousand faxes and emails to the Environmental Protection Agency (EPA) in response to a successful call for action against proposals for relaxing rules on diesel fuel.

One interesting side effect of Environmental Defense's organizational reinvention points to likely future directions for Internet-enabled group politics: a new openness toward coalition building with other organizations. In 1999, the group played a central role in the launch of a new Save Our Environment Coalition. Consisting of sixteen national environmental groups, including the Sierra Club, Defenders of Wildlife, and the World Wildlife Fund, the Coalition began by pooling its supporter databases and establishing a website, the Save Our Environment Action Center (Save Our Environment Coalition, 2004). The site takes the model of affiliate membership to new heights. Citizens can join the network to receive information about campaigns by email newsletter or be called upon to sign petitions or write to their representatives, but the network only exists in a virtual form.

This example illustrates how traditional, even staid groups are changing their internal organization and building new networks among previously untapped reservoirs of citizen support. It suggests the ways in which Internet technologies facilitate the bridging of organizational boundaries, often in very short periods of time, for the sake of a particular campaign. By reorganizing their efforts in this way, some groups are able to reduce costs and increase their operational flexibility. In some ways, this diminishes the impact of accepted trends in group politics. For example, the costs of group campaigns in the United States increased steadily during the postwar period, so much so that by the 1990s many critics complained that poorly resourced groups were unable to launch even the most rudimentary campaigns. In 2000, the U.S. Direct Marketing Association estimated that a simple direct mail-out to one hundred thousand individuals would cost about $30,000. An email campaign could cost as little as a tenth of that sum (Bimber, 2003:100–11). Such reductions in the costs of campaign activity present new opportunities for underresourced groups. The Net often lowers entry costs and allows poorly funded groups to behave as if they have greater resources than they in fact possess. For instance, they are able to build networks using emails and websites and do not have to pay for permanent official staff in central offices, as the Save Our Environment Action Center demonstrates.

The example of Environmental Defense points to a future in which traditional groups adapt to Internet-mediated politics, but we should be cautious about drawing too many general conclusions. At the moment, such organizational innovation is far from universal. For example, a detailed empirical study of British trade unions reveals a lack of innovation and a general resistance to organizational change and ad hoc alliance formation along the lines Bimber identifies in his U.S. study (Ward and Lusoli, 2003). While almost all British unions have an online presence and use email for some of their internal communication, it is clear that they have not yet taken advantage of the Internet for mobilizing supporters around particular campaigns. In their research, Stephen Ward and Wainer Lusoli found that union leaders were becoming excited by the emergence of a service provision model, in which the organization becomes rather like a consumer group such as the Automobile Association. In many respects, this route diverges from the changes identified by Bimber: it still rests on the assumption that the maintenance of a dues-paying membership should be of paramount concern rather than mobilizing non- or affiliate members in specific campaigns. Similarly, in another area, health advocacy, Lori Brainard and Patricia Siplon (2002) reveal a growing divide between conservative establishment groups and newer, more radical, web-based groups.

Traditional groups tend to use the Internet in ways that fit with their historical approach: they fund-raise, recruit members, and align themselves with expert medical opinion on illnesses and are resistant to online strategies. On the other hand, the radical groups analyzed in their study focus on coalition building with other advocacy groups, providing solidary resources (Wilson, 1974) such as the ability to participate in online discussion forums or email lists and critiques of expert medical opinion that spring from self-empowerment values. Thus, it would appear that the overall pattern of adaptation for traditional groups remains mixed.

There are good reasons for this mixed pattern. After all, Internet campaigning is not without its problems. A significant downside comes in the form of "cheap talk" effects. These make it easier for policy makers to ignore Internet communication, such as form emails or electronic petitions, on the grounds that they have been transmitted at close to zero cost (Bimber, 2003:107). Of course, much of this predates the Internet. During the early 1990s, under the scrutiny of critics like William Greider (1992:36–54), these became mockingly referred to as "astroturf campaigns." Unlike genuine grassroots campaigns, which are generally poorly resourced in financial terms but well resourced in terms of volunteer numbers, astroturf campaigns use a range of expensive communication tools to give the impression of a groundswell of popular support around a particular issue. Ever since mass mail-ins became a feature of modern politics, legislators have been compelled to develop mechanisms for dealing with the flood of correspondence they receive each day. Research evidence suggests that members of Congress are more likely to value nonautomated correspondence, such as a personal handwritten letter, than they are a prewritten form letter or an email circular (Frantzich, 2003:37). Some groups have responded by attempting to make their form letters more diverse, by asking supporters to compile their own custom letters from several predefined templates, or, in the case of the international human rights group Amnesty International, by encouraging members to write physical letters (Lebert, 2003:216). Astroturf techniques were once thought to be the sole preserve of public relations consultancies acting on behalf of wealthy corporate clients, but the temptations are no longer restricted to such organizations. Email has leveled the playing field, transforming it into a new astroturf commons upon which even poorly resourced groups may graze.

The "cheap talk" effects of online campaign activity are rather paradoxical. Legislators are reacting to the increased electronic flow of opinion by dismissing much of it. This is perceived to be a function of the low costs to the citizen in producing a form letter email. High-cost forms of communication such as old-fashioned letters are more highly valued. Yet in terms of democratic theory, sheer numbers should, theoretically, count for something. In elections, for example, it is a basic principle that the aggregation of electoral preferences produces a desirable outcome: the winner has the support of the majority of the electorate (the vagaries of different electoral systems notwithstanding). In other words, in an election, it is the repetition of a single opinion that signals support for a candidate or policy. In the world between elections, however, despite the rise of email and other Internet-enabled campaign tools, due to the poor reputation of astroturf lobbyists, such repetition of opinion is not taken as seriously; it is citizen passion that may weigh more heavily in legislators' minds (Frantzich, 2003:38). Well-meaning groups who provide email forms for their supporters to send on could be doing more harm than good: they are giving the impression that their supporters do not hold a variety of positions or cannot be bothered to write their own emails. This might mask the extent to which a particular cause actually enjoys genuine grassroots support.

Despite such problems and contradictions, it is clear that many of the assumptions about how traditional groups organize and mobilize their support require cautious reappraisal. Membership of an organization over time becomes less important than the ability of the organization itself to use electronic networks to tap into groundswells of citizen opinion around particular events or online communities that build from the bottom up, based on common experiences. Rather than delegating their authority to the leadership of an organized group based upon a relatively fixed and stable conception of their interests, citizens increasingly appear to be voicing their concerns in more granular ways—on particular issues at particularly significant times, such as when specific pieces of legislation are before Congress, particular rules are going through the federal government's e-rule-making process, or street demonstrations are occurring. Citizens may also be mobilized by personal life events which drive them to seek out others, such as illness or an unpleasant experience with a professional, or by a large public or private sector organization. These are, in many ways, manifestations of the postindustrial politics outlined in chapter 2.

Organizational Hybridity: MoveOn

If the Internet has affected the way that traditional interest groups do business, it has also spawned new, hybrid types of political organization. An excellent example comes in the form of America's MoveOn, which was established in September 1998 by two Silicon Valley software designers.

Joan Blades and Wes Boyd, a husband-and-wife team who designed screen savers, computer games, and educational software, established MoveOn as a bipartisan reaction against the proceedings to impeach President Clinton in the wake of the Monica Lewinsky scandal of 1997–98. The couple were appalled at the mainstream media's obsession with Lewinsky and what they perceived as the insularity of Washington politics. The movement's initial website, set up at a cost of just $89, contained an online petition requesting that Congress pass a simple censure motion rather than go through impeachment hearings and "move on" to more pressing policy issues. The response was staggering. Within a month of its launch, the petition had amassed over quarter of a million signatories and MoveOn had recruited over two thousand volunteers. Also in its first month, these volunteers distributed twenty thousand paper comments to politicians and presented hard copies of the petitions to some two hundred twenty-six representatives (Brown, 1998). By Christmas 1998, the number of signatories had grown to four hundred fifty thousand (Clausing, 1999).

MoveOn's spontaneous mobilization is significant in itself, but the way in which the movement metamorphosed once the Lewinsky scandal died down illustrates the organizational flexibility of Internet-mediated group politics. Once a decision was reached to carry on the movement, MoveOn diversified its operations. In 2001, a peace campaign was launched by a Maine student, Eli Pariser, which took the form of an online campaign and petition calling for the United States to build a multilateral consensus in response to the terrorist attacks of September 11, 2001. Soon after the petition, MoveOn rapidly blossomed into a key coordinator of the U.S. antiwar protests in early 2003.

In alliance with other groups, it played a major role in funding an antiwar coalition (Win Without War), disseminating antiwar information, organizing over three thousand simultaneous candlelit vigils in 122 countries, and publicizing real-world demonstrations, such as the huge marches in hundreds of cities on February 15, 2003 (Hickey, 2004; Kahn and Kellner, 2004:88).

MoveOn was also able to make a seamless transition from transnational mobilization to involvement in the more prosaic aspects of U.S. electoral politics. It staged an unofficial Democratic online primary in June 2003, during which it also asked party members to make donations, volunteer, and provide their email addresses to their favored candidate. In two days, 317,000 members voted online—more than in the Iowa and New Hampshire primaries combined (Hickey, 2004). The email addresses of supporters were passed on to the Democratic candidates' campaign teams. Howard Dean's team received a large proportion of the 140,000 voters' email addresses. This alerted them to a reservoir of Internet support upon which they were able to capitalize later in the primary campaign (Hickey, 2004).

MoveOn also focuses on the local level. For example, in 2003 it held a number of simultaneous public meetings with Members of Congress in their districts (Hickey, 2004). These were used to exert lobbying pressure on a number of progressive causes. More controversially, MoveOn also runs the ancillary Political Action Committee (PAC) to selectively fund-raise and mobilize support for liberal candidates, its intention being to "encourage and facilitate smaller donations to offset the influence of wealthy and corporate donors" (MoveOn Political Action Committee, 2004a). Once it had fended off a Republican Party legal challenge based on the argument that it was flouting the 2002 McCain-Feingold regulations on soft money contributions for election campaigns, with Eli Pariser in charge, the MoveOn PAC supported John Kerry's 2004 Democratic presidential campaign. The movement focused on combining Internet fund-raising and localized efforts, often with startling success. Upon the announcement of its support for Kerry, it emailed its 2.1 million supporters, asking for donations. On a single Saturday in May 2004, for example, a MoveOn mass bake sale (labeled "Bake Back The White House") saw half a million Americans raise over $750,000.

How do we make sense of MoveOn? Is it an interest group, a social movement, or simply the progressive wing of the Democratic Party? While its membership (in early 2005) amounts to around 3 million (including some seven hundred thousand living outside the United States), its core staff is tiny: in the middle of 2003, it had just four paid employees (Von Drehle, 2003). Even at the height of the 2004 presidential campaign, the MoveOn PAC had just twenty staff members nationwide. In aggregating millions of small donations, the basic secret of the organization's success is not new. One thing is certain: it is categorically *not* a traditional membership-based interest group that has simply discovered the web. Although it obviously draws most of its support from progressive activists, it has no single, easily identifiable sectional interest or social constituency to represent. At the same time, however, its range of causes to date has not been so broad that it resembles anything approaching either an unofficial political party or populist movement. When it organizes meetings with members of Congress, often on highly specific pieces of legislation, it behaves a little like a Washington lobby group. It avoids outright alignment with the Democrats and an outright anti-Republican crusade. The MoveOn PAC exploits the now-familiar 527 tax loophole in U.S. finance regulations allowing independent or quasi-independent groups to campaign indirectly in favor of a candidate. But of the money it raised in 2004, less than half was earmarked for Democratic Party candidates. A further sum was used for a series of MoveOn advertisements aimed at voters in marginal districts, while the remainder went toward a "get out the vote" campaign (MoveOn Political Action Committee, 2004b). Crucially, MoveOn chimes in with the transformations undergone by traditional membership groups such as Environmental Defense. While it asks for volunteers and donations in its email newsletters and occasionally uses the term "member" to refer to its supporters, there is no fixed annual membership fee nor is there a formalized local branch structure to maintain. It is difficult to escape the conclusion that MoveOn is a genuinely novel form of hybrid political organization (Chadwick, 2005). Time will tell if it maintains this course in future, or indeed, whether it will undergo another metamorphosis.

TRANSNATIONAL E-MOBILIZATION

Up to now I have been mainly concerned with groups operating in a national context. We have seen, however, how the formation of intergroup alliances has been facilitated by the Internet and the new kinds of organizational flexibility it permits. These are themes that are even more important for transnational forms of e-mobilization. In recent years, the number and scope of political campaigns that involve a transnational element has increased (Tarrow, 1998:176–95). Explanations for this vary, as do assessments of the role of the Internet in facilitating or making a qualitative difference to such activity. But most scholars now have to come to terms with the fact that the Internet is an indisputable feature of contemporary social movements' strategies.

It may seem obvious, but we need to bear in mind the sheer physical quantity of communication that now routinely flows across national boundaries between substate political actors. There are historical examples of social movements communicating in this way, including, for instance, the nineteenth-century antislavery movement or the early-twentieth-century women's suffrage campaigns. But the levels of transnational cooperation and coordination that now occur as a matter of routine far exceed those of the pre-Internet era.

Lurking in the background of many accounts is the assumption that transnational politics is a creature of the increasing interdependency among nation-states caused by globalization processes (Keohane and Nye, [1977] 1989). Since the 1990s, at the state and substate levels, the tendency has been toward forming new transnational organizations that are often, in reality, little more than loose networks. While national political elites have shifted their focus toward a new global policy-making environment (Rosenau, 1992), leading some to question the power and accountability of organizations like the World Trade Organization (WTO), the International Monetary Fund (IMF), or the World Bank Group (WBG), it is equally the case that globalization has opened up new spaces for nongovernmental actors to press for change in an increasingly fluid environment. In this kind of context, collaboration among networks of groups and social movements often leads to a syncretic strategy: loose alliances of groups are often able to use the Internet to simultaneously mobilize and focus their efforts on different levels of politics, seamlessly shifting from the national to the transnational. There are several excellent examples of this.

The Zapatista Effect

> Marcos is gay in San Francisco, black in South Africa, an Asian in Europe,
> a Chicano in San Ysidro, an anarchist in Spain, a Palestinian in Israel . . .
> a pacifist in Bosnia, a housewife alone on a Saturday night in any neigh-
> borhood in any city in Mexico . . . a single woman on the Metro at 10 PM.
> Marcos is all the exploited, marginalized, and oppressed minorities,
> resisting and saying, "Enough."
>
> —ZAPATISTA SUBCOMMANDER MARCOS, QUOTED IN SIMON, 1994

Any student of e-mobilization cannot ignore Mexico's Zapatistas, and rightly so: their ongoing campaign for land rights conducted against the Mexican state is an excellent example of how a seemingly local issue can be radically transformed into a global concern almost overnight through the Internet. One of the most influential analysts of the information age, Manuel Castells, defines the Zapatistas as "the first informational guerrilla movement" (Castells, 2004:82).

On New Year's Day 1994, approximately three thousand indigenous Indian peasants from the impoverished state of Chiapas in southern Mexico declared themselves the Ejército Zapatista de Liberación Nacional (EZLN). They then engaged in an armed uprising, resulting in the capture of several towns and hundreds of ranches in the region. They were led by a group of urban revolutionary intellectuals, including an individual known as Subcommander Marcos, who would soon emerge as the figurehead of the EZLN. When the Mexican army moved in, the guerrillas retreated, but not before the deaths of over one hundred forty people during the ensuing battle. Within a few days, Subcommander Marcos had astutely crafted an online presence that was immediately seized upon by the major news media. A global network of websites, email, and Usenet discussion lists sprang up to disseminate information about the Zapatistas' cause, spurring hundreds of journalists to flood into Chiapas, eager to report on the story. On January 12, the Mexican president, Carlos Salinas de Gortari, declared a cease-fire before opening negotiations with the EZLN.

The Zapatista guerrillas take their name from Emiliano Zapata, the revolutionary leader of the peasant army of the 1910 Mexican Revolution, but conflict between indigenous peoples and the Mexican state has deep historical roots, dating back to the Spanish conquest of the sixteenth century. The principal source of tension is land. The Zapatistas drew their support from among peasant settlements in the Lacandon rainforest, created during the 1930s as part of a series of land reforms aimed at stabilizing Mexico's rural society. Over the course of the century, Indian groups were repeatedly forced to move and resettle, according to policies set down at the national level by Mexico's dominant party, the Partido Revolucionario Institucional (PRI), often acting under the influence of powerful economic interests.

The immediate causes of the uprising came in the early 1990s, when the Mexican government issued a decree abolishing the land-use rights of the Indian communities in Lacandon as preparations got underway for Mexico's entry into the North American Free Trade Agreement (NAFTA). Eager to attract inward investment to help its ailing economy, the Mexican government, under the direction of President Salinas, embarked upon a program of economic liberalization that would expose peasant agricultural communities to the harsh winds of global markets. The local rural economy in Chiapas is heavily dependent upon coffee, corn, cattle, and timber. When the NAFTA agreement forced the Mexican government to begin opening up the area to cheap imports of corn and to remove price guarantees on coffee, the local economy started to decline. The final straw came when the government amended Article 27 of the Mexican constitution, promptly abolishing communal ownership of agricultural land in Indian regions. The removal of restrictions on the land market was, again, required under the preconditions of NAFTA, further highlighting the impact of global capitalism on Mexico's poor. It was this awareness of the intertwined nature of the local and global contexts that lent itself to the Zapatistas' Internet strategy.

Claiming that the Zapatistas were a patriotic movement, Subcommander Marcos railed against the single-party state dominated by the PRI and celebrated what he claimed was the centuries-long struggle against inequality by indigenous peoples. But Marcos's critique also extended to the growth of global neoliberalism, exemplified by new trade regimes such as NAFTA and what was perceived as the pernicious influence of new international organizations such as the WTO. It therefore struck a chord among a diverse constituency of campaigners in developed and developing countries, including environmentalists, feminists, socialists, and anarchists, but also incorporated more centrist human rights– and development-focused non-governmental organizations (NGOs).

What role did the Internet play in the Zapatista uprising? Some writers have argued that a misleading mythology has built up around the movement's use of technology (May, 2002:86). For instance, it was mainly sympathizers outside Mexico that established the websites and paid for and maintained them on behalf of the guerrillas, and they could rely on academics such as Harry Cleaver of the University of Texas and advocacy groups such as the Texas-based National Commission for Democracy in Mexico, whose efforts in translating and distributing information was significant in generating interest in the United States and Europe (Kowal, 2002:113). Global "hacktivist" groups (discussed later), such as the Cult of the Dead Cow, Electronic Disturbance Theater, and Electrohippies, also deployed their technical expertise to coordinate acts of electronic civil disobedience against the Mexican government. Romanticized images of Subcommander Marcos firing off polemical emails from his laptop in the rainforest are clearly wide of the mark.

Nevertheless, the Zapatista uprising neatly crystallizes the changing nature of political action in an increasingly Internet-mediated, transnational environment. A grass-roots movement that had been marginalized and was unable to gain access to the political elite and mainstream media both in Mexico and abroad was able to use the Internet to disseminate information about its plight. The Zapatistas were able to construct an elaborate, decentralized but influential global network of supporters, many of whom were mobilized to engage in acts of electronic and direct civil disobedience or could be persuaded to lobby their own governments to take action at the international level. And it is equally misleading to suggest that none of the technological initiatives emerged from within Mexico. Between 1989 and 1993, an alternative computer network called La Neta was established with the support of the Catholic Church, the Institute for Global Communications in San Francisco, and a variety of women's NGOs. La Neta contributed toward getting local Chiapas groups online before the January 1 insurrection.

One of the main discussion lists, Chiapas-I, was hosted on servers at the National Autonomous University in Mexico City (Castells, 2004:84).

By demonstrating the potential of Internet technologies, the Zapatistas arguably created a long-term shift in global social movement politics. What Cleaver, an admittedly partisan commentator, labels the "Zapatista Effect" (Cleaver, 1998) is still being felt over a decade after the initial uprising. This effect may be understood principally in terms of the continued centrality of Zapatista-related websites for a global network of NGOs, ranging from women's groups to health-related campaigners and human rights organizations such as Amnesty International. The genesis of this transnational "movement of movements" was a series of "encounters" held in Chiapas during 1996 and Spain in 1997. Sponsored by the Zapatistas and coordinated by email and websites, these gatherings involved thousands of political activists involved in various campaigns against global neoliberalism (Cleaver, 1998:630). A sophisticated webmetric analysis, which maps the links between different websites and seeks to identify important nodal points in a network, demonstrates that the Zapatista cause binds together hundreds of global NGOs (Garrido and Halavais, 2003:181). In this sense, the Zapatistas' use of the Internet has not only assumed symbolic importance as one of the first examples of an online social movement; it also has material significance for the continuation of a global network of NGOs, allowing these disparate groups to "see" one another and others to make sense of how their causes are related. Over a decade later, despite having won considerable concessions from the Mexican state, the EZLN's campaign continues.

The influence of the Zapatista uprising radiated around the world during the late 1990s, leading other movements to adopt many of its strategies. On June 18, 1999, hundreds of thousands of protestors located in dozens of cities came together virtually and physically in what was termed a Carnival against Capitalism. The demonstrators represented a diverse array of causes, including environmentalism, labor activism, feminism, animal rights, socialism, anarchism, and antiwar movements. The largest events, in London and San Francisco, had been planned well in advance by groups such as Reclaim the Streets and Earth First, using email and the web. A somewhat cryptic website, j18.org, had been set up to provide information on meeting places as well as updates on events throughout the day.

Since J18, websites that parallel real-world demonstrations have become commonplace and are woven into the fabric of most international gatherings. The most infamous example occurred in 1999, when protests at the meeting of the WTO in Seattle were largely coordinated through cell phones, email, bulletin boards, and chat rooms. Of equal significance is the fact that protests were held simultaneously in over eighty major cities in dozens of countries. The timing and character of these were coordinated using the Net. In Seattle, for example, a group called the Direct Action Network established an ad hoc communication network comprising phones, wireless handheld computers, radio devices, police scanners, and laptops. They also used mobile devices to feed live video to the Internet as well as warnings about the movement of police through the city (Rheingold, 2002:161). When the police and FBI managed to cripple this network, the group responded by buying new mobile phones from supplier Nextel, with which they hastily built a new ad hoc mobile communications system.

Smart Mobs

The use of cell phones and wireless handhelds in the J18 protests has started to influence the dynamics of similar events. Such cases of ad hoc street-level coordination have been termed smart mobs (Rheingold, 2002). Probably the best example of a political smart mob comes from the so-called People Power II protests in the Philippines during 2001.

In January 2001, over a million people gathered at Epifanio de los Santos Avenue, a major highway in central Manila, the capital of the Philippines. The crowd were there to protest against the collapse of the impeachment trial of the president, Joseph Estrada. Estrada was accused of corruption, and his trial had been widely covered in the national and international news media. Because the evidence against Estrada was so overwhelming, the trial's failure was popularly attributed to his influence over several of the senators on his impeachment committee. Such was the shock and surprise at the trial's collapse, hundreds of thousands of ordinary people almost immediately went out on to the streets to register their contempt and to call for the president's resignation. These events became known as People Power II—named as a sequel to the original People Power uprising of 1986 which unseated the autocratic President Ferdinand Marcos. They were heavily dependent upon the protestors' use of mobile phones. By far the most prevalent form of communication was text messaging (Cabras, 2002).

Cell phones occupy a central place in Philippines society, largely due to unreliable, expensive landlines, the high cost of personal computers, a slow postal service, and overcrowded, congested towns and cities that make travel difficult (the capital, Manila, is home to 10 million). During the People Power II uprising, less than 1 percent of the population had Internet access at home, though cybercafés were very popular. However, around 13 percent of the population had a cell phone. Phones can be bought at low cost and maintained by prepaid cards. Text messaging is extremely popular, due to the relative expense of voice calls. Mobile communications have assumed a symbolic significance due to the ability of users to overcome the country's crumbling infrastructure, a feature of life in the Philippines that is popularly ascribed to state incompetence and corruption (Rafael, 2003:402).

In the space of just four days, President Estrada was forced to resign. There were reasons other than the protests that led to his downfall, most notably the withdrawal of support by the military, but the largely nonviolent demonstrations played a significant role in voicing citizen disquiet. Vicente Rafael suggests that mobile communication allowed individuals to organize as a spontaneous crowd while simultaneously coordinating their actions in ways that are not normally characteristic of crowdlike forms of behavior (Rafael, 2003:415).

Smart mobs indicate how mobile Internet technologies are likely to influence future political protest. Unlike traditional computers connected to the Internet, which are often used by solitary individuals sitting in a quiet corner, mobile technologies are deeply embedded in the context of everyday experiences. In the shopping center, the café, or the street corner, talking and texting are woven into the fabric of everyday social space in a way that large bulky computers will never be. In this sense, mobile use of the Internet is a much more obviously social form of technology. In their analysis of the 1999 Carnival against Capital, Alan Scott and John Street (2000) use the phrase "organized spontaneity" to capture this paradoxical blend of coordination and decentralization. Almost leaderless and often temporary forms of organization, smart mobs possess the spontaneity and physical presence of a crowd while also displaying the collective intelligence of a united, purposive group.

Blogging

The explosion of blogging has democratized access to the tools and techniques required to make a political difference through content creation. In the past, though the creation of basic websites could be a fairly simple task, it often required specialist knowledge of HTML and server configuration to create exciting sites that had interactive features like discussion boards, polling, and chat. Updating websites could also be a cumbersome process. Blogging software has changed the landscape of the Internet because it provides ordinary users with a personal publishing platform: the ability to create slick, dynamic, interactive websites that are easily updated. Moreover, using Extensible Markup Language (XML)[1] and other metadata classification techniques, bloggers can easily link their blogs to others, creating a virtual community of opinion based on ongoing dialogue and debate. There are, of course, many millions of individual blogs that are completely devoid of political content. It is also the case that many blogs are nothing more than individual rants. However, many are increasingly collaborative, bringing groups of journalists—amateur or professional—together in virtual public spaces to comment on daily news events in ways that may reproduce the economies of scale that can be found in larger media production systems such as newspapers.

Aside from their impact on mainstream election campaigns and news production (see chapters 7 and 12), bloggers have also started to exert an influence in the more diffuse transnational environment. For example, during the initial phases of the Iraq conflict in the spring of 2003, Salam Pax, a resident of Baghdad who became known as the "Baghdad Blogger," risked his life to produce daily reports on his blog Dear_Raed. News of Pax's blog rapidly spread around the Net, but its influence on perception of the events in Iraq massively increased when stories from Pax's site began to be syndicated in the United Kingdom's *Guardian* newspaper (Pax, 2003, 2004). Although, as we shall see in chapter 7 (on parties and election campaigning), blogging has been appropriated by mainstream politicians as a way of fund-raising, there are tentative signs that it will also become an established means of Internet-mediated mobilization.

HACKTIVISM

In the introduction to this chapter I outlined a third form of e-mobilization: direct action that exploits the technical properties of the Internet itself to achieve a set of political goals (see exhibit 6.1). Politically motivated hacking, or "hacktivism," draws upon

---

[1]**Extensible Markup Language (XML)** is designed to make it easier for different types of computer systems to process information contained within documents. It achieves this by applying data tags to discrete pieces of information in, for instance, a web page or a web-based application form that are then able to be used by all parties in an electronic "chain" of processes.

EXHIBIT 6.1. HACKTIVIST TECHNIQUES

- **Defacing:** breaking into and altering the content of a website to change its content. The most common form of hacktivism.

- **Distributed denial of service attacks:** aims to physically disrupt a network by flooding it with simultaneous requests for data from thousands of computers connected to the Internet. These might be the result of deliberate action taken by individuals sitting at their computers, perhaps using hacktivist software such as Electrohippies' Tactical Floodnet. Alternatively, an attack may be orchestrated by a small group of hackers who take advantage of "zombie" computers that have been preinfected with a trojan—a type of virus that enables the hackers to direct traffic from such machines to a specific target.

- **Ping storms:** an attack which uses the Internet "ping" program (used to test the presence of a computer in a network) to overload a server by flooding it with "ping" requests.

- **Email bombing:** using automation software to inundate an email mailbox with thousands of messages in a matter of minutes, with the aim of crippling an organization's email capabilities.

- **Malicious code attacks:** deliberately attempting to destabilize an organization by introducing, for example, a virus which erases data, a worm (a self-replicating virus) that may cause high volumes of network traffic, or a trojan that allows a hacker to easily break into a system, perhaps to use the bandwidth for a distributed denial of service attack.

- **Redirects:** intercepting web traffic destined for a particular site and redirecting it elsewhere.

Sources: Summarized from Conley, 2003; Glave, 1999; Lemos, 2001; Taylor, 2001; Vegh, 2003; Weisenburger, 2001; Yes Men, 2004.

the resources of the hacker community and hacker culture. Much hyperbole surrounds hacking; the meaning of the term is widely disputed (Nissenbaum, 2004), and the very idea of a single community of hackers that share a common culture has been difficult to sustain since computers and the Internet became so widespread.

In the past, the term "hacker" had fairly narrow connotations. It generally referred to those who used their skills to break into a computer system or modify hardware or software in ways that displayed their expertise. For early hackers, the aim was to gain information about how a piece of software worked, to expose its design flaws as a step on the way to improving it, or to bring together disparate pieces of hardware or code to work around problems. Paul Taylor argues that the term originated at Massachusetts Institute of Technology in the 1950s and was used to refer to the ad hoc technique of "hacking together" solutions to the problems presented by large, unstable mainframes or obsessively "hacking through" difficult programming tasks (Taylor, 1999:14). Historically, hackers have often simply reveled in the mischief of bringing down a computer system. But it is important to stress that hacking has often been combined with broader social and political goals. Central to these are critiques of "bogus" authority figures, closed, centralized systems of control, and attempts to restrict access to information through intellectual property law. Steven Levy, a renowned commentator in the area, devotes a chapter of his influential book *Hackers* to what he terms the "hacker ethic" (Levy, 1984 [2001]:39–49):

- Access to computers—and anything which might teach you something about the way the world works—should be unlimited and total. Always yield to the Hands-On Imperative!
- All information should be free
- Mistrust Authority—Promote Decentralization
- Hackers should be judged by their hacking, not by bogus criteria such as degrees, age, race, or position
- You can create art and beauty on a computer
- Computers can change your life for the better

In many respects, by focusing on political goals, hacktivism represents "the contemporary refashioning of the hacker ethic" (Taylor, 2001:59; see also Jordan and Taylor, 2004). Yet combined with its relatively enlightened tenets are ideas drawn from cyberpunk subculture. Derived in part from the bleak vision of the near future in the science fiction of William Gibson, especially his highly influential novel *Neuromancer* (1984), cyberpunk stresses the role of hacker antiheroes in struggling against the dehumanizing effects of "technological systems they nevertheless yearn to immerse themselves in" (Taylor, 2000:43). For this reason, hacker culture is often portrayed as extremely individualistic, though when it comes to politically motivated hacking, group collaboration is often the norm.

Part of the problem with hacktivism is the mythology and sensationalism that surrounds computer hacking in general. Since the mid-1980s, stories of hacking have been a mainstay of established media, with particularly celebrated cases such as the 1998 arrest of Kevin Mitnick, who was considered so dangerous that he was imprisoned and, when released, forbidden from laying his hands on a computer keyboard (Thomas, 2000:30). When Mitnick demonstrated that his compulsion was under control, he was permitted to use a computer but forbidden from touching a modem! Hackers have been portrayed as deviants, criminals, or both. But although the dominant media discourse is one of demonization, historically hackers have collaborated to make many valuable contributions to the development of specific technologies, not least of which is the Internet itself (Nissenbaum, 2004:211). Given this background, it should not be surprising that hackers should occasionally emerge as active political participants.

The most renowned example of hacktivism to date came in the form of online action in support of the Zapatistas. Instrumental in orchestrating the campaign was a group known as the Electronic Disturbance Theater (EDT). During the mid to late 1990s, EDT coordinated several different politically motivated hacks against the Frankfurt stock exchange, the U.S. Pentagon and Federal Communications Commission, and the website of Mexico's president Zedillo. EDT's main weapon was to flood web servers with thousands of simultaneous requests from individual computers connected to the Internet, thereby bringing the server down. The group created its own software application, Tactical FloodNet, which it distributed freely to those wanting to join in the attacks (it has since been used by other groups and in other online protests). EDT labeled its action "electronic civil disobedience," a term which properly encapsulates such protests when they involve crippling web servers, because this is an act that has now been criminalized in many countries. Other notable examples of politically motivated hacking are summarized in exhibit 6.2. The examples considered here deliberately exclude instances in which politically motivated hacking forms part of an ongoing military conflict. These are considered in chapter 11, where we examine the Internet's role in national security.

EXHIBIT 6.2. EXAMPLES OF HACKTIVISM

In September 1999, the racist Ku Klux Klan organization's website is hacked and all of its traffic redirected to the site of antiracist group Hatewatch.

In December 1999, activists establish a protest site with the domain name www.seattlewto.org, in an attempt to attract traffic away from the official site for that year's WTO meeting, www.wtoseattle.org. Later, during the meeting itself, Electrohippies Collective, a group based in the United Kingdom, launches a four-hundred thousands strong attack on the WTO website to coincide with the street demonstrations in Seattle.

In 2000, at the World Economic Forum (WEF) meeting, its website is duplicated and parodied by a hacktivist group named the Yes Men. The group releases an ingenious piece of software entitled Reamweaver (a mischievous play on the popular Dreamweaver web design package). The software quickly copies a website, allowing it to be placed on a different server. Activists choose sites with similar domain names to fool casual web browsers and the occasional journalist. The software makes it easy for users to change the duplicate site, enabling the insertion of critical and satirical content.

In September 2001, in a move timed to coincide with the Prague meeting of the IMF, a French group named the Federation of Random Action releases Protest Online Chat—software that allowed protestors to chat while electronically bombarding the web servers of the IMF and the World Bank.

In January 2002, the meeting of the WEF in New York is disrupted by a virtual sit-in involving one hundred sixty thousand online protestors. EDT organizes a distributed denial of service attack using its Tactical FloodNet software. The attack takes the WEF site down for two days.

In July 2002, Stefan Puffer, a Houston computer security consultant and "war driver," is indicted under the Computer Fraud and Abuse Act for hacking into the Harris County, Texas, district clerk's wireless network but is later acquitted by a jury as an ethical, or "white hat," hacker trying to demonstrate the vulnerability of the county's networks to a reporter from the local newspaper. Wireless LANs, which became popular in the early 2000s, have relatively weak security and can be hacked into by those with a little patience, a basic receiver inside a Pringles potato chip canister, and widely available software such as Netstumbler. "War driving," which originated with a body known as the Bay Area Wireless Users Group, refers to the practice of driving around city centers and even suburban neighborhoods "sniffing" for unencrypted wireless LAN packets that indicate the presence of an unsecured network. If such a network is located, war drivers can raid corporate servers for free software, make use of the free Internet connection and bandwidth, and often post the details of the LAN onto war-driving websites. Alternatively, in a practice inspired by the homeless travelers of the U.S. Great Depression but which became popular in London and other U.K. cities, hackers will use chalk to scribble the wireless LAN station ID onto nearby walls, alerting bypassers to the availability of free bandwidth.

In December 2002, on the eighteenth anniversary of the 1984 Bhopal, India, chemical plant disaster, the Yes Men hacktivists establish a protest site at the domain www.dow-chemical.com. The site is registered under the name and real address of the son of Dow's CEO. Dow fights back by wresting control over the domain from the Yes Men.

In February 2003, Cult of the Dead Cow release a peer-to-peer application, 6/4. Taking its name from the date of the Tiananmen Square massacres of 1988, the hacktivist group describes it as "a new protocol standard for decentralized peer-to-peer networks . . . [making] state-sponsored censorship based on either host-based access controls or content filtering ultimately impossible."

In 2004, the Yes Men's Reamweaver software is used to create a parody of the World Trade Organization site at the domain wtoo.org. At first glance, the site is remarkably similar to the real WTO site (at wto.org). However, a closer look reveals that much of the content has been altered to highlight the perceived role of the WTO in contributing to global inequalities.

Sources: Adapted from Conley, 2003; Cult of the Dead Cow, 2004; Glave, 1999; Lemos, 2001; Taylor, 2001; Technology Bytes, 2002; Vegh, 2003; Weisenburger, 2001; Yes Men, 2004.

There is conflict within the hacktivist community over the appropriateness of particular methods. Some groups, such as the Cult of the Dead Cow (CDC), concentrate on circumventing restrictions on freedom of speech and are against attacks that bring down web servers or deface sites on the grounds that they constitute an abrogation of First Amendment free speech rights. On the other hand, another major group, the Electrohippies, argue that web server attacks and site defacing are legitimate forms of electronic civil disobedience. It is akin to civil disobedience in the offline world, which derives its force from the very fact that the law is being broken (Weisenburger, 2001). Despite the high esteem in which the CDC is held, since the vast bulk of hacktivist exploits involve distributed denial of service attacks or defacing, the majority of hacktivists are aligned with the Electrohippies perspective.

Despite a reputation for deviance, subversion, and anarchy, much of which derives from low-level moral panics created by Hollywood films such as *War Games* (1984) or *Swordfish* (2001), some research suggests that most true hackers are not driven by political or financial motivation (Skibell, 2002). However, hacktivists have made efforts to make their software and techniques open to nonexpert users, and, in recent years, hacking has been partially democratized as the Internet itself has acted as a vast distribution network for simplified, even user-friendly versions of the tools of the hacker trade, such as the EDT's Tactical FloodNet application. The emergence of what have been termed "script kiddies"—a pejorative term to describe those who spread malicious code by running simple programs that require no expert knowledge—has exposed some of the mystique surrounding hacking. Similarly, the forms of collective action characteristic of hacktivism depend upon large numbers of participants, the vast majority of which are ordinary computer users with few if any specialist skills.

ASSESSING THE IMPACT OF THE INTERNET ON GROUP AND MOVEMENT POLITICS

We have considered a range of examples from the world of group and movement politics. In this final section, I try to tease out the difference the Internet makes to political mobilization.

To begin, for some scholars it makes little difference. Mario Diani, for example, argues that the Internet reinforces preexisting organizational structures. In this perspective, "sustained collective action is unlikely to originate from purely virtual ties" (Diani, 2000:394). So-called professional protest movements such as Greenpeace depend heavily upon a core of full-time employees funded by a largely passive membership base. Greenpeace's activity mainly centers upon attention-grabbing symbolic demonstrations that are carried out by a relatively small number of dedicated individuals. Although the Internet is being used by Greenpeace to communicate with its membership as well as to distribute in-depth material relating to its various campaigns, it achieves these goals in a somewhat standardized fashion, and its website does not function as a place for online discussion and deliberation for its membership. From the reinforcement perspective, the fundamental organizational characteristics of Greenpeace are such that the fostering of a strong identity among its supporters is secondary to the goal of achieving tight integration at the center backed by mass-membership funding. Thus, the Internet contributes to the preexisting "professionalization" processes already underway. Even in the transnational environment, in this perspective, computer-mediated communication is most often likely to extend the capacity of existing networks rather than create completely new ones, because there is a physical international policy arena which promotes face-to-face interaction among such groups.

In many respects, this reinforcement approach is appealing and intuitive. But not all scholars agree that we can explain recent developments by simply referring back to the pre-Internet organizational forms of a group. As we saw earlier in our discussion of Bruce Bimber's work, organizational change is itself occurring under the weight of Internet technologies. Another writer who has established a framework for answering this question is Lance Bennett (2004, 2003a, 2003b). Drawing upon and extending some of his themes, here I outline several facets of the Internet difference.

Creating Permanent Campaign Networks

While some scholars have questioned the permanence of Internet-enabled forms of political mobilization (Lin and Dutton, 2003:132), global citizen activism is now a "political way of being" (Castells, 2004:154), not just for those activists involved but also for established political elites who must confront their opponents at regular intervals. After the Zapatista uprising of 1994 and the "battle in Seattle" of 1999, many commentators argued that such protests were nothing more than flashpoints that would soon disappear. While the levels and intensity of protest have undoubtedly diminished, of more importance in the long term are what we might call the sedimentary traces of these high-profile events. These exist in the form of loose but integrated infrastructures of communication on the Internet, and despite the absence of obvious leaderships, they persist over time. This is the transnational Zapatista effect identified by Cleaver (1998), but it may also be observed at the national level. The early examples of e-mobilization in the United States demonstrate this. The networks established in the MarketPlace campaign were later used in the Clipper Chip protests, and the threads could (literally) be picked up again in the late 1990s during the campaign against unique hardware identifiers in Intel processors. And as we saw, MoveOn was able to put down virtual roots that have nourished its diversification into new campaign areas.

As new networks develop, both within and across national boundaries, perhaps one of the biggest shifts is occurring almost behind the scenes. While online mobilization of the kinds achieved in the cases examined throughout this chapter did involve, to greater or lesser degrees, town hall forms of online deliberation, it is equally likely that the effectiveness of the protests and campaigns was also dependent upon the creation of basic information networks and the sense of collective enterprise brought about by simple hyperlinking rather than grand and detailed debates about substantive issues.

Equally, however, these forms of mobilization necessitate online issue networks that consist of trusted sources of information, and collaborative endeavor and visible signs of online deliberation increase the trustworthiness of an organization because they give the appearance of openness. In most cases of online mobilization, the requisite trust is much less likely to be the product of single, authoritative sources, such as group leaders, scientific experts, and certainly not government bodies. Indeed, in the examples of "organized spontaneity," leaders are difficult to identify. Instead, what emerges is what we might term "distributed trust"—that is, trust becomes a by-product of the discursive context of the issue network itself, the extent to which organizations encourage deliberative spaces as well as how they link to one another.

Reducing the Impact of Ideological Fragmentation

While the episodes of transnational mobilization such as J18 and Seattle involved disparate groups and movements creating ad hoc alliances, it seems clear that mobilization can occur without ideological coherence. This point clashes to some extent with one of the major assumptions of social movement theory, which stresses the importance of ideology for contributing to shared identities that are precursors to mobilization. At the transnational level, however, there is a patchwork of multiple and overlapping public spheres, each containing any number of groups and movements. This makes ideological integration difficult to achieve. Bennett argues that the Internet overcomes some of these difficulties, making it possible for groups to form horizontally integrated transnational networks based on email, discussion sites, and information repositories, even if they lack a persistent common cause (Bennett, 2003a; Leizerov, 2000:468). It is also the case that the Internet overcomes fragmentation for those transnational groupings that may have national identity in common but little else, such as immigrants and diasporic communities (Mitra, 2001:30).

The campaign against Microsoft is a particularly interesting example here. Initiated in the early 1990s by labor activists, it spread to incorporate a radically diverse network of supporters. Between 1997 and 2001, the main coordinating organization was a body known as Netaction. This was, in reality, little more than a network of actors who could contribute information and commentary on Microsoft's activities, including reports on issues such as privacy, open-source software, intellectual property, consumer rights, security, and business ethics. The network coalition against Microsoft contained left-wing activists eager to expose the abuse of corporate power, but it also contained a number of companies such as Netscape, Oracle, and Sun Microsystems, not to mention the republican senator Orrin Hatch. But while this diversity could be seen as a strength, it ultimately proved to be a weakness. As Bennett argues, Netaction's nonideological character was a liability in the U.S. Justice Department's eventual antitrust case of 1999, because its members found it difficult to agree on what would constitute an acceptable settlement (Bennett, 2003a:154). The Internet may be making possible looser, more diverse political campaigns, but this is no guarantee that they will be any more successful in achieving their goals than traditional, more ideologically coherent campaigns based around traditional groups such as labor unions.

In addition to its role in overcoming ideological fragmentation, the Internet can bring to the surface latent ideologies that previously lacked institutional concentration. As Lori Brainard and Patricia Siplon's research on health advocacy groups convincingly argues, the speed, flexibility, and distance-reduction effects of the Net fostered a new, radical, rights-based ideology of individual empowerment and a suspicion of professional power that serves as a bond and a springboard for policy discussion for those with long-term illnesses (Brainard and Siplon, 2002:146). Although health advocacy is an area in which self-help support networks are more prevalent than any other, what is particularly interesting about this argument is that it goes beyond simple efficiency claims, to suggest that the Internet can create qualitative shifts in the values as well as the strategies and relative power of groups and movements.

Increasing Organizational Flexibility

The Internet makes it much more likely that existing organizational forms will be reconfigured on the fly, in response to new demands or a perceived desire to shift focus to new campaigns. Internet-enabled organizations often lack the bureaucratic structures that make rapid change so difficult for traditional groups and movements, such as established leaders, a permanent administrative staff, and physical headquarters.

A radical extension of these trends comes in the form of smart mobs. Mobilization of the kind that occurred in Seattle in 1999 and the Philippines in 2001 relies on the convergence of mobile computing and communications, commitment to an immediate common cause, and co-location in the form of a street protest or other public, symbolic act. Rheingold (2002) and others use theory drawn from some of the wilder fringes of the natural sciences to argue that new forms of emergent behavior are likely to become more prevalent in political and social organization. In this view, spontaneous coordination occurs through the use of communication technologies. But it is not simply brought about through a broadcasting model—the transmission and reception of a common message to which all then adhere. The rapidity with which changes in strategy occur in such examples of mobilization—often in the space of a few minutes—means that they could not possibly operate on the assumption of a leader issuing all-knowing commands from above. While it would be an exaggeration to say that the events of Seattle and the Philippines were fully leaderless, it is nevertheless the case that the protestors' strategies emerged through "a dynamically shifting aggregation of individual decisions." For Rheingold, coordination in such contexts is achieved through "flocking" behavior, or what Kevin Kelly calls "swarm systems" (Kelly, 1994). Kelly and other writers, including Steven Johnson, argue that networks are able to leverage a kind of collective intelligence to achieve tasks that are beyond the capacity of individuals. They are characterized by an absence of centralized control and relatively autonomous but highly connected subunits (Rheingold, 2002:176, 178). On a similar note, Jackie Smith's 2001 analysis of the Seattle protests demonstrates how a sophisticated division of labor was rapidly established, that saw local and national protestors engage in the physical acts of mobilization on the ground, while those groups with existing transnational links used their positions to frame the meaning of the events for the mainstream media and protestors outside the United States. Research on Internet audio "pirates" reveals the same capacity for creating organizational effectiveness online (Cooper and Harrison, 2001). The Internet therefore reinforces what theorists such as Alberto Melucci identified as a new organizational experimentalism among groups and movements in the 1980s (Melucci, 1989:208).

New Media Goes Old Media

A common thread running through many recent protests is the way in which traditional media have picked up stories that first appeared online. The rise to prominence of blogs, do-it-yourself journalism, as well as ordinary websites, email, text messaging, and chat communication gives news a viral character that seems difficult for even the most staid of traditional media veterans to resist. There are several analyses of this "new media goes old media" phenomenon, including local mobilization such as the Stop the Overlay campaign against the introduction of new telephone area codes in west Los Angeles in the late 1990s, documented by Lin and Dutton (Lin and Dutton, 2003). But probably the best example to date is the now famous case of MIT graduate student Jonah Peretti and his personal "culture jamming" email campaign against Nike (Peretti with Micheletti, 2004).

Responding to Nike's offer to allow customers to personalize their footwear, Peretti requested that the word "sweatshop" be printed on his new trainers. When Nike refused, an email exchange began in which Peretti pointed out the contradiction between Nike's offer and its attempts at censorship. The story, which first appeared on a little-known website, shey.net, was quickly picked up by the San Jose Mercury News, the nearest there is to a local paper for Silicon Valley, but soon spread to the *Village Voice,* the British *Independent,* the *Wall Street Journal, USA Today,* and many other mainstream news media over the following weeks (Bennett, 2004:111; Bennett, 2003a:161; Shey, 2004). The effects of Peretti's campaign were not immediate, but the ideas behind it gradually diffused into public discourse, so much so that by the late 1990s mainstream press coverage of Nike was dominated by stories about its employment practices. "The Nike Product has become synonymous with slave wages, forced overtime and arbitrary abuse" said the company's CEO in 1998 (quoted in Bennett, 2003b:33). Thus, although web-enabled mobilization could be said to disintermediate established media and political actors, allowing grassroots activists to bypass political elites and established institutional processes, the more successful campaigns have recognized the value of using the web to set the mainstream media's agenda.

Fusing Politics and Culture

The Nike sweatshop email campaign drew upon strategies that had been popularized by other cases of "culture jamming," many of which used the Internet. In the late 1990s, privacy campaigners' action against Intel's decision to include unique hardware identifiers in the design of its Pentium III chip involved turning the company's Intel Inside logo into one that read, "Big Brother Inside." Anti–Coca Cola "subvertisements" were created by a transnational group of media and advertising sector activists known as the Adbusters Media Foundation. Culture jamming has developed into an important subcurrent of Internet political culture as the activists involved are often drawn from the new media, graphic design, or advertising industries. Spurred on by the rediscovery and 1999 updating of the *First Things First Manifesto*—a statement by 1960s graphic designers critical of the ethical neutrality of the advertising industry—a number of anti-commercial campaigns such as Buy Nothing Day have been launched which skillfully tap into and subvert current advertising industry branding attempts (Adbusters, 2004; Lasn, 2000; Meikle, 2002:131–34; Soar, 2002). In 2004, in a continuation of earlier campaigns in which it had asked supporters to paint over the logos on their sportswear, Adbusters launched their own "brand" of unbranded, ethically produced, $40 Black Spot sneakers. The aim was to hit Nike where it hurt, by eating into its market share. These cases display similar characteristics: low-level, individual forms of protest quickly blossom into widely known viral campaigns due to the nature of the Internet and the ease with which symbolic forms like logos and photographs can be manipulated in the digital realm.

Of course, cultural politics are not only the preserve of progressives. The Internet makes it much easier for extremist conservative groups to fuse cultural and political ideas. In the United States, members of the far right militia movement were early adopters of Internet technology. In Germany, the far right presents itself as a counter-cultural movement and uses the Net to appeal to disaffected youngsters. Neo-Nazi websites sell celebratory books, T-shirts, DVDs, CDs, and video games and host MP3 files produced by white supremacist bands. Excluded from formal political participation, the producers of countercultural sites attempt to influence politics through shaping youth culture (Chroust, 2000:116). For such groups, the Internet offers the same set of advantages as it does to progressives—interconnectivity, low cost, the circumvention of a hostile mainstream media—but it also adds others, such as relative anonymity and covert communication (Whine, 2000:239–42).

Reducing Collective Action Problems

Many of the impacts just considered boil down to the ways in which the Internet softens collective action problems. Until recently, the majority of research on political mobilization tended to assume that it is dependent upon strong, face-to-face ties between the members of a group. One of the leading authors in the field, Sidney Tarrow, maintains that this is the case, even for cases of action in which there is a transnational element (Tarrow, 1998:193; see also Diani, 2000:394). Such assumptions jell with an early strand of research on online social networks which argues that computer-mediated communication lacks the richness of real-world interactions, is flawed as a means of communicating emotional or complex ideas, and is likely to produce isolation or conflict rather than social solidarity (Kraut et al., 1998). Much of the skeptical literature on online activism is based on the assumption that physical proximity enhances collective identity and therefore collective action, but it is significant that one of the most influential early studies of the isolating effect of the Internet by Robert Kraut and colleagues has now been reversed by the original authors. They speculate that changes in the medium itself, as more interactive applications have arisen, now mean that it has "generally positive consequences" (Kraut et al., 2002:68). This illustrates the dangers of generalizing too broadly on the basis of psychological snapshots.

Increasingly, the assumption that face-to-face ties are necessary for political mobilization appears to be under threat, not only by the numerous examples in which distance effects were significantly reduced but also by a competing body of social network research. Proximity is much less important for the creation of social identity than is often assumed. For example, in their work on German environmental activists, Tom Postmes and Suzanne Brunsting (2002:294) argue that

> social behavior does not just stem from the immediate proximity of other individuals: we internalize many aspects of our social world and incorporate these into the social identities that we may take on even when we are isolated from others . . . individuals' behavior and cognitions can be highly social despite the fact that they are isolated from the direct influence of others in their group.

Moreover, two features of online political contexts are arguably just as likely to contribute to greater collective cohesion as they are to fragmentation. First, the relative anonymity of the online world renders individuals less accountable for their actions. They feel empowered to speak up against more powerful actors because they have less fear of punishment. Second, the absence of physical markers in the online world reduces the likelihood of splits and factions developing within a group. In their pioneering study of email, Lee Sproull and Sara Kiesler (1986) argued that it may be unsuited to creating strong ties, but by reducing some of the common anxieties of communication, such as fear of embarrassment or rejection, it reduces inhibitions and creates greater numbers of useful weak ties as well as making communication among strangers more effective by reducing the need for extraneous social pleasantries.

We also need to revisit our discussion of weak ties theory (see chapter 5) to consider why strong ties should be considered to be inherently better than weak ones. As we saw in that chapter, this theory holds that, for tasks like acquiring new information, weaker ties are in fact better because they increase the size of the information pool from which an individual can draw when deciding how to act. As Mark Granovetter (1973:1378) put it: "weak ties, often denounced as generative of alienation are . . . indispensable to individuals' opportunities and to their integration into communities; strong ties, breeding local cohesion, lead to overall fragmentation" (see also Bennett, 2003a:146; Constant et al., 1996). There is less likelihood that new resources will flow into a tightly knit, face-to-face or local community. Also, Caroline Haythornthwaite has elaborated on the importance of "latent ties"—those that are technically possible but "not activated by social interaction" (Haythornthwaite, 2002:389). Individuals belonging to the same organization or electronic network such as an email list have latent ties established for them by the communication infrastructures of the organization. Such theories of weak and latent ties seem particularly applicable to the case of Internet-enabled mobilization, especially in a transnational context, where the sharing of information among those who have never met face-to-face is required for simultaneous protests in multiple towns and cities and for the creation of organizational innovation and flexibility in the absence of permanent leaderships.

A further challenge to the assumption that the Internet makes no difference to collective action is provided by threshold theory. In seeking to explain why individuals decide to join in with collective action, such as a riot, a strike, or even the spreading of a rumor, Granovetter argues that in conditions of uncertainty or danger, an individual's propensity to join in is based on her assessment of the risks of doing so (1978:1422). In brutally simple terms, threshold theory recognizes that many instances of direct action involve "you first" and "safety in numbers" scenarios. But it is a powerful explanation of why individuals get involved in potentially risky forms of collective action. For example, those with relatively high thresholds are only likely to join a strike if the risks (like losing one's job) are relatively low. In terms of this theory, instances of collective action in which the Internet plays a major role could be said to reduce threshold effects for some individuals, making collective action more likely to occur. This is because the Internet functions as a highly efficient way of simultaneously informing many others that you are engaging or are about to engage in action (Rheingold, 2002:176). In some circumstances, this can lead to incredible accelerations in mobilization, as occurred in the case of cell phone use in the Philippines, considered earlier in this chapter, because safety in numbers is much easier to achieve.

Some writers have started to reappraise classic theories of collective action in political science, especially Mancur Olson's influential work from the 1960s, in light of the Net (Lupia and Sin, 2003; Olson, 1965). Olson argued that forming groups is very difficult for some sections of society. He begins from the rational choice assumption that individuals are rational actors seeking to maximize their individual utility. When an individual decides to join a group, she weighs up the personal benefits she might receive from the existence of such a group. Then, she assesses the likelihood that joining the group will be decisive in determining the group's success. The final calculation is of the membership costs involved in joining. Will I have to pay expensive subscription dues? or Will I be tied up in boring meetings every evening?

Olson developed his argument by stating that most interest groups are set up to secure what economists call "public goods." A public good is nonexcludable: it is available to everyone, however much or little they contribute to its creation. For example, in a factory, a wage rise is usually given to every employee, whether he or she is a union member or not. A union may have spent many months campaigning for a pay rise for its members, but all employees in the factory get the raise. Nonunion members therefore "free ride" on the backs of union members, because union members pay dues, attend meetings, or even strike, usually at some personal cost. The effects of the free-rider problem also differ according to group size. Olson argued that large groups can be very difficult to organize because individuals tend to think that joining is not going to make much of a difference to its chances of success and they will receive the benefits in any case, through free riding. An individual will think: "Why should I bother to join? There are plenty of other members, my free riding will go unnoticed, and I'll still get the benefits in the long run." Large groups are also more expensive to organize.

For Olson, the end result of such collective action problems is that some "latent" groups will never form, and if they do, they will always struggle to recruit and mobilize members. Successful groups either coerce people to join or entice them by offering selective incentives—benefits that are only available to group members. Many associations give members benefits like cheap accident and unemployment insurance or free legal representation. If a group can provide a package of benefits which offset the costs of an individual joining and supporting activities, Olson argues that it will survive.

Olson's theory has been hugely influential for many years. However, in a recent interpretation of some of its central themes, Arthur Lupia and Gisela Sin (2003) claim that the Internet and related technologies have changed some of the dynamics of group mobilization, with broadly positive consequences. First, because it reduces the costs of communication, the Internet overcomes some of the disadvantages faced by large, non-elite groups in recognizing their supporters, building an organization, and mobilizing at key times. Second, because many online environments make nonparticipation much easier to spot, the Internet can reduce free-rider effects. For instance, an online donation drive can match actual contributors against a database of potential supporters, enabling the group's staff to tailor selective incentives to the particular interests of nondonors.

Even hacktivists employ technology to circumvent the kinds of collective action problems that have traditionally plagued weak or poorly resourced groups. Hackers share their expertise with other hackers and with nontechnical activists who wish to participate. By doing so, they are providing those who wish to engage in collective action with the resources that they themselves lack. Indeed, this interpretation may also be applied to many other forms of Internet-enabled mobilization in which groups and movements now routinely engage (Leizerov, 2000:465). These include providing email templates, simple web forms that aggregate opinion before dispatching the results to elected representatives, or subversive symbolic resources like the altered graphics and logos that appear in culture jamming protests. These activities produce public goods that can reduce some of the individual costs of political participation (Samuel, 2001).

Hacktivism may also be understood in the context of a well-established tradition of writing about "repertoires" of collective action (Tilly, 1978; Traugott, 1995), or the ways in which the organizational form and tactics of a group, such as the way it makes decisions, become symbolic of its goals (Melucci, 1989:206–7). In other words, repertoires play a role in sustaining collective identity. They are not just tools to be adopted but come to shape what it means to be a participant in a group or social movement. Excellent examples here include environmental groups, whose methods of organization and decision making have traditionally been self-consciously nonhierarchical, consensual, and participatory. Recent research suggests a symbiosis between these values and their approach to Internet technologies (Pickerill, 2003).

One final—and often forgotten—aspect of collective action is its high-risk nature. In the case of hacktivism, of course, the Net reduces threshold effects because the perceived risks of physical injury or getting caught are hugely diminished. But those who engage in action which carries the risk of arrest, personal injury, or even death are most often members of close-knit personal networks where trust levels, for good or ill, are high. Computer-mediated communication is relatively low risk and therefore a relatively blunt instrument for developing trust among strangers. Although the forging of a collective identity through online means may be easier among those who share a common goal or interest, this is a world away from the intense relationships that exist in terrorist organizations, for instance (Diani, 2000:397). Thus, although terrorist organizations are a type of movement that also appear to be making use of the Internet for their internal communications (see chapter 11), it is arguably less likely that high-risk group action will be initiated solely by Internet communication.

Conclusion

When Internet use started to expand during the mid-1990s, there were many overly optimistic accounts of events such as the Zapatista uprising, which pointed to a bright new future of global citizen activism that would tame some of the pernicious aspects of neo-liberalism. By the early 2000s, a strongly pessimistic backlash had set in, where the best we could hope for was a reinforcement model in which the Net does not fundamentally reconfigure group and movement politics. This chapter has tried to paint a more complex picture. Spectacular examples of mobilization, whether transnational or national, now need to be situated within the context of more prosaic but still significant organizational and strategic innovations among traditional interest groups. Again, however, there are countless groups upon which the Internet has had little effect, apart from spurring them to establish a simple web page. Many groups and movements have not fundamentally changed their organizations and strategies. Yet at the same time we should not be blind to genuinely novel forms of citizen action like hacktivism or hybrid forms such as MoveOn. It is not hyperbolic to state that these were unimaginable before the Internet.

The most straightforward argument that the Internet makes a difference to mobilization derives from the technology's perceived role in reducing the costs of communication (Klein, 1999). While these cost-reduction effects are crucial, this chapter has also sought to demonstrate that the effects have often gone beyond this by bringing together previously isolated political support networks. By "changing who says what to whom" (Lin and Dutton, 2003:133), Internet-enabled forms of mobilization have reconfigured political action. This is a thread running through many of the examples discussed here. While the Internet's capacity to oil the machinery of politics is crucially important in its own right, perhaps the biggest challenge for students of this area of Internet politics lies in making the links between the emergence of the Internet as a tool for communication and shifts in qualitative values that it may have caused or encouraged. In other words, how the repertoires of collective action are being shaped by the medium itself.

New, more fluid types of organizational membership have emerged which allow some groups to mobilize individuals as actors in key online information networks. Some are also able to raise money without suffering from collective action problems. Yet much depends upon the level and focus of their efforts. A group wishing to raise funds to create a network of volunteers might find email a solution to the prohibitive costs of a mass paper mail-out and may be able to get by on a small core of technically literate staff. But in a campaign environment such as a presidential election or high-profile senate race, television is more likely to predominate; this requires professional skills and imposes huge costs. It is notable, for instance, that Howard Dean's 2003–2004 Democratic primary campaign used the bulk of the funds raised via the Internet to pay for huge amounts of television advertising. But this takes us into the realm of the Internet's impact on election campaigning—the subject of the next chapter.

Discussion Points

- How have traditional interest groups adapted to the Internet?
- Do the effects of the Internet on interest groups and social movements go beyond simply increasing the efficiency of communication?
- Is hacktivism a form of political action?
- Could hybrid forms of political organization such as MoveOn have existed before the Internet?
- Must political mobilization rest upon face-to-face interaction?

Further Reading

The best place to begin is undoubtedly Bruce Bimber's book (2003), but Brainard and Siplon, 2002, Leizerov, 2000, Lupia and Sin, 2003, and Postmes and Brunsting, 2002, are all thoughtful.

An insight into the early Internet campaigns in the United States can be found in Gurak, 1997, while Castells, 2004, is excellent on the Zapatista uprising.

Tarrow, 1998, is an enduring approach to social movements, but for an excellent argument situating transnational mobilization in the context of the Internet, see the superb cluster of essays by Lance Bennett (2004, 2003a, 2003b). For cultural politics online, see Lasn, 2002, Peretti with Micheletti, 2004, and Scott and Street, 2000.

Research on new movements like MoveOn is in its infancy, but there is a useful essay by Hickey (2004) and a paper by Chadwick (2005). Research on hacktivism is similarly embryonic, but there is now a useful book by Tim Jordan and Paul Taylor (2004).

Some of the wilder fringes of this subject are covered in Rheingold, 2002.

PARTIES, CANDIDATES, AND ELECTIONS

E-campaigning

We listen. We pay attention. If I give a speech and the blog people don't like it, next time I change the speech. . . . What we've given people is a way to shout back, and we listen—they don't even have to shout anymore.

—HOWARD DEAN, *Quoted in* Wired, *January 2004*

CHAPTER OVERVIEW

Here I consider the impact of the Internet on parties and election campaigning. Following a contextual discussion of recent challenges to political parties I examine the evolution of online campaigning in the United States and the United Kingdom. An extended case study of the 2003–2004 primary and presidential campaigns illustrates several key shifts in this area. Finally, I assess how and why the Internet might be reconfiguring this area by focusing on three themes: party competition, power diffusion, and institutional adaptation.

During the summer of 2003 stories began to filter through to the mainstream American media about Howard Dean, liberal former governor of Vermont, possibly securing the Democratic Party's presidential nomination. As we shall see, Dean and his staff were proving highly successful in using the Internet to fund-raise and mobilize support. Dean eventually failed in the primaries, but the new grassroots campaigning techniques his staff and volunteers pioneered had an immediate impact on the rest of the presidential race—and on the campaign of the eventual Democratic nominee, John Kerry, in particular.

Yet the upsurge was unexpected. Before Dean and the "Deaniacs," Internet campaigning was widely regarded as dead and buried. This assumption is now less secure. Here, we examine the evolution of the Internet's impact on election campaigning. The chapter focuses mainly on the United States, which has been in the vanguard in this area and the subject of most detailed studies. However, it also looks across the Atlantic, to Britain, a country where parties are historically much stronger, where the political system differs in important respects from that in the United States, but which nevertheless has recently been undergoing much soul searching about the decline of political participation and the rise of "professional," media-driven forms of politics—the very trends against which the Dean supporters reacted. Given the remarkably high voter turnout in the 2004 U.S. presidential election, these may perhaps be undergoing decisive shifts.

CONTEXT: DIAGNOSING THE ELECTORAL MALAISE

Debates about the impact of the Internet on election campaigning do not exist in a vacuum but must be viewed within the context of a number of significant themes in the political science of elections and party systems. These themes apply strongly to the United States and the United Kingdom but also touch on the politics of many other liberal democracies.

First and foremost, in the United States and the United Kingdom but also in many other liberal democracies, voter turnout has been in decline. In the United States, until the 2004 presidential election turnout of 61 percent (6 percent up on 2000), it had almost become a cliché to observe this fact. In 1964, turnout in the U.S. presidential election reached 63 percent before taking a slow but inexorable drift downward. Congressional elections have always experienced low turnout, but there, too, the trend is gently downward, with some occasional shock years, like 1998, when only 35 percent voted—the lowest figure for the entire postwar period (International Institute for Democracy and Electoral Assistance, 2004). Declining participation among the young is also well established. In 2000, only 37 percent of eighteen-to-twenty-four-year-old Americans voted. Between 1972 and 2000, turnout among eighteen-to-twenty-four-year-olds fell by around 15 percent (Center for Information and Research on Civic Learning and Engagement, 2004). Early estimates of the youth turnout in 2004 indicate that the proportion of eighteen-to-twenty-four-year-old voters in the whole electorate remained broadly the same. Meanwhile in the United Kingdom, where electoral participation has historically been much higher, the 2001 general election caused great alarm, when turnout fell to just 59 percent. More worryingly, some estimates suggest voting among the eighteen-to-twenty-five age group fell to less than 40 percent (Coleman and Gøtze, 2001:5). The 2005 general election, a closer contest, saw the figure rise to just 61 percent, indicating a basic downward trend. Declining citizen participation in one of the basic rituals of liberal democratic politics provides a backdrop to many of the themes below.

Second, there is an ongoing debate about the decline of parties, particularly their social bases of support (Dalton, 2000). Many argue that postindustrial societies no longer contain the large social classes and other homogeneous groups that gave rise to political parties during the nineteenth and early twentieth centuries. As societies have become more socially fragmented, parties have seen their social bases wither or become riddled with cross-cutting social cleavages. As a consequence, weakening party identification—the extent to which electors see a party as naturally "theirs," based upon feelings of loyalty and social tradition—has caused a decline in party membership and a rise in the volatile politics of issue voting (Himmelweit et al., 1985). Voters are now much more likely to float free of party identification and make more "rational" assessments of the parties' policy platforms and record in office in their voting decisions (Rose and McAllister, 1986).

Third, some argue that participation in parties has fallen not because there are less people participating in politics overall, but because more choose to participate in interest groups, single-issue organizations, new social movements, and extremist or protest parties (Jordan, 1998). In the past, citizens' political preferences were much more stable and easy to predict. Now, however, political identities seem less fixed. Citizens demand more flexible and complex ways of expressing their diverse political views and no longer see political parties as solely capable of accommodating such ideological diversity (Norris, 1999). The overall results are paradoxical, with lower levels of voter turnout in national and local elections but the rise of single-issue campaigns, short-term volunteering, and Internet participation.

Fourth, many writers have identified decisive shifts in parties' strategies and organizational structures over the last thirty years. Probably the most influential thesis in this area is Otto Kircheimer's historical theory of the transition from "mass" to "catch-all" parties (1966). Mass parties were dominant throughout Europe (not the United States, or at least not in the same form) between the late nineteenth and mid-twentieth centuries. They tended to have coherent ideologies, established organizations such as local branches and, in the case of social democratic parties, tried to integrate their social base of voters by incorporating associations such as trade unions into their structures (Duverger, 1954; Lipset and Rokkan, 1967). Classic examples include the British Labor Party before the 1990s or the Swedish and German Social Democrats.

Followers of Kircheimer now argue that mass parties have given way to catch-all parties. These are characterized by a ruthless focus on electoral success, a reduced emphasis on participation in the local party structures by the rank and file, weak or vague ideological stances that are designed to attract as many voters as possible, an emphasis on the personal charisma of the leader, and the use of modern communication techniques, such as targeting the mass media rather than relying upon ordinary party activists to mobilize support at the grass roots. Catch-all parties do not rely upon a specific social group, such as the working class, but deliberately keep their messages vague enough to appeal to the center ground. Over time, in electoral arenas where there are simple Left-Right divisions in important policy areas (such as economic policy), catch-all parties that are serious about winning elections must converge on what Anthony Downs famously termed the "median voter"—the person whose views are hypothetically at the center of the political spectrum (Downs, 1957). While this may satisfy the majority of voters, because they are clustered around the center ground, those whose views are located on the Left or Right of the political spectrum, where there are fewer votes to be won, will find their opinions marginalized. Downs argued that median voter convergence is an ingenious means of ensuring that the preferences of the majority of the electorate are satisfied. But for those on the Left or the Right or those whose political views cannot be mapped simply onto a Left-Right spectrum, such as an ethnic or religious group, the overall outcome may be a party system that does not adequately cater to their beliefs.

Although the catch-all party model has been highly influential, it is sometimes seen as having less relevance for the United States, principally because Kircheimer based his analysis on European examples, where it was relatively easy to discern a transition away from ideological coherence and participatory organizational structures. However, U.S. parties are excellent examples of the catch-all party, so long as we recognize that there are certain contradictory tendencies at work in the U.S. system (Gunther and Diamond, 2003:186). In the U.S. case, the rise of professionalized, media-focused campaigning, personality driven politics, and the weakening of parties' relationships with their traditional social bases has been matched by the spread of primary elections. Primaries have arguably weakened party elites and have distributed the power to select candidates among the broader electorate.

A fifth theme of the electoral malaise is professionalization. Some writers argue that the period since the 1960s has witnessed a paradigm shift in election campaigning. The rise of television, in the eyes of critics, has led to campaigns dominated by personality contests, dumbed-down or packaged political messages, the centralized control of information, spin doctors, soundbites, and "infotainment." Professionalization has created a new class of political communications specialists such as opinion pollsters, advertising agencies, journalists, and now Internet consultants, whose role is to sell candidates and policies in much the same way that businesses sell products (Davis, 2002; Franklin 2004; Gitlin, 1994; Scammell, 1995; Wring, 2004). This has increased levels of voter cynicism about the electoral process. These attitudes are reinforced by mainstream styles of journalism that focus on the campaign "game" (and often the journalists' own roles as game players) rather than substantive issues—a phenomenon termed "metacommunication" (Esser et al., 2001; see also Cappella and Jamieson, 1997). Professionalization also incorporates the concept of the permanent campaign, which refers to the ways in which parties and candidates in office are perpetually focused on building media profiles and visibility with an eye to the next election rather than trying to create policy successes while in government (Blumenthal, 1980; Heclo, 2000). Critics of professionalization argue that parties no longer function as effective organs of citizen participation but are dominated by party elites in top-down fashion. Although the argument that parties are elitist is far from new (Michels, 1915; Ostrogorski, 1902), some claim that oligarchic tendencies have recently intensified in the new era of political communication (Davis, 2003; Hallin, 2000; Heffernan and Stanyer, 1998). In this view, party elites can now make direct appeals to the electorate; they are less dependent upon grassroots activists to spread the gospel, raise funds, and mobilize voters on election day. Reducing this dependency upon the party rank and file allows leaders relative autonomy from democratic control but also ruthless control of the communication of political messages. The outcome is a media-driven environment in which political and communication elites talk to one another without much in the way of popular input. Ordinary party activists are there to hear and cheer but little else.

Finally, there is the issue of party funding. In the United States and the United Kingdom, huge increases in campaign spending over the last thirty years have led many commentators to criticize the role played by wealthy donors in the political process. Large corporate donations make candidates less dependent upon the grassroots. Parties can buy more airtime or advertising space in the press and use it to communicate directly with those undecided voters in key constituencies or swing states that are crucial for electoral success. In other countries, concerns have arisen over the rise of so-called cartel party systems (Katz and Mair, 1995). These exhibit collusion between the major parties in establishing electoral rules, such as the electoral system or the party funding regime. The veneer of party competition often conceals the reality, which is that parties fear new entrants into the political marketplace and will do all that they can to ensure that this does not occur. Although the cartel argument is most relevant for European countries, especially systems that feature state funding for parties, it is also of some relevance for the United States. Recent presidential elections have featured historically strong though still unsuccessful third-party candidates such as Ross Perot and Ralph Nader, bringing into focus how the electoral system and the funding regime affect electoral outcomes.

THE POTENTIAL IMPACT OF THE INTERNET: KEY CLAIMS

As the discussion of these six contextual themes reveals, debates about the impact of the Internet in this area are growing in fertile soil. Let us briefly consider the kinds of claims that have been made about the Internet's impact on the electoral malaise (Browning, 1996; Corrado and Firestone, 1996; Grossman, 1995; Morris, 1999; Rash, 1997; Selnow, 1998; Trippi, 2004).

Party Competition

The most well-known set of arguments focuses on the Internet's capacity to increase party competition. It potentially allows previously marginalized or even new parties to emerge and compete with established players or perhaps facilitates nonparty or even antiparty political movements. Parties and candidates that either lack the financial resources to buy advertising space or whose views mean that they are marginalized by mainstream media may be able to circumvent these restrictions by using the Internet as a cheaper, more efficient way to reach out to voters. They may bypass traditional media altogether or may use alternative spaces on the web to try to influence the mainstream media's framing of events. The overall outcome is a more pluralistic and competitive party system in which new parties are more likely to emerge and enjoy success. Citizens are more likely to be energized, and voter turnout will increase. Because it massively increases the amount of information available to voters and party activists, the Internet undermines the gatekeeping role of traditional media by creating a vast ocean of always-available "raw" news about candidates. This is in stark contrast to the environment created by television news—a medium that revolves around easily digestible chunks of information in the form of two-minute stories. Motivated voters are now able to examine candidates' voting records, campaign donations, and previous speeches online. In the past, access to these resources was in practice reserved for journalists, lobbyists, and campaign professionals. Not only does the sheer quantity of political information increase, its production and circulation becomes democratized as more citizens start to publish political information and commentary through devices such as blogs.

Power Diffusion

The second set of arguments centers upon how the Internet may increase grassroots control over candidates and party leaderships, resulting in new, participatory campaigns featuring larger memberships operating in decentralized, horizontal network structures that depart from the hierarchical structure typical of the catch-all party. Continuous interaction between candidates and their supporters will enhance democratic control by the grass roots, it is claimed, serving to undermine recent trends toward elitism. Candidates will tailor their programs to voters' interests in much more refined ways and will "narrowcast" messages to discrete groups in the electorate. These forces will diffuse out into the broader party system as citizens become more adept at monitoring campaigns. Groups of grassroots activists will be empowered to make strategic interventions at decisive moments in the campaign, such as organizing quickfire donation drives. Meanwhile, psychologically disempowered spectators will feel their political efficacy increase, not only by physically turning out to rallies and meetings but by contributing to and learning from a much richer online public debate (Bucy and Gregson, 2001). Remote voting over the Internet will pull greater numbers into the electoral process, especially the young and the elderly, due to the convenience it provides. The solemn procession to the polling place will become a thing of the past.

At first glance, this summary might appear rather hyperbolic. But it is—believe it or not—a fairly understated distillation of what a number of commentators have been arguing since the mid-1990s. Probably the most well-known exponent of the view that the Internet will effect a major power shift is Dick Morris, former advisor to president Clinton and founder of the online opinion poll website Vote.com. Consider his checklist of transformations (exhibit 7.1). As you can see, Morris's claims are gargantuan. But he is far from a lone voice in the wilderness. In fact, more recently there have been important newcomers to the optimists' camp, caused largely, as we shall see below, by the Democratic primary campaign of Howard Dean in 2003–2004 (Trippi, 2004).

Institutional Adaptation

Yet the incredible optimism of Morris has been countered by what has come to be known as the normalization thesis, which is perhaps best labeled the institutional adaptation model (Davis, 1999; Margolis and Resnick, 2000; Margolis et al., 1997; Resnick, 1998). In this perspective, as regular politics moves online, it tames the democratic potential of the Net. A whole new stratum of web designers and other assorted new media workers have slotted in with spin doctored and packaged politics. These are seen as lamentable but inescapable features of contemporary liberal democracies. The "egalitarian" Net of the pre-1990s has been replaced by slick websites targeted at specific audiences: politics as usual moves online. In this perspective, the Internet will not change the fundamental dynamics of election campaigning. Party competition will not increase, because the wealthier parties and candidates will be able to make more effective use of Internet techniques: they will have better websites, more talented staff, and more advanced back-end technologies; they will also be able to converge their television campaigns with their online presence. Parties and campaigns will not become more participatory but will continue to be dominated by elites. In fact, the Internet may intensify political inequalities. In the words of Richard Davis (1999:119), "the main beneficiaries among the electorate will be the politically interested." The catch-all party will adapt to the new Internet environment.

To see the tension between these three dynamics in action, consider the evolution of online campaigning.

EXHIBIT 7.1. THE TRANSFORMATION
OF THE ELECTORAL PROCESS?

- The Internet will lead to de facto government by referendum, dramatically reining in leaders. Soon, tens of millions of people will register their opinions on the Net and compel the attention of elected representatives.

- Internet voting will usurp the media's role in handicapping elections and anointing frontrunners.

- As more people switch from television and newspapers to the Internet, money will not be effective in reaching them.

- The new voters—the X generation—will assert its power. As campaigns are waged over the Net, younger voters will reshape the national agenda.

- The media's emphasis on ratings and reach will be replaced by the Internet's focus on depth. The power of the media establishment will erode as all stations and newspapers become equally available to every Internet user.

- Television advertisements reach an audience involuntarily while voters on the Internet receive political messages only if they want them. This difference will force a change in the way campaigns are waged.

- Television campaigning emphasizes thirty-second messages endlessly repeated. On the Internet, it will be the most interesting campaigns that will attract the biggest audiences.

- The Internet will permit a candidate to target his message to distinct voting groups. The interactivity of the Internet will tell candidates—and their managers—what is working and what isn't.

- Email campaigns will be crammed into the final hours before election day as last-minute appeals for voters volley back and forth.

- Voting over the Net will increasingly replace traditional polling. This will let voters initiate ideas and assume an active role in the dialogue.

- Party-line voting in Congress will diminish, as will the parties' role as fundraisers. Party organizations will wither.

- The members of the Fourth Estate—journalists and broadcasters—are the most obvious losers in this new paradigm. With fewer people reading, watching, or listening to the big three networks and more citizens using cable television or the Internet to get direct, unfiltered news, the Fourth Estate is losing its power.

- A decade from now, politics could revolve around one-on-one virtual conversations between candidate and voter. The cybercandidate will be a composite of stored video images with preprogrammed responses.

Source: Quoted and adapted from Morris, 1999.

THE EVOLUTION OF ONLINE CAMPAIGNING:
THE UNITED STATES

The U.K. and U.S. party systems share many common features, but they also differ in important respects. This is not the place to explore these in any detail, but it is worth mentioning some salient ones as a brief prologue to our story of how the two systems have experienced the impact of the Internet. This is important because it is arguable that the candidate-centered nature of the U.S. party system has made it much more open to being reconfigured by the Internet.

In basic terms, when it comes to national elections, both are historically embedded two-party systems: only two parties have a realistic chance of securing executive power; single-party executives are the norm at the national level (not at the devolved level in the United Kingdom); and parties take turns controlling the executive. Both countries have a simple plurality electoral system based on geographical constituencies, and this reinforces the two-party system.

Yet British parties, the party system, and its typical campaigning patterns differ from those in the United States in several important respects. In the United Kingdom, parties are coherent and disciplined both inside and outside the legislature. Parties have a life outside of election campaigns; they are organs of policy and participation and have fairly stable (though declining) memberships. There is no primary system in the United Kingdom; therefore levels of internal competition between contender candidates are low (or rivalry takes place behind the scenes) and campaigns are much shorter and less expensive. But U.K. parties do have internal procedures which, to varying extents, involve mass memberships in the selection of national leadership positions. Permanent local constituency associations select their local party candidates, subject to the final approval of central staff.

In the United States, however, the following generalizations usually apply. First, party discipline is often erratic in Congress, especially in the Senate, where there is some degree of fluidity from issue to issue. Second, U.S. politics is candidate centered. Parties have very little life outside of Congress and election campaigns. Support networks must be built between elections. U.S. parties are often described as shell organizations, whose principal function is to fund-raise and mobilize support. There is no system of individual membership, though there is a chance for ordinary party supporters to play a role in the selection of candidates through the primary system. U.S. elections are also fragmented: the president and members of Congress are elected separately, whereas in the United Kingdom, the prime minister and cabinet are drawn from the members of Parliament elected at the general election.

The 1996 U.S. Campaign: A False Start?

In the United States, commentators have continually prophesied the coming of the "first Internet election" since the 1992 presidential campaign, when Bill Clinton's staff placed the texts of a few speeches and some basic biographical sketches on a primitive gopher server located at the University of North Carolina–Chapel Hill. That was before the adoption of HTML and the graphical browser. The material was publicized around

Usenet newsgroups, but such a small proportion of the public had Internet access that it had no discernible impact on the campaign.

The Clinton campaign's online efforts of 1992 were eclipsed by what occurred in 1996. By then, Internet use among the general public had started to take off. Around 30 percent of Americans had regular Internet access, and it has been estimated that 10 percent of voters used the Internet for election news during the year. Surveys also showed that Internet users were more likely to vote, creating the impression that targeting them would be a highly efficient means of mobilizing support (Davis, 1999:88). During the televised candidate debate of 1996, Republican hopeful Bob Dole ended by awkwardly stating the address of his website—a move which caught the media's imagination and quickly became symbolic of the Internet's political arrival. Political websites mushroomed during the campaign. Republican presidential candidate Lamar Alexander held online discussions with supporters during the primaries. The Democrats and Republicans both launched national campaign sites that would serve as the prototypes for today's much more sophisticated and interactive versions. The fluidity of the environment made measurement difficult, but Richard Davis's survey found that 521 congressional candidates had their own sites by the time of the November poll (1999:87–88).

Nonmainstream parties, especially the Greens, the Libertarians, the Natural Law Party, and the Reform Party, quickly established their own sites. Suddenly, outsider candidates in the primaries found their sites listed alongside those of the main contenders in the burgeoning portals and directories. A glance at the Yahoo! directory for October 1996 reveals the Republicans' listing standing shoulder to shoulder with the Reform's and Socialist Party's (Yahoo!/Internet Archive, 2004). While this seemingly created the impression of increasing party competition, less wealthy candidates were less likely to create websites, or if they did, they were insubstantial (Klotz, 2004:68). Minor parties were usually squeezed out of the media coverage that appeared on major news sites such as CBS, CNN, and ABC. It has also been suggested that advantage flowed to incumbents, who could use their official congressional sites to increase their visibility (Davis, 1999:94–95). Overall, though, the evidence is mixed. For example, despite the translation of incumbency effects into the online environment, Bill Orton, Democratic representative for Utah's third district, was beaten by Chris Cannon. While Orton did not create a campaign site, Cannon invested heavily in his. It is impossible to tell whether this made a difference to the result, but such a contrast is unlikely to have helped Orton's chances.

Much was expected of candidate websites during the 1996 campaign. With hindsight, however, it appears that candidates, campaign managers, and the media were just beginning to feel their way around the new medium. Most sites were infrequently updated. While many contained substantial detail on policy positions, they often adopted the now-familiar "brochureware" model. They were simple HTML versions of campaign literature that had been produced for the offline campaign. Some sites did offer digital resources, such as banners and logos that citizens were encouraged to place on their own sites or print out and pin to noticeboards. The majority of sites also gave out details of how to volunteer, but anecdotal evidence indicates that very few citizens provided their details through online channels (Davis, 1999:108). Indeed, what little evidence there is indicates that the audiences for most candidate sites were very small. For example, the site of Julia Carson, Democratic representative for Indiana's seventh district, was accessed just twenty times a day during the most intensive campaign period (Davis, 1999:113).

Levels of interaction between candidates and voters were also generally low in 1996 (Klinenberg and Perrin, 2000). Three-quarters of sites contained email links, but few voters took the opportunity to use email to contact candidates, and few candidates gave the impression that they would even reply. Around one in ten contained online opinion poll facilities, but often the results of these remained private. In any case, they were blunt instruments because no effort was made to restrict responses to those living in the relevant constituency. Only a handful of sites created discussion forums designed to facilitate citizen-to-citizen discussion. President Clinton's site contained a Be Your Own Pundit section, but messages were censored (Klotz, 2004:70). There were some pioneers, such as Ken Poston, Democratic candidate for Georgia's ninth district, who held monthly online discussions in a virtual "town hall" filled with avatars (Davis, 1999:90). It is also significant that some candidates started to construct their own networks of links to other organizations, such as interest groups, even though many were reluctant to endorse other sites for fear of being associated too closely with them (Davis, 1999:101). However, in 1996, the only glimmer of what would come with the 2004 campaign was a finding by a consulting firm, Campaign Solutions, that candidate websites were attracting significant numbers of new volunteers. A survey of those who volunteered online via Republican candidates sites found that 90 percent of the volunteers were new to the campaign and some 55 percent were first-timers (Klotz, 2004:71)

Online fund-raising efforts in the 1996 campaign now seem prehistoric. Less than half of the candidates even asked for donations on their sites, and those who did seldom got beyond providing addresses for campaign offices or a printable form that could be returned with a check. Secure servers for credit card transactions were almost nonexistent. It has been estimated that the Clinton campaign raised just $10,000 from people who responded to a website request (Davis, 1999:109). Aside from the fact that secure server technology was in its infancy, a gray area in campaigning laws meant that candidates would not be able to secure matching funds for money raised online. These problems had melted away by the 2000 election. By then, e-commerce had become mainstream and the Federal Election Commission (FEC) had issued a ruling permitting funds raised online to be considered for the matching program. These changes had a decisive impact on U.S. elections, as we shall see later.

Did the Internet create more substantive, issued-focused debate, or did it reinforce trends toward negative campaigning? Interestingly, negative strategies were generally few and far between in the online environment in 1996. Only around a third of candidates used negative strategies against their opponents (Klotz, 2004:70). This trend continued through the 1998 midterm elections but, as we shall see, tailed off after 2000, when "going negative" became as prevalent online as it is in other media in U.S. campaigns.

The 1998 midterm campaigns evolved gently from those of 1996, but one highlight stands out: Jesse Ventura's famous victory in the Minnesota gubernatorial campaign. Ventura, a charismatic native Minnesotan and ex-professional Wrestler, actor, and radio talk show host, ostensibly stood as a candidate for Ross Perot's now-defunct Reform Party, though his policies were generally idiosyncratic. Knowing that he would face an uphill struggle in a tight three-way contest dominated by two high-profile and high-spending opponents, Norm Coleman and Hubert "Skip" Humphrey, Ventura and his small campaign team decided to experiment with the Internet. He established an incredibly basic but, as it transpired, highly effective website. The site cost just $200 to establish and $30 per month to maintain. The campaign team created a simple discussion board to allow supporters to communicate with each other, but this effectively served as an announcement page for Ventura himself, especially during the closing stages of the campaign when he undertook a seventy-two-hour drive across Minnesota. The tour stops were posted on the discussion board, and supporters were asked to turn out to hear Ventura speak (Stromer-Galley, 2000b:122). The website also urged unregistered younger voters to register late in the campaign—a factor which contributed to his overall success (Klotz, 2004:71). Ventura took the governorship without an organized party, having spent just $650,000, compared with the $15 million spent by his opponents (Stromer-Galley, 2000a:44).

The Year 2000: Another False Start?

Despite the false starts of the 1996 campaign, the 2000 elections promised to be much more Internet driven. The context had shifted. Most surveys indicated that around 50 percent of the U.S. public now had Internet access (Bimber and Davis, 2003:37). Around three-quarters of Senate and House candidates had specific campaign sites in the 2000 races (Schneider and Foot, 2002:45). Robert Klotz (2004) argues that financially disadvantaged candidates (defined as those with less than half of their opponents' campaign funds) were in fact more likely to have a campaign website in 2000, indicating that the electoral website digital divide had apparently disappeared. In the lead-up to the fall campaign, many commentators likened the sense of anticipation to the first television election of 1960. Ventura's Minnesota triumph, though in many ways a freak result, seemed to herald a new era.

Some, but by no means all, of this promise was fulfilled. There were genuine innovations during the 2000 campaign, but the overall message was decidedly mixed. Given what occurred in 2004, the 2000 elections are best seen as a transitional stage on the way to something much more significant, especially in the spheres of fund-raising and voter mobilization.

Most of the significant developments came during the primary season rather than the main campaign. Following a 1999 FEC ruling which relaxed the regulations on online fund-raising, candidates immediately saw the potential of the Internet for securing donations. In a taste of what was to come in Howard Dean's campaign during the 2003–2004 primaries, Democratic candidate Bill Bradley flooded the web with banner advertisements asking: "Tired of Politics as Usual?" Republican candidate John McCain—unexpected victor in the New Hampshire primary—reportedly received around $1.4 million in online donations during just three days. At one stage, donations flooded in at around $18,000 per hour. By the close of the primaries, McCain had raised around $6 million and Al Gore, around $10 million online (Bimber, 2003:183). However, despite expectations that online contributions would continue to rise during election year, they tailed off after the party conventions (Bimber and Davis, 2003:39). The main presidential contenders did raise substantial sums in comparison with their 1996 counterparts, but these represent small proportions of the overall campaign funds.

Support for McCain drifted away during the rest of the primaries, and George Bush emerged as the favorite. McCain's campaign did, nevertheless, indicate that from now on candidates could use the Internet to raise and access funds very quickly, provided they could get the technology in place and a sense of momentum established. This was perhaps most graphically illustrated by what happened during the protracted Florida recount. Conscious that campaigning would have to continue lest either side be perceived as having given up the fight, both parties issued urgent online requests for extra donations. Greg Sedberry, web campaign manager for Bush, recorded over ten thousand online donations during the week after election day (Sedberry, 2001:9).

The 2000 primaries also demonstrated the Internet's capacity for mobilizing volunteers—a factor largely absent from the 1996 campaign. At one stage, Republican contender Steve Forbes claimed to have recruited thirty thousand volunteers through the web and email. So began a now-familiar technique. Campaign managers started to send out targeted emails to a few thousand people, usually requesting help. They would find that dozens of volunteers would arrive at their campaign headquarters. Those who were not keen to engage in physical campaigning were pointed in the direction of advice and resources for organizing, letter writing, and local fundraising. These kinds of effects, especially the impact of email, led to something of a scramble to gather email addresses and segment them by demographics and constituency (Bimber and Davis, 2003:41). In 2000, most websites contained email newsletter sign-up boxes, but the viral nature of email was also exploited, as supporters were encouraged to circulate messages to friends and family. Websites contained downloadable form letters, but Ralph Nader's website also contained broadcast-quality audio files that supporters were encouraged to distribute to local and Internet radio stations (Schneider and Foot, 2002:50). The Internet thus started to facilitate a large, cheap, volunteer distribution network.

By 2000, candidate websites had also evolved away from the brochureware model that had proved remarkably resilient during the 1996 and 1998 campaigns (Kamarck, 1999). A quarter of the primary and presidential candidate sites featured interactive elements such as discussion forums for citizen-to-citizen communication and occasional real-time (though heavily moderated) online chats with candidates. Al Gore's site was exemplary, providing an instant messaging feature that could be used among visitors. Some candidates asked supporters to email stories about their campaign experiences for inclusion on the website, and there were other attempts to create an online community ethos that had been distinctly lacking in previous elections. Techniques from e-commerce sites such as Amazon also started to leak into campaign sites. For instance, Al Gore's site allowed readers to select their interests from a range of twenty-two issue areas and voter groups. The site would then automatically generate a customized page and encourage the reader to dispatch a link to the page to ten other email addresses (Schneider and Foot, 2002:50).

Despite these innovative trends, other features of the 2000 campaign indicate the incursion of politics as usual, or rather, televised politics as usual (Novotny, 2002). First, surveys revealed that only around one in ten Americans used the Internet for information about the campaign. As table 7.1 shows, traditional media retained their dominance in this area.

Second, though online campaigning was highly issues focused and positive in 1996, by 2000, this had started to change: going negative became more prominent. As

Table 7.1. Media Sources of Campaign News in U.S. Elections, 2000

Media	Percentage
Television coverage	70
Newspapers	39
Radio	15
Internet	11
Magazines	4

Source: Extracted from Pew Internet and American Life Project, 2000.

Table 7.2. The Evolution of Negative Online Campaigning in U.S. Elections (in percentages)

Characteristic	1996	1998	2000	2002
Some negative campaigning	34	48	63	68
Negative campaigning on main page	16	38	55	65
Extensive negative campaigning	8	18	31	35

Source: Extracted from Klotz, 2004:77.

Note: Sample is all Democratic and Republican U.S. Senate candidates. "Extensive" negative campaigning = devoting over 1000 words to criticism of opponent.

table 7.2 shows, by the 2002 midterms, it had seemingly become an entrenched feature of the online campaign. Indeed, one empirical study (Wicks and Souley, 2003) revealed that the levels of negative attack messages on candidate websites during the 2000 campaign directly mirrored those on television.

Yet by far the most unusual development in 2000 appeared in the shape of Internet-enabled "vote trading" (Worley, 2001). Toward the end of the campaign it became clear that the result would be close. The presence of Ralph Nader as a third candidate caused the Democrats great concern, the fear being that Nader's supporters would unwittingly split the anti-Republican vote in key marginal states, gifting the victory to Bush. On the other hand, the realistic goal for Nader supporters was to secure 5 percent of the popular vote—a figure that would guarantee them public financial support in the 2004 campaign. Those familiar with British election campaigns, where close three-party contests occur quite frequently, instantly recognized the potential for tactical voting in this scenario. In the United Kingdom, many Labor voters in seats where their favored candidate stands little chance will vote Liberal Democrat to prevent the Conservative candidate winning the seat. In fact, earlier in the campaign, Nader had urged Green supporters to be "strategic" in their voting (Worley, 2001:35). But tactical voting in a constituency is one thing; coordinating that across an entire country (because Nader required 5 percent of the *national* popular vote) is incredibly difficult (see exhibit 7.2).

Of course, in the final analysis, vote trading did not affect the outcome of the election, nor did it succeed in securing the hallowed 5 percent of the popular vote for Nader. In the state where it really mattered—Florida—hanging chads aside, Gore lost by five hundred thirty-seven votes (according to the official final count), so Nader's twenty thousand votes dented Gore's chance of taking the state (Merolla, 2002). Yet these sites added a new element to U.S. elections, where tactical voting has historically been relatively weak. As we shall see, these innovations quickly spread to the United Kingdom. Yet overall, the 2000 campaign is best seen as a staging post. There were hints at what

EXHIBIT 7.2. VOTE TRADING IN THE 2000 U.S. ELECTION

The emergence of vote-trading websites was originally inspired by hacktivist James Baumgartner, a graduate student from upstate New York. Baumgartner established a satirical online auction site, voteauction.com, in mid-August 2000. The site would supposedly allow individuals to sell their votes. The scheme was to auction blocs of votes, and no money would change hands until absentee ballots had been checked following the election (Worley, 2001:33). Sale of votes is, of course, illegal. When the New York elections board contacted Baumgartner, despite the fact that the site was organized by hacktivist group ®™ark as a commentary on corporate dominance in U.S. politics, he closed the site down and sold it to an overseas company.

Yet the idea of using the Internet to mobilize a tactical voting campaign clearly sparked the imagination of many others. The first website to emerge was founded by Steve Yoder, a Washington, D.C., Nader supporter. Voteexchange.org appeared on October 1, 2000. Three weeks later, another site emerged. Cleverly named Nadertrader.org, it was founded by Jeff Cardille, an environmental studies graduate student at the University of Wisconsin–Madison. The site called on those living in marginal states to "contact a Gore-voting friend in a strongly Bush-leaning state and informally agree that your friend will vote for Nader, while you will vote for Al Gore" (quoted in Worley, 2001:37).

Yoder's and Cardille's sites were given free publicity on October 24, when an American University law professor, James Raskin, published an article in *Slate* outlining the theoretical elegance of the Nader trader scheme and how it could be automated using vote-matching software. This led to the rapid proliferation of similar sites, such as winwincampaign, voteswap2000, and tradevotes.com. Around sixteen sites emerged, which between them registered hits running into the several millions. In the period of just over two weeks through to polling day, Cardille's Nadertrader site received seven hundred fifty thousand hits (Worley, 2001:37).

Despite multiple legal challenges to these sites, it has been estimated that by election day, trading sites registered around sixteen thousand swapped votes. In Florida, the pivotal marginal, around fourteen hundred Floridian Nader supporters pledged to transfer their vote to Gore.

Source: Summarized from Worley, 2001.

was to come with interactivity, mobilization, and fund-raising in 2004, but traditional media strategies were dominant throughout.

EMULATION OR INNOVATION?: THE UNITED KINGDOM

The first U.K. general election to feature Internet campaigning occurred in 1997, when Tony Blair and the Labor Party achieved a landslide victory over John Major and the Conservatives. Yet if the 1996 U.S. election was something of a damp squib, its U.K.

counterpart was truly dire. Levels of Internet access were much lower in the United Kingdom. At the time, around 10–15 percent of the British public had access. Such low levels were a major factor in influencing campaign managers' views of the Internet's potential to reach out to voters. This did not, however, prevent them from establishing basic online presences. The major U.K. parties started to move online in 1994 and 1995, and by 1996, Labor, the Conservatives, and the Liberal Democrats had functional websites (Bowers-Brown, 2003:104). In the absence of external demand, it would appear that party leaders wished to appear dynamic, modern, and in touch with the younger segments of the electorate. They could also not afford to be offline if their competitors were online. Almost all fringe parties had sites in the 1997 campaign. Overall, however, British parties fumbled around, not really knowing what to make of the new medium, treating it a little like an electronic newspaper and succumbing to the familiar charms of the brochureware approach (Ward and Gibson, 2003:191). Research undertaken in 1998 concluded that British party websites "contain only limited opportunities for interactivity" (Gibson and Ward, 1998:31). Blair's slick, media-focused campaign made expert use of television (Scott and Street, 2000) and seems to have perfected old technologies like telephone canvassing but made little attempt to integrate the Internet, except perhaps as a means of more efficiently providing information like press releases to journalists or local party staff. Connecting with voters was way down the list of priorities—perfectly rational given the low numbers of Internet users. It has been estimated that the Labor Party site received just one thousand hits a week during the 1997 campaign (Gibson and Ward, 1998:32).

It was not until the 2001 general election that the Internet started to have an impact on British campaigning. By this time, access levels had reached around 40 percent, with around 35 percent connecting from home (U.K. Office of National Statistics, 2004b). These levels were still lower than those during the U.S. election of 2000, but as the numbers approached the 50 percent mark, party leaders started to invest significant resources in their online strategies. British parties' online campaigning in 2001 owed much to the U.S. experience of a few months earlier. In fact, U.K. campaign managers eagerly followed the presidential contest in an effort to "learn lessons" (Gibson et al., 2003:51). The web made it easier to continue a long-term process of information sharing and emulation that has gone on between the countries for many years.

National campaign websites in 2001 made much more obvious effort to connect with voters. Like their U.S. counterparts, they established email lists, asked site visitors to sign up for email newsletters, and targeted key sections of the electorate, whom it was assumed would be "turned on" by the Internet (Labor launched a widely criticized site aimed at young voters—RU UP 4 IT?). The three major parties distributed daily campaign emails. At one stage, the Labor Party's list contained around thirty-five thousand subscribers (Coleman and Hall, 2001:11).

Although discussion forums were less prevalent than the fairly ambitious approach adopted by Gore in the United States, some U.K. sites did ask citizens to send in their comments via email forms, and there were some online question-and-answer sessions with senior politicians. Multimedia made its way into the national web campaigns; both party leaders did webcasts and made audio and video files available for download. Both even had special sections of their site designed for access via mobile phone and handheld computers.

There were also reasonably sophisticated targeting features, such as a facility on the Labor site allowing a voter to type in a postal code to find out what "Labor's done in your area." The Labor site would create an automated response detailing some geographically specific policy achievements. The Conservatives' similar MyManifesto initiative returned different policy areas depending upon the demographic profile entered. These kinds of features, which sometimes require quite sophisticated back-office skills and databases, indicated that the major parties' online campaigns were starting to evolve.

Internal party communication using email and secure intranets also became more important during the 2001 campaign. Parties were much more likely to use the Net to distribute campaign materials to local constituency parties (Ward and Gibson, 2003:192). For instance, the Conservatives issued around one hundred documents per day via their party intranet. Most of these were press releases, advice on how to respond to journalists, and digital resources like leaflets (Coleman and Hall, 2001:11).

Still, a major difference between the United States and Britain was Britain's low number of candidate sites. From their comprehensive survey, Stephen Ward and Rachel Gibson (2003:195) found that only around a quarter of candidates had sites that genuinely tried to reach out to the voters during the campaign, with the third party, the Liberal Democrats, as the most active. That these figures are lower than the United States, where the focus is much more on candidates rather than the national parties, is not surprising. But the sheer size of the difference is significant. Part of the problem is U.K. electoral law, which forbids members of Parliament from using their Westminster Parliament sites or from even referring to themselves as members of Parliament during the final four weeks of the campaign (Ballinger and Coleman, cited in Ward and Gibson, 2003:195). There is some evidence that marginal constituencies increased the level of online campaigning, but there also appears to have been a general unwillingness on the part of candidates to use the Internet during the 2001 campaign because it was a medium used by less than 50 percent of the public. Many local candidate sites were standard brochureware or consisted of material copied from the national party sites.

On the positive side, email links now appeared on almost all local candidate sites, 14 percent included online opinion polls, and there were a handful of experiments with live chats, such as those held by Peter Lilley, Conservative member of Parliament for Hitchen. Asynchronous discussion features were, however, very few and far between. Ward and Gibson estimate that only around 8 percent of sites contained these features (Ward and Gibson, 2003:199). Indeed, the Conservative Party did not have discussion boards on *any* of its candidates' sites. Even where forums did exist, they were sparsely populated and very rarely featured posts by the candidate.

Yet, as with the U.S. 2000 election, there were interesting cases of online innovation. The do-it-yourself nature of many of the unofficial sites is noteworthy—a new and different kind of citizen-produced information ecosystem developed away from the major party sites. There is also some evidence that parties managed to recruit members and donations via their national websites, though data is impossible to acquire and campaign spending is in any case much more tightly controlled in the United Kingdom (parties may spend a maximum of £30,000 [$57,000] per parliamentary constituency in the twelve months prior to election day, effectively limiting the national campaign spending to just over £15 million [$29 million]. Perhaps most significantly, however, supporters who were not party members could more easily make donations via websites—a trend that intensified in the 2005 general election.

There were other notable innovations in 2001. In the United Kingdom, many more people own cell phones than have access the Internet. In 2001, cell phone ownership, at 67 percent, was much higher in the United Kingdom than the United States (U.K. Office of National Statistics, 2004a). Labor sent out four mass text messages to around one hundred thousand phone numbers in their database. In a remarkable example of narrowcasting aimed at younger voters, a batch of text messages promising that Labor would relax pub opening hours was dispatched at closing time on the last Friday night of the campaign. The party was hoping to encourage cell phone users to start a viral campaign. During the final week, Labor invited visitors to its website to choose from a list of different messages that the site would then send to a specified cell phone number (Coleman and Hall, 2001:13).

The phenomenon of online vote trading also made its way across the Atlantic (Buckley, 2001). British voters are used to tactical voting in three-party races, but the policy is officially frowned upon by the party leaderships. Tacticalvoter.net aimed to "make sure that 2001 is another win-win election for the center left" (Tacticalvoter.net/Internet archive, 2004). Other sites sprang up, but probably the most significant was votedorset.net, established by Labor-supporting singer Billy Bragg. Its self-described mission can be found in exhibit 7.3.

EXHIBIT 7.3. VOTE TRADING IN THE 2001 UK ELECTION: VOTEDORSET.NET

"votedorset.net—recycle your wasted vote

In 1997, two Conservative MPs were elected to represent the West Dorset and South Dorset constituencies, despite the fact that the majority voted against them. To avoid this happening again, Labor supporters in West Dorset could make a tactical vote for the Liberal Democrats, whilst in South Dorset, LibDem supporters could reciprocate by voting for the Labor candidate.

In order that votes cast might better reflect the democratic will of voters in our area, we are providing an online voter matching service which will pair Labor supporters in West Dorset with Liberal Democrat supporters in South Dorset to facilitate dialogue about tactical voting in the forthcoming general election.

To be matched, fill in the appropriate form below. You will receive the e-mail address of a match in your neighboring constituency. Your match will receive your e-mail address. Your details will not be compiled and stored on a database and will only be released to your designated match.

Tactical voting posters and bumper stickers for the West Dorset and South Dorset constituencies are available to download free from tacticalvoter.net

Votedorset.net is not affiliated to nor funded by any political party."

Source: Quoted from Votedorset.net/Internet archive, 2004.

As in the United States, vote-trading sites were the subject of formal complaints. For example, the member of Parliament for Dorset South complained (unsuccessfully) to the U.K. Information Commissioner about Votedorset. When that failed, the site was hacked by Conservative supporters and had to change its format to an online discussion forum. There is some evidence that vote trading might have worked but only in two constituencies. In Cheadle, the Conservatives lost by just 33 votes. Tacticalvoter.net had 47 recorded trading pledges in that constituency. Similarly, in Dorset South, the Conservatives again lost by 153 votes, which was less than the 185 pledges that trader sites had recorded (Coleman and Hall, 2001:18). Neither of these outcomes made any difference to the overall election result—another Labor landslide.

Did the Internet promote more substantive discussion of issues and undermine trends toward negative campaigning? We have no systematic data of the kind that exists for the United States, and negative campaigning is a less salient feature of British electioneering in any case. However, the impression given by the main party sites is that going negative was part of the overall approach. Labor's typical strategy during the campaign was to place banners linking to other stories at the bottom of the party home page. This provided a counterbalance to the positive stories more prominently displayed at the top of the page. Negative stories were, however, to the fore on the Conservatives' national site, which featured huge banner graphics and numerous bullet points detailing Labor's deficiencies. It has also been argued that the technical sophistication and visual appeal of the main British party sites closely rivaled those in the United States. This suggests an increasing emphasis on glitz and presentational professionalism in U.K. parties' web strategies (Gibson et al., 2003:66).

Overall, however, the Internet had little decisive impact on the 2001 election. Only 7 percent of respondents claimed to have used it to look for election information, compared with 74 percent for newspapers and 89 percent for television. It appears to have played only a marginal role in influencing how individuals decided to vote, as the following data from a MORI survey of July 2001 reveal (see table 7.3).

While it is not surprising to find television and newspapers ahead of the Internet in this poll, the margins are unexpectedly huge. It is particularly strange to find that billboard advertisements (party-funded television advertisements are forbidden in the United Kingdom) had more impact than online sources in the minds of voters. Still, it needs to be recalled that unlike the 2000 U.S. campaign, the 2001 U.K. election was not

Table 7.3. Media Influences on Voting Decision in the 2001 U.K. General Election (in percentages)

Media	Great Deal	Fair Amount	Not Very Much	None at All	Don't Know
Television coverage	13	36	20	30	1
Newspapers	8	30	22	39	1
Television election broadcast	6	16	20	57	1
Radio	5	17	18	58	3
Billboard advertisements	2	8	17	72	1
Canvass call	2	6	9	80	3
Internet	1	3	5	87	4

Source: MORI, 2001.

Note: The question was "Please tell me how much influence, if any, each of the following had on your decision about what you would do on the day of the General Election?"

a close race. It had been obvious for many months before the campaign that Labor would win. As ever, we should be cautious about concluding too much from opinion polls, but these data nevertheless help to put the Internet's fledgling status in U.K. election campaigns in context. Indeed, in the lead-up to the U.K. poll of May 2005, little appeared to have changed (see chapter 13).

THE FIRST REAL U.S. INTERNET ELECTION: THE 2003–2004 PRESIDENTIAL CAMPAIGN

Here it is, the end of 2003, and we're actually on top, ahead in the polls, in the process of raking in more than $50 million, $15.8 million in this fundraising quarter alone—a record—most of it from small donations of $100 or less. And whose fundraising record are we beating? Our own! From the quarter before. We have an army of almost 600,000 fired up supporters, not just a bunch of chicken-dinner donors, but activists, believers, people who have never been politically involved before and who are now living and breathing this campaign.

—JOE TRIPPI, *The Revolution Will Not Be Televised,* xi

The presidential campaign of 2003–2004 was the first real Internet election in the United States. A reader picking up this book in ten years time will probably chuckle at that sentence, but from the earliest stages of the extraordinary primary campaign of 2003 through to election day in November 2004, the Internet was often central to mainstream U.S. politics in a way that had been almost unimaginable after the events of 2000—and the equally lackluster midterms of 2002 (Cornfield et al., 2003). It is difficult not to get swept away on the tide of enthusiasm reflected in Joe Trippi's comment, quoted in the epigraph. (Trippi was campaign manager for Democratic Party candidate Howard Dean.) It will take some time for the hard analyses to emerge, but let us try to tease out the central themes of the primary and presidential campaigns and start to assess their significance.

Much like 2000, many of the Internet-driven surprises occurred during the primaries. Howard Dean started the campaign in last place. An obscure former governor of Vermont, in early 2003 he had virtually no campaign funds and only around four hundred known supporters. Yet within a year, going into the primary vote season, he was widely regarded as the front-runner. He had raised over $40 million—around eight times more than John Kerry—and had more than half a million supporters across the country. What role did the Internet play?

The 2004 campaign was the first in which the online and offline environments genuinely merged. The primary and presidential candidates effectively used the web to bring people together in real-world meetings. During the winter of 2003, Dean's staff negotiated with Scott Heiferman, the owner of an obscure website called Meetup.com. The purpose of Meetup was very simple. Rather than using the web to bring people together in virtual communities, the plan was to get them to meet in physical places, like bars, coffee shops, and restaurants. Individuals could register their names and locations on the site and establish local Meetup groups based on their interests. Heiferman, who had been inspired by Robert Putnam's "bowling alone" thesis (see chapter 5), saw Meetup as a way of using the Internet to create real-world social networks (Wolf, 2004).

The idea of using Meetup for political gatherings arose from discussions involving several political bloggers and Dean's campaign manager, Joe Trippi. In February 2003, no more than a few hundred attended five Meetups. But within a month, political blog sites had started to publicize the campaign. In March 2003, there were 79 Meetups in 14 cities across the United States (Dodson and Hammersley, 2003). By the end of the year, the Dean group on Meetup had 140,000 members, there were 800 meetings scheduled for the month of December (Wolf, 2004), and around 2,000 comments a day were being posted to the official Dean blog (Gillmor, 2004:97). This stood in stark contrast with John Kerry's Meetup supporters, which numbered only 18,900 going into the primary voting round (McCullagh, 2004). Dean's campaign team recognized early on that it could not possibly retain central control over the Meetups and largely devolved this to local organizers. Dean said of Meetup: "They built our organization for us before we had an organization" (Wolf, 2004).

Yet there was organization from above. The web campaign team came of age in 2004. Dean's staff included three full-time programmers and a network of over one hundred volunteer coders (McCullagh, 2004). Trippi also bought in a suite of software tools from Convio, an Austin, Texas, company that specializes in what it calls "online constituent relationship management"—essentially software tools aimed at nonprofit organizations. In early 2003, many nonprofits had started to notice sizeable increases in their online donations (Hardy, 2004). The Dean campaign wanted to capitalize on what it saw as a new willingness by people to donate money and keep informed about campaigns via email.

The campaign was also adept at linking with other political movements and positioning itself in existing online political networks. What some termed "peer-to-peer politics" actually had something of a precedent. In South Korea's presidential election of December 2002, winner Roh Moo-Hyun benefited greatly from a network of around 80,000 supporters who were very active in discussion forums and chat rooms (Elledge, 2003). The extent to which the Dean campaign borrowed some of Roh's techniques is uncertain, but there is a marked similarity between the two campaign styles. Online protest movement MoveOn (see also chapter 6) staged an unofficial Democratic online primary in June 2003, during which it also asked members to provide their email addresses to their favored candidate, make donations, and volunteer. Dean's team received a large proportion of his 140,000 voters' email addresses, alerting it to a reservoir of Internet support upon which they were able to capitalize later in the primary campaign (Hickey, 2004). Dean was also supported by a dense network of bloggers. Foremost among these was Markos Moulitsas Zúniga, whose blog the Daily Kos had been a magnet for left-of-center Democrats since 2002. By May 2004, the Daily Kos was attracting 150,000 visitors per day (Zetter, 2004). These online volunteers banded together to form the Dean Defense Force, whose role was to send quick-fire rebuttals to television and newspaper editors accused of misleading coverage.

The high numbers of volunteers working in the key primary states allowed the Dean campaign to develop relatively close links with voters. They organized thousands of small-scale neighborhood meetings. These mostly took place in individual homes and were inspired by similar tactics used for mobilization among farm workers in California during the 1970s. At the end of the meetings, which were described as the political equivalent of Tupperware parties, campaign staff would ask attendees if they

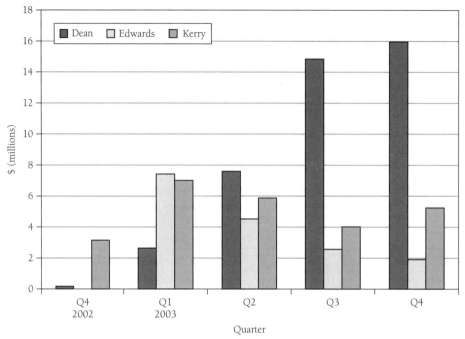

Figure 7.1. Democratic Party primary campaign contributions, 2002–2004. *Sources:* Analysis and adaptation of data from Anstead, 2005; U.S. Federal Election Commission, 2005.

would agree to host other house meetings. In Deerfield, New Hampshire, there had been six house meetings in the town by December 2003. The first one alone attracted 150 people, in a town of just 3,600 (Nagourney, 2003). The campaign also mobilized supporters from areas outside of the key early primary states, such as California, to send handwritten letters to voters in Iowa and New Hampshire (Dodson and Hammersley, 2003). An estimated 3,500 volunteers flooded into Iowa during the final week of the campaign (McCullagh, 2004).

But probably the most significant element of the primaries was the genuine emergence of the Internet as a fund-raising weapon. Figure 7.1 shows the official amounts filed with the FEC—the body that oversees campaign donations—between the final quarter of 2002 and the end of 2003. The figures reveal an astonishing turnaround by Dean in the middle of 2003 and a huge lead over the other main contenders, John Kerry and John Edwards.

But in many respects, these figures do not reveal some of the outstanding fund-raising moments of the campaign. For example, the day following Al Gore's public backing of Dean in early December 2003, the Dean website placed a button on its home page asking supporters to "thank Al" by donating money. In four days, that site feature alone raised half a million dollars (Dodson and Hammersley, 2003). Gathering accurate data in this area is very difficult, but there is evidence to suggest that Dean secured large numbers of small donations (McCullagh, 2004). It has been calculated that at one stage 280,000 individuals had contributed to a $40 million running total (a Democratic party primaries record), which makes the average contribution $143 (Singel, 2004).

Yet by the end of January 2004, Dean's campaign was over. He had finished third behind Kerry and Edwards in Iowa and a poor second to Kerry in New Hampshire. Just like John McCain in 2000, Dean failed to generate support where it counts—at the ballot. Trippi resigned from the campaign in early February 2004.

It is clear that the Internet did not make up for shifting contexts and traditional political gaffes of the kind that can very quickly derail a candidate. The capture of deposed Iraqi leader Saddam Hussein a few weeks before the caucus vote in Iowa went some way toward denting Dean's criticism of the Bush administration's handling of the war. Dean's now-famous "scream" of defiance—a reaction to defeat in Iowa—was widely and repeatedly televised and, ironically, encoded as an MPEG video file before being distributed to hundreds of thousands of people across the Internet in a matter of hours. His refusal to open to the public the sealed files from his period as governor of Vermont contradicted the transparency symbolized by his campaign techniques. Trippi complained about the lack of experience among the Dean supporters, a factor which hindered him when among those primary voters that did not necessarily share the Internet evangelism (Trippi, 2004:xii). A further problem—one that still hangs over all attempts to use the Internet for political campaigning—concerns its suitability for reaching out to undecided voters. The fervor of the Deaniacs turns out to have been based partly on self-reinforcement. It seems that a lot of talking and storytelling was going on at the Meetups but not all of it was focused on getting out the vote. Meetups made getting supporters to attend meetings easier, but this is not the same as voting and may have created a false sense of security among supporters (Shirky, 2004). The extent to which the Dean Internet campaign pulled in those who were not already supporters is debatable.

A survey of participants in twenty-four Dean Meetups across fifteen states during one night in October 2003 reveals mixed evidence (Williams and Gordon, 2003). The percentage of participants that indicated that they had voted in 2000 was very high—89 percent. The view that the Meetups were pulling in the politically apathetic is difficult to sustain on these figures. At the same time, however, some of the data do reveal an important mobilizing effect (tables 7.4 and 7.5).

Table 7.4. Volunteer Commitment Among Dean Meetup Participants, U.S. Primary Campaign, 2003

Will get much more involved following Meetup	31%
Get somewhat more involved	42%
No change	22%
Get less involved	<1%
Don't know	6%

Source: Williams and Gordon, 2003. n = 579. Figures rounded.

Table 7.5. Level of Support Among Dean Meetup Participants, U.S. Primary Campaign, 2003

Much stronger support following Meetup	22%
Somewhat stronger support	30%
No change	44%
Weaker support	<1%
Don't know	4%

Source: Williams and Gordon, 2003. n = 579. Figures rounded.

Clearly, the Dean Meetups did have an impact on participants' perceptions of their future levels of involvement and support, with around a third stating that they were much more likely to get involved in the campaign following a Meetup and just over a fifth reporting stronger levels of support.

Evidence from a more comprehensive two-stage survey of the Deaniacs conducted before and after the November poll by the Pew Center for the People and the Press reveals some interesting findings. The popular image of the Deaniacs as dominated by young people is not fully borne out. In fact, their age distribution does not differ substantially from that of Democrat supporters in the population as a whole. Dean supporters were also wealthier, more highly educated, and less ethnically diverse than Democrats as a whole. However, there was a significant "engagement effect" among younger citizens: 42 percent of the Dean activists stated that this was their first involvement in a presidential campaign, while 36 percent claimed that they were more actively engaged than in previous campaigns (Kohut, 2005:2).

Despite Dean's failure to secure the nomination, the new style of campaigning had an immediate impact on the rest of the campaign and a significant long-term impact on U.S. politics. For one, it sent shock waves through the Democratic Party establishment, and it also spurred the Republicans to place more emphasis on the web. By the primary voting season, the other main contenders, John Kerry and John Edwards, had borrowed many features from Trippi's Internet strategy. They had blogs and a presence on Meetup and started to bring in online donations—many from former Dean supporters. The Pew Center survey found that two-thirds of those who had volunteered for or donated money to the Dean campaign went on to do the same for Kerry (Kohut, 2005:2). Once Kerry secured the party nomination, through the spring and summer of 2004, the intensity of online campaigning increased, as did the funds.

The Bush campaign was also compelled to enhance its web profile. In the spring of 2004, it appointed Michael Turk, a former worker on the E-government Program in the Office of Management and Budget, as e-campaign manager. Turk introduced several innovations. Some were borrowed from the Democrats, but others signaled intriguing differences. The Bush campaign claimed it had six million email subscribers to its news alerts, compared with Kerry's one million (Witt, 2004). It also targeted specific groups of voters, particularly those that spend more time online, such as working mothers (Boutin, 2004). As a rival to Meetup, Turk encouraged a series of nationwide "parties for the president," Supporters were asked to "join Laura Bush" as well as each other in "partying." These were a success. By the time of the Democratic Convention in July, over seventeen thousand parties had been held (Bush-Cheney 2004).

Interactivity was less prominent in the Bush web campaign. There was no site discussion board, though they did hold regular chat sessions involving party elites. They had a blog, but it was not interactive and consisted largely of press releases. However, during the later stages of the campaign, Kerry's discussion groups were occasionally removed from his site and the blog was tightly edited. The Republicans had "Barbara and Jenna's Journal," featuring the Bush's daughters, who announced, "we have decided to start campaigning for our Dad." Kerry's site broke supporters up by zip code and asked them to write letters to their local media. However, the Bush campaign went further, using Microsoft mapping technology to identify newspapers and television stations close to their homes (Witt, 2004). Overall, Bush's site had more-diverse content and was more feature-rich. It had better online tools and back-office data integration, but it lacked some of the interactivity provided by the Kerry site.

Yet it was in the area of fund-raising where the Dean campaign's influence was most keenly felt. By the time Kerry accepted the nomination at the Democratic Convention on July 29, his personal campaign alone had raised around $185 million, compared with Bush's $226 million (Dwyer et al., 2004). Around $82 million of Kerry's funds—more than a third of his total—were raised online (Justice, 2004a; 2004b). Bush managed $9 million online. During just one day in late July 2004, Kerry raised $5.7 million via Internet donations (Justice, 2004b). The effects of this are significant. Online funds can be accessed much more quickly and are much cheaper to collect than traditional methods. Luxurious dinner events aimed at wealthy donors can cost 25 percent of the funds raised. Telephone or direct mail, which accounted for around $12 million less than the amount Kerry raised over the Net, can cost around 15 percent to collect. Only around 3 percent of Internet donations is lost in administrative costs (Dwyer et al., 2004). Between early spring and the Democratic Convention in late July, e-commerce company Amazon.com helped out with processing small online donations, its website proclaiming that it would "take the friction out of grassroots contributions to presidential candidates," and make it "as easy for people to contribute as it is to buy the latest Harry Potter book" (Amazon, 2004). The explosion of online fund-raising did much to reduce the traditional gap between Democratic and Republican candidates that has long been a feature of U.S. presidential elections.

Kerry, of course, failed to unseat Bush. So how significant was the Internet in 2004? At the time of writing (early 2005), it is too early to draw more than a few tentative conclusions. First and foremost, it needs to be recalled that Howard Dean did not even make it past the primaries. In terms of outcomes, therefore, his team's online innovations had no effect, and Dean could be seen as the political equivalent of a burned-out dotcom. But we need to look beyond this, to consider the effect on future assumptions about how to run an election campaign. These effects are not likely to be restricted to the United States but will radiate outward across many countries over the coming years. The significance of the Dean campaign lies not in the outcome but in the campaigning methods, the grassroots networks it created, and above all, the subversion of the professional campaign model and the rise of a new type of civic engagement. The most basic indication of this is that voter turnout increased to 61 percent. And these effects were not restricted to the Democrats' campaign but almost certainly helped the Republicans mobilize their own supporters as well.

Yet there is an ambiguity here about the role of the Internet vis-à-vis traditional media. Television and the press started to pay attention to Dean when the donations started to flood in. This in turn focused attention on the Meetups, which in turn increased their number. The fact that two powerful trade unions, the American Federation of State, County, and Municipal Employees and the Service Employees International Union, gave their backing also helped raise his profile. Dean also used a large quantity of the money raised online to pay for traditional television advertising, with which he flooded Iowa and New Hampshire during the final weeks of the campaign. Thus, Internet-only campaigns are clearly unsustainable. They may be useful for fund-raising but are less useful for targeting and mobilizing voters. Similar themes run through all of the U.S. and U.K. elections since the mid-1990s. This now seems to be an established trend.

ASSESSING THE INTERNET'S IMPACT ON PARTIES AND ELECTIONS: THE BIGGER PICTURE

The Internet now has an entrenched position in U.S. electoral politics and is steadily evolving in the United Kingdom. During the 1990s, much discussion tended to focus on the presence or absence of candidate websites. Such approaches now seem quaint. The issue is no longer whether parties campaign online but how and with what effects. Let us revisit the three main themes I outlined earlier in the chapter: party competition, power diffusion, and institutional adaptation.

Party Competition Effects

Is the Internet intensifying the process of party competition? In a very basic sense, party competition has been affected, but so far the effects have mainly been felt in the online environment itself. There is a huge discrepancy between the online party system and the real world of electoral contests. In her survey of 2000, Pippa Norris found that the United States, the bastion of two-party systems, had sixty-seven "digital" parties. Other countries with (basically) two-party systems and simple plurality electoral systems, such as Canada and the United Kingdom, also possessed large numbers of online parties—more than forty-five in those two cases (Norris, 2001:154). Green parties were more likely to have a well-developed online presence, and there was some limited evidence that fringe parties were taking advantage of the Net. Minor party websites can and often do outperform their major rivals. Stephen Ward and colleagues have argued that major parties dominate cyberspace during election campaigns, but fringe parties can catch up between elections. They also found that there is no intrinsic connection between party resources and the level of sophistication of a party site (Ward et al., 2003:24).

Much has been made of the impact of resource inequalities on parties' online competition. It has often been argued that wealthier candidates have been able to employ staff to create glitzier, more high-tech websites and that this gives them an advantage. Four points can be made about this assumption. First, evidence from usability studies indicates that effective sites often have pared-down designs. Flashy graphics do not make a site more effective (Nielsen, 1999). Second, we need to be wary of generalizations about the richness of detail offered by party websites. Density of information does not, by itself, produce openness and transparency. The British Labor Party's site contained "thousands upon thousands of apparently relevant performance indicators, every one of which the party can claim illustrates the success of its policies . . . everything appeared to be getting better everywhere" (Dorling et al., 2002:477). Third, the real inequalities in this area may only now be starting to appear, as compressed digital video becomes more widespread. The increasing convergence of media forms will open up a divide between rich and poor candidates. Only the wealthy will be able to afford the much higher cost technologies and staff required, not to make video available for download but to produce slick television advertisements and promotional films that must be created before they even come near a website. Finally and most obviously, we need to distinguish between the Internet itself as a forum for party competition and the larger party ecosystem. As we have seen, the Internet is still just one of several campaign media. Minor parties and marginal wings of the major parties are still at a disadvantage because the majority of the electorate still seek their political news from non-Internet sources. Even the Dean campaign used the vast bulk of the money it raised online to target traditional media, especially television.

Party competition effects are undoubtedly occurring due to the presence of a more pluralistic sphere of ideas during the campaign. Election campaigns have long featured new websites, like electorales.com (for Hispanics) in the United States or zindagee.co.uk (for Asians), that are aimed at specific segments of the public. Existing lifestyle sites such as Planetout.com produce specially tailored election content (Coleman, 2001:40; Coleman and Hall, 2001:18). Blogs were also crucial for the 2004 campaign. That citizens are increasingly drawn to such sites was a major finding of Michael Cornfield and colleagues' survey of the U.S. 2002 midterms (Cornfield et al., 2003:4). Perhaps it is not surprising that these have emerged, given that mainstream online news sites have often been as reluctant as politicians to create venues for citizen-to-citizen deliberation during campaigns (Singer and Gonzalez-Velez, 2003). Whether such sites are pulling in previously disengaged citizens, creating a greater plurality of voices in the political system, or influencing how parties appeal to voters is difficult to discern. We might theorize that parties will increasingly try to link to such sites as a means of targeting specific sets of voters, and there is much anecdotal evidence from the 2004 elections that this occurred. But what systematic research there is so far reveals that that linking is not treated as strategically as we might assume (Foot et al., 2003).

In the area of fund-raising, at the moment the United States and the United Kingdom appear to be diverging quite radically. In the United States, where we would expect to see candidates focus efforts on fund-raising, before the 2004 primaries and presidential campaigns, it had become almost commonplace to dismiss the importance of the Internet as a tool for raising money (Ward et al., 2003:20). Although John McCain's unsuccessful 2000 campaign generated some excitement, he only raised around $3.5 million online. After Kerry raised $82 million, these assumptions are less convincing. The Democrats' incredible success in this sphere closed the gap between them and the Republicans in the 2004 race. It is, however, extremely unlikely that these patterns will be replicated in many European or Scandinavian countries, where parties are often state funded (Ward et al., 2003:20). It will be interesting to see how parties in countries without state funding, such as the United Kingdom, react to the American experience. We can already see subtle but significant changes. Both Labor's and the Conservatives' websites now contain "Donate" buttons in their navigation bars, and these were made more prominent in the build-up to the 2005 general election (see also chapter 13).

Power Diffusion Effects

Is the Internet decreasing voter apathy, making connections between candidates and voters, pulling more people into the electoral process, and empowering grassroots activists? Before the 2004 U.S. campaign, the answer to this question would have been "no" or, at best, "maybe." However, following the momentous primary season, matters are more complex. Perhaps many commentators missed warning signs from farther afield, such as South Korea, where the Net played a major role in the 2002 presidential election. There is some evidence of demand for greater interactivity between representatives and citizens. A MORI poll in the United Kingdom during 2001 discovered that 39 percent of respondents wished to see their members of Parliament hold online meetings, 32 percent wished to contact them via email, and 20 percent desired "consultation forums" in which constituents could express their views to their representative (Coleman and Gøtze, 2001:21). Surveys for the Pew Center in the United States have consistently revealed that citizens wish to use the Net to interact with politicians (Cornfield et al., 2003; Pew Internet and American Life Project, 2000).

The jury is also still out over the extent to which the Internet contributed to the large increase in voter turnout in the U.S. elections of 2004. It is difficult to ignore the hypothesis that it made a difference, but there are of course many other substantive issues that affect turnout in any election. The bitter partisan divide was certainly a contributory factor, as was the context of the war in Iraq and the unexpected salience of moral issues like gay marriage and abortion, which deeply polarized (and mobilized) the electorate. An earlier study found that Internet use does not affect the propensity to vote (Bimber, 2001). (Interestingly, however, in a finding that foretold events of 2004, that research also found that Internet users were more likely than others to donate money to candidates.) In their analysis of responses by politically interested web users to questionnaires distributed during the 1996 and 2000 U.S. campaigns, Thomas Johnson and Barbara Kaye (2003) found that Internet use significantly enhances citizens' interest in politics, their perceptions of their political efficacy (how they rate their influence on politics), and their likelihood of voting. Web usage was far more closely associated with political interest than newspaper, radio, or television use. Indeed, newspaper use was found to *decrease* political involvement. Self-efficacy increased significantly between 1996 and 2000, as did the relationship between web use and self-reported voter turnout (Johnson and Kaye, 2003:25). Respondents stated that they spent an average of fourteen hours a week looking for political information during the 2000 campaign. Men were more likely than women to use the Internet for politics. However, trust in politicians did not increase with political Internet use.

Unfortunately, it is impossible to generalize from these results. They are drawn only from surveys of politically interested web users and therefore exhibit the common problem of circularity: by focusing on already interested individuals, it is impossible to tell whether the Internet is having independent effects or if it is merely making it easier for those already motivated to participate. Despite these weaknesses, they nevertheless illustrate some important trends. Johnson and Kaye argue that scholars are not likely to find large structural shifts occurring at the level of the political system; it is far more likely that effects will be felt at the individual level. They write: "The web politically empowers individuals and increases their feelings of self-efficacy, levels of political involvement, political interest, campaign interest, and likelihood of voting. Rather than it having a direct effect on the larger political system, its influence may be working indirectly by first strengthening the constituency" (2003:28). If this is the case, such effects are likely to become more politically significant as Internet use increases. The longer term (i.e., five to ten years) impact may be significant. Indeed, these findings have been bolstered by Caroline Tolbert and Ramona McNeal's (2003) analysis of the 2000 U.S. National Election Survey data, which found that Internet access increases voter turnout by as much as 12 percent, even after controlling for demographic variables.

Such findings may however be undermined by studies that go beyond self-reported perceptions about Internet use. For instance, based on analysis of two months of website usage logs obtained from audience measurement company Nielsen/Netratings, David Tewksbury (2003) has argued that Internet users are less likely to seek out political news stories than has previously been assumed. During his survey period—which coincided with the 2000 primary campaigns—more than half of the readers did not access any public affairs news online (defined as sections of sites that cover politics, international affairs, local news, U.S. national news, and opinion pieces) but much preferred sports, financial, and entertainment news. The advantage of Tewksbury's approach is that it relies not on self-reporting by citizens but on reasonably objective measurements of how people actually behave online.

What about online interaction between candidates and the public? As we saw above, citizen-to-candidate and citizen-to-citizen modes of communication have always been poor relations in parties' online strategies. This would appear to be a global trend. A 2001 analysis of over three hundred party websites around the world found that the majority were lacking in interactive features. Although 79 percent of sites contained email addresses of party officials, the vast majority provide basic information such as brief histories (78 percent), candidate biographies (60 percent), press releases (70 percent), or descriptions of the party organization. Only around a third (35 percent) contained invitations to join a discussion forum or email list (Norris, 2001:162). When the figures for EU-member countries are isolated, much more impressive levels of interactivity were found (Norris, P., 2003), perhaps suggesting the beginnings of a move away from the brochureware approach and toward greater efforts to engage citizens in policy discussion. The next few years of elections in major European liberal democracies may therefore exhibit some of the features of the 2004 U.S. campaign. Time will tell.

Despite the trend toward greater interaction on candidates' websites, this strategy is fraught with pitfalls. Some experimental studies have argued that introducing too much interactivity reduces positive impressions of a candidate. Interactive sites take longer to navigate and convey disorganization and a lack of clarity (Sundar et al., 2003). Some suggest that interactivity is discouraged because it means that candidates lose control by having to respond to agendas set by others (Davis, 1999:82). In the classic Downsian perspective, parties will seek to reduce the costs to the individual voter of acquiring information about their platforms (Downs, 1957). They will shy away from presenting the electorate with detailed policy information, instead favoring vague but easily identifiable brand images. Over the nearly half-century since the publication of Downs's book, political scientists have used this insight to explain party competition in liberal democracies. Once they accommodated themselves to the new demands of televised politics, party leaders have become increasingly adept at using the medium to brand themselves. But the Internet destabilizes this relatively controlled environment. Information abundance reduces the costs of information seeking for the citizen, increasing the demand for more detailed policy statements, thereby making it more difficult for party leaders to control their brand images.

While the types of interaction and the quality of deliberation vary greatly, it is possible to generalize about the overall effects of devices like blogs and discussion forums. A series of exchanges in a deliberative environment is likely to produce a more elaborate explanation and defense of policy than a simple presentational website. This creates its own problems for candidates seeking to aggregate votes, especially in majoritarian two-party systems such as the United States, where candidates often "fudge" divisive issues for fear of alienating a large section of the electorate. An example is the issue of legal abortion in the United States (Stromer-Galley, 2000a:53).

One way of dealing with this risk of losing control of what is an important part of news management is to simply exclude discussion forums from a campaign site (Stromer-Galley, 2000b). Indeed, George W. Bush's online team decided to do precisely this during the early stages of his 2004 reelection campaign. But how do we explain the proliferation of forums, candidate blogs, and real-time chats that has recently occurred? It is possible that a different strategy for dealing with the loss of control also presents itself in the form of distancing—or "passing the buck" to participants in online deliberative environments. For example, early in the 2004 presidential race, John Kerry's site contained a relatively lively (though still moderated) online forum. Subdivided along policy lines, the forum contained a section on women's issues, which was dominated by discussion on abortion.

Kerry's position in the 2004 campaign was pro-choice, though the precise details of his stance were rarely elaborated upon, a prime characteristic of candidate strategies on this issue in contemporary U.S. politics (Stromer-Galley, 2000a). At the same time, however, in the Women's Issues Discussion Forum, supporters and opponents of Kerry were busy arguing among themselves in ways that revealed myriad positions, including the technical requirements of the law. Kerry's online team was, consciously or unconsciously, defusing the issue by allowing a genuine debate to take place on the Kerry site but in such a way that did not jeopardize the official Kerry stance. Thus, what appears at first glance to be a high-risk strategy can actually work in a candidate's favor, because Kerry could give the impression of encouraging debate on his site while still retaining his overall position. The costs of "losing control" may therefore be exaggerated.

This interpretation might lend some credence to accounts that point to underlying shifts in the campaign environment. Steven Schneider and Kirsten Foot (2002) argue that elections now offer a distinct sphere of appealing online citizen actions (Schneider and Foot, 2002). The Internet provides citizens with opportunities to organize their offline engagement in campaigns through physical attendance at rallies and fund-raising events, but it also provides a potentially rich number of online political behaviors: email, discussion forums, and instant messaging. The key point in this perspective is that the distinction between being a citizen offline and being one online has started to dissolve. Television-era campaigning relied upon physical but highly staged meetings between candidates and supporters. The interaction that occurs in those environments is for the benefit of the cameras and the viewers at home. Internet-enabled interaction may not be face-to-face but it is in many ways more real and rewarding than the average campaign rally.

Yet there are still many reasons why increasing grassroots influence over party leaders will be difficult to achieve (Ware, 1987:150–72). First, problems of scale and complexity mean that activists cannot always be included in decision making. Second, party leaders have the power of patronage. Their ability to hire and fire puts them in a superior position in most circumstances. Third, party leaders can and do often go over the heads of party activists to gain votes from the wider electorate. They can do so without losing too many of the votes of their natural supporters. Finally, party leaders often have to make rapid strategic changes during an election campaign. These may involve marginalizing grassroots opinion. These factors constitute a formidable set of obstacles to the Internet's ability to diffuse power in this area.

Institutional Adaptation Effects

What evidence is there for the claim that institutional adaptation is the dominant trend?

First, it seems clear that the Dean campaign would have been impossible had it not been for a number of recent structural shifts in the professional political communication industry. The market for political information now exhibits greater diversity. The emergence and steady institutionalization of Internet campaign consultants has brought a new group of technically skilled professionals into the political sphere. These players are often one step ahead of the traditional media and sometimes even their political "masters" (Farrell et al., 2001). They are able to manipulate the vast quantities of data now collected by parties and build software systems that can exploit that data (Howard, 2003). The likelihood is that these U.S. trends will migrate because the global demand for such skills is likely to increase throughout the liberal democratic world—and beyond—over the coming years.

Those who lament the rise of the professional model of campaigning tend to assume that "dumbed-down" television coverage has displaced more erudite press coverage as the chief source of political information. This is said to reduce the educational benefit to citizens of election campaigns. But where the Internet ought to be located in the information ecosystem is a matter of debate. Are campaign websites more like newspapers or television? We saw previously recent trends toward the convergence of television and the Internet as television advertisements increasingly find their way online. This would suggest that the Net will become more like television in the future. On the other hand, most political websites also contain relatively rich sources of textual information about a candidate's policies. In fact, the waters are muddied still further by a school of thought which suggests that television is not the impoverished communication tool critics decry (Graber, 2001), and a recent empirical study suggests that educative effects do not substantially differ by medium (Norris and Sanders, 2003). Television, newspapers, and party websites all increase citizens' political knowledge during a campaign.

A long-standing claim about the Internet is that it allows parties to narrowcast messages to segments of the electorate, but we need to unpack what this means. Using market research techniques to segment a customer base in much the same way as private businesses seek to do before creating specific chunks of website content designed to tap into these specific market segments is a form of narrowcasting, but it is not a very politically efficient one. A major problem for candidates in political systems with strong local constituency traditions or localized voting systems, such as the United States and the United Kingdom, is that candidate websites are blunt instruments for reaching the people that matter: those who are eligible to vote in the candidate's constituency or a decisive swing state. Even devices like online opinion polls cannot easily be restricted to a group of constituents. Narrowcasting is much easier to achieve using email, where it is possible to create distribution lists of relevant voters, but even here public awareness of junk email can dilute its effects.

It could be that arguments about democracy are misplaced. As Colton Campbell and David Dulio argue, for some, online campaigning can be used to "engineer the most efficient victory with the least public involvement" (2003:11). Much of what parties now do online falls within the domain of what Steven Schier (2000) has termed "activation." Contrary to "mobilization," which Schier sees as a relic of the late nineteenth century when parties were active and U.S. voter turnout high, "activation" refers to the methods that "candidates employ to induce particular, finely targeted portions of the public to become active in elections, demonstrations and lobbying." While mobilization is "inclusive, seeking to arouse all possible voters to vote in response to a direct partisan message," activation is "exclusive by design" (Schier, 2000:7–8). Narrowcasting, where it can occur, is therefore perfectly compatible with an institutional adaptation perspective.

In many respects, candidates use their websites not just to reach out to voters, but to attract newspaper and television journalists looking for fresh content (Lipinski and Neddenriep, 2004). That they are able to do this much more rapidly and efficiently may speed up the campaign environment. Significant developments in this sphere include the trend toward using knowledge management systems to generate rapid rebuttals to claims by the opposition. These are now posted on party websites and emailed to journalists in a matter of minutes. But this kind of communication may not bring new actors into the process. It simply speeds up the existing interaction among political and media elites.

The impact of blogs on these dynamics is also ambiguous. On the one hand, it could be argued that they undermine the traditional gatekeeping role of large news organizations and democratize journalism, making it more about issues and less about metacommunication (Esser et al., 2001) regarding the game of politics. A good example of this came in September 2004, when CBS news anchor Dan Rather was forced to apologize for running a story about Bush's National Guard service based on evidence from forged documents. Republican bloggers exposed the story as a fake and hounded Rather and the CBS news team (Dorroh, 2004). Yet on the other hand, blogs could be interpreted as an extreme form of metacommunication. Bloggers tend to be political "junkies" obsessed with every nuance of the game. The most popular blogs tend to be written by political insiders or professional journalists. The Internet perhaps intensifies preexisting trends toward what Larry Sabato terms "feeding frenzy" and "attack" styles of journalism (Sabato, 1991). The multiplication of available news channels has massively increased competition in the sphere of news gathering. The news media increasingly feed off each other and tend to "pack" together for fear of missing a story. Competition also leads to a "salami-slicing" approach, as minor elements of a story get released over time to give the impression of newness. The chief characteristics of attack journalism include gossip and rumor as news, attempts to expose "unacceptable" previous personal conduct by politicians, ever-greater intrusions into politicians' private lives, and the elevation of journalists to the status of grand inquisitor. All of these behaviors exist in the "blogosphere."

Of course, one way of adapting to the Internet is to ignore it. Surveys of U.K. party websites have found that only around a quarter of local constituency organizations were online during the 2001 general election—up from around 10 percent in 1998 (Ward et al., 2003:30; Ward and Gibson, 2003:195). The local party website scene in the United Kingdom is patchy at best. This suggests reluctance on the part of central office to impose structure from above. But why bother? At present, the Internet is arguably less effective than television in reaching undecided voters (Klotz, 2004:64). Such voters are less likely to be motivated to seek out political information using a "lean forward" medium. As a "lean back" medium, television is likely to increase the rate of serendipitous encounters voters have with candidates, such as "incidentally" viewing a political advertisement in the middle of a movie, a talk show, or where advertisements are banned (the U.K.), political coverage sandwiched in between lighter content during an evening news program. This is hardly the stuff of participatory politics romanticized by e-democrats, but the reality is that winning elections, especially when the race is close, is all about raising candidate visibility among undecided voters in key marginal constituencies. Television is still widely regarded as the best means of doing this.

Conclusion

Was 2004 the end of the broadcast era of political communication, as some (Trippi, 2004) have claimed? In the United States, election campaigning has arguably moved into the Internet age. But what the "Internet age" actually means in the context of electoral politics is problematic. If the Internet continues to evolve along its present lines, it is quite likely that the broadband effect will make it much more like the televisual experience so lamented by the organizers of the Dean campaign. It will also be interesting to see if the energy and momentum established online in 2003–2004 will be maintained through the next round of U.S. elections and beyond. After all, the most high-profile recent election campaign in the United States, aside from the presidential contest, saw movie star Arnold Schwarzenegger win the California governorship in the autumn of 2003. The "Governator" campaign made little use of the Internet but preferred to use tried-and-true television spots (Gillmor, 2004:90).

The vast bulk of research in this area consists of surveys of websites, questionnaires of party staff, or individual-level opinion surveys. There is a dearth of literature that tries to link features of a political system, such as the electoral system, type of legislature, strength and number of parties, and political culture, with Internet-related developments, though this type of research is beginning to emerge (e.g., March, 2004; Zittel, 2004). It seems likely that such nuanced approaches will in future be able to account for the remarkable watershed of the 2004 U.S. campaigns while still explaining why countries with less candidate-centered political systems, like Britain, only selectively adopt Internet strategies from across the Atlantic.

Developments are also likely to evolve along with the diffusion of the Internet. Globally, the strongest predictor of party presence online is level of Internet use among the population (Norris, 2001:166). For parties in countries where Internet diffusion is low, there is little incentive to go online. This is likely to change, but the overall impact of the Internet will also continue to be shaped by the features of a country's political system.

Discussion Points

- Has the early potential of the Internet been realized in the area of election campaigning?
- Why has the United States witnessed greater levels of online campaigning than the United Kingdom?
- Assess the long-term significance of the Dean campaign of 2003–2004.
- Is online interaction with citizens too risky for politicians?
- Have parties successfully adapted to the Internet?
- Evaluate the claim that the Internet will combat voter apathy.

Further Reading

The literature on the electoral malaise is massive, but good places to begin are Dalton, 2000, Franklin, 2004, and Schier, 2000.

For enthusiastic predictions of the Internet's effects, Morris, 1999, is hard to beat.

On the United States, see Davis, 1999, for earlier campaigns and Bimber and Davis, 2003, for a thorough analysis of the 2000 campaign. For the United Kingdom and other European cases, Gibson et al., 2003, is a very useful collection, edited by some of the pioneers of the empirical mapping of this area. The essay by Coleman and Hall (2001) is a lively chronicle of the online election of 2001 in the United Kingdom. Cornfield et al., 2003, is a good overview of the state of play just prior to the 2004 campaign in the United States.

Wolf's 2004 article in *Wired* combines journalistic flair with some thoughtful theoretical reflections on the significance of the Dean campaign. For a wonderful insider account of the 2003–2004 primaries, see Trippi, 2004. Williams and Gordon (2003) gathered some preliminary survey data on the primary campaign, while the Pew Center (Kohut, 2005) has published a comprehensive profile of the Deaniacs.

Stromer-Galley, 2000b, is thoughtful on why candidates have traditionally avoided interaction via the web, though this appears a less secure theory after 2004. Schneider and Foot (2002) dissect the opportunities for meaningful action online during elections, while Johnson and Kaye (2003) demonstrate a link between Internet use and political engagement. Tewksbury (2003) has an innovative methodology but is more skeptical.

EXECUTIVES AND BUREAUCRACIES

E-government

CHAPTER OVERVIEW

In the last of our chapters on the Internet's impact upon political institutions, we examine e-government. First, I consider the origins of e-government in the new public management ideas of the 1990s. Second, I analyze some of its tensions and paradoxes by concentrating on four main themes: cost reduction, coordination, effectiveness, and democratization. The last of these is particularly important: is e-government about better government or better democracy? The chapter concludes by discussing some interpretations of how the Internet may be reconfiguring power relations, both within bureaucracies and between bureaucracies and other parts of political systems.

In 2003, the U.S. federal government spent more than $50 billion on information technology. (GEIA, 2002). Government websites consistently feature in the top ten most-visited online destinations. In July 2004, the government came sixth, behind Microsoft Network, Time Warner, Yahoo!, Google, and eBay, with 43 million unique visitors each spending an average of twenty-five minutes on a government site (Nielsen/Netratings, 2004). But why did government go online in the first place? In whose interests is it to increase government's online presence, and whose interests might it jeopardize? What kind of ideological claims are made about the potential of electronic service delivery and how have administrative structures been transformed by these developments, if at all? Are they leading to new forms of democracy and greater individual freedom and empowerment within the public sector or are they having a detrimental (or even negligible) impact? This chapter explores the issues surrounding the most lauded and high-profile political uses of Internet technology to date: e-government.

THE ORIGINS OF E-GOVERNMENT:
POLICY DISCOURSE IN TWO PIONEER STATES

In Western states, the presence of government departments and agencies on the web is now taken for granted. Matters are different in the developing countries, though there is some evidence of catch-up. The core ideas and techniques associated with putting government online emerged in the most technologically advanced countries, especially those whose populations were pioneers in using the Internet in the 1990s. However, there is no straightforward correlation between the levels of e-government and the existence of established liberal democratic traditions of information transparency and freedom of speech. E-government has brought up significant problems of access, privacy, and surveillance, especially in the United Kingdom and the United States. But authoritarian regimes, such as Singapore and even China, for instance, have also been quick to develop their own distinctive e-government programs.

Despite the fact that the rest of the world is catching up, the United States, Canada, Australia, and the United Kingdom have blazed the trail by establishing a basic informational form of web presence in the mid-1990s and by developing more ambitious and integrated programs later on—what we now recognize as e-government (see exhibit 8.1). The European Union (EU), as a supranational body with an increasing amount of influence on the administrative machinery of its member states, has also been an important actor in defining the scope and purpose of public sector use of the Internet since the 1990s, principally under the auspices of the European Commission's Information Society Project Office.

Early government responses to the Internet often went little further than placing information on the web in a simple electronic version of traditional paper-based means of dissemination. The arrival of e-government, which signaled the acceptance of Internet connectivity as a tool that could be used to improve efficiency, cut costs, and change the way governments have traditionally interacted with citizens, constitutes a dramatic shift in the dominant ethos of public policy and administration. Whether putting public services online marks a transition from a primarily managerial model of governance toward a consultative and even participatory approach is less certain, but, even taken on its own terms, the nature of the public sector has undoubtedly changed in many countries in recent years and seems set to evolve along technologically influenced lines for some time to come.

But how and why did e-government emerge? A useful way of understanding the development of public policy and administrative reforms, at least in those political systems that exhibit genuine policy debates, is to unravel and analyze the ideas that proved dominant at key stages of the policy process. When it comes to an area such as administrative technologies, this process is even more firmly rooted due to the fact that most government departments and agencies now lack the resources (both technical and financial) to build systems and hardware from scratch. They have long outsourced software development to private firms and now buy the vast bulk of their hardware from private suppliers, often in off-the-shelf forms. This means that in practice, governments have spent much of their energy on defining the uses to which new technology is put, because administrative elites realize that once the "raw materials" required for electronic service delivery

EXHIBIT 8.1. DEFINING E-GOVERNMENT

Creating a brief, workable definition of e-government seems almost impossible, not only because it is in a constant state of evolution but also because its meaning differs according to one's normative perspective. There are also different national interpretations of the term, though it undoubtedly crosses borders with remarkable ease, making it one of the fastest spreading ideas for public sector change in history (Jaeger, 2003:324). The influential Gartner Group consultancy describes e-government as "the continuous optimization of service delivery, constituency participation, and governance by transforming internal and external relationships through technology, the Internet, and new media." Mark Forman, former associate director for information technology and e-government at the U.S. Office of Management and Budget (OMB), defines it as "the use of Internet technology and protocols to transform agency effectiveness, efficiency, and service quality" (both quoted in Seifert, 2003:2).

Despite the difficulties of aiming at a moving target, a usefully clear exposition has been provided by Paul Jaeger:

"From a technical standpoint, e-government initiatives usually involve several types of electronic and information systems, including database, networking, discussion support, multimedia, automation, tracking and tracing, and personal identification technologies. Depending on the nation, e-government can span local governments, state or provincial governments, and the national government, with the levels having separate or interconnected e-government sites. . . .

The goals for e-government websites are as diverse as the governments that are creating them. E-government, if implemented properly, can improve current government services, increase accountability, result in more accurate and efficient delivery of services, reduce administrative costs and time spent on repetitive tasks for government employees, facilitate greater transparency in the administration of government, and allow greater access to services due to the around the clock availability of the Internet. E-government also allows governments to offer enhanced services by creating new ways to interact with the government, such as email, online meetings and forums for voicing opinion, online transactions, and online voting. E-government is even used in some locations as a method to reduce corruption in government functions.

E-government activities can be examined in terms of the interactions between sectors of government, businesses, and citizens. Government-to-government (G2G) initiatives facilitate increased efficiency and communication between parts of a government. G2G initiatives can improve transaction speed and consistency, while reducing the time employees must spend on tasks. G2G interactions can also allow for much more proficient sharing of vital information between parts of the government. Government-to-business (G2B) initiatives, involving the sale of government goods and the procurement of goods and services for the government, have benefits for both businesses and governments. For businesses, G2B interactions can result in increased awareness of opportunities to work with the government and in cost savings and increased efficiency in performing transactions. For governments, G2B interactions offer benefits in reducing costs and increasing efficiency in procurement processes. . . .

Though e-government has clear benefits for businesses and governments themselves, citizens may actually receive the widest array of benefits from e-government. Government-to-citizen (G2C) initiatives can facilitate involvement and interaction with the government. For the citizen, e-government can offer a huge range of information and services, including information for research, government forms and services, public policy information, employment and business opportunities, voting information, tax filing, license registration or renewal, payment of fines, and submission of comments to government officials. By giving geographically isolated citizens a greater chance to connect with the government and other citizens, e-government offers a new way to facilitate citizen participation in the political process."

Sources: Quoted from Jaeger, 2003:323–24. See also Seifert, 2003.

have been procured, they must work with what they have. Getting the ideas right in the first place—framing the purpose of technological deployment—becomes crucial. Guidelines and priorities become embedded within contractual agreements between governments as purchasers and companies as providers of the technological means and soon become distributed within the broader political system and public debate. With these issues in mind, let us briefly consider the policy origins of e-government in two pioneer states: the United States and the United Kingdom (Chadwick and May, 2003).

The United States

The U.S. federal government has been in the vanguard of e-government policy developments since the early 1990s. It was one of the first countries to explicitly link new technologies with a more general program of administrative reform under the auspices of its National Performance Review, which began in 1993 and lasted through to the late 1990s. The Democratic administration of the 1990s, led by Bill Clinton and Al Gore, made many appeals to the transformative power of information technology, and in the summer of 2000, this culminated in the federal government's launch of Firstgov—the first government portal of its kind. Initially little more than a Yahoo!-style directory rather than the more ambitious government gateway U.S. citizens were promised, it was further developed by the Bush administration between 2001 and 2004.

The application of information and communication technology was at the heart of the National Performance Review (U.S. National Performance Review, 1993b). This was coordinated by Al Gore's Office of the Vice President, and Gore in particular was quick to emphasize how the Internet could be harnessed to broader objectives of cost cutting and increases in productivity that were at the center of the debate on re-engineering government that emerged among public administration scholars in the early 1990s (Osborne and Gaebler, 1992). Importantly, the e-government agenda in the United States, in common with the other lead countries, was heavily dominated by the executive branch. The Executive Office of the President, chiefly through the Office of Management and Budget (OMB) and the General Services Administration (GSA), took the lead.

The aims of the main National Performance Review report of 1993 were explicit:

> Our goal is to make the entire federal government both less expensive and more efficient, and to change the culture of our national bureaucracy away from complacency and entitlement toward initiative and empowerment. We intend to redesign, to reinvent, to reinvigorate the entire national government. . . . We need a federal government that treats its taxpayers as if they were customers and treats taxpayer dollars with the respect for the sweat and sacrifice that earned them. (U.S. National Performance Review, 1993a: introduction)

In the 1997 update on the National Performance Review, *AccessAmerica* (U.S. National Partnership for Reinventing Government, 1997), the Clinton administration was unambiguous in its view that the Internet could be used to re-engineer the relationship between government and citizens.

A major issue at the time was how existing government technologies might fit in with the National Performance Review agenda. The Review argued that current systems could be modernized in ways that would allow their inherent properties to be used more intensively. Increased automation was the order of the day (U.S. National Performance Review, 1993a: preface). E-government was thus perceived as a continuation of a computerization of government agenda that began back in the 1960s. But the emulation of new private sector management practices was also at the forefront of the program. Government in the "Information Age," as the report termed it, was to adapt in the way that large, vertically organized corporate bureaucracies had been forced to adapt. The creation of entrepreneurial organizations was dependent upon new working practices. The Internet would assist in the creation of customer-focused public bureaucracies (see exhibit 8.2).

In a theme that was to find similar expression in demands for "joined-up government" in Britain, Canada, and many other countries, the National Performance Review established the idea of "virtual agencies" as a means of coordinating efforts across what was seen as a large and rambling administrative machine. In the future, it was suggested, customers would not need to have knowledge of the structure of government but would instead be able to transact on the basis of a number of clearly identifiable service themes (U.S. National Performance Review, 1993b: section IT01). These would supposedly be based on intuitively expressed customer demand rather than the producer-driven needs of a department or agency. Customers would transact with several different agencies without realizing it, while those agencies involved would find it easier to share information and make decisions.

The U.S. e-government program was heavily oriented around introducing new ways for customers to transact with government. The benefits system, which includes the administration of food stamps, unemployment benefit, Medicare, Medicaid, child support, and related Social Security benefits, has shifted to a system of electronic transfer. Customer inquiries are increasingly automated or handled more efficiently through the use of call centers and one-stop shops. Millions of individuals now file their tax returns online. Electronic kiosks have been placed in benefits offices and other public buildings, allowing access to government information sites and the submission of electronic forms. Email use has been radically expanded across the federal government;

EXHIBIT 8.2. CUSTOMERS OR CITIZENS?: E-GOVERNMENT AND THE NEW PUBLIC MANAGEMENT

E-government was very much a product of a public sector reform agenda that exploded in the early 1990s—the so-called new public management. For instance, the U.S. National Performance Review stated:

> "By 'customer' we do not mean 'citizen.' A citizen can participate in democratic decision-making; a customer receives benefits from a specific service. All Americans are citizens. Most are also customers. . . . In a democracy, citizens and customers both matter. But when they vote, citizens seldom have much chance to influence the behavior of public institutions that directly affect their lives: schools, hospitals, farm service agencies, social security offices. It is a sad irony: citizens own their government, but private businesses they do not own work much harder to cater to their needs." (U.S. National Performance Review, 1993a: section 5).

This is a classic piece of new public management ideology. Individuals were to have influence over government services as customers but not as citizens. It could have been possible to discuss mechanisms beyond the customer service approach, which might have involved citizens *as citizens* using technology to influence policy and service delivery, but this was not considered necessary or appropriate.

now even the most senior officials publicize their email addresses. A national network for law enforcement and public safety has been established to enable communication within the criminal justice system and emergency services, a development which made the transition to the new homeland security information policy in the wake of 9/11 much easier to achieve by President Bush.

The ways in which e-government was originally framed went on to have a decisive influence, but progress on targets was slower than expected. As a consequence, President Clinton issued an executive memorandum in December 1999, calling upon agency heads to accelerate e-government. Of particular concern was the failure to introduce coordinating mechanisms that would make it easier for customers to access services irrespective of the originating agency—a principle which found expression in the FirstGov portal, launched in September 2000 (U.S. National Partnership for Reinventing Government, 2000). FirstGov is at once significant yet unremarkable. The portal concept, which was seen as the holy grail for the private Internet sector in the mid-1990s, is now commonplace. There is, therefore, little novelty in applying this concept to government websites. However, FirstGov was the first easily navigable interface to government and public services, and it had a distinct emphasis on the individual consumer. Each of the ways in which it was possible to transact with government was laid out in celebratory list fashion, with four organizing sections: Shop Online, Apply, File, Register or Print Forms Online, Check Performance Online, and Let the Government Know (FirstGov, 2000). FirstGov is important for what it represents in the broadest sense—the ubiquity of the Internet and its associated protocols, file formats, and "look and feel" as a medium.

The United Kingdom

During the 1990s, the U.S. e-government program was a good five years ahead of Britain's, but the National Performance Review's framing of it in terms of its contribution to service delivery had a profound impact. In common with the approach adopted in the United States, Britain's development of e-government was spearheaded by the Cabinet Office, specifically from the Central Information Technology Unit (CITU), which was folded into the Office of the E-envoy in 1999 (now the Cabinet Office E-government Unit).

Tony Blair's Labor government, elected in May 1997, claimed that its e-government reforms were developing a new approach to state-citizen interaction. In fact, they owed a great deal to the previous Conservative government's green paper of November 1996—*Government Direct*. This set out three basic aims: "to provide better and more efficient services to business and to citizens; improve the efficiency and openness of government administration, and secure substantial cost savings for the taxpayer" (U.K. CITU, 1996: par. 4.1). As with the U.S. National Performance Review, the new form of state-citizen interaction was to be based on "providing information, collecting taxes, granting licenses, administering regulations, paying grants and benefits, collecting and analyzing statistics, and procuring goods and services" (U.K. CITU, 1996: par. 1.4). The Conservatives' green paper also similarly conflated the terms "citizen" and "customer" (U.K. CITU, 1996: par. 5.2). Several other dominant themes of the new public management were in evidence early in the British government's plans, notably the need for "efficiency through rationalization" (cost cutting), but these did however exist in tension with some optimistic statements about the potential for the Internet and intranets to provide extra connections, coherence, and coordination across government. There was little consideration of how the Net might provide for greater citizen influence on policy making.

When the Labor Party came to power, most of these earlier plans were incorporated into the broader *Modernizing Government* white paper of early 1999. There were important shifts in emphasis, as themes such as "joined-up government" became central to the new vision (though even that can be found in the older proposals). But the dominant theme of individual consumers and business benefiting from improved service delivery was retained. Again, the principal framework of the white paper is established by an emphasis on "modernization," "efficiency," and "quality" (U.K. Cabinet Office, 1999: sec. 4). The key aim here was for government to emulate those private-sector practices which involve innovative use of technologies in "knowledge management." Government was to become a "learning organization" (U.K. Cabinet Office, 1999: sec. 5). Internet and internal networking technologies, such as the new Government Secure Intranet, it was argued, have the potential to integrate a diverse range of information sources and improve the "business of government" by bringing departments together in "on-line meetings and discussion groups" (U.K. CITU, 2000:21).

The *Modernizing Government* white paper was a relatively ambitious agenda for public-sector reform. The perception that disaggregating and decentralizing the British

EXHIBIT 8.3. THE U.K. APPROACH: *MODERNIZING GOVERNMENT*

E-government would:

- make it easier for business and individuals to deal with government;

- enable government to offer services and information through new media like the Internet or interactive television;

- improve communications between different parts of government so that people do not have to be asked repeatedly for the same information by different service providers;

- give staff at call centers and other offices better access to information so that they can deal with members of the public more efficiently and helpfully;

- make it much easier for different parts of government to work in partnership: central government with local authorities or the voluntary sector, or government with third-party delivery channels such as the post office or private sector companies;

- help government to become a learning organization by improving access to and organization of information.

Source: Adapted from U.K. Cabinet Office, 1999: sec. 5.

civil service during the Thatcher era of the 1980s had led to fragmentation hung heavily over the document. E-government was seen as one way to reintegrate the administrative machine, but in ways that were dynamic and subtle enough to accommodate the principles of the new public management and, at the rhetorical level at least, avoided "going back" to the old "public service" values that had characterized the British state during the last period when Labor had been in office in the 1970s. The British government provided one of the clearest visions of what e-government might look like in the section entitled "Information Age Government" (see exhibit 8.3).

But with the possible and partial exception of the last category of benefits, these all stand squarely within the accepted parameters of public-sector managerialism. Businesses and citizens as consumers would come to transact with government in a number of ways: they would book driving tests, look for employment, or submit tax returns (U.K. Cabinet Office 1999: sec. 5). But citizens as political participants would be able to do very little. They hardly appeared in the white paper. Nowhere did attempts to consult directly with the public through electronic networks appear as a path of possible development. By the time of the British *E-government* document of 2000—arguably the most coherent statement produced by any government to date—it proved relatively straightforward to frame the reforms in terms of "better services for citizens and businesses and more effective use of the Government's information resources" along with "the application of e-business methods throughout the public sector" (U.K. CITU, 2000:1). This reveals one of the major tensions within e-government: is it about better government or better democracy?

THE PROMISES AND PARADOXES OF E-GOVERNMENT

While e-government, with its emphasis on the interface between government and external networks, is genuinely new, the basic use of computers inside public sector organizations has a long history. Scholars have always been fascinated by the effects of computer systems on organizational power structures, and some of the pioneering research in this area dates from the 1970s and early 1980s, when writers took stock of the computerization of the public sector that began in earnest during the 1950s (Danziger et al., 1982; Laudon, 1974; Simon, 1965, 1973; see also Bellamy and Taylor, 1998). The 1970s and 1980s were in many respects the golden age of organizational computing, when the promises of efficiency gains and more rational, scientific forms of policy making were heralded as the positive benefits of introducing routine task automation and what were, at the time, sophisticated information management techniques. But this period was also characterized by an increasingly volatile public debate about the risks associated with computerization in dangerous environments like defense and nuclear power as well as the more subtle effects of computers in the workplace, like de-skilling, worker alienation, and management surveillance.

At the level of government operations, among the systems that proved popular by the 1970s were databases of public employees, welfare recipients, and criminals; financial management systems that allowed for oversight across departments and agencies; fiscal impact budgeting systems, which allowed local planners to model different planning scenarios according to hypothetical levels of taxation and public expenditure; and a whole range of computerized inventories of government property and possessions. Automation and rapid retrieval were the order of the day, especially at the level of local governments. Aside from the technical virtues of such systems, some political scientists, such as Anthony Downs, considered the possibility that computers would cause power shifts in both corporations and government bureaucracies. Downs argued that the introduction of information technology would cause "redistribution of the benefits of decision-making" (Downs, 1967, quoted in Danziger et al., 1982:171). In other words, computerization produces new winners and losers, and almost all of the thorny issues that were first raised by social scientists during the golden age of organizational computing remain with us in the twenty-first-century era of Internet-enabled e-government.

Our brief examination of the policy origins and main features of e-government in our two case study countries—the United States and the United Kingdom—reveals that it has been fairly narrowly defined as a program of managerial administrative reform rather than a means of revitalizing democracy and citizenship. Enhancing deliberation, participation, and citizen influence on policy seems to have been little more than an afterthought to improving efficiency and cutting costs inside government departments and agencies (Chadwick and May, 2003; Musso et al., 2000). In part, this reflects the origins of e-government itself: many of the ideas have been developed away from the scholarly domain. An enormous gray literature of white papers, consultation documents, consultancy reports, corporate documents, and league tables has emerged, many of which are of limited scholarly value (e.g., Accenture 2001; Bertelsmann Foundation, 2002; Deloitte Consulting, 2000; EDS and Neaman Bond Associates, 2002; United Nations Department of Economic and Social Affairs, 2003; but for good exceptions see

U.K. National Audit Office, 1999, 2002). Political scientists have been rather slow to engage with the emerging agenda. The problem with the league tables approach adopted in so much of the gray literature is that it often pays little attention to the underlying significance of e-government for political power in the public sector.

In fact, the use of new communication technologies to transform the public sector rests upon a number of key claims, all of which have implications for power relations, both within executive branches and between executives and other components of political systems. E-government visionaries differ in their emphases, but it is possible to discern a set of reform goals that are shared across the board (Bacon et al., 2002; Byrne, 1997; Curtin et al., 2004; Holmes, 2001; Lawson, 1998; Silcock, 2001). These outcomes might appear to be compatible at first glance, but on closer inspection certain contradictory pressures become evident. Let us now scrutinize the main claims made for e-government: cost reduction, coordination, effectiveness, and, most importantly, democratization.

Cost Reduction

Reducing administrative costs has been central to the e-government agenda since the early statements of the 1990s, but this theme was given even greater prominence following the downturn in the commercial technology sector of the early 2000s, especially in the United States and the United Kingdom, where "value for money" reemerged as a powerful criterion for assessing the success of new government IT projects. It has been argued that the cost savings from e-government are "potentially enormous" (Fountain, 2001:4). It is claimed that most of the savings—up to 50 percent in some cases—will arise from a shift from paper-based to web-based payments systems and from paper-based to web-based document management. Potential savings may also be made by replacing traditional paper-based tendering procedures with web-based e-procurement-governments will seek to emulate the successes of private sector organizations that have reportedly reduced costs and improved competition down the supply chain by moving purchasing online. In the United States, the federal government spent $10 billion in online purchases in 2000 (Holmes, 2001:37). In Britain, the Office of Government Commerce has been at the forefront of e-procurement, effecting cost savings through, for example, its online stationery system (Mathieson, 2003). When we add less easily quantifiable savings in time, travel, and human effort to such figures (Fountain with Osorio-Urzua, 2001), it becomes apparent that e-government has the potential to outstrip traditional cost-cutting programs of public sector reform, such as administrative devolution and partnerships involving public and private sector actors. The cost-reduction benefits of e-government have also been seized upon by some developing countries, such as India, Mexico, and South Africa, as a means to tackle public sector corruption (Polikanov and Abramova, 2003:47). Even authoritarian states such as China have launched e-government programs to reduce the huge costs of the public sector, which in China consumes 20 percent of GDP annually on administrative goods (Zhang, 2002:166).

Perhaps the most important cost-reduction effect of e-government is the perceived reduction in staff levels that will result following increased automation and disintermediation through the introduction of technologies such as "zero-touch" administrative processing. Zero-touch has been used to great effect in companies like Amazon.com, and in the United Kingdom, the National Audit Office has consistently argued that sophisticated automation ought to be at the forefront of the e-government cost-cutting drive (U.K. National Audit Office, 1999).

The problems with e-government as a cost-cutting mechanism are, however, manifold. For one, there is immense pressure on departments and agencies to increase rather than reduce investment in their web presence in order to improve their e-government services (U.K. National Audit Office, 1999:4). Second, there are surprisingly few rigorous analyses in this area, and gathering accurate and focused data on cost savings in government is notoriously difficult. It is doubly difficult demonstrating savings produced by the introduction of new technology. Those who have explored the issue have tended to conclude that costs have risen or have broadly remained static. Paul Henman's analysis of social security computerization found that the number of clients each agency staff member dealt with remained the same after computerization, and the percentage of an agency's total costs taken up by administrative costs actually increased over time (Henman, 1996; see also Margetts, 1991). This is primarily due to the significant initial costs of new hardware, software, and systems, not to mention service contracts. While this might be seen by some as a desirable effect of the reforms for domestic economies—especially at a time when private sector buying of technologies is in the doldrums—headline-grabbing savings need to be balanced against the medium- and long-term costs. But the difficulties do not end there. Problems with high-bandwidth services can soon escalate as agencies become victims of their own success. In 2002, the British government's attempt to put its historical census data online proved a spectacular failure, as the servers were flooded with millions of simultaneous requests. In November 2004, probably the worst information technology disaster in British history occurred when one hundred thousand desktop computers in the Department for Work and Pensions were automatically upgraded with the wrong software patch, causing a huge backlog in benefit payments (Maguire, 2004). This came on top of a weighty legacy of high-profile government information technology failures in the United Kingdom, where recent problems include glitches in the Passport Agency (Silcock, 2001:97) and the Child Support Agency.

A fundamental issue here is whether private sector experiences with e-commerce are really analogous with those in the world of government and the public services. The craze for corporate restructuring, which took off in the 1980s and culminated in the dotcom boom, was in part fueled by expectations of efficiency gains brought about by strategic use of new communication technologies. It presented a relatively clear relationship between technological use and beneficial outcomes: greater efficiency meant higher profit margins. Although efficiencies became a by-word for job losses, from the perspective of private sector managers, increased profits, rising share prices, and the expansion of the company provide rewards to those fortunate enough to be left with employment. But in the public sector the gains are less clear. Civil servants risk becoming victims of their own success, as efficiency gains often mean job losses, pay freezes, reductions in promotion opportunities, de-skilling, and threats to agency autonomy through mergers. For example, in 2002 it was estimated by the British House of Commons' Public Accounts Committee that the Inland Revenue could cut thirteen hundred jobs if half of its tax returns were submitted online (U.K. Public Accounts Committee, 2002:14). Such conclusions inspired the U.K. Treasury to embark upon a massive program of civil service job cutting during 2004 and 2005, with over one hundred thousand civil servants likely to be shed after several agency mergers (Poole, 2004). Much of this has been spurred by faith in e-government.

Moreover, in the developing world, the parameters of debate are often different. As Richard Heeks (2002:100) argues, in many African countries, where public sector wages are less than a tenth of those in the West and where technology costs are two to three times higher, automation means replacing cheap civil servants with costly hardware. Nor is there an automatic relationship between the introduction of e-government and the reduction of corruption. For example, in their research on sub-Saharan Africa, Kimberly Barata and Piers Cain (2001:256) reveal that electronic financial management systems have done little to improve accountability. Computer programmers are a relatively rare commodity, possessing specialist skills that make them the target of bribes. Electronic transfer systems also make money laundering more difficult to detect.

In the same vein, technologies such as zero-touch workflow are not without pitfalls. Automation works down at the lower levels of the administrative hierarchy, where the complexity of information requests is kept to a minimum, but it has been difficult to implement in those environments that involve going beyond simple responses to cues in electronic forms. Any form of extended textual data, which, in electronic form is the likely replacement for face-to-face conversation, is incredibly difficult to process in an automated system. Automated decision making in the benefits system often relies upon artificially restrictive textual content which reduces flexibility. Despite the rise of knowledge management software, whose advocates claim can quickly trace patterns in large amounts of textual information, zero-touch in its present incarnation is yet to radically transform workflow in the public sector. Nor, given the amount that governments must invest in such technologies, has it generated quick cost savings.

Coordination

For around fifty years, management theorists have argued that private sector organizations could benefit from the improved internal communication provided by computer networks (Leavitt and Whisler, 1958). But in the early 1990s, it became the received wisdom that large firms could dramatically improve their internal coordination by sharing and managing knowledge, best practices, and planning mechanisms (Davidow and Malone, 1992; Drucker, 1988, 1993; Fulk and DeSanctis, 1995; Hammer and Champy, 1993; Scott Morton, 1991). Administrative models which placed flexibility, dynamism, and teamwork at the center of their approach became the celebrated ideals, and these soon started to seep into the public sector (Ronfeldt, 1992; Swinden and Heath, 1994). E-government takes up and energizes these themes by promising IT-enabled teams working across government agencies to counteract the long-lamented effects of the "silo" (or "stovepipe") culture, in which departments engage in unhealthy competition for information resources that could be shared or unknowingly engage in developing information banks (and even policies) that overlap with those of other departments. Joining up government, it is argued, also provides a means of solving problems that cut across existing agency boundaries and avoids policy failures, especially in "megatask" areas (Alkadry, 2003:187) that are beyond individual comprehension or require multiagency responses, such as, for instance, taxation, criminal justice, welfare, and environmental policy.

On top of this shift in management philosophy, by the turn of the century, knowledge of some of the less desirable effects of the new public management reforms of the 1990s had increased. The fragmentation of the public sector caused by the disaggregation and devolution of administrative tasks has made executive coordination more difficult. New public management reformers promised greater efficiency through increased specialization, but this came at a price: executive agencies involved in the rapid processing of high-volume data have arguably contributed to a general deskilling of substantial sections of the public sector workforce. E-government provides a means of integrating diverse components of the state bureaucracy through networked teamwork while simultaneously empowering workers by enhancing their ability to make decisions based on the evidence made available by databases, what Shoshana Zuboff terms "reskilling" (1988:57).

The coordination claims made for e-government also stem from the recognition that the Internet changes the nature of government IT (Landsbergen and Wolken, 2001:207). This has been a crucial foundation of e-government initiatives to date, with their multipurpose portals designed to integrate departments and services and present unified, user-friendly "front-ends" accessible by various means, including, in the British case, interactive digital television (implemented in April 2002), mobile devices, and public electronic kiosks in various locations such as libraries, supermarkets, and railway stations. The strategy has been made more achievable through the new interoperability brought about by the use of a new data-tagging standard, XML—a means of defining data which enables cross-platform integration within government and less troublesome integration with the wider Internet (U.K. CITU 2000; McGill, 2000). The days of inward-facing, byzantine, tailor-made systems which rapidly outdate are perhaps coming to an end. XML also constitutes an intriguing example of policy convergence across national boundaries. In the United States, President Bush's flagship "24 e-government projects," announced in 2002, make much of XML. The development of the tagging standards (or XML schemas, as they are known) relies increasingly on international collaboration between e-government agencies. In December 2002, an international committee composed of representatives of the U.S., U.K., Danish, and Canadian e-government agencies, together with a range of private sector actors, including Microsoft, Sun Microsystems, and Fujitsu, was founded to develop specific e-government schemas (Frank, 2002; Lisagor, 2002).

One of the more influential gray literature interpretations of the coordination thrust of e-government is consultancy firm Deloitte's six-stage model of e-government progress. This has arguably had a huge effect on the mindset of e-government reformers around the world (see exhibit 8.4).

At first glance, e-government, in the enthusiastic vision promoted by Deloitte, offers a neat solution to the difficulties of coordinating effort in large organizations. In the United States, the concept of the virtual agency has been celebrated as a key element in this. Virtual agencies may have no obvious jurisdictional existence but integrate "information, decisionmaking processes, and flows across organizational boundaries" (Fountain, 2001:26). Far more than the simple presentation of information on the web by a single agency, they are characterized by the sharing of information held in databases and work patterns based on networks of problem-solving teams, often involving public and private actors. Such virtual agencies have grown in number in recent years,

EXHIBIT 8.4. DELOITTE'S SIX-STAGE MODEL OF E-GOVERNMENT PROGRESS

- **Stage 1: Information Publishing/Dissemination.** Individual governmental departments set up their own websites that provide the public with information about them, the range of services available, and contacts for further assistance. At this stage, governments establish an electronic encyclopedia that reduces the number of phone calls customers need to make to reach the appropriate employee who can fulfill their service requests.

- **Stage 2: "Official" Two-Way Transactions.** With the help of legally valid digital signatures and secure websites, customers are able to submit personal information to—and conduct monetary transactions with—individual departments. At this stage, customers must be convinced of the department's ability to keep their information private and free from piracy.

- **Stage 3: Multipurpose Portals.** This is the point at which customer-centric governments make a big breakthrough in service delivery. Based on the fact that customer needs can cut across department boundaries, a portal allows customers to use a single point of entry to send and receive information and to process monetary transactions across multiple departments. In essence, governments expand the concept of one-stop delivery to meet the broader array of customer needs both within and outside government services.

- **Stage 4: Portal Personalization.** Through stage 3, customers can access a variety of services at a single website. In stage 4, government puts even more power into customers' hands by allowing them to customize portals with their desired features. To accomplish this, governments will need much more sophisticated web programming that allows interfaces to be user manipulated. The added benefit of portal personalization is that governments will get a more accurate read on customer preference for electronic versus nonelectronic service options.

- **Stage 5: Clustering of Common Services.** Stage 5 is where real transformation of government structure takes shape. As customers now view once-disparate services as a unified package through the portal, their perception of departments as distinct entities will begin to blur. They will recognize groups of transactions rather than groups of agencies. To make it happen, governments will cluster services along common lines to accelerate the delivery of shared services. Long-standing territories and funding streams will constitute just a subset of the barriers to creating a new organizational model.

- **Stage 6: Full Integration and Enterprise Transformation.** What started as a digital encyclopedia is now a full-service center, personalized to each customer's needs and preferences. At this stage, old walls defining silos of services have been torn down and technology is integrated across the new enterprise to bridge the shortened gap between the front and back office. In some countries, new departments will have formed from the remains of predecessors. Others will have the same names, but their interiors will look nothing like they did before e-government.

Source: Quoted and adapted from Deloitte consulting, 2000:22–24.

especially in the United States. Prominent examples include the U.S. Business Advisor (www.business.gov), which provides a variety of information and transaction services; AccessAmerica for Seniors (www.seniors.gov), which integrates a range of information sources of relevance to the elderly; and FirstGov for Consumers (www.consumer.gov).

Virtual agencies mark a significant departure from previous approaches to service delivery. They signal a recognition that the identities of users of public services are rarely monolithic and that a detailed knowledge of the structures of the federal administration should not be a prerequisite for access to its services. By conceiving of the user base of such services as highly segmented, in much the same way as does the private e-commerce sector (Bellamy and Taylor, 1998:21; Van Everen, 2002), e-government strategists argue that improved customer service can be delivered to those who are perceived to be most in need. In time, so the argument runs, decisive organizational change will occur, as the virtual agency cannibalizes the "real" agencies out of which it grew. The implementation of such projects across government, especially in the United States, has expanded massively under the Bush administration since 2000, with the addition of www.grants.gov, www.kids.gov, www.students.gov, and www.export.gov, to name but a few.

Yet despite the promise of increased coordination, some scholars have argued that when technologies become embedded in institutional settings like government departments and agencies, there is no guarantee that their innate potential will be exploited. In Jane Fountain's terms, we need to distinguish between raw, or "objective," technology and technology as it is actually used, or "enacted" (2001:10–14). Technologies often have unintended consequences, and these vary according to institutional context. Just because the Internet and intranets allow for communication across organizational boundaries does not necessarily mean that this will occur. Virtual agencies, for example, have proved difficult to implement because they may involve job losses, or, for those who are fortunate enough to retain their job, they may take the power of decision away from previously important managers. There are also long-standing problems with counteracting the silo culture that are not going to disappear with the introduction of new technologies. The Office of the E-envoy in the United Kingdom experienced significant problems with spreading the gospel of e-government throughout British central and local government. Much the same may be said for the OMB in the United States. A major hurdle has been excessive departmentalism, but it must also be recognized that public bureaucracies in these countries are not the relatively monolithic entities that they were twenty years ago. The situation is compounded by the differing technological demands of individual departments and agencies and the fact that some, in effect, "go it alone" with their own projects. The latter has largely been the case with the implementation of e-government in British local government—developments led by the Office of the Deputy Prime Minister rather than the Office of the E-envoy (Cross, 2002). By introducing new delivery channels, e-government may thus increase competition within and between organizations (Borins, 2004), increasing fragmentation rather than reducing it. Some public lawyers have even argued that integration across government is steaming ahead without proper regard for the constitutional implications of joining up previously separate functions (Morison, 2003). Thus, there are several obstacles to the vision of e-government as increasing coordination.

Effectiveness

A third major claim is that e-government will improve the effectiveness of public sector organizations. Effectiveness is a nebulous concept, but in this context it may be defined simply as the extent to which a department or agency's policy and administrative objectives are achieved (James, 2003:9). Increasing effectiveness obviously reduces policy and administrative failure. A major theme here is the way in which e-government is said to contribute to the "flattening" of hierarchical command structures. Many aspects of this debate owe their origins to the postbureaucracy thesis of Charles Heckscher and Anne Donnellon's influential anthology on the changing nature of business organizations in the 1980s and '90s (1994). They argued that the introduction of new technologies not only fostered more rapid communication, it also caused fundamental long-term shifts in internal power structures. Vertically integrated hierarchies of command and control were being displaced by looser, more flexible, horizontally integrated networks. The boundaries of organizations were becoming blurred as firms outsourced functions and established ad hoc alliances with other firms to fund the development of new products. Many of the features of postbureaucratic business organization have been identified as being at the heart of Silicon Valley's success (Saxenian, 1994).

E-government rests in part upon a claim that managers and front-line staff could be empowered, their creative impulses liberated in collaborative relationships with other workers and "knowledge entrepreneurs." The diffusion of technologies throughout an organization is said to provide individuals with the tools necessary for self-organization, reflection, and greater creativity (Holmes, 2001:57–84; Leadbeater, 1999:93–107). Access to centralized databases allows for rapid retrieval of information necessary for good decision making. In this perspective, e-government goes beyond simple task automation and chimes in with broader debates about "post-Fordist" organizational forms. Despite claims that e-government will automate a great number of tasks, it can also be interpreted as contributing to the supersession of rigid, deskilled work patterns of the past. Networked collaboration and knowledge sharing are central to this post-Fordist vision of the public sector organization. This warrants further attention because it highlights many of the underlying dynamics of e-government (see exhibit 8.5).

It would, however, be too simplistic to explain e-government as a post-Fordist administrative paradigm. Transformations in technologies themselves have not, of course, always been mirrored by changes in governments' and citizens' attitudes as to how they might be used. The use of database applications for information retrieval and electronic filing, coupled with an emphasis on automating routine tasks, has been at the center of public sector use of computers since the late 1960s (Bellamy and Taylor, 1998:38–46; Garson, 1999; Margetts, 1999). The demands generated by the creation and expansion of welfare states in Western liberal democracies found a natural response in such solutions; they held out the promise of speeding up information processing and response times, especially in information-intensive agencies, such as those dealing with benefit payments, criminal justice, and health care. The mass-provision, Fordist model of welfarism, enacted by silo-based public bureaucracies staffed by unambiguously public civil servants, necessitated large-scale data-processing systems. Thus, the fact remains that much of what governments do with computers will continue to be based in silos and will involve automation, information retrieval, and management: the domain of

EXHIBIT 8.5. WEBER, FORD, AND TAYLOR: THEORISTS AND ARCHITECTS OF MODERN BUREAUCRACY

Max Weber's model of bureaucracy underpins the vast bulk of academic research on the administrative structures of the modern state. Its elements range across a number of his works, but the ideal type bureaucracy for Weber was as follows:

- Jurisdictional areas are fixed, official, and ordered by laws and rules
- There is a firmly ordered hierarchy, which ensures that lower offices are supervised by specified higher ones within a chain of command
- Business is managed on the basis of written documents and a filing system
- The authority of officials is impersonal and stems entirely from the post they hold, not from personal status
- Bureaucratic rules are strict enough to minimize the scope of personal discretion
- Appointment and advancement within a bureaucracy are based on professional criteria, such as training, expertise, and administrative competence (Heywood, 2002:359).

Fordism is a concept used across the social sciences but especially in political science, geography, economics, sociology, and management studies. It originally refers to the principles of work organization pioneered by the car manufacturer Henry Ford at his Highland Park, Michigan, factory in 1914. Based upon increased mechanization and the intensification of the division of labor in tightly controlled moving assembly lines, Ford's methods produced greater productivity and made the cheap mass manufacture of standardized products more viable (for good surveys, see Rupert, 1995, 2002; Webster, 2002:75–82). Ford's methods were copied around the world and became the standard template for industrial organization for most of the twentieth century, and, despite the rise of what has been termed "post-Fordism," they remain dominant to this day.

Taylorism is a closely related set of principles with origins in the early twentieth century. Taking its name from F. W. Taylor, a U.S. engineer obsessed with increasing worker efficiency, it aims to reduce the amount of labor time spent per individual product unit (Taylor, 1911). Much like Fordism, this involves mechanization and increased specialization through a rigorous division of labor, but Taylor also argued that close disciplinary control and monitoring of the work environment was required. By carefully employing "time and motion" studies of how workers behaved, Taylorism aimed to divide up tasks and, in a sense, automate them by assigning very narrow and specific roles to individuals who were mostly forbidden from stepping outside of their predefined position in the production process. Taylorist principles were exported around the world with as much success as Fordism.

Taylorism and Fordism have not, of course, been restricted to the sphere of industrial production: they have also been influential in white-collar organizations, including classic public sector bureaucracies, where repetitive, high-volume tasks are often the norm.

By the 1980s, however, theorists of post-Fordism were forecasting the death of such approaches, and a new theory of work organization was born, based upon creative individualism, short-run production, flexible specialization, contracting out, team working, innovative networks, and the end of mass standardization (Aglietta, 1979; Amin, 1994; Burrows and Loader, 1994; Lipietz, 1997).

data entry, electronic archives, databases, and one-dimensional applications. Hardly the stuff of empowering post-Fordism.

When it comes to increasing organizational effectiveness through flattening hierarchies and enhancing public sector creativity, the counterargument is that there is mixed evidence that the introduction of information and communication technologies in the public sector has produced these effects in the past (Margetts, 1999). Indeed, what is evident, especially in Jane Fountain's influential study (2001:164), is a rather uneasy blend of the old and the new; a "dual system . . . that combines pockets of networked creativity and openness with large areas of traditional command and control." Governments' information-processing requirements have far from disappeared. In fact, they may well have increased under the influence of citizen demand. Health, welfare, and criminal justice agencies play pivotal roles in most Western states and, crucially, involve administrative coordination at—and between—both national and local levels. At the same time, even if the technological barriers to joined-up government are being overcome by the implementation of new, more interoperable networks, where information sharing around government is supposedly made easier, as David Landsbergen and George Wolken have argued in their study of officials in the United States, there is no guarantee that information sharing will actually occur (2001:208; see also Drake et al., 2004). This confirms earlier findings from studies of the introduction of groupware (software that allows groups to collaborate across networks) in large organizations. For example, Wanda Orlikowksi (1993) argues that those at the top and bottom of an organizational hierarchy are more willing to share information than those in middle management, because middle managers see information as a precious commodity that will help them move up the career ladder.

Even large private companies have been reluctant to empower workers. During the height of the dotcom boom, new companies such as the celebrated Yahoo! were mythologized as examples of workplace equality and relative freedom from managerial control. However, as the high-tech sector began to return to normal in 2001, not only did Yahoo! and others start to "get real" about the amount of autonomy they allowed their workers, it soon became clear that the established major players that would survive the downturn in the technology sectors—large companies such as IBM, Microsoft, EDS, and Oracle, for example—had deeply entrenched hierarchical structures, particularly in creative fields, and core functions such as bringing in new business (Greenwood, 2001). Critics point to the ways in which technologies are simply "bolted on" to existing ways of working or how potentially empowering technologies are subverted by managers or elected politicians.

More depressingly, there is an ongoing debate about the role of technologies in workplace surveillance (Fernie and Metcalf, 1998), as managers find that new forms of communication can in fact be monitored more closely than traditional forms. Claims that the interdepartmental sharing of information using intranets and databases will empower formerly de-skilled staff lower down the administrative hierarchy may also be treated with skepticism if placed in the context of broader debates about the impact of technology on frontline workers in large organizations. There is an inevitable tension between automation and autonomy. Neo-Marxist perspectives on workplace technologies emphasize their role in squeezing every last drop of productivity from the workforce and the hyperefficient automation of older command-and-control hierarchies (Braverman, 1974). Decision-making systems may provide ready-made templates which require nothing more complicated than choosing from a range of preprogrammed options (Snellen, 2003; Warhurst and Thompson, 1998). Furthermore, research on "telework" demonstrates how individual workers interacting with such systems can be monitored much more easily by managers (Bryant, 1995; Fernie and Metcalf, 1998; Stanworth, 1998, 2000), and those performing at what managers consider to be a suboptimal level are confronted, not with the potentially sensitive judgment of a human supervisor but the "hard" aggregate data easily retrieved from the system itself. Although such interpretations have been criticized as exaggerated and misleading (Bain and Taylor, 2000), as managers become more knowledgeable about such possibilities, it is possible that they will increasingly request such features to be built into the systems they purchase for routine administration.

At issue here is our understanding of the very nature of organizational networks, especially if we make a distinction between those that are formed between theoretically independent organizations or groups of actors and those that are formed from groups of actors within single organizations (Fountain, 2001:60–64). While the former may be characterized by creativity, fluidity, and the relative absence of stifling command-and-control structures and may indeed allow groups to coalesce in a relatively ad hoc fashion to solve common problems through pooling resources, the latter—internal organizational networks—are often very different. Internal networks have always existed in public sector organizations, but they may in fact be better understood as hierarchies. The exchange of resources between actors in a virtual organization may appear on the surface to be taking place in a network, but on closer inspection, the type of task or inequalities of power, status, and prestige that in practice shape these relationships may in fact render them hierarchical (Ahuja and Carley, 1998). Although the decentralizing properties of Internet-based communication may soften some of these effects, this is not always the case, as Nicholas Ducheneaut's sophisticated analysis of how email is used in organizational "power games" demonstrates (2002). The capacity of the Internet to facilitate collaborative networked interaction between independent organizations is easier to understand than its capacity to change internal organizational hierarchies. There are no guarantees that the new networks created by e-government reforms are not simply mapping on to preexisting power structures.

Finally, there are several further significant political, economic, and technical barriers to the development of government as a more effective learning organization in which information flows freely, empowering both public officials and citizens. In conventional political terms, the sophisticated sharing of data by disparate government agencies presents threats to individual privacy that have been heavily criticized, especially as citizens become more aware of new risks such as identity theft and surveillance techniques that are being developed in response to electronic communication (for broader coverage of this see chapter 11). In the United Kingdom, for example, there has been much resistance to the idea of a national identity card that would provide authentication for e-government services. In countries such as Sweden, where ID cards are long established, such problems are less pronounced (Silcock, 2001:96). In the United States, the drive toward placing ever greater amounts of information on the web in the name of transparency has taken repeated knocks. For example, in the aftermath of the 9/11 attacks, the Department of Homeland Security insisted that many government agencies remove sensitive information from their websites, while at the local level, in Hamilton County, Ohio, the Clerk of Courts site, considered exemplary for its open information policy, was forced to restrict access to documents after being sued by a victim of identity theft whose Social Security number had been taken from the site (Perry, 2004). E-government enthusiasts bemoan the difficulties of implementing data sharing across government, not only because there is a consensus that improving response times and reducing costs is dependent upon removing task duplication across government through such means, but also because private sector contractors who sell their systems to private sector organizations rarely come up against the kinds of political opposition that will usually greet such developments in the public sector. A further problem concerns the fear among senior agency officials of massive public scrutiny and dramatic increases in requests for information and what we might term political "leakage," a process whereby conflict resolution previously handled within legislatures and in the tensions between legislatures and executives oozes into administrative agencies themselves (Landsbergen and Wolken, 2001:209). And finally, in technical terms, the problem of joining up many different preexisting government "legacy" systems has always proved a problematic element in government computing and hangs heavily over e-government reforms, as does the issue of how different agencies define and categorize individual data in the first place.

E-GOVERNMENT AS DEMOCRATIZATION

In his critique of bureaucracy, Ralph Hummel (1977) argues that a common "bureaucratic experience" envelops all those who work within large, modern organizations. Hummel describes how bureaucrats become divorced from the wider social contexts in which they work. Because they are rooted in disproportionately optimistic assumptions about the importance and efficacy of technical formal rules, the norms which govern life in a bureaucracy are different from those that would prove acceptable in ordinary social interaction. This leads to a general ignorance of the views of citizens outside the bureaucracy and an unhealthy conformity to the rationalized procedures within it. Bureaucratic organizations are therefore bound, in Hummel's view, to be unresponsive to citizens (Alkadry, 2003). Is e-government reconfiguring this "bureaucratic experience," and what are the implications of such changes?

Government Websites: Interactivity and Opportunities for Citizen Deliberation

An important aspect of e-government is its potential to facilitate interaction between citizens and the whole government apparatus, not just the legislative branch. This

Table 8.1. Interactive Features on Government Websites, 2004 (global)

	2001	2002	2003	2004
Provide email addresses	73	75	84	88
Provide areas to post comments	8	33	31	16
Offer email updates	6	10	12	16
Offer website personalization	—	1	1	2

Source: Adapted from West, 2004.

Note: All numbers given in percentages.

points to a potential reshaping of the relationship between public bureaucracies and those whom they serve. Citizens are able to be citizens, not just consumers, in their interactions with departments and agencies and are thus able to augment the tasks of scrutiny and accountability performed by legislatures. Much of this depends, however, upon the levels of interactivity provided by government websites (Hacker, 1996). To what extent are government departments and agencies becoming more interactive, and do they provide citizens with opportunities for political deliberation? Obviously this is a huge question, and we can only skim the surface here. A major problem is the lack of available evidence.

An early attempt to assess the interactivity of government websites found that U.S. and Canadian sites were clearly ahead of the game, providing more opportunities for citizen engagement and deliberation than their western European counterparts (Chadwick with May, 2001). However, across all policy sectors, the scores for interaction and potential for deliberation were found to be low. Social services websites in the United States and Canada achieved fairly impressive results early on along with other sectors, such as communications, finance, science and technology, and government operations. But others, such as defense and, perhaps more surprisingly, education, exhibited poor levels of interactivity and potential for citizen deliberation.

More recently, a series of studies from the Center for Public Policy at Brown University assessed the current state of e-government in 198 countries worldwide. One of the measures they use is "public outreach," defined as "interactive features that facilitate communication between citizens and government" (West, 2004:9). Table 8.1 summarizes the findings since 2001.

Of course, there are limitations to these forms of analysis. Nevertheless, they provide a broad overview of the state of e-government. The verdict: while e-government is contributing to the opening up of government departments, the story differs quite strongly across countries, policy sectors, and channels of communication. But the increasing use of email and comment areas detailed in table 8.1 suggests that e-government may be reconfiguring the "bureaucratic experience." Let us explore this in more detail.

Outward-Facing Networks

Some authors have argued for a radical extension of e-government in order to involve citizens more fully in regular policy making and administrative processes. Such perspectives, which are particularly strong in Canada and Australia, go beyond simple electronic service delivery and seek to use the Internet to incorporate citizens' deliberation into the initial stages of policy development or the very process of continually re-engineering public services (Coe et al., 2001; Lenihan, 2002; Lenihan and Alcock, 2000; see also Milward and Snyder, 1996; Taylor, 1995). In its most ambitious guise, this form of e-government entails a radical overhaul of the modern administrative state, as regular electronic interaction involving elected politicians, civil servants, and citizen groups becomes standard practice in all stages of the policy development process and routine administration. It seeks a thorough transformation of public bureaucracies to reflect not only the advances in networking achieved since the rise of the Internet but also wider shifts toward more deliberative modes of policy making (Kelly, 2004; Mintrom, 2003). The Internet thus offers the potential to increase political participation and reshape the state into an open, interactive, network form as an alternative to both traditional, hierarchical, bureaucratic organizations and more recent market-driven forms of service delivery. In some ways, this kind of approach extends Alvin Toffler's model of "prosumption"—a conflation of "production" and "consumption" used to describe the ways in which the lines between consumers and producers of goods become blurred when technologies make it easier to bring consumers into the production process itself (Toffler, 1981:271; see also Bellamy and Taylor, 1998:83; Tapscott, 1995:62). A good example of how a private company has effectively operationalized prosumption can be found in the way in which Dell Computer Corporation sells its PCs online in highly configurable versions.

Proponents of this model argue that widespread use of the Internet means that the traditional application of computers in public bureaucracies, originally based around inward-facing mainframe systems originating in the 1960s, should now be superseded by outward-facing networks in which the boundaries between an organization's internal information processing and its external users effectively melt away (Lenihan, 2002; Andersen, 1999). In this view, government is able to respond to the needs of its citizens, who are able to exert influence via rapid, aggregative feedback mechanisms like email and interactive websites. A recent example of this is the online questionnaire used by the U.K.'s National Health Service website NHSDirect, which was used as a source of information to restructure the site itself (Nicholas et al., 2002).

In contrast with older Fordist technologies, e-government requires a flexible, build-and-learn approach, characterized by teamworking across departmental boundaries via intranets and various forms of groupware (U.K. National Audit Office, 1999; Peled, 2001). Irrespective of whether this enhances direct citizen control over the design and delivery of public services or, more pessimistically, enhances the power of professional and expert groups (Rowe and Shepherd, 2002), the overall vision is of improved policy making. Furthermore, e-government offers an opportunity for public servants to experiment with new communication technologies in ways that have previously proved difficult, even impossible. With ownership and use of personal computers in the home at their highest-ever levels in the United States and Europe, more white-collar workers are familiar with web browsers, the layout of web pages, and the expectations of convenience and relative ease of use that the Internet provides in the home. This form of what we might term "tacit skilling" provides grist to the mill for those who argue that empowerment of public servants as "knowledge workers" is what will inevitably be a part of putting public services online.

The Blurring of Executive and Legislative Functions

E-government potentially blurs the distinctions between executive and legislative functions. As we saw in chapter 5, the U.S. federal government has blazed a trail in this area with its e-rule-making program, designed to allow citizens to comment on agency rules as they are being developed (Coglianese, 2004a, 2004b; Shulman et al., 2003). But perhaps the best example of this blurring of functions occurred during an online consultation in the Netherlands, involving the minister for inner city problems and civil servants from his department in a series of chats and web forums. Significantly, civil servants became involved in the discussions, were openly identifiable, and were speaking on behalf of the government. This diluted the Netherlands' usually strong norm of ministerial responsibility (which it shares with the United Kingdom), whereby ministers are the funnels through which accountability flows between Parliament and the government (Coleman and Gøtze, 2001:40). Such initiatives therefore bring up their own issues of accountability as well as the idea that elected representatives may become disintermediated.

A further contribution to the disintermediation of representative institutions derives from how e-government reinforces new forms of public sector accountability that have arisen since the new public management boom of the 1990s: the phenomenon of "regulation inside government" (Hood et al., 1999). Internal accountability through administrative supervision in the form of regular audits, efficiency reviews, inspections, service agreements, and other devices of managerial oversight are heavily dependent upon the gathering and analysis of information (Bekkers and Homburg, 2002). The growth of such processes across governments in the West creates a new and different climate of accountability, as bureaucracies increasingly police themselves using internal administrative mechanisms. Traditional forms of political accountability involving elected representatives become less important to the production of "quality."

Choice, Voice, and the Politics of Convenience

For many of its most enthusiastic advocates, e-government exposes public services to the same kinds of stringent tests as private sector firms operating within the realm of e-commerce. In this market-driven model, over the long term, governments will become more responsive to the demands of their "customers," more able to quickly adapt to changes in operational policy, rapidly process individual requests, clamp down on fraud, and play leading roles in the provision of credible, high-quality information to citizens suffering from information overload. In this comparatively narrow but still important sense, e-government brings government closer to the people by meeting the increasing expectations of citizens regarding convenience, accessibility, and timeliness. We can see at work in e-government reforms—and in governments' new electronic faces more generally—the kind of consumerism that exists all over cyberspace (Chadwick, 2001). In seeking to emulate the private sector by capitalizing on shifts in consumption patterns, e-government reformists forecast the demise of monolithic and cumbersome state provision. In its stead will emerge a newly flexible and dynamic model of the public sector which will give users, in all their post-Fordist diversity, what they want, when they want it, at the lowest possible cost in terms of time and effort. Customers not only have a greater choice but come to play a role in coproducing the design and delivery of public services themselves: in short, how those choices are presented in the first place (Mintrom, 2003). Utilizing user feedback mechanisms to improve public services is by no means a new idea, but the simplicity, immediacy, and transparency gained by using Internet-based approaches that allow public services to directly integrate user opinion are new, as is the sheer volume of basic information about government activity available to those sufficiently motivated to seek it out.

In conditions of relative abundance (relative, that is, to nations outside the developed world), the consumerist politics of convenience are becoming increasingly important determinants of governance structures, electoral change, and party strategy. The effects of these developments, according to some writers (Norris, 2000), are not the erosion of citizenship values but their metamorphosis into forms more suited to post-industrial politics (see also chapter 2). Of course, it may be objected that the politics of convenience have nothing whatsoever to do with democracy, electronic or otherwise, that choice should not be confused with voice. It may depend in large part upon the extent to which one is convinced by broader postindustrial arguments about the proliferation of nontraditional repertoires of political activity and whether they can be stretched in this way (Inglehart, 1997, 1990; Mintrom, 2003; Norris, 2002b).

The Democratization of Design

A fourth, perhaps less obvious area in which e-government contributes to democratization concerns the context in which e-government technologies are designed. Such systems are not neutral; they shape and constrain the types of behavior in which it is possible to engage while interacting with government and other citizens online. A debate has now emerged across the public sector about the benefits of open source compared with proprietary software (Mathieson, 2003). For example, in early 2003, the Department for Work and Pensions in the United Kingdom launched an e-procurement system, Purchase and Pay, running on the free Linux operating system. Open-source software design is predicated on the argument that cooperative and collaborative sharing of expertise results not only in technically better software but also in socially and politically progressive technologies that are more flexible, transparent, and cost effective to maintain. Its chief architect, Richard Stallman, founder of the Free Software Foundation and one of the originators, along with Linus Torvalds and many others, of Linux, argues that the public and nonprofit sectors are at risk of being hamstrung by costly and inflexible proprietary systems over which they have little control (GNU Project–Free Software Foundation, 2003). In this perspective, the democratic values of open source, which would potentially involve technicians and nonexperts inside and outside government in continuous dialogue to develop and refine systems, would align the public sector with an already existing culture of voluntarism that exists in cyberspace. By involving service users, it could also counter accusations of technocratic bias that have plagued government technology projects in the past. One example of an area crying out for open-source style negotiation and collaboration is data sharing and the protection of privacy, especially in light of concerns over the record of proprietary software companies on consumer privacy. The voluntarist ethic of open source could not only generate cost savings (always important for the public and nonprofit sectors) and more refined software; it will also empower public sector technicians to modify and adapt systems as they see fit and, through online discussions, inject citizens' views on how these systems should operate.

CONCLUSION

When large organizations first started to implement computer systems, the dominant orthodoxy was that they were apolitical, neutral tools. This tied in with the rise of so-called scientific administration and a general current in the social sciences toward what was known as the "end of ideology" thesis (Bell, 1960). Computing was seen as a part of the end of ideology because it held out the promise of information abundance as a pragmatic route to objectively better solutions to social and economic problems rather than policy guided by "irrational" belief systems. Writers such as Herbert Simon (1973) dissected but also celebrated new forms of information management within bureaucracies as the first step on the road to what they believed would be a form of bureaucracy that would better serve the public interest.

However, these assumptions were steadily revised (Danziger et al., 1982; Dutton, 1999; Kling and Iacono, 1989; Kraemer and King, 1986). Some writers claimed that in most cases technology's impact on power relations could best be understood in terms of how dominant coalitions of actors could shape outcomes, irrespective of who, on the surface, appeared to own or control computing resources: "computing will *reinforce* the power and influence of those actors and groups who already have the most resources and power in the organization," wrote Nick Danziger and colleagues (1982:18). For instance, cities with strong mayors would most likely see the mayor's position enhanced by computerization. In contrast, the computerization of local governments that were fragmented tended to reinforce decentralization, thus favoring groups who could make the most of such an environment—agencies and departments away from the center. Taking budgeting systems as another example, it was found that what appeared on the surface to be a neutral piece of scientific management turned out to be based very firmly on ideological priorities, public relations, and the short-term political demands of elected officials (Danziger et al., 1982:190–92).

The reinforcement approach is useful for focusing attention on the often contingent nature of e-government reforms. Despite the wide range of ambitious claims made by promoters, as we have seen in this chapter, these are refracted through the prisms of pre-existing variables. In the United Kingdom, several authors have argued that a close-knit policy community has heavily influenced decisions on the use of computers in government since the 1980s, with the result that service delivery rather than more democratic considerations has prevailed (Bellamy et al., 1995; Pratchett, 1999). In the United States, research on local government websites by Juliet Musso and colleagues concludes that an entrepreneurial model of e-government as service delivery has prevailed over a civic model which stresses access to decision making or community building (2000; see also Weare et al., 1999). A comparison of policy ideas in the EU, the United Kingdom, and the United States concludes along the same lines (Chadwick and May, 2003), while case studies of the U.S. federal government reveal a complex mixture of selective technology adoption and use, not unlike the findings of the reinforcement model (Fountain, 2001;

see also Grafton, 2003; Norris, D., 2003). Thus, the process of institutionalizing new communication technologies can often reshape the technologies themselves (D. Norris, 2003:420). The overall outcome is deeply contradictory.

As we saw, however, there are serious claims that e-government will democratize the public sector. If, as I have outlined above, one of the central visions of e-government is of a post-Fordist public sector governance with networkers empowered by information sharing across departmental boundaries, the reinforcement model will perhaps require revision. Although it has great relevance for understanding e-government, an inescapable problem with the reinforcement approach is that it was crafted during a period when the outward-facing networks of government were not developed. E-government challenges many of its assumptions. The emphasis on interfacing with groups outside government has already had an influence on internal organizational forms, as evidenced in the development of virtual agencies and portal websites. Flatter hierarchies of more creative and cooperative officials permanently plugged in to wider informational networks that include online citizen groups and affected interests is one possible outcome of e-government.

On the other hand, perhaps this is missing the fundamental point of e-government. Another more critical interpretation focuses on the concept of legitimacy, in particular, how the increased potential for governments to control what they communicate to the public about their actions gives communication professionals, or spin doctors, much wider opportunities to frame political messages. E-government offers political elites a new, previously unavailable electronic face. This is controlled by government itself and is subject to the central demands of contemporary politics, namely presentational professionalism, disingenuous statistical detail (Dorling et al., 2002), and softer forms of strategic communication such as imagery, symbolism, and strategic language use (Chadwick, 2001). In Britain, for example, where the Labor government's intensification of spin-doctored, sound-bite politics is now such a taken-for-granted part of national life that it is hardly commented on at all, the Strategic Communications Unit controls the executive's web presence, and it shows. In the United States, the Department of Defense now publishes transcripts of major interviews with journalists not in the interests of openness, but to counter in advance misquotation by the press (Gillmor, 2004:66). The rather amateurish, patchy, and utilitarian government websites of the 1990s have now been replaced by a more professional approach, which ties in with broader communication strategies. This is undoubtedly a product of the general increase in Internet usage among electorates, but it also represents an increasing awareness of the properties of the web as a medium and how this may contribute to the symbolic dimension of government activity.

Executive websites provide new avenues for government self-publicity, allowing them to bypass hostile news media. The symbolic architecture of a government's Internet presence is likely to be just as important in the future as it has been in the past, but the emerging techniques point to a more complex relationship between rulers and ruled, one that will be based upon immediacy of contact, a more direct appeal to lifestyle concerns and entertainment values. Many executive websites, with their virtual tours and celebrity pets, are typical of the infotainment genres which are the stock-in-trade of the more commercial frontiers of the web. The Internet thus offers political elites many opportunities to intensify and diversify the ways in which they sustain themselves in positions of power.

A significant side effect of putting public services online has been the change in what citizens expect of public sector organizations and, in turn, how those organizations see their own role in the new environment. Functions of representation and deliberation that are supposed to be the preserve of legislative bodies are being usurped by public bureaucracies. Whether such initiatives are the creatures of executives or of legislatures matters a great deal for how e-government will evolve. If government departments and agencies continue to establish their own online discussion forums, legislatures will find themselves increasingly marginalized. Awareness of this is, not surprisingly, growing in legislatures that are already comparatively weak for old, nontechnological reasons—in the United Kingdom and Canada, for example. Time will tell, but unless legislatures seize the initiative, departments and agencies may go their own way in developing managed consultation processes that give legislation the veneer of enhanced legitimacy.

Discussion Points

- What are the policy origins of e-government?
- Is e-government about better government, better democracy, or both?
- How is e-government different from previous government computerization initiatives?
- Is e-government the ultimate form of professionalized political communication?
- Does e-government change power relations with public bureaucracies?
- Does e-government redistribute power within a political system?

Further Reading

Enthusiastic introductions to the ideas underlying e-government are provided by Holmes, 2001, and Bacon et al., 2002. Of the voluminous gray literature in this area, Deloitte's report (2000) stands out. Jaeger, 2003, is scholarly but still accessible. Fountain's book (2001) is probably the most influential full-length academic study of e-government to date.

Brown University's Center for Public Policy website contains downloadable versions of its annual e-government surveys (http://www.insidepolitics.org). Chadwick and May, 2003, compares the United States, the United Kingdom, and the EU.

On the interpretation of e-government as democratization, Lenihan, 2002, is thought provoking. Mintrom, 2003, thoughtfully contextualizes these ideas. See also Chadwick, 2003. The technology as empowerment thesis is well-stated by Zuboff, 1988.

An accessible account of the contradictions between centralization and decentralization is provided by Peled (2001), who in some respects updates the influential work of Danziger et al. (1982). Bellamy and Taylor (1998) covered many of the important themes before the term "e-government" was invented.

ISSUES AND CONTROVERSIES

CONSTRUCTING THE GLOBAL INFORMATION SOCIETY

The global information society is evolving at breakneck speed. The accelerating convergence of telecommunications, broadcasting multimedia and information and communication technologies is driving new products and services, as well as ways of conducting business and commerce. At the same time, commercial, social and professional opportunities are exploding as new markets open to competition and foreign investment and participation. The modern world is undergoing a fundamental transformation as the industrial society that marked the 20th century rapidly gives way to the information society of the 21st century. This dynamic process promises a fundamental change in all aspects of our lives, including knowledge dissemination, social interaction, economic and business practices, political engagement, media, education, health, leisure and entertainment. We are indeed in the midst of a revolution, perhaps the greatest that humanity has ever experienced. To benefit the world community, the successful and continued growth of this new dynamic requires global discussion.

—WORLD SUMMIT ON THE INFORMATION SOCIETY ANNOUNCEMENT,
NOVEMBER 2003

CHAPTER OVERVIEW

This chapter examines the recent emergence of a new global information society regime. This is composed of a range of international organizations, nongovernmental actors, and business associations whose main aim is to influence the frameworks within which Internet policy discussions will occur over the coming years. At present, the global agenda is split between those who argue that the Internet and other information and communication technologies should form part of a socially responsible approach to development and those who wish to open up markets in developing countries for information technology and e-commerce companies in the developed world to exploit. Many of these organizations appear at various points throughout chapter 10—"The rise of Internet Governance."

This chapter identifies and discusses an array of international organizations and forums that are arguably constructing a new global information society regime. As the strategic importance of Internet connectivity has increased throughout the world, a diverse set of actors is attempting to influence its future development through programs of research and education, myriad pilot projects, summits, conferences, and ad hoc bodies involving states and nonstate actors, such as the European Union (EU) Information Society Project, the G8's Digital Opportunity Taskforce (G8 DOT Force), the United Nations Information and Communication Technology Taskforce (UNICT), the Global Information Infrastructure Commission (GIIC), and many others. On the surface, these activities might not appear to have regulatory power. But in a rapidly developing global policy environment often lacking legally enforceable rules, such actors are increasingly important (Chayes and Chayes, 1995; Haas, 2002). As I discussed in chapter 2, they constitute what some international relations scholars term "governance without government." As Rosenau (1992:4) puts it:

> Governance is not synonymous with government. Both refer to purposive behavior, to goal oriented activities, to systems of rule; but government suggests activities that are backed by formal authority, by police powers, to insure the implementation of duly constituted policies, whereas governance refers to activities backed by shared goals that may or may not derive from legal and formally prescribed responsibilities and that do not necessarily rely on police powers to overcome defiance and attain compliance. Governance, in other words, is a more encompassing phenomenon than government. It embraces governmental institutions, but it also subsumes informal, non-governmental mechanisms whereby those persons and organizations within its purview move ahead, satisfy their needs, and fulfill their wants.

Due to the Internet's status as a global network of networks that allows communication to flow across national borders with relative ease, Internet policy problems require a multilateral response. Even if it was in its interests to do so, a single nation-state is incapable of exercising hegemonic control over the Internet. At the same time, single nation-states cannot, by themselves, protect their citizens from what may be perceived as the undesirable effects of completely unregulated communication, such as cultural imperialism, economic monopoly, privacy threats, and terrorism, to name a few. This creates a context of "complex interdependence" (Keohane and Nye, 1989) that is ripe for attempts to construct an international policy regime. Oran Young (1999:22) identifies a "governance gap" at the international level, into which a range of new public and private actors are now flooding. As we shall see in this chapter, this certainly appears to capture the essence of what has occurred in recent years. More radically, Manuel Castells writes of the recasting of individual states' sovereignty into a highly fluid, complex, and overarching global "network state, formed by nation-states, regional and local governments, and non-governmental organizations" (Castells, 2004:364). The Internet requires but also creates the conditions for the fluid nature of international governance.

Scholarly research that focuses specifically on attempts to construct a regime for the global information society is in its infancy (but see Braman, 2004; Cogburn, 2004; Marsden, 2000; and 6, 2002). Yet over the last decade, the proliferation of global initiatives has created powerful trends toward the establishment of a number of governance mechanisms. Some now argue that we are witnessing the emergence of a new, highly complex, "global information policy regime" (Braman, 2004). Because it is increasingly based upon the convergence of previously distinct functional areas such as telecommunication, computing, and broadcast media, the Internet is central to such a regime. Overall, however, the diffusion of the Internet is still highly dependent upon the establishment of a suitable infrastructure with global reach. The hardware and other physical structures that developed countries take for granted are patchy or nonexistent in less-developed areas. The dominant approach among bodies such as the UN has been to point to the economic advantages of developing countries' integration into the global information society. But what might appear at first glance to be a common sense attempt to spread the benefits of the Internet to developing countries is, as we shall see, contested.

COMPLEX INTERDEPENDENCE AND INTERNATIONAL REGIMES

In the field of international relations, much discussion currently focuses on two big ideas: complex interdependence and regime theory. These are useful tools for trying to make sense of how, in the absence of a single sovereign entity, a highly fluid set of actors and organizations can come to shape policy at the international level.

Robert Keohane and Joseph Nye, who first defined the concept of complex interdependence, argue that international relations have moved into an era where state and nonstate actors are increasingly enmeshed in reciprocal relationships that transcend national borders (1989). Interdependence has emerged as a result of an increasing number of transactions—"flows of money, goods, people and messages"—that now involve some sort of transnational element (Keohane and Nye, 1989:8). States find it increasingly difficult, if not impossible, to stand alone in the international system. They find military means of asserting their power increasingly ineffective and are thus constantly seeking to develop other ways of regulating activity in the international sphere. But in the absence of a global sovereign power, argue Keohane and Nye, the normal mechanisms for regulating conduct are little more than loose networks of organizations, based on agreements, treaties, conferences, and summits involving public and private actors. Occasionally, some states may fall back on military force and may be able to integrate powerful private actors such as transnational corporations to enhance their power. But in many respects, structures of global governance exist in the minds of the actors involved. Without general acceptance of their legitimacy—which is often very fragile—these institutions would find it incredibly difficult to exist, let alone achieve their objectives. Yet they exist because states have decided to create them. They largely rely on competition among actors using soft, or persuasive, forms of power rather than hard forms of power such as military coercion or direct economic sanctions (Keohane and Nye, 1998:86).

Ultimately, despite what might appear to be a bewilderingly complex set of disconnected institutions and behaviors in the international sphere, over time, these networks may become sedimentary, forming the bedrock of assumptions about how to develop policy. Ideas about how to govern the information society—even the very idea itself—do not spring from thin air but are constructed over time through multiple channels involving many different actors, largely using soft power resources: ideas. The Internet itself enables more rapid diffusion of ideas as soft power and increases competition among providers of the ideas that influence global policy. While states retain their superiority in areas such as intelligence and surveillance, they and large corporate actors find their credibility as information providers under threat and are forced to compete with nonstate actors that are increasingly able to challenge official versions of events and present alternative perspectives (Risse, 2004:309; Scholte, 2004). The proliferation of international organizations and initiatives dealing not just with the Internet but with many other areas of global concern in part reflects the fact that there are simply more players at the global level than ever before.

However, while the idea of interdependence might seem to indicate that all actors have equal power, this is not the case. Keohane and Nye argue that some actors are more vulnerable to dependence on others, and this creates asymmetrical interdependencies. For example, the leading role of the United States in the global hardware, software, and entertainment industries allows it to assert its power in the international sphere. Yet the United States is still dependent upon the actions of other states in the international system (Rogerson, 2000:422–23). For one, states can refuse to integrate their Internet infrastructures with those of the rest of the world, or they can restrict access to their physical territories. In the case of countries with huge (and rapidly growing) markets such as China, these restrictions can have a significant impact on the fortunes of U.S. companies and the U.S. government. The rise of the Internet has increased the fluidity of the international environment, eroding some of the power of large organizations to control information flows, opening up the field to "loosely structured network organizations and even individuals" (Keohane and Nye, 1998:83). But the developed states still need to integrate developing states into the global system if they are to maintain their dominant position.

A second useful tool for conceptualizing the global information society comes in the form of regime theory. This seeks to understand and explain how and why new rules develop at the international level to govern specific policy areas. Probably the most influential definition of an international regime has been put forward by Stephen Krasner, who defines them as "principles, norms, rules, and decision-making procedures around which actor expectations converge in a given issue area" (1982:185). This is a deliberately loose definition that can cover a range of actors and institutions, including, in the eyes of some scholars, private bodies like firms, business associations, or even organized criminal gangs. As Rodney Bruce Hall and Thomas Biersteker have argued, "private sector markets, market actors, non-governmental organizations, transnational actors, and other institutions can exercise forms of legitimate authority" (2002:5; see also Ronit, 2001).

When it comes to the Internet, it could be argued that the nearest we have to an international regime is what scholars have termed the telecommunications regime. This, however, covers only some aspects of Internet communication and is now seen as increasingly under threat (Cogburn, 2003; Drake, 2000). While the old regime was dominated by an intergovernmental body called the International Telecommunication Union (ITU) and predicated upon a relatively simple set of agreements among states (largely because many of them owned their respective telecommunication infrastructures), the new regime is characterized by the privatization of telecommunication infrastructures, the influx of a large number of private actors, and new services related to the convergence of computing, telecommunication, and entertainment (Drake, 2000). Hence the attempts to construct a much broader global information society agenda based around the Internet and mobile communications in recent years.

When an old regime no longer functions effectively, a new one must be built. How can this happen in the absence of central direction? An interesting perspective on regime emergence is constructivism. This is a wide-ranging and ambitious set of theories, but, put simply, a constructivist approach would argue that the development of Krasner's "principles, norms, rules, and decision making procedures" at the international level is largely a matter of how different actors construct their own interests and the interests of others in an ongoing process of interaction. Central to this process are ideas, knowledge, and language as tools actors use to try to establish meanings that are favorable for the achievement of their goals. Crucially, however, these goals themselves come to be modified in the multiple processes of interaction that occur in international organizations and forums (Ruggie, 1998; Wendt, 1992; see also Risse, 2004). In other words, in a context of incessant technological change, the very idea of a global information society has to be constructed, or given meaning through discussions involving a range of actors and institutions, including nongovernmental organizations (NGOs) (Boli and Thomas, 1999; Rodgers, 2003), before principles, norms, rules, and decision-making procedures can become effective.

THE GLOBAL INFORMATION SOCIETY REGIME: MAPPING THE KEY PLAYERS

In recent years, a plethora of global information society initiatives has emerged. Some have developed as part of much broader approaches to financial, trade, social, and development issues. Others are highly specific programs in the area of information and communication technologies. But what unites the vast majority of these is the view that the information society is a positive force that should be encouraged in a global context. Collaborative networks at the international level are now common in this area. For instance, the UNICT has worked closely with the G8 DOT Force and the World Economic Forum (WEF) (UNICT, 2003a).

Many keyboards have been worn out by attempts to pin down the idea of the information society, but this is not the place to enter into detailed definitional discussion (see May, 2002; Webster, 2002). At the risk of oversimplification, I have presented what I regard as the core themes of the current policy agenda on the global information society (see exhibit 9.1; for a more detailed account, see also Venturelli, 2002). Following that, I map out the most important ingredients in this acronym soup of actors involved in trying to establish a global information society regime. Key actors and initiatives are italicized.

EXHIBIT 9.1. THE GLOBAL INFORMATION SOCIETY: CORE THEMES

- **Liberalizing and privatizing infrastructures** to increase competition, reduce costs, and increase demand.

- **Encouraging private investment** to create new communications infrastructure and high-technology sectors.

- **Creating standards** for areas like privacy and data security.

- **Protecting intellectual property rights** of those who innovate in information-based products and services.

- **Promoting administrative modernization** through e-government.

- **Promoting diversity of applications and online content** tailored to specific localities.

- **Promoting universal access** to information services.

- **Promoting global cooperation in technological research and development.**

Sources: Heavily adapted from Cogburn, 2003, and Venturelli, 2002.

INTERGOVERNMENTAL ORGANIZATIONS

The United Nations (UN)

The UN is a vast organization, and several of its sections have been active in this area. The most significant is the *International Telecommunication Union (ITU)*. A specialist agency of the UN, it already had an established presence in the international regulation of telecommunication (it was originally founded in 1865 to develop common standards and regulations for the burgeoning global telegraph networks [ITU, 2003a]). Over the course of the twentieth century it evolved with the telecommunication environment, but it still describes itself as an "impartial, international organization within which governments and the private sector . . . work together to co-ordinate the operation of telecommunication networks and services and advance the development of communications technology" (ITU, 2003b). It consists of 190 member states and over 600 nonstate bodies. Every four years the ITU holds the World Telecommunications Development Conference. By getting more involved in debates about the global information society, the ITU wishes to assert itself in a rapidly changing global telecoms market experiencing a shift away from nationalized analog networks toward a more uncertain, deregulated future of mobile technologies and the Internet (Drake, 2000:164).

Another specialist UN agency, the *World Intellectual Property Organization (WIPO)*, was formed in 1970. Consisting of 177 member states, it seeks to protect the "rights of creators and owners of intellectual property . . . worldwide." By seeking to create "a stable environment for the marketing of intellectual property products, it also oils the wheels of international trade" (WIPO, 2003). The WIPO works globally to protect the interests of intellectual property holders. It does so by administering a number of treaties and agreements that regulate intellectual property in those states that have agreed to enforce them within their own territories. The most significant of these is the Trade Related Agreement on Intellectual Property Rights (TRIPS), jointly forged with the World Trade Organization (WTO) in 1994. This greatly enhanced the WIPO's influence in the global arena. The growing power of the WIPO is a reflection of the growing importance of intellectual property disputes for the future of the Internet (see also chapters 10 and 12).

The UN has also been the most prominent actor in the sphere of technologies for development, launching *UNICT* in November 2001. UNICT is a creature of the UN's Economic and Social Council—a powerful presence in the UN administration (around 70 percent of the UN's resources are devoted to its operation). The origins of the UNICT in the Council gives an indication of its social welfare emphasis. Its goal is "the harmonious development of a global network society." To achieve this, it seeks to put "technologies at the service of development . . . [by] harnessing the potential of the information and communication technology revolution for development for all, for the reduction of poverty, and for the empowerment of those who are currently marginalized" (UNICT, 2003a).

Thus, UNICT, as befits a UN entity, is concerned with using information and communication technologies to promote social and economic development. It is, in several respects, a pioneering project: it is the first of its kind to explicitly include a membership, comprised of governments, other UN agencies, NGOs, academics, and private sector actors, all of whom possess formally equal decision making power; and it rests upon international collaboration through the development of a number of partnerships with other organizations, particularly the G8, the WEF, and the Global Business Dialogue on E-Commerce (GBDE).

The UNICT has an ambitious range of objectives, including the fostering of participation by developing countries in information society policy-making bodies; the promotion of low-cost wireless connectivity in less-developed countries; the development of localized digital content and software; support for programs of training and education, especially in Africa; encouraging entrepreneurial activity in the technology sector as a means of creating employment to reduce poverty; and the deployment of information and communication technologies in health-care systems combating HIV/AIDS and other diseases (UNICT, 2003b). However, much of what UNICT does merely involves the coordination of activities initiated elsewhere. It has a very small core budget for its first three years ($5 million) and does not have any "operational or implementing capacity" of its own—features that weaken its organizational power, both within the UN and in the larger context of governance in this area (UNICT, 2003b). Nevertheless, its role as a coordinating body involves raising funds (around $50 million in the first three years) from some of its wealthier partner organizations and channeling these into the program set out in its Plan of Action.

The European Union (EU)

If the UN has been a prime mover at the global level, the most powerful regional organization is undoubtedly the EU. Information and communication technologies have been a priority area for the *European Commission*, the executive arm of the EU, since the early 1990s, when the Bangemann Report sparked off several initiatives aimed at spreading technology use throughout the EU. The report attempted to locate Europe at the center of global markets in the high-tech sector, largely as a means of countering competition from Japan and the United States (European Council, 1994). Stressing the importance of free markets, the Bangemann Report listed "ten applications to launch the information society": teleworking; distance learning; a network for universities and research centers; telematic services for small- and medium-sized enterprises; road traffic management; air traffic control; health-care networks; electronic tendering; a trans-European administration network; and city-information highways (European Council 1994). The report explicitly urged the European Union member states to have "faith in market mechanisms as the motive power to carry us into the Information Age" (European Council, 1994:2; Kaitatzi-Whitlock, 2000:53–54). The *Information Society Project Office*—a coordinating agency which pulled together a range of different actors spread across the EU institutions—was established in 1994.

Between 1998 and 2002, the EU conducted the *Information Society Program*, aimed at spreading the Internet gospel and investigating its economic, social, and political impact. More recently, a new *Information Society Directorate General* was created and the *eEurope* initiative launched, with an emphasis on e-commerce, mobile telecommunication, broadband, media convergence, and e-government (European Commission, 1999; Simpson, 2000). While the bulk of the EU's work in this area is aimed at the member states, it increasingly looks to enhance what it calls "Europe's role and visibility within the global dimension of the Information Society," though the latter is predominantly framed as a global market rather than an arena for social development (European Commission, 2003; Goodwin and Spittle, 2002). In addition to these initiatives, the EU has been keen to push a pro-European perspective in opposition to what it perceives as U.S. dominance in Internet policy. Perhaps more than any other program of administrative reform, e-government has been popularized by the EU, especially by the Commission (Chadwick and May, 2003), not only because it sees it as a way to integrate programs of administrative reform across the EU's member states, but also because government use of technology has been seen as providing stimulus to European IT companies competing with those in the United States and the Far East.

The Organization for Economic Co-operation and Development (OECD)

Though it has much less institutional power than the EU, the OECD plays an important role in creating the background research upon which many of the key global information society initiatives have been based. The OECD consists of thirty countries that "share a commitment to democratic government and the market economy," though it now incorporates several advisory committees that bring in representatives from civil society organizations, especially business and trade union groups (OECD, 2004a). Founded in 1945 as a means to implement the U.S.-backed Marshall Plan for postwar reconstruction, its remit now is to produce research, recommendations, and internationally agreed-upon rules to assist multilateral initiatives to "build strong economies in its member countries, improve efficiency, hone market systems, expand free trade and contribute to development in industrialized as well as developing countries"

(OECD, 2004b). The OECD's Internet-related work largely funnels through its *Directorate for Science, Technology, and Industry*, but its *Directorate for Public Governance and Territorial Development* places much emphasis on e-government. In 1998, it hosted the influential *Ministerial Meeting on E-Commerce* in Ottawa, Canada, which played a major role in stoking up interest in the new economy among governments in developed countries.

The G7/8

The G7/8 (which is formally composed of the world's eight leading economies: Canada, France, the United States, Britain, Germany, Japan, Italy, and Russia) has also been a key player in diffusing ideas about e-commerce. At a 1995 conference at Brussels, which had substantial private sector involvement, it outlined a number of themes for the development of a global information society. In 2000, the G7/8 countries and a range of international organizations met in Okinawa, Japan, to establish the Charter on the Global Information Society. One of the outcomes was the creation of the *G8 DOT Force*. Its initial membership consisted of government representatives, private sector actors, and nonprofit bodies from the G7/8 countries, together with similar personnel from a small selection of developing countries (Bolivia, Brazil, Egypt, India, Indonesia, Senegal, South Africa, Tanzania) as well as other international organizations, including the World Bank Group (WBG) and the ITU (G8 DOT Force, 2002b).

Officially ended in 2002, the G8 DOT Force turned out to be a short-lived affair. But during that time it played a central role in a number of technology-for-development initiatives and quickly expanded to include thirty countries and twenty projects. Most of these were in the same areas as UNICT—involving developing countries in global policy forums; improving Internet infrastructure and access in poor rural areas; establishing education and training programs; creating locally relevant web content; using the Internet for health care; improving accountability and reducing corruption through e-government; and promoting entrepreneurialism through e-commerce. Its most important substantive programs to date include the Italian government's *E-government for Development* initiative and a $6.5 million project carried out by the French government for the establishment of community Internet access stations in French-speaking Africa. Other notable projects include the implementation of "Edu-telecentres" in Malawi, Kenya, Uganda, and Zambia to support teacher training and distance learning and the creation of a Health InterNetwork portal to provide information to public health workers (G8 DOT Force, 2002b). The DOT Force's role was to kick-start a series of programs, and its agenda has essentially been passed down to UNICT and other organizations.

In common with the UNICT, the G8 DOT Force explicitly recognized the importance of participation by developing countries in the global Internet policy sphere. As a result, along with the Markle Foundation, a U.S.-based charitable organization, it set up a *Partnership for Global Policy Participation* in 2002 (G8 DOT Force, 2002a). The Partnership identifies a number of problems with inequality of access to global policy forums and aims to redress these with programs to raise awareness and develop expertise in developing countries, together with more prosaic but significant matters such as providing funding for representatives from poorer nations to attend international meetings.

Asia-Pacific Economic Co-operation (APEC) and the Association for South East Asian Nations (ASEAN)

Not surprisingly, regional associations other than the EU have tried to assert their identities in this area. APEC is an unusual organization but is also symptomatic of the kind of governance structures that have become more common in recent years. Consisting of twenty-one member economies of the Asia-Pacific region (including the United States, Canada, and Australia), which together constitute around a half of global GDP, the APEC does not issue binding agreements but merely serves as a discussion and consensus-building forum. The APEC's principal emphasis has been on trade and investment liberalization, mainly with a view to increasing export levels in its member economies (APEC, 2004b). This emphasis is strongly present in its *Telecommunications and Information Working Group*, which is mainly composed of business representatives. Following a ministerial meeting in 2002, the APEC issued a *Telecommunications and Information Action Plan*, aiming at a "fully liberalized telecommunications sector" in the APEC region (APEC, 2004a). Although it focuses largely on infrastructural issues, APEC's activities cover many other areas, especially Internet-related piracy, which involve a mission to strengthen the WTO in the global system. The other main regional organization in Asia, the ASEAN, consisting of Indonesia, Malaysia, Philippines, Singapore, Thailand, Brunei Darussalam, Vietnam, Laos, Burma, and Cambodia, aims to increase economic cooperation and create a free-trade area. In 2000, the organization launched an E-ASEAN initiative covering mainly infrastructure and e-commerce, but it also includes some e-government initiatives (ASEAN, 2004).

The World Trade Organization (WTO)

The WTO is widely regarded as one of the most influential international organizations shaping the global information society regime. Established in 1995, it currently consists of 144 member states. It has placed Internet policy at the center of its concerns since an addition to the General Agreement on Trade in Services (GATS) in 1997, outlining principles for opening up global markets for electronic services (among many others). In the context of GATS, since 1998 it has taken a close interest in e-commerce (WTO, 1998), with ministerial declarations in the area in 1999 and 2001 and an ongoing project to develop rules for the regulation of services delivered electronically across national boundaries (Aronson, 2000; Moore, 2000). The WTO's work touches on many areas of relevance, but its most significant activity to date has been its role in policing treaties and agreements to protect intellectual property rights—an area in which the developed nations have huge advantages in the global economy (Thomas, 1999). In tandem with the WIPO (see previous discussion, under the UN heading), the WTO plays a significant role in enforcing and monitoring the TRIPS agreement, introduced in 1994. TRIPS contains a number of rules to which member states are required to adhere to protect intellectual property rights in the international trading system. These are mainly aimed at harmonizing the ways in which different states handle copyright and patent infringements. TRIPS was an explicit recognition of the importance of the service sector in the global economy, especially the provision of digital products such as software, which could easily be reproduced and circulated, and online "knowledge services" which easily cross borders and often require no physical exchange of goods, lowering the barriers to piracy. However, technological convergence on the Internet as a means for the delivery of audiovisual goods now means that whole swathes of electronic products that were not previously protected or were only vaguely regulated are being brought under the umbrella of the WTO (Pauwels and Loisen, 2003).

The WTO's decisions are legally binding upon member states. It has already emerged as a powerful and controversial player in the global system, as witnessed by the force of protests against its activities in the Seattle meeting of ministers in November 1999 (Vegh, 2003; see also chapter 6) and its resultant attempts to increase the involvement of civil society groups and developing countries in its operations as a means of enhancing its legitimacy (Ford, 2003; Wilkinson, 2002). Some argue that the WTO has been captured by commercial interests, resulting in an international intellectual property regime that benefits large corporations by upholding their ownership rights rather than stressing the open transfer of knowledge as a means to assist developing states, in the area of software, pharmaceuticals, or agriculture, for example (Drahos with Braithwaite, 2002). The WTO is also a major player in the developing Internet governance regime (see chapter 10).

The World Bank Group (WBG)

The WBG is an equally controversial global player. Much like the WTO, the World Bank has attracted fierce criticism in recent years, often from online activists, for the liberalization conditions it attaches to its loans and what is perceived as its reluctance to reduce the debt burden of developing countries (Vegh, 2003). Consisting of 183 member states, its general role in the international system is as a provider of loans, share capital, financial expertise, training programs, and technical assistance to governments in developing countries. Through its *Global Information and Communication Technologies Department* it has long attempted to encourage the modernization of telecommunication infrastructure in developing countries by promoting free markets and competition, with varying degrees of success (Støvring, 2004). In 1997, the WBG, together with the Canadian government, organized a Global Knowledge Conference. This has now developed into the *Global Knowledge Partnership,* a multistakeholder initiative which still involves the WBG, along with many other players. In recent times, this activity has broadened to encompass all aspects of technology policy, including investing in start-up companies around the world. The WBG spends an estimated $1.5 billion on information- and communication technology–related activities each year (Daly, 2001:1).

Through its *Information for Development Program (InfoDev),* the WBG has also established its own presence as a technology-for-development player. InfoDev awards grants, funded principally from donations by nation-states, though large corporations like IBM are also contributors (World Bank Information for Development Program, 2003). However, with an annual budget of only $10–15 million per year, InfoDev represents a tiny proportion of World Bank spending (Daly, 2001:1).

Nongovernmental Organizations

So far we have considered the role of intergovernmental organizations in shaping the global information society regime. It is not surprising that long-established bodies like the UN, the OECD, or the EU have moved into the field. But we also need to include several important nongovernmental organizations. Most of these represent business interests, while others are socially progressive advocacy networks.

The Internet Corporation for Assigned Names and Numbers (ICANN)

ICANN's purpose, since its creation in 1998, is to administer the Internet's Domain Name System (DNS) "for the benefit of the Internet community as a whole" (ICANN articles of incorporation, quoted in Kleinwachter, 2003a:1103). ICANN, working in tandem with the WTO, makes global public policy on who deserves property rights in domain names. It imposes sanctions on those who refuse to comply through removing sites from the DNS and thus from the Internet itself. Chapter 10 is devoted to understanding and explaining the emergence of what some describe as a global government for the Internet. Yet ICANN deserves mention here because it is increasingly involved in the larger global information society regime through its links with the WTO and the WIPO. Indeed, most of the organizations covered in this chapter work with ICANN either directly or indirectly. As we shall see, there is much dispute over the precise nature of ICANN, but at this stage, it is probably best understood as a quasi-nongovernmental organization.

The World Economic Forum (WEF)

The WEF originated in the early 1970s as an annual meeting of chief executives from the world's most powerful corporations. Over the last thirty years it has played an increasingly important role in defining global economic policy agendas. During the late 1990s, its meetings of heads of government and the "1000 foremost corporations worldwide," as the Forum describes its membership, became key events. In common with the WTO, the WEF has also been the target of protestors campaigning against global neoliberalism. The 2000 meeting in particular was marked by violent clashes between protestors and the Swiss authorities. The WEF responded by broadening participation in its meetings to include academics and some civil society groups.

Many of those who participate in the WEF meetings are drawn from media, Internet, telecommunication, or software sector corporations, and this tends to shape its public profile. Microsoft's founder, Bill Gates, for example, used the Davos meeting of 2002 to announce a massive ($50 million) charitable donation to be spent on HIV/AIDS programs in Africa (World Economic Forum, 2003). In common with the other organizations described here, many of the WEF's initiatives are aimed at setting the global agenda. Foremost among these are its *Global Competitiveness*, *Global Digital Divide*, and *Global Governance* programs. Members of those bodies involved in Internet governance and regulation attend WEF meetings. A significant chunk of what it does in the global arena is determined by the large transnational corporations that constitute its membership (Thomas, 2002). It is thus an important form of private authority in the global system that can be used to exert leverage over nation-states.

The Global Business Dialogue on E-commerce (GBDE) and the Global Information Infrastructure Commission (GIIC)

While the WEF has a broad remit to promote business interests, in recent years, new, more-focused private actors have emerged. Describing itself as "one of the world's leading private sector voices on e-commerce policy," the GBDE is made up of twenty-five of the world's largest transnational technology corporations. Its membership roster includes companies such as HP, France Telecom, Alcatel, Fujitsu, Hitachi, Nokia, Siemens, and NTT (GBDE, 2004). It lobbies national governments and other international organizations in five main areas: security, e-government, intellectual property rights, junk email, taxation, and trade, though it mainly emphasizes the role of the WTO in developing rules for free trade in e-commerce goods and services.

The GIIC is a confederation of chief executives of around fifty firms, most of which are based in the technology sector. Its commissioner staff also includes a small number of representatives from other international organizations, such as the World Bank Group and the UN. Major companies include Cisco Systems, Fujitsu, Deutsche Telekom, Sprint, NEC, Toshiba, Nokia, Cable and Wireless, and Oracle. In seeking to "strengthen the leadership role of the private sector," it covers many of the same issues as the GBDE but places greater emphasis on broadband infrastructure and investment in developing countries (GIIC, 2004).

The Internet Society (ISOC)

The ISOC was established in 1992 by many of the technicians involved in the early development of the Internet. It is an international nonprofit organization and now contains the *Internet Engineering Task Force (IETF)*, an important voluntary standards development body consisting largely of technicians. The IETF is arguably the most influential organization in defining Internet network standards (particularly TCP/IP). It holds regular online and offline meetings that are open to all comers. In the early days these gatherings tended to be dominated by computer scientists, but now many nontechnical delegates attend. The ISOC was initially designed to provide legal protection for Internet engineers, but it now plays a much broader role. It has evolved into an interest group–come-professional network whose remit extends to the "growth and evolution of the worldwide Internet, with the way in which the Internet is and can be used, and with the social, political, and technical issues that arise as a result" (quoted in Froomkin, 2003:788). Establishing an institutional presence in the international arena for Internet technicians allows them to deal with other standards-setting institutions like the ITU (Mueller, 2002:95). In the 1990s, the Internet Society was an obvious contender for some sort of jurisdictional role in Internet governance (see chapter 10). The context of convergence arguably enhances its influence still further.

The Association for Progressive Communications (APC)

There are many different civil societal groups attempting to shape the global information society, but the APC is arguably the most important. Established in 1990, it emerged as a major civil society actor during the late 1990s. It defines itself as

> a global network of non-governmental organizations whose mission is to empower and support organizations, social movements and individuals in and through the use of information and communication technologies to build strategic communities and initiatives for the purpose of making meaningful contributions to equitable human development, social justice, participatory political processes and environmental sustainability. (Association for Progressive Communications, 2004)

The Association acts as a loose umbrella organization for a range of networks around the globe. In 2004, its global membership stood at thirty-six organizations based in twenty-nine countries. The majority of these are themselves umbrella groups representing internal country networks, such as the U.K.'s Greennet, which combines environmentalism with a commitment to open-source software, antisurveillance campaigns, and progressive development, or South Africa's Women'sNet, which provides information and support in areas such as HIV/AIDS, violence against women, women's health, and the gender gap in South African politics.

A GLOBAL INFORMATION SOCIETY REGIME?

Do these organizations and forums constitute a new global information society regime (see figure 9.1 on pp. 222–223)? In terms of Krasner's (1982:185) classic definition outlined in the introduction to this chapter—"principles, norms, rules, and decision-making procedures around which actor expectations converge in a given issue area"—the answer would appear to be a cautious "yes." However, as Sandra Braman (2004:7) argues, this regime is only in the early stages of development. Which institutions will emerge as powerful in future is far from clear, and there is a (remote) possibility that the regime may atrophy.

In fact, many argue that states continue to hold the trump card. While it is simplistic to assume that a single nation-state—the United States—can, at present, assume hegemony in the area of Internet policy, individual nation-states continue to play hugely important roles in producing and implementing policies for their own economic development (Hirst and Thompson, 1999; Wade, 1996; Weiss, 1998). And since the terrorist attacks of September 2001, the United States has reasserted its interests in the international arena; it is undoubtedly the most powerful single nation-state (Castells, 2004:344–55). The weakening of multilateralism will fuel already existing differences in approaches to regulating the information society, not just between the United States and the developing countries, but also between the United States and the rest of the developed world, particularly the EU states (Newman and Bach, 2004).

Another factor here is that the relative influence of these actors varies significantly. Some of these bodies have skeletal structures with very few permanent staff members. Others are not in any position to generate their own budgets. Some of the international meetings end with funding commitments; many do not. Perhaps the strongest emerging intergovernmental actor is the WTO, whose rulings are binding on member states. However, not all states are members, rulings can still be circumvented, and they are often difficult to implement, as Christopher Hughes (2002) demonstrates in relation to China's formal accession to the WTO in 2000. China has been very resistant to implementing WTO directives. As another example, if we consider one of the key objectives of the global information society regime, particularly in the eyes of the WBG—privatization of telecommunication—it is obvious that it is far from being achieved. According to the ITU, ninety of its member states still have state-owned infrastructures, while many of those that have privatized ended up creating private monopolies or duopolies. Moreover, the evidence that privatization of telecommunication actually increases Internet diffusion (outside the OECD countries) is weak (Guillén and Suárez, 2001:351). The example of South Korea, where broadband Internet penetration currently stands at around 70 percent, is often cited as an example of the power of liberalization and privatization. Yet as Heejin Lee and colleagues have shown, the Korean success story is as much reliant upon public promotion by government and cultural factors as it is competition in the telecommunication market (Lee et al., 2003). If the existence of a regime is measured by its direct policy effectiveness, the evidence is currently patchy.

Despite these qualifications, a development that lends support to the regime formation interpretation is the fact that all of these organizations, in addition to countless others, have now been brought together under the umbrella of the World Summit on the Information Society (WSIS). Organized in two distinct stages (2003 and 2005), the first of which set out a declaration and action plan, the WSIS is a fascinating illustration of the way in which Internet policy has been thrust into the limelight. It is not without significance that the ITU was the main organizer of the summit and was responsible for coordinating a range of other activities in the build-up to and the aftermath of the first meeting in Geneva, held during December 2003. By adopting this responsibility, the ITU was competing for the position of chief global player. The significance of WSIS also stems from its relatively open structure and the prominence of civil societal groups in its proceedings. Participants are drawn from governments, the private sector, civil society, and many of the UN organizational family in a way that bears many of the hallmarks of contemporary global governance structures. All of the organizations identified in this chapter are involved. The official list of participants in the Geneva round was immense, stretching to 192 pages, and no doubt will increase by the Tunisia meeting in November 2005 (WSIS, 2003b). Scores of other participants do not appear on the official list, and an array of parallel events, both real and virtual, took place alongside the first main summit. Some of these were of the kind that have sprung up alongside other global meetings in recent times: highly critical websites and mailing lists, public protests, and online activist tactics like virtual sit-ins and alternative running commentaries via blogs.

Yet the WSIS agenda, or what passes for an agenda given the huge diversity of interests involved, is deeply controversial. In the preparatory phase, civil society groups, disenchanted with what they perceived as the corporate-driven nature of the summit, started work on their own separate declaration, which was eventually issued alongside the official version. A "counterevent"—the World Forum on Communication Rights, organized by activists arguing that the WSIS was paying insufficient attention to development issues—coincided with the first round (World Forum on Communication Rights, 2003).

The WSIS conflict, which is similar to those exhibited in other multistakeholder initiatives (Koenig-Archibugi, 2004:255), illustrates some more general problems with ascribing too much influence to such events. Conferences on the information society have typically produced countless action plans, agreements, and memoranda of understanding.

Figure 9.1. The Global Information Society Regime.

Entity	Type				PRINCIPAL FOCI				
		Liberalizing and Privatizing Infrastructures	Encouraging Private Investment	Creating Standards	Protecting Intellectual Property Rights	Promoting Diversity of Applications and Content	Administrative Modernization	Promoting Universal Access	Promoting Global Co-operation in Technology Research and Development
International Telecommunication Union (ITU)	Global intergovernmental			*		*		*	*
World Intellectual Property Organization (WIPO)	Global intergovernmental			*	*				
UN Information and Communication Technology Task Force (UNICT)	Global multi-stakeholder					*	*	*	*
European Union (EU)	Regional intergovernmental	*	*	*	*		*		*
Organization for Economic Co-operation and Development (OECD)	Intergovernmental	*	*				*		*
G7/8	Intergovernmental	*	*				*		
Asia-Pacific Economic Co-operation (APEC)	Regional intergovernmental	*	*	*	*				*
Association for South East Asian Nations (ASEAN)	Regional intergovernmental		*			*	*		
World Trade Organization (WTO)	Global intergovernmental	*	*	*	*				

Organization	Classification							
World Bank Group (WBG)	Global intergovernmental	*	*	*			*	
Internet Corporation for Assigned Names and Numbers (ICANN)	Global quasi-nongovernmental	*		*				
World Economic Forum (WEF)	Global nongovernmental	*		*				*
Global Business Dialogue on E-commerce (GBDE)	Global nongovernmental	*	*	*			*	
Global Information Infra-structure Commission (GIIC)	Global nongovernmental	*		*		*		
Internet Society (ISOC)	Global nongovernmental			*	*	*	*	*
Association for Progressive Communications (APC)	Global nongovernmental			*	*	*	*	*

Sources: Analysis and adaptation of data from organizational websites, July 2004: http://www.itu.int, http://www.wipo.int, http://www.unicttaskforce.org, http://europa.eu.int/ispo, http://www.oecd.org, http://www.g8online.org, http://www.apec.org, http://www.aseansec.org, http://www.wto.org, http://www. infovdev.org, http://www.icann.org, http://www.weforum.org, http://www.gbde.org, http://www.giic.org, http://www.isoc.org, http://www.apc.org.

More rarely, they may establish new organizational structures and secure financial resources. From an optimistic perspective, it could be argued that the frequent and multiple interactions that now occur at the global level help create publicity, generate new policy frameworks, and over time, will "socialize" developed states into creating a new global information society regime more sensitive to the needs of developing countries. This argument has been made in relation to analogous areas, such as global environmental regulation, for instance (Haas, 2002:75). However, even these optimistic assessments must be tempered by the reality that many of the organizations and initiatives described above have very fragile institutional bases. These are often ad hoc, short-term projects that disappear or change as rapidly as they emerge once specific proposals are mentioned (Dutton et al., 1995). Isolated international meetings are unlikely to produce lasting policy change. When meetings occur frequently and regularly, an organization is likely to have greater power. Unfortunately, most of the global information society organizations that meet frequently are either representatives of the developed countries, such as the G8, the OECD, the International Monetary Fund (IMF), and the World Bank, or private corporations. As Peter Haas says of summitry: "It is difficult to measure directly the effects . . . and the record of states in complying is mixed or uncertain. The goals are often ambiguous. State reporting about compliance is generally weak and incomplete, and few provisions for verification of state compliance are made at the conferences" (Haas, 2002:80). While the recent WSIS initiative gives the appearance of dynamism, there are huge divisions running through the program, especially between those who see the Internet as a means of enhancing social welfare and those who see it as a way to open up new markets for transnational corporations based in the developed world. And to date very few important funding commitments have emerged from the WSIS (see also chapter 13).

Conferences and other international gatherings may also be dominated by competition among specific groups of elites organized in "epistemic communities." This concept refers to networks of "professionals with recognized expertise and competence in a particular domain and an authoritative claim to policy-relevant knowledge within that domain or issue-area" (Haas, 1992:3). In the international sphere, where formal mechanisms of power are more difficult to identify, epistemic communities are arguably the lifeblood of rule-making regimes. However, though they may compete, some epistemic communities are more powerful than others. They may exclude certain actors, or they may choose to rely on certain types of knowledge to deliberately exclude others (Risse, 2004:311). Wealthier governments and large corporations may enjoy more nodal positions in relevant networks and have greater information resources at their disposal than governments in developing countries and NGOs (Cogburn, 2004). Technocratic elites may find that they are relatively unconstrained by public pressures, leading to calls for new forms of accountability (Slaughter, 2004:164). Epistemic communities may be seen as a threat to nation-states because they are networks that develop a common interest away from the interests of any single state. At the same time, however, they may be seen as serving states if the members of the network are drawn mainly from among representatives of interests that happen to be geographically concentrated, like the e-commerce or software industries, for example, in an individual state or small group of states.

The divisions weakening the WSIS project arguably go back a long way. An ideological schism has continually weakened global information society initiatives

(Cogburn, 2004; see also Servaes and Heinderyckx, 2002). According to Derrick Cogburn, there have been two competing visions of the Internet's contribution to the global economy and how it ought to be steered at the global level: a social welfare approach and an e-commerce approach. The social welfare approach stresses public forms of regulation to overcome the digital divide but is also based upon the Net's potential to promote welfare and increase levels of socio-economic development, particularly in the developing countries but also among the poorer sections of developed societies. This view is mainly held by developing countries and an assortment of civil society groups such as the APC. It is also prevalent in certain international institutions that have recently become more open to the influence of developing countries, such as the ITU and other "technology-for-development" bodies in the UN. Taken together, these are attempting to form a social welfare regime.

The second vision, the e-commerce approach, is preoccupied with economic development. This much narrower approach stresses private forms of self-regulation and the importance of opening up developing countries to e-commerce by providing the tools and infrastructure necessary to compete in the global market for electronic information services, allowing inward investment by financial institutions and transnational technology corporations and, most crucially, by using the power of the WTO and the WIPO to safeguard the intellectual property interests of companies in developed states (Thomas, 1999). This vision is strongly promoted by developed countries, especially the United States, but it is also dominant in a range of international organizations, most notably the OECD, ICANN, parts of the European Commission, and global business organizations like the WEF, the GBDE, and the GIIC. This network of institutions and actors is attempting to establish an economic development regime.

While these two visions have long existed in tandem, critics like Cogburn argue that social welfare is now being forced to take a backseat to economic development (Cogburn, 2004; see also Stolfi and Sussman, 2001). Bodies such as the GIIC have quietly dropped their emphasis on socially beneficial technologies and have aligned themselves with the United States and other governments in "making the world safe" for e-commerce. They seek to marginalize the ITU, which they perceive as being captured by the interests of developing countries. It follows that the emergent regime is likely to focus on "information and communications infrastructure development, electronic payment systems, financial services, customs and taxation, security and encryption, a global uniform commercial code, technical standards and interoperability, and consumer protection," when it could be developing e-government, telemedicine, knowledge sharing, universal access to telecommunication, community-building projects, and the development of local media content (Cogburn, 2004:158). In this critical interpretation, the global agenda is skewed because developing countries and NGOs are unable to make decisive contributions to the often-hidden policy discussions that precede the major international meetings. For example, the WSIS declaration of December 2003 was effectively written during a number of preparatory meetings (called Prepcoms) held before the conference. Now standard before most international meetings, prepcoms are small groups of government representatives, technical specialists, affected interests, and lawyers who come together to effectively write the conclusions of a meeting in advance. By so doing, of course, they set the agenda for the meeting itself. Many civil society organizations were unable to participate due to the costs of attendance, or they refused on democratic grounds. Cogburn also argues that the economic development through e-commerce model has greater international influence because it is more narrowly focused in comparison with the rather more diffuse social welfare approach.

This line of critique has been extended by others. For example, Robert Wade (2002) discerns a new system of "digital dependence" in which developing countries become locked in to continual hardware and software upgrades for technologies that are in any case tangential to their basic needs, while business actors increasingly call the shots in the forums that matter, such as standards-setting bodies like the WTO and ICANN. This is reinforced by the advantage developed countries have in establishing information services such as the World Bank's Development Gateway, aimed at spreading the liberalization gospel, which, in rival interpretations, runs counter to the interests of many developing countries. For example, developing countries may have an incentive to introduce administrative modernization through e-government as a way of demonstrating the liberal-democratic credentials of openness and transparency that are often preconditions of receiving funds. But they do not have the capacity to develop their own e-government systems; they must buy them from firms based in the developed world. The result is likely to be a convergence of organizational forms (DiMaggio and Powell, 1983:154) that over the long term can only benefit the powerful economic players. While on the surface this might resemble progress, it introduces a new form of dependency for developing states (Wade, 2002:461).

These are powerful arguments, but there are also less pessimistic accounts. If we bear in mind the context of complex interdependence outlined at the beginning of this chapter, the competition between these two visions might not turn out to be a zero-sum game. The global diffusion of e-commerce cannot take place in the absence of Internet infrastructure and standards. An optimistic interpretation would hold that social welfare could piggyback on the economic development approach. Developing countries will attempt to ensure that infrastructural investment assists socially beneficial projects as well as creates a market for goods produced in developed states. In addition, network standards are often public goods available to all and, once established, may be molded to more socially beneficial ends. Evidence from China's "twin track" approach, which combines traditional industrialization with an emphasis on information services (Dai, 2002), and recent cross-country studies of e-commerce diffusion (Gibbs et al., 2003) and the PC industry (Hart and Kim, 2002) suggests that nationally specific economic development strategies are possible, despite forces pushing countries into global market networks. In Southeast Asia, despite significant pressures to liberalize from the World Bank and the IMF, some states continue to own and centrally plan their telecommunication sectors (Kalathil and Boas, 2003:72). Some scholars have gone further, arguing that among NGOs, a dominant social development model has emerged that is concerned with "addressing social implications of technology, enhancing social well-being through technology, or promoting industrial, social and economic progress in developing countries through technology" (Luo, 2000:149). Indeed, it is arguable that socially progressive NGOs see the piggyback model as viable, and the Internet provides new public spheres in which they can assert it at the global level (Rodgers, 2003). These trends suggest difficulties for any international regime that does not include at least some social welfarist elements and a recognition of national diversity.

CONCLUSION

This chapter has provided a map of an emergent, fragile international governance regime centered upon devising principles, norms, rules, and decision-making procedures on the Internet and its related, often convergent technologies. It has also discussed a number of different interpretations of the likely effects of this regime for the relations between developed and developing countries. It is important to stress that this is a *emergent* regime (Braman, 2004; Curtis, 2003). The WSIS process is still in flux, and its remit is so vast that it is likely to play a role in setting the agenda at the global level for many years to come. The extent to which it will translate into concrete policies backed by funding and sanctions for noncompliance is in some doubt (see chapter 13). The gulf between the two principal competing visions of the global information society—the social and the economic—is either likely to weaken policy or to be resolved by the ascendancy of one vision over the other. The signs are that the economic vision is likely to prove dominant. Participation by developing countries is taken for granted in the structures of this new global governance regime. Yet participation is by itself no guarantee of policy influence (Slaughter, 2004:171). Some might wish to conceive of the Internet as a subfield of telecommunication policy. However, as convergence continues apace, it is arguable that developing a regulatory regime for the Internet itself is likely to emerge as a much more important—perhaps *the* most important—area in its own right. It is to this issue that we now turn.

Discussion Points

- Why is it possible to argue that there is a global information society regime?
- What are the central principles of the global information information society? Are they sufficient?
- Is the global information society regime likely to serve the interests of some states more than others?
- Which ought to prevail: the social or the economic vision of the global information society?
- Should nongovernmental actors be able to set global policy agendas on information and communication technologies?
- What is digital dependence? Is it a useful concept?

Further Reading

Strong but quite specialized works include the collections of essays edited by Braman (2004) and Marsden (2000). Cogburn, 2004, provides a highly readable overview of the contradictions of the global information society regime.

Good general introductions to global governance include the collection of essays edited Held and McGrew (2002) and the 2004 special edition of the journal *Government and Opposition* 39(2).

The rise of private forms of authority in the global system is covered by Hall and Biersteker, 2002. Keohane and Nye (1998) provide a brief update to their theory of complex interdependence focusing on the Internet. For skepticism about global governance and the notion of digital dependence, see Wade, 1996 and 2002.

THE RISE OF INTERNET GOVERNANCE

We reject kings, presidents, and voting. We believe in rough consensus and running code.

—DAVID CLARK, *Internet Engineering Task Force, 1997*

Although the Internet allows a high degree of decentralized activities . . . co-ordination of the . . . operation of the Domain Name System (DNS) root must be co-ordinated by a central entity.

—INTERNET CORPORATION FOR ASSIGNED NAMES AND NUMBERS, 2001

CHAPTER OVERVIEW

This chapter examines recent international attempts to provide a governance structure for the Internet, particularly the emergence and current workings of what many commentators perceive to be a new regulatory regime or even a "global Internet government": the controversial Internet Corporation for Assigned Names and Numbers (ICANN). I trace the emergence of Internet governance from a policy crisis in the late 1990s involving a range of different political actors: the U.S. government, the European Union (EU), the International Telecommunications Union (ITU), the Internet Society (ISOC), and the World Intellectual Property Organization (WIPO). I consider how the emerging system is being shaped, how actors in the global system are increasingly attempting to regulate and steer the Internet, and some of the implications for its future development.

Recent years have witnessed the emergence of a new global governance regime for the Internet, centered mainly but not exclusively around a body known as the Internet Corporation for Assigned Names and Numbers (ICANN). Contrary to the old argument that the Internet is inherently ungovernable, it is now evident that the formation of a body like ICANN, in addition to the increasing interest taken by established actors in the international system sketched out in the previous chapter, has created potentially powerful points of control and influence over this most decentralized of communication media. This chapter explores this new global politics of Internet governance.

LAW AND GOVERNANCE IN CYBERSPACE

It is often stated that the Internet "cannot be regulated" or that it is "uncontrollable." Former U.S. president Bill Clinton famously said that controlling the Net is like "trying to nail Jell-O to the wall" (quoted in Wacker, 2003:58). John Gilmore, one of the founders of the cyberlibertarian Electronic Frontier Foundation (EFF), put it like this: "The Net interprets censorship as damage and routes around it" (quoted in Boyle, 1997:1). These are among the most often repeated statements about the Internet. But are they accurate?

In chapter 3 we examined the Internet's core technological building blocks. Foremost among these was TCP/IP—the set of elegant and flexible protocols that allow information to move around global networks. TCP/IP is often celebrated as a highly decentralized and relatively anonymous method of network organization, and there is no doubt that compared with prior forms of networking computers, it does offer many advantages. The global spread of the Internet—perhaps the fastest-ever instance of technological diffusion—is being enabled by the ease with which additional computers may be added to existing networks. The seamlessness of TCP/IP, which can connect many different types of machines together—from mobile hand-held devices through to massive supercomputers—has ensured its popularity and longevity.

These characteristics have led many commentators to argue that the Internet should not, and never will be, susceptible to regulation by national governments. Advocates of this view not only maintain that traditional forms of national regulation are impossible with a decentralized, distributed medium not based in any single nation-state, they go one stage further to argue that even international organizations might not be able to offer any meaningful way of steering the Internet. Prominent legal scholars in this area contend that the Net's technical evolution, developed, as we have seen, in large part through the voluntary activities of individuals, teams of researchers, and scientists in loose bodies like the Internet Engineering Task Force (IETF), provides the closest approximation to a model of governance that will work in cyberspace (Froomkin, 2003; Johnson and Post, 1996; Post, 1997). This self-governance approach, rooted in the ideas of the late-eighteenth- and early-nineteenth-century U.S. thinker (and president), Thomas Jefferson, is based upon what has become known in the Internet community as "rough consensus." The precise meaning of this term is difficult to pin down, but it essentially refers to an informal but rigorous style of decision making that has characterized the development of the Internet's technical architecture since the early 1970s. In the early days, the Internet's technical community ascribed status and influence to those individuals who provided the best solution to technical problems. In other words, there were always arguments about the best way to proceed with the development of technical standards, but in the end those who developed the best code and could implement it quickly usually won out (Gould, 2000:205). "Rough consensus" has been criticized for its elitism but it still exerts a romantic hold over many involved in the debates about establishing regulatory power over the Internet.

David Johnson and David Post's interpretation of cyberspace (1996) has been influential in shaping the contours of the debate, particularly in the United States, where there is a strong and distinctive tradition of federalism. The federal nature of the U.S. system of government, and federalist theory more generally, is important for understanding their argument because they borrow elements from these to make a case for self-governance by the Internet's diverse community of "Netizens." At the root of this perspective is the difference between laws that have a meaningful existence within geographically defined territories, and laws that "govern" cyberspace. Johnson and Post argue that the modern territorial basis of law derives from four principal features: power, effects, legitimacy, and notice. The problem with these four territorial determinants of law is that they often do not apply in cyberspace, or if they do, we must stretch the concepts or bring in caveats to make them work.

- **Power:** law must be enforced, which ultimately requires physical control over a given territory. The Internet weakens the link between territory and behavior.
- **Effects:** historically, most forms of behavior have specific effects on local populations. Laws emerge that are designed to have an effect on those specific forms of behavior rather than behavior in other jurisdictions. The Internet makes the geographical effects of behavior more difficult to predict and control.
- **Legitimacy:** since the emergence of nation-states as the main form of political entity, a development which (loosely) dates from the seventeenth to the nineteenth centuries, it has become widely accepted that legitimate government (that is, government that rests, ultimately, on the consent of the governed, however that may be defined) is conducted in geographically delimited spaces. The Internet erodes this geographical limitation, causing nation-states and other actors to try to establish their legitimacy in new, non-territorial ways.
- **Notice:** in a world of recognizable boundaries, it is relatively simple to recognize when we pass from one jurisdiction to another. Geographical borders are signposts that play an important role in allowing us to distinguish between different systems of law. The Internet renders these boundaries much less visible; it is difficult to tell which kinds of rules apply in which settings.

Consider some examples of this lack of territoriality when it comes to regulating behavior in cyberspace. There is no "natural" connection between the physical location of a computer connected to the Internet and the kind of activity for which it may be used. When an email sent to a colleague on the desk next to yours arrives at the same speed as one sent thousands of miles around the world and which may travel through the network created by hundreds of other computers situated in many different countries, you are unable to know, and arguably cease to care, about the geographical spaces through which the data flows. When the material on a website hosted in Britain can be simultaneously accessed by people all over the world, it is sometimes meaningless to assume that the content on that site has a greater impact on the British than it does on those who access it from other countries. The sheer volume of information that flows across geographical boundaries means that states cannot possibly hope to intervene without completely isolating themselves from participation in global markets (Kobrin, 2002). In the cases where states have sought to exert total control of information exchange, as, for instance, in China or North Korea, such efforts have proved difficult because dissidents can use technology, such as proxy servers, to preserve anonymity (Keller, 2000; Wacker, 2003). These problems are not restricted to authoritarian states. In 2002, Spain's Basque separatist party was officially outlawed by a Spanish court. Upon attempting to close down the party's website, the Spanish government found that it was unable to do so: the site was registered by an Australian firm and hosted on a server in California (Kleinwachter, 2003b:19). And when it comes to the legitimacy of governing bodies, at the moment it is not possible to identify a geographical entity that has the legitimate authority to make binding rules for all Internet users at all times. Participants engaged in online behavior, such as those, for instance, involved in Usenet discussions, may reside anywhere. What brings them together is not their territorial identity (except in the case of communities whose end is to discuss such matters) but common interests that often transcend national boundaries.

How, then, can we conceptualize the global governance of the Internet? The answer, for some, is to see cyberspace as a distinct "place," with structures, rules, and behaviors that often differ from those in the offline world. Only then can we start to design laws that effectively and fairly regulate the online world. The Net is, after all, highly *self*-regulated. The borders and boundaries of the Internet may not be geographical but they are physical; to go online you must physically connect via an Internet Service Provider (ISP). To use a particular Internet service or site, you must physically "point" your computer to its resources, and you may need to pay a subscription fee or enter a password. We do not enter cyberspace as completely free Netizens, because we are constrained by the terms of use of our ISP, by particular websites we visit, by the rules that may be established in online communities, or by the software architecture that enables some types of behavior and proscribes others. As Lawrence Lessig (1999:6) has argued: "In real space we recognize how laws regulate—through constitutions, statutes and other legal codes. In cyberspace we must understand how code regulates—how the software and hardware that make cyberspace what it is *regulate* cyberspace as it is." This is perhaps the closest approximation to law in cyberspace.

What happens, in this perspective, when the laws of cyberspace conflict with those of nation-states? In the absence of territoriality, the relevant political units are not nation-states but self-defined groups of users who construct rules for the online spheres in which they participate. Different sets of rules will develop in different areas of cyberspace, and, in the federalist perspective, governments should delegate regulatory powers to groups, even when group members may reside in other nation-states. Where geographically defined laws conflict with the laws of cyberspace, Johnson and Post suggest that the principle of the comity of nations should apply: a mechanism widely used in international law to regulate the relations between nation-states where formal treaties or other agreements may not provide strict guidance. This would permit Netizens from outside a geographical jurisdiction to have a say in developing rules that may apply in areas that affect their interests but which involve changing the laws of countries other than their own. While this may appear on the surface to go against the tenets of national sovereignty, Johnson and Post argue that the principle of comity has a long and distinguished history that will serve it well in regulating the conflict between cyberlaw and national law.

This may sound straightforward, but in reality the "comity of nations" idea is deeply problematic. It was tested in 2000, when a French court asked Yahoo! to close Nazi propaganda websites hosted on its servers. The company took the case to a U.S. court, claiming that the French courts did not have the authority to prevent a U.S.-based company from operating, and won (Kleinwachter, 2003b:19). At the same time, other writers such as Jack Goldsmith (1998) have argued that territorially based national laws provide all we need to regulate the online world.

The argument in favor of self-regulation by groups who have powers delegated to them by nation-states draws upon Thomas Jefferson's ideas about the importance of limiting the power of central government. Jefferson argued for devolving decision making as far as possible to what he perceived as an innately democratic citizenry (Post, 1997). It also draws inspiration from the contemporary political philosopher Michael Walzer, specifically his argument that in order to achieve greater equality, societies must be understood as consisting of different spheres of activity (or "spheres of justice") in which different sets of rules should apply (Walzer, 1983). In an interesting twist, David Post contrasts this Jeffersonian/Walzerian model of governance with a Hamiltonian alternative which sees the answer to regulating the Internet as involving the development of *centralized* institutions which impose uniform rules on nation-states and Netizens (Post, 1997). Unlike Jefferson, Alexander Hamilton's contribution to constitutional debates during the early years of the United States stressed the need for centralized control and mechanisms of government such as the Supreme Court, which he believed would provide a useful buffer between a flawed, "passionate" people and their more "enlightened" representatives.

On the surface, this battle of ideas over Internet governance may seem far-fetched, because it treats law not as strictly codified rules, but as something that emerges from interactions between Internet users in cyberspace. In reality, though, it is not so far removed from the way in which law in the real world develops. All laws emerge from decisions designed to regulate human interaction at some stage or other. They are not conjured out of thin air but from shared understandings of the problems at the time relevant judgments are issued. Ultimately, this approach simply maps this expanded understanding of how real-world law develops onto human interactions in cyberspace—a "place" that shares many features in common with offline interactions but which also has many of its own unique characteristics. As such, the projected conflict between centralized Hamiltonian and decentralized Jeffersonian models crystallizes many of the important issues at stake in the future of Internet governance. If the Hamiltonian approach wins out, we can expect to see the development of a range of new institutions designed to regulate and control behavior in cyberspace, because Jeffersonian self-government, in this perspective, will lead to chaotic, dysfunctional, and ineffective forms of regulation.

Yet while the model of law employed above may not be unreasonable, there are other aspects that we might want to consider. It is one thing to paint a picture of the world as one would like it to be and quite another to describe and analyze it as it actually is. In other words, much of the writing on Internet governance collapses the distinction between normative and explanatory arguments. We might wish to see the Internet as an ungovernable sphere of communication, but the reality is more complex. The Internet is comparatively free; yet, as we shall see, it contains weak points at which regulatory pressure may be applied, and, like all areas of activity, it is susceptible to being defined and shaped in ways that favor powerful interests and actors. These include existing nation-states, who may simply and effectively use domestic laws where they can be applied (Goldsmith, 1998). Powerful nation-states may try to ensure that their legal norms are simply writ large at the international level. Or entirely new international regulatory regimes may appear which might often transcend and limit the actions of individual nation-states. As we shall see below, all of these dynamics can be observed in Internet governance.

THE CONDITIONS OF GLOBAL INTERNET GOVERNANCE AND REGULATION

At the end of the twentieth century it became increasingly obvious that the Internet was growing at a phenomenal rate. It was equally obvious to governments (especially the U.S. government), international organizations, and business corporations that it was a relatively wild and untamed sphere of communication. As a result, these actors started several new initiatives aimed at shaping the future of the Net. These were attempts to build a stable regulatory regime for the Internet itself, largely pursued through a self-governance model, first introduced via ICANN in 1998 but involving organizations such as the ITU, the IETF, the ISOC, and the WIPO. This form of regulation has gone through decisive changes since it was first established, including experiments with global democratic elections, an increase in the role of states in its procedures, and the institutionalization of a quasi-judicial role in Internet-generated intellectual property disputes.

By the late 1990s, the question of whether—and how—this new global network of networks could be regulated loomed large. In the words of Dan Hunter, in the 1990s, the United States "realized it was faced with an international diplomatic problem and a regulatory nightmare. It effectively owned the Internet, by virtue of the Department of Commerce's control over IP address and domain name allocation" (Hunter, 2003:1172). These functions are known colloquially as the root. Almost all of the Internet governance and regulation issues at the global level revolve to some extent around the problem of the root (Mueller, 2002). Why?

The Root

As we saw in chapter 3, the Internet could not function without TCP/IP. Every major application Internet users take for granted—email, web browsers, chat, audio, video, in fact any service that makes use of the Internet in some way—runs on top of this suite of software protocols first implemented in the early 1970s. But what is less commonly understood is that for TCP/IP to function properly, there must exist some form of managing the allocation of IP addresses and the resources to which they point, in particular the process by which obscure numerical addresses, such as http://212.187.244.16, are translated into identifiable domain names, such as http://www.whitehouse.gov. This set of functions, known as the Domain Name System (DNS), has been described as "the root" of the global Internet: "the point of centralization in the Internet's otherwise thoroughly decentralized architecture" and "the top of the hierarchical distribution of responsibility that makes the Internet work" (Mueller, 2002:6; see also Klein, 2002). Problems with the functioning of the root may take several days to have an impact on the global Internet, because the data contained in the DNS system is duplicated on many hundreds of different computers at any one time and, as Mueller points out, establishing a new DNS would not be an insurmountable task for a major ISP (Mueller, 2002:48). The DNS is therefore a distributed database which can route around blockages or missing data. Nevertheless, the costs of losing the root, in terms of network instability, would soon become economically and politically significant, and, contrary to Mueller's argument that another entity would be likely to create its own DNS, this neglects the inevitable free-rider effects (the tendency to try to minimize one's own effort by capitalizing on the effort of others) that would deter any single company, or even a group of companies, from stepping in to create what had previously been taken for granted by all. A grossly simplified model of what the root does is presented in figure 10.1.

When governments seek to regulate a particular activity, they tend to do so at the easiest entry point. Consider the regulation of economic life through direct taxation, for example. This is one of the most efficient ways of affecting how businesses and individuals behave, not only by removing opportunities for investment or the spending of disposable income but also by allowing the government itself to provide different goods and services to citizens directly, financed by public expenditure. Now, if we consider this feature of regulation and apply it to the Internet, it is soon evident that the DNS root constitutes the Net's weakest point. Without an efficiently functioning means of handling IP addresses and domain names, the Net would not function. This vulnerability has become especially acute since the explosion of the web in the 1990s, because domain name servers—the hardware and software that handles how IP addresses are resolved into more easily recognizable domain names (e.g., www.shopping.com)—have been fundamental to the commercial models of corporations seeking new online markets.

The analysis of Internet governance and regulation are by no means exhausted by consideration of the root. But it is essential to bear in mind that many other issues at the global level, such as concerns over jurisdiction, freedom of expression, privacy, surveillance, intellectual property, economic monopoly, harmful content, standards, taxation, consumer protection, and security, are dependent to varying extents on what happens in the sphere of the DNS. Root-dependency scenarios, some real, some as yet hypothetical, are presented in figure 10.2.

Who Should Rule the Root?

There is an inevitable tension between the desire to protect and govern the root as a global public resource and the fear of handing over centralized control to a single agency, such as a national government, an international organization, or a set of powerful but unaccountable business corporations. The situation is even more complex because the root plays a pivotal role in a global system of communication. Some regulatory problems with which we are more familiar—those that are confined to a single nation-state or, in a stretch, perhaps a politically defined supranational entity such as the EU—do not transfer easily into rule making for the Internet, which must always be understood in a fully global context. This is how the debate about Internet governance began.

But the regulation of important global resources, especially in the field of communications, is not new. Previous technologies—from the postal system through the telegraph, the telephone, radio, and satellite to aviation and shipping—have all required

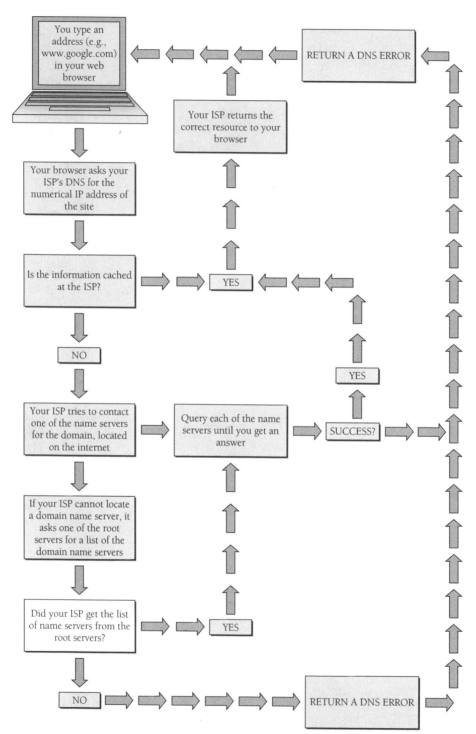

Figure 10.1. How the DNS root works (root functions in unshaded box). *Source:* Adapted from Zoneedit, 2003.

Figure 10.2. No DNS Entry, no Website: Why the Root Matters.

Problem	DNS Root Dependency Scenario
Jurisdiction	The most important DNS hardware is located in the United States. The United States decides to restrict the DNS by closing its servers.
Freedom of expression versus harmful content	Specific governments call for international regulation of content. Offending sites are removed from the DNS.
Privacy, surveillance, and national security	The DNS includes a database of domain name registrants, published openly on the web (called WhoIs?). Government agencies try to map terrorist networks by using data mining techniques to analyze WhoIs? (see also chapter 11).
Intellectual property rights	A person establishes a website with a domain name that implies criticism of another organization. The organization claims that this infringes its intellectual property because it uses its name in the domain name. The site is removed from the DNS.
Concentration of ownership	A startup e-commerce company in an African country tries to register a .com domain name in the hope of tapping into global markets, only to find that the name has been taken by a U.S. firm.
Taxation of transnational e-commerce	Governments make subjection to a new form of e-commerce tax a condition of DNS visibility.

some form of coordination that stretches beyond the grasp of a single nation-state. The usual path to a legitimate regulatory settlement involves a mixture of existing institutions and declarations—nation-states, industry standards bodies, trade associations, and specialist intergovernmental agencies or sections of existing international bodies such the UN—often under the aegis of treaties. In the debates about Internet governance, this established model has often been rejected on the grounds that the Internet is something entirely new that requires its own distinctive form of self-governance—one able to cope with rapid expansion and a hugely diverse global constituency of producers and consumers in a range of business and nonbusiness sectors.

Network Effects and Standards

But what the Internet *does* have in common with these other forms of communication are network effects. These have a huge impact on the success or failure of a particular technology or standard. Consider the example of a company that wishes to make profit from a new invention. Consider, at the same time, a customer who wishes to make use of that invention, but in order for her to do so, others must use it in broadly the same way. It follows that the more users there are, the more utility each individual will gain. In order for the company and the user to both get more of what they want, there must be more than one user. In other words, there must be a network. This increases what economists Stan Liebowitz and Steve Margolis (1998) have termed "synchronization value"—the extra utility that results from belonging to a network of other users.

If we consider a real-world example of network effects, we can start to appreciate the importance of common technological standards like the DNS. There are many throughout history, but a classic case is the tussle between rival computer operating systems during the 1980s and '90s—the legendary Apple versus Microsoft era. Irrespective of the technological properties of different computer hardware (in this case Apple's computers versus IBM's and IBM "clone" PCs running the Microsoft Windows operating system), the utility of a machine, from the viewpoint of the end user, was determined in large part by the network effect. In other words, when purchasing a new computer, users not only asked themselves: "Which is the better machine?" They also asked: "Which machine will enable me to communicate and work easily with other computer users?" A more recent example—one that may become as much of a classic as Apple versus Microsoft—is the rate of adoption of video-enabled mobile devices that run on high-speed "third-generation" telecommunication networks. What use is a mobile video-phone if no one else has one? Phone and telecommunication companies are busy establishing standards that ensure different companies will be able to link their networks together, thus making it more attractive for consumers to use videophones. But unless there is a critical mass of such phone users, no amount of technical wizardry is going to establish a market by itself.

Network effects and standards are phenomena which we will revisit in chapter 12, because the political economy of the Internet is conditioned by them in a variety of different ways, though their precise role is a matter of debate among economists (Liebowitz and Margolis, 1998). In the case at hand—Internet governance—their importance lies in the fact that convergence on a single set of standards has at the present time made it very difficult to imagine an alternative technical means of running the Internet (Marsden, 2000:16–18; Mueller, 2002:55). By the 1990s, the DNS was the established standard for translating domain names into IP addresses, and all Internet service providers became reliant on it. The exit costs of setting up an alternative system are too high. Users around the globe are dependent upon the beneficial network effects created by the common standard of the DNS, but this provides an entry point for those interested in regulating the Internet.

During the late 1990s, technical management of the root and the broader issues of Internet governance and regulation were often conflated. Despite protestations by many that technical management and content regulation were completely distinct, those involved soon began to realize that they were not. It is possible to argue that technical standards bodies should restrict themselves to "the plumbing not the people," in Internet pioneer Esther Dyson's words (quoted in Mueller, 2002:8). But dig a little deeper and it soon becomes obvious that standards bodies have long had effects on the structure and content of their particular industries. In radio and television, frequency scarcity has long enabled governments to influence who has the right to broadcast and who does not. Given the limited amount of physical bandwidth available for FM radio broadcasting, for example, it becomes necessary to manage the airwaves through the granting of licenses. ("Pirate" radio stations are simply those that are not officially licensed.) In practice, such licenses are not available to all comers and certainly not on the first-come-first-served basis on which, as we shall see below, Internet domain name registrations were handled until the late 1990s. Licensing bodies tend to spend much of their time imposing minimum standards on broadcasters as a means of protecting consumers but also as a form of political management, by pursuing social goals such as promoting access to "good" information and restricting access to content considered "harmful" (Collins, 2000). Even after the rise of digital satellite broadcasting, frequency scarcity still exists and continues to allow national regulatory bodies to restrict content through a backdoor means. Precisely the same can be said for mobile communication. In the United Kingdom, the mobile frequency spectrum license auction of 2000, in which telecommunication companies were invited to submit bids to run mobile voice and data networks, was predicated on the very idea of limiting the range of successful bidders to maximize infrastructural investment by a few key players (BBC News Online: Business, 2000).

Thus, standards are highly political, not only in the way they shape behaviors, but also because they always need to be adhered to in some way, whether through voluntary cooperation or due to fear of government sanctions. In the early days of the Internet, during the 1970s and '80s, as we saw in chapter 3, the development of standards took place in informally organized groups such as the Network Working Group or the IETF. Indeed, the latter continues to exist and plays an important role, alongside other standards organizations like the World Wide Web Consortium (W3C). But in 1998, the creation of a new standards body with pretensions to global regulatory powers changed forever a part of the Internet that once operated on a relatively informal and relatively depoliticized basis. Thus, ICANN has, on the surface, a standards body role, but this very role generates concern about the possible regulatory outcomes of its actions.

Scarcity and Common Pool Resources

Another set of phenomena we need to understand if we are to come to grips with Internet governance relates to the formation of property rights and common pool resources. Milton Mueller (2002) has argued that the rise of Internet governance is effectively an attempt to institutionalize a set of rules for the commercial management of global networks. The development, in this case, of new economic and political opportunities—the commercial exploitation of domain names (especially .com) as part of an e-commerce strategy of selling goods and services online, and the expansion of a new medium of communication with potentially subversive effects—led to intense conflict between economic and political actors. In the early stages of the Internet's expansion, no strong institution existed to enforce an agreed-upon set of rules about how property rights in domain names should be implemented and regulated.

In a seminal work, the political scientist Elinor Ostrom (1990) calls this type of collective action problem a "common pool resource" issue. Where there exists, for example, a common natural resource, such as a grazing pasture, a forest, or an ocean, assuming that individuals are rational, the tendency is for economic actors to exploit that resource to the point of exhaustion and contribute nothing to its maintenance. Unless governance arrangements are created that resolve conflicts between the different actors and which prevent the resource from being exhausted, the end result in such cases is likely to be perpetual conflict, wasteful duplication of activity in the short term, and the depletion of the resource in the long term. Ostrom demonstrated that governance arrangements in such cases tend to revolve around one of three alternatives: privatization through the creation and regulation of a market based on property rights; centralized control by governments; or, in Ostrom's favored solution, the development of voluntary rules for self-governance of the resource by those involved in its exploitation.

A complicating factor in the case of Internet governance once again derives from its global character. Traditionally understood, institutions which regulate and enforce property rights are national in their orientation. Consider the role played by national courts or government agencies, for example. Even supranational entities such as the EU can only act decisively within their territorial jurisdiction, and the EU itself is a player in a wider global system. Faced with the need for settling global disputes over property rights, nation-states have tended to collaborate to develop what are known as international regimes. As we saw in the previous chapter, these are institutional frameworks based upon agreed rules and procedures that are usually, but not always, the outcome of some bargaining process. Yet in the case of the Internet, the global network mainly developed at arm's length from national governments and their regulatory agencies. This creates problems when it comes to institutionalizing a common pool resource like the root. States had very few existing powers that they could project into the international arena. Even the United States, which has always maintained ultimate authority over the DNS due to the origins of the Internet in the Department of Defense, has been unwilling to take direct control. Should it attempt to do so, other states and supranational actors like the EU would not simply stand aside while the United States asserted its hegemony. The complex mixture of actors involved in staking a claim to the root makes it that much more difficult to simply assign the task to pre-existing international organizations (Mueller, 2002:67). Let us explore this controversy in a little more detail by examining the formation and role of ICANN.

THE DOMAIN NAME WARS AND THE RISE OF A GLOBAL GOVERNANCE REGIME FOR THE INTERNET

Between 1994 and 1998, a protracted, often bitter debate took place between government officials, technicians, corporations, lawyers, and representatives of existing international standards bodies over the future management of the DNS root. The domain name wars, as they have now become known, eventually led, in 1998, to the foundation of ICANN and the Internet governance regime that exists today and which will continue to influence the Net's development for the foreseeable future. Formally, ICANN is a private organization responsible for overseeing the registration of domain names and for ensuring the smooth running of the DNS. Informally, it has been described as the "government of the Internet," though this perhaps obscures more than it reveals about the way it actually works. Either way, the domain name wars serve as a useful entry point for understanding the wide-ranging politics of Internet governance today.

A whole range of policy issues swirled around during the domain name wars, but the main areas of controversy (Mueller, 2002:8–10) were as follows:

- How and by whom should the DNS ultimately be controlled—the U.S. government, telecommunication providers, the Internet technical community, international institutions like the UN, or an entirely new regime?

- To what extent should the registration of domain names be regulated by existing national laws and international treaties relating to intellectual property and trademark protection, and to what extent should these be allowed to restrict freedom of expression in cyberspace?

- Domain name scarcity can be solved by the creation of lots of new domains (e.g., .web, .kids, or .shop). However, increasing the number of domains makes it more difficult for companies to protect their intellectual property and their market share because it lowers barriers to entry into online markets. Should such scarcity continue?

- The hardware on which the root servers run is mostly concentrated in the United States, with all but three of the thirteen servers being located there (the others are in Britain, Sweden, and Japan). Is it desirable that such an important global resource be physically located in a few nation-states?

Prior to the expansion of the Internet in the 1980s, the addressing system used to connect computers was small scale and relatively informal. So long as the Net remained the preserve of academics and government-sponsored researchers, the inelegant nature of numerical addressing did not pose significant problems. However, the rise in the number of connected computers in the mid-1980s led some technicians to call for a new system that could cope with network expansion without having to be constantly redesigned. In a number of Request for Comments documents circulated among members of the loosely organized bodies established by ARPANET technicians between 1981 and 1984, the shape of the DNS began to emerge, and it was formally launched in January 1985 (Paré, 2003:15). Convergence on the DNS, widely seen as the best solution for the sustaining the Internet's growth, created powerful network effects. To understand why controversy over Internet governance persists and is likely to do so for many years to come, we need to appreciate two facets of the old regime: its informal and trust-based nature and the pragmatic and often unthoughtful granting of monopoly powers to organizations that turned out to have played a hugely important strategic role in the Internet's development. We also need to identify the diverse range of affected interests involved in the struggle to establish a new regulatory regime for the Internet in the 1990s.

The Old Regime: Informality and Trust, Monopoly without Legitimacy

Much of the architecture of the contemporary Internet was established with the DNS in the 1980s: the link between domain names and institutions or countries; the importance of particular identifying domain suffixes (e.g., .com, .edu) as a crude indication of site content; a system for registering new domains, administered on a daily basis by a body known as the Stanford Research Institute–Network Information Center, based at Stanford University, California; and a system for assigning IP numbers, based at the Information Sciences Institute (ISI) at the University of Southern California but officially carried out at the behest of the U.S. Defense Communications Agency. In 1985, think.com, the first .com domain, and .uk, the first country-code domain, were both registered. But what appeared on the surface as a complex set of technical and institutional arrangements worked out very differently in practice, because the policy and large segments of the administration of the DNS was effectively left up to one man—Jon Postel (Weinberg, 2000:194). Postel had played an important role in the development of ARPANET in the 1970s and was highly regarded for his technical expertise and energy. From 1972 on, Postel had been responsible for assigning and distributing network numbers. He continued to play this role until his unexpected death in 1998, by which time the domain name wars were in full swing. So long as ARPANET remained a restricted academic and government network, this informal system, based essentially upon other network users' trust of Postel, kept the potentially explosive issue of domain name registration and administration firmly in the technical realm.

In 1988, Postel invented a new institution—the Internet Assigned Numbers Authority (IANA)—but this was in practice nothing more than a fancy name for his own individual function as the administrator of the DNS (Mueller, 2002:93; Paré, 2003:17). There was no obvious controversy at the time, but Postel had effectively constituted a regulatory body that was not recognized in law but which had technical legitimacy and the potential to expand as quickly as the Internet itself. The "guy with long hair and a beard and sandals who lives overlooking Marina del Rey," as David Clark fondly described Postel in 1997, was almost single-handedly responsible for the smooth running of a crucial part of a rapidly expanding global communications network (Clark and Zittrain, 1997). Nobody complained about this arrangement, because it worked.

Yet during the 1990s, this informal system came under massive pressure. As the commercial value of an online presence became more evident, new Internet users, particularly businesses, sought to establish a more formal and legally accountable institution to oversee the expansion of the Internet in general and the development of standards and the allocation of domain names in particular.

Alongside the informal, trust-based system led by Postel/IANA, the 1990s saw the development of administrative institutions that effectively came to enjoy monopoly control over the registration of domain names. Between 1991 and 1993, the U.S. National Science Foundation (NSF) started to shift many of the functions of root administration from the education and research environment to the private sector. In 1993, an obscure Virginia-based company founded in 1979, Network Solutions, Inc., together with the telecommunication giant AT&T and a company named General Atomics, were granted a five-year U.S.-government-sanctioned monopoly over large functional areas of domain name registration (Paré, 2003:19). At this stage, the registration of names did not incur a fee, making the monopoly position of Network Solutions relatively unproblematic. In addition, the terms of the agreement with the NSF stipulated that the IANA (effectively Jon Postel) would continue to exert its authority over the DNS, though the terms of the relationship between the two were never clearly delineated.

The combination of these two fundamental features of what we can only loosely term Internet governance before ICANN was precisely what caused such political conflict from the mid-1990s on. Technicians, researchers, and the small minority of Internet enthusiasts accepted these informal arrangements not only because they seemed to work, but also because they jelled with an ideology of libertarianism which, as we saw in chapters 2 and 3, suffused the Net.

But as the Internet gained in popularity in the mid-1990s, the nature of these governance arrangements was increasingly called into question. The main spark was a scarcity of commercially desirable names in the .com domain, primarily caused by the initial stages of the dotcom gold rush that reached its climax in the spring of 2000. As companies and private individuals sought prestigious "dotcom real estate," it became obvious that conflict over property rights in domain names would ensue and that the whole process required, at least in the minds of those who were trying to stake their claims in cyberspace, a heavier regulatory touch.

The early policy for handling domain name scarcity was stark and brutally simple: first come, first served. While this might have suited an environment of technical collaboration with a libertarian ethos, it turned out to be ill-suited to the realities of global capitalism in the mid-1990s. The advent of the World Wide Web and the graphical browser transformed the Internet experience, making it accessible to nontechnical users for the first time. Once individuals could type an easily identifiable address into their browser, domain names suddenly became a hugely significant and valuable economic resource. By 1995, what was meant by the word "Internet" had changed.

The policy of first come, first served effectively turned domain names into a common pool resource (Ostrom, 1990; Mueller, 2002:67). Not regulating access to the registration of names created a frenzy of acquisition, as people sought to register names, especially short, simple names in the .com domain (like shopping.com). Businesses and individuals eager to establish an online presence often found, to their disgust, that their favored domain names—usually .com addresses that clearly identified their company and which had instant global reach because they were not tied to a country-code domain, such as www.mcdonalds.com—had been preregistered by nonassociated individuals or other companies. Such early, and often multiple, registrations occurred for various reasons, from blatant profiteering ("cybersquatting" in the hope of eventually selling the name back to its "rightful" owner for a high fee) to legitimate uses such as fan sites or customer information material (see exhibit 10.1).

In many cases, corporations were surprisingly slow to realize the potential commercial value of controlling their own domain name. However, a number of high-profile legal cases put the spotlight on the issue and led to several copycat lawsuits. As a means of exercising some leverage over what they perceived to be an arbitrary and unaccountable set of institutions operating outside of the bounds of law, companies in several countries began litigation designed to demonstrate trademark and other intellectual property infringements. Postel's and Network Solutions' policy on such infringements had, again, been very clear but also very naive; it simply stated that domain name registrants should check that they were not infringing trademarks, but nothing would be done by these bodies to settle disputes where they should arise (Paré, 2003:22). This policy proved inadequate.

Intellectual Property Interests Close In

Postel/IANA and Network Solutions found themselves under heavy pressure by the mid-1990s. In an attempt to bolster their untenable position as well as to protect themselves from the threat of lawsuits, they changed their policy on allocating domain names. First come, first served would continue, but domain name registrants had a responsibility to formally declare that their name did not infringe the intellectual property rights of another entity. Intellectual property was defined in this case as a preexisting, federally registered trademark. Further, Network Solutions from now on reserved

EXHIBIT 10.1. THE DOMAIN NAME WARS: AN INTELLECTUAL PROPERTY LAND GRAB

The McDonalds.com domain was registered in 1994 by a *Wired* magazine journalist, Joshua Quittner, partly as a publicity stunt for his column but also as a means of demonstrating the frailties of the registration system. Quittner apparently called to warn McDonald's HQ in advance of the registration, only to find that nobody cared about his registering a potentially lucrative domain name without incurring charges. McDonald's subsequently purchased the domain name from Quittner in exchange for a charitable donation to a public school in New York City.

Dennis Toeppen, an Illinois-based self-styled domain name entrepreneur, registered around two hundred domain names in 1995, including famous brands such as the clothing retailer Eddie Bauer. Toeppen hoped to sell these back to the real companies for a profit.

Others attempted to attract traffic to their sites and generate advertising revenue by deliberately registering names that were one slip of the keyboard away from a well-known brand site. Yahoo! was a particular victim of this, as literally dozens of Yahoo! lookalike domains were registered by those hoping to capitalize on typing errors. More infamously, since 1997, the owners of an adult site, www.whitehouse.com, have attracted large amounts of stray traffic from users trying to access the U.S. presidential site, www.whitehouse.gov.

There were also celebrated cases of deception, such as when the domain name peta.org, which in the United States would be most freely associated with the site of the pressure group People for the Ethical Treatment of Animals, was registered by an individual whose site was titled People Eating Tasty Animals. The site was taken down following a lawsuit initiated by the original PETA. Eventually the U.S. courts came down heavily against such practices, but it all added to the feverish context.

Many companies launched their own desperate attempts to register almost any imaginable domain name that might one day prove commercially useful for its association with their product. Procter and Gamble and Kraft/General Foods registered two hundred names describing various aspects of biological frailty, including badbreath.com.

Conflicts over desirable .com domain names were soon accompanied by disputes of a less predictable nature. The expansion of the Internet in the mid-1990s saw the addition of all of the remaining country codes (like .uk, .ca) to the DNS root. The reference document used by Jon Postel and the IANA for assigning such codes was the UN's official list of country abbreviations. All of the major country codes had been established in the 1980s, but many of those belonging to smaller, often developing nations were now up for grabs. Jon Postel was the principal guardian of the process, but he was increasingly unable to intervene in cases where individuals or companies in small nations sought to exploit their "natural resource." Famous examples include Tuvalu, a group of islands in the South Pacific, whose UN country code happened to be .tv. The .tv domain was sold for $50 million and is now owned by Verisign, who markets .tv domain names for as much as $1 million each.

Sources: Summarized from Mueller, 2002:115–20; Quittner, 1994; Simms, 2001; .TV Corp, 2003.

the right to withdraw a domain name upon receipt of an order from a U.S. court claiming such an infringement (Mueller, 2002:120). With this decision, the IANA and Network Solutions were effectively granting companies and individuals who claimed intellectual property infringements the ability to suspend the DNS functions for those websites that were the target of their litigation. Suspend the DNS, and a website effectively does not exist.

This was a highly controversial policy switch. Not only did it appear that Postel/IANA and Network Solutions were bowing to the pressure of business interests, they were also translating existing U.S. intellectual property law into a new area that had not been fully tested in the courts and were doing so without any legal or political legitimacy. By acceding to the demands of those companies unable to register their favored dotcom names, Postel and Network Solutions made it easier for intellectual property law to "stick" in this uncharted territory; they were effectively doing the work of the business groups for them.

The upshot of this policy change was a whole swathe of cases in which companies that had earlier missed out on their favored domain either paid the first registrant substantial amounts of money to buy the domain or launched legal action based on trademark infringement. Appeals on behalf of trademark holders flooded in, leading to the suspension of thousands of domain names between 1995 and 1998. The new policy has been described as "a highly significant development in Internet governance" due to the fact that it constituted the first attempt by a registration body (Network Solutions) to bypass existing national laws (Mueller, 2002:124).

Controversy during the early phase of the domain name wars also revolved around the financial benefits of the monopoly role that Network Solutions, Inc., enjoyed in the early 1990s. As domain name registrations started to soar in 1995 and the associated administrative costs spiraled, the company started charging a domain name registration fee. Not surprisingly, its revenue started to increase dramatically and soon ran into the hundreds of millions. This caused uproar among fledgling Internet companies, network operators, civil libertarian groups, and those private citizens who hitherto had not had to pay for this free service. Fee charging appeared to them as the thin end of the wedge. It was only a matter of time, they believed, before access to domain names would be controlled by a few dominant business players who could effectively rig the market in their own interests by artificially inflating prices. Onlookers questioned this U.S. government-created monopoly's legitimacy, calling for the introduction of competition to reduce end-user costs.

As the domain name wars continued, the whole issue of jurisdiction over the Internet's root functions was thrown into the melting pot. Four main sets of institutional actors sought to establish positions of authority over the Internet during this period of flux: the ISOC, the ITU, the U.S. government, and the WIPO.

As we saw in chapter 9, the ISOC is an international nonprofit organization and contains the IETF, an extremely important voluntary standards development body consisting largely of network technicians. It allows Internet engineers to deal with other standards-setting institutions like the ITU (Mueller, 2002:95). In the 1990s, the ISOC was an obvious contender for some sort of jurisdictional role in Internet governance.

In contrast, the ITU, a specialist agency of the UN, already had an established presence in the international regulation of telecommunication. By getting more involved in the debate on the future of the DNS, the ITU wished to assert itself in a new global Internet market (Drake, 2000:164).

Postel wished to see his functions transferred to the ISOC. However, the plan attracted strong criticism from those who argued that the U.S. government should continue to hold overall jurisdiction over the root. Matters were complicated by the messy reality of the DNS, which made the government's jurisdictional claim problematic. Network Solutions had only been granted the license to administer one of the thirteen root servers, albeit the most important one (server A). The others were administered by a range of organizations within and outside the United States. It was difficult to see how a single nation-state, albeit a hugely important one in the Internet's development, could claim authority over the whole root. Institutionalization of this function would prove to be much less straightforward than it seemed.

The U.S. government was also being strongly lobbied by commercial interests. As the problem of domain name scarcity intensified, several new solutions were suggested. Most of these included the introduction of new top-level domains (like .med, .ltd, .web or .xxx, .music, or .fun) and the setting up of multiple rival registry agencies to compete with Network Solutions. In fact, if purely technical considerations had held sway, the introduction of a large number of new domain suffixes would have been an elegant solution, flooding the market with lots of new virtual real estate. But these ideas were pushed aside. The creation of new domain names was bitterly opposed by those business interests who wished to protect their intellectual property rights. They argued that new domains simply made it easier for individuals and companies to "illegally" register names and would make it even more difficult for companies to prevent trademark infringements and other forms of "piracy." Such interests began to argue for a cooling off period once a domain name registration had been filed. This would allow time for an investigation to determine whether a registration was in breach of intellectual property law.

The increasingly intractable problem led the ISOC to establish an investigative committee in late 1996. This was given the task of finding an internationally workable solution. Its membership consisted of representatives from the International Trademark Association (a professional association that serves to protect the interests of trademark holders in the global economy), the ITU, the NSF, individuals from large information technology and telecommunication companies such as IBM and Telstra, and last but by no means least the WIPO. The entry of the WIPO into the field of Internet governance was highly significant. It was both a reflection of the growing importance of intellectual property disputes for the future of the Net and the first indication that a new global regulatory regime might emerge as a solution to the domain name wars.

In February 1997, the ISOC's committee published its final report. The recommendations were highly controversial due to their perceived capitulation to commercial interests. The committee proposed the introduction of just seven new domain names rather than taking the bold step of radically opening up the market by creating many more. These recommendations were widely criticized not only for their content, which was perceived as giving in to wealthy trademark holders, but also for the manner in which the deliberations had been conducted. The committee, contrary to the spirit of the Internet's development, met in secret and did not publish summaries of its discussions. An additional Memorandum of Understanding was suggested as a first step on the way to finding a general set of principles for Internet governance. The MoU, as it soon became known, provided for the establishment of a new international committee to regulate the root. Its membership was to be principally composed of representatives of the ISOC, Postel/IANA, the ITU, the WIPO, the International Trademark Association, and the new Council of Registrars representing domain name registries. The committee also sought to defuse intellectual property disputes by recommending a complex arbitration procedure that was, significantly, to be overseen by the WIPO.

Intervention by the U.S. Government and the Formation of ICANN

Despite continuing criticisms of the powers that the MoU granted to bodies such as the ISOC, the ITU, and the WIPO, moves toward establishing it as the new Internet governance framework began. But in the summer of 1997, the U.S. government dropped a bombshell. This took the form of the Framework for Global Electronic Commerce, calling upon the U.S. Department of Commerce to "create a contractually-based self-regulatory regime [for the Internet] that deals with potential conflicts between domain name usage and trademark laws on a global basis without the need to litigate" (quoted in Kleinwachter, 2003a:1110). The U.S. Department of Commerce effectively ignored the previous efforts organized by the ISOC and instead issued its own consultation on how domain name registration should be handled. This was undoubtedly an assertion of U.S. hegemony over the Net. However, it was also a reflection of the views of Ira Magaziner, President Clinton's senior advisor on Internet issues. Magaziner went on to argue that the U.S. government believed that a private sector–led self-governance model should emerge as the solution to the problem of the Internet.

Yet in the short period of just a couple of years, the number of actors with a stake in the future of Internet governance had radically increased. This greatly complicated matters, as a range of different interests competed against each other in a highly fluid global environment. We can identify at least ten distinct groups that attempted to influence the outcome of the U.S. government's consultation process (see exhibit 10.2). Out of this diversity emerged a dominant coalition of interests that were able to forge the ICANN settlement between 1998 and 2000.

Central to the self-regulation agenda favored by the U.S. government was a grouping of large telecommunication and e-commerce companies, spearheaded by IBM and MCI-Worldcom (group 5 in exhibit 10.2). Operating through an umbrella organization, the Global Internet Project (founded in 1996 by senior executives of sixteen major firms), IBM and MCI-Worldcom sought to prevent international regulation of the Internet. Arguing that regulation would impede the growth of e-commerce, they lobbied strongly that Internet governance would have to be shaped in such a way that it would not harm the interests of the private sector. The Global Internet Project played a leadership role for the global IT sector, which included the powerful Information Technology Association of America and the World Information Technology and Services Alliance (Mueller, 2002:169).

At the same time, IBM was busy lobbying the Clinton administration to develop a new framework for e-commerce that would rest on self-regulation by the industry. As events unfolded, it became clear that IBM and MCI-Worldcom wished to play a major role in the development of Internet governance. Both were appalled at the potential for instability in the current system. If e-commerce was to thrive, they argued, the Net

EXHIBIT 10.2. INTERNET GOVERNANCE STAKEHOLDERS DURING THE RISE OF ICANN

1. The U.S. government, which was heavily lobbied by business interests but which also wished to avoid a policy crisis and acceding too much influence to foreign interests and international institutions, especially the EU and the UN.

2. Network Solutions, Inc., the domain name registration authority for .com, .org, and .net domains, which controlled over 70 percent of the global market. Wished to assert its control over the intellectual property in its registration database and to continue making profit.

3. The formally and informally organized Internet technical community. This was composed of the original ARPANET technicians, Jon Postel/IANA, the ISOC, and its IETF. Wanted to retain control over the DNS and the future development of technical standards through "rough consensus" decision making.

4. Trademark and intellectual property interests. Major corporations opposed to the creation of new top-level domains on the grounds that they would be even more difficult to police. Wanted an easier way to monitor domain name registration and legally enforce their rights. Included groups such as the International Trademark Association, the Motion Pictures Association of America, but also the WIPO.

5. Corporations involved in telecommunication and e-commerce. The main players were IBM, MCI-Worldcom, AT&T, AOL, France Telecom, and Deutsche Telekom. Sought a stable regulatory environment for the Internet with maximum private control. Operated through umbrella trade organizations such as the Global Internet Project.

6. Prospective domain name registrars seeking entry into the lucrative .com markets, including small companies and entrepreneurs outside the United States. Also individuals and groups wanting to establish new domains.

7. Local and regional ISPs and their trade associations, such as Commercial Internet Exchange and the European Internet Service Providers Association. Wanted much the same as group 5 but had less power over telecommunication infrastructure.

8. Country-code registries. A diverse group ranging from large nonprofit consortiums in Germany and Britain to registries run in government ministries in other countries. All with de facto property rights in top-level domains, such as .uk, .ca, .de, and so on.

9. Civil liberties/progressive groups in civil society such as the Electronic Frontier Foundation, Computer Professionals for Social Responsibility, the Domain Name Rights Coalition, and the American Civil Liberties Union who were concerned with freedom of expression and opposed to the expansion of intellectual property rights by businesses.

10. International organizations and national governments. The European Commission and some national governments, particularly France and Australia, sought to counter U.S. economic and political dominance of the Internet. The ITU and the WIPO sought new roles in Internet governance.

Source: Adapted from Mueller, 2002:68, 166–67.

required a solid architecture—one controlled by major economic stakeholders. These views were also acceptable to the EU, which was keen to avoid the extension of U.S. government influence over the net and wished to involve itself and European business actors in the development of the new regime (Burkert, 2003; Gould, 2000:201; Kleinwachter, 2003a:1111). Between January and September 1998, largely behind closed doors, the new shape of Internet governance was agreed, as Ira Magaziner, President Clinton's adviser, forged a coalition including Jon Postel and other key technicians, trademark interests, and large technology firms.

In June 1998, the U.S. government issued its policy in the form of a white paper: *Management of Internet Names and Addresses*. This made the case for a new private non-profit corporation to regulate the DNS but left the formation of the new body to private sector stakeholders. In other words, IBM's and MCI-Worldcom's views had been influential in shaping the white paper. Corporate concerns were met: no new domains would be created and a global trademark arbitration body located in the WIPO would be established. The white paper declared that the new regulatory body was to be operational by October 2000. Based in the United States, it would have a representative board of directors drawn from among the major global Internet stakeholders, would be run on transparent lines, and, significantly, would not include any government officials.

The publication of the Department of Commerce plans rapidly met with a response in the form of the International Forum on the White Paper, consisting of a wide range of different actors, from industry experts, ISPs, lawyers, web developers, and trademark holders to civil society groups and ordinary citizens from over fifty countries. The Forum held an ongoing online debate, during which five contending drafts of potential new governance arrangements were discussed. Participation in the four major real-world Forum meetings was open to all-comers. The chaotic but momentous atmosphere of the meeting in Reston, Virginia, the home of the ISOC and the epicenter of the U.S. high-tech/government nexus, was notable, reflecting the "rough consensus" that had long been established as a decision-making method in Internet policy circles. It has been described as "a revolutionary legislative process, akin to international law-making" (Kleinwachter, 2003a:1113).

As it turned out, events moved beyond the scope of the Forum, and its overall influence on the ICANN settlement was marginal. In September 1998, when the time came to draw the International Forum's ideas together in a proposal document, Postel/IANA and others refused to participate. They had negotiated their own deal with the U.S. Department of Commerce, the ISOC, the dominant business coalition, and the European Commission. The institutional details and interim membership of a new body called the Internet Corporation for Assigned Names and Numbers (ICANN) were released at the end of the month. Thus, the short-lived international direct democracy of the International Forum on the White Paper drew to a close.

The ICANN proposals were immediately attacked by cyberlibertarian pressure groups such as the Electronic Frontier Foundation (EFF) and a number of trade bodies, including the European Internet Service Providers Association. The ITU was also reluctant to support the proposals but in the end chose to do so on the basis that it could exert more influence inside ICANN. Critics argued that the democratic procedures of the International Forum had been swept aside. They also criticized the undemocratic nature of ICANN, suggesting that it would prove to be unaccountable and likely to be hijacked by corporate interests. In what was seen as a token gesture, the U.S. government stipulated that ICANN's first task was to create a structure that would provide for the election of its nine board members (Paré, 2003:35). ICANN duly made these revisions. But its first (nonelected) board of directors was drawn almost exclusively from among those who had forged the settlement with the Department of Commerce. In the eyes of critics, its legitimacy as the new international organization responsible for ruling the root was tainted from its inception.

INTERNET GOVERNANCE SINCE ICANN

That is the story of the emergence of a new regulatory regime for the Internet. But is ICANN really a new government for the Net, as some have claimed? This phrase might have an appealing ring to it, but it obscures more than it reveals. It is more accurate to describe ICANN as an important component of a complex and emergent system of global governance for the Internet. Legally, it is "a nonprofit public benefit corporation . . . organized under the California Nonprofit Public Benefit Corporation Law for charitable and public purposes." Its purpose, since its creation in 1998, is to act "for the benefit of the Internet community as a whole" (ICANN articles of incorporation, quoted in Kleinwachter, 2003a:1103). Its structures are very similar to those used in modern business corporations. It has a chief executive officer, a board of directors, and a range of different supporting organizations lower down the hierarchy (Hunter, 2003:1155).

At the same time, ICANN's operation stretches beyond what business corporations normally do because it regulates the Internet, through its quasi-judicial role in deciding on disputes over domain names, its veto on the creation of new domains, and its general policy remit to maintain the Net's stability and viability through the enforcement of standards. In short, ICANN makes global public policy on who deserves property rights in domain names. It imposes sanctions on those who refuse to comply by removing sites from the DNS and thus from the Internet. Regulatory decisions in these areas affect the financial interests of tens of millions of individuals worldwide and the economic and political relations between states in the international system. Disputes over the future development of the DNS, such as the roll-out of new domains, continue apace. What ICANN does is therefore deeply political and will become more so as the Internet continues to diffuse around the globe. Moreover, given the increasing influence of states and supranational organizations such as the EU in its affairs, ICANN's political role is being reinforced in such a way that it is starting to resemble a more traditional regulator with executive powers.

Given the contested and deeply politicized context of its emergence, it should come as no surprise that ICANN has been widely criticized on the grounds that it lacks legitimacy. A number of groups, such as ICANNwatch.org and ICANNatlarge.com, have sprung up to monitor its activities, report on its decisions, and mobilize against any extension of its powers. These initiatives stem in part from the restricted, often secretive nature of the decision-making processes which led to its creation. But some critics continue to maintain that there is no real consensus about how to govern the Internet and that the new settlement is a betrayal of the voluntarist, libertarian ethos upon which it was originally based (Froomkin, 2003; Mueller, 2002; Post, 1999). From the perspective of democratic theory, the formation of a governance and regulatory body in a crucial area of policy in the international system, where most of the important decisions are taken behind closed doors, is simply politics as usual. From the perspective of international political economy, which seeks to identify the underlying economic factors that shape and constrain international politics, ICANN is business as usual. Dominant corporate interests, most of whom are transnational, are eager to protect their trademarks and the telecommunication infrastructure—assets crucial for profitable business in the early twenty-first century. Such business groups are now able to exert their influence over the technical community and the U.S. Department of Commerce and can rely on existing international institutions such as the WIPO, itself widely regarded as the protector of the West's dominant intellectual property interests (Drahos with Braithwaite, 2002; May, 2000:67–71). Freedom of expression takes second place to the comfortable expansion of existing offline commercial interests into the new e-commerce environment.

Direct versus Functional Representation

The fiasco of the ICANN elections (see exhibit 10.3) combined with the ongoing criticism from the at-large members of the board have led to a fundamental reappraisal of ICANN's role and an ongoing program of reform (Stuart Lynn, 2002). New draft ICANN bylaws in December 2002 removed at-large representatives from the Board of Directors altogether. The only popular input from Internet users will now come in the form of the At-Large Advisory Committee, which can send one nonvoting member to the Board of Directors. The pioneering democratic experiments would appear to be over. Any vestigial remains of citizen participation are now filtered through a corporatist model some argue was always planned, had ICANN not been forced into holding elections to the Board by activists (Hunter, 2003:1156). This corporatist model is predicated on the idea of functional representation: those with a functional role or interest in the running of the Internet are incorporated in an advisory capacity in ways that allow views to be fed up to a powerful Board of Directors. This marks a shift away from the experiment with direct representation using a theoretically global constituency of Netizens.

Some argue that the debate about using democratic structures to govern the Internet is entirely misplaced. Instead of trying to mimic liberal democratic institutional features like legislatures, this perspective suggests that the Internet requires a corporate model of governance. In this approach, Internet governance should be treated in the same way as we treat businesses. The question we should ask is not. "Is ICANN democratic?" but "Is it well managed?" Thus Tamar Frankel (2002) suggests that the regulations that have built up around corporate governance should apply, as should mechanisms such as external review, the regular publication of results and budgets, formal planning, conflict of interest declarations, and other forms of public reporting and audit. The problems with this are manifold, but perhaps the biggest flaw is that ICANN lacks shareholders. In corporate governance, shareholders can sometimes play an important role as an internal constituency whose interests are tied to those of the business, even if they are seldom

EXHIBIT 10.3. ICANN ELECTIONS: GRAND EXPERIMENT IN GLOBAL DEMOCRACY OR GRAND FARCE?

As a means of defusing criticism and enhancing ICANN's legitimacy, the U.S. government has been keen to make sure that ICANN's bylaws provide for various representative mechanisms designed to incorporate communication from below. Three primarily technical supporting organizations and an at-large membership of ordinary interested Internet users were supposed to do the job of fostering consensus-based policy making. The supporting organizations each nominate three members of ICANN's Board of Directors. Nonbusiness groups are given very little influence in these organizations.

As for the at-large membership, this innovation was greeted with immense excitement when first announced in 2000. It seemed to herald a genuinely new form of experimental international organization—one that would routinely hold democratic elections and be accountable to a burgeoning global civil society organized around the issues of Internet governance. Nine at-large members of the ICANN Board of Directors were to be elected to represent the interests of the global Internet community. This was an extraordinary move, unprecedented in the history of international relations.

There were, however, significant problems with the 2000 elections. Initially, nine members of the nineteen-strong Board of Directors were to be elected from the global at-large constituency. But ICANN's Board delayed the introduction of what it perceived as an unnecessary distraction. In 2000, a global election was held which allowed five constituencies of Internet users (North America, Latin America, Europe, Asia and Australia, and Africa) to elect just five board members. The other four were internally appointed. It was proposed that the elections would be held biannually from then on. The results are in table 10.1.

As we can see, what might have been a massive global experiment in representative democracy and a possible model for other international organizations turned out to be something of a damp squib. Some aspects of the elections were genuinely innovative. Candidates were required to restrict their online campaigning to preapproved web page formats, and a month-long online discussion forum was set up to allow them to answer questions on their platforms. Other aspects of the elections were heavily criticized. Individuals could register to vote so long as they had an email address and a verifiable residential address. Due to fears about the security of online voting, however, the election was mostly held offline. This required a huge global

Table 10.1.   ICANN Global At-Large Election Results, 2000

Region	Number of Candidates	Membership	Votes Cast	Turnout
Asia/Pacific	5	38,397	17,745	46.21%
Europe	7	23,519	11,309	48.08%
North America	7	10,694	3,449	32.25%
Latin America	5	3,571	1,402	39.26%
Africa	3	321	130	40.50%
Total	27	76,502	34,035	44.49%

mailing of ballot slips with PIN numbers that an individual then had to input before being permitted to vote online. ICANN ran out of funds for running the election, stopped sending out the slips, then took the online registration system down during the closing stages of the registration period. The turnout, at 34,035, was pitifully small. Africa returned a total of just 130 votes. Even Europe's turnout was only a little over 11,000. The elections were not widely publicized, but other, more fundamental explanations of the poor turnout have been suggested by Dan Hunter (2003:1179): "most of the world does not have access to the Internet, those who do have access do not know about ICANN, and those who do know about ICANN do not care about how it is run." The results of the first election did, however, indicate widespread dissatisfaction with ICANN itself, as highly critical candidates easily defeated ICANN's nominees.

Sources: Election.com, 2003; Hunter, 2003; Klein, 2001, 2002; Kleinwachter, 2003a; Markle Foundation, 2001; Marlin-Bennett, 2001; Weinberg, 2000.

genuinely active. ICANN may occasionally look like a business, but it is not. It is a nonprofit corporation with no shareholders, and it has competence in a politically important area where "rough consensus" and libertarianism have been the dominant approach. This is precisely the reason why elections and other representative mechanisms were introduced.

The Increasing Presence of Governments

There are unresolved and fundamental issues over ICANN's jurisdiction. The U.S. government still has the final authority over the root, even though ICANN was supposed to take over this role (Kleinwachter, 2003a:1118). In 2002, the ITU claimed that that it was responsible for substantive policy matters with regard to the Internet, such as "stability, security, freedom of use, protection of individual rights, sovereignty, competition rules and equal access for all" (quoted in Kleinwachter, 2003a:1120). This was an indirect attack on ICANN. Meanwhile, the EU has developed policy on what it terms the "International management of the Internet," which involves working through the ICANN Governmental Advisory Committee (GAC) to apply pressure from an EU perspective (Burkert, 2003:1208–11). The EU has also been keen to establish a .eu domain that may act as a European alternative to .com, which is perceived as giving U.S. companies an unfair advantage in global markets.

Although it was envisaged that ICANN would not include government officials, they have found a place to exert influence as members of ICANN's GAC (Mueller, 2002:207). Although the ICANN board has had great difficulty in persuading governments that they should enter into international contractual agreements with it, the potential involvement of around two hundred governments in the GAC points towards a future in which political actors will have a greater say in regulating the Internet via this "*de facto* inter-governmental Internet organization" (Kleinwachter, 2003a:1116). Even though the Committee lacks legitimacy, with only around thirty states regularly participating in its meetings, this is a significant departure from the model of industry self-governance that was heralded during the late 1990s.

The involvement of national governments in ICANN has also been spurred on by unforeseen external shocks to the international system. The terrorist attacks of 9/11 radically altered the terrain of Internet governance and the DNS, bringing into sharp relief the importance of global communications for national security, particularly in the United States, where, as we shall see in the next chapter, the Bush administration placed the Internet at the center of its plans to combat terrorism. In late 2001, at the first ICANN meeting following 9/11, the security of the root was called into question. The response has been to allow governments a much bigger role through the GAC. Governments increasingly see the relative freedom of Internet communication as a threat to their national security—a phenomenon of which private actors involved in a self-governance institution might not be as acutely aware. Indeed, ICANN's reforms give much greater power to its GAC, which may now send representatives to the Board of Directors and other ICANN advisory committees, albeit in nonvoting capacities. More significantly, governments now have influence over Board decisions because the Board is required to notify the GAC of any proposals that raise "public policy issues." The GAC also has the right to "put issues to the Board directly" (ICANN, new bylaws 2002, quoted in Kleinwachter, 2003a:1120–21).

Links with the WIPO

A final, persistently controversial area concerns the role of the WIPO. Only seven new domains were created in the first five years of ICANN's founding, and existing trademark holders were given prior access to these through the so-called sunrise policy, which allowed businesses to preregister their favored names in the new .info, .biz, .pro, .name, .aero, .coop and .museum domains before they were released to the general public in 2001. The central causal factor in the domain name wars—scarcity—has thus been maintained because it satisfies companies seeking to lower the costs of policing the domain name system through the courts.

While governments are playing a greater role in ICANN, other international organizations like the WIPO are also muscling in. Intellectual property protection and Internet governance are now explicitly linked as a matter of policy and procedure. This is where ICANN almost plays the role of an international court, but it does so only in alliance with other important global agencies. In consultation with the WIPO in 1998 and 1999, it invented a new procedure to deal with intellectual property disputes. This gives ICANN and the WIPO new powers to protect trademarks because it provides a number of relatively cheap arbitration forums for complainants to lodge claims against infringements such as cybersquatting. Analyses of its decisions have demonstrated bias in favor of established intellectual property interests: those complainants with larger market shares are more likely to win a case than less powerful actors (Mueller, 2000). Trademark holders are also granted heavy influence over deliberations about the introduction of new domain names, and they get cheap access to the global register of domain names for marketing purposes, irrespective of the threats to individual privacy that this entails.

CONCLUSION

The establishment of ICANN marked a watershed in the history of the Internet. Although it lacks legitimacy, the new institution regulates the Net and goes far beyond the role of a technical standards body. It provides a quasi-judicial function that maintains legally binding contracts. It provides a deeply flawed but nonetheless significant element of representation for what passes for the global Internet community through its at-large membership. It provides an arena for national governments to influence policy through the GAC and thus shares features in common with other international organizations. At the same time, ICANN has sole responsibility for maintaining an economic climate of domain name scarcity that arguably undermines freedom of expression and centralizes control over a hugely important global resource (Mueller and McKnight, 2003).

A central problem for ICANN is that it is essentially a private body that exercises regulatory functions traditionally reserved for public institutions. Moreover, it does so in an ever-expanding, highly complex, international environment where national jurisdiction does not have much impact and where there is a unique clash of values. Some see the Internet as a public resource in the broadest sense; others see it primarily as a means of generating profit. A further constituency resists all attempts to exert control, whether in the public or the private interest, because they are perceived to be a betrayal of the Internet's libertarian roots. But even this approach has problems because it is seen as politically naive, elitist, and technocratic.

The onward march of the Internet continues apace, and this expansion will require the implementation of new standards. For example, a new version of the Internet Protocol, IPv6, is under development. The emergence of mobile communications and other forms of convergence whose success depends upon network effects has arguably made Internet governance and regulation even more important than it seemed during the dizzy days of the domain name wars. ICANN is, however, a deeply contested international institution. While it possesses many novel and experimental features, which, its defenders and critics alike would say, derive from its atypical origins in the Internet community, the fact remains that it presides over a tightly regulated system for the control of domain name registration and the administration of the root. Critics organized around free speech and other civil society groups argue that ICANN is unrepresentative, unresponsive to the needs of end users, and beholden to large corporate interests, either directly or indirectly through its links with other international institutions such as the WIPO.

As we saw in chapter 9, alongside the emergence of ICANN, recent years have also witnessed a proliferation of projects, programs, and forums at the global level that position Internet technologies at, or close to, the center of their concerns. Long-standing Internet players like the ITU are staking a claim. Established international organizations like the UN are rapidly expanding their activities. (The future of ICANN emerged as one of the main themes in the run up to the first round of the World Summit on the Information Society in December 2003.) New or recently formed entities like the WTO and the WIPO are closing in, while private or semi-private entities like the World Economic Forum are also attempting to set the global agenda. The present regime is in transition and can best be characterized as one of "public-private co-regulation" (Kleinwachter, 2003b:18). By involving themselves in international organizations with a focus on regulating the Internet, however minimally, nation-states have started to develop agendas which are likely to lead to greater political control over what was previously a relatively depoliticized medium based around "rough consensus" decision making in technical standards bodies. Internet governance is likely to remain a deeply controversial area for many years to come.

Discussion Points

- Can the Internet be regulated?
- How and why did a regulatory regime for the Internet emerge?
- Does self-governance work, or should nation-states take control of strategically important resources such as global communication networks?
- Is democratic participation in international organizations like ICANN possible? If so, what forms should it take?
- Which international organizations are influential in Internet governance?

Further Reading

Easily the best account of the rise of Internet governance to date is Milton Mueller's 2002 book, which goes into much more detail than is possible here.

Much of the literature in this area has so far been published in law journals, but nonlawyers should not be put off by this: a great deal of the discussion borrows heavily from political theory. See the special issue of the *Loyola of Los Angeles Law Review* 36 (3), 2003. On matters relating to the democratic legitimacy (or otherwise) of ICANN, Dan Hunter's essay in the *Loyola* collection is a clear and provocative read (Hunter, 2003).

A reasonably dispassionate account of the extraordinary ICANN elections of 2000 can be found in the Markle Foundation's report (2001), while the special issue of the journal *Info* 3 (4) 2001 contains some excellent analysis.

SURVEILLANCE, PRIVACY, AND SECURITY

In the twenty-first century, surveillance is seldom a personal hailing, a face-to-face matter, a one-off event. It is continuous, general, routine, systematic, impersonal, and ubiquitous.

—DAVID LYON, 2003

You have no privacy. Get over it.

—SCOTT MCNEALY, *Quoted in* Wired News *January 26, 1999*

CHAPTER OVERVIEW

This chapter explores how the Internet is reconfiguring the relationship between surveillance, privacy, and security. It considers state-initiated surveillance in two distinct though interrelated forms. Intrastate surveillance concerns attempts by states to monitor the Internet use of their populations as a way of dealing with harmful content, crime, subversion, and terrorism. Interstate surveillance concerns states' roles in the international sphere, where they attempt to monitor external threats to national security by intercepting global Internet communications or defending themselves against (or even launching their own) cyberwarfare attacks. While intrastate and interstate surveillance are distinct, they increasingly overlap in a globalized environment of blurred territorial boundaries. Recent developments, most notably the terrorist attacks on the United States of September 2001, rendered such boundaries even more porous. Yet if states continue to be the most significant actors in the landscape of surveillance, they are increasingly joined by corporations. This chapter also considers how businesses use the Net to gather, process, match, and integrate personal information. The line between state and corporate surveillance is itself blurring as states seek to extend their reach through methods such as data mining. The Internet is implicated in all of these areas, either as an object of surveillance or as part of the infrastructure which allows law enforcement and corporate actors to more efficiently distribute information around these systems. Such developments have important implications for individual privacy.

New communication technologies have often heralded greater political freedom. In nineteenth-century Britain, the rise of the popular press led to premature predictions of the end of aristocratic political dominance. In 1989, Chinese student dissidents' occupation of Tiananmen Square took place in a new context of global satellite television broadcasting. But there is, of course, another side to this history: technologies of freedom have also been technologies of control. Since ancient times, communication and surveillance have gone hand in hand. During times of perceived crisis, the links between them are stronger still. Thus, surveillance long predates the Internet. This, despite repeated misquotation and misinterpretation, is what Sun Microsystems CEO Scott McNealy meant when he infamously remarked that we "have no privacy" (Sprenger, 1999; SFGate.com, 2003).

But if it is wise to place current concern over electronic surveillance in historical context, we also need to acknowledge how the Internet complicates issues that were once more easily disentangled. Internet-enabled surveillance must be situated within a broad thematic context of state security, privacy, freedom of expression, corporate power, and social discrimination. As Gary T. Marx (2003:370) has argued:

> In many settings privacy and surveillance are different sides of the same nickel. Privacy can serve as a nullification mechanism for power offered by surveillance. Surveillance seeks to eliminate privacy in order to determine normative compliance or to influence the individual for its own ends.

In this chapter I use three themes—surveillance, privacy, and security—as a way of integrating a range of issues and controversies about the Internet's role in this area.

What Is Surveillance?

Surveillance permeates modern life. It transcends the physical monitoring of people by people or the simple covert interception of mediated communication, though these remain some of its most important dimensions. David Lyon (2003:5) defines it as

> routine ways in which focused attention is paid to personal details by organizations that want to influence, manage, or control certain persons or population groups. It occurs for all kinds of reasons, which can be located on a continuum from care to control. Some element of care and some element of control are nearly always present, making the process inherently ambiguous.

Lyon's definition is useful for capturing the everyday nature of contemporary surveillance but also its role in promoting socially beneficial and socially damaging outcomes. In Lyon's terms, the effects of surveillance can be "social care" or "social control" (2001:3). While a deep-seated dislike of being monitored appears to be the norm in most cultures, there are many areas of life in which surveillance is beneficial. For example, since the rise of state welfare programs, gathering personal information about individuals has been a part of the social contract upon which the provision of care often depends. This is surveillance as social care. But when police and military agencies increase the scope of their monitoring, as has occurred under new legislation such as the 2001 USA PATRIOT Act and similar post-9/11 laws in many other countries around the world, concerns begin to be raised about the negative effects: mutual suspicion, invasions of personal privacy, the possibility that errors will lead to the incarceration of innocent people, or, worse still, that governments may be tempted into quick-fix responses to terrorist acts in order to be seen to be doing something decisive. The "care" to "control" continuum alerts us to the political justifications that often undergird the extension of surveillance, especially during times of real or perceived crisis. Moreover, surveillance as a social practice now seems to penetrate deep into societies, such that we are all, to some extent, involved in monitoring others, either through attempts to protect others from social harm, such as when a parent installs filtering software on a child's computer to oversee her web browsing through to the kind of mistrust and near panic of the informal racial profiling that was widespread in many countries during the winter of 2001.

Perspectives differ on the social and political consequences of surveillance, ranging from those who justify it as an absolute necessity on the grounds of national security through to those who claim that it dilutes social trust, leads to a culture of suspicion which unfairly impacts upon ethnic and religious minorities, permits unacceptable infringements of privacy, and creates a general chilling effect that discourages criticism of government. Many of the recent developments in state-initiated surveillance, such as the intensification of data mining, biometrics, and the integration of previously separate databases, are in fact based upon trends that stretch back to the beginning of the cold war. Yet 9/11 undoubtedly had a huge impact on thinking in this area—a shift that has been reinforced by fragmentary revelations about the ways in which terrorist organizations such as Al Qaeda have themselves used Internet communication (Fielding, 2004; Verton, 2003). Responses to 9/11 have not only been overwhelmingly technological in their approach; they have been conspicuously global. These characteristics inevitably focus attention on the Internet as both a source of threats and a component of modern military strategy.

Such disputes are likely to intensify as the Internet diffuses around the globe and becomes even more important for everyday life in the developed countries. This is because electronic surveillance, whether we like it or not, involves the continuous monitoring of those who are doing nothing illegal. It may be objected that the innocent have nothing to fear, and there is, of course, much truth in this. However, for some, the fundamental issue is not the impact of surveillance at the individual level as much as its socially aggregated effects—its role in classifying, sorting, and discriminating against certain social groups; the issue of why some social groups are more surveilled than others; our ability to control what others can know about our social and political interactions; and the penetration of increasing areas of our lives by commercialism. Thus, while law-abiding individuals may claim that they are not harmed by ever-present electronic surveillance, such socially aggregated forces do have the potential to exert strong effects at the individual level. Ultimately, the politics of surveillance, privacy, and security is about who knows what, when, how, and why. This inevitably involves thinking about power.

SURVEILLANCE THEORY

Surveillance is a perennial theme in modern social and political theory. While snooping and eavesdropping are probably as old as humanity, surveillance in the form of systematic and routine forms of state and private sector monitoring of the population are usually associated, at least in the West, with the rise of the modern state and the emergence of the capitalist economy, from broadly the sixteenth century onward (Dandeker, 1990; Giddens, 1985; Lyon, 1994). Numerous writers have developed theories and metaphors to capture the role and function of surveillance as well as to criticize and resist it, but for our purposes these can be summarized under four main headings: totalitarianism, panopticism, surveillant assemblage theory, and legalism. These provide a useful backdrop to the concrete examples discussed in this chapter. Almost all writing on surveillance adopts one or more of these four theoretical approaches. Even those who might not claim to be rooted in any grand theoretical tradition often have distinctive assumptions. Lawyers specializing in privacy cases, for instance, and those who look to constitutional provisions to protect citizens' privacy generally hold the assumption that the law is an effective weapon that can be used to shield individuals from an over-mighty state. Indeed, such legalism, as I term it here, is the mainstream policy response to the problem of surveillance in liberal democratic states. But as we shall see, there are other more radical and disturbing approaches.

Totalitarianism

Probably the most enduring theory of surveillance takes its cue from George Orwell's famous dystopian novel *Nineteen eighty-four* (Orwell, 1949). Honed by many in their critiques of Nazi Germany in the 1930s and Stalinist forms of communism throughout the cold war era, visions of an ever-watchful Big Brother backed by a huge state bureaucracy and omnipresent monitoring technologies have been highly influential in defining how we conceive of modern surveillance (e.g., Friedrich and Brzezinski, 1965). Orwell's insidious telescreen device, which simultaneously monitors and communicates propaganda, can be read as a metaphor for the contemporary Internet.

While the totalitarian approach often lapses into cliché, it does highlight several important trends in contemporary surveillance: the centralization of power, the unobtrusive interception of private communications, the climate of fear and social mistrust, and the way in which attempts to legitimize the state's actions are often bound up with its attempts to monitor and shape reactions among the population, enabling subtle forms of social control and mobilization. But despite its influence, totalitarian theory has several limitations for making sense of Internet surveillance. Orwell focused his attention exclusively on the nation-state acting in a simple top-down fashion, whereas surveillance now involves private corporations on a grand scale and is a highly decentralized yet globalized phenomenon that does not always respect national boundaries (Lyon, 1994:61).

Panopticism

The term "panopticon," meaning "all-seeing place" (a neologism derived from Greek), stems from political philosopher Jeremy Bentham's famous architectural design for a new, highly efficient prison (see exhibit 11.1). Published in 1791, Bentham's proposal was never put into practice in its entirety, but its principles have informed many kinds of surveillance technologies and processes, from Closed Circuit Television (CCTV) to

EXHIBIT 11.1. DISCIPLINARY SURVEILLANCE IN BENTHAM'S PANOPTICON

"The Panopticon, as designed, would be a many-sided construction with a central observation tower. Each cell would be supplied with two windows, one to provide backlighting for the occupant, the other to allow the observer in the tower unimpeded visual access. Unlike the dungeon, which locked prisoners away in darkness, the panoptic design provided control through complete visibility. Because each occupant of a cell would be isolated from others, it would reduce the possibility of the collective, co-operative, or infectious spread of problematic conditions or behavior. . . . All could be managed more efficiently if isolation and surveillance could be facilitated. In Bentham's design, power would operate because it was both visible and unverifiable. The central tower, visible at all times, would be a constant reminder that an unseen observer might be watching at any time. The Panopticon would be efficient because it would require fewer guards or supervisory personnel. In one sense, the system was self-monitoring in that residents would soon come to expect continuous surveillance or, at the very least, would always be uncertain about when the next glance would fall on their cell. The likelihood of periodic observation would operate like random reinforcement in conditioning each person to his status. . . . In an age of electronic networks, virtual memory, and remote access to distributed intelligence and data, disciplinary surveillance is no longer limited to single buildings, and observation is no longer limited to line of sight."

Source: Quoted from Gandy, 1993:22.

supermarket loyalty cards through to company managers' enthusiasm for instant messaging technologies.

The relevance of the panopticon for understanding modern societies arose mainly due to the work of the social and political theorist Michel Foucault. Foucault argued that the panopticon was an archetypal product of the eighteenth-century Enlightenment. In other words, it was part of a broader ideological shift toward the rationalization of society, based upon principles of scientific measurement and control through empirical observation rather than brute force (Foucault, 1977; see also Lyon, 1994:62). Foucault also argued that the panoptic principle permeates major institutions, such as schools, workplaces, the military, and state bureaucracies.

In recent years, a body of scholars has used panopticism to illustrate the ways in which modern consumerism depends upon electronic surveillance. It is no longer simply a matter of how we interact with government. Indeed, the interlinking of government, police, and corporate-sector databases is deeply controversial. In Oscar Gandy's (1993:15) theory of the panoptic sort, electronic forms of automated surveillance

> involve the collection, processing, and sharing of information about individuals and groups that is generated through their daily lives as citizens, employees, and consumers and is used to co-ordinate and control their access to the goods and services that define life in the modern capitalist economy.

In other words, highly efficient electronic forms of surveillance have a socially discriminatory effect, categorizing some groups as worthy of special treatment and others as the subjects of social discipline. Consider, for example, the racial profiling that is now commonplace as part of the process of seeking to identify potential terrorists.

Paradoxically, we are often willing participants in this process: by volunteering personal information when we buy consumer goods, use financial services, or apply for welfare benefits, we become subjects of what Mark Poster terms the "superpanopticon": a massive grid of personal information flows (Poster, 1990). Yet although we may initially be willing, over time we might seek to exercise greater control over the information that resides in databases. It is socially useful to have control over what others can know about us because publicly available information may be inaccurate, partial, or decontextualized. This, too, can lead to socially damaging stereotyping and the restriction of choice (Rosen, 2001:9; see also Elmer, 2003). Given the massive increase in data storage, the Internet also reduces what Jean-François Blanchette and Deborah Johnson (2002:33) identify as "the social benefits of forgetfulness": the idea that in the course of a lifetime societies benefit from giving individuals a second chance, a fresh start. Areas of the law regulating bankruptcy, juvenile crime, and credit reports recognize this principle by building in limits to the length of time information may be stored and retrieved. Cheap electronic storage obviously reduces such costs, increasing organizational incentives to hold on to information for much longer periods.

Panopticism alerts us to five crucial features of electronic surveillance: efficiency through automation; impersonality; ubiquity; preemption; and social discipline. This is a significant departure from the Orwellian totalitarian model because it reveals the ways in which surveillance becomes so deeply embedded in social behavior that we come to police ourselves in the expectation (or fear) that we are constantly being monitored. We often have no way of knowing when we can act with genuine freedom.

The Surveillant Assemblage

Totalitarian and panoptic theories have their strengths, but some argue that they fail to capture the decentralized, networked nature of surveillance since the rise of the Internet. Drawing upon the work of social theorists Gilles Deleuze and Félix Guattari, Kevin Haggerty and Richard Ericson (2000) conceptualize surveillance as an assemblage of information flows. In this perspective, surveillance is a matter of tapping into these flows at strategic points, but it is seldom a simple case of the state or large corporations acting upon us in the top-down manner assumed by Orwell and, to a lesser extent, Foucault. Haggerty and Ericson liken contemporary surveillance to the ways in which rhizomic plants spread their structures horizontally under the ground. Rhizomes (e.g., the ginger plant) are remarkably resilient, throwing out new shoots in a continuous process of subterranean expansion. Rhizomic surveillance does not originate in a single technology, institution, or even set of institutions such as a state bureaucracy but derives from "multiple connections across myriad technologies and practices." It spreads through societies through flows of personal information concerning individuals' "habits, preferences and lifestyle from the trails of information which have become the detritus of everyday life" (Haggerty and Ericson, 2000:609, 611). These fragments of information are continually reassembled by organizations that wish to use data for the purposes of selling products by authenticating our identities as worthy recipients of goods and services.

While the concept of the surveillant assemblage might seem a little abstract, it usefully captures the essence of the Internet's role. Like the totalitarian and panoptic models, it is predicated upon unobtrusive observation, preemption, and the internalization of disciplinary forms of power. But by highlighting the interconnected, organic nature of horizontal information flows, it draws our attention to the quiet expansion of network technologies and their role in tying together discrete pieces of data from across those multiple areas of society which rely upon personal information to function: government agencies, security services, or corporations. A further advantage of this approach is that it does not assume that surveillance depends on hierarchy. Indeed, modern surveillance technologies also enable distributed voyeurism on a grand scale. Thomas Mathiesen (1997) terms this "synopticism"—the watching of the few by the many. Not even the powerful can completely escape the surveillant gaze. The Internet opens up new possibilities for those who lack formal political power to track and monitor political and economic elites (Haggerty and Ericson, 2000:618; see also Wall, 2003:121). Illustration of this potentially subversive and empowering aspect of the Internet can be seen in Lord Hutton's 2004 inquiry into the death of the British government's scientific adviser Dr. David Kelly. In this case, the vast majority of evidence—some of it extremely damaging to the Blair administration in the United Kingdom—took the form of rhizomic trails of archived emails. Modern surveillance thus appears unavoidable. We are monitored in so many areas of our lives that it is impossible to stand outside it.

Legalism

It should be clear by now that there are some radical, if rather gloomy, interpretations of the role and function of surveillance. If we subscribe to the theory of the surveillant assemblage, for example, it becomes almost impossible to imagine that there are areas of our lives that can be identified as truly private. Yet mainstream political discourse in liberal democracies continues to be dominated by privacy talk. I term this kind of approach legalism, not in a pejorative sense, but merely to indicate that it involves appeals to laws and constitutional protections against what are seen as unacceptable intrusions into the private sphere. Legalism assumes that we have meaningful choices in resisting unwarranted surveillance. It rests on the liberal idea of constant political negotiation between competing objectives: national security; the profitability of companies; and the right to privacy of individuals eager to prevent personal information gleaned in one context from being used in another.

Many have argued that privacy is necessary for the healthy functioning of liberal democratic politics. Thus, the problem with ubiquitous electronic surveillance is not that we have a simple dislike of being watched (though many of us undoubtedly do); it is that the distinction between private and public expression allows us to exert some control over how we would like the world to see us. As Jeffrey Rosen puts it: "Privacy is necessary to protect all of us from . . . misinterpretation. A liberal state respects the distinction between public and private speech because it recognizes that the ability to expose in some contexts parts of our identity that we conceal in other contexts is indispensable to freedom" (2001:11). As ever greater parts of our lives move online, the potential for loss of control over what others can know about us increases.

Herman Tavani makes a useful distinction between four commonly held views of privacy: nonintrusion, or the idea that we ought to be left alone; seclusion, which maintains that we can only enjoy privacy while in the actual condition of being alone; control, which holds that we enjoy privacy only if we can exert control over the information that an organization or other individual can hold about us; and finally limitation, which stresses different zones of privacy, where personal information ought not to be made available (Tavani, 2000:66). Most legal systems in liberal democracies seek to enshrine several of these types of privacy by offering constitutional safeguards to protect citizens from arbitrary actions against them by government or corporations. Legal approaches to the problem of surveillance, security, and privacy attempt to grapple with the effects of technological change by reinterpreting existing law or by calling for new law and policy. They are an indispensable element of contemporary political discourse about the Internet.

THE PROBLEM AND POTENTIAL OF THE INTERNET: AUTHENTICATION, INTEGRATION, AUTOMATION, AND PREEMPTION

Having briefly explored some of the ways in which surveillance theory can shed light on electronic communication, it is useful at this stage to take stock of the difference the Internet makes in this area. This boils down to four main themes: authentication, integration, automation, and preemption.

In face-to-face communities, individual identity is established by clearly visible markers, such as physical appearance. These markers of identity are much more problematic in the relatively fluid, large-scale urban communities of modern life. In a city such as Los Angeles or London, a large proportion of the interactions that take place on a daily basis involve strangers. In the kinds of environments in which most of us now live, features have been developed by both private companies and governments to regulate behavior and access. These may be relatively simple, such as car license plates, or more technologically advanced, such as ATM cards, but what they have in common is the ability to authenticate an individual as a person entitled to a good or service. Once these kinds of technologies of authentication exist, their usefulness and credibility must be maintained by legal frameworks. Driver's licenses look the way they do (with photographs) and contain the information they do (with date of birth) because policy choices have been made about how best to authenticate individual drivers. The circumstances under which you can apply for such a document as a driver's license are fairly tightly controlled. Thus, all manner of public and private institutions will ask you to produce your license to prove that you are who you say you are, safe in the knowledge that your credentials have been checked when the authorities issued your license.

If such methods of identification and authentication are one place removed from the old-fashioned process of actually knowing another person or knowing what she looks like, interactions that take place over the Internet present a much larger problem. In the absence of real physical markers, behavior in cyberspace becomes much more difficult to regulate (Lessig, 1999:33). In the real world it is impossible to hide all of your physical and mental characteristics; on the Internet it is a relatively simple matter to pretend to be something you are not. In fact, pseudonymity, while frowned upon in the real world, is one of the most widely accepted practices in cyberspace. Both government and online businesses are almost totally dependent upon methods that verify a customer's identity and his ability to pay for or be entitled to goods and services. The interests of government and business thus converge on an architecture that allows individuals to be authenticated and online behavior to be monitored in indirect though highly effective ways (Lessig, 1999:44, 99). In many respects, the legislative responses to terrorism in the United States have exploited the increasingly "regulable" nature of cyberspace, though, as we shall see, these have been fiercely resisted.

If authentication poses a challenge to those who wish to surveille the Internet, such drawbacks can be partly offset by the Net's power to integrate and automate. As we saw in chapter 8, a major driver of e-government is the perceived benefit of joining-up government agencies. When it comes to surveillance, the Internet provides highly efficient automated means of bringing together discrete pieces of information to inform decision making. Indeed, at the level of surveillance systems themselves, the holy grail is to have intelligent software agents use algorithmic techniques to make decisions "on their own."

Even video surveillance through relatively old technologies like Closed Circuit Television (CCTV) can now be operated from remote locations via Internet networks. CCTV may also be partly automated using motion detection and image recognition software. London's Automatic Numberplate Recognition System for criminal and antiterrorist detection rests upon such techniques, as does the city's traffic congestion charging scheme. These systems automate the matching of vehicle license plates with the British Police National Computer Database (C. Norris, 2003:270). Despite problems with facial recognition pilot schemes, such as those undertaken in the London Borough of Newham in the United Kingdom and Tampa Bay, Florida, manufacturers are continuing to refine the technologies (Wood et al., 2003:147). When linked with such biometric information, networked digital CCTV becomes a powerful integrator of information sources. The technologies are not new, but the ways in which they can be easily and cheaply networked are new and allow those with access the ability to use the Internet to remotely view and immediately redistribute images gleaned from CCTV monitors. A scenario here might involve British intelligence officers viewing a protest march in London while communicating with their U.S. counterparts, who are also watching in real time (C. Norris, 2003:269–72). With ever-increasing storage capacity meaning that data trails can linger for many years, these processes take the idea of preemption— surveillance in advance—to new levels of sophistication.

The idea of preemptive monitoring is deeply controversial in most liberal democracies. For example, in the United States, the Fourth Amendment to the Constitution, dealing with search and seizure (in common with similar laws elsewhere) increases the hurdles that government or private actors must overcome before they are able to interfere with personal belongings. Although all manner of exceptions have been incorporated within such legal frameworks over time, the basic principle that the authorities require specific warrants in order to enter a citizen's home, based upon a specific and reasonable suspicion of criminality, is deeply embedded in many political cultures. Warrants, though flawed and often weak protection, at least provide a means by which citizens must be warned in advance that their private possessions and communications are about to be surveilled. If the authorities go beyond the terms of a warrant, an individual has legal recourse. Even in the absence of a specific warrant, those who search an office or apartment will, unless they are extremely careful, leave a physical trail.

Yet in a world in which so much information circulates around electronic networks, there are some importance changes to this familiar scenario. With electronic surveillance, as Lawrence Lessig has demonstrated, the hurdles to effectiveness are much easier to overcome and the physical traces of an electronic search less easy to trace. Lessig uses the hypothetical example of a Federal Bureau of Investigation (FBI) worm that is deliberately propagated across the Internet with the aim of finding a particular document on the hard disks of vulnerable computers. If the worm finds the document, it sends a message back to its creators. If it does not, it destroys itself without trace. All of this is done without the knowledge of the computer owner. If fears of breaching the Fourth Amendment surface, the FBI responds by ensuring that it secures judicial sanction before proceeding to place the worm on specific computers. But at the same time, legislation is passed that requires that computer networks be designed in such a way that FBI worms can operate freely on them in the future. From now on, the preemptive searching via this worm is designed in to the architecture of the Net. In such a form of electronic search, the costs of searching are dramatically reduced while the efficiency of the method is dramatically increased (Lessig, 1999:17–19). As we shall see, concerns over the designed-in nature of preemptive Internet surveillance underpin much of the debate about recent legislation such as the USA PATRIOT Act of 2001.

With these four themes—authentication, integration, automation, and preemption—in mind, let us consider some recent examples and trends in corporate, intrastate, and interstate surveillance.

Corporate Surveillance

In the immediate aftermath of 9/11, a group of large technology companies, including Oracle, AOL Time Warner, Hewlett-Packard, and AT&T, approached the U.S. government to offer their assistance in the war against terror. Government has turned to technology providers to build new security systems, such as the three-year, $3 billion contract awarded to Unisys to provide systems for the new Transportation Security Administration for airports. A clutch of other companies has emerged to provide surveillance solutions, such as Dynago's data-mining services that will retrieve word patterns from vast quantities of text or Imagis's casino CCTV technology that has been purchased by the FBI (Lyon, 2003:67, 78). This is understandable, given the ways in which the corporate sector has spent many years refining its own techniques of information acquisition, storage, retrieval, and integration. Consider some examples.

In 2004, during the U.S. Super Bowl halftime show, a performance involving musicians Janet Jackson and Justin Timberlake went wrong due to an infamous "wardrobe malfunction." Timberlake grabbed Jackson as part of a dance move, causing a piece of material from the front of her costume to fall away. The incident rippled through news reports for several weeks, but the most interesting story came from the press office of TiVo—the manufacturers of the interactive set-top box known as a personal video recorder. TiVo proudly announced that the halftime show was its "most replayed moment" of all time. How did it know? The company had been monitoring the advertisement-viewing behavior of twenty thousand of its subscribers during the game and was able to identify a 180 per cent spike in replays of that moment (TiVo Corporation, 2004).

On a similar theme, in September 2000, it emerged that the online retailer Amazon.com was using technology based on cookies[1] to discriminate between returning and new customers. Customers who returned to Amazon's site and logged in to their accounts were presented with higher prices than first-time visitors (McCarthy, 2000). The scheme caused a public outcry and was quickly dropped, but not before it had led to heightened awareness of the potential for cookies to infringe individual privacy.

Perhaps the most notorious Internet privacy cases to date concerned the online advertising agency Doubleclick and Microsoft's .NET Passport. Doubleclick formerly paid websites to have its clients' advertisements displayed as banners. The problem, however, was that pages containing Doubleclick advertisements dumped cookies on users' hard drives. This allowed the company to collect data from across a wide range of websites (so long as they contained Doubleclick advertisements) and to pull this together to refine its own advertising strategy—selling the right "eyeballs" to clients or to sell on to others. Matters were brought to a head in 1999 when Doubleclick merged with Abacus—a traditional market research company that maintained a wide-ranging database of consumers' mail-order purchases. A protest by privacy advocates led Doubleclick to drop plans to merge its online database with Abacus's catalog database (Rosen, 2001:164). The controversy over cookies eventually led Microsoft to include new features in its Internet Explorer web browser. These allow users to control which cookies they are willing to accept and to block or delete others. However, Microsoft itself became the focus of controversy in 2002 when it announced its new .NET Passport service. The company marketed .NET as a convenient service for customers. The idea was to provide a single point of authentication that would allow users access to a range of secure e-commerce and online content sites. Each user would be assigned a unique electronic identifier that would "follow" them around the .NET system. However, this violated EU data protection legislation, and the company was forced to modify its scheme (Reidenberg, 2004:7).

The cases of TiVo, Amazon, Doubleclick, and .NET are excellent examples of how the Internet allows forms of surveillance to be efficiently and invisibly automated—what Oscar Gandy (1993) terms "the panoptic sort." This operates in a variety of discriminatory ways. For instance, geodemographic systems match data on consumer behavior with location. Localities are distinguished by the characteristic consumption

---

[1]**Cookies:** small text files that are downloaded to a user's computer during a visit to a website. They contain information about how the user has clicked through the site, as well as other variables. The data is stored on the computer's hard disk but can be retrieved by the website if the person goes back to the site.

patterns that occur among their population. Visit the British website www.upmys-treet.com, which ties in with a geodemographic database provided by a private data-mining company, and after entering your postal code you may find, like me, you live in a "middle income, home owning area" among "managers and skilled workers" that like to "play golf, go walking, or enjoy fishing." While these details may seem innocuous or inaccurate (I don't golf or fish), in fact, such systems are increasingly used by companies and local planners when making decisions about where to establish premises or infra-structural improvements. Critics thus argue that data mining (see exhibit 11.2) and geodemographic systems reinforce preexisting spatial segregation between "viable" wealthy neighborhoods and "less viable" deprived areas (Phillips and Curry, 2003).

While browser changes and software fixes have defused concerns over cookies, disputes over new forms of corporate Internet surveillance started to ramp up as com-panies began to look for new revenue streams following the collapse of the dotcom bubble in 2000. The most high-profile disputes have occurred over so-called spyware (Bruening and Steffen, 2004; Klang, 2003). Spyware is significant not just because it in-conveniences consumers and violates their privacy but also because several of the tech-niques exploited in spyware programs are similar to those used by both criminals and law enforcement agencies in their attempts to surveille the Internet. Cookies could per-haps be viewed as a simple form of spyware, but they are not executable programs and as such are relatively "dumb" (but still powerful) ways of collecting information about Internet users. In contrast, the most heavily criticized forms of spyware are keystroke loggers (keyloggers) or similar programs that detect passwords and other personal data before sending them back to a specified computer. Keyloggers have been found bundled in virus and trojan files and are part of the armory of law enforcement officers.

Far more common forms of spyware are programs that piggyback on seemingly le-gitimate software and websites or those which openly engage the user in consenting to allow information about browsing habits to be transmitted back to companies that have poor privacy policies governing how that information may be used and sold (Bruening and Steffen, 2004:4). Examples of these two types abound: many "freeware" file-sharing programs like Bearshare, Limewire, or Kazaa have, at various stages, sought to generate revenue by bundling spyware with their programs. More insidious programs install themselves by exploiting security loopholes in browser software, by requiring that a user click the "OK" button on a popup box, for instance. Upon starting up their browser, an individual may find that their home page has been hijacked by a pornogra-phy site or, worse still, that they have unwittingly downloaded a hacked "dialer" that automatically calls a premium-rate phone number without consent (dialers are a com-mon way of paying for adult content).

Spyware is problematic because it falls between the cracks in existing privacy leg-islation. The U.S. Congress has considered a number of bills, but none were enacted (Volkmer, 2004). A major problem here are the license agreements that may adequately forewarn users about the privacy implications of installing a piggyback program but which most of us click through without reading. These difficulties are also compounded by the transient nature of the free-/shareware software market and the transnational or-ganization of online criminal networks that exploit dialers, for example (Klang, 2003).

Methods such as data mining and spyware have now also found their way into political campaigning. A political action committee (PAC) known as United Campaigns

EXHIBIT 11.2. DATA MINING

Data mining refers to a range of statistical techniques derived from artificial intelligence technologies. The aim is to discover hidden patterns and relationships between pieces of information in very large databases. Data-mining companies seek to identify new social or consumer categories and to make decisions and predictions about the future behavior of social groups based upon aggregated knowledge of how that behavior has occurred in the past. This is achieved by developing profiles based upon the data trails that we leave when we perform transactions or simply browse around the Internet. Unlike conventional databases, which are built around categories that the user knows in advance, data mining seeks to reveal patterns in the data that cannot be known in advance due to its volume and apparent complexity.

Examples of data mining in action include attempts to deter credit card fraud through the automated identification of anomalous purchases and Amazon.com's well-known product recommendation feature, which offers shoppers similar items based upon how they have clicked through the site or product combinations that have tended to occur in the past. Less pleasant examples include insurance data mining which identifies "risky" behavior patterns that generate higher premiums for certain social groups or the recently abandoned Computer Assisted Passenger Prescreening System (CAPPS II) in the United States. Meant to be installed at airline check-in desks, CAPPS II was conceived as a means of identifying known terrorists and criminals but also of assigning risk scores to individuals based upon "commercially available data and current intelligence information" (U.S. Department of Homeland Security, 2004). It would rapidly mine data from a range of sources, including the FBI, the Internal Revenue Service, the National Crime Information Center, the Social Security Administration, the State Department, credit reference agencies and banks, among others.

Before the widespread use of the Internet, data mining was relatively cumbersome and mainly centered on transactional information. Today, data is mined from websites through the use of web forms, server log files, cookies, and other forms of "clickstream" monitoring. Artificial intelligence technology has inspired the creation of "intelligent" software agents that are able to "learn" and refine their data mining models over time.

The market for data-mining technologies has increased dramatically in recent years, largely due to the reduction of the costs of storing, retrieving, and transmitting data; the growth of e-commerce and more sophisticated models of customer market segments; as well as the heightened security environment post-9/11. The most significant criticism of data mining is that it removes the ability of the individual to truly consent to how personal information is ultimately used.

Sources: Summarized from Cavoukian, 1998; Gandy, 2000, 2003; Hunter, 2002; Lyon, 2003; Tavani, 2000; U.S. Department of Homeland Security, 2004.

(a pseudonym) acts as a form of Internet consultant to U.S. senators and representatives, nonprofit groups, and other campaigns. The organization maintains a large database of individual-level political information, such as online donation records linked with specific demographics. United Campaign's clients use these data to identify potential supporters and donors. These techniques are of course the bread and butter of traditional political campaigning. But there the similarities end. United gathers much of its database from a free email service provider which requires customers to fill out forms and questionnaires as a condition of the service. These include data such as "age, gender, income, expected major purchases, hobbies, interests, family size, and education" that are cross-referenced with the 150 million U.S. voter registration records and 50 million records from Departments of Motor Vehicles. Although many U.S. states forbid the use of voter records for private gain, United circumvents these regulations due to its formal status as a PAC. It runs a not-for-profit Internet Service Provider (ISP), which it uses to gather subscriber information via cookies and legal forms of spyware. These track web use and spawn targeted advertising campaigns to drive traffic to clients' sites. It also trades data with other organizations. According to researchers Philip Howard and Tema Milstein, it covers "more than 75% of the voting public" in the United States (2003:8–9).

The idea of privacy selling may seem an attractive means of using free goods and services, but it is unpalatable for many, as the case of Google's botched launch of its GMail service illustrates. In the spring of 2004, the search engine and web services company announced plans for its new free email system, GMail, to a furor among privacy activists. The "price" of free GMail for users was permitting Google to scan and index keywords and phrases in email messages using its search algorithm. The results would be used to serve targeted text advertisements as "sponsored links" alongside users' messages. Although Google insisted that its system was entirely automated and did not contain personally identifiable information, pressure group Privacy International filed complaints in seventeen European countries as well as Canada and Australia, severely delaying GMail's official launch.

At the root of such controversy is a clash of values over privacy itself. In one long-established perspective, privacy is an inalienable right which deserves protection independently of any particular economic context such as a market for property rights. Such a perspective is highly critical of the notion of introducing market relations as privacy selling into this sphere of activity, not only because this is seen as morally suspect, but also because market relations are far from equal. Even with ways of automating customer privacy preferences such as cookie controls, some market sectors are relatively unfree, because they are dominated by a few big players. In such markets the exit costs for consumers are usually high. There may be very few or even no other companies providing the good or service for which they must forfeit their personal information. It has been countered that gaps in the market will create new opportunities for companies that pride themselves on not requesting, retaining, or selling personal information. But this ignores the fact that monopoly or near-monopoly markets are the way that they are because they evolved in more naive times, when the protection of personal information in an online environment was not as pressing a problem as it is today.

If corporations monitor consumers, they increasingly do the same to their employees. Electronic workplace surveillance is now common. A host of software can be bought off the shelf by managers wishing to monitor email and web-browsing habits.

Keyloggers are now commonplace in many customer call centers. The increase in tele-working has created new demand among managers keen to oversee their far-flung workers. Most large companies now insist that workers connect from home using Virtual Private Network (VPN) connections—a secure "tunnel" of communication that encrypts data sent across the Internet, keeping it from prying eyes. The advantages of VPN extend beyond security, however, because it allows managers to track employee activity, such as when they logged on to the VPN, for how long, and which websites they visited. Similarly, instant messaging software has become wildly popular in the corporate sector, not only because it offers quick and convenient communication, but also because it can alert bosses when a worker goes offline or is not responding to requests. Instant messaging has also moved into mobile communications, as cell phones with Windows Mobile operating systems have a messaging client built in.

Yet there are reasons other than worker discipline that drive companies to monitor the Internet communication of their workforce. Fear of sexual harassment lawsuits has been a major driver in the United States, where employers defend monitoring on the grounds that they wish to avoid being found negligent in harassment cases. Thus, employee privacy may be infringed for the broader social goal of reducing sexual discrimination. And employers have so far been relatively unconstrained by the law. A landmark 1985 Supreme Court ruling on the case of Magno Ortega, a psychiatrist at a northern Californian hospital whose private things in his office had been seized as part of an investigation into his behavior, ruled in favor of his employer. The court argued that Ortega should have had no expectation of privacy in the working environment and therefore should have realized that rifling through his personal belongings was legitimate.

The problem with this interpretation is that it has empowered employers to press ahead with Internet monitoring schemes protected by the circular argument that employees can expect little right to privacy if the technical means by which it can be denied are in place. Thus, employers may monitor email because employees *know* that their email is being monitored and thus have no expectation of privacy.

One of the best-known applications of this bizarre principle was the case of *Smyth v. Pillsbury Corp* (1996). Pillsbury had consistently espoused the policy of email confidentiality and had apparently promised that no worker should suffer discrimination as a result of his email being intercepted. But when an employee, Michael Smyth, wrote to one colleague of wanting to "kill the back-stabbing bastards" in the sales division of the company, Pillsbury's managers proceeded to pull out all of Smyth's email correspondence that month before firing him. In the legal case that followed, Smyth's claim was dismissed on the (Ortega case) grounds that he had no expectation of privacy when communicating across the company's email network (Rosen, 2001:66–74).

Still, if the architecture of cyberspace can be designed in ways that cause concerns over privacy, this needs to be balanced against the mechanisms that can protect personal information. We should not lose sight of the facts that make the Internet so difficult to regulate in the first place: the many possibilities for anonymity, the subversive use of pseudonymity, the lack of identifying geography, the use of encryption, the ease of access, and the radically reduced costs of publication. All of these are taken for granted in interactions in cyberspace. They have made it possible for forms of expression and behavior that are on the margins of acceptability in liberal democracies to flourish.

Intrastate Surveillance

I turn now to what I term intrastate surveillance: attempts by states to monitor the Internet use of their populations as a way of dealing with harmful content, crime, supervision, and terrorism.

Early debates about state surveillance of the Internet centered upon online pornography in the United States. In the minds of civil libertarians, the issue essentially boils down to freedom of speech and privacy of personal communication. If law enforcement bodies are to bring to justice those who break the law by creating and distributing illegal child pornography, for instance, they must be permitted to surveille the perpetrators and ultimately censor content. But while child pornography is illegal in almost all jurisdictions around the world, pornography depicting adults, so long as it falls within the scope of legally agreed-upon definitions, is widely permitted. Questions then inevitably revolve around the breadth of such legal definitions and how law enforcement agencies may apply methods of surveillance to operationalize these in criminal investigations. Civil libertarians fear that, if left unchecked, criminal surveillance methods have a tendency to spill over into other areas.

The online pornography saga began in 1996 when the Communications Decency Act (CDA) was passed with little congressional debate. Now regarded as something of a knee-jerk reaction to a moral panic about Internet pornography, the CDA was promoted by socially conservative bodies like the National Coalition for the Protection of Children and Families but heavily criticized for its vagueness by civil liberties organizations. The act was designed to prevent the transmission to children (wittingly or unwittingly) of "patently offensive" representations of sexual activities. The American Civil Liberties Union (ACLU) quickly launched a legal challenge in a district court on the grounds of violation of First Amendment speech rights. The government lost, and the case was passed up to the Supreme Court. In June 1997, in a landmark ruling (*ACLU vs. Reno*), the justices declared the CDA in violation of the First Amendment. Their decision was based upon the breadth of the act. Terms such as "patently offensive" were not adequately defined, for example, while the act would supposedly apply to the whole Internet without defining whether some activities would be more worthy targets than others. Interestingly, as Robert Klotz observes, the court also argued that the Internet should be treated on the same grounds as print media (Klotz, 2004:145; see also Weaver, 2000). The justices maintained that unlike broadcasting, the Net required a high degree of intentionality on the part of readers. It was therefore less likely that children would be accidentally exposed to pornographic material. This is an important distinction that has conditioned the debate ever since and has made it much more difficult for conservative campaigners to tighten restrictions on online pornography. Similar criticisms of definitional breadth and theories of intentionality undergirded federal courts' decisions to rule against "CDA II"—the Child Online Protection Act—in 2000 and 2002 (Jaeger and McClure, 2004; see also Strossen, 2000).

Of course, a common personal response to the problem of restricting access to online pornography takes the form of desktop filtering software. While this may be acceptable in the confines of the home, when such filters are used in the public sphere, they instantly become politically controversial. Following the failure to pass the CDA, and thus to target the suppliers of online pornography, supporters of pornography censorship increasingly looked to institutionalize software filtering in public places, such as schools and public libraries. The result was the Children's Internet Protection Act (CIPA) of 2000, introduced by Republican senator of Arizona John McCain. This required all public schools and libraries to install filtering software to prevent users viewing pornographic images. This was to be achieved by making federal subsidies to public bodies for Internet connectivity—the so-called e-rate program—conditional upon the installation of the filters.

The legislation was immediately challenged by civil liberties groups, once again on the grounds that it was too cumbersome. Filtering software has repeatedly been shown to be imperfect and likely to block many legitimate sites. However, in June 2003, the Supreme Court (in a six to three decision) ruled that the CIPA would prove effective and was in accordance with the First Amendment. The act requires the blocking of three types of content that have been legally defined in previous U.S. law: "obscenity," "child pornography," and content "harmful to minors" (those under eighteen). However, the third category of expression—that deemed "harmful to minors"—is most controversial. This is because it covers material of a sexual nature that may be of "serious literary, artistic, political, or scientific value" *to adults*. This might include scientific works, literature, art, photography, or educational materials about sexual health (Jaeger and McClure, 2004). Critics, such as the American Library Association, not only consider the technology of filtering to be crude and ineffective, they also argue that the producers of material that is "harmful to minors" but of value to adults are having their speech rights infringed, and the readers of that material are being preemptively surveilled when they use the Internet in public places. At the time of writing (early 2005), the CIPA remains intact, though it is likely to undergo further legal challenge.

Groups such as the National Coalition for the Protection of Children and Families have also campaigned for the installation of filtering technologies in network access packages provided by ISPs. Many large ISPs, such as AOL, have included user-configurable filters in their products. But for critics, the introduction of Internet content filtering by ISPs or any other body implies surveillance and the interception of Internet communication that threatens First Amendment speech rights. Filtering could easily be applied to other forms of online speech, or it could be invisibly extended. It is also subject to the wisdom of the agency that defines the filters. It thus sets a dangerous precedent (Lessig, 1999:179).

As the example of online pornography demonstrates, the most widespread response to surveillance—at least in liberal democracies—is privacy law. But here traditions differ. In western Europe, the protection of individual privacy has been won mainly through the introduction of new legal rules governing how information may be stored and used. Responses to new environments, such as the Internet, create new rules that account for new commercial practices, electronic networks, and storage systems. This rules-based approach has not been as prevalent in the United States, where companies' property and free speech rights in the data they collect have tended to override individual privacy rights (Cain, 2002; Phillips, 2003:15). There, the preference has been for self-regulation through industrywide codes of practice and enforcement through liability rules. This means that if companies' own attempts to secure consumer privacy are found wanting, a person can seek redress for privacy infringements through the courts, but only *after* the infringement has occurred. In such a context, an individual has little preemptive control over how her personal information may be used. She can later sue for damages, but this is costly and cumbersome. And the problem with voluntary schemes is that they may be ineffective in the face of the rapid changes being wrought by e-commerce, particularly the massive range of privacy policies and problems such as spyware that exist across the commercial Internet.

This is not to say that the United States lacks a legislative framework for protecting individual privacy. The Privacy Protection Act of 1980 shields authors and publishers from unreasonable intervention by law enforcement agencies. Similarly, the 1994 Privacy Act requires that individuals explicitly consent to the circulation of government-held information, such as their Social Security numbers, photographs, fingerprints, or even voiceprints (Cain, 2002:24). But aside from the anomalous cable television and video rental sectors, the United States has very little legislative protection for individual data held by corporations. Financial, medical, employment, and telephone records are routinely passed around without the explicit consent of the individuals concerned (Steinke, 2002:197).

The competing European and U.S. approaches to privacy came into conflict in the late 1990s, following the EU's 1998 Data Protection Directive stipulating how companies ought to deal with personal information (see exhibit 11.3). U.S. companies refused to comply with the directive, but after a series of negotiations, a "safe harbor" agreement was established which exempted U.S. firms from full compliance. Harmonization of privacy policy in the sphere of e-commerce appears to be some way off (Regan, 2003), though some U.S. analysts have called for European-style data protection legislation as the answer to what are seen as weak attempts at self-regulation by companies—a view that is widely resisted in the U.S. e-commerce sector (Strauss and Rogerson, 2002). Indeed, EU law was strengthened in 2002 by the new Directive on Privacy and Electronic Communications covering all Internet communication, though it is unclear whether this will make much difference to problems like spyware and the abuse of cookies, largely because of the due notice requirements that are met by click-through license agreements and website privacy policies (European Union, 2002; King, 2003).

"Crypto": Privacy-Enhancing Technologies

In the absence of a strong, European-style legislative framework in the United States, civil libertarians have responded to Internet surveillance by arming themselves with privacy enhancing technologies. These take a number of forms. Near-anonymous web browsing can be achieved through the skilful use of proxy servers that make a computer's IP address difficult (though not impossible) to trace. More refined tools, such as Anonymizer, make users virtually invisible to website owners (though not to ISPs or the law enforcement authorities, should they seek to seize Anonymizer.com's log files) (Tavani, 2000:84). Along the same lines, much stronger but more difficult to use forms of protection are based upon an emerging technology known as onion routing. This is a technical protocol which allows a sender to add several layers of encryption to message packets. As the packets travel through the many routers on the way to their destination, layers of encryption are gradually removed, but the IP addresses of these routers are

EXHIBIT 11.3. STRONG PRIVACY LAW: THE EUROPEAN UNION

Since the 1960s, privacy has been a matter of political controversy in many western European countries. Germany and the United Kingdom in particular have often been at the forefront of attempts to devise data protection legislation. Attempts to create a common environment for data protection at the level of the European Union (EU) came to a head in 1998, with the implementation of the EU Data Protection Directive. As Steinke has argued, the main features of this are:

- "An organization must inform individuals about the purposes for which it collects and uses information about them, how to contact the organization and the types of third parties to which it discloses the information.

- An organization must offer individuals the opportunity to 'opt out' of whether their information can be used for a purpose besides the one for which it was originally gathered. For sensitive information such as medical conditions, racial or ethnic origin, political opinions, etc., consumers must be given a specific 'opt in' choice before the information is disclosed to a third party.

- Each organization handling personal data must take reasonable steps to ensure its security and integrity.

- Individuals must have access to their personal information and be able to correct it. There must also be mechanisms to assure compliance with the EU Directive, recourse for individuals who are affected by non-compliance and consequences for the organization when the directive is not followed.

- Corporations and governments are forbidden from using most personal records for any purpose other than the original one, without explicit permission.

- The directive also requires the creation of government data protection agencies, registration of databases with those agencies, and sometimes even prior approval before certain data may be processed.

- Personal data on EU citizens may only be transferred to countries outside the EU that adopt these rules or are deemed to provide 'adequate protection' for the data."

Source: Quoted from Steinke, 2002:195.

protected until the very last router stage. In 2004, the U.S. Navy commenced development on Tor, its own variation of onion routing (Harrison, 2004). While not guaranteeing complete anonymity, Tor makes it much more difficult for snoopers to identify the precise origin and destination of Internet communications.

Yet by far the most significant and controversial privacy-enhancing technology is public key encryption. For ordinary citizens and consumers, but also for criminals, terrorists, and military adversaries, public key is potentially a very powerful means of evading the prying eyes of corporations, the law enforcement authorities, and the enemy. Herein lies the political controversy.

Before the invention of public key in the mid-1970s, encrypting a message meant producing an encryption key that is used to encode and decode a message. Simple encryption, for example, might involve replacing all letters in a phrase with those alphabetically prior to them (so "Peter" becomes "Odsdq"). In this case, both sender and receiver of a communication need to know that the key to the encryption involves rearranging the letters, but a (very) casual observer might fail to spot this, scratch his head, and move on. Real keys are of course much more sophisticated than this, but the big problem with simple encryption is obvious: it all depends on keeping the key secret. If the key is revealed to the world, either by code breaking (someone who has the mental agility, time, and tenacity to break the code) or by simple theft, communications can be intercepted, decoded, and altered at will by anyone. The high-stakes process of code breaking is famously conveyed by the story of mathematician Alan Turing and his colleagues' cracking of the German Enigma code, used to communicate information about the location of U-boats during the Second World War.

Public key encryption addresses the fundamental weakness of simple encryption by using two interrelated keys—one public and one private. This chapter is not the place to explore this in detail, but the basics need to be grasped to understand why it is so powerful and has proved so controversial. If I wanted to send you a message using public key encryption, I would use your public key (which is known to everyone) to encrypt it. You would then use your private key to decrypt it. However you and only you will be able to decrypt the message, because only you have the unique private key that corresponds with the public key that you broadcast to the world.

The beauty of public key encryption is that it removes the need for a common key that is used by both sender and receiver. So long as you and I keep our (different) private keys secret, the communication will be secure. If a digital signature is added to the communication, you can also be confident that the communication has not been intercepted and modified by some third party. Further, if a digital certificate authority—a trusted outside body—is added to the chain, you can verify that I am actually the owner of my public key. This is basically the technology that enables secure e-commerce transactions.

Public key encryption is very difficult to crack. Though the public and private keys must be mathematically related, the way in which the algorithm works makes it incredibly difficult to reverse engineer a private key from a public key. Today, code breakers often attempt to discover encryption keys using "brute force" techniques. They use a powerful computer and a program designed to test all possible number sequences until the key is found. In the case of 40-bit encryption, this might be achieved in a few hours. But recently, the development of more sophisticated 128-bit and 256-bit encryption algorithms means that it may take many years, rendering the task itself practically meaningless.

During the late 1990s, a struggle over encryption standards took place between private corporations, the U.S. government's intelligence and law enforcement agencies, and a group of cyberlibertarian hackers (Levy, 2002). Known as the crypto wars, the main issue was whether strong (128-bit) forms of encryption should be made available for use by the general public and whether software companies should be granted export licenses for their sale and distribution overseas. The government was eager to restrict the spread of strong encryption because it feared that it would fall into the hands of criminals, terrorists, and rogue states. This would make global intelligence gathering much more difficult. But from the perspective of corporations such as Microsoft and IBM, having their products rely on weak encryption would prove a disadvantage in the global marketplace; it would allow companies based in countries without such restrictions to get one step ahead in providing businesses with the tools they required to secure their global Internet communications. Meanwhile, the so-called cypherpunk community, with support from groups like the Electronic Frontier Foundation (EFF), argued that encryption was an essential tool in securing citizens' communications in the face of what they perceived to be the Orwellian tendencies of U.S. agencies such as the FBI, the Central Intelligence Agency (CIA) and the National Security Agency (NSA). They claimed that First Amendment constitutional rights to freedom of speech were being infringed. In any case, they argued, strong crypto was already widely available on the Internet—it was pointless trying to stop it. The government favored a scheme based on key escrow, meaning that communications could be encrypted but the government would hold a master key.

Following a number of legal challenges and failed legislation, finally, in 2000, the government announced that it would relax the rules on the export of 128-bit encryption, a decision which paved the way for the incorporation of strong privacy-enhancing technologies to be enshrined in many kinds of software tools, including Microsoft's Windows 2000 and XP operating systems (Bowden and Akdeniz, 1999; Levy, 2002:310). The problem for the United States and other governments, of course, is that strong public key encryption is now widely available to all. However, recent developments have tended to overshadow such concerns.

The Impact of 9/11 on Intrastate Surveillance

The terrorist attacks of September 2001 have led to a raft of Internet surveillance initiatives. Six weeks after 9/11, the U.S. Congress enacted the Providing Appropriate Tools Required to Intercept and Obstruct Terrorism (PATRIOT) Act. This provided security and law enforcement bodies with an array of new powers to surveille and investigate U.S. citizens. The act, which built upon and extended existing legislation, granted the FBI court-ordered powers to monitor communications believed to be related to terrorism. It also streamlined the process of obtaining the warrants that allow the FBI to wiretap telephones (including cell phones) and Internet accounts. In the past, each account had to be covered by a separate court order, but now all accounts can be covered by just one. Announcing the legislation, Attorney General John Ashcroft defined a new era of "roving" surveillance, which "permits the use of devices that capture senders' and receivers' addresses associated with communications on the Internet" (quoted in Verton, 2003:219). Emails have been intercepted under search warrants for many years, but PATRIOT extended this to computerized voice mail messages and provided law enforcement agencies with the power to obtain credit card transaction information from e-commerce purchases and bank account details. The act also encourages ISPs to voluntarily disclose customer records by protecting them from liability in cases where disgruntled individuals might sue a company for breaching its privacy policies (Phillips, 2003:7). This gives ISPs much more of an incentive to comply with requests for information (Reidenberg, 2004:14). In late 2002, the new Department of Homeland Security was established—the first in U.S. history with a specific brief to prevent domestic terrorist attacks. The Domestic Security Enhancement Bill of 2003—an even more radical extension to PATRIOT—was delayed, though it may be resurrected. The reelection of President Bush and the strengthened Republican grip on Congress in 2004 will provide such initiatives with a renewed stimulus.

PATRIOT built upon existing surveillance systems, most notably the FBI's DCS1000 monitoring system. First established in 1999 with the codename Carnivore, DCS1000 integrates FBI computers with ISP servers. FBI investigators must obtain court orders to run keyword searches designed to catch criminals and terrorists. Agents install a packet sniffing workstation in ISP server headquarters before running the DCS1000 software to capture the flow of data, including instant messaging, email, web browsing, and FTP transfers. Data is analyzed using a suite of software tools called Dragonware. A central feature of DCS1000 is that it may be used to access the full content of communication, not just simple identifiers like sender and receiver locations or time and frequency of messages.

Despite its rather sinister connotations and the protests of privacy groups, DCS1000 was actually a tightly circumscribed method of Internet surveillance. It was dependent upon the granting of specific warrants and could only be used if the FBI demonstrated to a federal judge probable cause of criminality. Those being monitored had to be notified that their communication had been intercepted—though, for obvious reasons, this often occurred afterward (U.S. Department of Justice, 2000; Mencik, 2001). However, the PATRIOT Act greatly reduced the legal friction involved in establishing DCS1000 Internet wiretaps. The FBI no longer requires probable cause that a crime has occurred, only that the surveillance is relevant to an ongoing investigation, and in the majority of cases, officers are not required to inform those being monitored (Mencik, 2001).

The PATRIOT measures were greeted with widespread criticism by civil liberties groups such as the ACLU, the EFF, and the Washington, D.C., based Electronic Privacy Information Center. They argue that the legislation had been passed in haste during a period of crisis, on the mistaken assumption that further terrorist attacks were imminent. They also argued that the definition of behavior that would attract surveillance was too broad and could even include peaceful civil disobedience.

These views have not prevented legislation akin to PATRIOT from being introduced in other countries, most notably the United Kingdom, where the Regulation of Investigatory Powers Act (RIPA) 2000 and the Anti-terrorism, Crime, and Security Act (2001) grant the home secretary relatively open-ended powers to issue warrants to authorize ISP wiretaps. This legislation also requires all telecommunication providers (including fixed line and mobile ISPs) to retain selected billing and call data for a period determined by the government. RIPA established a new legal regime for police and security services to intercept Internet communications, including email correspondence, websites, and newsgroup visits. From what we know, the process works in a similar fashion to DCS1000: law enforcement officers, acting under warrant from the home secretary, install black box terminals in ISP server buildings. These are used to intercept Internet traffic.

One of the most controversial aspects of the U.K.'s RIPA legislation is the requirement that suspects surrender encryption keys or face two years in prison. While these parts of the act were diluted following a sustained campaign by an alliance of corporate

ISPs and civil libertarian groups such as Liberty, the Foundation for Information Policy Research, and Stand.org.uk, the act retained the key surrender clauses. Critics argue that RIPA subtly shifts the burden of proof away from investigators and onto individuals, who must demonstrate that they have done all they can to surrender their encryption keys, even in cases where they may have been lost or forgotten. Suspects are also forbidden from informing others that they are under investigation and face a five-year prison sentence for doing so (Fitzpatrick, 2002:365).

Under Britain's post-9/11 equivalent of PATRIOT—the Anti-terrorism, Crime, and Security Act (2001)—a "voluntary code of practice" on data retention was drawn up in consultation with telecommunication providers, but the home secretary may overrule this at any time. This is still fiercely resisted by the umbrella association for U.K. ISPs (ISPA U.K.), which objects to the increased costs of maintaining logs as well as the threats to privacy. The U.K. information commissioner, Richard Thomas, whose role is to oversee the workings of data protection and freedom of information legislation, has also criticized the act. However, despite a special parliamentary review of the legislation in 2003, which pointed out the potential for abuse of creating huge databases that may be accessed by a swathe of government and law enforcement bodies, it remains in place (U.K. Privy Counsellor Review Committee, 2003:96).

Formal legislative action like the PATRIOT Act and their British equivalents at least have the advantage of being open to public scrutiny, unlike some of the other initiatives that have followed 9/11. A program that sought to capitalize on the Internet's capacity for distributed voyeurism was the FBI's Terrorism Information and Prevention System (TIPS). This asked those who come into contact with the public in their daily jobs to report suspicious behavior to the FBI using a toll-free phone number or a web form at the FBI's site. TIPS was a small component of a much larger program, Total Information Awareness (TIA), located, somewhat ironically, in the Advanced Research Projects Agency (ARPA)—the body which had such an influence on the development of the Internet during the early 1970s (see chapter 3). Led by John Poindexter, one-time national security advisor to President Reagan, TIA was inspired by the revealing investigation of Al Qaeda organizer Mohammed Atta's movements before the 9/11 attacks (see exhibit 11.4). The Pentagon was keen to extend its surveillance capabilities to encompass the huge amounts of electronically stored data that exist in the commercial sector. The aim was to use data-mining techniques to find patterns in seemingly unrelated pieces of information, such as car rental and hotel receipts, online credit card purchases, and medical, banking, driving, and educational records. The idea of opening up consumer databases to the Department of Defense and permitting cross-referencing with public databases proved extremely controversial with civil liberties organizations and provoked much resentment among sections of the public (Verton, 2003:222). As a result, Congress cut funding for the TIA program in September 2003, but the White House has refused to accept this (EFF, 2004). As with the extensions to the PATRIOT Act, TIA initiatives could make a comeback under the second Bush administration.

Concerns about increases in intrastate surveillance in the Anglo-American liberal democracies seem justified, but they must also be placed in the broader context of what has been possible elsewhere. Consider the example of China, where Internet surveillance is endemic.

EXHIBIT 11.4. THE NETWORKED INTEGRATION OF SURVEILLANCE

"Some rather telling television images circulated after September 11th. They depicted Mohammed Atta, the alleged leader of the 9/11 conspirators, in the days leading up to the attacks. He could be seen on grainy CCTV film footage entering a motel, paying for fuel at a gas station, picking up supplies in a convenience store, and so on. Not only were there images; his transactional data had been retrieved, showing his online air ticket purchase, his phone calls, his email use. Each detail was logged by airlines, phone companies and service providers. His trail was easy to follow, and after the event, yielded quite a detailed picture of his activities, and those of his colleagues.

These items did not initially form a police record or an intelligence report. They are merely the electronic footprints left by an (extra)ordinary consumer, a trail of transactions. They are unremarkable, taken-for-granted aspects of everyday life in a world of credit cards, bank machines, and the Internet. What is striking about them is how quickly the authorities were able to pull the bits of consumer data together, to construct a jigsaw of pieces which, when assembled, made up a partial portrait. Although policing and intelligence have always relied on such snippets and fragments of ordinary life activities, the crucial factor today is that they are so readily and instantly available."

Source: Quoted from Lyon, 2003:88.

Authoritarian States: China

China's approach to the Internet is deeply paradoxical. While the communist regime has sought to harness its potential for economic development, it has also been fearful of the politically destabilizing effects of greater freedom of communication. The regime has sought technology-driven economic development via its market reform strategy but has maintained, indeed tightened, its grip on the internal and external flow of Internet communication. The Chinese case demolishes many of the myths about the "uncontrollable" nature of the Internet.

Historically, the Maoist regime of the 1950s to the 1970s was based upon the "transmission belt" model of communication. Borrowed from Leninism, this conceived of the media as a tool for mobilizing the population for achieving nationally proscribed social and economic goals. This was enabled by a media and telecommunication system that was only open to key regime personnel. The market reforms that began in the late 1970s have produced a media and telecommunication sector less saturated with official ideology, but tight restrictions are nevertheless maintained (Kalathil and Boas, 2003:17–42). In 1999, the president of China, Jiang Zemin, declared the struggle to control the Internet a "battlefield without bloodshed" before claiming that the West was using it to launch a "peaceful revolution" against the "socialist countries" (quoted in Zhang, 2002:168).

Internet surveillance in China is based upon extensive technical mechanisms. In the mid-1990s, the regime took the decision to establish two levels of Internet access. Users may connect to the domestic Internet network reasonably freely, but international traffic must pass through a limited number of state-controlled backbone networks run by various state ministries (Kalathil and Boas, 2003:21). This ingenious system has allowed the state to let domestic ISPs and online media providers flourish while retaining extensive control and surveillance powers. And even though the domestic ISP market appears pluralistic, it too is in practice tightly controlled via the Ministry of Information Industry's monopoly over the important ChinaNET backbone. ISPs that are affiliated with the ChinaNET enjoy preferential leasing rates denied to independent ISPs. Around 90 percent of China's ISPs simply resell ChinaNET connections. This obviously gives the Ministry of Information Industry huge leverage over the supposedly free-market domestic ISP sector.

These infrastructure level controls are bolstered by a combination of software filtering, simple regulations, and coercion. Access to dissident sites, such as those run by human rights campaigners or supporters of the illegal Falun Gong religious sect, are restricted through firewall ban list filters regularly maintained by the Ministry of State Security, among others. The Ministry of Information Industry laid down rules in 2000 requiring ISPs to restrict the flow of dissident political views and to report those whose accounts were used for this purpose. As a result, content providers routinely monitor websites and bulletin boards and quickly remove sensitive comments. Local Internet cafés are required to cooperate with local security bureaus by installing monitoring software that allows local Internet police divisions to monitor individual browsing patterns.

These infrastructural, software, and physical methods have proved remarkably successful. In the late 1990s, the fledgling China Democracy Party was effectively quashed after its members were jailed for sending emails to dissidents overseas (Kalathil and Boas, 2003:30). Falun Gong, a transnational religious movement with bases throughout the Far East, has often sought to use the Internet to coordinate activities, but the Chinese police have targeted Falun Gong email accounts, making it difficult for internal supporters to make contact with those overseas, though there is still scope for using pay phones (Kalathil and Boas, 2003:30). It is difficult to estimate the number of arrests for online dissidence, but a well-known case involved a schoolteacher being jailed for two years for a message on the Nonchong city website, stating: "We all think about one sentence that none of us will say: overthrow the Communist Party" (Kalathil and Boas, 2003:26). And in 1999, a software developer, Lin Hai, was imprisoned for two years for distributing a list of thirty thousand email addresses to a Washington, D.C., based pro-democracy newsletter, *VIP Reference,* while in 2001, a subscriber was given a three-year prison sentence for forwarding the same publication to his friends (Klotz, 2004:209).

Despite the ubiquity of Internet surveillance in China, and, perhaps more significantly, its translation into punitive action and coercion, there is little sign that the communist regime is about to crumble under the weight of Internet freedoms. There may be scope for getting around software filtering using proxy servers or privacy protecting peer-to-peer programs like Peek-a-Booty, invented by members of the hacktivist group Cult of the Dead Cow, but there is little evidence that this activity is widespread (Kalathil and Boas, 2003:29). And, as Shanthi Kalathil and Taylor Boas (2003) have persuasively argued, the state has allowed the domestic ISP and content production sectors to expand. Among those business leaders seeking to make money from the Internet, there is a pragmatic attitude to surveillance and censorship. The state has so far been quite successful in producing a culturally and ideologically specific Internet experience for the vast majority of its population. Rules prevent any wholly foreign-owned company from acting as an online content provider. When (or if) China conforms to the full requirements of its World Trade Organization (WTO) membership, it will open up its ISP and content provider market to foreign firms. But China has yet to formally implement many WTO directives.

The experience of China hints at the ways that the Internet blurs the distinction between internal and external communication flows. Awareness of this increasing fluidity has spurred states to develop interstate forms of monitoring, to which I now turn.

INTERSTATE SURVEILLANCE

Regular interception of Internet communications at the international level has occurred for many years. The precise details of these programs are classified, but it now seems quite clear that emails, faxes, even voiceprints are routinely monitored and sifted by states under the auspices of various communications intelligence initiatives, many of which have their origins in the early cold war period (Lyon, 2001:95). Foremost among these is the ECHELON system, which began in the 1970s. ECHELON is a product of the UKUSA agreement on the interception of global telecommunication that also involves Australia, Canada, New Zealand, and thirty other countries but which is based in the U.S. NSA—one of the most secretive parts of the federal government. Unlike the FBI's DCS1000 system, discussed previously, public details of ECHELON are hazy. However, most accounts state that it intercepts satellite, microwave, and land-line telecommunication, principally by tapping into data and analog voice flows, before matching these against existing keyword databases. While the system is designed to counter terrorism, it also functions as a means of monitoring diplomatic communications as well as arms trading networks and those involved in economic espionage. The NSA and Britain's equivalent—the General Communications Headquarters (GCHQ)—reportedly act as hubs in the ECHELON network by sifting information before sending it out to the scheme's member states. Recently, the EU Commission publicly objected that ECHELON was in fact being used to acquire information that would help U.S. firms win European business contracts (Verton, 2003:215).

Privacy groups argue that initiatives such as ECHELON inevitably monitor the online activities of ordinary law-abiding citizens, while law enforcement agencies respond that this is impossible to avoid. But why do states surveille international Internet communications? Increasingly, it would appear that the answer lies in the perceived threats of cyberwarfare and cyberterrorism.

Cyberwarfare and Cyberterrorism

There has been much discussion about the use of the Internet by terrorist organizations, and therefore a strong health warning is necessary here. This is a world of intrigue, rumor, and hype, qualities which should encourage us to be cautious and focus on what we know from the public record rather than speculation.

The earliest publicized case of cyberwarfare involved the Tamil Tiger separatist group's attacks on Sri Lankan embassies' email servers in 1997. These took the form of "email bombs," in which servers were bombarded by thousands of simultaneous messages. Another early example took place in the context of the East Timor separatists' campaign against the Indonesian government in 1999. In December 1997, East Timor announced its "virtual independence" from Indonesia and marked this with the launch of a new "country" domain, .tp, and a website, www.freedom.tp, whose pages were actually based on servers hosted in Ireland. In early 1999, Indonesian hackers succeeded in disabling the .tp domain in a coordinated attack launched from (trojan-infected) zombie computers in multiple countries, including Australia, Japan, the Netherlands, and the United States. This effectively destroyed the separatists' presence on the web, though the domain was later reinstated and is still used (Nuttall, 1999; Vegh, 2003:78). The attacks were widely reported as being the work of the Indonesian government, though this is still unproven.

In areas of the world where long-term military and political conflict has become the norm, it is not surprising to find that cyberwarfare is part of the strategies of protagonists. Notable examples here include the dispute between India and Pakistan over the contested territory of Kashmir and the Arab-Israeli conflict. In 1998, the Indian Army's Kashmir website fell victim to Pakistani hackers, while in 2001 the Middle East conflict took a new turn when Palestinian hackers distributed a range of viruses, trojans, and worms aimed at crippling the Israeli government's information infrastructure (Vegh, 2003:80).

Cyberwarfare methods have also contributed to the fragile diplomatic relations between the United States and China for almost a decade. In 1999, when NATO forces mistakenly destroyed the Chinese embassy in Belgrade, Chinese hackers aimed their sights on U.S. government websites, defacing many with slogans and photographs of three Chinese journalists who died in the attack, as well as launching distributed denial of service attacks and email bombs (Kellan, 1999). In the spring of 2001, in response to the accidental collision of a U.S. surveillance plane and a Chinese fighter jet, U.S. hackers defaced over three hundred Chinese websites, only to see their Chinese counterparts respond by releasing a worm designed to deface U.S. sites by exploiting security holes in web servers (Vegh, 2003:80).

The proliferation of hacking attacks has forced states to step up their Internet surveillance as a means of preempting such threats. While most attacks cost money to fix and cause confusion and political embarrassment, they are largely symbolic acts designed to draw international attention to an issue. But another, arguably more serious, form of action involves targeting critical infrastructures.

Developed countries are heavily dependent upon the smooth functioning of major utilities. Clean water, constant electricity supplies, and rapid telecommunication networks are taken for granted. One of the biggest problems in the aftermath of the 9/11 attacks on New York City was repairing the communication infrastructure upon which large sections of the U.S. and global financial sectors depend. According to analysts such as Dan Verton (2003), the problem is that utilities like water purification, electricity supplies, and telecommunication are now linked together in a variety of ways through networked monitoring and control systems that are often automated or can be operated from a distance. These, known in the IT industry as supervisory control and data acquisition systems, are commonly used by private energy companies to manage fluctuations in the demand for natural gas and electricity, for example. While most of these systems are kept away from the open Internet, Verton maintains that many are not, and in any case skilled and motivated hackers would not necessarily find this an impediment. Terrorist hackers would be more likely to infiltrate such systems from the inside, by becoming an employee of a power company, for instance, or by using what hackers term "social engineering" techniques, such as simply asking someone for their network username and password. Alternatively, a protagonist may simply seek to physically destroy a strategically important computer system.

Successive U.S. administrations seem to have taken seriously the threat of cyberterrorist attacks. In 1997, an exercise named Eligible Receiver saw the U.S. Joint Chiefs of Staff hire a team of "white hat," or ethical, hackers to test the Pentagon's and other critical networks' security. The hackers drifted across the United States over a number of weeks, gradually acquiring network access allowing them to launch denial of service attacks, alter emails, and change account details. The outcome shocked the Pentagon, leading it to appoint a new chief information officer who sits alongside the secretary of defense for command, control, communications, and intelligence (Verton, 2003:33). The urgency of the problem was underscored in 1998, when President Clinton signed a directive outlining a new cybersecurity policy, and again, in 2000, when a new national plan was announced. In late 2001 and early 2002, large amounts of sensitive information, such as the position of nuclear plants, was scrubbed from U.S. government websites in an attempt to stymie intelligence gathering by terrorists. In 2003, the chief of the Department of Homeland Security, Tom Ridge, announced two new national strategies to "secure cyberspace" and "protect critical infrastructures."

It also appears that terrorist networks, particularly Al Qaeda, have used the Internet to co-ordinate their activities. The 2004 Report of the US National Commission on 9/11 details the routine role of web searches, emails and instant messaging in preparation for the 9/11 attacks. Mohammed Atta, described as the operational leader and the hijacker pilot of American Airlines flight 11, which crashed into the north tower of the World Trade Center, left a detailed trail of emails (later picked up by the FBI) and communicated via instant messaging up to the day before the attacks (U.S. National Commission on Terrorist Attacks, 2004:249).

How do we assess such developments? The Internet does potentially alter the usual risk and reward structures associated with terrorism. It is much less likely that an attacker will be identified and apprehended if she or he is operating from the other side of the globe. But much caution is required in interpreting cyberterrorism's real impact. This is made all the more difficult due to the secretive nature of the law enforcement and military spheres and the high political stakes of the reaction to 9/11. In the case of Al Qaeda, there appears to be no substantial evidence that the 9/11 attackers used specialist techniques such as encryption to secure their communications. Indeed, their use of the Internet was nothing out of the ordinary. The central figure, Mohammed Atta, used it to research U.S. flight schools from a base in Hamburg, Germany, but it is difficult to see why such behavior would raise suspicion in advance and how it could be prevented in future. And it seems clear that Osama Bin Laden made extensive use of anonymous faxes and difficult-to-trace satellite phones in the late 1990s (Verton, 2003:89–91), but there is little evidence that he commands the Al Qaeda network using the Internet. There are international hacker groups aligned with Al Qaeda, such as the AQTE Al Qaeda Network or the Al Qaeda Muslim Alliance, which have been responsible for bringing down congressional websites or releasing malicious code with Islamic fundamentalist themes, such as the VBS.OsamaLaden@mm worm (Verton, 2003:105–7). But at this point in time, there appears to be little hard, publicly available evidence that suggests that such groups are coordinated via the Internet.

Perhaps the most significant effect of the perceived threat of cyberterrorism will be a shift in how states themselves seek to combat international criminal or terrorist networks. According to Joel Reidenberg (2004), states have already increased their electronic means of enforcement in the online environment, largely due to the absence of viable alternatives. The destructive power of viruses, trojans, and worms may be harnessed for fighting international crime (by launching a denial of service attack on a server known to be hosting child pornography, for instance). While such actions will likely infringe many states' domestic laws regarding computer crime, they may be framed as legitimate acts of war, as some commentators described the hacking of Arab news station Al Jazeera's website during the early stages of the 2003 Iraq War, the perpetrators of which are yet to be revealed. Whatever the future holds, it does seem clear that states are taking such threats seriously, and are reacting in the form of domestic legislation and international cooperation that will only increase Internet surveillance.

CONCLUSION

At the level of practical politics in those liberal democracies that are the main focus of this book, the United States and the United Kingdom, legalism still constitutes a powerful defense against encroachments upon privacy. The crypto wars (discussed previously) demonstrate some of the complexities of balancing national security, the needs of corporations eager to protect their communications or to make profits selling encryption to consumers, and the privacy and free-speech arguments voiced by cyberlibertarians. The latter constituency claimed a victory in the crypto wars, but its nature and effects are uncertain. Privacy-enhancing technologies may empower individuals, but only those who have the expertise, patience, and tolerant context required to use them. Opinion poll evidence gathered over many years suggests that most people are willing to give up some privacy if they get something in return. Though there are signs that attitudes are hardening (Westin, 2003), it is still naive to expect the majority of computer users to avail themselves of the various tools and techniques required to protect communications. In short, there is no technical fix for the expansion of surveillance, there are only political and legal solutions.

And of course, cypherpunk ideas assume a very strong normative perspective in favor of a right to privacy, whereas the reality is that those committing a criminal act, such as distributing child pornography, arguably deserve no protection from police surveillance. Any technology that makes criminal investigation and antiterrorism more difficult will therefore continue to provoke controversy. In those cases where the police have had some degree of success, such as Operation Ore, an international child pornography investigation involving police agencies from the United Kingdom and the United States, there has proved to be a weak link, such as a credit card payments system that carried individual subscriber details (Tendler, 2002). It seems unlikely that such criminals will be as easy to detect in future, though the PATRIOT Act has made it much easier to cast the net of suspicion wider.

Of course, there are contexts in which private, encrypted communication takes place as a matter of course, not among criminals but among dissident critics of an authoritarian regime. When some of the early crypto tools began to spread in the mid-1990s, political dissidents seized upon them. Phil Zimmerman, the founder of Pretty Good Privacy, has something of a cult status among dissidents in China, Burma, and many other countries, even if the "walled garden" of hardware and software controls employed in China would appear to counter the view that encryption can be an effective weapon (Godwin, 2003:170).

Indeed, we can expect to see more creative solutions to filtering, blocking, and surveillance in liberal democratic states. Recent examples that point the way ahead include the state of New York's attempts to restrict its residents' access to online gambling by striking agreements with credit card companies or Pennsylvania's filtering of child pornography. Gambling is illegal in New York state—a fact which makes Internet casinos all the more attractive for some of its residents. It has so far proved extremely difficult to police access to offshore gambling sites. However, in 2002, the state attorney general negotiated with major credit card providers and online payments service Paypal to get them to block payments originating from residents of the state. This was a technical means of enforcing the existing law—a translation of the physical power of injunction into the online environment (Reidenberg, 2004:8). Meanwhile, in a more controversial move, Pennsylvania passed a state law in 2002 that enabled it to block child pornography flowing into ISP servers based in its jurisdiction, effectively preventing the material from ever reaching end users. This is precisely the same technique used by authoritarian states such as China and Saudi Arabia (Zittrain, 2003). The legislation was ruled unconstitutional by a Pennsylvania district court in September 2004, both on First Amendment (free speech) grounds and because it was interpreted as a restriction on interstate commerce (*Center for Democracy and Technology et al. vs. Pappert*, 2004). The filtering mechanisms, which were found to be far from perfect, also blocked large amounts of legal online content. However, governments in countries with weaker constitutional protections are likely to be impressed with the Pennsylvania scheme.

We can also expect to see the branching out of surveillance into the new frontier of the Internet: mobile communications. Cell phone services already rely upon geographical positioning, either through a technique known as triangulation, which pinpoints a caller's location in relation to the three nearest mobile communication towers, or through the more well-known Global Positioning System, which uses orbital satellites. As the diffusion of mobile Internet connected devices continues, ISPs, cell phone operators, and online content providers will increasingly come together to offer consumers a range of location-based services. In many western European countries, these are already established.

Since the early 1990s, the FBI has become increasingly concerned that it would be unable to effectively install wiretaps in cell phone networks. This led to the passing of the Communication Assistance for Law Enforcement Act (CALEA) in 1994, which requires that telecommunication companies maintain logs of when and where cell phone calls begin and end. These logs must be disclosed to investigative agencies upon request. However, because CALEA did not encompass Internet communications, provisions were inserted into the PATRIOT Act dealing with this. As we saw above, PATRIOT relaxed restrictions on the seizure of ISP logs and the interception of communications. This information includes temporarily assigned IP addresses, which already contain geographical information but which, in the near future, are likely to include much more specific locational data due to the convergence of Internet and cell phone networks and the proliferation of Internet-connected mobile devices (Phillips, 2003:10). Meanwhile, new methods of wirelessly tracking consumer goods based around Radio Frequency Identification (RFID) chips have been introduced by retailers and logistics companies. These work by transmitting data to RFID reader devices. Some schools in the United States have introduced RFIDs as a means of monitoring student attendance. In late 2004, both the United Kingdom and the United States were considering including the chips in passports.

I began this chapter by considering four theories of surveillance: totalitarianism, panopticism, surveillant assemblage theory, and legalism. Each offers a distinctive interpretation of the relationship between surveillance, privacy, and security. But in light of the ever-evolving evidence, perhaps the most convincing approach is the theory of the surveillant assemblage (Haggerty and Ericson, 2000). This manages to capture the decentralized but pervasive nature of Internet surveillance, characteristics which are only likely to intensify as mobile uses of the Internet become more widespread.

One of the themes of this chapter has been the ways in which corporate surveillance jells with the requirements of marketing and e-commerce. For some radical critics, the issue is not so much individual privacy as the broader economic structures underlying surveillance (Andrejevic, 2002, 2004). This highlights issues in the political economy of Internet media, to which I now turn.

Discussion Points

- Is surveillance socially and politically harmful?
- Is surveillance made easier or more difficult by the Internet?
- How can corporate forms of Internet surveillance be challenged?
- Are the methods of Internet surveillance used by China applicable to liberal democracies?
- Assess the threat of cyberterrorism.
- Are privacy-enhancing technologies essential tools for citizens?

Further Reading

For the lineage of the concept of surveillance, Lyon's 1994 overview is hard to beat, while his provocative essay (2003) on the effects of 9/11 highlights how the politics of electronic surveillance have shifted in recent years.

Good coverage of recent developments in corporate Internet surveillance can be found in Phillips and Curry, 2003, and Bruening and Steffen, 2004.

Rosen, 2001, is a superbly written introduction to the problem of online privacy, while Lessig, 1999, is perennially useful for thinking about the constitutional aspects.

For a hands-on illustration of privacy-enhancing technologies, Waste is a free piece of software that is quite simple to set up and allows you to chat and send documents across a peer-to-peer network using a form of public key encryption (see http://waste.sourceforge.net).

For a subtle and detailed account of the struggle by authoritarian states to come to terms with the Internet, see Kalathil and Boas, 2003.

Dan Verton's 2003 account of the threat of cyberterrorism is written with a nonacademic audience in mind but contains useful nuggets of information, as does the massive 9/11 Commission Report (U.S. National Commission on Terrorist Attacks, 2004).

The Political Economy
of Internet Media

It is only in legends that David beats Goliath.

—BEN BAGDIKIAN, 2004

Your voice matters. Now, if you have something worth saying, you can be heard.

—DAN GILLMOR, 2004

CHAPTER OVERVIEW

This chapter considers whether the Internet is changing the political economy of the media and entertainment industries. This is a potentially vast area, so I focus on three particularly controversial themes: ownership in the Internet media sector; the production and distribution of news; and the politics of intellectual property. To illuminate these areas, the chapter adopts a critical political economy perspective. Traditionally, this type of analysis focuses on how economic inequalities based upon ownership serve to narrow the range of media content available in market-based societies. My overriding question is whether the Internet is reinforcing or threatening established economic inequalities in the broader media. Is it having a leveling effect, by creating opportunities for new market entrants to spoil the party of the big media companies? Is it creating a newly diverse and pluralistic media landscape? Or are Internet media simply "business as usual"?

How is the Internet changing the economic structures of the media and entertainment industries? This is an expansive area, so in this chapter I explore developments in terms of three controversial themes: Internet media ownership; news production and distribution; and intellectual property. My three guiding questions are:

- To what extent does the Internet media sector mimic the long-established patterns of concentrated ownership in the broader print and broadcast media?

- To what extent has it altered the processes shaping a central area of media content: news production and distribution?

- What has been the effect of the phenomenon of Internet file sharing, the rise of open-source software, and other intellectual property disputes?

While the first two themes are long established, the recent rise to prominence of policy problems relating to intellectual property is arguably a direct result of the Internet's mass diffusion in the developed world. But all three of these themes are related: at stake is whether the Internet is altering some of the key power structures that characterize contemporary media. Thus, throughout this chapter we will consider some of the economic realities that shape the Internet.

THE POLITICAL ECONOMY APPROACH

My approach here is inspired by a theoretical tradition in media and communication studies known as critical political economy. Traditionally, this type of analysis focuses on how economic inequalities based upon ownership and control serve to narrow the range of media content available in market-based societies. While there are liberal political economy scholars who use a consumer sovereignty approach to assess the extent to which competition in media markets provides individuals with genuine choices about the kinds of media they consume (Compaine and Gomery, 2000), most critical research in this field seeks to demonstrate that the media operate as part of a complex system of economic and social relations and play a crucial ideological role in legitimizing the status quo (Garnham, 1990; Golding and Murdock, 1991; Herman and Chomsky, 2002; McChesney, 1999, 2000, 2004). Consumer sovereignty, in the critical political economy perspective, is often a myth; the reality is owner sovereignty, as "owners and managers, seeking advertisements, decide what is to be offered, and the public must choose among these" (Herman and Chomsky, 2002:xix). The idea that free-market competition promotes diversity of media content is seen by critical political economy as a complacent and inaccurate depiction of the oligopolistic media sectors that exist in the majority of countries around the globe.

Critical political economy scholars usually have strong normative perspectives on how the media and entertainment industries should be reorganized to promote greater democracy, citizenship, social equality, and self-realization (Murdock, 2004). In this sense, they subscribe to the eighteenth-century Enlightenment ideal of a rationally created "good society" which, it is argued, ought to feature a lively and pluralistic public sphere of political and cultural expression. While critics have suggested that this approach, especially in its Marxist flavors, may rest upon an inflexible theory of economic influence, it has the advantage of offering a set of principles to judge how communication structures contribute to broader social, economic, and political inequalities. As the latest in a long series of new forms of communication, it should come as no surprise that scholars have begun to interpret how the Internet may be reconfiguring or reinforcing preexisting economic inequalities in the production and distribution of media content.

Critical political economy approaches vary, but three broad schools can be identified: strong, weak, and instrumental.

The strong political economy approach insists that media should be seen as directly servicing a wider system of material production. In other words, they are not just residual, leisure phenomena. Advertising, for instance, has been essential for modern consumer capitalism. Thus the circulation of symbolic values in contemporary advertising becomes intertwined with the circulation of commodities; the ideological and the economic are locked in a symbiotic relationship. For example, Nicholas Garnham has argued that "a newspaper article or a television program is the way it is and carries one set of meanings, and by doing so excludes another set, because of the way in which production is organized" (1990:15). In other words, the kinds of media messages we are able to consume can, in this perspective, be directly related to the economic context in which they were produced. In Western societies, ideas which challenge the social, economic, and political status quo are less likely to appear in the mainstream media because the very definition of mainstream implies that they are in the hands of a small group of wealthy business elites (Bagdikian, 2004). Opinions that implicitly or explicitly question the values of business advertisers, in this view, are unlikely to appear in commercially funded media.

Many political economy treatments subscribe to a less forthright, or weak, theory of economic influence. For example, Graham Murdock and Peter Golding avoid the imagery of permanent and immovable economic structures and give more credit to the individuals involved in media production and the ways in which social groups actively construct their own lifestyles and identities through consumption (Murdock and Golding, 1989; Golding and Murdock, 1991). This theory of economic determination gives greater prominence to cultural and subcultural counters to mainstream media versions of events.

The instrumental approach, which is probably the best known in the Anglo-American countries, focuses on how owners and political elites are said to use the media directly as "instruments in campaigns of ideological mobilization" (Herman, 1986:175; see also Herman and Chomsky, 2002). Herman and Chomsky's propaganda model maintains that since the American media are highly concentrated enterprises run as conglomerates, they necessarily rely (as businesses do) on formal and informal links with other businesses (especially potential advertisers) as well as a close relationship with key political elites. This assumes that the normal state of affairs involves media cooperating with government and dominant economic interests in order to manage public opinion. As they put it: "the same underlying power sources that own the media and fund them as advertisers, that serve as primary definers of the news . . . also play a key role in fixing basic principles and the dominant ideologies" (2002:xi).

Herman and Chomsky can be criticized on several grounds, but most damaging is the view that their approach implies some form of instrumental or conscious action on behalf of the media, political elites, and corporate leaders. The propaganda model would have problems coming to terms with those who point, quite justifiably, at the occasions on which the media have directly challenged governments as well as the historical tendency for even the most unequal capitalist societies to create oppositional media forms such as the alternative press and now, of course, the wilder shores of the Internet.

While there are important differences between these three schools of thought, critical political economy scholars broadly share a common vision of what a healthy media environment, one relatively free from the distorting effects of market concentration, might look like. A useful set of normative principles has been advanced by Murdock and Golding (1989:182–83):

- "People must have access to the information, advice and analysis that will enable them to know what their rights are in other spheres and allow them to pursue those rights effectively."

- "They must have access to the broadest possible range of information, interpretation and debate on areas that involve political choices, and they must be able to use communications facilities in order to register criticism, mobilize opposition, and propose alternative courses of action."

- "They must be able to recognize themselves and their aspirations in the range of representations offered within the central communications sectors and be able to contribute to developing those representations."

Applying these norms involves a useful focus on both production and consumption. On the production side, maximum diversity and accountability should be promoted. As for consumption, they imply universal access to the media. In terms of media content, they would translate into a radical plurality of voices and styles. Of course, these are very demanding principles to judge media systems. But an advantage is that they can just as easily apply to the tools, including software, that power the Internet and allow social groups to express their identities. Here, the political economy approach would assume that democratizing access to such tools is essential if the Internet is to evolve as a freer medium than the traditional print and broadcast media. As we shall see, it is far from certain that the Internet is contributing to the development of such a diverse and pluralistic media landscape.

OWNERSHIP PATTERNS IN THE INTERNET MEDIA SECTOR

Concentration of ownership is a perennial theme in the political economy of the media. Dominance of the Internet media sector by a few major players will come as no surprise to those who have studied such trends in television, radio, and the press. Ben Bagdikian, one of the most prominent critics of U.S. ownership patterns, argues that since the mid-1980s, the number of dominant U.S. media companies has shrunk from fifty to just five (2004:28). Bagdikian's research has focused mainly upon how the "big five" global conglomerates dominate traditional media but has recently been updated to take account of the Internet. These claims have been contested by less critical authors such as Benjamin Compaine and Douglas Gomery, who point to churn among the top U.S. companies. But even Compaine is forced to concede that the top two companies increased their share of industry revenues by more than 50 percent between 1986 and 1997 (2000:562). The big five are AOL Time Warner, Walt Disney Company, Viacom, Bertelsmann (based in Germany), and News Corporation, owned by Rupert Murdoch (Bagdikian, 2004:3). (AOL Time Warner has undergone several name changes in its brief history, and its official label differs according to the jurisdiction. A single label is used here for the sake of simplicity.)

The key point about each of these concerns is not that they are powerful in any single sphere, such as the music industry or newspapers (though most of them are); it is that they are dominant across a range of media sectors, technologies, and distribution chains in many different locations around the globe. Of equal significance is the extent to which the various divisions of these five conglomerates collaborate with each other, through investing in new companies, funding the development of new technologies, exchanging assets, or even managing each others' concerns through interlocking board memberships. For instance, News Corporation is a joint investor with the rest of the big five in over sixty different television and print companies (Bagdikian, 2004:9). The effects of concentration of ownership, according to Bagdikian, are ideological bland-ness, as sources tend to converge on the right of the political spectrum, and a situation in which new market entrants often have to face the harsh reality that they must sell their businesses to established players or risk being crushed.

A graphic example of the effects of concentration of ownership are the recent changes to the U.S. radio sector (McChesney, 2004:230–31). The 1996 Telecommuni-cations Act removed restrictions on the ownership of national radio stations. This encouraged a land grab by major media companies, including Viacom and, most notori-ously, Clear Channel Communications. Before the act, Clear Channel's share of revenue in the radio sector was just 1.3 percent. By 2001, this had soared to 20 percent, and the company now owns over twelve hundred radio stations, covering over 60 percent of the rock and pop audience. Clear Channel has used its market power to increase advertiser revenues and the amount of airtime devoted to the broadcast of advertisements, but it and Viacom have also been responsible for a decline in local radio content following the introduction of their national distribution system. This allows the companies to simul-taneously broadcast content to many different local radio stations from a national base. Clear Channel has also strengthened its ties with independent promotion companies, whose role is to stay just to the right side of the laws regarding "pay for play" (payola) by channeling money to radio station owners in return for influence over station playlists (Boehlert, 2001).

To what extent are we seeing similar dynamics in the Internet media sector? Dur-ing the height of the dotcom boom of the late 1990s, it was often said that the Internet would radically destabilize the traditional media marketplace. It would have a leveling effect, by creating opportunities for new market entrants to spoil the party of the big global media companies (Compaine and Gomery, 2000:574). A few years on, it would appear that this dream has yet to become reality. The dotcom bubble was stimulated by genuine entrepreneurialism and technological change, but it was also underpinned by what Alan Greenspan, the chair of the U.S. Federal Reserve since 1992, termed "irrational exuberance." It was also aided by a climate of "easy" financing, especially in the form of venture capital (Noam, 2003:1). There are success stories in which brand-new companies have been able to secure a foothold as a result of the Internet. These include web retailer Amazon.com, search engine Google, auction site eBay, or directory and web services company Yahoo!. But it is also obvious that the traditional media giants were quick to react to the threat of dotcom. While the diversity of content avail-able in the online environment clearly does outpace that in the traditional media sector, as Deborah Howcroft (2001:198) has argued: "the scalability and flexibility of the Internet yields similar advantages for both large firms and small niche players." In other words, the big have stayed big, and those firms that have managed to establish powerful positions in the Internet economy have tended to retain that dominance over time.

There are several ways of illustrating these trends. One vivid picture is portrayed in table 12.1, which shows the ten most visited websites by parent company and brand in the United States during mid-2004. It clearly reveals that familiar names dominate the production and distribution of web content. Microsoft's dominance in the pre-Internet software sector has easily transferred over to the web era with its MSN portal. AOL was

Table 12.1. Top Ten U.S. Websites by Parent Company, Month of July 2004

Parent Company	Unique Audience (in millions)	Time Spent Per Person (hrs.:mins.)
1. Microsoft	106	2:01
2. Time Warner	94	5:11
3. Yahoo!	92	2:49
4. Google	61	0:32
5. eBay	48	1:40
6. U.S. government	44	0:25
7. InterActiveCorp	37	0:21
8. Amazon	35	0:18
9. RealNetworks	32	0:49
10. Walt Disney Internet Group	32	0:48

Source: Adapted from Nielsen/Netratings, 2004. Figures rounded.

once a new entrant in the media marketplace, until it merged with industry giant Time Warner in 2000 in a deal worth (on paper) $182 billion—the largest merger in history and one that led to the creation of the largest media company in the world (Bagdikian, 2004:4). Disney Corporation's pivotal role in the offline entertainment sector, including film, publishing, and merchandising, gives it an advantage on the web. And the position of InterActiveCorp is also telling, because it is a transnational conglomerate composed of twenty-eight Internet companies, including Expedia.com, Match.com, RealEstate.com, TripAdvisor.com, and many other high profile e-commerce sites.

Another brief illustration of trends involves examining what makes for a popular website. It is now clear that a major economic driver of the Internet sector is search. The portal sites, such as Yahoo! and MSN, rely in part upon visitors turning to their sites for the prominently displayed search boxes. Since it became obvious in the late 1990s that search sites regularly appeared in the top ten most visited Internet destinations, the big five media conglomerates have undergone a frenzy of acquisition of search engines. A good example is Disney, which bought early search leader Infoseek in 1998 before folding it into its Go.com search site and portal (Blevins, 2002:106). While market leader Google (which had 42 percent of the U.S. search market in 2004) has yet to fully yield to the allure of paid-for search, which ranks results according to how much advertisers are willing to pay for placement, the majority of competing search engines contain varying degrees of paid-for elements (SearchEngineWatch, 2005). The best example of this is Overture, which started out as an independent company but was quickly gobbled up by Yahoo!. Overture is probably the purest example of paid-for search, since it ranks search results according to how much advertisers are willing to bid for a prominent place in the listings. Moreover, Overture provides search technology for multiple partner sites, including InfoSpace, AltaVista, MSN, CNN.com, and others. Concentration of content is compounded by the fact that just four sites, Google, Yahoo!, MSN, and AOL, account for almost the *whole* of the U.S. market for search—and AOL's search is actually provided by Google (SearchEngineWatch, 2005).

These are important indicators of market concentration in Internet media, but it is possible to go beyond such relatively straightforward measurements as website visits. One helpful approach has been suggested by Eli Noam of Columbia University, who is conducting an ongoing investigation of market concentration in both new and old media in the United States (Noam, 2003, 2005). Noam suggests that the Internet media sector may be defined as the "core industries that provide instrumentalities and infrastructure components underlying the Internet's basic functioning." These include "Internet backbones; Internet Service Providers (ISPs); broadband providers; portals; browser software; search engines; media player software; and Internet Protocol (IP) telephony" (Noam, 2003:1–2). Omitted from Noam's definition is general online content, though pivotal sites in the form of portals and search engines, the most popular destinations according to table 12.1, are included.

Market concentration is a measure of the competitiveness of a market sector. In highly competitive markets, large numbers of firms compete for market share, and there are no obviously dominant players. Markets with low levels of competition are characterized by oligopolistic structures: two or three firms will typically dominate. Analyzing market concentration can be a vexed process, but probably the most widely accepted measure is the Herfindahl-Hirschman Index (HHI). The HHI is used by many government bodies (most notably the U.S. Department of Justice when it approaches antitrust regulation) for basic snapshots of market concentration. HHI scores are calculated according to a simple formula: the market share for each company is squared, and these figures are added together to create an overall score. Thus, in a hypothetical example (taken from the Department of Justice's own guidelines), for a market in which Firm A has 30 percent, Firm B has 30 percent, Firm C has 20 percent, and Firm D has 20 percent, the HHI score is $30^2 + 30^2 + 20^2 + 20^2 = 2600$. It is generally accepted that markets which score over 1800 are concentrated; those that fall between 1000 and 1800 are moderately concentrated; while those under 1000 are not concentrated (U.S. Department of Justice, 2004).

Noam's twenty-year study uses the HHI to assess market concentration in the Internet media sector. The results are quite unexpected. The data reveal that the sector did become more competitive from the late 1980s to the mid-1990s, but during the period when we would expect competition to intensify—the late 1990s dotcom bubble—it actually slightly declined. Indeed, the HHI scores reveal that the Internet sector has *never* been highly competitive (see figure 12.1).

How does the Internet sector compare with traditional media? Again, somewhat surprisingly, Noam's data indicate that the broadcasting, print media, and cable/satellite sectors all exhibit *lower* HHI scores, indicating that they are more competitive overall. And while the cable/satellite market has become more concentrated since 1996, the print and broadcasting markets are fairly unconcentrated and have remained broadly the same for the last twenty years (Noam, 2003:4). Noam concludes that the popular image of the Internet sector as a dynamic market filled with innovative small-to-medium-sized companies is a myth. In the near future, he predicts, we are likely to move to a sector dominated by large, profitable companies. There is no reason to believe that the Internet will be any different from other media.

Such findings are perhaps less surprising if we consider two particular aspects of the Internet's infrastructure: the telecommunication "backbones" that are predominantly owned by large, often long-established companies like AT&T (now owned by SBC), Sprint, and GTE/Bell Atlantic in the United States or BT in the United Kingdom; and key end-user software applications that are largely controlled by a handful of major companies.

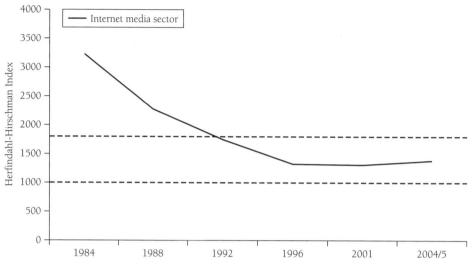

Figure 12.1. Market concentration in the Internet media sector (United States). *Source:* Noam, 2005.

Ownership of telecommunication backbones has made it relatively simple for traditional telecommunication operators to move into the Internet market (McChesney, 1999:160). In Britain, for example, BT's grip on the ISP market has proved controversial for many years. Regulatory pressure has gradually weakened its dominance, but its refusal to reduce its wholesale broadband prices (the prices at which it sells access to its lines to other ISPs) between 2001 and 2003 enabled it to squeeze many startup ISPs out of the market while it prepared for its own rollout of broadband.

When it comes to software applications, Microsoft's market dominance is legendary. The U.S. Department of Justice launched antitrust action against the company in 1998 and 1999. In those early days, the issue was primarily the position of the Internet Explorer web browser at the heart of the Windows operating system. Critics claimed that bundling in the browser gave Microsoft an unfair advantage because it was impossible to remove without damaging key parts of the operating system and this made it much less likely that users would install a competitor product. Since then, Microsoft has been in trouble with the European Commission for similar bundling of its Windows Media Player software and for refusing to publish elements of the code for Windows that allow it to interface with other software. The European Commission ruled in March 2004 that the secrets of Windows server software should be published and that Microsoft's Media Player should be removed from the Windows operating system, before announcing a record fine of $613 million for "abusing its market power in the EU" (European Commission, 2004). Microsoft immediately appealed, and it is likely that the legal challenge will continue for several years.

Despite its dominance in the operating system, office, and corporate networking sectors, Microsoft has been comparatively conservative in its attempts to diversify. Other companies have taken much more radical approaches, most often along the lines of horizontal and vertical integration.

Horizontal and Vertical Integration

Perhaps the best example of how traditional media companies have been successful in asserting their dominance in the new media environment is the AOL Time Warner merger of 2000. This brought together AOL, the ISP, portal, and content provider, with Time Warner, the owner of vast swathes of the publishing, film, music, television, and now Internet sectors. Time Warner alone owned such assets as HBO, CNN, Castle Rock, Warner Home Video, Turner Home Satellite, *Time*, *Sports Illustrated*, *Parenting*, and over fifty different record labels, to name just a few of its concerns. AOL, in 2000, had 22 million subscribers to its ISP service and web content. At the time, both individual companies were valued at well over $100 billion. The idea behind the merger was that AOL, desperate for valuable content for its websites, would gain access to all of the established Time Warner products. At the same time, Time Warner would secure a new distribution channel: the Internet. By the time the new company had been formed, it sprawled across 292 different concerns and partnerships in over sixty countries and brought together, through various alliances, companies such as eBay, HP, Sony, Bertelsmann, 3Com, and Amazon.com (Bagdikian, 2004:30–32; Blevins, 2002:97; Chan-Olmsted and Chang, 2003). AOL Time Warner currently has a vast network of tens of thousands of discrete websites.

The typical goals of media concentration of the kind that occurred with the AOL Time Warner merger are horizontal and vertical integration. Horizontal integration can refer to the practice of merging or acquiring companies that are based in the same media sector, such as a newspaper company that owns several different papers aimed at different market segments. Alternatively, a more overt form of horizontal integration may involve a company that owns other companies across a range of different but related media. All of the big five media and entertainment companies exhibit horizontal integration in both of these forms.

In contrast, vertical integration refers to the process whereby a company seeks to control as many aspects of the production and distribution process as possible. For instance, Rupert Murdoch's News Corporation owns newspapers (e.g., *The Times* and *The Sun* in the United Kingdom) and satellite television platforms and stations (e.g., Fox, Sky Movies in the United Kingdom, DirecTV in the United States). But it also owns a major Hollywood studio (Twentieth Century Fox). This often allows it to use its newspapers and television stations to market and air the films it has produced in its own film studio. Another example is Disney, which allows its intellectual property rights in famous brands (e.g., Mickey Mouse) to be used in its film studios (including Disney, Touchstone, Miramax), television (Disney Channel, ABC Network, ESPN), radio stations (ABC Radio Network), websites (the Go.com portal, Disney Online), retail stores, tourism schemes, and theme parks. Disney is able to use any part of its empire to push products that have been created in any of its other parts (Blevins, 2002:99; Flew and McElhinney, 2001; Wayne, 2003). While integration may give the appearance of increasing diversity, the overall impact is to narrow the range of media products, as branded goods become endlessly recycled or repackaged according to the medium through which they are to be promoted.

The Internet arguably accelerates both horizontal and vertical integration. This is largely due to trends toward convergence as well as its relatively low distribution costs and long reach: facets which make it an ideal medium for promoting content delivered through other channels and across national boundaries (see also chapter 1). The Internet has started to bring together previously separate arenas of production and distribution, and this is likely to intensify as broadband connectivity continues to diffuse. While the large media conglomerates are much more cautious about the profit-making potential of the Internet than they were during the late 1990s boom, the likes of Time Warner, Disney, and News Corp have undoubtedly seen the potential for meshing together the textual and audio-visual products they previously sold through discrete channels. For some, this points to a future in which the Internet converges on a broadcasting market model where entry barriers are so high (due to the high production values of the "best" Internet services) that content diversity is likely to wither on the vine (Gandy, 2002; Roscoe, 1999). It is also likely to intensify recent trends toward merger and acquisition in the U.S. telecommunication, cable, satellite, and Internet sectors (McChesney, 1999:123).

For transnational media conglomerates, the Internet's potential global reach by-passes some of the distribution risks they typically face, such as lack of local knowledge, differing national regulatory conditions, and cultural resistance on the part of some governments, for example France's legislative attempts to restrict the influx of Hollywood content. In other words, the Internet makes it easier to diversify in geographical terms without necessarily diversifying products. Hence the eagerness of the top global media conglomerates—Sony, AOL Time Warner, Bertelsmann, Vivendi, News Corporation, Disney, and Viacom—to develop the Internet as a distribution channel for music, movies, and other content as well as to develop strategic alliances in unfamiliar territories (e.g., AOL allowing Bertelsmann to own a 50 percent stake in its European ISP business in the late 1990s) (Chan-Olmsted and Chang, 2003:217–18; McChesney, 1999:180).

While convergence allows established players to translate their dominance over into a new sector, it has also meant the entry of many traditionally nonmedia players, such as software companies, telephone companies, ISPs, and other information providers like financial institutions and even travel agents or supermarkets. For example, while it has recently retreated from the sector by selling its 23 percent stake in U.K. cable provider Telewest, Microsoft still owns large stakes in several cable operators in the United States (Comcast), Canada (Rogers), the United Kingdom (NTL), the Netherlands (UPC), and other countries. It also provides software for several satellite and cable providers' set-top boxes (Charny, 2003).

Overall, however, it is often difficult to generalize about the impact of some of these new developments. Taking the ISP sector as an example, the market remains surprisingly vibrant, with well over a hundred continuing to do business in the United Kingdom, and around two hundred fifty national ISPs in the United States (Yahoo! Directory, 2004a, 2004b). There are undoubtedly market leaders. AOL, with 23 million subscribers, enjoys a 24 percent share of the U.S. market. The next competitor, United Online, is far behind, with 7 million subscribers and 7 percent of the market (see figure 12.2). There have also been a number of high-profile mergers and acquisitions in the U.S. telecommunication sector following its deregulation under the Telecommunications Act of 1996 (Winseck, 2002) as well as recent decisions by the U.S. FCC to end the common carrier requirement that cable and phone operators allow rival ISPs to provide broadband services over their lines (Krim, 2005; McChesney, 2004:219). Market concentration is also evident in the United Kingdom, and near-monopoly telecommunication provider BT has been largely successful in translating its business to

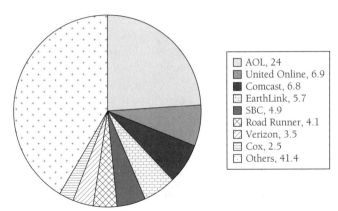

Figure 12.2. Residential market share of Internet Service Providers (United States), 2004 (by percent). *Source:* Goldman, 2004. Figures rounded.

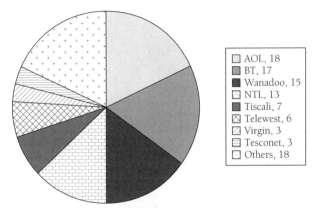

Figure 12.3. Residential market share of Internet Service Providers (United Kingdom), 2004 (by percent). *Source:* U.K. Office of Communications, 2004.

the Internet sector. But again, the pattern is contradicted by the fact that in the United Kingdom there is no clear leader comparable with AOL in the United States, as four major ISPs (including AOL itself) currently compete for top position (see figure 12.3). Though complete data for the ISP sectors are unavailable, it is nevertheless clear that the HHI scores in both the United States and the United Kingdom are likely to be well below 1000, indicating low levels of market concentration. It is also likely that competition in the ISP sector will intensify as wireless (WiFi) modes of access become more widely available in local communities, though in the United States there have already been attempts by the major broadcasting and telecommunication companies to restrict access to the frequency spectrum required for the widespread rollout of WiFi (McChesney, 2004:218).

Clearly, there are pockets of substantial market concentration in the Internet media sector, but there are also very competitive subsectors. Much of this indeterminacy can be explained by the paradox of the dotcom bust of 2000. The decline of investment in e-commerce companies and the dramatic fall in their market values allowed the big five media conglomerates to cherry pick from among them. But these forces of market concentration have been tempered by a widespread skepticism among traditional media owners and managers about the long-term economic impact of the Internet. Taking newspapers as a brief example, the savings in production and distribution costs gained by moving online may be very real, but only if it is assumed that the readership figures and therefore advertising revenues stay the same for a wholly online publication (Picard, 2002:64). Evidence so far would suggest that few consumers are willing to have *all* of their news delivered online. Online news divisions can actually *increase* costs for media companies, forcing them to find new opportunities for generating revenue. There are many examples of traditionally respected news providers, such as the United Kingdom's *Financial Times* or the United States' *New York Times*, placing infotainment or open e-commerce and sponsorship deals rather than quality news at the center of their online strategies. And the mixed results, to date, of the AOL Time Warner merger have compounded the fragile context of uncertainty and risk underpinning Internet media.

It is also increasingly clear that the Internet media sector is now firmly on regulatory agency agendas in most developed countries. A spectacular illustration of this came during the summer and fall of 2003, when the U.S. Federal Communications Commission (FCC) announced proposals for relaxing restrictions on the ownership of broadcasting companies. The chair of the FCC, Michael Powell, explicitly framed the proposals in terms of a new context of media diversity which, he argued, had been created by the proliferation of alternative sources of content on the Internet. However, not everyone agreed with Powell's analysis, and the public protests reached fever pitch during late 2003. Groups such as the Consumers Union spearheaded the campaign, but an estimated three-quarters of a million U.S. citizens complained to the FCC using email, fax, letters, and petitions, and the vast majority were opposed to any relaxation of the ownership rules (Calabrese, 2004:108; McChesney, 2004:282). Many of these were mobilized by the hybrid online grassroots movement MoveOn.org (see chapter 5), which also launched a targeted phone and petition campaign aimed at key members of Congress. At the time of writing (early 2005), a stalemate had been reached, as a federal court of appeal found the FCC's decision to be based on faulty reasoning (Krim, 2005).

News Production and Distribution

Our second major theme is news production and distribution. Forecasts of the demise of traditional printed newspapers proliferated during the dotcom era. But while it is undoubtedly the case that the Internet provides a huge range of material that was previously unavailable, it also appears that many of the established systems of news production and distribution remain firmly intact. Daily newspaper circulation has been in decline in many developed countries during the postwar era, yet traditional papers, magazines, and books do not show many signs of disappearing. Some recent insider research on online news operations reveals that managers, editors, and journalists may hold very different preconceptions about the need for taking advantage of the interactive capabilities offered by the Internet. Put simply, many journalists see the online version of a newspaper as simply an electronic mirror image of the print version, and there are organizational constraints upon breaking out of this approach (Boczkowski, 2004).

Pessimists claim, with much justification, that established news media have managed the transition to cyberspace with ease. A major dent in the argument that the Internet is leveling the news playing field is that the production of timely, relevant, high-quality news is an expensive business. Major news providers are typically large organizations with firmly entrenched hierarchical and bureaucratic structures (Epstein, 2000; Schlesinger, 1987). They are this way for a reason. Most alternative online news sites, like the countless blogs or the Indymedia network, rely primarily on volunteer labor (McChesney, 2004:220).

A disturbing trend in the online news sector is source concentration. Major traditional news media have long relied upon international news agencies, most notably Reuters and Associated Press (AP), for significant proportions of their content. This is especially the case in coverage of international events, where resource constraints mean that many organizations are unable to gather their own stories. The dominance of Reuters and AP in the global news industry means that even casual readers will notice similarities in content across major daily newspapers. In theory, of course, the Internet should reduce source concentration by enabling a diverse range of new players to enter the marketplace, creating new opportunities for editors to break free of news agency dependency. But according to research conducted by Chris Paterson (2005), this is a myth: the online news audience is subjected to even *greater* amounts of agency news content than the offline audience. This is for two principal reasons. First, as table 12.2 shows, when it comes to online news, readers tend to gravitate to the usual suspects: Yahoo!, MSN, AOL Time Warner, Google, Disney, and so on. Second, the bulk of these sites are heavily reliant upon the Reuters and AP agencies for their news content. From a comparative analysis of fifteen major news stories, Paterson found that 85 percent of news on the popular portal sites (Yahoo!, Lycos, Excite, and AOL) was simply duplicated news agency content. Moreover, those sites that claim to be independent producers of news (CNN, ABC, MSNBC, CNBC, CBS, and others) also exhibited surprisingly high levels of agency dependence. For these sites, the average amount of purely copied text was 43 percent.

Clearly these data do some damage to the idea of the Internet as an open and pluralistic sphere of news media. But while they may give a broad overview, they are not, of course, the whole story. In other respects, the Internet has spawned a new style of do-it-yourself journalism which arguably threatens the dominance of the major media organizations. Two examples—the Indymedia network and blogs—illustrate this trend.

Table 12.2. Leading Online News Sites (United States), 2004

1. Yahoo! sites, with key news channel, news.yahoo.com
2. MSN-Microsoft sites, with news channels MSNBC (in partnership with General Electric), and CNBC
3. AOL Time Warner, with news brands AOL, CNN, Time, Netscape News
4. Google, with news brand news.google.com
5. Terra Lycos, with news channel news.lycos.com
6. Excite Network, with news channel news.excite.com
7. Walt Disney Internet Group (WDIG), with news channels ABCnews.com, Go, and others
8. Viacom Online, with news channel cbsnews.cbs.com

Source: Paterson, 2005.

Indymedia.org

An excellent example of the new do-it-yourself journalism is the Indymedia network (see exhibit 12.1). Initially focused on reporting the activities of social movement activists, Indymedia now covers the whole range of news, from the local to the global level. It maintains its progressive bias, however, and has established a reputation as a first port of call for those seeking news on protests, marches, and other forms of demonstration which seldom feature in the mainstream press and broadcasting schedules. Indymedia represents an important departure from traditional models of news gathering and distribution as practiced by global news agencies such as Reuters and AP. Although the latter pride themselves on their breadth of coverage and

---

EXHIBIT 12.1. INDYMEDIA.ORG

Indymedia started out as a single media center but it has since grown into a global network of 135 news websites, many of which have their own devolved structure of local sites geared to specific towns and cities within their jurisdiction. While most of the Indymedia centers (103 in early 2004) are based in the United States, Canada, and Europe, there are 15 sites in Latin American countries, 9 in Oceania, 5 in Africa, and a small number in other regions (Indymedia.org, 2004). The first center was established in Seattle in 1999, in anticipation of the protests against the World Trade Organization (WTO) that year. The aim was to provide coverage of the issues and events that the mainstream media would likely ignore. The run-up to the 1999 WTO meeting had been given cursory treatment by major news providers. Using borrowed computers and an initial donation of just $30,000, Indymedia volunteers set about aggregating news items from around the globe, as well as commissioning context pieces from the personal viewpoints of street protestors to economic and scientific analyses of the impact of the WTO on world trade and development.

Despite its highly professional and polished electronic face, Indymedia remains true to its origins among anti-globalization protestors, radical journalists, web designers, and other Internet media professionals willing to volunteer their time and technical skills. Journalists are crucial—without them there would be little or no content. However, more significant is the alliance between ordinary eyewitness reporters, journalists, and the software engineers who maintain the network of sites. Many of these are involved in other Internet-related campaigns, such as the open-source software movement. They have used their skills to provide Indymedia with highly developed audio and video streaming together with a sophisticated system of "open publishing," which allows contributors to file stories, and submit comments, supplementary material, and foreign-language translations of existing news stories from any location using a simple web-browser interface.

Sources: Summarized from Bennett, 2003a; Downing, 2003; Dueze, 2003; Indymedia, 2004; Kahn and Kellner, 2004; Kidd, 2003; Postmes and Brunsting, 2002.

real-time reactions to unfolding events, until Indymedia's covergence of content with technological means, there were very few opportunities to launch an enterprise that would match the commercial news providers' features while shifting the focus onto grassroots and protest politics. Part of the genuine novelty of Indymedia reportage is its contributors' style of interventionist videography, which usually involves mingling among the protestors themselves rather than remaining behind the police lines (Downing, 2003:251).

The broader significance of Indymedia is thus threefold. First, it represents a direct and viable challenge to the mainstream media's portrayal of important international events. Second, it constitutes a new mode of news production and distribution that could never be replicated within the confines of a traditional news firm and not even in the global collaborative networks that are now common in the commercial news world. The Indymedia network is highly devolved. It features thousands of contributors across 135 portal sites which are country or city specific, but these sites are themselves subdivided into sections devoted to specific issues and locations. The internal organization is democratic and consensus based, in the traditions of new social movement organizing and the Internet's founders. It holds international meetings online and has a large number of email lists and discussion sites covering the main internal and organizational issues. The paradox of Indymedia is that its main site and portals offer a global perspective but one which allows readers to drill down to local content very quickly. Although many of the sites have a common electronic face, this is due mainly to a need to keep the technology simple; there is no direct overall editorial control in the Indymedia network (Downing, 2003:251). Finally, Indymedia's significance lies in its "open publishing" technology and the ways in which this genuinely makes a difference (Meikle, 2002:88–112). Without it, this kind of activity would be restricted to the 1980s paradigm of desktop publishing, at best, or it would simply not exist.

Variants of the Indymedia model have also started to spread. For example, in South Korea, Ohmynews.com acts as an online newspaper site but also resembles a huge news agency due to the way it solicits and manages its content. The publication, which uses the slogan "every citizen a reporter," will allow anyone to sign up as a contributor. Each day its staff sifts through several hundred submissions before selecting the best stories for publication. A system based on story prominence provides the freelance "citizen-journalists" with payment. Entry paths into mainstream Korean journalism have long been tightly restricted by professional training and accreditation systems. Ohmynews set out to bypass these and has had significant success, with twenty-six thousand reporters having signed up by 2003 (Gillmor, 2004:126).

Blogs and the "Former Audience"

The most strident claims that the Net has genuinely changed the underlying structures of news production point to the proliferation of blogs. (Ashbee, 2003; Drezner and Farrell, 2004; Gillmor, 2004; Hansard Society, 2004; Matheson, 2004; McKenna and Pole, 2004). In the eyes of the optimists, such as Silicon Valley journalist Dan Gillmor, blogging has dented the power of big media to the extent that what we once thought of as the audience are now the "former audience": ordinary individuals are becoming active producers of the news in a way that was impossible to imagine before the Internet provided the tools and networks. Gillmor argues that the romantic image of investigative journalists working slowly and carefully to unearth the big stories has been steadily undermined by the forces of commercialism. However, such in-depth reporting now increasingly occurs in the "blogosphere," away from the established news institutions upon which citizens previously relied (Gillmor, 2004:xv).

A major factor shaping the popularity of blogging is the very cheap and usable nature of the major software platforms like Userland, Typepad, or Blogger. These allow individuals or groups to post news items quickly and easily using a simple web-browser interface. No knowledge of web design is needed to produce a slick and effective blog. The freshness and immediacy of the many blogs is enhanced by the format: the vast majority order content in reverse chronological order, and most blogs provide very simple means by which readers can post reactions to each item. Equally important is the ability to provide readers with search functions, elaborate systems of categorization, and cross-referencing. This is because many blog platforms are essentially databases with web interfaces. This reinforces the view that blogs have leveled the news production playing field, because in the early phases of Internet growth, from the mid to late 1990s, it was obvious that the major media companies were developing huge, sophisticated news sites with large archives. Individual political commentary sites and email lists existed, of course, but the vast majority looked amateurish in comparison with the big media company sites. While most blogs (deliberately) do not resemble the slick presentational formats of the major news sites, the most popular ones use similar technologies, such as metadata protocol RSS (Really Simple Syndication). This allows bloggers to automate the sharing of news and blog entries and partly explains the amazing speed with which breaking stories now spread around the blog sites. Collective campaigning on blogs such as Instapundit contributed to the pressure on Senate majority leader Trent Lott to resign following remarks he made at veteran Republican senator Strom Thurmond's retirement party in 2002 (Ashbee, 2003). A similar storm in the blogosphere contributed to the decision by the editor of the *New York Times* to resign in the wake of the story fabrication scandal involving Jayson Blair in 2003 (Kahn and Kellner, 2004:92).

But are blogs really creating long-term changes in the news environment? For a start, some blogs are obviously having a strong quantitative impact; the popular sites receive around two hundred thousand hits per day (McKenna and Pole, 2004:4). However, some argue that there have also been qualitative shifts because the collaborative endeavor that characterizes political blogging has brought forth a new style of "distributed" journalism, in much the same way that mobile technologies have facilitated new forms of protest mobilization (see chapter 6). These interpretations point to blog news sites such as Slashdot.org or Kuro5hin.org, which have decentralized fact checking, and aggregate rating mechanisms that give readers powers to decide whether a story sinks or swims. Similar decentralized forms of what Yochai Benkler (2002:375) terms "Commons-based peer production" fuels the growth of "wikis": sites containing content that anyone may collaborate on in editing using a basic web-browser interface. And, as we shall see below, these are central characteristics of open-source software production.

However, other studies have argued that blogs have little decisive impact on their own but only come to play key roles when they frame issues and events for the mainstream media. As Daniel Drezner and Henry Farrell argue, "They are less important because of their direct effects on politics than their indirect ones—they influence important actors within mainstream media who in turn frame issues for a wider public" (2004:23). There is also the issue of long-term viability. While enthusiasm about "new business models" (Gillmor, 2004:155) might be overblown, some popular blog sites have invited appreciative readers to make small donations via virtual "tip jars" through micropayment services like Paypal. Such donations, in conjunction with advertising, are likely to generate enough income to cover the bandwidth costs of the popular blogs, but they are not likely to rival the salaries offered by major media organizations for those willing, talented, and lucky enough to be recruited to mainstream journalism. Even optimists such as Benkler argue that large organizations continue to have the resources necessary for in-depth background research.

At the same time, however, talk of economic viability might be missing the key point about do-it-yourself journalism: it is most often pursued with little expectation of financial reward, and the costs of production and distribution are low in comparison with traditional media (Shirky, 2003). Consider other types of news-making activities in which the "former audience" are engaging, such as "hyperlocal" coverage. Many small-to medium-sized U.S. cities are poorly served by mainstream media. But while there are plenty of personal websites that discuss local issues, these can never provide enough coverage to make the experience compelling for local residents. However, with blog platforms, local news sites can be run on a volunteer basis. An excellent example of this is GoSkokie.com, a hyperlocal site for the town of Skokie, Illinois. All content on the site, including everything from hard news to commentaries to restaurant reviews, is submitted by local volunteers (Gillmor, 2004:134; GoSkokie.com, 2004).

One sphere in which do-it-yourself news production and distribution using the Internet has undoubtedly altered the established game is coverage of international events. International news has long been a target for critics of the media. For example, Herman and Chomsky's political economy approach (2002) attacked U.S. media companies for failing to accurately reflect what they saw as the reality of U.S. military adventurism. Eager to learn the lessons of the Vietnam War, during the Gulf War of 1990–91, the authorities exerted incredibly tight control over journalists' movements and access to information. But by the Iraq conflict of 2003 the media environment had shifted once again, not only because the Internet emerged as a decisive weapon in the armory of Al Qaeda terrorists and resistance factions in Iraq's major cities, but also because it was a means by which antiwar groups in the United States and Europe could disseminate critical information. A steady stream of audio and video messages from Osama Bin Laden and other Al Qaeda figures has been published online. Iraqi kidnapping groups have used the Net to publish horrific video footage of their civilian captors. The photographs of U.S. military personnel humiliating Iraqi prisoners of war at the Abu Ghraib jail were rapidly distributed across blogs, Usenet, and email. Ironically, the first photographs had been sent to friends and relatives in the United States by email before an anonymous source sent them on to journalists at the *Washington Post,* CBS, and the *New Yorker* in spring 2004 (Reid, 2005).

The Politics of Intellectual Property

Our third major area is intellectual property. Before the mass diffusion of the Internet, this was hardly the hot policy topic that it is today. This is not to say that copyright, patents, and trademarks have not been seen as economically significant. Unauthorized copying of goods is an ancient practice—one that came into its own during the spread of new mass market recording and reproduction technologies during the nineteenth and early twentieth centuries. Over the last decade, however, legal and political debate over the meaning and scope of intellectual property has intensified to such an extent that it is one of the most important aspects of Internet politics and policy. Such disputes are producing new forms of political activism aimed at protecting creative freedoms perceived to be under threat due to the fusion of corporate capitalism and digital technologies. The most high-profile conflicts to date have focused upon the issue of copyright, which provides the main focus of my discussion here.

The emergence of the Internet has led some to argue that the concept of intellectual property is meaningless and that attempts to protect it in the same way as other types of property are ultimately futile in an era of perfect digital reproduction (Barlow, 1996). At the same time, however, there are those who see in the Internet the technological means to extend the control of intellectual property in digital information goods. This has led critics to argue that the balance between the rights of individual creators (or the companies that own their creations) and the benefit to societies of free access to information is being reshaped (Lessig, 2004).

If intellectual property law is now widely criticized as a weapon of corporate control, its historical origins are rather different. Patents, copyrights, and trademarks were originally designed to balance the interests of individual creators with those of society. In this view, restricting the uses of a creator's work for a limited time incentivizes programmers, authors, musicians, artists, and so on to produce works, safe in the knowledge that they will receive some reward. But the idea of building in qualifications to this protection in the form of specific time limits and usage permissions is that the works will eventually enter the public domain, allowing future creators to draw freely upon them in their own work. Creative works based upon information derive this extra value from their status as public goods. To release this value by allowing information to enter the public domain has usually been seen as economically beneficial to society as a whole. For contemporary critics, the issue is not whether intellectual property ought to be discarded; it is about shifting the balance away from corporate control toward a regime which contributes to society's economic and cultural development (Lessig, 2004:xiv).

These principles may look straightforward. But when applied to Internet media, two problems arise. The first derives from the economic nature of information. Unlike tangible goods, information cannot be exclusively owned. In other words, my having information does not prevent you from having it, and if a website distributes information, once the initial costs of establishing a site and producing the information are met, potential bandwidth bottlenecks aside, it makes little difference if one or one million individuals access it. The Internet therefore amplifies the status of information as a public good. In contrast, if you take my newspaper away, you have a new newspaper and I have none, and if I want to buy another newspaper, when I do so I will also be paying the costs that a newspaper company incurred when producing and distributing my new copy (Compaine and Gomery, 2000:550).

The second problem is that in the predigital environment, copying was either too expensive or resulted in unacceptable loss of quality. These facts did not prevent the unauthorized reproduction of copyrighted works, but they did at least keep the practice under some sort of basic control. The means of distribution in the analog world are, primarily, physical (tapes, paper, vinyl). Digital reproduction allows perfect copies of an original book, song, or film to be made *and distributed* at radically reduced costs. If compression technologies are used, such as the MP3 codec for music or the DivX codec for video, the distribution of files becomes even easier. Some quality may be lost when compared with the original, but most users cannot discern the difference, and the reduced costs of distribution (bandwidth, processor time) and consumption (not having to rent or purchase a film) usually make up for such quality loss. Digital methods of reproduction existed long before the Internet took off, and unauthorized physical copying of CDs is as old as the format itself. But what makes the Internet different is the ease with which copies can be circulated and recirculated at virtually no cost to individual users. Gradual improvements in both the technologies of reproduction and communication resulted, by the end of the 1990s, in an Internet awash with unauthorized copies of software programs, music files, e-books, films extracted from DVDs, scanned photographs, even needlepoint patterns. Any digital object can be duplicated with no loss of quality or perhaps with some loss for the sake of creating smaller files that are easier to move around the Net.

This new technological context has understandably led to a diverse array of responses by those companies whose business relies upon intellectual property. But such responses have led critics to point to a crucial paradox: rather than sweeping intellectual property away, the Internet can actually make it easier to control and exploit. Many companies have coded new, highly restrictive means of preventing the unauthorized reproduction and distribution of copyrighted works. The very characteristics of digital creations that make them so susceptible to "piracy" simultaneously allow copyright holders, should they wish, to control access to their creations in ways that have never before been possible. In short, digital technologies allow information goods to be treated in a way that puts them on a par with tangible forms of property. How is this possible?

The answer turns on a distinction between copyright enforcement before and after the rise of digital technologies. Lessig provides the example of the book (1999:128; 2004). If you buy a book in hard form, though you cannot, according to copyright law, copy it whole and sell it, there are many other things that you are able to do that are perfectly permissible in most countries. You can buy it fairly anonymously, using cash as the payment method. You can read it as many times as you wish, and you can lend it to your friends or family members. Under what are known as fair-use rights, you can reproduce excerpts from it in your own writing. You have the right of first sale, meaning that you can sell it secondhand. Copyright law allows an individual to use a copyrighted work (for which they have paid) in a diversity of ways. The framework that guides such uses is fundamentally legal rather than technological.

Now, consider this same scenario in the light of the example of the e-book. The vast bulk of e-books published by major publishers are protected by so-called Digital Rights Management (DRM) encryption. DRM, though far from perfect, is an attempt by publishers (as well as record companies and film studios) to restrain unauthorized reproduction and distribution. They can work in a variety of ways, but what they have in common is restricting use of an e-book to the person who initially paid for the privilege to read it. They usually achieve this by technically removing the ability to copy the e-book file to another computer. This is a basic but mostly effective means of preventing the proliferation of copy-protected e-books. Yet it is only one use of DRM technology. The same technology can be used to introduce all manner of gradations of e-book usage, at different price levels and with different customers in mind. E-books can be made available for a selected period of time, may or may not allow text to be copied from them, and often do not permit pages or sections to be printed. Online e-book distribution sites, for example, will allow you to download an e-book to your PC, but DRM technology will likely give you a window of time, perhaps a few weeks, within which you must read the book, unless you subscribe to a permanent account giving you unrestricted access. Leave it too long and you will find that the book has been automatically erased from your hard disk or rendered unreadable. Thus fundamentally technological means of restricting access and use of an e-book—in ways that are much more stringent than would have been possible in the analog world—come to displace legal means.

Resistance to such technological threats to ideas as public goods has led in recent years to the emergence of a movement for a "creative commons." Its supporters argue that as the Internet emerges as the primary means by which creative works are distributed, new forms of copyright protection like DRM will increasingly threaten the social utility function of sharing information and ideas (Creative Commons, 2004).

Napster, Peer-to-Peer, and the Internet Gift Economy

Probably the most notorious area of dispute over the Internet's impact on intellectual property revolves around the idea that it has facilitated a new mode of economic activity. The idea of an online gift economy—one not based upon monetary exchange and direct reciprocity but simple altruism—was originally applied to the idea of personal advice and information. In many ways, Usenet newsgroups in which individuals could gain information and emotional support were the original online gift economy.

Yet almost as soon as Usenet became popular, Internet users began to share other forms of information goods—software, music, video, pictures, and word-processed books and training manuals. The newsgroups that carried this content were labeled "binaries" groups, to indicate that they contained files rather than textual messages. The problem with binaries newsgroups is that they are difficult to access and difficult for ISPs to maintain. They cannot be searched very easily, and content that is posted tends to "roll off" the major news servers in a short period of time to make space for new messages and files. At the same time, though sharing files did occur across the open web in the late 1990s, this route was also plagued by problems such as the costs of storage and bandwidth and the ease with which the authorities could monitor web traffic. Other routes to file sharing that were quite widespread before the proliferation of peer-to-peer networks involved setting up simple personal servers using the File Transfer Protocol

(FTP) or using chatrooms. But these were notoriously unreliable; individuals would take their FTP servers down for long periods without giving any notice, and chatrooms were forbidding places for the uninitiated.

In 1999, Shawn Fanning, an undergraduate at Northeastern University, Boston, sought to get around these problems by designing a network and PC software that would allow people to share music files on their own computers with others without the need to upload the files to a server (Alderman, 2001). The idea was that each user would run a program that would index the files on her machine, and logs of these indexes would be collated in a number of Napster servers dotted around the Internet. When a user logged on and conducted a search, the index servers would return a list of results pointing to the files on other users' computers. Clicking on a song would make a direct connection with the individual who had the file on her hard disk. Because it relied on index servers, Napster was not a pure peer-to-peer program, but its ease of use and relative reliability made it massively popular almost overnight. Conservative estimates suggest Napster's user base peaked at around 13 million in early 2001. Napster's founders claim that numbers reached around 70 million during some periods (Goldstein, 2003:166).

By the end of 1999, it was obvious that Fanning had unleashed a major force. Major record companies, operating with the backing of their trade association, the Recording Industry Association of America (RIAA), launched a lawsuit against Napster with the aim of shutting the service down. The global music industry has long been dominated by five major recording companies (all but one are part of a media conglomerate): Bertelsmann Music Group (owned by Bertelsmann), EMI (independent), Universal Music Group (owned by Vivendi Universal), Warner Music Group (owned by AOL Time Warner), and Sony Music (owned by Sony Corporation). Indeed, in 2004, the big five became the big four, as Bertelsmann and Sony merged their music divisions to create the largest recording company, with around 25 percent of global market share (BBC News Online, U.K. edition, 2004).

The big five and the RIAA argued that Napster was deliberately established to enable copyright infringement and that its use was harming CD sales. It was impossible to make a case on the grounds that Napster itself was infringing copyright directly, because the files were not hosted on its own servers but stayed on individual subscribers' computers. However, the RIAA argued that Napster was guilty of "contributory infringement" by creating the conditions in which individuals could share protected files. Defenders of Napster used the argument that it was simply a file indexer and could be used to share any content, including legally acquired MP3s from unsigned artists. Broader arguments about the program's impact on the music industry continued, with supporters suggesting that it stimulated CD sales and opponents claiming that it reduced them. The Napster legal tussle continued through to September 2002, but in the final analysis, the U.S. courts came down on the side of the record companies' arguments.

However, the huge growth of Napster inspired many other Napster clones, such as Morpheus and Kazaa. In fact, since Napster's demise and ultimate metamorphosis into a legitimate download site, peer-to-peer software has become much more widespread, with literally hundreds of different options, the most radical of which use the Gnutella protocol, which removes the need for central index servers. Apple's portable digital music player, the iPod, also became popular as a means by which people could store their MP3s (both legal and illegal). While Apple's entry into the legitimate music download market has been successful, the iPod has also spurred the growth of "illegal" peer-to-peer networks.

Faced with a general failure to close down Napster clones, in 2003, the record companies changed their strategy to one of targeting college campuses and individual file sharers by issuing civil lawsuits for copyright infringement. In the spring of 2003, the RIAA sued two students at Rennselaer Polytechnic Institute, one at Princeton, and one at Michigan Technological University on the grounds that they had established peer-to-peer services on campus networks (Dean, 2003a). Between September and December 2003, the RIAA sued around four hundred individuals who were sharing one thousand music files or more (Dean, 2003b). The vast majority of these cases were settled out of court through the payment of variable fines.

While these lawsuits succeeded in temporarily reducing the traffic on peer-to-peer networks, by late 2004 it became obvious that the RIAA could not possibly target large numbers of file sharers because the record companies seemed unwilling to waste resources doing so. In any case, by that stage the game had shifted once again, as the major media companies changed tack by launching their own legitimate download sites. The hope now is to normalize the idea of paying for music downloads in the hope that this will reduce piracy. The music files are protected by DRM restrictions governing the number of times a song may be duplicated, moved to another device, or copied to a CD. This makes them difficult to share across the open peer-to-peer networks.

File sharing has generated a debate, not only about the changing nature of the music industry but also about the broader economic impact of the Internet. In one corner stand those who argue that peer-to-peer file sharing constitutes a form of civil disobedience, an alternative creative community, or even a progressive new social movement that subverts some of the established practices of corporate media (Barbrook, 2000; Dyer-Witheford, 2002; Vaidhyanathan, 2004). In the other corner stand the skeptics—those who argue that challenges to intellectual property regimes like file sharing are either apolitical or likely to be defeated or coopted by the mainstream media as they adapt by extracting value from new business models based on digital distribution and ever-tighter restrictions on intellectual property (Drahos with Braithwaite, 2002; May, 2002; McLeod, 2001).

There is evidence for both interpretations. A generation of young people for whom file sharing appears normal has emerged. The social practices in which they are routinely engaged are not likely to disappear overnight. Many of the early Napster adopters were ideologically committed to challenging the power of the big five (now the big four) record companies on the grounds that their conglomerate structures restricted diversity, treated struggling new artists unfairly, and drew large revenues from back-catalog sales. Many advocates of file sharing have visions of a future media industry in which large conglomerates are no longer able to control the distribution of products. In its place will emerge a direct relationship between artists and their community of fans, as artists come to distribute their music directly to their audiences and are no longer obliged to surrender a cut to the record company. The aim, in other words, is to expose the record companies as symbols of broader issues of concentration of ownership and unfair restrictions on the dissemination of creative works. Writers like Nick Dyer-Witheford and Siva Vaidhyanathan take this approach further still by arguing that the battle between peer-to-peer networks and the media industry represents a fundamental clash of ideologies—"anarchy versus oligarchy," in Vaidhyanathan's words (2004:23). Such progressive optimists maintain that the politics of access to information has become a central struggle in an information society, and peer-to-peer has raised awareness of the role played by intellectual property in maintaining inequalities at many levels, not just with the entertainment industry but also with the pharmaceutical, agricultural, and engineering sectors, where patents, trademarks, and copyrights are used by corporations to restrict competition and artificially inflate prices. Such broader thrusts lay behind the popularity of new licensing models for the sanctioned sharing of copyrighted content, such as the Creative Commons license (Creative Commons, 2004).

On the other hand, despite the existence of an ideologically inspired core of file sharers, there are many for whom the experience has little or no political relevance. Many are undoubtedly attracted to the possibility of acquiring music without purchasing a CD and have no agenda beyond this consumerist one. It has also been argued that the everyday micropolitics of intellectual property might be significant in reshaping social practices, but they have thus far failed to radiate out into a macropolitics of sustained political campaigns against media conglomerates (May, 2002:103). As for the broader critique of intellectual property put forward by Vaidhyanathan, there are few signs that a private interest conception of intellectual property law has been upstaged by a new public interest model (Drahos with Braithwaite, 2002:169–86).

In any case, the media industry has rapidly adapted to the threat of the Internet. For example, between 2002 and 2005, numerous commercial music download sites emerged. The vast bulk of these were backed by one or more of the big four record labels. Napster has itself been reborn as a legal download site with an emphasis on monthly music rental subscriptions which allow users to listen to unlimited tracks, so long as they maintain their subscription (with numerous retail and hardware alliances struck, including one with that most conservative of British institutions—the Post Office). While DRM technologies can always be circumvented, the aim, as with all previous forms of copyright protection, is to make infringement less convenient, either by increasing the risk of getting caught or the amount of time it takes to evade the protection. If online music distribution takes off—and there are many signs that it will, if Apple's record at selling over 1 million tracks a day during 2004 is anything to go by (McCue, 2005)—the irony is that, just as with the e-book example given previously, DRM technologies will restrict what individuals can do with their legally purchased music and movies to a greater extent than if they had bought a physical CD. This future scenario was brought home to many in 2003, when a person attempted to sell on a "secondhand" iTunes download on eBay, only to have it removed by the auction site for violation of its "downloadable media policy" (Smith, 2003). Under rights of "first sale," no such difficulties would have been encountered in trying to sell a physical CD.

In the end, there are several good business reasons why the music and film industries are moving into legitimate online distribution. These mainly center on the cost savings generated by shifting from the relatively expensive production and distribution of physical media (CDs, DVDs, and video and audio tape) to cheaper digital forms. For example, around half of the income from the sale of a CD is soaked up in getting the product to the shelf and does not reach the record company, music publisher, or artist. Online distribution creates new costs such as the creation and maintenance of websites and managing bandwidth, but it is highly unlikely that these would approach the costs of physical production and distribution through stores. Digital downloads therefore offer media companies a choice: they can either pass on these cost savings to the consumer, give more back to artists in the form of royalties, or, most likely, they can enjoy higher profit margins (Picard, 2002:58). Hardly the stuff of major upheavals in the global media sector.

The Free and Open-Source Software Movement

The second major focus of debates about the Internet gift economy is the free and open-source software movement (FOSS). While many collapse the distinction between "free" and "open source," it is more accurate to distinguish between the two. The free software movement, in which "free" stands for "freedom" rather than "free of charge," was initiated by Richard Stallman, a software writer, in 1984. The idea was to create software that was robust, flexible, yet relatively inexpensive. But more important, such programs would be a deliberate challenge to the power of dominant corporations like IBM and Microsoft. Stallman and his supporters have consistently argued that closed source, or proprietary, software is inimical to human freedom because it denies access to common resources, in this case software source code that could be built upon and improved for the benefit of society. Stallman is therefore doctrinally opposed to all forms of proprietary software development. The broader open-source movement is based upon similar principles but tends to be more pragmatic, often advocating a blend of open and proprietary development. FOSS is potentially a major challenge to the established players in the Internet media sector. Why?

First, in the eyes of some, it poses an ideological and practical threat to the economic power of large companies, especially Microsoft. This basic point bears repeating because it would appear that FOSS is steadily becoming more popular as the quality and accessibility of programs develops and it gains more widespread recognition (see exhibit 12.2). A future in which Microsoft has less control over the desktop and server markets would be one in which there is greater diversity of products and less ideological influence in the hands of powerful individuals like Bill Gates.

Second, for some optimistic commentators, FOSS represents the pinnacle of the online gift economy by demonstrating the viability of a postcapitalist form of social and economic organization. As Steven Weber (2004:7) describes them, FOSS zealots see it as a "libertarian reverie, a perfect meritocracy, a utopian gift culture that celebrates an economics of abundance instead of scarcity, a virtual or electronic existence proof of communitarian ideals, a political movement aimed at replacing obsolete nineteenth-century capitalist structures with new 'relations of production' more suited to the Information Age." As Weber himself points out, it is an exaggeration to claim that FOSS is ushering in such a new era, not least because there are many FOSS advocates who insist that it is a profitable business model. But, as with file sharing, some FOSS projects, particularly the Linux operating system, have been a chink in the armor of free market principles (Benkler, 2002).

Third, FOSS challenges many of the traditional assumptions about property rights and how to reward individuals for their labor in a market-based society (Weber, 2004:5). Free and open-source software is mostly developed through unpaid voluntary

EXHIBIT 12.2. EXAMPLES OF POPULAR FREE AND OPEN-SOURCE SOFTWARE

- **Apache:** web server.
- **Bittorrent:** peer-to-peer file sharing.
- **FreeBSD:** operating system.
- **GNU Emacs:** text editor.
- **Jabber:** instant messaging.
- **Linux:** operating system.
- **Media Player Classic:** multimedia player.
- **MediaWiki:** online collaborative content production.
- **Mozilla Firefox:** web browser.
- **Mozilla Thunderbird:** email.
- **Ogg Vorbis:** audio compression (like MP3).
- **OpenGroupware:** network collaboration and scheduling.
- **OpenOffice:** office suite.
- **phpBB:** discussion forum and online polling.
- **WordPress:** blogging.

Source: Adapted from Wikipedia, 2005.

collaboration online in virtual communities. While there are many individuals who earn a living from selling service and support for open-source software, like Linux, most free and open-source developers do not secure direct material gains from their efforts. The vast majority of projects are voluntary. They involve programmers curious about a particular problem and who wish to see an elegant and widely recognized solution to it. Proprietary software is not developed in this way. In large software houses like Microsoft, source code development takes place behind closed doors. It involves teams of individuals internal to the firm developing a program before it is released to users. The key point is that the "recipe" for key applications like Microsoft's Office suite, for instance, is kept secret and is heavily protected by intellectual property law: patents, copyrights, trademarks, and end-user licenses. In contrast, open-source projects deliberately publish the underlying recipe for all to see. Due to the way open-source software licensing works, all are free to use, modify, and distribute the source code, so long as they do not restrict access to it or any modified form of it.

Given this context, the real conundrum is why free and open-source software exists at all. Answering this question gives us some insight into the nature of the Internet gift economy more generally. Conventional economic wisdom would have it that property rights in source code are what incentivize people to develop new code. The reason why Microsoft holds onto the secrets of its code is that it wishes to have exclusive rights to extract value from the fruits of its labor. No such incentives exist in much of the FOSS arena, yet many programs that are developed and maintained in this way, such as the Apache servers, which power around two-thirds of the web, are hugely successful. Steven Weber convincingly argues that a complex system of incentives does in fact exist in FOSS development communities and to perceive them as based on pure altruism is wrong: developers seek forums in which they can enjoy themselves by creating new things and demonstrate their prowess; good software also requires a large user base of beta testers to report bugs; FOSS communities often consist of thousands of willing end users upon whom developers may draw as a resource for moving software forward; and they also share common values, such as the hacker ethic (see chapter 5), and common enemies (e.g., Microsoft) which bind them together (Weber, 2004:128–56).

Fourth, the FOSS movement also challenges conventional wisdom about organizational structure and coordination (Weber, 2004:10). Software development is an incredibly complex business. Many of the popular office programs run several million lines of code. The development process has evolved to the extent that it is usually impossible for a single individual to create a program in its entirety. Large companies have reacted by developing hierarchical industrial models of production in which instructions come from the top and discrete tasks are allocated to teams of workers in a strict division of labor with the aim of satisfying market demand. But FOSS takes another approach: it relies upon relatively decentralized, voluntary systems of co-operation in which authority is often murkily defined or nonexistent and in which the division of labor is based upon what people want to do rather than what they are instructed to do or believe the market demands. There is something unusual about the fact that FOSS collaborators stick together in pursuit of the same goal. We would normally expect projects to fall apart as a result of internal bickering, individual laziness, duplication of effort, or lack of strategic direction. Projects do, of course, fall apart, but many do not. Why?

The principal reason is that it would be inaccurate to portray successful FOSS projects this way, because the major developments, such as Linux, have long relied upon the expertise and gatekeeping abilities of small groups of talented individuals (in Linux's case, its originator, Linus Torvalds). Many FOSS projects are actually modular, meaning that they are disaggregated into small chunks. This makes it easier to develop new features without altering the stable core of a project. FOSS communities also make use of many of the familiar mechanisms of social sanctioning online: they publicly flame one another and refuse to work with rivals. In many cases the exit costs of leaving a FOSS project are higher than the costs of loyalty or voicing criticism. Projects such as Apache have also relied upon formal governance mechanisms such as email voting and polling (Weber, 2004:157–89).

Finally, the FOSS movement also has a broader relevance for Internet media regulation. Creations such as Linux stand in stark contrast with the centralized production processes that lead to proprietary software, and the networks of code writers in open-source communities cannot be so easily regulated. The fact that over 90 percent of the computers around the globe use Microsoft operating systems makes the company an obvious target of regulation. Governments tend to try to regulate at the point at which it will be perceived they will have most effect and incur the least cost. Thus, requiring Microsoft, for instance, to make changes to its software is a highly efficient means of indirectly regulating the behavior of large numbers of Internet users. One could argue that users who were disgruntled with the government's proposals, and Microsoft's compliance, could simply switch to a different operating system. However, the exit costs in such a case are likely to be extremely high for the average user. There is new expertise to be gained, perhaps new hardware to be purchased. There are also all-important network effects that make switching difficult because the utility of a piece of software increases as its user base increases (see also chapter 10).

The kind of dynamic we see here produces a form of regulatory lock-in, in which the interests of government coincide with those of major software and hardware manu-facturers—those who produce the architecture or code on which the Internet depends. It is a structural dynamic based on interdependency. Governments are dependent upon large software firms for economic reasons, such as their contribution to a healthy do-mestic economy and so on. But in the relatively new sphere of Internet media, govern-ments can also pursue social goals through the requirement that companies engineer-in features of their applications that enable regulation. At the same time, from the per-spective of the companies, a closed model of software development has traditionally been seen as the route to profitability. Moreover, companies must ensure that they re-main on good terms with government because it will lead to a helpful economic context without burdensome regulation. Proprietary software thus provides advantages to both the company and government regulators; FOSS disturbs this comfortable arrangement.

CONCLUSION

Drawing conclusions in this area is particularly difficult because the Internet media sec-tor is in a state of perpetual flux. This has created some surprising predictions. Even the most seemingly pessimistic writers such as Ben Bagdikian are nevertheless sanguine about the future, pointing to a new generation of Internet journalists and technologists eager to overturn the old, big media order (2004:133). On the other hand, as we would expect, the critical political economy approach has its fair share of pessimists keen to point out that the early promise has been sidelined by commercialization (Herman and Chomsky, 2002:xvi).

As we have seen throughout this chapter, contradictory forces are at work, and these differ according to context. For instance, we can identify market concentration in the Internet media sector, especially in the ISP, portal, and operating systems markets. There are even signs that it is less competitive than the traditional media sectors. We can also see how the Internet has helped already powerful media conglomerates like AOL Time Warner and Disney expand their horizontal and vertical integration strategies. There is no doubt that the online experience of the average Internet user in the two countries from which most of the examples in this book are drawn—the United States and the United Kingdom—seems to consist of a fairly predictable diet of mainstream media sites that are owned by large conglomerates. Content that does not come into this category tends to originate with long-standing information technology companies, such as Microsoft, or pure Internet success stories, such as Yahoo! or Google. The likes of Yahoo! and Google have grown so rapidly that they already have substantial market power and are likely to retain it for many years to come.

If we examine our second major theme—the production and distribution of news—though disturbing trends like source concentration are evident, new develop-ments such as Indymedia and blogging have arguably started to disturb the ecosystem.

It is highly unlikely that most Internet users will give up visiting CNN.com (for example) in favor of a diet of blogs, but at the margins, do-it-yourself journalism seems likely to continue to play a role, even if this is often indirect, as mainstream journalists increasingly pick up stories from the blogosphere. In this sense, the Internet does appear to be contributing to a more pluralistic public sphere of communication—one less constrained by commercial values.

Reflecting finally on our third major area, the politics of intellectual property, once again we see contradictory trends. Those who forecast a spontaneously emerging gift economy that will displace market relations are wide of the mark, but there have been marginal shifts. The long-term impact of peer-to-peer technologies is in the balance, as the music, film, and software industries attempt to establish their own legitimate alternatives to widespread piracy. But even if they succeed, peer-to-peer file sharing is unlikely to disappear; the same can be said of open-source software.

Overall, judged in terms of a political economy approach, the Internet has unleashed contradictory forces. Some of these reinforce the economic status quo; some challenge it. Though there appears to be little evidence at this stage for Joel Amernic and Russell Craig's view that the Net is "in danger of being controlled by a few mega-corporations" (2004:21), it will be interesting to see how these contradictions are resolved in future.

Discussion Points

- Is there market concentration in the Internet media sector?
- Has the Internet changed the economics of news production?
- How has the Internet reshaped the politics of intellectual property?
- How significant is the Internet gift economy?
- What are the social, economic, and political consequences of free and open-source software?

Further Reading

Excellent introductions to the critical political economy approach can be found in the work of McChesney (1999, 2000, 2004). Noam's 2003 study of market concentration in the Internet sector is concise and to the point. Blevins, 2002, is a useful distillation of the impact of the Internet on one media conglomerate: Disney.

On news, Gillmor, 2004, contains much information on the rise of blogging and is highly readable. Downing, 2003, is a thoughtful analysis of Indymedia.

On how the Internet is being used to tighten corporate control over intellectual property, see Lessig, 2004. Provocative accounts of the online gift economy include Barbrook, 2000, and Vaidhyanathan, 2004. The best book-length treatment of free and open-source software is written by a political scientist, Weber (2004), but see also Benkler, 2002.

CONCLUSION

The Future of Internet Politics

The future is already here. It's just not very evenly distributed.
—WILLIAM GIBSON, 1999

CHAPTER OVERVIEW

In this final chapter I take a brief look at the likely short- to medium-term future of Internet politics. My strategy is to attempt to trace forward some of the key developments that we have encountered throughout the book.

What does the future hold for Internet politics? This is a risky question, because the medium has an uncanny knack of defying even the most cautious predictions. However, my strategy throughout the book has been to combine concrete empirical examples with consideration of the major scholarly interpretations of the Internet's impact on political life. Thus, rather than trying to pluck predictions out of thin air, my approach here is to try to trace, in thematic fashion, some likely short- to medium-term trends on the basis of what has been discussed in each substantive chapter. I organize the discussion around the book's three main sections: contexts, institutions, and issues.

CONTEXTUAL FUTURES

While it makes sense to see Internet technologies as having some innate properties that shape political action (see chapter 2), precisely which of these are dominant in any given institutional or policy context is a matter for investigation, not casual assumption. As this book has demonstrated, the Interent is a deeply contradictory medium. A large part of the problem derives from rapid change, not only in the technologies themselves but, perhaps more importantly, in popular assumptions about how to use the technologies in political ways. This tends to create an environment within which particular Internet technologies appear to lie dormant—perhaps for several years—before they are seized upon, developed, and thrust into the political mainstream. Blogging is an excellent example. The technologies of blogging have been around since the late 1990s, but it was only during the U.S. presidential campaign of 2003–2004 that their political potential was recognized. The era of personal publishing that was predicted in the mid-1990s—largely on the back of the explosion of simple websites—has turned out rather differently due to the influence of blogs. And it is of course highly likely that blogging itself will continue to evolve (or even decay), as broadband increasingly allows writers to integrate images, audio, and video. Indeed, some blog sites already resemble do-it-yourself television or radio stations.

The case of blogging illustrates some wider trends in the evolution of the basic technological building blocks of the Internet itself. As we saw in our prehistory of the Internet (chapter 3), the basic features of Internet communication such as TCP/IP make it a highly flexible and decentralized medium. Despite the rise of slick presentational websites, these characteristics continue to constrain government and corporate attempts to exert greater control over Internet content. Nevertheless, the battle for the future of the Internet is in many respects a battle over standards. Older technological advances, such as the invention of the browser and HTML, while fundamental, are likely to seem like the naive products of a bygone era of scientific endeavor when compared with future developments. Organizations such as the World Wide Web Consortium (W3C), the main standards body for the web, contain technicians, but they also contain business interests eager to ensure that the basic properties of the Internet render it an environment suitable for the ruthless exploitation of commerce. This constituency aims at the commodification of as many aspects of the online environment as possible, and this is likely to involve tussles over what may appear as minor, fine-grained details in the short term but which, in the medium term, turn out to be decisive in favoring commercial interests.

A good example of this is the ongoing implementation of IPv6, a new version of the Internet Protocol (the "IP" in TCP/IP). First defined as a standard by the Internet Engineering Task Force (IETF) in 1998, IPv6 is technically designed as a solution to the future exhaustion of numerical IP address space. However, it will enable many more devices, especially mobile handsets, to connect to the Internet and communicate with each other. The idea of a fully mobile Internet is likely to be made much easier with IPv6, as is the ultimate dream of a fully converged media/telecommunication/computing environment. This is essentially because the protocol allows many different devices to be assigned their own unique IP address, whether they are televisions, cameras, music players, DVD players, games consoles, mobile phones, and even "white goods" appliances. Hence the alliance of large telecommunication, hardware, and software companies pushing for the protocol's early implementation—in such a way that can be exploited commercially.

The implementation of IPv6 is likely to generate increasing controversy over the next few years, as the public becomes aware of its potential for increasing both corporate and state surveillance as well as the fact that a major driver of its adoption appears to be its suitability for military applications. Yet at the same time, in some respects IPv6 represents an intensification of the original principles underlying TCP/IP. For some, the idea of massive interoperability is faithful to the original libertarian values of the Internet, and IPv6 can just as easily be used to subvert control from above as facilitate it by making do-it-yourself forms of peer-to-peer networking much easier to establish

(Poppe, 2004). This clash of ideas can be seen quite clearly running through the recent high-profile summits and conferences, such as the U.S. IPv6 Summit at Reston, Virginia, home of the Internet Society (ISOC), in December 2004 (U.S. IPv6 Summit, 2004).

If corporate interests are pushing for the development of new protocols that will shape the Internet for a generation, they are being resisted by a progressive global agenda to tackle the digital divide: the World Summit on the Information Society (WSIS). As we saw in chapter 4, even in terms of simple physical access to the Internet, there are signs that the divide between developing and developed countries may be widening as a result of long-established structural factors. The WSIS commits the United Nations and other international institutions to developing a coherent program for tackling the global digital divide. With a second summit meeting in November 2005, the WSIS is likely to set the global agenda for possibly up to a decade.

However, two major problems are likely to bedevil the WSIS: lack of focus and coherence and weak financial commitment from developed countries. The first problem in part reflects the ubiquity of information and communication technologies in the developed world. The fact that vast swathes of social, economic, and political activity involves the Internet and related technologies creates a potentially huge array of issues and interests. And the idea of the developing world catching up in terms of Internet diffusion rests upon a static definition of technology. The digital divide is a moving target due to rapid technological change. The second problem—financial commitment— is nothing new in the sphere of international summitry. But the WSIS has had particularly bad problems in this area. A Task Force on Financial Mechanisms was established in 2004 with a brief to report to the second round summit meeting on how best to raise funds for development programs. However, the report goes little further than restating the problem and suggests no concrete means of raising money (WSIS Task Force on Financial Mechanisms, 2004). It is difficult to escape a pessimistic forecast in this area.

Prospects for narrowing country-level digital divides in the developed world are arguably better. As we saw in chapter 4, many countries had Internet diffusion rates that exceeded 50 percent in 2002. The next five years are likely to see many more countries reach this milestone. Yet, as our case study of the United States demonstrates, it is clear that Internet diffusion is slowing quite considerably, leading some to forecast that it will take many years to reach the penetration levels characteristic of other new media technologies like cable and satellite television. Indeed, it is possible that the market for Internet access from home might already be at saturation point in the United States. If this is the case, it requires a shift of focus to consider not only how people are actually able to make use of the Internet in purposive ways but also how new inequalities are being opened up by differences in connectivity. Broadband users tend to create their own content and tailor and manage the content of others according to their own needs (Horrigan and Rainie, 2002). In other words, the broadband versus dial-up divide reinforces the divide between those who are actively involved in creating web pages and blogs, contributing to discussion forums, sharing files, managing their own news feeds via news aggregator software, and so on and those for whom the Net is a much more disjointed, passive experience.

As with so many other aspects of Internet politics, there is some scope for voluntaristic solutions. Moves are already underway to establish large-scale wireless networks covering entire neighborhoods or even cities based on established WiMAX standards (fast, wide-ranging wireless networks). Such schemes are currently sponsored by a mixture of local governments, public-private partnerships, and charitable bodies. Over the next few years, conflict between these projects and fully commercial telecommunication operators is likely. An indication of this comes in the form of Philadelphia's wireless Muninet. By the end of 2006, the city government will aim to spend $10 million on the creation of a 135-square-mile "data cloud" that will provide heavily subsidized broadband Internet access for homes, businesses, and nonprofits, including, importantly, the poorer neighborhoods of west Philadelphia. Not surprisingly, traditional telecommunication providers are worried about such citizen-based schemes. In fact, they have already moved to quash their further development. Verizon, the largest operator in the state of Pennsylvania, successfully lobbied the state legislature to ban the further development of Muninets across the state (Dodson, 2005). If broadband continues to diffuse unevenly, and the signs are that it will, given the stubbornly high subscription charges in the United States and most European countries (Britain included), such responses to the broadband divide are likely to move further up policy agendas.

INSTITUTIONAL FUTURES

Contextual factors like the technological building blocks of the Internet and the digital divide shape Internet politics, but as the second section of the book demonstrates, existing institutions and practices are equally important. We considered four major areas in which an institutional impact is being felt: e-democracy, e-mobilization, e-campaigning, and e-government. On the basis of what we observed, what are likely future trends in these areas?

In the area of e-democracy (chapter 5), it is already possible to identify a steady shift away from the older emphasis on community networks and small-scale experiments of the past toward further integration of online deliberative forums in real-world policy-making processes at both local and national levels. The case studies of e-rule making in the U.S. Federal government and the U.K.'s Commbill forum that ran alongside a parliamentary committee would indicate that executives and legislatures are beginning to shed some of their earlier skepticism. Some countries, notably Canada, Australia, and New Zealand, now have fairly well-established professional expertise in the area of e-consultation. A new generation of public servants and commercial consultants eager to provide the software tools and training required for successful online discussions is fast emerging. This kind of expertise was simply not available during the Internet's early expansion, and it is likely to have a significant practical effect on elected politicians' perceptions of the viability of using Internet technologies. There will always be the temptation to continue with limited experiments, however, and time will tell if such schemes as the U.K. government's local e-democracy project, which ran through to the spring of 2005, will create lasting structures or whether the e-democracy specialists move into safer areas of business and public service (U.K. Office of the Deputy Prime Minister, 2005).

The impact of the Internet on interest groups and social movements is likely to move in a similar direction. During recent years, much excitement has been generated by new forms of action such as hacktivism and by the rise of new transnational social movements built upon loose networks. Thus, in chapter 6, for example, we examined how the Zapatistas' local campaign for land rights in southern Mexico became transformed into a global campaign involving activists and hacktivists from dozens of countries. Such activity will undoubtedly continue to proliferate and will be spurred by global initiatives like the WSIS.

Likely to be just as significant in the long term, however, are incremental but decisive shifts in the organizational strategies of traditional groups as well as the proliferation of new hybrid forms of mobilization like MoveOn. As our case study of Environmental Defense (drawn from Bimber, 2003) demonstrates, the group has effectively reinvented its organization based around a web, email, and database strategy. It has also established virtual alliances with other environmental groups without having to commit significant resources. Even more remarkable is the success of MoveOn, a hybrid combination of independent lobby group, leftist Democratic Party grassroots movement, mass petition site, and political action committee that also has an overseas membership (Chadwick, 2005). In the near future, I would argue that we can expect to see variants of the MoveOn model exported to other countries as well as the continual metamorphosis of the original organization: in early 2005 the movement shifted its focus to Social Security reform.

Questions of exportability obviously loom large in the sphere of election campaigning. As we saw in chapter 7, following several false starts in the United States, the 2003–2004 primary and presidential campaigns put the Internet center stage. Howard Dean's campaign may have burned out, but the methods it pioneered went on to shape both the Democrats' and the Republicans' online strategies. In the area of fund-raising in particular, it seems highly likely that the Internet is a weapon that cannot be ignored in the future at all levels of U.S. electoral politics. And though the hard evidence is yet to appear, it is likely that Internet campaigning played at least some role in the historically high voter turnout—up 6 percent on the 2000 contest.

But a major issue for the future is the extent to which the features of the U.S. campaign are going to influence elections elsewhere. Many of the major western European liberal democracies have state-funded political parties, making the issue of fund-raising less politically charged. Our other major case study in chapter 7, the United Kingdom, does not have state funding but has only selectively adopted and adapted features of U.S. online campaigning. Britain was in the final throes of a general election in May of 2005, just as this book went into production. While the Internet presence of candidates was an improvement over 2001, it was clear that the Internet did not play the role it did in the 2004 U.S. campaign. Online fund-raising is now a more prominent part of British parties' web strategies, yet the party-centered nature of British politics means that their greater institutional presence and continuous membership basis does not create as many pressures to continually rebuild campaign machines in the manner of their U.S. counterparts. In many respects, the Internet is better suited to the relatively fluid context of U.S. primary campaigning. It is notable that in the United States, most of the innovations have occurred during the primary season. Primaries, however loosely defined, are largely absent from European party systems. In the United Kingdom, parliamentary candidates are selected by a combination of central party elites and small committees of local constituency activists. Also, there is historical resistance to the idea of candidates "floating free" of a party.

There is evidence that some British members of Parliament may be using the Net to reach out to supporters outside the traditional structures of party. For instance, some appear to use email distribution lists for at least some of the functions performed by blogs (Jackson, 2004), though there is a difference between what is essentially a one-to-many device and the many-to-many features of blogs. We can perhaps expect to see campaign blogs appearing on central party websites in the future, but authentic individual party-leader blogs are probably unlikely to take off in the United Kingdom. There is greater scope for constituency-level blogging: around fifty parliamentary candidates blogged during the 2005 campaign (Kimber, 2005). But recent experience during a high-profile by-election in the northeast of England, where one of the candidates, Jody Dunn, used her blog to make mildly derogatory remarks about the character of the local town that were instantly pounced upon by the mainstream media, would indicate the risks, certainly from the viewpoint of party central office (Aitkenhead, 2004). And there is every possibility that Republican-style noninteractive blogs will emerge as the dominant model, as illustrated by the case of Kevin Davis, the British Conservative Party challenger for Kingston and Surbiton in 2005 who removed the comments facility from his three hundred hits-a-day campaign blog due to what he termed "inappropriate and slanderous comments . . . from political opponents" (Davis, 2005). It is too soon to say with any certainty, but overall, the lack of enthusiasm by mainstream British politicians for using the Internet to engage citizens, when compared with their U.S. counterparts, may partly explain the comparatively small increase in voter turnout in the U.K. general election of 2005. There, turnout improved by just 2 percent, compared with a 6 percent increase in the United States in 2004.

There is much less uncertainty about the spread of e-government—the focus of our final institutional analysis (chapter 8). This is the most obvious and tangible way in which the impact of the Internet has been felt on the mainstream business of government and politics. As we saw, e-government offers many advantages for politicians, bureaucrats, and, potentially, citizens. However, to date it has been defined in peculiarly narrow terms. It is first and foremost about managerial control and cost reduction. In many respects, the next few years are crucial in the evolution of e-government. One scenario is that the prospects for democratic uses of e-government will increase as politicians and citizens start to see the potential for opening up new channels of communication between civil society and government. In this future, e-government programs start to integrate some of the e-democratic experiments of recent times. Another scenario is that the current obsession with efficiency and electronic service delivery comes to dominate all aspects of e-government reform. There are signs that this shift is already occurring in the early-adopter countries. In the United States, the second Bush administration is likely to intensify the emphasis on cost reduction that began early in the first administration. The United Kingdom's e-government program is currently undergoing a period of change as it becomes central to the implementation of a new round of efficiency savings spurred by a major Treasury review in 2004. The e-democracy element of the United Kingdom's program, which was never considered to be a central plank, has been downgraded still further (Chadwick, 2003).

Such developments might suggest that the major liberal democracies will soon converge on a Singapore-style model. The authoritarian city-state has long been perceived as the acme of managerial e-government, with a ruthless focus on using IT to stamp out waste and duplication. However, perhaps this assumption is misleading, because even Singapore has recently developed the successful online Government Consultation Portal, featuring a large range of active discussions on topics directly related to policies, such as plans to extend smoking bans and compulsory HIV testing (Singapore Government Consultation Portal, 2005). This outshines several of the experiments attempted by e-government programs in liberal democracies to date.

ISSUE FUTURES

If making predictions about the Internet's role in shaping political institutions is difficult, thinking about the future of Internet policy issues is almost impossible. Nevertheless, in chapters 9 through 12 we examined four areas that have been consistently problematic: attempts to establish some form of global information society agenda at the international level; the controversy over Internet governance; the role of the Internet as a new arena for state and corporate surveillance; and finally, the political economy of the Internet media sector. It seems likely that these four areas will continue to be significant for many years to come.

As we saw in chapter 9, an array of international organizations and forums are arguably constructing a new global information society regime. As the strategic importance of Internet connectivity has increased throughout the world, a diverse set of actors is attempting to influence its future development through programs of research and education, pilot projects, summits, conferences, and ad hoc bodies involving states and nonstate actors, such as the European Union (EU) Information Society Project, the G8's Digital Opportunity Taskforce, the United Nations Information and Communication Technology Taskforce (UNICT), the Global Information Infrastructure Commission (GIIC), and many others. This regime is only in an embryonic phase and in certain respects lags behind the diffusion of technological innovation being driven by market forces. But the ideological struggle between an economic and a social development model is set to shape the evolution of the regime for some time to come. While pessimists may see the economic model as already dominant, in fact, the ongoing WSIS is testament to the continued relevance of the social development model. A core issue looking to the future will be the extent to which the diffuse bands of progressive nongovernmental organizations (NGOs) mobilized around the WSIS agenda will be able to offset the power of established international actors, not only by directly challenging the interests of business but also by aligning themselves with progressive factions within the United Nations, especially the International Telecommunication Union (ITU).

The role and influence of the United Nations is also increasingly central to the future development of Internet governance (chapter 10). During 2004 and early 2005, a debate arose about the involvement of UN member governments either in the established Governmental Advisory Committee of the Internet Corporation for Assigned Names and Numbers (ICANN), or possibly through a new mechanism. Part of the problem with Internet governance at the international level is that the nearest we have to a governance institution—ICANN—lacks legitimacy because there is no consensus on how the Internet ought to be governed. ICANN was founded both as an alternative to governance by the U.S. state and any preexisting international institution. It was also hatched at a time when notions of self-governance were in the ascendancy. But since ICANN's foundation, it would appear that there have been at least three different conceptions of Internet self-governance, and these are highly likely to clash in future, not only with each other but also with any agenda to establish governmental control via some specially created UN division. First, there is the older view of self-governance by "rough consensus and running code"—Internet technician David Clark's description of how early decision making in technical standards bodies, particularly the IETF, took place. This approach suggests that those with the motivation and ability to develop the technical features of the Internet ought to be the ones who govern it. A second conception, which often but not always overlaps with the first, is self-governance by those private sector concerns with a stake in the Internet business sector: the Internet Service Providers (ISPs), telecommunication providers, hardware and software companies, and media content companies. This approach implies that the major commercial players should be able to exert most leverage because innovations that benefit end users will only emerge if companies can make the Internet pay as a business. The third conception, which we might term citizen self-governance, rarely overlaps with the second but may overlap with the first as a fused form of techie and democratic libertarian ideology. This approach suggests that ordinary Netizens—or those with sufficient motivation at any rate—should organize and collaborate through civil associations and that their views should be funneled into international bodies like ICANN through proper democratic mechanisms. This conception suffered a severe setback in 2000 when the ICANN global election descended into chaos, but it remains a powerful normative perspective which unites many of the progressive NGOs buzzing around the WSIS.

The continuing clash of perspectives at the level of ICANN—a body which, to confuse matters further, usually denies that it has any substantive policy-making role—may turn out to be distracting attention from another trend: the increasing involvement of national and even subnational governments in directly governing and regulating the Internet through decisive technological interventions like targeting local ISPs. This leads us to the future of our third major policy area: surveillance, security, and privacy (chapter 11).

The near-term future of Internet surveillance is likely to be dominated by two themes: the impact of mobile technologies, and states' capacity for developing new forms of surveillance based upon a more sophisticated understanding of the vulnerability of certain aspects of Internet networking to strategic intervention. The first of these—mobile technologies—presents new surveillance opportunities both to state and corporate actors. Wireless Radio Frequency Identification (RFID) chips are proliferating at a rapid rate and will soon find their way into many areas of life, from passports to supermarket shelves or even clothing. GPS technologies are now finding their way into mobile phones and other hand-held devices. For cell phone providers, the vision is of a totally integrated Internet and phone network powered by GPS services that will pinpoint an individual's precise location and deliver timely information based in part upon user selected preferences but also data-mining technologies. While the legislative frameworks required for government agencies to access this data are only in an embryonic stage, over the next few years the sheer amount of locational, demographic, and behavioral data that can be physically stored, processed, and transmitted will massively increase, creating a major problem in the eyes of civil libertarians. Once again, convergence is likely to drive events, making Internet communication more central to policy than ever.

Yet it would be unwise to assume that the increasingly mobile nature of the Internet is going to radically disturb some of the basic practices of communications interception. As our brief case study of China's Internet surveillance regime demonstrates, infrastructural controls are surprisingly easy to install and maintain, given the political will and a suitable legal context (chapter 11). Nor are these measures exclusive to authoritarian regimes. Pennsylvania's Internet Child Pornography Act of 2002 enabled it to block content flowing into ISP servers based in its jurisdiction, effectively preventing the material from ever reaching end users. Though the legislation was ruled unconstitutional by a Pennsylvania district court in September 2004, both on First Amendment (free speech) grounds and because it was interpreted as a restriction on interstate commerce, this type of intervention is likely to prove much more common from now on, especially in countries that lack robust constitutional speech protections.

Our final chapter (12) dealt with the Net's impact on the economic structures of the media and entertainment industries. As we discovered, the mythology of dotcom created several dubious assumptions about the competitiveness of the Internet media sector as well as its likely effects in leveling the media playing field more generally. Most of the major subsectors of the Internet sector are now characterized by levels of market concentration typical of other media sectors. It seems clear that average Internet users derive much of their online diet of information, entertainment, and shopping from a handful of well-known sources. The major telecommunication providers have mainly transferred their dominance into the Internet sector, and though there have been difficulties, for instance with the AOL Time Warner merger, it appears that old media conglomerates are successfully adapting to the online environment.

There are, nevertheless, important signs of change that perhaps point to a less certain future for big media. The rise of blogging is democratizing news production and distribution, while the two principal elements of the online gift economy—file sharing and free and open-source software (FOSS)—may cause dents in the future convergence strategies of major entertainment and software firms. Overall, however, this chapter revealed deeply contradictory trends, and there are few signs that these contradictions will be resolved in the short term.

Indeed, the Internet media sector is evolving rapidly, as the dotcom era fades but the Net enters the fabric of everyday life. It is now becoming commonplace for even the most zealous of dotcom boosters (e.g., *Wired* magazine) to speak of a "post-dotcom era." Though this is ill-defined, it seems to imply an online environment in which there is some sort of evolving balance between commercial and noncommercial activity. The spread of noncommercial "social software" and "blogware"—meaning broader online content creation platforms that make it much easier for groups to create their own virtual communities—is only likely to augment online political activity. Much of the impetus will come from the FOSS movement, which is currently enjoying unprecedented popularity following high-profile successes like the Firefox web browser. And it is likely that the elective affinity between the values of the FOSS community and those progressive and libertarian strands of Internet political activism will continue to feed its development in the short to medium term.

In the field of news production, there are early signs that mainstream media and private corporations are beginning to reign in the blogosphere, either by appropriating some of its stylistic conventions or by more direct means like legal challenges. Mainstream newspaper websites are starting to incorporate the blog format into their regular content. A good example is the British *Guardian*'s online blog. Similarly, IT and Internet companies, including Microsoft, Google, and Sun Microsystems, have been quick to see the potential of blogs for publicizing their products. Bloggers in part owe their success to the fact that they are less constrained by the norms and standards of mainstream journalism. Thus, possibly more serious in the longer term are legal challenges which involve targeting individual blogs in attempts to shut them down. In March 2005, a Santa Clara County superior court decision ruled that bloggers were not entitled to the same First Amendment protections as regularly employed journalists. The case involved Apple Computer's subpoenaing of three gossip blog owners on the grounds that the sites published trade secrets about forthcoming Apple products. The company sought the names of the sites' insider sources (Borland, 2005). The fact that these blogs act as wonderful free publicity for the company seems to have escaped their notice, but the longer-term implications for more overtly political blogs could be significant. The next few years may witness the imposition of further legal restraints.

Attempts at legal restraint have, of course, been a major part of the entertainment media's attempts to minimize the damage caused by the online gift economy based upon file sharing. As we saw in chapter 12, though it took them several years, the major media corporations have finally woken up to the commercial potential of legal digital distribution. The next few years are likely to witness the replacement of legal strategies by more attractive commercial ones. File sharing is not going to disappear. There is always likely to be a flourishing "darknet" (Lasica, 2005) of peer-to-peer activity; the central issue is how large and economically powerful it is allowed to become.

CONCLUSION

As this chapter and, indeed, the book as a whole has shown, Internet politics is a fast-moving field characterized by uncertainty, paradox, overstatement and understatement. This fluidity is what makes it a fascinating area of study. When trying to make generalizations, perhaps the best we can hope for is an appreciation of the radically contingent nature of the field, and there is little likelihood that this facet is going to change in future. If anything, the explosion of social scientific research on the Internet over the last few years—much of it covered herein—has only complicated matters still further. But in the end, it is the deeply contradictory nature of Internet politics that defines it as a subject. A more categorical conclusion at this stage is unwise.

Discussion Points

- How does increased mobility change the way we use the Internet for political activity?
- Should government become more involved in the provision of Internet services?
- How important are hybrid political organizations such as MoveOn likely to be in future?
- Is e-government likely to end with electronic service delivery?
- Should there be increased intervention at the global level to make the Internet available to all?
- Should Netizens control and regulate the Internet?
- What are the arguments for and against further commercialization of the Internet?

BIBLIOGRAPHY

6, P. (2002) "Global Digital Communications and the Prospects for Transnational Regulation." In Held, D., and McGrew, A. (eds.), *Governing Globalization: Power, Authority and Global Governance* (Polity, Cambridge), pp. 145–70.

Abouchar, K., and Henson, J. (2000) "The World Wide Web as Political Public Space." Paper presented to the Western Political Science Association Annual Meeting, March.

Abramson, J. B., Arterton, F. C., and Orren, G. R. (1988) *The Electronic Commonwealth: The Impact of New Media Technologies on Democratic Politics* (Basic Books, New York).

Accenture (2001) *E-government Leadership: Rhetoric versus Reality—Closing the Gap* (Accenture, New York).

Adbusters (2004) "Black Spot Sneaker." Black Spot Sneaker website at http://www.blackspotsneaker.org (accessed June 10, 2004).

Aglietta, M. (1979) *A Theory of Capitalist Regulation* (Verso, London).

Agre, P. E. (2002) "Real-Time Politics: The Internet and the Political Process." *Information Society* 18 (5), pp. 311–31.

Ahuja, M. K., and Carley, K. M. (1998) "Network Structure in Virtual Organizations." *Journal of Computer-Mediated Communication* 3 (4) at http://www.ascusc.org/jcmc/vol3/issue4/ahuja.html (accessed May 28, 2004).

Aitkenhead, D. (2004) "Today Hartlepool, Tomorrow . . ." *The Guardian,* September 28. Also available at http://www.guardian.co.uk/g2/story/0,3604,1314297,00.html (accessed February 21, 2005).

Alderman, J. (2001) *Sonic Boom: Napster, MP3 and the New Pioneers of Music* (Perseus Press, Cambridge, MA).

Alkadry, M. G. (2003) "Deliberative Discourse between Citizens and Administrators: If Citizens Talk, Will Administrators Listen?" *Administration and Society* 35 (2), pp. 184–209.

Amazon (2004) "Presidential Candidates." Amazon.com website at http://www.amazon.com/gp/misc/flag.html/ref=gw_pres_cand/104-0808610-4235114 (accessed July 20, 2004).

Amernic, J., and Craig, R. J. (2004) "The Rhetoric of a Juggernaut: AOL Time Warner's Internet Policy Statement." *Prometheus* 22 (1), pp. 21–41.

Amin, A. (1994) *Post-Fordism: A Reader* (Blackwell, Oxford).

Andersen, K. V. (1999) "Reengineering Public Sector Organizations Using Information Technology." In Heeks, R. (ed.), *Reinventing Government in the Information Age: International Practice in IT-Enabled Public Sector Reform* (Routledge, London), pp. 312–30.

Andrejevic, M. (2002) "The Work of Being Watched: Interactive Media and the Exploitation of Self-Disclosure." *Critical Studies in Media Communication* 19 (2), pp. 230–48.

——— (2004) *Reality TV: The Work of Being Watched* (Rowman and Littlefield, Oxford).

Anstead, N. (2005) "The Significance of the Dean Campaign." Master's diss., Royal Holloway, University of London.

Aronson, J. D. (2000) "After Seattle: Trade Negotiations and the New Economy." In Marsden, C. T. (ed.), *Regulating the Global Information Society* (Routledge, London), pp. 178–90.

Arterton, F. C. (1987) *Teledemocracy: Can Technology Protect Democracy?* (Sage, London).

Ashbee, E. (2003) "The Lott Resignation, 'Blogging' and American Conservatism." *Political Quarterly* 74 (3), pp. 361–70.

Bibliography

Asia-Pacific Economic Co-operation (APEC) (2004a) "2002 APEC Ministerial Meeting on Telecommunications and Information Industry." APEC website at http://www.apec.org/apec/ministerial_statements/sectoral_ministerial/telecommunications/2002/annex_a.html (accessed August 7, 2004).

———— (2004b) "About APEC." APEC website at http://www.apec.org/apec/about_apec.html (accessed August 7, 2004).

Association for Community Networking (2004) "Background and History of the AFCN." Association for Community Networking website at http://www.afcn.org/node/view/29 (accessed July 11, 2004).

Association for Progressive Communications (2004) "The APC Mission." APC website at http://www.apc.org/english/about/index.shtml (accessed May 14, 2004).

Association for South east Asian Nations (ASEAN) (2004) "The E-ASEAN Initiative." ASEAN website at http://www.aseansec.org/7659.htm (accessed August 6, 2004).

Bacon, K., Wesling, C., Casey, J., and Wodinsky, J. (2002) E-government: The Blueprint (Wiley, Chichester, UK).

Bagdikian, B. (2004) The New Media Monopoly, rev. ed. (Beacon Press, Boston).

Bain, P., and Taylor, P. (2000) "Entrapped by the Electronic Panopticon?: Worker Resistance in the Call Centre." New Technology, Work and Employment 15 (1), pp. 2–18.

Bakardjieva, M., (2003) "Virtual Togetherness: An Everyday-Life Perspective." Media, Culture and Society 25 (3), pp. 291–313.

Bakardjieva, M., and Feenberg, A. (2002) "Community Technology and Democratic Rationalization." Information Society 18 (3), pp. 181–92.

Baker, P. M. A., and Ward, A. C. (2002) "Bridging Temporal and Spatial 'Gaps': The Role of Information and Communication Technologies in Defining Communities." Information, Communication and Society 5 (2), pp. 207–24.

Bannon, L. J., and Griffin, J. (2001) "New Technology, Communities and Networking: Problems and Prospects for Orchestrating Change." Telematics and Informatics 18 (1), pp. 35–49.

Barata, K., and Cain, P. (2001) "Information, Not Technology, Is Essential to Accountability: Electronic Records and Public Sector Financial Management." Information Society 17 (4), pp. 247–58.

Barber, B. (1984) Strong Democracy: Participatory Politics for a New Age (University of California Press, London).

———— (1988) "Pangloss, Pandora or Jefferson?: Three Scenarios for the Future of Technology and Democracy." In Plant, R., Gregory, F., and Brier, A. (eds.), Information Technology: the Public Issues, Fulbright Papers, vol. 5 (Alden Press, Oxford), pp. 177–90.

———— (1997) "The New Telecommunications Technology: Endless Frontier or the End of Democracy." Constellations 4 (2), pp. 208–28.

Barbrook, R. (2000) "Cyber Communism: How The Americans Are Superseding Capitalism in Cyberspace." Science As Culture 9 (1), pp. 5–40.

Barbrook, R., and Cameron, A. (1996) "The Californian Ideology." Richard Barbrook's website at http://www.hrc.wmin.ac.uk/theory-californianideology.html (accessed April 13, 2004).

Barlow, J. P. (1996a) "A Declaration of the Independence of Cyberspace." Electronic Frontier Foundation website at http://www.eff.org/~barlow/Declaration-Final.html (accessed April 14, 2004).

———— (1996b) "Selling Wine without Bottles: The Economy of Mind on the Global Net." EFF website at http://www.eff.org/pub/Publications/John_Perry_Barlow/HTML/idea_economy_article.html (accessed July 25, 2000).

Basu, S. (2004) "E-government and Developing Countries: An Overview." International Review of Law, Computers and Technology 18 (1), pp. 109–32.

Bauer, J. M., Berne, M., and Maitland, C. F. (2002) "Internet Access in the European Union and the United States." Telematics and Informatics 19 (2), pp. 117–37.

BBC News Online: Business. 2000. "UK Mobile Phone Auction Nets Billions." BBC News Online: business section website at http://news.bbc.co.uk/1/hi/business/727831.stm (accessed October 20, 2003).

BBC News Online, U.K. Edition. 2004. "Brussels Objects to Sony-BMG Deal." *BBC News Online:* U.K. edition website, May 25, at http://news.bbc.co.uk/1/hi/business/3744825.stm (accessed December 21, 2004).

Beck, U. (1999) *What Is Globalization?* (Polity, Cambridge).

Bekkers, V., and Homburg, V. (2002) "Administrative Supervision and Information Relationships." *Information Polity* 7 (2–3), pp. 129–41.

Bell, D. (1960) *The End of Ideology* (Free Press, New York).

―――― (1973) *The Coming of Post-industrial Society: A Venture in Social Forecasting* (Basic Books, New York).

Bellah, R. N., Madsen, R., Sullivan, W. M., Swidler, A., and Tipton, S. M. (1985) *Habits of the Heart: Individualism and Commitment in American Life* (University of California Press, Berkeley).

Bellamy, C., and Taylor, J. A. (1998) *Governing in the Information Age* (Open University Press, Buckingham, UK).

Bellamy, C., Horrocks, I., and Webb, J. (1995) "Community Information Systems: Strengthening Local Democracy?" In Van De Donk, W. B. H. J., Snellen, I. Th. M., and Tops, P. W. (eds.), *Orwell in Athens: A Perspective on Informatization and Democracy* (IOS Press, Amsterdam), pp. 79–95.

Benhabib, S. (ed.) (1996) *Democracy and Difference: Contesting the Boundaries of the Political* (Princeton University Press, Princeton).

Benkler, Y. (2002) "Coase's Penguin, or Linux and the Nature of the Firm." *Yale Law Journal* 112 (3), pp. 369–446.

Bennett, W. L. (1998) "The Uncivic Culture: Communication, Identity and the Rise of Lifestyle Politics." *PS: Political Science and Politics* 31 (4), pp. 741–61.

―――― (2003a) "Communicating Global Activism: Strengths and Vulnerabilities of Networked Politics." *Information, Communication and Society* 6 (2), pp. 143–68.

―――― (2003b) "New Media Power: The Internet and Global Activism." In Couldry, N., and Curran, J. (eds.), *Contesting Media Power: Alternative Media in a Networked World* (Rowman and Littlefield, Oxford), pp. 17–37.

―――― (2004) "Branded Political Communication: Lifestyle Politics, Logo Campaigns and the Rise of Global Citizenship." In Micheletti, M., Follesdal, A., and Stolle, D. (eds.), *Politics, Products and Markets: Exploring Political Consumerism, Past and Present* (Transaction Publishers, London), pp. 101–25.

Berners-Lee, T. (1999) *Weaving The Web: The Past, Present and Future of the World Wide Web* (Orion, London).

Berra, M. (2003) "Information Communications Technology and Local Development." *Telematics and Informatics* 20 (3), pp. 215–34.

Bertelsmann Foundation (2002) *Balanced E-government: E-government—Connecting Efficient Administration and Responsive Democracy* (Bertelsmann Foundation, Gütersloh).

Bimber, B. (2001) "Information and Political Engagement in America: The Search for Effects of Information Technology at the Individual Level." *Political Research Quarterly* 54 (1), pp. 53–67.

―――― (2003) *Information and American Democracy: Technology in the Evolution of Political Power* (Cambridge University Press, Cambridge).

Bimber, B., and Davis, R. (2003) *Campaigning Online: The Internet in US Elections* (Oxford University Press, Oxford).

Blacksburg Electronic Village (2004) "History of the BEV." Blacksburg Electronic Village website at http://www.bev.net/about/history.php (accessed July 11, 2004).

Blanchette, J., and Johnson, D. G. (2002) "Data Retention and the Panoptic Society: The Social Benefits of Forgetfulness." *Information Society* 18 (1), pp. 33–45.

Blaug, R. (1997) "Between Fear and Disappointment: Critical, Empirical and Political Uses of Habermas." *Political Studies* 45 (1), pp. 100–17.

Blevins, J. L. (2002) "Source Diversity after the Telecommunications Act of 1996: Media Oligarchs Begin to Colonize Cyberspace." *Television and New Media* 3 (1), pp. 95–112.

Blumenthal, S. (1980) *The Permanent Campaign: Inside the World of Elite Political Operatives* (Beacon Press, Boston).

Blumler, J. G., and Coleman, S. (2001) *Realizing Democracy Online: A Civic Commons in Cyberspace* (IPPR, London).

Boczkowski, P. J. (2004) "The Processes of Adopting Multimedia and Interactivity in Three Online Newsrooms." *Journal of Communication* 54 (2), pp. 197–213.

Boehlert, E. (2001) "Pay for Play." *Salon.com* website at http://dir.salon.com/ent/feature/2001/03/14/payola/index.html (accessed December 21, 2004).

Boli, J., and Thomas, G. M. (eds.) (1999) *Constructing World Culture: International Non-governmental Organizations since 1875* (Stanford University Press, Stanford, CA).

Bonfadelli, H. (2002) "The Internet and Knowledge Gaps: A Theoretical and Empirical Investigation." *European Journal of Communication* 17 (1), pp. 65–84.

Borins, S. (2004) "A Holistic View of Public Sector Information Technology." *Journal of E-government* 1 (2).

Borland, J. (2005) "Cheers, Jeers for Ruling on Apple Bloggers." March 11, *CNet News* website at http://news.com.com/Cheers,+jeers+for+ruling+on+Apple+bloggers/2100-1030_3-5611908.html (accessed April 17, 2005).

Borsook, P. (2000) *Cyberselfish: A Critical Romp through the Terribly Libertarian World of High-Tech* (Little Brown, New York).

Bouras, C., Katris, N., and Triantafillou, V. (2003) "An Electronic Voting Service to Support Decision-Making in Local Government." *Telematics and Informatics* 20 (3), pp. 255–74.

Boutin, P. (2004) "Net-Savvy Campaign Boosts Bush." June 23, Wired News website at http://www.wired.com/news/politics/0,1283,63942,00.html (accessed July 29, 2004).

Bowden, C., and Akdeniz, Y. (1999) "Privacy II: Cryptography and Democracy." In Liberty (ed.), *Liberating Cyberspace: Civil Liberties, Human Rights and the Internet* (Pluto Press, London), pp. 81–124.

Bowers-Brown, J. (2003) "A Marriage Made in Cyberspace?: Political Marketing and UK Party Websites." In Gibson, R., Nixon, P., and Ward, S. (eds.), *Political Parties and the Internet: Net Gain?* (Routledge, London), pp. 98–119.

Boyd, J. (2002) "In Community We Trust: Online Security Communication at eBay." *Journal of Computer Mediated Communication* 7 (3) at http://www.ascusc.org/jcmc/vol7/issue3/boyd.html (accessed July 28, 2004).

Boyle, J. (1997) "Foucault in Cyberspace: Surveillance, Sovereignty, and Hard-Wired Censors." James Boyle's website at http://www.law.duke.edu/boylesite/foucault.htm (accessed November 28, 2003).

Brady, M. (2000) "The Digital Divide Myth." *E-commerce Times* website at http://www.ecommercetimes.com/story/3953.html (accessed April 18, 2005).

Brainard, L., and Siplon, P. (2002) "Cyberspace Challenges to Mainstream Nonprofit Organizations." *Administration and Society* 34 (2), pp. 141–75.

Braman, S. (2004) "Introduction: The Process of Emergence." In Braman, S. (ed.), *The Emergent Global Information Policy Regime* (Palgrave-Macmillan, Basingstoke, UK), pp. 1–11.

Brants, K., Huizenga, M., and Van Meerten, R. (1996) "The New Canals of Amsterdam: An Exercise in Local Electronic Democracy." *Media, Culture and Society* 18 (2), pp. 233–47.

Braverman, H. (1974) *Labor and Monopoly Capital: The Degradation of Work in the Twentieth Century* (Monthly Review Press, London).

Brown, J. (1998) "MoveOn Moves Offline." *Salon.com* website, at http://archive.salon.com/21st/log/1998/10/27log.html (accessed April 28, 2004).

Browning, G. (1996) *Electronic Democracy: Using the Internet to Influence Politics* (Pemberton Press, Wilton, CT).

Bruening, P. J., and Steffen, M. (2004) "'Spyware': Technologies, Issues and Policy Proposals." *Journal of Internet Law* 7 (9), pp. 3–8.

Bryant, S. (1995) "Electronic Surveillance in the Workplace." *Canadian Journal of Communication* 20 (4), pp. 505–21.

Buckley, J. (2001) "Vote Swapping Online." In Coleman, S. (ed.), *2001: Cyber Space Odyssey: The Internet in the UK Election* (Hansard Society, London), pp. 28–29.

Bucy, E. P., and Gregson, K. S. (2001) "Media Participation: A Legitimizing Mechanism of Mass Democracy." *New Media and Society* 3 (3), pp. 357–80.

Budge, I. (1996) *The New Challenge of Direct Democracy* (Polity, Cambridge).

Burkert, H. (2003) "About a Different Kind of Water: An Attempt at Describing and Understanding Some Elements of the European Union Approach to ICANN." *Loyola of Los Angeles Law Review* 36 (3), pp. 1185–238.

Burrows, R., and Loader, B. (eds.) (1994) *Towards a Post-Fordist Welfare State?* (Routledge, London).

Burstein, P. (1998) "Interest Organizations, Political Parties, and the Study of Democratic Politics." In Costain, A. N., and McFarland, A. S. (eds.), *Social Movements and American Political Institutions* (Rowman and Littlefield, Oxford), pp. 39–56.

Burstein, P., and Linton, A. (2002) "The Impact of Political Parties, Interest Groups, and Social Movement Organizations on Public Policy: Some Recent Evidence and Theoretical Concerns." *Social Forces* 81 (2), pp. 381–408.

Bush-Cheney 2004 (2004) "Party for the President." Bush-Cheney 2004 website at http://www .georgewbush.com/Party (accessed July 29, 2004).

Byrne, L. (1997) *Information Age Government: Delivering the Blair Revolution* (Fabian Society, London).

Cabras, A. (2002) "Beyond the Internet: Democracy on the Phone?" In Mazarr, M. J. (ed.), *Information Technology and World Politics* (Palgrave-Macmillan, Basingstoke, UK), pp. 85–99.

Cain, R. M. (2002) "Global Privacy Concerns and Regulation—Is the United States a World Apart?" *International Review of Law, Computers and Technology* 16 (1), pp. 23–34.

Cairncross, F. (1997) *The Death of Distance: How the Communications Revolution Will Change Our Lives* (Harvard Business School Press, Boston).

Calabrese, A. (2004) "Stealth Regulation: Moral Meltdown and Political Radicalism at the Federal Communications Commission." *New Media and Society* 6 (1), pp. 106–13.

Campbell, C. C., and Dulio, D. A. (2003) "Campaigning along the Information Highway." In Thurber, J. A., and Campbell, C. C. (eds.), *Congress and the Internet* (Prentice Hall, Upper Saddle River, NJ), pp. 11–30.

Canada Department of Foreign Affairs and International Trade (2004) "Canadian International Policy: Policy Discussions." Department of Foreign Affairs and International Trade website at http://www.dfait-maeci.gc.ca/cip-pic/participate/menu-en.asp (accessed November 19, 2004).

Cappella, J. N., and Jamieson, K. H. (1997) *Spiral of Cynicism: The Press and the Public Good* (Oxford University Press, Oxford).

Carvin, A. (2002) "Mind the Gap: The Digital Divide as the Civil Rights Issue of the New Millennium." In Bucy, E. P. (ed.), *Living in the Information Age: A New Media Reader* (Wadsworth-Thomson, London), pp. 251–54.

Casalegno, F. (2001) "On Cybersocialities: Networked Communication and Social Interaction in the Wired City of Blacksburg, VA, USA." *Telematics and Informatics* 18 (1), pp, 17–34.

Castells, M. (2000) *The Rise of the Network Society: The Information Age: Economy, Society and Culture,* vol. 1, 2nd ed. (Blackwell, Oxford).

———— (2004) *The Power of Identity: The Information Age: Economy, Society and Culture,* vol. 2, 2nd ed. (Blackwell, Oxford).

Cavoukian, A. (1998) *Data Mining: Staking a Claim on Your Privacy* (Office of the Information and Privacy Commissioner, Ontario). Also available at http://www.ipc.on.ca/docs/datamine.pdf (accessed October 20, 2004).

Center for Information and Research on Civic Learning and Engagement (CIRCLE) (2004) "Quick Facts—Youth Voting." CIRCLE website at http://www.civicyouth.org/quick/youth_ voting.htm (accessed July 24, 2004).

Chadwick, A. (2001) "The Electronic Face of Government in the Internet Age: Borrowing from Murray Edelman." *Information, Communication and Society* 4 (3), pp. 435–57.

———— (2003) "Bringing E-democracy Back in: Why It Matters for Future Research on E-governance." *Social Science Computer Review* 21 (4), pp. 443–55.

———— (2004) Anonymous interview with senior official, U.S. Environmental Protection Agency (EPA), March 16.

_____ (2005) "The Internet, Political Mobilization and Organizational Hybridity: 'Deanspace,' MoveOn.org and the 2004 US Presidential Campaign." Paper presented to the Political Studies Association of the United Kingdom Annual Conference, University of Leeds, Leeds, April 5–7, 2005, PSA website at http://www.psa.ac.uk/2005/Pdetails.asp?panelid=117 (accessed April 7, 2005).

Chadwick, A., with May, C. (2001) "Interaction between States and Citizens in the Age of the Internet: 'E-government' in the United States, Britain and the European Union." Paper presented to the American Political Science Association Annual Meeting, San Francisco, August–September.

Chadwick, A., and May, C. (2003) "Interaction between States and Citizens in the Age of the Internet: 'E-government' in the United States, Britain and the European Union." *Governance* 16 (2), pp. 271–300.

Chambers, S. (1996) *Reasonable Democracy: Jürgen Habermas and the Politics of Discourse* (Cornell University Press, Ithaca, NY).

Chan-Olmsted, S. M., and Chang, B-H. (2003) "Diversification Strategy of Global Media Conglomerates: Examining Its Patterns and Determinants." *Journal of Media Economics* 16 (4), pp. 213–33.

Charny, B. (2003) "Microsoft Loses £1.58 billion in Telewest Deal." *CNET News* website at http://news.zdnet.co.uk/business/0,39020645,2135358,00.htm (accessed December 21, 2004).

Chayes, A., and Chayes, A. H. (1995) *The New Sovereignty: Compliance with International Regulatory Agreements* (Harvard University Press, London).

Christensen, W., and Suess, R. (1989) "The Birth of the BBS." *Chinet.com* website at http://www.chinet.com/html/cbbs.html (accessed August 14, 2002).

Chroust, P. (2000) "Neo-Nazis and Taliban Online: Anti-modern Political Movements and Modern Media." In Ferdinand, P. (ed.), *The Internet, Democracy and Democratization* (Frank Cass, London), pp. 102–18.

Clark, D., and Zittrain, J. (1997) "On the Issue of Domain Names: Transcript of a Dialogue between Jonathan Zittrain and David Clark." Berkman Center website at http://cyber.law.harvard.edu/jzfallsem/trans/clark (accessed October 1, 2003).

Clark, T. N., and Hoffman-Martinot, V. (eds.) (1998) *The New Political Culture* (Westview Press, Boulder).

Clausing, J. (1999) "Anti-impeachment Website Tallies Millions in Pledges." *New York Times*, January 8. Also available at http://emoglen.law.columbia.edu/CPC/archive/campaigns/move-on-website-gets-pledges.html (accessed April 28, 2004).

Cleaver, H. (1998) "The Zapatista Effect: The Internet and the Rise of an Alternative Political Fabric." *Journal of International Affairs* 51 (2), pp. 621–40.

Coe, A., Paquet, G., and Roy, J. (2001) "E-governance and Smart Communities: A Social Learning Challenge." *Social Science Computer Review* 19 (1), pp. 80–93.

Cogburn, D. L. (2003) "Governing Global Information and Communications Policy: Emergent Regime Formation and the Impact on Africa." *Telecommunications Policy* 27 (1–2), pp. 135–53.

_____ (2004) "Elite Decision-Making and Epistemic Communities: Implications for Global Information Policy." In Braman, S. (ed.), *The Emergent Global Information Policy Regime* (Palgrave-Macmillan, Basingstoke, UK), pp. 154–78.

Coglianese, C. (2004a) "E-rulemaking: Information Technology and Regulatory Policy: Regulatory Policy Program Report RPP-05." Kennedy School of Government website at http://www.ksg.harvard.edu/press/E-Rulemaking_Report.pdf (accessed July 20, 2004).

_____ (2004b) "Information Technology and Regulatory Policy: New Directions for Digital Government Research." *Social Science Computer Review* 22 (1), pp. 85–91.

Cohen, G. A. (1995) *Self-Ownership, Freedom and Equality* (Cambridge University Press, Cambridge).

Cohill, A., and Kavanaugh, A. L. (2000) *Community Networks: Lessons from Blacksburg, Virginia* (Artech House, Norwood, MA).

Coleman, S. (2001) "The 2001 Election Online and the Future of E-politics." In Coleman, S. (ed.), *2001: Cyber Space Odyssey: The Internet in the UK Election* (Hansard Society, London), pp. 1–6.

——— (2004) "Connecting Parliament to the Public via the Internet." *Information, Communication and Society* 7 (1), pp. 1–22.

Coleman, S., and Gøtze, J. (2001) *Bowling Together: Online Public Engagement in Policy Deliberation* (Hansard Society, London).

Coleman, S., and Hall, N. (2001) "Spinning on the Web: E-campaigning and Beyond." In Coleman, S. (ed.), *2001: Cyber Space Odyssey: The Internet in the UK Election* (Hansard Society, London), pp. 7–24.

Collins, R. (2000) "Realizing Social Goals in Connectivity and Content: The Challenge of Convergence." In Marsden, C. T. (ed.), *Regulating the Global Information Society* (Routledge, London), pp. 108–15.

Compaine, B. M. (2001) "Declare the War Won." In Compaine, B. M. (ed.), *The Digital Divide: Facing a Crisis or Creating a Myth?* (MIT Press, Cambridge, MA), pp. 315–35.

Compaine, B. M., and Gomery, D. (2000) *Who Owns the Media?: Competition and Concentration in the Mass Media Industry* 3rd ed. (Lawrence Erlbaum, Mahwah, NJ).

Computer Industry Almanac (2004) Press releases. Computer Industry Almanac website at http://www.c-i-a.com/pr_info.htm (accessed September 4, 2004).

Conley, D. (2003) "Is Activism Dead?" *Newsweek*, June 5. Also available at http://thehacktivist.com/archive/news/2003/IsActivismDead-Newsweek-2003.pdf (accessed May 10, 2004).

Constant, D., Kiesler, S. B., and Sproull, L. S. (1996) "The Kindness of Strangers: The Usefulness of Electronic Networks and New Media in Organizations." *Organization Science* 7 (2), pp. 119–35.

Cooper, J., and Harrison, D. M. (2001) "The Social Organization of Audio Piracy on the Internet." *Media, Culture and Society* 23 (1), pp. 71–89.

Cornfield, M., Rainie, L., and Horrigan, J. B. (2003) *Untuned Keyboards: Online Campaigners, Citizens and Portals in the 2002 Elections* (Pew Internet and American Life Project, Washington, D.C.).

Corrado, A., and Firestone, C. M. (eds.) (1996) *Elections in Cyberspace: Toward a New Era in American Politics: A report of the Aspen Institute Communications and Society Program and the American Bar Association Standing Committee on Election Law* (Aspen Institute, Washington, D.C.).

Creative Commons (2004) Creative Commons website at http://www.creativecommons.org (accessed December 21, 2004).

Crocker, S. (1969) ARPANET Network Working Group Request for Comment 1, April 7, at http://rfc.sunsite.dk/rfc/rfc1.html (accessed July 2, 2002).

Cross, M. (2002) "E-genda for Britain." *The Guardian*, October 24, p. 17.

Cult of the Dead Cow (2004) Hacktivismo website at http://www.hacktivismo.com (accessed June 3, 2004).

Curran, J. (1991) "Mass Media and Democracy: A Reappraisal." In Curran, J., and Gurevitch, M. (eds.), *Mass Media and Society* (Edward Arnold, London), pp. 82–117.

Curtin, G., Sommer, M. H., and Vis-Sommer, V. (eds.) (2004) *The World of E-government* (Haworth Press, New York).

Curtis, T. (2003) "The International Telecommunication Regime in the Information Age." *Prometheus* 21 (4), pp. 399–414.

Dahl, R. (1989) *Democracy and Its Critics* (Yale University Press, New Haven).

Dahlberg, L. (2001a) "Extending the Public Sphere through Cyberspace: The Case of Minnesota E-democracy." *First Monday* 6 (3) at http://firstmonday.org/issues/issue6_3/dahlberg (accessed March 7, 2001).

——— (2001b) "The Internet and Democratic Discourse: Exploring the Prospects of Online Deliberative Forums Extending the Public Sphere." *Information Communication and Society* 4 (1), pp. 615–33.

Dahlgren, P. (2000) "The Internet and the Democratization of Civic Culture." *Political Communication* 17 (4), pp. 335–40.

Bibliography

Dai, X. (2002) "Towards a Digital Economy with Chinese Characteristics?" *New Media and Society* 4 (2), pp. 141–62.

Dalton, R. J. (2000) "The Decline of Party Identifications." In Dalton, R. J., and Wattenberg, M. P. (eds.), *Parties without Partisans: Political Change in Advanced Industrial Democracies* (Oxford University Press, Oxford), pp. 19–36.

Daly, J. A. (2001) "The Information for Development Program: Encouraging the Use of ICTs in Developing Countries." World Bank Information for Development Program website at http://www.infodev.org/library/WorkingPapers/dalywp.pdf (accessed November 26, 2003).

Dandeker, C. (1990) *Surveillance, Power and Modernity: Bureaucracy and Discipline from 1700 to the Present Day* (Polity, Cambridge).

Danziger, J. N., Dutton, W. H., Kling, R., and Kraemer, K. L. (1982) *Computers and Politics: High Technology in American Local Governments* (Columbia University Press, New York).

Davidow, W. H., and Malone, M. S. (1992) *The Virtual Corporation* (HarperBusiness, New York).

Davis, A. (2002) *Public Relations Democracy: Public Relations, Political Communications and the Mass Media in Britain* (Manchester University Press, Manchester).

——— (2003) "Whither Mass Media and Power?: Evidence for a Critical Elite Theory Alternative." *Media, Culture and Society* 25 (5), pp. 669–90.

Davis, K. (2005) "Ending the Abuse." Kevin Davis for Kingston and Surbiton website April 12, at http://kevindavis.blogspot.com/2005/04/ending-abuse.html (accessed April 17, 2005).

Davis, R. (1999) *The Web of Politics: The Internet's Impact on the American Political System* (Oxford University Press, New York).

Dean, K. (2003a) "RIAA Hits Students Where It Hurts." April 5, *Wired News* website at http://www.wired.com/news/digiwood/0,1412,58351,00.html (accessed December 18, 2004).

——— (2003b) "Tis the Season for RIAA Lawsuits." December 3, *Wired News* website at http://www.wired.com/news/digiwood/0,1412,61454,00.html (accessed December 18, 2004).

Dedrick, J., Kraemer, K. L., and Palacios, J. J. (2001) "Impacts of Liberalization and Economic Integration on Mexico's Computer Sector." *Information Society* 17 (2), pp. 119–32.

Deloitte Consulting (2000) *At the Dawn of E-government: The Citizen as Customer* (Deloitte, New York).

Dewey, J. (1927) *The Public and Its Problems: Lectures Delivered for the Larwill Foundation* (George Allen and Unwin, London).

Diani, M. (2000) "Social Movement Networks: Virtual and Real." *Information, Communication and Society* 3 (3), pp. 386–401.

DiMaggio, P. J., and Powell, W. W. (1983) "The Iron Cage Revisited: Institutional Isomorphism and Collective Rationality in Organizational Fields." *American Sociological Review* 48 (2), pp. 147–60.

Docter, S., and Dutton, W. H. (1998) "The First Amendment Online: Santa Monica's Public Electronic Network." In Tsagarousianou, R., Tambini, D., and Bryan, C. (eds.), *Cyberdemocracy: Technology, Cities and Civic Networks* (Routledge, London), pp. 125–51.

Dodson, S. (2005) "All Wired Up." *The Guardian*, March 3. Also available at http://www.guardian.co.uk/online/story/0,3605,1428626,00.html (accessed March 3, 2005).

Dodson, S., and Hammersley, B. (2003) "The Web's Candidate for President." *The Guardian*, December 18. Also available at http://www.guardian.co.uk/online/story/0,3605,1109026,00.html (accessed July 29, 2004).

Doheny-Farina, S. (1996) *The Wired Neighborhood* (Yale University Press, New Haven).

Dorling, D., Eyre, H., Johnston, R., and Pattie, C. (2002) "A Good Place to Bury Bad News? Hiding the Detail in the Geography on the Labor Party's Website." *Political Quarterly* 73 (4), pp. 476–92.

Dorroh, J. (2004) "Knocking Down the Stonewall." *American Journalism Review* December/January. Also available at http://www.ajr.org/index.asp?artType=2 (accessed December 6, 2004).

Downing, J. D. H. (2003) "The Independent Media Center Movement and the Anarchist Socialist Tradition." In Couldry, N., and Curran, J. (eds.) (2003) *Contesting Media Power: Alternative Media in a Networked World* (Rowman and Littlefield, Oxford), pp. 243–57.

Downs, A. (1957) *An Economic Theory of Democracy* (Harper and Row, New York).

• 335 •

Drahos, P., with Braithwaite, J. (2002) *Information Feudalism: Who Owns the Knowledge Economy?* (Earthscan, London).

Drake, D. B. (2004) "Information Sharing in and across Government Agencies: The Role and Influence of Scientist, Politician and Bureaucrat Subcultures." *Social Science Computer Review* 22 (1), pp. 67–84.

Drake, W. J. (2000) "The Rise and Decline of the International Telecommunications Regime." In Marsden, C. T. (ed.), *Regulating the Global Information Society* (Routledge, London), pp. 124–77.

Drezner, D. W., and Farrell, H. (2004) "The Power and Politics of Blogs." Paper presented to the American Political Science Association Annual Meeting, Chicago, August–September.

Drori, G. S., and Jang, Y. S. (2003) "The Global Digital Divide: A Sociological Assessment of Trends and Causes." *Social Science Computer Review* 21 (2), pp. 144–61.

Drucker, P. F. (1988) "The Coming of the New Organization." *Harvard Business Review* 66 (1), pp. 45–53.

———— (1993) *Post-capitalist Society* (HarperBusiness, New York).

Ducheneaut, N. B. (2002) "The Social Impacts of Electronic Mail in Organizations: A Case Study of Power Games Using Communication Genres." *Information, Communication and Society* 5 (2), pp. 153–88.

Dueze, M. (2003) "The Web and Its Journalisms: Considering the Consequences of Different Types of Newsmedia Online." *New Media and Society* 5 (2), pp. 203–30.

Dutton, W. H. (1992) "Political Science Research on Teledemocracy." *Social Science Computer Review*, 10 (4), pp. 505–22.

———— (1999) *Society on the Line: Information Politics in the Digital Age* (Oxford University Press, Oxford).

Dutton, W. H., Blumler, J. G., Garnham, N., Mansell, R., Cornford, J., and Peltu, M. (1995) "The Politics of Information and Communication Policy." In Dutton, W. H. (ed.), *Information and Communication Technologies: Visions and Realities* (Oxford University Press, Oxford), pp. 387–405.

Dutton, W. H., and Guthrie, K. (1991) "An Ecology of Games: The Political Construction of Santa Monica's Public Electronic Network." *Informatization and the Public Sector* 1 (4), pp. 1–24.

Duverger, M. (1954) *Political Parties: Their Organization and Activity in the Modern State* (Methuen, London).

Dwyer, P., Hof, R. D., Kerstetter, J., and Vickers, M. (2004) "The Amazing Money Machine." August 2, *BusinessWeek* website at http://www.businessweek.com/magazine/content/04_31/b3894011_mz001.htm (accessed August 2, 2004).

Dyer-Witheford, N. (2002) "E-capital and the Many-Headed Hydra." In Elmer, G. (ed.), *Critical Perspectives on the Internet* (Rowman and Littlefield, Oxford), pp. 129–63.

EDS and Neaman Bond Associates (2002) *The E-state of the Nations* (EDS/Neaman Bond, London).

Election.com (2003) "Results of ICANN 2000 At-Large Membership Vote." Election.com website at http://www.election.com/us/icann/icannresult.html (accessed November 21, 2003).

Electronic Frontier Foundation (EFF) (2004) "Total/Terrorism Information Awareness (TIA): Is It Truly Dead?" EFF website at http://www.eff.org/Privacy/TIA/20031003_comments.php (accessed October 20, 2004).

Eley, G. (1992) "Nations, Publics and Political Cultures: Placing Habermas in the Nineteenth Century." In Calhoun, C. (ed.), *Habermas and the Public Sphere* (MIT Press, Cambridge, MA), pp. 289–339.

Elledge, J. (2003) "South Korea Takes E-campaigning to New Heights: How Young Voters Used Keyboards and Keypads to Make Their Voices Heard." PoliticsOnline NetPulse website at http://netpulse.politicsonline.com/soundoff.asp?issue_id=7.01 (accessed August 1, 2004).

Ellul, J. (1964) *The Technological Society* (Knopf, New York).

Elmer, G. (2003) "A Diagram of Panoptic Surveillance." *New Media and Society* 5 (2), pp. 231–47.

Ennis Information Age Town (2004) Ennis Community website at http://www.ennis.ie (accessed July 11, 2004).

Epstein, J. E. (2000) *News from Nowhere: Television and the News* (Ivan R. Dee, Chicago).

Esser, F., Reinemann, C., and Fan, D. (2001) "Spin Doctors in the United States, Great Britain, and Germany: Metacommunication about Media Manipulation." *Press/Politics* 6 (1), pp. 16–45.

Etzioni, A. (ed.) (1995) *New Communitarian Thinking: Persons, Virtues, Institutions and Communities* (University Press of Virginia, London).

Etzioni, A., Laudon, K. C., and Lipson, S. (1975) "Participatory Technology: The Minerva Communications Tree." *Journal of Communications* (summer), pp. 64–74.

European Commission (1999) *E-Europe: An Information Society for All* (European Commission, Brussels). Also available at http://europa.eu.int/combm/information_society/eeurope/index_en.htm (accessed December 23, 1999).

————— (2003) "About This Site." EU Information Society website at http://europa.eu.int/information_society/basics/aboutus/index_en.htm (accessed November 26, 2003).

————— (2004) "Commission Concludes on Microsoft Investigation, Imposes Conduct Remedies and a Fine." Press release, March 24, European Commission website at http://europa.eu.int/rapid/pressReleasesAction.do?reference=IP/04/382&format=HTML&aged=1&language=EN&guiLanguage=en (accessed December 22, 2004)

European Council (1994) *Europe and the Global Information Society. Recommendations to the European Council* (European Commission, Brussels). Also available at http://www.ispo.cec.be/ida/text/english/bangemann.html (accessed November 11, 2000).

European Union (2002) "Directive on Privacy and Electronic Communications" (2002/58/EC). European Union website at http://europa.eu.int/eur-lex/pri/en/oj/dat/2002/l_201/l_20120020731en00370047.pdf (accessed October 28, 2004).

Farrell, D., Kolodny, R., and Medvic, S. (2001) "Parties and Campaign Professionals in a Digital Age: Political Consultants in the United States and Their Counterparts Overseas." *Press/Politics* 6 (4), pp. 11–30.

Feenberg, A. (1999) *Questioning Technology* (Routledge, London).

Ferlander, S. (2003) "The Internet, Social Capital and Community." PhD diss., University of Stirling, University of Stirling website at http://www.crdlt.stir.ac.uk/Docs/SaraFerlanderPhD.pdf (accessed July 12, 2004).

Ferlander, S., and Timms, D. (2001) "Local Nets and Social Capital." *Telematics and Informatics* 18 (1), pp. 51–65.

Fernie, S., and Metcalf, D. (1998) *(Not) Hanging on the Telephone: Payments Systems in the New Sweatshops* (Centre for Economic Performance, London School of Economics, London). Also available at http://cep.lse.ac.uk/pubs/download/dp0390.pdf (accessed July 5, 2004).

Fielding, N. (2004) "Al Qaeda Betrayed by Its Simple Faith in High-Tech." *Sunday Times*, August 8, pp. 14–15.

FirstGov (2000) "Electronic Transactions Offered by US Government Agencies." Firstgov website at http://firstgov.gov/featured/transact.html (accessed October 3, 2000).

Fishkin, J. S. (1991) *Democracy and Deliberation: New Directions for Democratic Reform* (Yale University Press, London).

Fitzpatrick, T. (2002) "Critical Theory, Information Society and Surveillance Technologies." *Information, Communication and Society* 5 (3), pp. 357–78.

Flew, T., and McElhinney, S. (2001) "Globalization and the Structure of New Media Industries." In Lievrouw, L. A., and Livingstone, S. (eds.), *The Handbook of New Media* (Sage, London), pp. 304–19.

Foley, M. W., and Edwards, B. (1999) "Is It Time to Disinvest in Social Capital?" *Journal of Public Policy* 19 (2), pp. 141–73.

Foot, K. A., Schneider, S. M., Dougherty, M., Xenos, M., and Larsen, E. (2003) "Analyzing Linking Practices: Candidate Sites in the 2002 US Electoral Web Sphere." *Journal of Computer-Mediated Communciation* 8 (4) at http://www.ascusc.org/jcmc/vol8/issue4/foot.html (accessed May 20, 2004).

Ford, J. (2003) *A Social Theory of the World Trade Organization: Trading Cultures* (Palgrave-Macmillan, Basingstoke, UK).

Fortner, R. S. (1995) "Excommunication in the Information Society." *Critical Studies in Mass Communication* 12 (2), pp. 133–54.

Foucault, M. (1977) *Discipline and Punish: The Birth of the Prison* (Allen Lane, London).

Fountain, J. E. (2001) *Building the Virtual State: Information Technology and Institutional Change* (The Brookings Institution, New York).

Fountain, J. E., with Osorio-Urzua, C. (2001) "Public Sector: Early Stage of a Deep Transformation." In Litan, R. E., and Rivlin, A. M. (eds.), *The Economic Payoff from the Internet Revolution* (The Brookings Institution, New York), pp. 235–68.

Frank, D. (2002) "E-gov XML Committee Formed." *Federal Computer Week*, December 6. Also available at http://www.fcw.com/fcw/articles/2002/1202/web-xml-12-06-02.asp (accessed February 4, 2004).

Frankel, T. (2002) *Accountability and Oversight of ICANN: Report to the Markle Foundation* (Markle Foundation, 2002). Also available at http://www.markle.org/news/ICANN_fin1_9.pdf (accessed November 21, 2003).

Franklin, B. (2004) *Packaging Politics: Political Communications in Britain's Media Democracy,* 2nd ed. (Arnold, London).

Frantzich, S. E. (2003) "RepresNETation: Congress and the Internet." In Thurber, J. A., and Campbell, C. C. (eds.), *Congress and the Internet* (Prentice Hall, Upper Saddle River, NJ), pp. 31–51.

Fraser, N. (1992) "Rethinking the Public Sphere: A Contribution to the Critique of Actually Existing Democracy." in Calhoun, C. (ed.), *Habermas and the Public Sphere* (MIT Press, Cambridge, MA).

Friedland, L. A. (2001) "Communication, Community and Democracy: Toward a Theory of the Communicatively Integrated Community." *Communication Research* 28 (4), pp. 358–91.

Friedrich, C. J., and Brzezinski, Z. K. (1965) *Totalitarian Dictatorship and Autocracy,* 2nd ed. (Harvard University Press, Cambridge, MA).

Froomkin, A. M. (2003) "Habermas@Discourse.net: Toward a Critical Theory of Cyberspace." *Harvard Law Review* 116 (3), pp. 749–873.

Fulk, J., and DeSanctis, G. (1995) "Electronic Communication and Changing Organizational Forms." *Organization Science* 6 (4), pp. 1–13.

G8 Digital Opportunity Task Force (G8 DOT Force) (2002a) "Global Policy-Making for Information and Communications Technologies: Enabling Meaningful Participation by Developing-Nation Stakeholders." Markle Foundation website at http://www.markle.org/globalpolicy/assets/roadmap_report.pdf (accessed November 26, 2003).

———— (2002b) "Report Card: Digital Opportunities for All." G8 DOT Force website at http://www.dotforce.org/reports/DOT_Force_Report_V_5.0h.pdf (accessed November 26, 2003).

Gamson, J. (2003) "Gay Media Inc.: Media Structures, the New Gay Conglomerates and Collective Sexual Identities." In McCaughey, M., and Ayers, M. D. (eds.). *Cyberactivism: Online Activism in Theory and Practice* (Routledge, London), pp. 255–78.

Gandy, O. H. (1993) *The Panoptic Sort: A Political Economy of Personal Information* (Westview, Oxford).

———— (2000) "Exploring Identity and Identification in Cyberspace." *Notre Dame Journal of Law, Ethics and Public Policy* 14, pp. 1085–111.

———— (2002) "The Real Digital Divide: Citizens versus Consumers." In Lievrouw, L. A., and Livingstone, S. (eds.), *The Handbook of New Media* (Sage, London), pp. 448–60.

———— (2003) "Data Mining and Surveillance in the Post-9/11 Environment." In Ball, K., and Webster, F. (eds.), *The Intensification of Surveillance: Crime, Terrorism and Warfare in the Information Age* (Pluto Press, London), pp. 26–41.

Garnham, N. (1990) *Capitalism and Communication: Global Culture and the Economics of Information* (Sage, London).

Garrido, M., and Halavais, A. (2003) "Mapping Networks of Support for the Zapatista Movement: Applying Social-Networks Analysis to Study Contemporary Social Movements." In McCaughey, M., and Ayers, M. D. (eds.), *Cyberactivism: Online Activism in Theory and Practice* (Routledge, London), pp. 165–84.

Garson, G. D. (ed.) (1999) *Information Technology and Computer Applications in Public Administration: Issues and Trends* (Idea Group, Harrisburg, PA).

Gates, B. (2000) "Speech to the Digital Dividends Conference," Seattle, October 18. Available at http://www.microsoft.com/billgates/speeches/2000/10-18digitaldividends.asp (accessed September 15, 2004).

Gershuny, J. (2003) "Web Use and Net Nerds: A Neofunctionalist Analysis of the Impact of Information Technology in the Home." *Social Forces* 82 (1), pp. 141–68.

Gibbs, J., Kraemer, K. L., and Dedrick, J. (2003) "Environment and Policy Factors Shaping Global E-commerce Diffusion: A Cross-Country Comparison." *Information Society* 19 (1), pp. 5–18.

Gibson, R. K., Margolis, M., Resnick, D., and Ward, S. J. (2003) "Election Campaigning on the WWW in the USA and the UK." *Party Politics* 9 (1), pp. 47–75.

Gibson, R. K., Nixon, P., and Ward, S. (eds.) *Political Parties and the Internet: Net Gain?* (Routledge, London).

Gibson, R. K., and Ward, S. (1998) "UK Political Parties and the Internet: 'Politics as Usual' in the New Media?" *Press/Politics* 3 (3) pp. 14–38.

Gibson, W. (1999) "The Science in Science Fiction." Interview on National Public Radio, November 30. Also available at http://www.npr.org/templates/story/story.php?storyId= 1067220 (accessed April 2, 2005).

Giddens, A. (1985) *Contemporary Critique of Historical Materialism*, vol. 2, *The Nation-State and Violence* (Polity, London).

––––––– (1991) *Modernity and Self-Identity: Self and Society in the Late Modern Age* (Polity, Cambridge).

Giese, K. (2003) "Internet Growth and the Digital Divide: Implications for Spatial Development." In Hughes, C. R., and Wacker, G. (eds.) *China and the Internet: Politics of the Digital Leap Forward* (RoutledgeCurzon, London), pp. 30–57.

Gillies, J., and Cailliau, R. (2000) *How the Web Was Born: The Story of the World Wide Web* (Oxford University Press, Oxford).

Gillmor, D. (2004) *We the Media: Grassroots Journalism, By the People, for the People* (O'Reilly, Cambridge).

Gitlin, T. (1994) *Inside Prime Time,* 2nd ed. (Routledge, London).

Glave, J. (1999) "Ku Klux Klan Korrected." September 10, *Wired News* website at http://www .wired.com/news/culture/0,1284,21687,00.html (accessed May 10, 2004).

Global Business Dialogue on Electronic Commerce (GBDE) (2004) "Membership." GBDE website at http://www.gbde.org/members.html (accessed August 20, 2004).

Global Information Infrastructure Commission (GIIC) (2004) "About the GIIC." GIIC website at http://www.giic.org/about (accessed February 5, 2004).

GNU Project–Free Software Foundation (2003) Copyleft website at http://www.gnu.org/copyleft (accessed April 9, 2003).

Godwin, M. (2003) *Cyber Rights: Defending Free Speech in the Digital Age,* rev. ed. (MIT Press, Cambridge, MA).

Golding, P., and Murdock, G. (1991) "Culture, Communications and Political Economy." In Curran, J., and Gurevitch, M. (eds.), *Mass Media and Society* (Edward Arnold, London), pp. 15–32.

Goldman, A. (2004) "Top US ISPs by Subscriber: Q3 2004." Jupiter Research/Internet.com website at http://www.isp-planet.com/research/rankings/usa.html (accessed November 25, 2004).

Goldsmith, J. (1998) "Against Cyberanarchy." *University of Chicago Law Review* 65 (4). Also available at http://cyber.law.harvard.edu/property00/jurisdiction/cyberanarchy.html (accessed December 1, 2003).

Goldstein, P. (2003) *Copyright's Highway: From Gutenberg to the Celestial Jukebox,* rev. ed. (Stanford University Press, Stanford, CA).

Goodwin, I., and Spittle, S. (2002) "The European Union and the Information Society: Discourse, Power and Policy." *New Media and Society* 4 (2), pp. 225–49.

GoSkokie.com (2004) GoSkokie.com website at http://www.goskokie.com (accessed December 21, 2004).

Gould, M. (2000) "Locating Internet Governance: Lessons from the Standards Process." In Marsden, C. T. (ed.), *Regulating the Global Information Society* (Routledge, London), pp. 193–210.

Government Electronics and Information Technology Association (GEIA) (2002) *13th Annual Five-Year Forecast of the Federal Information Technology Market and Opportunities* (GEIA, Washington, D.C.).

Graber, D. (2001) *Processing Politics: Learning from Television in the Internet Age* (University of Chicago Press, Chicago).

Grafton, C. (2003) "'Shadow Theories' in Fountain's Theory of Technology Enactment." *Social Science Computer Review* 21 (4), pp. 411–16.

Granovetter, M. S. (1973) "The Strength of Weak Ties." *American Journal of Sociology* 78 (6), pp. 1360–80.

——— (1978) "Threshold Models of Collective Behavior." *American Journal of Sociology* 83 (6), pp. 1420–43.

Greenleaf, W. H. (1983) *The British Political Tradition, vol. 2, The Ideological Heritage* (Methuen, London).

Greenwood, L. (2001) "Loss-Making Yahoo Mulls Lay-Offs." *BBC News Online* website October 10 at http://news.bbc.co.uk/1/hi/business/1592341.stm (accessed June 29, 2004).

Greider, W. B. (1992) *Who Will Tell The People? The Betrayal of American Democracy* (Simon and Schuster, New York).

Grossman, L. K. (1995) *The Electronic Republic: Reshaping Democracy in the Information Age* (Penguin, London).

Guillén, M. F., and Suárez, S. L. (2001) "Developing the Internet: Entrepreneurship and Public Policy in Ireland, Singapore, Argentina and Spain." *Telecommunications Policy* 25 (5), pp. 349–71.

Gunther, R., and Diamond, L. (2003) "Species of Political Parties: A New Typology." *Party Politics* 9 (2), pp. 167–99.

Gurak, L. J. (1997) *Persuasion and Privacy in Cyberspace: The Online Protests over Lotus Market-Place and the Clipper Chip* (Yale University Press, New Haven).

——— (1999) "The Promise and the Peril of Social Action in Cyberspace: Ethos, Delivery and the Protests over MarketPlace and the Clipper Chip." In Smith, M. A., and Kollock, P. (eds.), *Communities in Cyberspace* (Routledge, London), pp. 243–63.

Gurak, L. J., and Logie, J. (2003) "Internet Protests, from Text to Web." In McCaughey, M., and Ayers, M. D. (eds.), *Cyberactivism: Online Activism in Theory and Practice* (Routledge, London), pp. 25–46.

Haas, P. M. (1992) "Introduction: Epistemic Communities and International Policy Co-ordination." *International Organization* 46 (1), pp. 1–35.

——— (2002) "UN Conferences and the Constructivist Governance of the Environment." *Global Governance* 8 (1), pp. 73–91.

Habermas, J. ([1962], 1989) *The Structural Transformation of the Public Sphere* (Polity, Cambridge).

Hacker, K. L. (1996) "The Role of the Clinton Whitehouse in Facilitating Electronic Democratization and Political Interactivity." Paper presented to the Political Communication division of the Speech Communication Association, November. Available at http://web.nmsu.edu/~comstudy/pc1.htm (accessed June 20, 2001).

Hacker, K. L., and Van Dijk, J. (2000) "What Is Digital Democracy?" In Hacker, K. L., and Van Dijk, J. (eds.), *Digital Democracy: Issues of Theory and Practice* (Sage, London), pp. 1–9.

Hafner, K., and Lyon, M. (1996) *Where Wizards Stay Up Late: The Origins of the Internet* (Simon and Schuster, New York).

Haggerty, K. D., and Ericson, R. V. (2000) "The Surveillant Assemblage." *British Journal of Sociology* 51 (4), pp. 605–22.

Hall, R. B., and Biersteker, T. J. (2002) "The Emergence of Private Authority in the International System." In Hall, R. B., and Biersteker, T. J. (eds.), *The Emergence of Private Authority in Global Governance* (Cambridge University Press, Cambridge), pp. 3–22.

Hallin, D. C. (2000) "Commercialism and Professionalism in the American News Media." In Curran, J., and Gurevitch, M. (eds.), *Mass Media and Society,* 3rd ed. (Arnold, London), pp. 218–37.

Hammer, M., and Champy, J. (1993) *Reengineering the Corporation* (HarperCollins, New York).

Hampton, K. N. (2003) "Grieving for a Lost Network: Collective Action in a Wired Suburb." *Information Society* 19 (5), pp. 417–28.

Hansard Society (2000) *Women Discuss: Parliamentary Domestic Violence Internet Consultation* (Hansard Society, London).

——— (2003) "E-democracy Program." Hansard Society website at http://www.hansard-society .org.uk/edemocracy.htm (accessed April 3, 2003).

——— (2004) *Political Blogs: Craze or Convention?* (Hansard Society, London).

Hardy, I. (2004) "Web Campaigning." *BBC World News* website July 1 at http://bbcworld.com/ content/clickonline_archive_26_2004.asp?pageid=666&co_pageid=3 (accessed July 30, 2004).

Hargittai, E. (1999) "Weaving the Western Web: Explaining Differences in Internet Connectivity Among OECD Countries." *Telecommunications Policy* 23 (10–11), pp. 701–18.

Harrison, A. (2004) "Onion Routing Averts Prying Eyes." *Wired News* website August 5, at http://www.wired.com/news/privacy/0,1848,64464,00.html (accessed October 15, 2004).

Hart, J. A., and Kim, S. (2002) "Explaining the Resurgence of US Competitiveness: The Rise of Wintelism." *Information Society* 18 (1), pp. 1–12.

Hauben, M., and Hauben, R. (1997) *Netizens: On the History and Impact of Usenet and the Internet* (IEEE Computer Society Press, Los Alamitos, CA). Also available at http://www.columbia .edu/~hauben/netbook/index.html (accessed July 1, 2002).

Hayek, F. A. (1944) *The Road to Serfdom* (Routledge and Kegan Paul, London).

Haythornthwaite, C. (2002) "Strong, Weak, and Latent Ties and the Impact of New Media." *Information Society* 18 (5), pp. 385–401.

Heckscher, C., and Donnellon, A. (eds.) (1994) *The Post-bureaucratic Organization: New Perspectives on Organizational Change* (Sage, Thousand Oaks, CA).

Heclo, H. (2000) "Campaigning and Governing: A Conspectus." In Ornstein, N., and Mann, T. (eds.), *The Permanent Campaign and Its Future* (The Brookings Institution, Washington, D.C.), pp. 1–37.

Heeks, R. (2002) "E-government in Africa: Promise and Practice." *Information Polity* 7 (2–3), pp. 97–114.

Heffernan, R., and Stanyer, J. (1998) "The Enhancement of Leadership Power: The Labor Party and the Impact of Political Communications." In Pattie, C., Denver, D., Fisher, J., and Ludlam, S. (eds.), *British Elections and Parties Review, vol. 7* (Frank Cass, London), pp. 168–84.

Held, D., and McGrew, A. (eds.) (2002) *Governing Globalization: Power, Authority and Global Governance* (Polity, Cambridge).

Held, D., McGrew, A., Goldblatt, D., and Perraton, J. (1999) *Global Transformations: Politics, Economics and Culture* (Polity, Cambridge).

Helmers, C. T. (1975) "What Is Byte?" *Byte* 1, September, pp. 4–6. Also available at http://www. digibarn.com/collections/mags/byte-sept-oct-1975/one/index.html (accessed August 6, 2002).

Henman, P. (1996) "Does Computerization Save Governments Money?" *Information Infrastructure and Policy* 5 (4), pp. 95–106.

Herbst, S. (1994) *Politics at the Margin: Historical Studies of Public Expression outside the Mainstream* (Cambridge University Press, Cambridge).

Herman, E. S. (1986) "Gatekeeper vs Propaganda Models: A Critical American Perspective." In Golding, P., Murdock, G., and Schlesinger, P. (eds.) *Communicating Politics: Mass Communications and the Political Process* (Holmes & Meier, New York).

Herman, E. S., and Chomsky, N. (2002) *Manufacturing Consent: The Political Economy of Mass Media,* 2nd ed. (Pantheon, New York).

Herring, S., Job-Sluder, K., Sheckler, R., and Barab, S. (2002) "Searching for Safety Online: Managing 'Trolling' in a Feminist Forum." *Information Society* 18 (5), pp. 371–84.

Hervé-Van Driessche, K. (2001) "Parthenay, the Digital Town: Myth or Reality." *Telematics and Informatics* 18 (1), pp. 5–15.

Heywood, A. (2002) *Politics,* 2nd ed. (Palgrave, Basingstoke, UK).

Hickey, R. (2004) "Onward Deaniacs." TomPaine.com website at http://www.tompaine.com/feature2.cfm/ID/10111 (accessed June 8, 2004).

Hill, K. A., and Hughes, J. E. (1998) *Cyberpolitics: Citizen Activism in the Age of the Internet* (Rowman and Littlefield, London).

Himmelweit, H., Humphreys, P., and Jaeger, M. (1985) *How Voters Decide: A Model of Vote Choice Based on a Special Longitudinal Study Extending over Fifteen Years and the British Election Surveys of 1970–1983, 2nd ed.* (Open University Press, Milton Keynes).

Hirst, P. (ed.) (1989) *The Pluralist Theory of the State: Selected Writings of G. D. H. Cole, J. N. Figgis and H. J. Laski* (Routledge, London).

Hirst, P., and Thompson, G. (1999) *Globalization in Question,* 2nd ed. (Polity, Cambridge).

Hollander, R. (1985) *Video Democracy: The Vote-from-Home Revolution* (Lomond Press, Mt. Airy, MD).

Holmes, D. (2001) *Egov: Ebusiness Strategies for Government* (Nicholas Brealey, London).

Hood, C., Scott, C., James, O., Jones, G., and Travers, T. (1999) *Regulation inside Government: Waste Watchers, Quality Police and Sleaze-Busters* (Oxford University Press, Oxford).

Horrigan, J. B. (2004) "Pew Internet Project Data Memo: 55 per cent of Adult Internet Users Have Broadband at Home or Work." Pew Internet and American Life Project website at http://www.pewinternet.org/pdfs/PIP_Broadband04.DataMemo.pdf (accessed September 16, 2004).

Horrigan, J. B., and Rainie, L. (2002) *The Broadband Difference: How Online Americans' Behavior Changes with High-Speed Internet Connections at Home* (Pew Internet and American Life Project, Washington, D.C.). Also available at http://www.pewinternet.org/pdfs/PIP_Broadband_Report.pdf (accessed September 16, 2004).

Horrigan, J. B., Rainie, L., and Fox, S. (2001) "Online Communities: Networks That Nurture Long-Distance Relationships and Local Ties." Pew Internet and American Life Project website at http://www.pewinternet.org/pdfs/PIP_Communities_Report.pdf (accessed July 7, 2004).

Howard, P. N. (2003) "Digitizing the Social Contract: Producing American Political Culture in the Age of New Media." *Communication Review* 6 (3), pp. 213–45.

Howard, P. N., and Milstein, T. J. (2003) "Spiders, Spam and Spyware: New Media and the Market for Political Information." In Consalvo, M. (ed.), *Internet Studies 1.0,* available at Dr Philip N. Howard's website, Department of Communication, University of Washington, http://faculty.washington.edu/pnhoward/publishing/articles/howardmilstein.pdf (accessed October 3, 2004).

Howcroft, D. (2001) "After the Goldrush: Deconstructing the Myths of the Dotcom Market." *Journal of Information Technology* 16 (4), pp. 195–204.

Hughes, C. R. (2002) "China and the Globalization of ICTs: Implications for International Relations." *New Media and Society* 4 (2), pp. 205–24.

Hummel, R. P. (1977) *The Bureaucratic Experience* (St. Martin's Press, New York).

Hunter, D. (2003) "ICANN and the Concept of Democratic Deficit." *Loyola of Los Angeles Law Review* 36 (3), pp. 1149–83.

Hunter, R. (2002) *World without Secrets: Business, Crime and Privacy in the Age of Ubiquitous Computing* (John Wiley and Sons, New York).

Indymedia.org (2004) Indymedia.org website at http://www.indymedia.org (accessed May 6, 2004).

Inglehart, R. (1997) *Modernization and Postmodernization: Cultural, Economic and Political Change in Forty-three Societies* (Princeton University Press, Princeton).

——— (1999) "Postmodernization Erodes Respect for Authority, but Increases Support for Democracy." In Norris, P. (ed.), *Critical Citizens: Global Support for Democratic Governance* (Oxford University Press, Oxford), pp. 236–56.

Innis, H. A. (1951) *The Bias of Communication* (University of Toronto Press, London).

Internet Corporation for Assigned Names and Numbers (ICANN) (2001) "ICP-3: A Unique, Authoritative Root for the DNS." ICANN website at http://www.icann.org/icp/icp-3.htm (accessed November 26, 2004).

International Institute for Democracy and Electoral Assistance (IDEA) (2004) "Voter Turnout: United States." IDEA website at http://www.idea.int/vt/country_view.cfm (accessed July 24, 2004).

International Telecommunication Union (ITU) (2003a) "ITU Digital Access Index: World's First Global ICT Ranking." ITU website at http://www.itu.int/newsarchive/press_releases/2003/30.html (accessed September 9, 2004).

———— (2003b) "ITU Overview—History." ITU website at http://www.itu.int/aboutitu/overview/history.html (accessed November 17, 2003).

———— (2003c) "ITU Overview—Purposes." ITU website at http://www.itu.int/aboutitu/overview/purposes.html (accessed November 17, 2003).

———— (2003d) "World Indicators—Television." ITU website at http://www.itu.int/itunews/issue/2002/04/table4tv.html (accessed November 13, 2003).

———— (2004a) "ITU Internet Indicators." ITU website at http://www.itu.int/ITU-D/ict/statistics (accessed September 7, 2004).

———— (2004b) *Yearbook of Statistics: Telecommunication Services Chronological Time Series, 1993–2002* (ITU, Geneva).

———— (2005) "Key Global Telecom Indicators for the World Telecommunication Service Sector." ITU website at http://www.itu.int/ITU-D/ict/statistics/at_glance/KeyTelecom99.html (accessed April 26, 2005).

Internet Systems Consortium (2005) Domain survey. Internet Systems Consortium website at http://www.isc.org/index.pl?/ops/ds (accessed April 25, 2005).

Jackson, N. (2004) "Email and Political Campaigning: The Experience of MPs in Westminster." *Journal of Systemics, Cybernetics and Informatics* 2 (5), pp. 1–6.

Jaeger, P. T. (2003) "The Endless Wire: E-government as a Global Phenomenon." *Government Information Quarterly* 20 (4), pp. 323–31.

Jaeger, P. T., and McClure, C. R. (2004) "Potential Legal Challenges to the Application of the Children's Internet Protection Act (CIPA) in Public Libraries: Strategies and Issues." *First Monday* 9 (2) at http://firstmonday.org/issues/issue9_2/jaeger (accessed October 27, 2004).

James, O. (2003) *The Executive Agency Revolution in Whitehall: Public Interest versus Bureau-Shaping Perspectives* (Palgrave-Macmillan, Basingstoke, UK).

Jensen, J. L. (2003) "Virtual Democratic Dialogue: Bringing Together Citizens and Politicians." *Information Polity* 8 (1–2), pp. 29–47.

Johnson, D. R., and Post, D. G. (1996) "Law and Borders: The Rise of Law in Cyberspace." *Stanford Law Review* 48. Also available at http://www.temple.edu/lawschool/dpost/Borders.html (accessed October 18, 2003).

Johnson, T. J., and Kaye, B. K. (2003) "A Boost or Bust for Democracy? How the Web Influenced Political Attitudes and Behaviors in the 1996 and 2000 Presidential Elections." *Press/Politics* 8 (3), pp. 9–34.

Jones, A. (1994) "Wired World: Communications Technology, Governance and the Democratic Uprising." In Comor, E. (ed.), *The Global Political Economy of Communication: Hegemony, Telecommunication and the Information Economy* (Macmillan, Basingstoke, UK).

Jordan, G. (1998) "Politics without Parties." *Parliamentary Affairs* 51 (3), pp. 314–28.

Jordan, T. (2001) "Language and Libertarianism: The Politics of Cyberculture and the Culture of Cyberpolitics." *Sociological Review* 49 (1) pp. 1–17.

Jordan, T., and Taylor, P. (2004) *Hacktivism and Cyberwars: Rebels with a Cause?* (Routledge, London).

Jung, J., Qiu, J. L., and Kim, Y. (2001) "Internet Connectedness and Inequality: Beyond the 'Divide.'" *Communication Research* 28 (4), pp. 507–35.

Justice, G. (2004a) "Clicking into the Kerry Coffers for a One-Day Online Record." *New York Times,* July 2. Also available at http://www.nytimes.com/2004/07/02/politics/campaign/02donate.html?ex=1246593600&en=379352858367d47d&ei=5090&partner=rssuserland (accessed July 30, 2004).

—— (2004b) "Fund-Raising: Kerry Kept Money Coming with the Internet as His ATM." *New York Times*, November 6. Also available at http://www.nytimes.com/2004/11/06/politics/campaign/06internet.html?ex=1100760171&ei=1&en=feeca50af99bab47 (accessed November 7, 2004).

Kahn, R., and Kellner, D. (2004) "New Media and Internet Activism: From the Battle of Seattle to Blogging." *New Media and Society* 6 (1), pp. 87–95.

Kaitatzi-Whitlock, S. (2000) "A 'Redundant Information Society' for the European Union?" *Telematics and Informatics* 17 (1–2), pp. 39–75.

Kakabadse, A., Kakabadse, N. K., and Kouzmin, A. (2003) "Reinventing the Democratic Governance Project through Information Technology? A Growing Agenda for Debate." *Public Administration Review* 63 (1), pp. 44–60.

Kalathil, S., and Boas, T. C. (2003) *Open Networks, Closed Regimes: The Impact of the Internet on Authoritarian Rule* (Carnegie Endowment for International Peace, Washington, D.C.).

Kamarck, E. C. (1999) "Campaigning on the Internet in the Elections of 1998." In Kamarck, E. C., and Nye, J. S. (eds.), *Democracy.com? Governance in a Networked World* (Hollis Publishing Co., Hollis, NH), pp. 99–123.

Katz, J. E., and Rice, R. E. (2002) *Social Consequences of Internet Use: Access, Involvement and Interaction* (MIT Press, London).

Katz, R., and Mair, P. (1995) "Changing Models of Party Organization and Party Democracy: The Emergence of the Cartel Party." *Party Politics* 1 (1), pp. 5–28.

Keane, J. (2000) "Structural Transformations of the Public Sphere." In Hacker, K. L., and Van Dijk, J. (eds.), *Digital Democracy: Issues of Theory and Practice* (Sage, London), pp. 70–89.

Keeble, L., and Loader, B. D. (2001) "Community Informatics: Themes and Issues." In Keeble, L., and Loader, B. D. (eds.), *Community Informatics: Shaping Computer-Mediated Social Relations* (Routledge, London), pp. 1–10.

Kellan, A. (1999) "Hackers Hit Government Web Sites after China Embassy Bombing." *CNN News* website May 11 at http://www.cnn.com/TECH/computing/9905/10/hack.attack.02 (accessed May 12, 2004).

Keller, P. (2000) "China's Impact on the Global Information Society." In Marsden, C. T. (ed.), *Regulating the Global Information Society* (Routledge, London), pp. 265–84.

Kellner, D. (1999) "Globalization from Below?: Toward a Radical Democratic Technopolitics." *Angelaki: Journal of the Theoretical Humanities* 4 (2), pp. 101–12.

Kelly, K. (1994) *Out of Control: The New Biology of Machines, Social Systems and the Economic World* (Perseus, New York).

Kelly, T. (2004) "Unlocking the Iron Cage: Public Administration in the Deliberative Democratic Theory of Jürgen Habermas." *Administration and Society* 36 (1), pp. 38–61.

Keohane, R. O., and Nye, J. S. (1989) *Power and Interdependence: World Politics in Transition*, 2nd ed. (Scott, Foresman, London).

—— (1998) "Power and Interdependence in the Information Age." *Foreign Affairs* 77 (5), pp. 81–94.

Kidd, D. (2003) "Indymedia.org: A New Communications Commons." In McCaughey, M., and Ayers, M. D. (eds.), *Cyberactivism: Online Activism in Theory and Practice* (Routledge, London), pp. 47–69.

Kimber, R. (2005) "UK General Election 2005: Election Blogs and Forums." Dr Richard Kimber's website at http://www.psr.keele.ac.uk/area/uk/ge05/electionblogs.htm (accessed May 6, 2005).

King, I. (2003) "Online Privacy in Europe—New Regulation for Cookies." *Information and Communication Technology Law* 12 (3), pp. 225–36.

Kircheimer, O. (1966) "The Transformation of the Western European Party Systems." In LaPalombara, J., and Weiner, M. (eds.), *Political Parties and Political Development* (Princeton University Press, Princeton), pp. 177–200.

Klang, M. (2003) "Spyware: Paying for Software with Our Privacy." *International Review of Law, Computers and Technology* 17 (3), pp. 313–22.

Klein, H. (1999) "Tocqueville in Cyberspace: Using the Internet for Citizen Associations." *Information Society* 15 (4), pp. 213–20.

_____ (2001) "The Feasibility of Global Democracy: Understanding ICANN's At-Large Election." *Info: Journal for Policy, Regulation and Strategy for Telecommunications* 3 (4), pp. 333–45.

_____ (2002) "ICANN and Internet Governance: Leveraging Technical Co-ordination to Realize Global Public Policy." *Information Society* 18, pp. 193–207.

Kleinwachter, W. (2003a) "From Self-Governance to Public-Private Partnership: The Changing Role of Governments in the Management of the Internet's Core Resources." *Loyola of Los Angeles Law Review* 36 (3), pp. 1103–26.

_____ (2003b) "Global Governance in the Information Age," *Development* 46 (1), pp. 17–25.

Klinenberg, E., and Perrin, A. (2000) "Symbolic Politics in the Information Age: The 1996 Republican Presidential Campaigns in Cyberspace." *Information, Communication and Society* 3 (1), pp. 17–38.

Kling, R., and Iacono, S. (1989) "The Institutional Character of Computerized Information Systems." *Technology and People* 5 (1), pp. 7–28.

Klotz, R. (2004) *The Politics of Internet Communication* (Rowman and Littlefield, Oxford).

Kobrin, S. J. (2002) "Economic Governance in an Electronically-Networked Global Economy." In Hall, R. B., and Biersteker, T. J. (eds.), *The Emergence of Private Authority in Global Governance* (Cambridge University Press, Cambridge), pp. 43–75.

Koenig-Archibugi, M. (2004) "Transnational Corporations and Public Accountability." *Government and Opposition* 39 (2), pp. 235–59.

Kohut, A. (2005) *The Dean Activists: Their Profile and Prospects* (Pew Research Center for the People and the Press, Washington, D.C.).

Kooiman, J. (ed.) (1993) *Modern Governance: New Government-Society Interactions* (Sage, London).

_____ (2002) "Governance: A Social-Political Perspective." In Grote, J. R., and Gbikpi, B. (eds.), *Participatory Governance: Political and Societal Implications* (Leske and Budrich, Leverkusen, Germany). Also available at http://www.ifs.tu-darmstadt.de/pg/heinelt/p_eu_2000-2002-kooiman.pdf (accessed August 13, 2002).

Kowal, D. M. (2002) "Digitizing and Globalizing Indigenous Voices: The Zapatista Movement." In Elmer, G. (ed.), *Critical Perspectives on the Internet* (Rowman and Littlefield, Oxford), pp. 104–26.

Kraemer, K. L., and Dedrick, J. (2001) "Liberalization of the Computer Industry: A Comparison of Four Developing Countries." *Information Society* 17 (2), pp. 83–90.

Kraemer, K. L., and King, J. L. (1986) "Computing in Public Organizations." *Public Administration Review* 46 (3), pp. 488–96.

Krasner, S. (1982) "Structural Causes and Regime Consequences: Regimes as Intervening Variables." *International Organization* 36 (2), pp. 185–205.

Kraut, R., Kiesler, S., Boneva, B., Cummings, J., Helgeson, V., and Crawford, A. (2002) "Internet Paradox Revisited." *Journal of Social Issues* 58 (1), pp. 49–74.

Kraut, R., Lundmark, V., Patterson, M., Kiesler, S., Mukopadhyay, T., and Scherlis, W. (1998) "Internet Paradox: A Social Technology That Reduces Social Involvement and Psychological Well-Being?" *American Psychologist* 53 (9), pp. 1017–31.

Krim, J. (2005) "FCC Chief Must Work Out Details." *Washington Post*, January 22. Also available at http://www.washingtonpost.com/wp-dyn/articles/A27673-2005Jan21.html (accessed January 24, 2005).

Lal, K. (2001) "Institutional Environment and the Development of Information and Communication Technology in India." *Information Society* 17 (2), pp. 105–17.

Landsbergen Jr., D., and Wolken Jr., G. (2001) "Realizing the Promise: Government Information Systems and the Fourth Generation of Information Technology." *Public Administration Review* 61 (2), pp. 206–18.

Lasica, J. D. (2005) *Darknet: Hollywood's War against the Digital Generation* (John Wiley and Sons, Chichester).

Lasn, K. (2000) *Culture Jam: The Uncooling of America* (William Morrow and Co., New York).

Laudon, K. C. (1974) *Computers and Bureaucratic Reform: The Political Functions of Urban Information Systems* (Wiley, New York).

———— (1977) *Communications Technology and Democratic Participation* (Praeger, New York).

Lawson, G. (1998) *Netstate: Creating Electronic Government* (Demos, London).

Lazarsfeld, P., Berelson, B., and Gaudet, H. (1944) *The People's Choice* (Columbia University Press, New York).

Leadbeater, C. (1999) *Living on Thin Air: The New Economy* (Viking, London).

Leavitt, H. J., and Whisler, T. L. (1958) "Management in the 1980s." *Harvard Business Review* 36 (6), pp. 41–48.

Lebert, J. (2003) "Wiring Human Rights Activism: Amnesty International and the Challenges of Information and Communication Technologies." In McCaughey, M., and Ayers, M. D. (eds.), *Cyberactivism: Online Activism in Theory and Practice* (Routledge, London), pp. 209–31.

Lee, H., O'Keefe, R. M., and Yun, K. (2003) "The Growth of Broadband and Electronic Commerce in South Korea: Contributing Factors." *Information Society* 19 (1), pp. 81–93.

Leiner, B. M., Cerf, V. G., Clark, D. D., Kahn, R. E., Kleinrock, L., Lynch, D. C., Postel, J., Roberts, L. G., and Wolff, S. (2000) *A Brief History of the Internet*, version 3.31, Internet Society website at http://www.isoc.org/internet/history/brief.shtml (accessed July 2, 2002).

Leizerov, S. (2000) "Privacy Advocacy Groups versus Intel: A Case Study of How Social Movements Are Tactically Using the Internet to Fight Corporations." *Social Science Computer Review* 18 (4), pp. 461–83.

Lekhi, R. (2000) "The Politics of African America Online." In Ferdinand, P. (ed.), *The Internet, Democracy and Democratization* (Frank Cass, London), pp. 76–101.

Lemos, R. (2001) "'Pimpshiz' Speaks with Pride." *ZDNet UK*, January 15, Hacktivist.com website at http://thehacktivist.com/archive/news/2001/Pimpshiz-ZDNET-2001.pdf (accessed May 10, 2004).

Lenhart, A., Horrigan, J. Rainie, L., Allen, K., Boyce, A., Madden, M., and O'Grady. E. (2003) *The Ever-Shifting Internet Population: A New Look at Access and the Digital Divide* (Pew Internet and American Life Project, Washington D.C.).

Lenihan, D. G. (2002) *E-government, Federalism and Democracy: The New Governance* (Centre for Collaborative Government, Ottawa).

Lenihan, D. G., and Alcock, R. (2000) *Collaborative Government in the Post-industrial Age: Five Discussion Pieces* (Centre For Collaborative Government, Ottawa).

Lessig, L. (1999) *Code and Other Laws of Cyberspace* (Basic Books, New York).

———— (2004) *Free Culture: How Big Media Uses Technology and the Law to Lock Down Culture and Control Creativity* (Penguin, New York).

Levine, P. (2002) "Can the Internet Rescue Democracy? Toward an On-line Commons." In Hayduk, R., and Mattson, K. (eds.), *Democracy's Moment: Reforming the American Political System for the 21st Century* (Rowman & Littlefield, Lanham, MD), pp. 121–37.

Levy, S. (2001) *Hackers: Heroes of the Computer Revolution* (Penguin, New York).

———— (2002) *Crypto: Secrecy and Privacy in the New Code War* (Penguin, London).

Licklider, J. C. R. (1960) "Man-Computer Symbiosis." *IRE Transactions on Human Factors in Electronics*, March, pp. 4–11. Also available at ftp://gatekeeper.research.compaq.com/pub/DEC/SRC/research-reports/SRC-061.pdf (accessed September 1, 2002).

Liebowitz, S. J., and Margolis, S. E. (1998) "Network Externality." In *The New Palgrave Dictionary of Economics and the Law* (Macmillan, London). Also available at http://wwwpub.utdallas.edu/~liebowit/palgrave/network.html (accessed September 30, 2003).

Lin, W., and Dutton, W. H. (2003) "The 'Net' Effect in Politics: The 'Stop the Overlay' Campaign in Los Angeles." *Party Politics* 9 (1), pp. 124–36.

Lipietz, A. (1997) "The Post-Fordist World: Labour Relations, International Hierarchy and Global Ecology." *Review of International Political Economy* 4 (1), pp. 1–41.

Lipinski, D., and Neddenriep, G. (2004) "Using 'New' Media to Get 'Old' Media Coverage: How Members of Congress Utilize Their Websites to Court Journalists." *Press/Politics* 9 (1), pp. 7–21.

Lipset, S. M., and Rokkan, S. (eds.) (1967) *Party Systems and Voter Alignments: Cross-National Perspectives* (Collier-Macmillan, London).

Lisagor, M. (2002) "XML Marks the Spot." *Federal Computer Week,* April 15. Also available at http://www.fcw.com/fcw/articles/2002/0415/cov-xml-04-15-02.asp (accessed February 4, 2004).

Loges, W. E., and Jung, J. Y. (2001) "Exploring the Digital Divide: Internet Connectedness and Age." *Communication Research* 28 (4), pp. 536–62.

Lucas, H. C., and Sylla, R. (2003) "The Global Impact of the Internet: Widening the Economic Gap between Wealthy and Poor Nations?" *Prometheus* 21 (1), pp. 3–22.

Lucas, R. E. (2000) "Some Macroeconomics for the 21st Century." *Journal of Economic Perspectives* 14 (1), pp. 159–68.

Luke, T. (2000) "Dealing with the Digital Divide: The Rough Realities of Cyberspace." *Telos* 118, (winter), pp. 3–23.

Luo, X. (2000) "The Rise of the Social Development Model: Institutional Construction of International Technology Associations, 1856–1993." *International Studies Quarterly* 44 (1), pp. 147–75.

Lupia, A., and Sin, G. (2003) "Which Public Goods Are Endangered?: How Evolving Communication Technologies Affect 'The Logic of Collective Action.'" *Public Choice* 117, pp. 315–31.

Lyon, D. (1994) *The Electronic Eye: The Rise of Surveillance Society* (University of Minnesota Press, Minneapolis).

———— (2001) *Surveillance Society: Monitoring Everyday Life* (Open University Press, Buckingham).

———— (2003) *Surveillance after September 11th* (Polity, Cambridge).

Mackenzie, D., and Wajcman, J. (eds.) (1999) *The Social Shaping of Technology,* 2nd ed. (Open University Press, Buckingham, UK).

Macpherson, C. B. (1977) *The Life and Times of Liberal Democracy* (Oxford University Press, Oxford).

Maguire, K. (2004) "Benefits System Hit by IT Chaos." *The Guardian,* November 26. Also available at http://society.guardian.co.uk/internet/story/0,8150,1360162,00.html (accessed November 26, 2004).

Mahara, S. (2002) "From Tea Sheds to Cyber Cafes: Could an Internet-Driven Modernization Strategy Succeed in India?" in Mazarr, M. J. (ed.), *Information Technology and World Politics* (Palgrave-Macmillan, Basingstoke, UK), pp. 133–44.

March, L. (2004) "Russian Parties and the Political Internet." *Europe-Asia Studies* 56 (3), pp. 369–400.

Margetts, H. (1991) "The Computerization of Social Security: The Way Forward or a Step Backwards?" *Public Administration* 69 (3), pp. 325–43.

———— (1999) *Information Technology in Government: Britain and America* (Routledge, London).

Margolis, M., and Resnick, D. (2000) *Politics As Usual: The Cyberspace "Revolution"* (Sage, London).

Margolis, M., Resnick, D., and Tu, C. (1997) "Campaigning on the Internet: Parties and Candidates on the World Wide Web in the 1996 Primary Season." *Press/Politics* 2 (1), pp. 59–78.

Märker, O., Hagedorn, H., and Trénel, M. (2001) "Internet-Based Citizen Participation in Esslingen: Relevance—Moderation—Software" (Mediakomm/German Institute of Urban Affairs, Cologne). Also available at http://www.mediakomm.net/documents/kongress/esslingen/maerker_en.pdf (accessed August 3, 2004).

Markle Foundation (2001) *Carter Center for Election Monitoring Report on the Global, On-line, Direct Elections for Five Seats Representing At-Large Members on the Board of Directors of ICANN* (Markle Foundation, New York). Also available at http://www.markle.org/News/Icann2_Report.Pdf (accessed November 21, 2003).

Marlin-Bennett, R. (2001) "ICANN and Democracy: Contradictions and Possibilities." In *Info: Journal for Policy, Regulation and Strategy for Telecommunications* 3 (4), pp. 299–311.

Marsden, C. T. (ed.) (2000) *Regulating the Global Information Society* (Routledge, London).

Martin, R. (1998) "Present at the Creation: An Oral History of the Dawn of the Internet." *PreText Magazine* 5 at http://www.pretext.com/mar98/features/story1.htm (accessed July 1, 2002).

Marx, G. T. (2003) "A Tack in the Shoe: Neutralizing and Resisting the New Surveillance." *Journal of Social Issues* 59 (2), pp. 369–90.

Matei, S., and Ball-Rokeach, S. (2003) "The Internet in the Communication Infrastructure of Urban Residential Communities: Macro- or Mesolinkage?" *Journal of Communication* 53 (4), pp. 642–57.

Matheson, D. (2004) "Weblogs and the Epistemology of the News: Some Trends in Online Journalism." *New Media and Society* 6 (4), pp. 443–68.

Mathiesen, T. (1997) "The Viewer Society: Michel Foucault's 'Panopticon' Revisited." *Theoretical Criminology* 1 (2), pp. 215–33.

Mathieson, S. A. (2003) "Government in Free-for-All." *The Guardian,* April 4.

May, C. (2000) *A Global Political Economy of Intellectual Property Rights: The New Enclosures?* (Routledge, London).

—— (2002) *The Information Society: A Sceptical View* (Polity, Cambridge).

McCarthy, K. (2000) "Amazon Makes Regular Customers Pay More." *The Register* website, September 6, at http://www.theregister.co.uk/2000/09/06/amazon_makes_regular_customers_pay (accessed October 22, 2004).

McChesney, R. W. (1999) *Rich Media, Poor Democracy: Communication Politics in Dubious Times* (University of Illinois Press, Chicago).

—— (2000) "The Political Economy of Communication and the Future of the Field." *Media, Culture and Society* 22 (1), pp. 109–16.

—— (2004) *The Problem of the Media: US Communication Politics in the 21st Century* (Monthly Review Press, New York).

McCue, A. (2005) "Apple Racks Up Quarter of a Billion iTunes Downloads." *Silicon.com* website at http://networks.silicon.com/webwatch/0,39024667,39127321,00.htm (accessed January 26, 2005).

McCullagh, D. (2004) "The Cyberbrains behind Howard Dean." *CNet News Online* website at http://news.com.com/2008-1028-5142066.html (accessed February 25, 2004).

McGill, S. (2000) "EXtensible Is So Comprehensible." *Computing,* September 14, pp. 53–54.

McIntosh, A., Robson, E., Smith, E., and Whyte, A. (2003) "Electronic Democracy and Young People." *Social Science Computer Review* 21 (1), pp. 43–54.

McKenna, L., and Pole, A. (2004) "Do Blogs Matter?: Weblogs in American Politics." Paper presented to the American Political Science Association Annual Meeting, Chicago, August/September.

McLaine, S. (2003) "Ethnic Online Communities: Between Profit and Purpose." In McCaughey, M., and Ayers, M. D. (eds.), *Cyberactivism: Online Activism in Theory and Practice* (Routledge, London), pp. 233–54.

McLean, I. (1989) *Democracy and New Technology* (Polity, Cambridge).

McLeod, K. (2001) *Owning Culture: Authorship, Ownership and Intellectual Property Law* (Peter Lang, New York).

Mead, G. H. (1930) *Mind, Self and Society,* edited by Morris, C. W. (University of Chicago Press, Chicago).

Meehan, E. (1993) *Citizenship and the European Community* (Sage, London).

Meikle, G. (2002) *Future Active: Media Activism and the Internet* (Routledge, London).

Mele, C. (1999) "Cyberspace and Disadvantaged Communities: The Internet as a Tool For Collective Action." In Smith, M. A., and Kollock, P. (eds.), *Communities in Cyberspace* (Routledge, London), pp. 290–310.

Melucci, A (1989) *Nomads of the Present: Social Movements and Individual Needs in Contemporary Society,* edited by Keane, J., and Mier, P. (Century Hutchinson, London).

—— (1996) *Challenging Codes: Collective Action in the Information Age* (Cambridge University Press, Cambridge).

Mencik, S. (2001) "The PATRIOT Act and Carnivore: Reasons for Concern?" SearchSecurity.com website at http://searchsecurity.techtarget.com/tip/1,289483,sid14_gci784713,00.html (accessed October 15, 2004).

Merolla, J. (2002) "www.nadertrader.org: Strategic Voting in the 2000 US Presidential Election." Paper presented to the Midwest Political Science Association Annual Meeting, Chicago, April.

Michels, R. (1915) *Political Parties: A Sociological Study of the Oligarchical Tendencies of Modern Democracy* (Jarrold, London).

Mills, C. W. (1956) *The Power Elite* (Oxford University Press, Oxford).

Milward, H. B., and Snyder, L. O. (1996) "Electronic Government: Linking Citizens to Public Organization through Technology." *Journal of Public Administration Research and Theory* 6 (2), pp. 261–75.

Minges, M. (2000) "Counting the Net: Internet Access Indicators." Presentation to the Internet Society Global Summit, Japan, Internet Society website at http://www.isoc.org/isoc/conferences/inet/00/cdproceedings/8e/8e_1.htm (accessed September 9, 2004).

Minnesota E-democracy (2004) "E-democracy Mission." Minnesota E-democracy website at http://www.e-democracy.org/mission.html (accessed July 15, 2004).

Mintrom, M. (2003) "Market Organizations and Deliberative Democracy: Choice and Voice in Public Service Delivery." *Administration and Society* 35 (1), pp. 52–81.

Mitchell, W. J. (1995) *City of Bits: Space, Place and the Infobahn* (MIT Press, Cambridge, MA).

Mitra, A. (2001) "Marginal Voices in Cyberspace." *New Media and Society* 3 (1), pp. 29–48.

Moore, M. (2000) Opening remarks, e-commerce conference, ITC. WTO News: Speeches, WTO website at http://www.wto.org/english/news_e/spmm_e/spmm40_e.htm (accessed November 27, 2003).

MORI (2001) "Attitudes to Voting and the Political Process Survey." MORI website at http://www.mori.com/polls/2001/elec_comm.shtml (accessed July 28, 2004).

Morison, J. (2003), "Analysis: Online Government and E-constitutionalism." *Public Law* 47 (1), pp. 14–23.

Morison, J., and Newman, D. R. (2001) "Online Citizenship, Consultation and Participation in New Labor's Britain and Beyond." *International Review of Law, Computers and Technology* 15 (2), pp. 171–94.

Morris, D. (1999) *Vote.com: How Big-Money Lobbyists and the Media Are Losing Their Influence, and the Internet Is Giving Power Back to the People* (Renaissance Books, Los Angeles).

Mossberger, K., Tolbert, C. J., and Stansbury, M., with McNeal, R., and Dotterweich, L. (2003) *Virtual Inequality: Beyond the Digital Divide* (Georgetown University Press, Washington, D.C.).

MoveOn Political Action Committee (2004a) Statement of Purpose. MoveOn Political Action Committee website at http://www.moveonpac.org/whoweare.html (accessed June 8, 2004).

———— (2004b) "What the Press Says about MoveOn PAC." MoveOn Political Action Committee website at http://www.moveonpac.org/presscoverage.html (accessed June 8, 2004).

Mowlana, H. (1997) *Global Information and World Communication,* 2nd ed. (Sage, London).

Mueller, M. L. (2000) "Rough Justice: An Analysis of ICANN's Uniform Dispute Resolution Policy." Syracuse University Convergence Center website at http://dcc.syr.edu/miscarticles/roughjustice.pdf (accessed October 20, 2003).

———— (2002), *Ruling the Root: Internet Governance and the Taming of Cyberspace* (MIT Press, Cambridge, MA).

Mueller, M. L., and McKnight, L. (2003) "The Post Dotcom Internet: Toward Regular and Objective Procedures for Internet Governance." Paper prepared for presentation at TPRC 2003 Research Conference on Communication, Information, and Internet Policy, Arlington, VA, September 2003, Syracuse University Convergence Center website at http://dcc.syr.edu/miscarticles/NewTLDs-MM-LM.pdf (accessed October 21, 2003).

Mumford, L. (1967) *The Myth of the Machine: Technics and Human Development* (Harcourt Brace Jovanovich, New York).

Murdock, G., and Golding, P. (1989) "Information Poverty and Political Inequality: Citizenship in the Age of Privatized Communications." *Journal of Communication* 39 (3), pp. 180–95.

Murdock, P. (2004) "Past the Posts: Rethinking Change, Retrieving Critique." *European Journal of Communication* 19 (1), pp. 19–38.

Musgrave, S. (2004) "The Community Portal Challenge: Is There a Technology Barrier for Local Authorities?" *Telematics and Informatics* 21 (3), pp. 261–72.

Musso, J., Weare, C., and Hale, M. (2000) "Designing Web Technologies for Local Governance Reform: Good Management or Good Democracy?" *Political Communication* 17 (1), pp. 1–19.

Mwesige, P. G. (2004) "Cyber Elites: A Survey of Internet Cafe Users in Uganda." *Telematics and Informatics* 21 (1), pp. 83–101.

Nagourney, A. (2003) "Dean Organizers Take Lessons from Labor." *New York Times*, December 5. Also available at http://query.nytimes.com/gst/abstract.html?res=F60D14F93F590C768CD DAB0994DB404482 (accessed July 29, 2004).

National Partnership for Reinventing Government (1997), *Access America: Reengineering through Information Technology 1997* (GPO, Washington, D.C.).

——— (2000) Electronic government statement, National Performance Review website at http://www.npr.gov/initiati/it/ (accessed October 3, 2000).

Naughton, J. (1999) *A Brief History of the Future: The Origins of the Internet* (Weidenfeld and Nicholson, London).

Nelson, T. (1975) *Computer Lib/Dream Machines* (Nelson/Hugo's Book Service, Chicago).

Ness, D. (2003) "Technology-Rich Metros Increase Their Distance from Others." MetaFactsUSA website at http://www.metafactsusa.com/pages/info/tup_dates/tupan03_msa_030501.pdf (accessed September 15, 2004).

Newman, A. L., and Bach, D. (2004) "Self-Regulatory Trajectories in the Shadow of Public Power: Resolving Digital Dilemmas in Europe and the United States." *Governance* 17 (3), pp. 387–413.

Nicholas, D., Huntington, P., Williams, P., and Jordan, M. (2002) "NHS Direct Online: Its Users and Their Concerns." *Journal of Information Science* 28 (4), pp. 305–19.

Nie, N. H., and Erbring, L. (2000) *Internet and Society: Preliminary Report* (Stanford Institute for the Quantitative Study of Society, Stanford University Stanford, CA). Also available at http://www.stanford.edu/group/siqss/Press_Release/Preliminary_Report.pdf (accessed July 14, 2004).

Nielsen, J. (1999) *Designing Web Usability: The Practice of Simplicity* (New Riders, Indianapolis).

Nielsen/Netratings (2004) "US Broadband Connections Reach Critical Mass, Crossing 50 Percent Mark for Web Surfers." Nielsen/Netratings website at http://www.nielsen-netratings.com/pr/pr_040818.pdf (accessed September 15, 2004).

Nissenbaum, H. (2004) "Hackers and the Contested Ontology of Cyberspace." *New Media and Society* 6 (2), pp. 195–217.

Noam, E. (2003) "The Internet: Still Wide Open and Competitive?" *Oxford Internet Institute Issue Brief 1* (Oxford Internet Institute, Oxford).

——— (2005) "Cybermedia Industries." Data kindly provided to the author by Eli Noam, Columbia Business School, Columbia University, New York.

Norris, C. (2003) "From Personal to Digital: CCTV, the Panopticon, and the Technological Mediation of Suspicion and Social Control." In Lyon, D. (ed.), *Surveillance as Social Sorting: Privacy, Risk and Digital Discrimination* (Routledge, London), pp. 249–81.

Norris, D. (2003) "Building the Virtual State . . . or Not? A Critical Appraisal." *Social Science Computer Review* 21 (4), pp. 417–24.

Norris, P. (1999) "Conclusions: The Growth of Critical Citizens and Its Consequences." In Norris, P. (ed.), *Critical Citizens: Global Support for Democratic Governance* (Oxford University Press, Oxford), pp. 257–72.

——— (2000) *A Virtuous Circle: Political Communications in Post-industrial Societies* (Cambridge University Press, Cambridge).

——— (2001) *Digital Divide: Civic Engagement, Information Poverty and the Internet Worldwide* (Cambridge University Press, Cambridge).

——— (2002a) "The Bridging and Bonding Role of Online Communities." *Press/Politics* 7 (3), pp. 3–13.

——— (2002b) *Democratic Phoenix: Reinventing Political Activism* (Cambridge University Press, Cambridge).

——— (2003) "Preaching to the Converted?: Pluralism, Participation and Party Websites." *Party Politics* 9 (1), pp. 21–45.

Norris, P., and Sanders, D. (2003) "Message or Medium: Campaign Learning during the 2001 British General Election." *Political Communication* 20 (3), pp. 233–62.

Noveck, B. S. (2000) "Paradoxical Partners: Electronic Communication and Electronic Democracy." In Ferdinand, P. (ed.), *The Internet, Democracy and Democratization* (Frank Cass, London).

Novotny, P. (2002) "Local Television, the World Wide Web and the 2000 Presidential Election." *Social Science Computer Review* 20 (1), pp. 58–72.

Nozick, R. (1974) *Anarchy, State and Utopia* (Blackwell, Oxford).

NUA (2004) "NUA Internet Surveys." NUA website at http://www.nua.com/surveys/how_many_online (accessed September 7, 2004).

Nuttall, C. (1999) "Virtual Country 'Nuked' on Net." *BBC News Online* website January 26 at http://news.bbc.co.uk/1/hi/sci/tech/263169.stm (accessed May 11, 2004).

Oldenburg, R. (1997) *The Great Good Place: Coffee Shops, Bookstores, Bars, Hair Salons, and Other Hangouts at the Heart of a Community,* 2nd ed. (Marlowe, New York).

Olson, M. (1965) *The Logic of Collective Action: Public Goods and the Theory of Groups* (Harvard University Press, Cambridge, MA).

Organization for Economic Co-operation and Development (OECD) (2004a) "About OECD." OECD website at http://www.oecd.org/about/0,2337,en_2649_201185_1_1_1_1_1,00.html (accessed August 7, 2004).

——— (2004b) "Overview of the OECD." OECD website at http://www.oecd.org/document/18/0,2340,en_2649_201185_2068050_1_1_1_1,00.html (accessed August 7, 2004).

Orlikowski, W. J. (1993) "Learning from Notes: Organizational Issues in Groupware Implementation." *Information Society* 9 (3), pp. 237–50.

Orwell, G. (1949) *Nineteen eighty-four* (Secker and Warburg, London).

Osborne, D., and Gaebler, T. (1992) *Reinventing Government: How the Entrepreneurial Spirit Is Transforming the Public Sector* (Addison Wesley, Reading, MA).

Ostrogorski, M. (1902) *Democracy and the Organization of Political Parties* (Macmillan, London).

Ostrom, E. (1990) *Governing the Commons: The Evolution of Institutions for Collective Action* (Cambridge University Press, Cambridge).

Oyelaran-Oyeyinka, B., and Adeya, C. N. (2004) "Internet Access in Africa: Empirical Evidence from Kenya and Nigeria." *Telematics and Informatics* 21 (1), pp. 67–81.

Paine, T. (1984) *The Rights of Man* (Penguin, Harmondsworth, UK).

Pal, L. A. (1998) "A Thousand Points of Darkness: Electronic Mobilization and the Case of the Communications Decency Act." In Alexander, C. J., and Pal, L. A. (eds.), *Digital Democracy: Policy and Politics in the Wired World* (Oxford University Press, Don Mills, Ontario).

Papacharissi, Z. (2002) "The Virtual Sphere: The Internet as a Public Sphere." *New Media and Society* 4 (1), pp. 9–27.

——— (2004) "Democracy Online: Civility, Politeness, and the Democratic Potential of Online Political Discussion Groups." *New Media and Society* 6 (2), pp. 259–83.

Paré, D. (2003) *Internet Governance in Transition: Who Is the Master of This Domain?* (Rowman and Littlefield, Oxford).

Pateman, C. (1970) *Participation and Democratic Theory* (Cambridge University Press, Cambridge).

Paterson, C. (2005) "News Agency Dominance in International News on the Internet." In Skinner, D., Compton, J., and Gasher, M. (eds.), *Converging Media, Diverging Politics: A Political Economy of News in the United States and Canada* (Lexington Books, Lanham, MD).

Pauwels, C., and Loisen, J. (2003) "The WTO and the Audiovisual Sector: Economic Free Trade vs Cultural Horse Trading?" *European Journal of Communication* 18 (3), pp. 291–313.

Pax, S. (2003) *The Baghdad Blog* (Guardian Books, London).

——— (2004) "Dear Raed" blog at http://dear_raed.blogspot.com (accessed June 4, 2004).

Peled, A. (2001) "Centralization or Diffusion? Two Tales of Online Government." *Administration and Society* 32 (6), pp. 686–709.

Peretti, J., with Micheletti, M. (2004) "The Nike Sweatshop Email: Political Consumerism, Internet and Culture Jamming." In Micheletti, M., Follesdal, A., and Stolle, D. (eds.), *Politics, Products and Markets: Exploring Political Consumerism, Past and Present* (Transaction Publishers, London), pp. 127–42.

Perry, K. (2004) "County Purges Website." *Cincinnati Post,* December 22. Also available at http://www.cincypost.com/2004/12/22/id122204.html (accessed April 18, 2005).

Peters, B. G. (2000) "Governance and Comparative Politics." In Pierre, J. (ed.), *Debating Governance: Authority, Steering and Democracy* (Oxford University Press, Oxford), pp. 36–53.

Pew Internet and American Life Project (2000) "Youth Vote Influenced by Online Information, Internet Election News Audience Seeks Convenience, Familiar Names." Pew Internet and American Life Project website at http://www.pewinternet.org/PPF/r/27/report_display.asp (accessed July 24, 2004).

———— (2004a) "Tracking Survey May–June." Pew Internet and American Life Project website at http://www.pewinternet.org/trends/DemographicsofInternetUsers.htm (accessed September 14, 2004).

———— (2004b) "Usage over Time." Pew Internet and American Life Project website at http://www.pewinternet.org/trends/UsageOverTime.xls (accessed September 15, 2004).

Phillips, D. J. (2003) "Beyond Privacy: Confronting Locational Surveillance in Wireless Communication." *Communication Law and Policy* 8 (1), pp. 1–23.

Phillips, D. J., and Curry, M. (2003) "Privacy and the Phenetic Urge: Geodemographics and the Changing Spatiality of Local Practice." In Lyon, D. (ed.), *Surveillance as Social Sorting: Privacy, Risk and Digital Discrimination* (Routledge, London), pp. 137–52.

Picard, R. G. (2002) *The Economics and Financing of Media Companies* (Fordham University Press, New York).

Pickerill, J. (2003) *Cyberprotest: Environmental Activism Online* (Manchester University Press, Manchester).

Pierre, J., and Peters, B. G. (2000) *Governance, Politics and the State* (Palgrave, London).

Pigg, K. E. (2001) "Applications of Community Informatics for Building Community and Enhancing Civic Society." *Information, Communication and Society* 4 (4), pp. 507–27.

Pinkett, R., and O'Bryant, R. (2003) "Building Community, Empowerment and Self-Sufficiency: Early Results from the Camfield Estates–MIT Creating Community Connections Project." *Information, Communication and Society* 6 (2), pp. 187–210.

Polikanov, D., and Abramova, I. (2003) "Africa and ICT: A Chance for Breakthrough?" *Information, Communication and Society* 6 (1), pp. 42–56.

Polletta, F. (1999) "'Free Spaces' in Collective Action." *Theory and Society* 28 (1), pp. 1–38.

Poole, O. (2004) "Civil Service Chaos as 200,000 Strike over Cuts." *Daily Telegraph,* November 6. Also available at http://www.telegraph.co.uk/news/main.jhtml?xml=/news/2004/11/06/ncivil06.xml&sSheet=/news/2004/11/06/ixhome.html (accessed November 7, 2004).

Poppe, Y. (2004) "The Peer 2 Peer Internet: Crossing the IPv6 Chasm to New Territories of Revenue Opportunities." Presentation to the U.S. IPv6 Summit, Reston, VA, December 7–10. Also available at http://usipv6.unixprogram.com/usipv6_reston_2004/wed/Poppe.pdf (accessed January 28, 2005).

Post, D. G. (1997) "Governing Cyberspace." *Wayne Law Review* 43. Also available at http://www.temple.edu/lawschool/dpost/Governing.html (accessed October 20, 2003).

———— (1999) "Governing Cyberspace, or Where Is James Madison When We Need Him?" Temple University website at http://www.temple.edu/lawschool/dpost/icann/comment1.html (accessed October 21, 2003).

Poster, M. (1990) *The Mode of Information* (University of Chicago Press, London).

Postmes, T., and Brunsting, S. (2002) "Collective Action in the Age of the Internet: Mass Communication and Online Mobilization." *Social Science Computer Review* 20 (3), pp. 290–301.

Pratchett, L. (1999) "New Technologies and the Modernization of Local Government: An Analysis of Biases and Constraints." *Public Administration* 77 (4), pp. 731–50.

Price, M. E., and Wicklein, J. (1972) *Cable Television: A Guide for Citizen Action* (Pilgrim Press, Philadelphia).

Putnam, R. D. (1993) *Making Democracy Work: Civic Traditions in Modern Italy* (Princeton University Press, Princeton).

———— (1995) "Bowling Alone: America's Declining Social Capital." *Journal of Democracy* 6 (1), pp. 65–78.

——— (2000) *Bowling Alone: The Collapse and Revival of American Community* (Simon and Schuster, New York).

Quan-Haase, A., and Wellman, B., with Witte, J., and Hampton, K. (2002) "Capitalizing on the Internet: Social Contact, Civic Engagement and Sense of Community." In Wellman, B., and Haythornthwaite, C. (eds.), *The Internet and Everyday Life* (Blackwell, Oxford), pp. 291–324.

Quittner, J. (1994) "Billions Registered." *Wired*, October. Also available at http://www.wired.com/wired/archive/2.10/mcdonalds.html (accessed October 2, 2003).

Rafael, V. L. (2003) "The Cell Phone and the Crowd: Messianic Politics in the Contemporary Philippines." *Public Culture* 15 (3), pp. 399–425.

Rainie, L. (2004) "Pew Internet Project Data Memo," April 13. Pew Internet and American Life Project website at http://www.pewinternet.org/pdfs/PIP_April2004_Data_Memo.pdf (accessed September 9, 2004).

Rainie, L., and Bell, P. (2004) "The Numbers That Count." *New Media and Society* 6 (1), pp. 44–54.

Randall, N. (1997) *The Soul of the Internet: Net Gods, Netizens, and the Wiring of the World* (International Thomson Computer Press, London).

Rash, W. (1997), *Politics on the Nets: Wiring the Political Process* (W. H. Freeman and Co., Basingstoke, UK).

Regan, P. M. (2003) "Safe Harbors or Free Frontiers? Privacy and Transborder Data Flows." *Journal of Social Issues* 59 (2), pp. 263–82.

Reich, R. B. (1991) *The Work of Nations: Preparing Ourselves for Twenty-first Century Capitalism* (Simon and Schuster, London).

Reid, T. R. (2005) "Guard Convicted in the First Trial from Abu Ghraib." *Washington Post*, January 14. Also available at http://www.washingtonpost.com/wp-dyn/articles/A9343-2005Jan14.html (accessed January 15, 2005).

——— (1998) "Lex Informatica: The Formulation of Information Policy Rules through Technology." *Texas Law Review* 76 (3), pp. 553–94.

Reidenberg, J. R. (2004) "States and Internet Enforcement." *University of Ottawa Law and Technology Journal* 1 (1), pp. 1–25. Also available at http://ssrn.com/abstract=487965 (accessed March 31, 2004).

Resnick, D. (1998) "Politics on the Internet: The Normalization of Cyberspace." In Toulouse, C., and Luke, T. W. (eds.), *The Politics of Cyberspace: A New Political Science Reader* (Routledge, London), pp. 48–68.

Rheingold, H. (1993) *The Virtual Community: Homesteading on the Electronic Frontier* (Addison Wesley, Reading, MA).

——— (2002) *Smart Mobs: The Next Social Revolution* (Perseus, London).

Richards, D., and Smith, M. J. (2002) *Governance and Public Policy in the United Kingdom* (Oxford University Press, Oxford).

Risse, T. (2004) "Global Governance and Communicative Action." *Government and Opposition* 39 (2), pp. 289–313.

Ritzer, G. (1993) *The McDonaldization of Society: An Investigation into the Changing Character of Contemporary Social Life* (Pine Forge, London).

Robison, K. K., and Crenshaw, E. M. (2002) "Post-industrial Transformations and Cyber-Space: A Cross-National Analysis of Internet Development." *Social Science Research* 31 (3), pp. 334–63.

Rodgers, J. (2003) *Spatializing International Politics: Analyzing Activism on the Internet* (Routledge, London).

Roe Smith, M., and Marx, L. (eds.) (1994) *Does Technology Drive History? The Dilemma of Technological Determinism* (MIT Press, Cambridge, MA).

Rogers, E. M. (1995) *Diffusion of Innovations*, 4th ed. (Free Press, New York).

Rogers, E. M., and Malhotra, S. (2000) "Computers as Communication: The Rise of Digital Democracy." In Hacker, K. L., and van Dijk, J. (eds.), *Digital Democracy: Issues of Theory and Practice* (Sage, London), pp. 10–29.

Rogerson, K. S. (2000) "Information Interdependence: Keohane and Nye's Complex Interdependence in the Information Age." *Information, Communication and Society* 3 (3), pp. 415–36.

Ronfeldt, D. (1992) "Cyberocracy Is Coming." *Information Society* 8 (4), pp. 243–96.

Ronit, K. (2001) "Institutions of Private Authority in Global Governance: Linking Territorial Forms of Self-Regulation." *Administration and Society* 33 (5), pp. 555–78.

Roscoe, T. (1999) "The Construction of the World Wide Web Audience." *Media, Culture and Society* 21 (5), pp. 673–84.

Rose, R., and McAllister, I. (1986) *Voters Begin to Choose: From Closed-Class to Open Elections in Britain* (Sage, London).

Rosen, J. (2001) *The Unwanted Gaze: The Destruction of Privacy in America,* rev. ed. (Vintage, New York).

Rosenau, J. N. (1992) "Governance, Order and Change in World Politics." In Rosenau, J. N., and Czempiel, E. (eds.), *Governance without Government: Order and Change in World Politics* (Cambridge University Press, Cambridge), pp. 1–29.

Rousseau, J-J. (1968) *The Social Contract* (Penguin, Harmondsworth, UK).

Rowe, R., and Shepherd, M. (2002) "Public Participation in the New NHS: No Closer to Citizen Control?" *Social Policy and Administration* 36 (3), pp. 275–90.

Ruggie, J. G. (1998) "What Makes the World Hang Together? Neo-utilitarianism and the Social Constructivist Challenge." *International Organization* 52 (4), pp. 855–85.

Rupert, M. (1995) *Producing Hegemony: The Politics of Mass Production and American Global Power* (Cambridge University Press, Cambridge).

———— (2002) "Fordism." Mark Rupert's website at http://www.maxwell.syr.edu/maxpages/faculty/merupert/Research/Fordism/fordism.htm (accessed November 6, 2002).

Ryfe, D. M. (2002) "The Practice of Deliberative Democracy: A Study of 16 Deliberative Organizations." *Political Communication* 19 (3), pp. 359–77.

Sabato, L. J. (1991) *Feeding Frenzy: How Attack Journalism Has Transformed American Politics* (Free Press, New York).

Salter, L. (2004) "Structure and Forms of Use: A Contribution to Understanding the 'Effects' of the Internet on Deliberative Democracy." *Information, Communication and Society* 7 (2), pp. 185–206.

Salus, P. H. (1995) *Casting the Net: From ARPANET to Internet and Beyond* (Addison-Wesley, Reading, MA).

Samuel, A. (2001) "Digital Disobedience: Hacktivism in Political Context." Paper delivered to the American Political Science Association Annual Meeting, 2001.

Save Our Environment Coalition (2004) Save Our Environment Action Center website at http://www.saveourenvironment.org (accessed June 7, 2004).

Saxenian, A. (1994) *Regional Advantage: Culture and Competition in Silicon Valley and Route 128* (Harvard University Press, Cambridge, MA).

Scammell, M. (1995) *Designer Politics: How Elections Are Won* (Macmillan, London).

Schalken, K. (2000), "Virtual Communities: New Public Spheres on the Internet?" in Hoff, J., Horrocks, I., and Tops, P. (eds.), *Democratic Governance and New Technology: Technologically Mediated Innovations in Political Practice in Western Europe* (Routledge, London).

Scheufele, D. A., and Nisbet, M. (2002) "Democracy Online: New Opportunities and Dead Ends." *Harvard International Journal of Press/Politics* 7 (3), pp. 53–73.

Schier, S. E. (2000) *By Invitation Only: The Rise of Executive Politics in the United States* (University of Pittsburgh Press, Pittsburgh).

Schlesinger, P. (1987) *Putting "Reality" Together: BBC News* (Methuen, London).

Schneider, S. M., and Foot, K. A (2002) "Online Structure for Political Action: Exploring Presidential Campaign Websites from the 2000 American Election." *Javnost/The Public* 9 (2), pp. 43–60.

Scholte, J. A. (2004) "Civil Society and Democratically Accountable Global Governance." *Government and Opposition* 39 (2), pp. 211–32.

Schramm, W., and Roberts, D. F. (1971) *The Process and Effects of Mass Communication,* rev. ed. (University of Illinois Press, Urbana).

Schudson, M. (1991) "Historical Approaches to Communications Studies." In Jensen, K. B., and Jankowski, N. (eds.), *A Handbook for Qualitative Methodologies for Mass Communications Research* (Routledge, London), pp. 175–89.

Schuler, D. (1996) *New Community Networks: Wired for Change* (ACM Press/Addison-Wesley, New York).

Scott, A., and Street, J. (2000) "From Media Politics to E-protest: The Use of Popular Culture and New Media in Parties and Social Movements." *Information, Communication and Society* 3 (2), pp. 215–40.

Scott Morton, M. S. (ed.) (1991) *The Corporation of the 1990s: Information Technology and Organizational Transformation* (Oxford University Press, Oxford).

SearchEngineWatch (2005) "Nielsen NetRatings Search Engine Ratings." SearchEngineWatch website at http://searchenginewatch.com/reports/article.php/2156451 (accessed January 18, 2005).

Sedberry, G. (2001) "First Impressions." In Coleman, S. (ed.), *Elections in the Age of the Internet: Lessons from the United States* (Hansard Society, London), pp. 8–10.

Seifert, J. W. (2003) *A Primer on E-government: Sectors, Stages, Opportunities and Challenges of Online Governance* (U.S. Congressional Research Service RL31057, Library of Congress, Washington, D.C.).

Selnow, G. W. (1998) *Electronic Whistle-Stops: The Impact of the Internet on American Politics* (Praeger, Westport, CT).

Selwyn, N. (2004) "Reconsidering Political and Popular Understandings of the Digital Divide." *New Media and Society* 6 (3), pp. 341–62.

Servaes, J., and Heinderyckx, F. (2002) "The 'New' ICTs Environment in Europe: Closing or Widening the Gaps?" *Telematics and Informatics* 19 (2), pp. 91–115.

Servon, L. J. (2002) *Bridging the Digital Divide: Technology, Community and Public Policy* (Blackwell, Oxford).

SFGate.com (2003) "On the Record: Scott McNealy." SFGate.com website at http://sfgate.com/cgi-bin/article.cgi?file=/c/a/2003/09/14/BU141353.DTL (accessed October 29, 2004).

Shah, D. V., Kwak, N., and Holbert, R. L. (2001) "'Connecting' and 'Disconnecting' with Civic Life: Patterns of Internet Use and the Production of Social Capital" *Political Communication* 18 (2), pp. 141–62.

Shah, D. V., McLeod, J. M., and Yoon, S. H. (2001) "Communication, Context and Community: An Exploration of Print, Broadcast and Internet Influences." *Communication Research* 28 (4), pp. 464–506.

Shamberg, M. (1971) *Guerrilla Television* (Holt, Rinehart and Winston, New York).

Shapiro, A. L. (1999) *The Control Revolution: How the Internet Is Putting Individuals in Charge and Changing the World We Know* (PublicAffairs, New York).

Shenk, D. (1997) *Data Smog: Surviving the Information Glut* (Harper Collins, New York).

Shey, T. (2004) "Department of Personal Freedom (Jonah Peretti/Nike emails)." Shey.net website at http://www.shey.net/niked.html (accessed May 18, 2004).

Shirky, C. (2003) "Fame vs Fortune: Micropayments and Free Content." Clay Shirky's website at http://www.shirky.com/writings/fame_vs_fortune.html (accessed January 5, 2005).

———— (2004) "Exiting Deanspace." Corante website at http://www.corante.com/many/archives/2004/02/03/exiting_deanspace.php (accessed July 29, 2004).

Shulman, S. W., Schosberg, D., Zavestoski, S., and Courard-Hauri, D. (2003) "Electronic Rulemaking: A Public Participation Research Agenda for the Social Sciences." *Social Science Computer Review* 21 (2), pp. 162–78.

Silcock, R. (2001) "What Is E-government?" *Parliamentary Affairs* 54 (1), pp. 88–101.

Silverstone, R. (2004) "Regulation, Media Literacy and Media Civics." *Media, Culture and Society* 26 (3), pp. 440–49.

Simms, A. (2001) "Farewell Tuvalu." *The Guardian,* October 29. Also available at http://www.guardian.co.uk/comment/story/0,3604,582445,00.html (accessed October 7, 2003).

Simon, H. A. (1965) *The Shape of Automation for Men and Management* (Harper and Row, New York).

———— (1973) "Applying Information Technology to Organizational Design." *Public Administration Review* 33 (3), pp. 268–78.

Simon, J. (1994) "The Marcos Mystery: A Chat with the Subcommander of Spin." *Columbia Journalism Review,* September/October. Also available at http://archives.cjr.org/year/94/5/marcos.asp (accessed May 24, 2004).

Simpson, S. (2000) "Intra-institutional Rivalry and Policy Entrepreneurship in the European Union: The Politics of Information and Communication Technology Convergence." *New Media and Society* 2 (4), pp. 445–66.

Singapore Government Consultation Portal (2005) Government Consultation Portal website at http://www.feedback.gov.sg (accessed March 1, 2005).

Singel, R. (2004) "Net Politics Down but Not Out." *Wired News,* at http://www.wired.com/news/politics/0,1283,62123,00.html (accessed July 30, 2004).

Singer, J. B., and Gonzalez-Velez, M. (2003) "Envisioning the Caucus Community: Online Newspaper Editors Conceptualize Their Political Roles." *Political Communication* 20 (4), pp. 433–52.

Skibell, R. (2002) "The Myth of the Computer Hacker." *Information, Communication and Society* 5 (3), pp. 336–56.

Slaughter, A. (2004) "Disaggregated Sovereignty: Towards the Public Accountability of Global Government Networks." *Government and Opposition* 39 (2), pp. 159–90.

Smith, J. (2001) "Globalizing Resistance: The Battle of Seattle and the Future of Social Movements." *Mobilization* 6 (1), pp. 1–20.

Smith, M. A. (1999) "Invisible Crowds in Cyberspace: Mapping the Social Structure of the Usenet." In Smith, M. A., and Kollock, P. (eds.), *Communities in Cyberspace* (Routledge, London), pp. 195–219.

Smith, M. A., and Kollock, P. (eds.) (1999) *Communities in Cyberspace* (Routledge, London).

Smith, T. (2003) "99c iTunes Song Auction Bids Top $100,000." September 4, *The Register* website at http://www.theregister.co.uk/2003/09/04/99c_itunes_song_auction_bids (accessed December 18, 2004).

Snellen, I. (2003) "E-knowledge Management in Public Administration: An Agenda for the Future." In Wimmer, M. A. (ed.), *Knowledge Management in Electronic Government: 4th IFIP International Working Conference Proceedings* (Springer-Verlag, Heidelberg), pp. 70–75.

Soar, M. (2002) "The First Things First Manifesto and the Politics of Culture Jamming: Towards a Cultural Economy of Graphic Design and Advertising." *Cultural Studies* 16 (4), pp. 570–92.

Sprenger, P. (1999) "Sun on Privacy: Get over It." *Wired News* website January 26 at http://www.wired.com/news/politics/0,1283,17538,00.html (accessed October 29, 2004).

Sproull, L., and Kiesler, S. (1986) "Reducing Social Context Cues: Electronic Mail in Organizational Computing." *Management Science* 32 (11), pp. 1492–1512.

Stanley, J. W., Weare, C., and Musso, J. (2004) "Participation, Deliberative Democracy and the Internet: Lessons from a National Forum on Commercial Vehicle Safety." In Shane, P. (ed.), *Democracy Online: The Prospects for Political Renewal through the Internet* (Routledge, London), pp. 167–79.

Stanworth, C. (1998) "Telework and the Information Age." *New Technology, Work and Employment* 13 (1), pp. 51–62.

——— (2000) "Women and Work in the Information Age." *Gender, Work and Organization* 7 (1), pp. 20–32.

Steiner, P. (1993) "On the Internet, Nobody Knows You're a Dog." *New Yorker,* July 5. Also available at http://www.unc.edu/depts/jomc/academics/dri/idog.html (accessed August 3, 2004).

Steinke, G. (2002) "Data Privacy Approaches from US and EU Perspectives." *Telematics and Informatics* 19 (2), pp. 193–200.

Sterling, T. D. (1986) "Democracy in an Information Society." *Information Society* 4 (1–2), pp. 9–47.

Stolfi, F., and Sussman, G. (2001) "Telecommunications and Transnationalism: The Polarization of Social Space." *Information Society* 17 (1) pp. 49–62.

Stolle, D., and Hooghe, M. (2004) "Consumers as Political Participants? Shifts in Political Action Repertoires in Western Societies." In Micheletti, M., Follesdal, A., and Stolle, D. (eds.)

Politics, Products and Markets: Exploring Political Consumerism, Past and Present (Transaction Publishers, London), pp. 265–88.

Støvring, J. (2004) "The 'Washington Consensus' in Relation to the Telecommunication Sector in African Developing Countries." *Telematics and Informatics* 21 (1), pp. 11–24.

Strauss, J., and Rogerson, K. S. (2002) "Policies for Online Privacy in the United States and the European Union." *Telematics and Informatics* 19 (2), pp. 173–92.

Streck, J. (1998) "Pulling the Plug on Electronic Town Meetings: Participatory Democracy and the Reality of the Usenet." In Toulouse, C., and Luke, T. W. (eds.), *The Politics of Cyberspace: A New Political Science Reader* (Routledge, London), pp. 18–47.

Stromer-Galley, J. (2000a) "Democratizing Democracy: Strong Democracy, US Political Campaigns and the Internet." In Ferdinand, P. (ed.), *The Internet, Democracy and Democratization* (Frank Cass, London).

⸻ (2000b) "Online Interaction and Why Candidates Avoid It." *Journal of Communication* 50 (4), pp. 111–32.

⸻ (2003) "Diversity of Political Conversation on the Internet: Users' Perspectives." *Journal of Computer-Mediated Communication* 8 (3) at http://www.ascusc.org/jcmc/vol8/issue3/stromergalley.html (accessed May 20, 2004).

Strossen, N. (2000) "Cybercrimes versus Cyberliberties." *International Review of Law, Computers and Technology* 14 (1), pp. 11–24.

Stuart Lynn, M. (2002) "President's Report: ICANN—The Case for Reform, 24 February 2002." ICANN website at http://www.icann.org/general/lynn-reform-proposal-24feb02.htm (accessed November 20, 2003).

Suchman, L. A. (2002) "Practice-Based Design of Information Systems: Notes from the Hyper-developed World." *Information Society* 18 (2), pp. 139–44.

Sundar, S. S., Kalyanaraman, S., and Brown, J. (2003) "Explicating Website Interactivity: Impression Formation Effects in Political Campaign Sites." *Communication Research* 30 (1), pp. 30–59.

Sunstein, C. (2001) *Republic.com* (Princeton University Press, Princeton).

Swinden, K., and Heath, W. (1994) *Wired Whitehall 1999* (Kable, London).

Tacticalvoter.net/Internet Archive (2004) Internet Archive website at http://web.archive.org/web/20010419223624/http://www.tacticalvoter.net (accessed August 1, 2004).

Tambini, D. (1999) "New Media and Democracy: The Civic Networking Movement." *New Media and Society* 1 (3), pp. 305–29.

Tapscott, D. (1995) *The Digital Economy: Promise and Peril in the Age of Networked Intelligence* (McGraw-Hill, New York).

Tarrow, S. (1998) *Power in Movement: Social Movements and Contentious Politics,* 2nd ed. (Cambridge University Press, Cambridge).

Tavani, H. T. (2000) "Privacy and Security." In Langford, D. (ed.), *Internet Ethics* (Macmillan, Basingstoke, UK), pp. 65–95.

Taylor, F. W. (1911) *The Principles of Scientific Management* (Harper, London).

Taylor, J. A. (1995) "Don't Obliterate, Informate! Business Process Reengineering for the Information Age." *New Technology, Work and Employment* 10 (2), pp. 83–88.

Taylor, P. A. (1999) *Hackers: Crime in the Digital Sublime* (Routledge, London).

⸻ (2000) "Hackers: Cyberpunks or Microserfs?" In Thomas, D., and Loader, B. (eds.), *Cybercrime: Law Enforcement, Security and Surveillance in the Information Age* (Routledge, London), pp. 36–55.

⸻ (2001) "Hacktivism: In Search of Lost Ethics." In Wall, D. S. (ed.), *Crime and the Internet* (Routledge, London), pp. 59–73.

Technology Bytes (2002) "Stefan Puffer Acquitted of Hacking Into Harris County Office." Technology Bytes website at http://www.geekradio.com/modules.php?name=News&file=article&sid=152 (accessed June 8, 2004).

Tendler, S. (2002) "1200 Arrested in British Paedophile Raids." *The Times,* December 18. Also available at http://www.timesonline.co.uk/article/0_2-517566,00.html (accessed September 20, 2004).

Tewksbury, D. (2003) "What Do Americans Really Want to Know?: Tracking the Behavior of News Readers on the Internet." *Journal of Communication* 53 (4), pp. 694–710.

Thomas, C. (2002) "Global Governance and Human Security." In Wilkinson, R., and Hughes, S. (eds.), *Global Governance: Critical Perspectives* (Routledge, London), pp. 113–31.

Thomas, D. (2000) "Criminality on the Electronic Frontier: Corporality and the Judicial Construction of the Hacker." In Thomas, D., and Loader, B. (eds.), *Cybercrime: Law Enforcement, Security and Surveillance in the Information Age* (Routledge, London), pp. 17–35.

Thomas, P. N. (1999) "Knowledge Regimes: The WTO, IP and Public Interests in India." *Telematics and Informatics* 16 (4), pp. 219–31.

Tigre, P. B., and Botelho, A. J. J. (2001) "Brazil Meets the Global Challenge: IT Policy in a Postliberalization Environment." *Information Society* 17 (2), pp. 91–103.

Tilly, C. (1978) *From Mobilization to Revolution* (Addison Wesley, London).

TiVo Corporation (2004) "Justin and Janet Top Super Bowl Show According to Annual TiVo Audience Measurement Analysis." Press release, February 2, TiVo Corporation website at http://www.tivo.com/5.3.1.1.asp?article=200 (accessed March 27, 2004).

Tocqueville, A. (2003) *Democracy in America* (Penguin, London).

Toffler, A. (1981) *The Third Wave* (Bantam, New York).

Tolbert, C. J., and McNeal, R. S. (2003) "Unraveling the Effects of the Internet on Political Participation." *Political Research Quarterly* 56 (2), pp. 175–85.

Tonn, B. E., and Petrich, C. (1998) "Everyday Life's Constraints on Citizenship in the United States." *Futures* 30 (8), pp. 783–813.

Tonn, B. E., Zambrano, P., and Moore, S. (2001) "Community Networks or Networked Communities?" *Social Science Computer Review* 19 (2), pp. 201–12.

Traugott, M. (ed.) (1995) *Repertoires and Cycles of Collective Action* (Duke University Press, Durham, NC).

Trippi, J. (2004) *The Revolution Will Not Be Televised: Democracy, the Internet and the Overthrow of Everything* (Regan Books, New York).

Turkle, S. (1996) *Life on the Screen: Identity in the Age of the Internet* (Weidenfeld and Nicholson, London).

.TV Corporation (2003) website at http://www.tv (accessed October 7, 2003).

U.K. Cabinet Office (1999) *Modernizing Government*, Cm 4310 (HMSO, London).

U.K. Central Information Technology Unit (CITU) (1996) *Government.Direct: A Prospectus for the Electronic Delivery of Government Services*, Cm 3438 (HMSO, London).

———— (2000) *E-government: A Strategic Framework for Public Services in the Information Age* (HMSO, London).

U.K. National Audit Office (1999) *Government on the Web: A Report by the Comptroller and Auditor General*, written by Dunleavy, P., and Margetts, H. (HMSO, London).

———— (2002) *Better Public Services through E-government* (HMSO, London).

U.K. Office of Communications (2004) *The Communications Market: October 2004 Quarterly Update* (U.K. Office of Communications, London). Also available at http://www.ofcom.org.uk/research/industry_market_research/m_i_index/cm/qu_10_2004/cm_qu_10_2004.pdf (accessed December 15, 2004).

U.K. Office of the Deputy Prime Minister (2005) "E-Government@Local Homepage." Office of the Deputy Prime Minister website at http://www.localegov.gov.uk/page.cfm?pageID=74&language=eng (accessed February 25, 2005).

U.K. Office of National Statistics (2004a) "Adult Mobile Phone Ownership or Use." U.K. Office of National Statistics website at http://www.statistics.gov.uk/StatBase/ssdataset.asp?vlnk=7202&Pos=&ColRank=1&Rank=272 (accessed July 28, 2004).

———— (2004b) "Internet Access." U.K. Office of National Statistics website at http://www.statistics.gov.uk/cci/nugget.asp?id=8 (accessed July 28, 2004).

U.K. Parliament Joint Committee on the Draft Communications Bill (2003) "Report," at http://www.publications.parliament.uk/pa/jt200102/jtselect/jtcom/169/16901.htm (accessed April 4, 2003).

U.K. Privy Counsellor Review Committee (2003) *Anti-terrorism, Crime and Security Act 2001 Review Report* (HMSO, London). Also available at http://www.homeoffice.gov.uk/docs3/newton_committee_report_2003.pdf (accessed October 29, 2004).

U.K. Public Accounts Committee (2002) *E-revenue,* HC 707 (HMSO, London).

United Nations Department of Economic and Social Affairs (2003) *World Public Sector Report 2003: E-government at the Crossroads* (United Nations, New York).

United Nations Information and Communication Technologies Task Force (UNICT) (2003a) "About." UNICT website at http://www.unicttaskforce.org/about/principal.asp (accessed November 24, 2003).

_____ (2003b) "Plan of Action." UNICT website at http://www.unicttaskforce.org/about/planofaction.asp (accessed November 24, 2003).

United Nations Statistical Division (UNSD) (2004) "Millennium Indicators Database." UN Statistical Division website at http://millenniumindicators.un.org/unsd/databases.htm (accessed September 9, 2004).

University of California, Los Angeles (UCLA), Center for Communication Policy (2003) *The UCLA Internet Report: Surveying the Digital Future* (UCLA Center for Communication Policy, Los Angeles).

U.S. Census Bureau (2004) *Income, Poverty and Health Insurance in the US: 2003* (U.S. Census Bureau, Washington, D.C.). Also available at http://www.census.gov/hhes/www/income03.html (accessed September 15, 2004).

U.S. Central Intelligence Agency (CIA) (2003) *World Fact Book,* at http://www.cia.gov/cia/publications/factbook (accessed November 5, 2003).

U.S. Department of Commerce/National Telecommunications and Information Administration (NTIA) (1995) *Falling through the Net: A Survey of the "Have Nots" in Rural and Urban America* (U.S. Department of Commerce, Washington, D.C.). Also available at http://www.ntia.doc.gov/ntiahome/fallingthru.html (accessed September 15, 2004).

_____ (1997) *Falling through the Net II: New Data on the Digital Divide* (U.S. Department of Commerce, Washington, D.C.). Also available at http://www.ntia.doc.gov/ntiahome/net2/falling.html (accessed September 15, 2004).

_____ (1999) *Falling through the Net: Defining the Digital Divide: A Report on the Telecommunications and Information Technology Gap in America* (U.S. Department of Commerce, Washington, D.C.). Also available at http://www.ntia.doc.gov/ntiahome/fttn99/contents.html (accessed September 15, 2004).

_____ (2000) *Falling through the Net: Toward Digital Inclusion: A Report on Americans' Access to Technology Tools* (U.S. Department of Commerce, Washington, D.C.). Also available at http://search.ntia.doc.gov/pdf/fttn00.pdf (accessed September 15, 2004).

_____ (2002) *A Nation Online: How Americans Are Expanding Their Use of the Internet* (U.S. Department of Commerce, Washington, D.C.). Also available at http://www.ntia.doc.gov/ntiahome/dn (accessed September 15, 2004).

U.S. Department of Homeland Security (2004) "Fact Sheet: CAPPS II at a Glance." Department of Homeland Security website at http://www.dhs.gov/dhspublic/display?content=3162 (accessed October 20, 2004).

U.S. Department of Justice (2000) "Illinois Institute of Technology Research Institute Independent Technical Review of the Carnivore System: Draft Report." Department of Justice website at http://www.usdoj.gov/jmd/publications/carniv_entry.htm (accessed October 20, 2004).

_____ (2004) "The Herfindahl-Hirschman Index." Department of Justice website at http://www.usdoj.gov/atr/public/testimony/hhi.htm (accessed December 18, 2004).

U.S. Federal Election Commission (2005) "FEC Electronic Filing Report Retrieval." U.S. Federal Election Commission website at http://www.fec.gov/finance/disclosure/efile_search.shtml (accessed April 19, 2005).

U.S. IPv6 Summit (2004) U.S. IPv6 Summit 2004 website at http://www.usipv6.com (accessed January 28, 2005).

U.S. Libertarian Party (2005) "Issues and Positions." U.S. Libertarian Party website at http://www.lp.org/issues/issues.shtml (accessed April 26, 2005).

U.S. National Commission on the Terrorist Attacks [the 9/11 Commission] (2004) *The 9/11 Commission Report* (GPO, Washington, D.C.). Also available at http://www.9-11commission.gov/report/index.htm (accessed October 22, 2004).

U.S. National Partnership for Reinventing Government (1997) *Access America: Reengineering Through Information Technology* (GPO, Washington, D.C.).

——— (2000) "Electronic Government." National Partnership for Reinventing Government website at http://www.npr.gov/initiati/it/ (accessed October 3, 2000).

U.S. National Performance Review (1993a) *From Red Tape to Results: Creating a Government That Works Better and Costs Less: Report of the National Performance Review* (GPO, Washington, D.C.).

——— (1993b) *Reengineering through Information Technology: Accompanying Report of the National Performance Review* (GPO, Washington, D.C.).

Vaidhyanathan, S. (2004) *The Anarchist in the Library: How the Clash between Freedom and Control Is Hacking the Real World and Crashing the System* (Basic Books, New York).

Van de Donk, W., Tops, P., and Snellen, I. (eds.) (1995) *Orwell in Athens: A Perspective on Informatization and Democracy* (IOS Press, Amsterdam).

Van Dijk, J., and Hacker, K. (2003) "The Digital Divide as a Complex and Dynamic Phenomenon." *Information Society* 19 (4), pp. 315–26.

Van Everen, D. (2002) "Customer Segmentation Strategies." *Line56: The E-business Executive Daily Website* at http://www.line56.com/articles/default.asp?ArticleID=4055 (accessed October 30, 2002).

Van Zoonen, L. (1992) "Feminist Theory and Information Technology." *Media Culture and Society* 14 (1), pp. 9–31.

——— (2002) "Gendering the Internet: Claims, Controversies and Cultures." *European Journal of Communication* 17 (1), pp. 5–23.

Vegh, S. (2003) "Classifying Forms of Online Activism: The Case of Cyberprotests against the World Bank." In McCaughey, M., and Ayers, M. D. (eds.), *Cyberactivism: Online Activism in Theory and Practice* (Routledge, London), pp. 71–95.

Venturelli, S. (2002) "Inventing E-regulation in the US, EU and East Asia: Conflicting Social Visions of the Information Society." *Telematics and Informatics* 19 (2), pp. 69–90.

Verba, S., Schlozman, K. L., and Brady, H. (1995) *Voice and Equality: Civic Voluntarism in American Politics* (Harvard University Press, Cambridge, MA).

Verton, D. (2003) *Black Ice: The Invisible Threat of Cyber Terrorism* (McGraw-Hill Osborne, London).

Volkmer, C. J. (2004) "Should Adware and Spyware Prompt Congressional Action?" *Journal of Internet Law* 7 (11), pp. 1, 12–18.

Von Drehle, D. (2003) "From Screen Savers to Progressive Savior." *Washington Post*, June 5. Also available at http://www.washingtonpost.com/ac2/wp-dyn?pagename=article&contentId=A14925-2003Jun4&notFound=true (accessed June 8, 2004).

Wacker, G. (2003) "The Internet and Censorship in China." In Hughes, C. R., and Wacker, G. (eds.), *China and the Internet: Politics of the Digital Leap Forward* (RoutledgeCurzon, London), pp. 58–82.

Wade, R. H. (1996) "Globalization and Its Limits: Reports on the Death of the National Economy Are Greatly Exaggerated." In Berger, S., and Dore, R. (eds.), *National Diversity and Global Capitalism* (Cornell University Press, Ithaca, NY), pp. 60–88.

——— (2002) "Bridging the Digital Divide: New Route to Development or New Form of Dependency? *Global Governance* 8 (4), pp. 443–66.

Wall, D. S. (2003) "Mapping Out Cybercrimes in a Cyberspatial Surveillant Assemblage." In Ball, K. A., and Webster, F. (eds.), *The Intensification of Surveillance: Crime, Terrorism and Warfare in the Information Age* (Pluto Press, London), pp. 112–36.

Walzer, M. (1983) *Spheres of Justice: A Defence of Pluralism and Equality* (Basic Books, New York).

Ward, S., and Gibson, R. K. (2003) "On-line and On Message? Candidate Websites in the 2001 General Election." *British Journal of Politics and International Relations* 5 (2), pp. 188–205.

Ward, S., Gibson, R. K., and Nixon, P. (2003) "Parties and the Internet: An Overview." In Gibson, R. K., Nixon, P. G., and Ward, S. J. (eds.), *Political Parties and the Internet: Net Gain?* (Routledge, London), pp. 11–38.

Ward, S., and Lusoli, W. (2003) "Dinosaurs in Cyberspace? British Trade Unions and the Internet." *European Journal of Communication* 18 (2), pp. 147–79.

Ware, A. (1987) *Citizens, Parties and the State: A Reappraisal* (Polity, Cambridge).

Warhurst, C., and Thompson, P. (1998) "Hands, Hearts and Minds: Work and Workers at the End of the Century." In Thompson, P., and Warhurst, C. (eds.), *Workplaces of the Future* (Macmillan, Basingstoke, UK), pp. 1–24.

Warschauer, M. (2003) *Technology and Social Inclusion: Rethinking the Digital Divide* (MIT Press, Cambridge, MA).

Wayne, M. (2003) "Post-Fordism, Monopoly Capitalism and Hollywood's Media Industrial Complex." *International Journal of Cultural Studies* 6 (1), pp. 82–103.

Weare, C., Musso, J. A., and Hale, M. L. (1999) "Electronic Democracy and the Diffusion of Municipal Web Pages in California." *Administration and Society* 31 (1), pp. 3–27.

Weaver, R. L. (2000) "Free Speech, Crime, and the Challenge of Advancing Technology." *International Review of Law, Computers and Technology* 14 (1), pp. 25–32.

Weber, L., Loumakis, A., and Bergman, J. (2003) "Who Participates and Why? An Analysis of Citizens on the Internet and the Mass Public." *Social Science Computer Review* 21 (1), pp. 26–42.

Weber, M. (1947) *The Theory of Social and Economic Organization* (Free Press, New York).

Weber, S. (2004) *The Success of Open Source* (Harvard University Press, Cambridge, MA).

Webster, F. (2002) *Theories of the Information Society*, 2nd ed. (Routledge, London).

Weinberg, J. (2000) "ICANN and the Problem of Legitimacy." *Duke Law Journal* 50, pp. 187–260.

Weisenburger, K. (2001) "Hacktivists of the World, Divide." SecurityWatch website at http://thehacktivist.com/archive/news/2001/Hacktivists-SecurityWatch-2001.pdf (accessed May 10, 2004).

Weiss, L. (1998) *The Myth of the Powerless State: Governing the Economy in a Global Era* (Polity, Cambridge).

Wellman, B., and Gulia, M. (1999) "Virtual Communities as Communities: Net Surfers Don't Ride Alone." In Smith, M. A., and Kollock, P. (eds.), *Communities in Cyberspace* (Routledge, London), pp. 167–94.

Wellman, B., Quan-Haase, A., Boase, J., Chen, W., Hampton, K., de Diaz, I. I., and Miyata, K. (2003) "The Social Affordances of the Internet for Networked Individualism." *Journal of Computer-Mediated Communication* 8 (3) at http://www.ascusc.org/jcmc/vol8/issue3/wellman.html (accessed May 20, 2004).

Wendt, A. (1992) "Anarchy Is What States Make of It: The Social Construction of Power Politics." *International Organization* 46 (2), pp. 391–425.

West, D. M. (2004) *Global E-government 2004* (Center for Public Policy, Brown University, Providence, RI). Also available at http://www.insidepolitics.org/egovt04int.pdf (accessed November 24, 2004).

Westin, A. F. (2003) "Social and Political Dimensions of Privacy." *Journal of Social Issues* 59 (2), pp. 431–53.

Whine, M. (2000) "Far Right Extremists on the Internet." In Thomas, D., and Loader, B. (eds.), *Cybercrime: Law Enforcement, Security and Surveillance in the Information Age* (Routledge, London), pp. 234–50.

Wicks, R. H., and Souley, B. (2003) "Going Negative: Candidate Usage of Internet Web Sites during the 2000 Presidential Campaign." *Journalism and Mass Communication Quarterly* 80 (1), pp. 128–44.

Wikipedia (2005) "List of Open Source Software Packages." *Wikipedia Free Encyclopedia* at http://en.wikipedia.org/wiki/List_of_open-source_software_packages (accessed January 15, 2005).

Wilhelm, A. G. (2000) *Democracy in the Digital Age: Challenges to Political Life in Cyberspace* (Routledge, London).

———. (2001) "From Crystal Palaces to Silicon Valleys: Market Imperfection and the Enduring Digital Divide." In Lax, S. (ed.), *Access Denied in the Information Age* (Palgrave, London), pp. 199–217.

Wilkinson, R. (2002) "The Contours of Courtship: The WTO and Civil Society." In Wilkinson, R., and Hughes, S. (eds.), *Global Governance: Critical Perspectives* (Routledge, London), pp. 193–211.

Williams, C., and Gordon, J. (2003) "Dean Meetups: Using the Internet for Grassroots Organizing." Department of Behavioral and Political Sciences, Bentley College, Bentley College website at http://ecampus.bentley.edu/dept/bps/Faculty/cwilliams.htm (accessed July 29, 2004).

Wilson, J. Q. (1974) *Political Organizations* (Basic Books, New York).

Winner, L. (1977) *Autononmous Technology: Technics Out of Control as a Theme in Political Thought* (MIT Press, Cambridge, MA).

――――. (1988) "Do Artifacts Have Politics?" In Kraft, M. E., and Vig, N. J. (eds.), *Technology and Politics* (Duke University Press, Durham, NC).

Winseck, D. (2002) "Illusions of Perfect Information and Fantasies of Control in the Information Society." *New Media and Society* 4 (1), pp. 93–122.

Winston, B. (1998) *Media Technology and Society: A History from the Telegraph to the Internet* (Routledge, London).

Witt, L. (2004) "Kerry Net Strategy Now on Voters." July 3, *Wired News* website at http://www.wired.com/news/politics/0,1283,64066,00.html (accessed July 29, 2004).

Wolf, G. (2004) "How the Internet Invented Howard Dean." *Wired*, January.

Wood, D., Konvitz, E., and Ball, K. (2003) "The Constant State of Emergency?: Surveillance after 9/11." In Ball, K., and Webster, F. (eds.), *The Intensification of Surveillance: Crime, Terrorism and Warfare in the Information Age* (Pluto, London), pp. 137–50.

World Bank Information for Development Program (InfoDev) (2003) "The InfoDev Mission." InfoDev website at http://www.infodev.org/about/prospectus.htm (accessed November 26, 2003).

World Economic Forum (WEF) (2003) "Initiatives." WEF website at http://www.weforum.org/site/homepublic.nsf/Content/Initiatives+subhome (accessed November 27, 2003).

World Forum on Communication Rights (2003) World Forum on Communication Rights website at http://www.communicationrights.org (accessed November 27, 2003).

World Intellectual Property Organization (WIPO) (2003) "General Information." WIPO website at http://www.wipo.org/about-wipo/en/gib.htm#P9_1980 (accessed November 17, 2003).

World Summit on the Information Society (WSIS) (2003a) "Declaration of Principles and Plan of Action." WSIS website at http://www.itu.int/wsis/documents/doc_multi.asp?lang=en&id=1161|1160 (accessed September 9, 2004).

―――― (2003b) "Official List of Announced Participants." WSIS website at http://www.itu.int/wsis/docs/geneva/draft_announced_summit_participants.pdf (accessed November 27, 2003).

World Summit on the Information Society (WSIS) Task Force on Financial Mechanisms (2004) "Report of the Task Force on Financial Mechanisms for ICT for Development." WSIS website at http://www.itu.int/wsis/docs2/pc2/off7.pdf (accessed February 1, 2005).

World Trade Organization (WTO) (1998) *Electronic Commerce and the Role of the WTO* (WTO, Geneva). Also available at http://www.wto.org/english/res_e/booksp_e/special_study_2_e.pdf (accessed November 27, 2003).

Worley, B. (2001) "Comment: Nader's Traders vs State Regulators: Examining the Controversy over Internet Vote Swapping in the 2000 Presidential Election." *North Carolina Journal of Law and Technology* 2 (1), pp. 32–66.

Wring, D. (2004) *The Politics of Marketing the Labor Party: A Century of Stratified Electioneering* (Palgrave-Macmillan, Basingstoke, UK).

Wyatt, S., Thomas, G., and Terranova, T. (2002) "They Came, They Surfed, They Went Back to the Beach: Conceptualizing Use and Non-use of the Internet." In Woolgar, S. (ed.), *Virtual Society? Technology, "Cyberbole." Reality* (Oxford University Press, Oxford), pp. 23–40.

Yahoo! Directory (2004a) "ISPs: National (US)" Yahoo! Directory website at http://dir.yahoo.com/Business_and_Economy/Business_to_Business/Communications_and_Networking/Internet_and_World_Wide_Web/Network_Service_Providers/Internet_Service_Providers__ISPs_/National__U_S_/ (accessed December 21, 2004).

―――― (2004b) "UK: ISPs." Yahoo! U.K. Directory website at http://uk.dir.yahoo.com/Regional/Countries/United_Kingdom/Business_and_Economy/Business_to_Business/Communications_and_Networking/Internet_and_World_Wide_Web/Network_Service_Providers/Internet_Service_Providers__ISPs_/ (accessed December 21, 2004).

Yahoo!/Internet Archive (2004) *Yahoo—Government: Politics,* October 23, 1996, Internet Archive website at http://web.archive.org/web/19961220185130/www.yahoo.com/Government/Politics (accessed July 26, 2004).

Yes Men (2004) Reamweaver website at http://www.reamweaver.com (accessed May 10, 2004).

Young, O. (1999) *Governance in World Affairs* (Cornell University Press, London).

Zetter, K. (2004) "Blogs Counter Political Plottings." May 5, *Wired News* website at http://www.wired.com/news/politics/0,1283,63334,00.html (accessed July 29, 2004).

Zhang, J. (2002) "Will the Government 'Serve the People'?: The Development of Chinese E-government." *New Media and Society* 4 (2), pp. 163–84.

Zittel, T. (2004) "Political Representation in the Networked Society: The Americanization of European Systems of Responsible Party Government?" *Journal of Legislative Studies* 9 (3), pp. 32–53.

Zittrain, J. (2003) "Internet Points of Control." *Boston College Law Review* 44 (2), pp. 653–88.

Zoneedit (2003) "Simplified Example of DNS." Zoneedit website at http://www.zoneedit.com/doc/dns-basics.html (accessed November 18, 2003).

Zook, M. A. (2001) "Old Hierarchies or New Networks of Centrality? The Global Geography of the Internet Content Market." *American Behavioral Scientist* 44 (10), pp. 1679–96.

Zuboff, S. (1988) *In the Age of the Smart Machine: The Future of Work and Power* (Basic Books, New York).

INDEX

The letters *e, f, and t* following entries denote exhibit, figure, and table, respectively.